Encyclopedia of Crime & Justice

Second Edition

EDITORIAL BOARD

Encyclopedia of Crime & Justice

Second Edition

Joshua Dressler, Editor in Chief

Volume 2
Delinquent & Criminal Subcultures—
Juvenile Justice: Institutions

MACMILLAN REFERENCE USA

GALE GROUP

THOMSON LEARNING

*New York • Detroit • San Diego • San Francisco
Boston • New Haven, Conn. • Waterville, Maine
London • Munich*

Macmillan Reference USA
An imprint of the Gale Group
300 Park Avenue South
New York, NY 10010

27500 Drake Road
Farmington Hills, MI 48331

Library of Congress Cataloging-in-Publication Data
Encyclopedia of crime and justice.—2nd ed. / Joshua Dressler, editor in chief.
    p. cm.
   Includes bibliographical references and index.
   ISBN 0-02-865319-X (set: alk. paper)—ISBN 0-02-865320-3 (v. 1: alk. paper)—ISBN 0-02-865321-1 (v. 2: alk. paper)—ISBN 0-02-865322-X (v. 3: alk. paper)—ISBN 0-02-865323-8 (v. 4: alk. paper)
    1. Criminology—Encyclopedias. 2. Criminal justice, Administration of—Encyclopedias. I. Title: Crime and justice. II. Dressler, Joshua.
HV6017 .E52 2002
364'.03—dc21

2001042707

Portions of "Delinquent and Criminal Subcultures" have been adapted in part from "The Code of the Street" by Elijah Anderson by permission of W. W. Norton & Company Inc.

Printed in the United States of America
Printing number
 2 3 4 5 6 7 8 9 10

D

DELINQUENT AND CRIMINAL SUBCULTURES

Subcultures consist of norms, values, interests—and artifacts associated with them—that are derivative of, but distinct from, a larger referential culture. The term also is sometimes used loosely to distinguish individuals, groups, or other collectivities based on their demographic characteristics (e.g., age, ethnicity, and regional location) or pattern of behavior (e.g., occupation or commitment to particular activities—birdwatching, stamp collecting, a delinquent or criminal behavior pattern, etc.). The critical element in defining a subculture, however, is the extent to which the shared values, norms, and identities associated with a membership category or a behavior pattern distinguishes the category or pattern of behavior from the larger, more inclusive, social and cultural systems with which it is associated.

Criminal or delinquent subcultures thus consist of systems of norms, values, interests, and related artifacts that support criminal or delinquent behavior. The extent to which delinquent and criminal behavior is "supported" by subcultures varies a great deal, as does the involvement of the many behaviors specified in law as criminal or delinquent. Some subcultures support particular criminal acts or a limited set of such acts (see Inciardi). Some criminal subcultures are simply opportunistic, embracing virtually any criminal opportunity (e.g., subcultures of "hustlers"; see Anderson, 1978; Valentine). To a large extent this is also the case with delinquent subcultures, where specialization is rare. In contrast, "professional criminals" take pride in their craft, organize themselves for the safe and efficient performance of the crimes in which they specialize, and generally avoid other types of criminal involvement that might bring them to the attention of authorities (Sutherland).

Subcultural theory

No general theory has emerged, despite many efforts to define the notion as a theoretical construct (but see Yinger, 1960; 1977). A large body of research documents an enormous range of subcultures. On the basis of illustration and analogy drawn from this research, several principles of subcultural formation have been identified.

The first principle is that culture is adaptive (see Sills, ed., entries under "Culture"). It follows that subcultures also are adaptive; and, as is true of social life in general, subcultures change in response to changing technologies and fashions and ecological, political, and economic conditions (see Shover).

A second fundamental principle is that "social separation produces cultural differentiation" (Glaser, p. 90). Groups or categories of persons that are socially separated from one another inevitably face different problems of living; hence, culturally different solutions to such problems also emerge. Social separation is not sufficient to explain subcultural adaptations, however. Albert Cohen, theorizing about "the delinquent subculture" argued that a "crucial condition for the emergence of new cultural forms is the existence, in effective interaction with one another, of a number of actors with similar problems of adjustment" (p. 59). "Similar problems of adjustment," of course, may involve quite conventional people whose special interests require communication and interaction with others who have these same interests (e.g., stamp collectors). However, Cohen viewed this condition as especially appropriate to subcultures associated with such non-utilitarian delinquent behaviors as vandalism and general "hell raising."

Observing that this type of behavior occurs most frequently among working-class boys, Cohen hypothesized that this type of delinquent subculture was formed in reaction to status problems experienced by working-class boys in middle-class institutions such as schools. Many working-class boys are inadequately prepared for either the educational demands or the discipline of formal education. As a result they perform poorly, and are evaluated accordingly, in terms of the "middle-class measuring rod" found in elementary and secondary schools. Working-class girls, who are subject to closer controls in the family and judged according to traditional female role expectations, experience less pressure in such middle-class contexts.

For some working-class boys, Cohen argued that the solution to status problems is to reject the performance and status criteria of middle-class institutions—in effect, turning middle-class values upside down. Cohen's theory did not seek to account for the behavior of individual delinquent boys, or for the behavior of all working-class boys. Most of the latter do not engage in serious delinquent or criminal behavior. Alternative adaptations are available for most young people, for example, the underachieving but essentially nondelinquent "corner boys" or the high-achieving "college boys" described in William Foote Whyte's classic book, *Street Corner Society* (1943).

The processes associated with alternative behavioral adaptations are not completely understood. There is ample evidence that working-class and lower-class boys and girls tend to be devalued and marginalized in middle-class institutional contexts, despite often well-intentioned efforts on the part of schools and other institutions. Institutions also develop subcultural adaptations in dealing with young people. Some of these are counterproductive, in effect enhancing the behaviors they are designed to control (see Devine). Marginalization of delinquents and criminals is even greater than that of persons who are devalued by virtue of their social class position. This is particularly true of persistent delinquents and criminals and those who commit serious crimes, in contrast to those who only rarely transgress the law and with little conse-

quence. When marginality is reinforced by labeling, stigmatization, or prejudicial treatment in schools and job markets, "problems of adjustment" magnify. The common ecological location of many delinquents, in the inner-city slums of large cities, and their coming together in schools, provides the setting for "effective interaction."

These principles converge, theoretically and empirically, in recent scholarship. Based on extensive research, William Julius Wilson argues compellingly that a permanent underclass—the "truly disadvantaged"—emerged in the United States during the 1960s and 1970s. Social isolation and concentration effects are especially evident among the ghetto poor who are African Americans. Both have increased at a time of unprecedented affluence in the larger society, exacerbating problems in every institutional sector and leaving in its wake a host of social ills, including poverty, drug abuse, crime, and delinquency.

Although criminal and delinquent subcultures have a long history in industrialized societies (Cressey; Schwendinger and Schwendinger), they continue to change in response to changing social and economic conditions. Among these subcultures, the emergence of a truly *youth subculture* has been a major influence. Coleman and colleagues trace this development to events occurring in the United States following World War II: the "baby boom" and increasing affluence, which combined to create a huge youth market; extension of formal education of the young; delaying labor force participation by young people; increased numbers of women entering the work force, further separating mothers from children in homes and neighborhoods; increased employment of adults in large organizations where young people were not present; and expansion of the mass media, increasingly focused on the youth market, catering to and shaping their fashions. Each of these broad social changes increased greatly in scope as the twentieth century drew to a close.

Thus, socially isolated from mainstream society, the young people of the underclass are nevertheless subject to the blandishments of youth fashion and its expensive artifacts. Mercer Sullivan, studying cliques of young men in Brooklyn, New York, observed that among these young men the "cultural meaning of crime was constructed in . . . interaction out of materials supplied from two sources: the local area in which they spend their time almost totally unsupervised and undirected by adults, and the consumerist youth culture promoted in the mass media" (p. 249). The result is a volatile mix of macro-level deprivation, individual concerns with status and survival, and group and interpersonal relationships that set the stage for violence.

American society as seen from ground zero

The transformation of American cities, from an economy based on manufacturing to one of service and high-tech industry, and the impact of an increasingly global economy has left many people in the inner city in the lurch. The result has been the emergence, in some inner city areas, of an urban underclass (Wilson). Residents in these areas suffer not only the grinding effects of poverty, but of alienation as well. Many are convinced that the agents and agencies of social control are firmly against them and others of their communities, and have come to see racism as one of the important facts of daily life. Such profound alienation is exacerbated by market forces that take well-paying jobs from inner cities and replace them with less well-paying, dead end, service jobs that must compete with illegal means of livelihood that appeal especially to those who are alienated. Trinkets such as cars, gold, and designer clothing are dangled in front of people as signs or accessible symbols of status in a highly circumscribed environment with very limited opportunities. In these circumstances, such symbols acquire special significance, particularly when they become associated with highly exaggerated notions of personal worthiness, status, and respect.

This problem is especially evident among inner-city black Americans—at ground zero— where neighborhood effects of poverty are most intense and prolonged and where there is an extremely strong desire for direct evidence of social well-being but with few legitimate employment opportunities available that would allow inner-city residents to improve their lot or make a decent living. And community residents easily see a racial connection in their plight. For instance, the citizenship of U.S. blacks antedates all but native Americans among minorities in the United States, yet they remain at the back of the job queue, competing not only with new immigrants but with overseas workers whose low wages attract manufacturers. Those at ground zero have little standing, and often feel they and their communities are largely written off by the authorities. The most desperate residents, including many decent people, then feel they are on their own, particularly in matters of personal security, and have to do what they can to survive. For many, especially the youth, this situation encourages profoundly alienated subcultural themes that are generally associated with crime and violence, particularly in the media. In response, the wider society readily defines inner-city residents as violent and crime prone, and not worthy of association, thus providing a rationale for further isolating them. A vicious cycle is thereby set in motion that has had a significant impact on the major metropolitan areas of the United States.

It is important to recognize that not everyone who lives in the inner cities is poor and alienated. Overwhelming numbers of people are poor but civil and decent to their neighbors. As indicated above, in order to protect themselves, "decent" parents and children must mimic the tough behavior of the alienated, showing all who enter their presence that they are capable of defending themselves and their loved ones, an extremely important value in the local community. Strikingly, such an accommodation to the conditions of the neighborhood often results in the "streeting down" of the community, that is, more and more people, out of self-defense, adopt a "street" demeanor simply to let others know in no uncertain terms that they are not to be trifled with. With such widespread isolation from mainstream institutions and culture, local groups of young men and women are encouraged to form street gangs, which at times become criminally or quasi-criminally active gangs.

A major difference between blacks and other ethnic groups in the United States is that alienation, inequality, and racialized crime have existed for so very long. This fact, together with the general sense of how remote prospects for advancement in mainstream society are, only heightens the significance of immediate gratification, particularly among the youth.

Moreover, such alienation diminishes the relevance of the wider society's values and the impact of its sanctions (Anderson, 1999). Those who engage in criminal activity may feel less constrained by the hopes, aspirations, and dreams that might be realized in mainstream society, and so they are freed to commit violence toward their fellow citizens. The angriest and most alienated people develop a heightened sensitivity to slight when disrespected by others, and are often required to defend their honor and "get back respect" in order to survive socially in the neighborhood and, too often, violence is the result. This critically important reality must be appreciated if the violence of young inner-city poor African Americans is to be understood.

The staging area

The combination of concentrated urban poverty, social isolation, and historical circumstances has contributed to a unique kind of area frequented by the poor and alienated. Young people in particular fill the vacuum left by societal neglect by congregating in places that allow them to act out roles that give them esteem and status among their peers. It is here, in *staging areas*, that street-oriented groups thrive and their members look for identity (Anderson, 1999).

The staging area, or as described by participants, a "hangout," is a public place where activities occur that set the stage for other activities, which may be played out either on the spot in front of all who have congregated there or (depending on the circumstances) in less conspicuous locations. A thought of burglary or robbery might materialize into a plan. A verbal altercation in a park may be settled with a fight, for example, down a side street. People gather here at all times of the night and day, "profiling" and "representing" the image of themselves by which they wish to be known: they try to present the most valued notion of who they are and how they stand in relation to others. Competition can be fierce, and consequential. Hence, boys and girls, and some "grown" people too, stand around, taking the measure of one another, "looking things over," as they say. In this hangout, "watch your back" takes on literal meaning. Friends bond and reassure one another ("I got your back"), for there are always people in the vicinity looking for opportunities to violate others or simply "to get away with something." In such settings public displays of decency get little respect, and "looking hard" or being taken as meaner than the next person becomes the dominant issue.

Apart from the school, which is in a category by itself (as will be discussed below), three types of staging areas can be distinguished. One is quite local, revolving around neighborhood establishments such as carry-outs, liquor stores, and bars. The staging area may be inside, on a street corner outside, or at a house party with little or no adult supervision (Short and Strodtbeck). Alcohol and drugs are available. A second type consists of business strips where stores cater to street-oriented working-class and poor people. Buzzing with activity, people are drawn from a larger area. The third type—multiplex theaters, sporting events, and concerts—brings together large crowds from throughout the city. These are the most volatile, especially at places such as roller-skating rinks or dances where music, alcohol, and drugs combine with rough crowds of young people inclined to "act out" what they have seen or heard others do, either in films, on recordings, or in person. Some young people are highly suggestive. People from other neighborhoods, outsiders, who come to a staging area and present themselves are said to be "representing" both who they are and the "world" or "hood" from which they hail.

To actively represent, one may be required to fight in public, in an effort that inevitably reflects on one's "name" or the reputation one is building. Moreover, to represent is to place one's area of the city on the line, to say to outsiders, "Hey, this is what's to me [what I am made of] and my neighborhood," compared with other neighborhoods of the city. At sporting events, a school's prestige may be on the line. It is at the staging area that the subculture of the street germinates and grows, nurtured by the tough conditions of this space, including the audiences that live by it, and thus are required to support it. For the boldest young people, it is sometimes necessary to in effect put a chip on one's shoulder and dare others to knock it off, to wage a campaign for respect, but with the added elements of dare and challenge. There are often enough young people in the staging area to provide an audience as well as the critical mass of negative energy necessary to spark violence, not just against people like themselves but also against others present in the staging area, at times creating a critical flashpoint for violence.

In staging areas around streetcorners and carryouts, where many drug dealers and corner boys hang out, because of the array of status symbols and their meanings, would-be aggressors are generally inclined to know who is who, who "can fight" and who cannot, who has nerve and heart and who is a chump. Around these settings, in various social arenas, and on the streets more generally, the chump gets little or no respect, and those who resemble this model most often get pushed around, picked on, tried or tested, and ultimately most often become frequent victims of robbery and gratuitous violence, serving a purpose for those who would campaign to stand superior.

Material things serve as profound symbols, playing an important and complicated role in establishing self-image while representing. Youths typically place a high premium on eyewear, leather jackets, expensive sneakers, and other items that take on significance as status symbols. An impoverished inner-city youth who can acquire these material things is able to feel big and impress others, who may then attempt to relieve him of his property in order to feel big themselves and to impress still others. The wise youths of the neighborhood understand that it is better not to opt for the more expensive items, because they realize that by doing so they make themselves into targets for theft and robbery. Not only must the young person display something of value, but he must also be able to hold on to it. Hence, simply visiting the staging area can be both satisfying and risky. One goes to the "block," the strip, or the concert to see the latest trends, what is happening, who is doing what with whom, who did what to whom, and when.

Further, the staging area is also a densely populated place where young people hang out and look to meet members of the opposite sex. Here young men and women out to be "with it" or "hip" smoke cigarettes or drink "forties" or other alcoholic beverages, or perhaps they are there to get high on "blunts" (drug-laced cigars). Young men may taunt others by joking with them, saying directly, "Now, start something!" as though they are ready for anything. At an event with large crowds from all over the city, heterogeneous groups vie for social position. People can become touchy, and a fight can start over seemingly minor incidents; but what may happen is hardly minor: an injury or death may result, the social order of groups may be altered, and the stage may be set for payback-inspired feuds. With so much at stake a person can easily feel disrespected by another who looks at him or her for "too long," or by simply being cut off in the concession line. Such a "cut," which might also be viewed as an advance at someone's girl- or boyfriend, may be taken as a "statement." Challenging the statement creates a "beef," and a confrontation can erupt. As the situation deteriorates, it may be very difficult for either party to back down, particularly if members of the audience have, or are understood to have, a significant social investment in who and what each participant pretends to be.

Staging area matters often involve retribution, or "payback," and to be prepared for anything, some people carry "equalizers" or "shit"—firearms or other weapons—to staging areas. Because of formal security, most will leave their shit elsewhere, hidden in accessible places to be retrieved when the need arises. A young man with a publicly known beef will feel there is a chance that he will have to go get his shit. His life does not have to be in immediate danger; pride, how he feels about his homies, low feelings, or having gotten the bad end of an altercation may be enough for him to prepare to settle things in order to avenge an earlier beating, or answer a perceived threat.

Although staging areas are often the places where beefs develop and fights to settle them occur, the code of the street germinates, emerges, and grows on the streets, in the alleys, and on the playgrounds of the inner-city neighborhood, where in the interests of social survival small children begin early in life their campaign for respect (Anderson, 1999).

The school as a staging area

In the toughest urban neighborhoods, the local school serves as an outpost of the traditions of the wider society as well as a focal point for local culture, a place where "the little traditions" of the local neighborhood and the "great traditions" of the wider society come together. Racially segregated and situated in an impoverished inner-city community in which violence, drugs, and crime are rampant, and sometimes ignored by the authorities, it is characterized by the street-decent dynamic. Defined by the young people themselves, youths who are viewed as decent are often not given much respect on the street, and those viewed as "street" are generally seen as tough, and therefore to be respected.

During their early years, most of the children accept the legitimacy of the school, and eagerly approach the task of learning. With the passage of time, however, the relentless campaign they wage for respect in their public environment requires that the street code be observed. By the fourth grade, enough children have usually opted for the code of the street that it begins to compete effectively with the culture of the school, and the code begins to dominate their public culture—in school as well as out—becoming a way of life for many, eventually conflating with the culture of the school itself. Under such circumstances, the school becomes a primary staging area for the campaign for respect.

In this process, for largely instrumental purposes, decent kids learn to "code switch," while street kids become more singularly committed to the street. The difference is strongly related to family background, available peers and role models, and just "how tough" the neighborhood is perceived to be. For many alienated young black people, attending school and doing well become negatively identified as "acting white," and to do so in this environment is to mark oneself as vulnerable. In an essentially racially black street-world, there is often a strong need to demonstrate one's ability to handle oneself socially and physically on the ghetto streets. This is a powerful community value in and of itself. "Street knowledge" is esteemed, and the quest for it and the consideration for those who have it begin to predominate, ultimately competing with and at times undermining the mission of the school.

As these neighborhood conditions persist, with each passing year the school loses ground as more and more students adopt a street orientation, if only for survival and self-defense in the neighborhood. But often what is out on the streets is brought into the classrooms, for largely more expressive purposes. Hence, some of the most troublesome students are then encouraged by peers to act out, to get over on the teacher, to test authority by probing for weaknesses. Particularly during mild weather, many students in the upper grades attend school sporadically or stop coming altogether, because street activities effectively compete for their time. Even while in school, they walk the halls instead of attending class, and their encounters there often mirror those on the street, marked by tension and fights.

The most troubled street-oriented kids may fight with teachers, bring guns and knives to school, and threaten people. In this highly competitive setting, deprivation and anger are combined. The most deprived youths, who can easily be made to feel bad, sometimes become envious and jealous of peers. Some compensate by lifting themselves up by putting others down. A common tactic is to "bust on" or "signify" at someone, verbally teasing the person, at times to the point of tears. Sometimes the prettiest girls can get beaten up out of jealousy. From so much envy and jealousy, beefs easily erupt, beginning with ritual "bumping" and ending in serious physical confrontations to settle things. Bumping rights are negotiated, determining who is allowed to bump whom, to pick on whom, and in what circumstances. In this process young people campaign for place, esteem, and ultimately respect.

In this way, the school becomes transformed in the most profound sense into a staging area for the streets, a place where people come to present themselves, to represent where they come from, and to stay even with or to dominate their peers. Violence and threats of violence are very often of an instrumental nature, and always a possibility, for the typically troubled school is surrounded by persistent poverty, where scarcity of valued things is the rule, aggravating an already highly competitive social environment. And authority, especially that of the police and other agents of social control, is very often questioned, and outright defiance may be seen as a virtue. In this campaign, young people must be prepared not only show a certain defiance of this authority, but at times to fight, or at least not to back down.

Moreover, young people must also take great care with their public appearance. To gain and maintain the respect of their peers, they must display the right look. And the right look means not wearing old or "bummy" clothes, or sneakers that are worn or dirty or out of style. Esteem is so precarious that it can be taken away with just a word, and kids are constantly challenged to defend what they have and who they want to be. Social life becomes a zero-sum scenario in which appearance and possessions may have the effect of diminishing others. In dealing with this setting, the decent kids often mimic the street kids, behaving in street ways that often confuse teachers (and also prospective employers and police who might be incapable of distinguishing the decent from the street). Some teachers are unable to differentiate between the two groups; they may become overwhelmed, unwilling, or unable to discern the often shy kid behind the "tough" facade.

As indicated, much of students' behavior may be purely defensive, requiring significant expenditures of social energy. The weakest players tend to be victimized and the business of the school is disrupted. In the toughest situations, the street element (and those who would be street) may dominate the school and its local terrain. Although most of the young people in these settings are inclined toward decency, when street elements rule, they must campaign for respect by adopting a street attitude, look, and presentation of self. The decent kids must struggle to maintain their credibility. One fifteen-year-old boy typically changed his "square" clothes for a black leather jacket (thereby adopting a street look) after he got around the corner from his home and out of his mother's view. In order to preserve his own self-respect and the respect of his peers, he would also hide his books under his jacket while walking to school, bidding to appear street. In school, as in the neighborhood, adolescents are concerned with developing a sense of who they are, what they are, and what they will be. They try on many different personas and roles, and they experiment with many scripts. Some work, others do not.

School authority is extremely important to young people, but too often authority figures are viewed as alien and unreceptive. Teachers and administrators are concerned that their own authority be taken seriously, and claims to authority are often up for grabs—even subject to out-and-out challenge. Although young people do not develop their identities based solely on privileges and rewards granted by teachers, this dynamic does exist. Often students perceive (more or less accurately) that the institution and its staff are utterly unreceptive to their street presentations. Mixed with their inability to distinguish the decent child from the street child, the teachers' efforts to combat the street may cause them to lump the good students with the bad, generally viewing all who display street emblems as adversaries.

In response, decent children place ever greater stock in their ability to code-switch, adopting one set of behaviors for inside the building and one for outside. In the heat of campaigning for respect, however, the two roles often merge. The resulting confusion undermines school discipline, particularly when some children "get away with it."

When students become convinced that they cannot receive their "props" (proper due) from teachers and staff, they turn elsewhere, typically to the street, encouraging others to follow their lead, particularly when the unobtainable appears to be granted only on the basis of acting white. A powerful incentive for young people then emerges, especially for those sitting on the cultural fence, to invest themselves in an oppositional subculture—which may be confused with "black identity." Such a resolution allows alienated students to campaign for respect on their own terms. In this connection, many students become smug in their lack of appreciation for the school and its connection with the wider traditions.

Education is thus gradually undermined as the mission of the school is realized to be incompatible with the more prevalent code of the street. For so many young people, to embrace the school is to give in and act white, neither of which is publicly acceptable. The values of decency and of education have not been deeply enough inculcated and explained to the children, to make them want to give up the ways of the street. Thus, the school, as an outpost of mainstream society, attempts to deliver its message in an environment that has little regard for that society. The code of the street, and by extension the oppositional subculture, competes very effectively with traditional values. Alienated black students take on oppositional roles so effectively that they may be viewed as models for other disaffected students.

The school is a microcosm of the community. Despite security measures, kids parade up and down the halls, socializing. Some buy and sell drugs inside the school as well as outside. Yet school remains a haven, a place where one can go, expect, and find relative order and peace. One of the implications of the reality here described speak to distinctions between the violence in middle-class suburban places like Columbine, Colorado, and that which occurs in the inner cities. Behavior in ground zero areas is often instrumental, a way people live to get along, and the violence is often retributive; people seek to visit retribution or to "get back" at those who violate them through transgressions or threats. And children and young adults as well as mature people abide by the code of the street, whereas in places like Columbine, the code of the street is not so necessary. For in such middle-class communities kids can travel to and from school and interact with their peers without the code. Staging areas exist among middle-class kids, but with less threat and violence (see Schwartz). The violence in middle-class communities is more likely to be expressive, perhaps mimicking what is seen on television and motion picture screens, which often present a glorified picture of violence, including that which takes place in the inner city. The issue of expressive versus instrumental violence speaks to the alienation occurring at ground zero.

Conclusion

Among delinquent groups and subcultures there is great variation in the nature and strength of group norms, values, and interests. Much, however, remains unknown. The extent to which delinquent behavior is attributable to group norms, values, or special interests is itself problematic, inasmuch as delinquent behavior of some highly delinquent gangs appears to result from the operation of group processes as much as from group norms (Short, 1997). Observations of street gangs suggest that, among even the most delinquent groups, relatively little of group life involves delinquent behaviors; and, when such groups participate in delinquent episodes, some members typically do not become involved. Subcultures consist of "collections of normative orders"—sets of rules and practices related to a common value (Herbert)—rather than norms oriented around a single value (such as being "macho," "cool," or exceptionally gifted in some way). Individuals typically associate with more than one subculture-witness the "decent" youth observed by Anderson (1999), for example. Simply being associated with a subculture thus is unlikely to be a good predictor of the behavior of any particular individual.

Cultures, subcultures, and the groups associated with them overlap, often in multiple and complex ways. To speak of a youth culture, for example, is to denote a subculture of the larger adult-dominated and institutionally defined culture. Similarly, delinquent subcultures contain elements of both youth and adult cultures. Williams's lower-class, minority "cocaine kids," for example, were entrepreneurial, worked long hours, and maintained self-discipline—all important elements in the achievement ideology of the American Dream (see Messner and Rosenfeld; also Fagan; Hagan, et al.). Most saw their involvement in the drug trade as a way to get started in legitimate business or to pursue other conventional goals, and a few succeeded at least temporarily in doing so. The criminal subculture with which they identified shared a symbiotic relationship with their customers (including many middle- and upper-class persons), who shared subcultural values approving drug use but who participated in the subculture of drug distribution only as consumers. For the young drug dealers, selling drugs was a way to "be somebody," to get ahead in life, and to acquire such things as jewelry, clothing, and cars—the symbols of wealth, power, and respect.

Sullivan's study of groups and young males in three Brooklyn communities—black, predominantly Latino, and white—is particularly significant in this regard. The young men in Mercer Sullivan's white group were able to find better jobs than were the black and Hispanic youth at all ages. Their stock of *human capital* had been reinforced by experience with the discipline of the workplace, while their *social capital* was enhanced by their ability to secure better-quality jobs as a result of the superior personal networks that they shared with the adult community (Sullivan).

The minority youth were disadvantaged, with respect to both human and social capital, in the family and in other ways (see Coleman). Both human and social capital are acquired through personal experience, and communities and neighborhoods vary in their stock of both, qualitatively and quantitatively.

Subcultures are dynamic and ever changing, influenced by both external and internal forces and processes. Substantial knowledge gaps exist at each level of explanation, and precisely how they relate to each other is not well understood. Subcultures both effect social change and adapt to it, and for this reason they are important theoretically, empirically, and as they reflect and influence social policy. The report by Robert Sampson and his colleagues that Chicago neighborhoods with higher scores on "collective efficacy" have lower rates of criminally violent behavior, for example, suggests that developing ways to encourage identification of neighbors with each other, and willingness to help one another in their common interest, will enhance local social control and help to weaken the influence of subcultures that encourage such behavior. Many such examples might be cited.

ELIJAH ANDERSON
JAMES F. SHORT

See also CRIME CAUSATION: SOCIOLOGICAL THEORIES; CRIMINAL CAREERS; DEVIANCE; JUVENILE AND YOUTH GANGS; JUVENILE STATUS OFFENDERS; ORGANIZED CRIME; PROSTITUTION.

BIBLIOGRAPHY

ANDERSON, ELIJAH. *A Place on the Corner.* Chicago: University of Chicago Press, 1978.
———. *Streetwise: Race, Class, and Change in an Urban Community.* Chicago: University of Chicago Press, 1990.
———. *The Code of the Streets.* New York: W.W. Norton, 1999.
COHEN, ALBERT K. *Delinquent Boys: The Culture of the Gang.* New York: Free Press, 1955.
COLEMAN, JAMES S. "Social Capital in the Creation of Human Capital." *American Journal of Sociology* 94 (Suppl. 1988): S95–S120.
COLEMAN, JAMES S.; BREMNER, ROBERT H.; CLARK, BURTON R.; DAVIS, JOHN B.; EICHORN, DOROTY H.; GRILICHES, ZVI; KETT, JOSEPH F.; RYDER, NORMAN B.; DOERING, ZAHAVA BLUM; and MAYS, JOHN M. *Youth Transition to Adulthood.* Report of the Panel of the President's

Science Advisory Committee. Chicago: University of Chicago Press, 1974.

CRESSEY, DONALD R. "Delinquent and Criminal Subcultures." In *Encyclopedia of Crime and Justice.* Edited by Sanford H. Kadish. New York: Free Press, 1983. Pages 584-590.

DEVINE, JOHN. *Maximum Security: The Culture of Violence in Inner-City Schools.* Chicago: University of Chicago Press, 1996.

FAGAN, JEFFREY. "Gangs, Drugs, and Neighborhood Change" In *Gangs in America,* 2d ed. Edited by C. Ronald Huff. Newbury Park, Calif.: Sage, 1996. Pages 39-74.

GLASER, DANIEL. *Social Deviance.* Chicago: Markham, 1971.

HAGAN, JOHN; HEFLER, GERD; CLASSEN, GABRIELE; BOEHNKE, KLAUS; and MERKENS, HANS. "Subterranean Sources of Subcultural Delinquency Beyond the American Dream." *Criminology* 36 (1998): 309–341.

HAGEDORN, JOHN M. "Gang Violence in the Post-Industrial Era." In *Youth Violence.* Vol. 24 of *Crime and Justice.* Edited by Michael Tonry and Mark H. Moore. Chicago: University of Chicago Press, 1998. Pages 365-419.

HAGEDORN, JOHN M., with MACON, PERRY. *People and Folks: Gangs, Crime, and the Underclass in a Rustbelt City.* Chicago: Lake View Press, 1987.

HERBERT, STEVE. "Police Subculture Reconsidered." *Criminology* 36 (1998): 343–369.

INCIARDI, JAMES A. "Vocational Crime." In *Handbook of Criminology.* Edited by Daniel Glaser. Chicago: Rand-McNally, 1974. Pages 299–401.

KLEIN, MALCOLM W. *The American Street Gang.* New York: Oxford University Press, 1995.

MESSNER, STEVEN F., and ROSENFELD, RICHARD. *Crime and the American Dream.* Belmont, Calif.: Wadsworth, 1994.

SAMPSON, ROBERT J.; RAUDENBUSH, S. W.; and EARLS, F. "Neighborhoods and Violent Crime: A Multilevel Study of Collective Efficacy." *Science* 277 (1997): 918–924.

SCHWARTZ, GARY. *Beyond Conformity or Rebellion: Youth and Authority in America.* Chicago: University of Chicago Press, 1987.

SCHWENDINGER, HERMAN, and SCHWENDINGER, JULIA SIEGEL. *Adolescent Subcultures and Delinquency.* New York: Praeger, 1985.

SHORT, JAMES F., JR. *Poverty, Ethnicity, and Violent Crime.* Boulder, Colo.: Westview, 1997.

———. "The Level of Explanation Problem Revisited—The American Society of Criminology 1997 Presidential Address." *Criminology* 36 (1998): 3–36.

SHORT, JAMES F., JR., and STRODTBECK, FRED L. *Group Process and Gang Delinquency.* Chicago: University of Chicago Press, 1965.

SHOVER, NEIL. *Great Pretenders: Pursuits and Careers of Persistent Thieves.* Boulder, Colo.: Westview, 1996.

SILLS, DAVID, ed. *International Encyclopedia of the Social Sciences.* New York: Macmillan and Free Press, 1968.

SULLIVAN, MERCER L. *"Getting Paid": Youth Crime and Work in the Inner City.* Ithaca, N.Y.: Cornell University Press, 1989.

SUTHERLAND, EDWIN H. *The Professional Thief.* Chicago: University of Chicago Press, 1937.

VALENTINE, BETTYLOU. *Hustling and Other Hard Work: Life Styles in the Ghetto.* New York: Free Press, 1978.

WHYTE, WILLIAM FOOTE. *Street Corner Society.* Chicago: University of Chicago Press, 1943.

WILLIAMS, TERRY. *The Cocaine Kids: The Inside Story of a Teenage Drug Ring.* Menlo Park, Calif.: Addison-Wesley, 1989.

WILSON, WILLIAM JULIUS. *The Truly Disadvantaged: The Inner City, the Underclass, and Public Policy.* Chicago: University of Chicago Press, 1987.

YINGER, MILTON. "Contraculture and Subculture." *American Sociological Review* 23 (1960): 625–635.

———. "Countercultures and Social Change." *American Sociological Review* 42 (1977): 833–853.

DETERMINATE SENTENCING

See SENTENCING: ALLOCATION OF AUTHORITY.

DETERRENCE

The concept

The narrow sense: fear of punishment. In a narrow sense, *deterrence* can be defined as the prevention of socially undesirable behavior by fear of punishment. A person who might otherwise have committed a crime is restrained by the thought of the unpleasant consequences of detection, trial, conviction, and sentence ("simple deterrence"). A distinction is often made between *general deterrence*, which signifies the deterrent effect of the threat of punishment, and *special deterrence* (or *individual deterrence*), which signifies the effect of actual punishment on the offender.

The basic phenomenon is the fear of punishment. This fear may be influenced by the experience of punishment. When an offender has been punished he knows what it is like to be prosecuted and punished, and this may strengthen his fear of the law. The experience may, however, work the other way. It is conceivable that the offender previously had exaggerated ideas of the consequences of being caught and now draws the conclusion that it was not as bad as he had imagined. In this case, the special deterrent effect of the punishment is negative. More important, probably, a person who has been convicted of a somewhat more serious crime, and especially one who was sentenced to imprisonment, will have less to fear from a new conviction, since his reputation is already tarnished. In practice, it will be difficult or impossible to isolate the deterrent effects of the prison experience from other effects of the stay in prison. What we can measure is how offenders perform after punishment, expressed in figures of recidivism.

The broad sense: the moral effects of criminal law. In a broad sense, *deterrence* is taken to include not only the effect of fear on the potential offender but also other influences produced by the threat and imposition of punishment. Criminal law is not only a price tariff but also an expression of society's disapproval of forbidden behavior, a fact influencing citizens in various ways. Most people have a certain respect for formal law as such. Moreover, the criminalization of a certain type of behavior may work as a moral eye-opener, making people realize the socially harmful character of the act ("the law as a teacher of right and wrong"). The moral condemnation expressed through the criminal law may also affect the moral attitudes of the individual in a less reflective way. Various labels are used to characterize these effects: the moral, the educative, the socializing, the attitude-shaping, or the norm-strengthening influence of the law. From the legislator's perspective, the creation of moral inhibitions is of greater value than mere deterrence, because the former may work even in situations in which a person need not fear detection and punishment. In the Scandinavian countries and Germany the moral component in general prevention is considered to be essential. For the moral effect of criminal law the perceived legitimacy of the system, rooted in the application of principles of justice, proportionality and fairness, are regarded as more important than severity of sentences.

General deterrence and general prevention. In continental literature *general prevention* is used as a technical term that denotes both the effect of fear and the moral effect of the criminal law. This is equivalent to *general deterrence* in the broad sense, but the term deterrence tends to focus on the effect of fear. Most American research papers on deterrence do not mention the question of definition but do in fact work with the broad concept, since they are concerned with all effects on crime rates of the system of criminal justice and make no effort to exclude effects produced through mechanisms other than fear.

Habituative effects of criminal law. Much law-abiding conduct is habitual, and the threat of punishment plays a role in this habit formation. It is sufficient to mention the response of drivers to traffic signals. In a broad sense *deterrence* can be taken to include also the habituative effects of the law. Habit formation is, however, a secondary phenomenon. For a habit to be established, there must first be compliance based on other sources, which may include fear and respect for the law. The habit is eventually formed through repetition of the law-abiding conduct.

A historical perspective

Historically, deterrence has been, along with retribution, the primary purpose of punishment. The deterrent purpose has often led to penalties that, to contemporary minds, seem cruel and inhuman. Capital punishment and corporal punishment were the backbone of the systems of criminal justice up to the late eighteenth century. Executions were made public spectacles, and cruel methods of execution were often invented in order to enhance the deterrent effect.

In the eighteenth century the writers of the classical school of criminal justice—notably Cesare Beccaria in Italy, Jeremy Bentham in England, and P. J. A. von Feuerbach in Germany—based their theory of criminal law on general deterrence. The central idea was that the threat of punishment should be specified so that in the mind of the potential lawbreaker the fear of punishment would outweigh the temptation to commit the crime. The penalty should be fixed by law in proportion to the gravity of the offense. The certainty of punishment was considered as more important than the severity of the punishment. According to the classical theory, the penalty in the individual case had as its primary function to make the threat of the law credible. Only occasionally did these writers mention the moral effects of the criminal law.

In the late nineteenth century and the first half of the twentieth century the idea of deterrence lost ground to the idea of treatment and rehabilitation. Criminologists and penologists voiced the view that the most important aim of punishment was to correct the offender and, if this proved impossible, to incapacitate him. Therefore, the penalty had to be adjusted to the needs of the individual offender. In the United States the *indeterminate sentence* was introduced. The idea of the indeterminate sentence is based on an analogy to medical treatment in a hospital. The offender should be kept as long as necessary in order to cure him, no shorter, no longer; and just as with a stay in a hospital, the duration should not be decided in advance but on the basis of the observation of progress. On the European continent, measures of safety and reform for certain categories of offenders were introduced, based on similar ideas. The idea of deterrence was often ridiculed as fictitious, outmoded, and the cause of much unnecessary suffering. The saying "Punishment does not deter crime" was often accepted as established truth.

Although these ideas were dominant in the professional literature up to the 1950s, legislators, prosecutors, and judges continued to have faith in deterrence. From the early 1960s a change in criminological thought began to take place and gradually gained momentum. Research into the differential effects of various sanctions led to great skepticism with regard to society's ability to rehabilitate offenders. It appeared that choice of sanction had very little effect when compared to the personality and background of the offender and to the social environment he went back to after his encounter with the machinery of justice. Moreover, it seemed that no one was able to tell when to release the offender in order to maximize his chances of a law-abiding life in the future. At least for the overwhelming majority of offenders, the hospital analogy does not work.

Two tendencies have emerged: a movement in favor of fixed sentences in proportion to the gravity of the offense, as demanded by the classical school of criminal law ("neoclassicism"); and a revival of interest in deterrence. When faith is lost in the idea of treatment and rehabilitation as the basis for a system of criminal sanctions, other aims of punishment come into focus. Up to 1965 the only empirical research in deterrence consisted of a few papers on the death penalty. Since the mid-1960s a series of books and a stream of research papers have been published on the subject, mainly in the United States, Canada, and Great Britain, but also in Germany, the Nether-

lands, and Scandinavia (see Beyleveld). Most research has been undertaken by either sociologists or economists. The economists, following the lead of Gary Becker, look upon the risk of punishment as a cost of crime and apply econometric methods to find out how a change in the price affects the rate of crime (Eide).

Empirical and ethical questions

In discussing deterrence one is confronted with two categories of questions. One category consists of empirical or factual questions: Does deterrence work, and if so, how well, in which fields, and under what circumstances? Another category consists of ethical questions: To what extent is the purpose of deterrence a valid moral basis for lawmaking, sentencing, and the execution of sentences? A penalty may be effective as a deterrent yet unacceptable because it is felt to be unjust or inhumane. The position on such questions as capital punishment, corporal punishment, and the length of prison sentences is dependent not only on views on efficacy but also on moral considerations. Even if it were possible to prove that cutting off the hands of thieves would effectively prevent theft, proposals for such a practice would scarcely win many adherents in the Western world today. Much of the discussion on deterrence has been of an emotional nature and has not separated the empirical questions from the value questions. Often people have let their views on empirical questions be heavily colored by their value preferences instead of basing them on a dispassionate scrutiny of the available evidence (Andenaes, 1974, pp. 41–44).

General deterrence: myth or reality?

The strongest basis for the belief in deterrence is the eminent plausibility of the theory from the viewpoint of common sense. That the foresight of unpleasant consequences is a strong motivating factor is a familiar experience of everyday life. It would be a bold statement that this well-known mechanism of motivation is of no importance in the decision to commit or not commit an offense. Most offenders, and even more so most potential offenders, are within the borders of psychological normalcy. There is no prima facie reason to assume that they are insensitive to negative inducements.

Historical experiences from police strikes and similar situations show that even a short breakdown of criminal justice leads to great increases in offenses such as burglary and robbery (Andenaes, 1974, pp. 16–18, 50–51). By introspection many know that the risk of detection and negative sanctions plays a role for their own compliance with rules about taxation, customs, drinking and driving, and other traffic offenses. It seems to be a universal experience that police regulations that are not enforced gradually cease to be taken seriously. Paradoxically, the consequences of police corruption can be mentioned as a demonstration of the deterrent impact that the criminal law has when the machinery of justice is working normally and properly (Andenaes, 1975, pp. 360–361). All available data indicate that organized crime flourishes most where the local police have been corrupted. Police corruption paralyzes enforcement and gives professional criminals a feeling of immunity from punishment. That crime flourishes when the criminal justice system is paralyzed through corruption is another way of stating that a criminal justice system that works normally does deter crime, or at least some forms of crime, to some degree.

It seems safe to conclude that criminal law and law enforcement play an indispensable role in the functioning of a modern, complex society. However, from a practical point of view, this insight is of limited value. Policymakers are not confronted with the choice of retaining or abolishing the whole system of criminal justice. The choices are of a much more narrow kind. The legislator sometimes has the choice between criminalization or decriminalization of a certain type of behavior, such as homosexual conduct, abortion, pornography, or blasphemy. More often the choice is between a somewhat stricter or milder penalty or between somewhat higher or lower appropriations for the police or other control agencies. For the police, the prosecutor, the judge, and the prison administrator the choices are still more limited. The questions of practical importance do not refer to the total effects of criminal law but to the marginal effects of this or that change in the level of punishment or the allotment of resources (Zimring and Hawkins, pp. 7–8). These effects are difficult to foresee. Decisions on whether to change or not to change are often made on the basis of overly simplistic assumptions.

Factors in deterrence

Severity and credibility of the threat. According to common sense, the motivating force of the threat of punishment will normally increase with the severity of the penalty and the risk of detection and conviction. It is a fair assumption that most offenses would not have been committed if the potential offender foresaw a 50 percent risk of being detected and receiving a severe prison sentence. Even in this situation there would, of course, be exceptions: cases of psychopathological crime, crime under extreme emotional stress, certain political crimes, and so on.

Since Beccaria it has been generally accepted that certainty of punishment is more important than severity, and research gives some support for this assumption. Such a simple formula needs qualifications. For example, in the field of white-collar crime a fine may be considered merely a business expense, whereas a prison sentence, through its stigmatizing character, may act as a strong deterrent. But if the level of penalties is already high, it seems probable that further increases in severity will yield diminishing returns. Moreover, excessively severe penalties may be counterproductive by reducing the risk of conviction. When the penalties are not reasonably attuned to the gravity of the violation, the public is less inclined to inform the police, the prosecuting authorities are less disposed to prosecute, and juries are less apt to convict.

Experience in Finland in the postwar years indicates that the general level of sentencing has a limited influence on deterrence. At the beginning of the 1950s the prison rate in Finland was about four times higher than in the Scandinavian neighboring countries (Denmark, Norway, Sweden). Since then the Finnish authorities systematically have endeavored to reduce the use of prison. Through decriminalization of offenses (most important public drunkenness), shorter sentences, more use of suspended sentences, community service, and heavy fines, the prison population has gradually decreased. In the 1990s it was on the same level as in the other Scandinavian countries, in which the prison rate has remained fairly stable (between 50 and 60 per 100,000 inhabitants).

Despite the great reduction of imprisonment in Finland the crime trend has been the same in all countries. The amount of crime has increased, but the curves are strikingly symmetric (Lappi-Seppälä, 1998). It should be added that the incapacitative effect of imprisonment plays a minor role in the Scandinavian countries as compared with the United States, which has much longer sentences and a prison population that is at least ten times higher (about 650 per 100,000 inhabitants in 1998).

The problem of communication. The motivating effect of criminal law does not depend on the objective realities of law and law enforcement but on the subjective perception of these realities in the mind of the citizen. A change that is not noticed can have no effect. If we intend, for example, to increase the deterrent effect in a certain field by more severe sentences or increased police activity, a crucial question will be whether people will become aware of the change. This aspect did not attract much attention in the classical theory of deterrence. It seemed to be tacitly assumed that there would be an accord between objective facts and subjective perceptions. Survey research into public beliefs and attitudes has demonstrated that this is far from the case. Smaller changes tend to go unnoticed whether they tend toward increased severity or leniency.

Types of offenses. The importance of deterrence is likely to vary substantially, depending on the character of the norm being protected by the threat of punishment. Common sense tells one that the threat of punishment does not play the same role in offenses as different as murder, incest, tax fraud, shoplifting, and illegal parking. One distinction of importance is between actions that are immoral in their own right, *mala in se*, and actions that are morally neutral if they were not prohibited by law, *mala prohibita*. In the case of *mala* per se, the law supports the moral codes of society. If the threat of legal punishment were removed, moral feelings and the fear of public judgment would remain as powerful crime-prevention forces. In the case of *mala prohibita* the law stands alone; without effective legal sanctions the prohibition would soon be empty words. There are, however, great variations within each of the two groups. As Leslie Wilkins stated, "The average normal housewife does not need to be deterred from poisoning her husband, but possibly does need a deterrent from shoplifting" (p. 322). A realistic appraisal of the role of deterrence demands a thorough study of the specific offense and the typical motivation of violators.

Differences among persons. People are not equally responsive to legal threats. Some are easily deterred, others may lack the intellectual or emotional ability to adjust their behavior to the demands of the law. Children, the insane, and the mentally deficient are for this reason poor objects of deterrence. The same holds true for people who lack the willpower to resist the desires and impulses of the moment, even when realizing that they may have to pay dearly for their self-indulgence. Individuals who are well integrated into the social fabric have more to lose by conviction than those on the margin of society. When experts and political decision-makers discuss the deterrent impact of the threat of punishment, there is always a risk that they may draw unjustified conclusions on the basis of experience limited to their own social groups.

Conflicting group norms. The motivating influence of the criminal law may become more or less neutralized by group norms working in the opposite direction. One may think of religious groups opposing compulsory military service, organized labor fighting against a prohibition of strikes, or a racial minority fighting against oppressive legislation. In such cases there is a conflict between the formalized laws of the state and the norms of the group. Against the moral influence of criminal law stands the moral influence of the group; against the fear of legal sanction stands the fear of group sanction, which may range from the loss of social status to economic boycott, violence, and even homicide. Experience shows that the force of the group norm often prevails. In an atmosphere of alienation and antagonism, any attempt at law enforcement, even a well-justified and lawful arrest, may be the signal for an outbreak of violence and disorder, as was the case with the Watts riot of 1965 (President's Commission, pp. 119–120).

Methods of research

In spite of the great importance accorded deterrence in lawmaking and sentencing, deterrence remained a neglected field of research until about 1970, in part because of ideology and in part because of great methodological difficulties. In subsequent years research activity has been intense. Most of the research falls under the following categories.

Comparison over time. The most straightforward method of exploring the effects of a change in legislation or enforcement on the rate of crime is before-and-after research. The great difficulty in such research is to identify the impact of the change among all the other factors that have been involved at the same time. Only abrupt and major changes can be expected to give clear statistical evidence of the effects. Changes introduced in the criminal justice system may be accompanied by changes in the tendency of the victims to report the crime or by changes in the practice of crime recording by the police, so that the statistics are not comparable. These difficulties can, to some degree, be overcome by victimization studies undertaken both before and after the reform.

Perhaps the best-known example of before-and-after research was conducted in Great Britain in connection with the Road Safety Act of 1967, which made it an offense to drive with a blood alcohol concentration of 0.08 percent or more. The penalty is normally a fine and loss of driving license for one year on the first offense. From the day the new legislation went into effect, there was a considerable drop in highway casualties as compared with previous years. For the first three months casualties were 16 percent lower than in the preceding year, and deaths were down by 23 percent. For the night hours casualties were reduced by about 40 percent. Unfortunately, it seems that most of the effect has gradually been lost. As time passed it became increasingly difficult to isolate the effects of the law, but H. Laurence Ross's conclusion seems well founded: the benefits produced by the legislation had largely been canceled by the end of 1970 (p. 77).

According to Ross, the explanation of this declining effect lies in a lack of enforcement. The publicity accompanying the law had given the public exaggerated and quite unrealistic ideas about the risk of apprehension and conviction, but little effort was made to enforce the law. The police did not perceive the law as defining an important task, and gradually the public learned that it had overestimated the risk.

The crucial importance of the risk of detection in this area is convincingly demonstrated by the effects of the Finnish reform of drinking-and-driving legislation in 1977 (Andenaes, 1988, pp. 42–63). Before the reform Finland had the most severe sentences for drunken driving among the Scandinavian countries, with prison sentences of several months. After the reform the great majority of offenders got fines or suspended prison sentences. At the same time a fixed limit of 0.05 percent blood-alcohol concentration was established, and the amount of random breath tests of drivers was drastically increased, from about 10,000 in 1977 to about 700,000 in 1984. Roadside surveys of a representative sample of drivers showed that the proportion of motorists driving under the influence of alcohol after the reform had been reduced to about half. The number of alcohol-related accidents also had diminished, although not to the same degree. The main reason for this probably is that many alcohol-related ac-

cidents are caused by drivers who have serious alcohol problems and do not react to the threat of punishment in the same way as average drivers.

Comparison between geographic areas. A second method is to compare areas with differences in legislation, in sentencing, or in law enforcement, to see whether these differences are reflected in crime rates. This method was used in research on capital punishment as early as the 1920s, by comparing murder rates in retentionist and abolitionist states. Beginning in the late 1960s the method of geographical comparison has been widely used for different types of crime, by both sociologists and economists, who have employed various statistical techniques in order to discover the effects of differences in certainty and severity of sanction. Most of the American studies use the individual states as units of comparison, are based on official statistics, and are limited to the seven index crimes (homicide, assault, rape, robbery, burglary, larceny, and auto theft, as enumerated by the Federal Bureau of Investigation).

The research has almost invariably found an inverse relationship between certainty of punishment (or rather certainty of imprisonment) and crime rates. Some, but not all, of the researchers have found a similar but mostly lower relationship between severity of punishment (normally measured in length of prison sentences) and crime rates. The findings are, however, difficult to interpret. A few points should be mentioned:

1. Many of the studies do not try to distinguish between effects of deterrence and effects of incapacitation. The effects they ascribe to deterrence may in fact be a result of the incapacitation of offenders sentenced to prison.
2. A correlation between crime rates and severity and certainty of sanction does not in itself say anything about the direction of causality. Crime rates may influence severity or certainty of sanction as well as the other way around. The correlation may also be the result of a third factor, for example, the normative climate in a society. Few of the studies tackle these problems in a wholly satisfactory way.
3. The statistical equations have certain built-in assumptions that are not necessarily true.
4. If a study does not find a correlation between crime rates and severity or certainty of sanction, this does not prove that the differences in severity or certainty are without effect but only that in the given sample the effect is not

of a sufficient magnitude to be statistically demonstrable.

5. As noted previously, official crime statistics fail to account for variations in rates of victim reporting and police recording of offenses. A low crime-reporting and/or recording rate tends to simultaneously lower the official crime rate, while raising the apparent rate of imprisonment; a high reporting or recording rate has the opposite effect. These variations naturally tend to produce a spurious inverse relationship between official crime rates and imprisonment rates.

For these and other reasons the comparative research should not be accepted uncritically. The highly technical character of such research also constitutes a barrier against practical application until a high degree of agreement among researchers is reached.

Survey research. Survey research can be of interest to the theory of deterrence in many ways. The simplest form of such research consists in collecting data on public knowledge and beliefs about the system of criminal justice. Studies have generally found that such knowledge is low and haphazard. Comparisons over time or between geographical areas of such surveys can be used to explore how perceptions of severity and certainty of punishment vary with actual severity and certainty.

The survey method seems especially suitable for research into the moral effects of criminal law. Attitude surveys in England before and after introduction of the blood-alcohol limit (Sheppard) showed that the new statute and the accompanying publicity did not have any tangible effect on the attitudes to drinking and driving. In contrast, a survey study from Norway, where similar but stricter legislation had been in force for forty years, indicated that the law had been successful in reaching the citizens with its message (Hauge). Thus, the two studies taken together give support to the view that the moral effect of the law depends on a longtime process.

Limits of research

The stream of research papers and the accompanying theoretical discussions have above all clarified the methodological problems and illustrated the limitations of different research methods. The research has produced fragments of knowledge that can be of use to check and supplement commonsense reasoning, which will have to be relied on for a long time to come. There is a long way to go before research can give quantitative forecasts about the effect on crime rates of contemplated changes in the system. Some researchers have tried to quantify their findings. The best-known example is Isaac Ehrlich's controversial work on the effects of capital punishment on the murder rate. According to Ehrlich, statistics on the use of capital punishment in the United States in the years from 1933 to 1969 indicated that each execution in this period had prevented seven to eight murders. The study has been severely criticized (see Beyleveld), and such quantitative assessments seem clearly premature.

It may be asked how far the problems of deterrence are at all researchable. The long-term moral effects of criminal law and law enforcement are especially hard to isolate and quantify. Some categories of crime are so intimately related to specific social situations that generalizations of a quantitative kind are impossible. One may think of race riots, corruption among politicians and public employees, and many types of white-collar crime. An inescapable fact is that research will always lag behind actual developments. When new forms of crime come into existence, as did hijacking of aircraft or terrorist acts against officers of the law, there cannot possibly be a body of research ready as a basis for the decisions that have to be taken. Common sense and trial and error have to give the answers.

Deterrence and public sentiment

Most serious students of crime and criminal justice probably would agree that the fluctuations in crime rates have more to do with social and economic changes than with changes in criminal law. However, the limited role of criminal justice has not become common knowledge. It seems that politicians as well as the general public tend to overestimate the deterrent effect of criminal law on crime rates. Moreover, in the political struggle more votes are won by promising to be tough on crime than by taking a moderate attitude. A complicating factor is that the invocation of deterrence may be a cloak for retributive feelings. This is most obvious with regard to the death penalty. In this field public sentiment in the United States contrasts sharply with that of the rest of the Western world.

JOHANNES ANDENAES

See also CAPITAL PUNISHMENT: MORALITY, POLITICS, AND POLICY; PUNISHMENT; SENTENCING: ALTERNATIVES.

BIBLIOGRAPHY

ANDENAES, JOHANNES. *Punishment and Deterrence*. Foreword by Norval Morris. Ann Arbor: University of Michigan Press, 1974.

———. "General Prevention Revisited: Research and Policy Implications." *Journal of Criminal Law and Criminology* 66 (1975): 338–365.

———. "The Scandinavian Experience." In *Social Control of the Drinking Driver*. Edited by Michael D. Lawrence, John R. Snortum, and Franklin E. Zimring. University of Chicago Press, 1988.

BECKER, G. S. "Crime and Punishment: An Economic Approach." *Journal of Political Economy* 76 (1968): 168–217.

BEYLEVELD, DERYCK. *A Bibliography on General Deterrence*. Aldershot, Hampshire, U.K.: Saxon House, 1980. The bibliography also gives summaries of and useful comments to the included studies.

BLUMSTEIN, ALFRED; COHEN, JACQUELINE; and NAGIN, DANIEL, eds. *Deterrence and Incapacitation: Estimating the Effects of Criminal Sanctions on Crime Rates*. Washington, D.C.: National Academy of Sciences, 1978.

EHRLICH, ISAAC. "The Deterrent Effect of Capital Punishment: A Question of Life and Death." *American Economic Review* 65 (1975): 397–417. For full references and commentaries to the controversy, see Beyleveld, pp. 184–201, 382–385.

EIDE, ERLING. *Economics of Crime. Deterrence and the Rational Offender*. North-Holland, Amsterdam, The Netherlands: Elsevier Science B.V., 1994.

GIBBS, JACK P. *Crime, Punishment, and Deterrence*. New York: Elsevier, 1975.

HAUGE, RAGNAR. "Drinking-and-Driving: Biochemistry, Law, and Morality." *Scandinavian Studies in Criminology* 6 (1978): 61–68.

LAPPI-SEPPÄLÄ, TAPIO. "General Prevention—Hypotheses and Empirical Evidence." *Ideologi og empiri i kriminologien*. Rapport fra NSfKs 37. forskerseminar, Sverige (1995): pp. 136–159.

———. *Regulating the Prison Population. Experience from a Long-Term Policy in Finland*. Helsinki: National Research Institute of Legal Policy, 1998.

President's Commission on Law Enforcement and Administration of Justice, Task Force on Assessment of Crime. *Task Force Report: Crime and Its Impact—An Assessment*. Washington, D.C.: The Commission, 1967.

ROSS, H. LAURENCE. "Law, Science, and Accidents: The British Road Safety Act of 1967." *Journal of Legal Studies* 2 (1973): 1–78.

SHEPPARD, D. *The 1967 Drink-and-Driving Campaign: A Survey among Drivers*. Road Research Laboratory Report LR230. Crowthorne, Berkshire, U.K.: Ministry of Transport, 1968.

VON HIRSCH, ANDREW; BOTTOMS, ANTHONY E.; BURNEY, ELIZABETH; and WIKSTRÖM, PER-OLOF. *Criminal Deterrence and Sentence Severity: An Analysis of Recent Research*. Oxford, U.K.: Hart Publishing Ltd., 1999.

WILKINS, LESLIE T. "Criminology: An Operational Research Approach." In *Society: Problems and Methods of Study*. Edited by A. T. Welford. London: Routledge & Kegan Paul, 1962. Pages 311–337.

ZIMRING, FRANKLIN E., and HAWKINS, GORDON J. *Deterrence: The Legal Threat in Crime Control*. Foreword by James Vorenberg. Chicago: University of Chicago Press, 1973.

DEVELOPING COUNTRIES, CRIME IN

At the beginning of the twenty-first century, the prevalent conception of societal change is still encapsulated by the term *development* (Escobar). Definitions vary, but many emphasize a relatively optimistic view of history (often called *modernization*) in which development refers to the increased use of technology, increased generation of wealth, and increased attention to democratic procedures and human rights in government. Even critical visions of history recognize the semantic dominance of the term, while disputing its content: Marxist scholars typically refer to *underdevelopment* to describe the negative consequences generated by the exploitative links between richer and poorer countries. Since the 1990s, much attention has focused on rapid increases in global interconnection, but the attendant conceptual framework—*globalization*—has yet to dethrone development as the dominant perspective on societal change.

When understood as modernization, development includes the growth of science, and therefore criminology. Indeed, historical and contemporary descriptions show that the evolution of criminology closely parallels the process of economic growth. Thus, the discipline came into existence as the industrial revolution was being born in western Europe, and subsequently spread as other parts of the world achieved economic progress. Social control, of course, is found in every society. But criminology—the application of scientific methods to the crime problem—has developed unevenly around the world. The bulk of research on crime is to be found in the wealthiest nations, although wealth is not a perfect correlate of criminological activity.

The concept of development not only serves to illuminate the history of criminology, but also provides a lens through which many criminologists see the world. Given the widely embraced goal of producing general explanations of crime, which hold across time and place, the comparative dearth of information on the poorer countries is a problem. In the rudimentary regional terminology common to developmental perspectives, explanations originating in the *developed* countries might not be valid in the *developing* countries; hence the need to test theories there. However, different levels of development also provoke an alternative approach to theorizing because they focus attention on the association between societal change and crime. Cross-national studies of development and crime offer the tempting possibility of theoretically significant findings based on samples of developed and developing countries, thereby avoiding the parochialism that apparently plagues much of the discipline.

Nevertheless, the cumulative result of criminological inquiry over the last twenty years reveals the problems of adopting a developmental perspective on crime. The simple division of the world into developed and developing countries is now beginning to look simplistic; the theoretical utility of development as an explanatory concept for crime seems limited. While the process of development is of central importance for understanding the rise of criminology, the concept of development is not of central importance for understanding crime. The continuing global diffusion of the discipline may be relatively unobjectionable, but the conceptual framework of development is likely to be discarded in the future.

Information on crime and criminal justice

The comparative state of information on crime and criminal justice around the world should not blind us entirely to absolute standards of evaluation. Thus, although data systems in the richest countries are well established, they are still inadequate in many ways (Lynch). Similarly, it is all too easy to assume that little or nothing exists in the developing world, a state of affairs belied by the growing volume of databases and edited collections that routinely include developing countries (e.g., Barak; Heiland et al.). Governments in developing countries have included at least basic information-gathering on crime and criminal justice as part of their bureaucratic routine for quite some time. Moreover, NGOs (non-governmental organizations) and other research groups have recently begun collecting more information on crime, partly in response to the perceived crisis in personal safety in many developing countries.

Nevertheless, there is no doubt that databases in the developing countries offer shorter time series, with larger gaps and fewer variables for the criminologist. The United Nations' Global Report on Crime and Justice, compiled with mainly official statistics in the late 1990s, was able to include ninety-one of the world's two hundred or so countries, but the developing countries were greatly underrepresented (Newman). The situation is similar if we examine the most important alternative to official statistics on crime and criminal justice: the International Crime Victim Survey (ICVS). The ICVS is a standardized survey asking questions about household and personal victimizations, reporting to the police, and subjects' fear of crime. Its first three sweeps (1989, 1992, 1996) included fifty-five countries, but the proportional representation of developing countries was much lower (van Dijk). Moreover, the sample frame in the developed countries was national, but in developing countries it was confined to a major urban area. While a global count of other victim surveys would be difficult to accomplish, there seems little reason to doubt that they have also been more abundant in the developed nations. Finally, self-report surveys of involvement in crime and delinquency appear to repeat the same pattern. The first International Self-Report Delinquency Study, asking males and females aged fourteen to twenty-one about involvement in common delinquent acts, was confined to thirteen developed countries, and other cross-national projects using this type of survey methodology are uncommon. Examples of single self-report studies from developing countries can be found, but far less frequently than in the developed countries.

The reasons for the comparative lack of data on crime in developing countries have not been systematically studied, but are probably not hard to find. Undoubtedly the scarcity of resources is a major contributing factor. With a sevenfold difference in gross national product between richer

516 DEVELOPING COUNTRIES, CRIME IN

and poorer countries, it is not surprising that governments in the developing world dedicate relatively little attention to information gathering. An additional reason may be that governmental social control is less salient in developing countries and therefore many crimes, and responses to crime, are unrecorded. Numerous studies describe patterns of crime and responses to crime in preliterate societies, rural communities, and low income urban neighborhoods where official intervention is rare (Abel). Finally, governmental crime control in many developing countries appears to make less use of planning, with its typical emphasis on the production of quality data for diagnosis, policy development, and evaluation. If decision-making is not based on systematic information, there is less interest in fostering data collection.

If these are the causes of the comparative lack of data in developing countries, it is evident that substantial improvements will not be rapid. It is by no means certain that poorer nations will get wealthier, that governments will penetrate and consolidate their hold over national territories, or that politicians will overcome their resistance to statistics. The most promising area for criminology is in international initiatives to encourage or support increased data gathering, such as the United Nations Surveys of Crime Trends and Operation of Justice Systems, which have been conducted every five years since 1977, or the growing number of cross-national studies supported by national or international funding agencies. The databases that result from these projects will help to provide better answers to the questions asked by both practitioners and theoreticians in criminology (Howard et al.).

Studies of crime in developing countries are not only hampered by missing cases and variables, but also by the often formidable difficulties involved in constructing comparisons for any international data set (Neapolitan). One problem involves varied legal definitions of crime. Burglary, for example, is recognized as a separate type of theft in common law countries, but not in civil code countries. A second problem involves varied perceptions of what constitutes a crime. Hitting a child, taking property without permission, and making gifts to public officials, for example, have no constant moral or legal status around the world. Third, levels of crime-reporting and police-recording diligence are also variable. Neuman and Berger's speculation that officially recorded crime rates are related to levels of development has received recent support from

data on reporting rates for common crimes: they are highest in the New World (North America, Australia, New Zealand) and Western Europe, lowest in Latin America and Asia (van Dijk).

Confronted by these problems, comparisons based on official statistics are best confined to homicide because its definition tends to be less varied than those of other types of crime, while the seriousness of murder leads to recording rates that are closer to 100 percent (LaFree). Official rates of other types of crime are better treated at face value (a measure of police knowledge of crimes), or at most as a surrogate measure of public demand for police intervention. Thus, if comparisons based on official statistics must be restricted to one of the least frequent offenses, alternative measures of crime are extremely important. While victimization surveys have considerable limitations, they are able to measure a range of common crimes and eliminate most of the legal, if not the cultural, variation in the definition of crime. For that reason, the relatively standardized information collected through the ICVS represents a notable recent addition to our knowledge about crime in developing countries, although it must be remembered that the samples are drawn exclusively from large urban areas.

Crime rates and trends in developing countries

Comparisons based on official homicide rates and ICVS data reveal quite similar regional patterns. Latin America and Africa lead the world in crime rates. Western Europe and the New World have relatively low crime rates, but not always the lowest, for those are also to be found—depending on the specific comparison—in the Arab or Asian countries. For common crimes (property crimes that affect households, and thefts, assaults, and sexual incidents involving individuals), the ICVS finds that the rate of victimization over the previous five years in urban areas is lowest in Asia (excluding Japan; 45.0%), highest in Latin America (76.6%) and Africa (74.0%), while both the New World and Western Europe are close to the mean (van Dijk). When broken down by type of victimization, this pattern is largely repeated, except for car related crimes (car theft, theft from cars, car vandalism), which are considerably more frequent in the New World and Western Europe, most probably reflecting the much larger number of cars in those countries.

Officially recorded homicide rates show a similar pattern. Rates are highest in Latin America and Africa, lower in North America, eastern Europe, and South Asia, and lowest in the Arab states and western Europe. However, the magnitude of these differences is greater than in the victimization data: the median homicide rate in Latin American countries is nearly nine times that of the Arab countries. White collar crime, as measured by a question in the 1996 ICVS about the solicitation of bribes by government officials during the previous year, was most prevalent in Latin America (21.3%), Africa (18.8%), and Asia (14.6%), moderately high in central and eastern Europe (10.7%), and lowest in western Europe and the New World (1% or less).

There is almost no comparative analysis of trends in crime rates in the developed and developing countries. However, van Dijk reports that victimization rates have declined in the most industrialized countries, while there is no evidence of a similar decline in other parts of the world. The relative recency of the ICVS means that this finding should be treated as provisional.

What these results suggest is that a simple division of the world into developed and developing countries, at least based on cross-sectional crime rates, is problematic. The fact that regions of the developing world tend to lie at both extremes on measures of prevalence indicates that differences between developing countries are greater than the differences between the developing and developed worlds. The long-standing but frequently ignored caution from criminologists to avoid oversimplified generalizations about regional crime patterns has not lost its relevance. Moreover, this finding also implies that attempts to link development and crime rates are likely to face uncooperative data.

Explaining crime in developing countries

Criminologists working in both developed and developing countries occasionally insinuate that crime in developing countries requires a separate explanation. However, such an enterprise contradicts the generally accepted goal of parsimony in theorizing. While every culture in the world has the potential for generating rich insights into the nature and causes of crime, any explanation of crime in developing countries should also be an explanation of crime in the developed countries.

The development of criminology has confined almost all theorizing to the developed world, thereby raising nagging doubts about the generality of its propositions (Beirne and Nelken). But the regional imagery inherent in developmental terminology obscures the complex relationship between theories and places. As with the state of data, the comparative progress of theory testing should not blind us to absolute progress. The tendency is to assume that theories originating in the developed world have received substantial empirical support there, making tests in developing countries the crucial arbiter of generality. In fact, tests in the developed world are neither numerous nor consistently supportive, such that the empirical validity of these theories is still an open—and global—question. For example, Travis Hirschi's control theory, one of the discipline's most influential perspectives, had been tested seventy-one times by 1991, all of them in developed countries. Yet many methodological difficulties had been encountered in those tests, and the validity of the theory has not been definitely confirmed or negated (Kempf). Thus, tests of criminological theories in the varied social and cultural environments of developing countries, while almost nonexistent, are of potentially great value.

An alternative route to theoretical progress, and one that starts by including at least some developing countries, has been the search for associations between diverse measures of development and the rate or type of crime in cross-national samples. Typical variables are urbanization, income inequality, unemployment, and age structure, and findings have varied quite substantially, due to the use of different developmental indicators, different measures of crime, different samples, and different statistical models (Bennett). The heterogeneous crime rates within the developing world, discussed in the previous section, also underline the difficulty of finding robust associations between development and crime.

Using data for forty-nine countries from the ICVS, van Dijk found that higher rates for the most serious household and personal victimizations were substantially accounted for by a greater proportion of the population living in larger cities, a higher proportion of young males who are dissatisfied with their household income, and a lower level of affluence. Victimization rates for all personal crimes were positively correlated with the proportion of young males dissatisfied with household income, the rate of gun ownership, and affluence; and negatively correlated with the average level of education. Studies of homicide tend to find that homicide rates are positively correlated with economic inequality and population growth, negatively related to economic development, industrialization, and urbanization, and unrelated to unemployment, social or cultural heterogeneity, and the proportion of young people in the population (LaFree). Overall, these findings reveal that the correlates of specific crime types are not the same, making it difficult to summarize the impact of development on crime.

Notwithstanding the variability in results, criminologists have attempted to link development and crime through recourse to several theories (Neuman and Berger). A common strategy starts from Durkheim's study of societal change, highlighting the relatively abrupt transition from traditional to modern social systems and the consequent disruption of normative standards. This leads to an argument that increased crime in developing countries results from weakened social controls. Other studies start from Durkheim's concept of *anomie* and postulate economic stress, or *strain*, as the primary explanation. Although they work from a different theoretical foundation, Marxist criminologists arrive at a similar hypothesis about the positive correlation between economic inequality and crime rates. Finally, some criminologists have adopted a situational perspective, arguing that development increases the opportunity for most forms of property crime, but decreases the ecological prerequisites for violent encounters.

Unfortunately, researchers are often vague about the theoretical link between development and crime. Probably a major reason for this is that measures of development are operationally distant from the two concepts that dominate criminology's efforts to explain crime: motivation and opportunity. For example, inequality is a measure of the concentration of income in a national population, which indicates nothing directly about the motivation to commit crime. Nevertheless, it has been used as a measure of both normative disruption and strain. Similarly, urbanization has been used as an indicator of both motivation and opportunity. When the same variable can be interpreted in different ways, its theoretical utility is greatly reduced. Given that developmental indicators are limited to those gathered by governments, covering basic demographic, economic, and social characteristics but nothing so sophisticated or abstract as criminal motivation and opportunity, the most that can be expected from the development and crime literature are informed speculations about the causes of crime in developing countries, but not the rigorous evaluation of theory.

Responses to crime in developing countries

The last two centuries have witnessed the diffusion of criminal justice models from developed to developing countries, initially through colonization, subsequently through technical missions and consultants (Gómez Buendía). In developing countries, criminal codes and procedures, models of police organization, and prison systems all bear signs of the influence of the developed countries—a situation that has prompted much research, often critical, into the assimilation process. Rather than simple organizational transfer, the evolution of criminal justice systems in developing countries has involved selective appropriation and frequent *creolization* (adaptation) of Western models of crime control (Salvatore and Aguirre).

Against this background of relatively slow institutional change, concerns over crime in the late twentieth century produced some important short-term responses in developing countries. Statistics indicate that citizens are making more demands for police services, as measured by the increasing numbers of crimes reported to the police, and that urban inhabitants are reporting high levels of concern about personal safety and the protection of property (Zvekic and Alvazzi del Frate). Support for legal punishment, especially imprisonment, and for dubiously legal actions such as police shootings of civilians, is comparatively high. However, criminal justice agencies are perceived as inefficient and sometimes threatening, leading to the selective expansion of informal social control, especially greater protective measures, together with the exercize of, or support for, direct action against offenders, such as lynchings. Crime, and the fear of crime, have come to dominate and shape the urban ambiance in many developing countries (Caldeira).

CHRISTOPHER BIRKBECK

See also COMPARATIVE CRIMINAL LAW AND ENFORCEMENT: CHINA; COMPARATIVE CRIMINAL LAW AND ENFORCEMENT: ISLAM; COMPARATIVE CRIMINAL LAW AND ENFORCEMENT: PRELITERATE SOCIETIES; CRIME CAUSATION: POLITICAL THEORIES; CRIME CAUSATION: SOCIOLOGICAL THEORIES; STATISTICS: HISTORICAL TRENDS IN WESTERN SOCIETIES.

BIBLIOGRAPHY

ABEL, RICHARD L., ed. *The Politics of Informal Justice: Comparative Studies*. New York: Academic Press, 1981.

BARAK, GREGG, ed. *Crime and Crime Control. A Global View*. Westport, Conn.: Greenwood Press, 2000.

BEIRNE, PIERS, and NELKEN, DAVID, eds. *Issues in Comparative Criminology*. Aldershot, U.K.: Dartmouth/Ashgate, 1997.

———. "Routine Activities: A Cross-National Assessment of a Criminological Perspective." *Social Forces* 70 (1991): 147–163.

CALDEIRA, TERESA P. *City of Walls: Crime, Segregation and Citizenship in Sao Paulo*. Berkeley, Calif.: University of California Press, 2001.

DURKHEIM, ÉMILE. *Selected Writings*. Cambridge, U.K.: Cambridge University Press, 1972.

ESCOBAR, ARTURO. *Encountering Development: The Making and Unmaking of the Third World*. Princeton, N.J.: Princeton University Press, 1994.

GÓMEZ BUENDÍA, HERNANDO, ed. *Urban Crime: Global Trends and Policies*. Tokyo, Japan: The United Nations University, 1989.

HEILAND, HANS-GÜNTHER; SHELLEY, LOUISE; and KATOH, HISAO, eds. *Crime and Control in Comparative Perspectives*. New York: Walter de Gruyter, 1992.

HOWARD, GREGORY J.; NEWMAN, GRAEME; and PRIDEMORE, WILLIAM ALEX. "Theory, Method, and Data in Comparative Criminology." In *Criminal Justice 2000, Volume 4: Measurement and Analysis of Crime and Justice*. Edited by David Duffee. Washington, D.C.: National Institute of Justice, 2000. Pages 139–211.

KEMPF, KIMBERLY L. "The Empirical Status of Hirschi's Control Theory." *Advances in Criminological Theory* 4 (1993): 143–186.

LAFREE, GARY. "A Summary and Review of Cross-National Comparative Studies of Homicide." In *Homicide Studies: A Sourcebook of Social Research*. Edited by M. Dwayne Smith and Margaret A. Zahn. Thousand Oaks, Calif.: Sage, 1998. Pages 125–145.

LYNCH, JAMES. "Crime in International Perspective." In *Crime*. Edited by James Q. Wilson and Joan Petersilia. San Francisco, Calif.: ICS Press, 1995. Pages 11–37.

NEAPOLITAN, JEROME L. *Cross-National Crime: A Research Review and Sourcebook*. Westport, Conn.: Greenwood Press, 1997.

NEUMAN, W. LAWRENCE, and BERGER, RONALD J. "Competing Perspectives on Cross-National Crime: An Evaluation of Theory and Evidence." *The Sociological Quarterly* 29, no. 2 (1988): 281–313.

NEWMAN, GRAEME, M., ed. *Global Report on Crime and Justice*. New York: Oxford University Press, 1999.

SALVATORE, RICARD D., and AGUIRRE, CARLOS. *The Birth of the Penitentiary in Latin America*. Austin, Tex.: University of Texas Press, 1996.

VAN DIJK, JAN J. M. "The Experience of Crime and Justice." In *Global Report on Crime and Justice*. Edited by Graeme Newman. New York: Oxford University Press, 1999.

ZVEKIC, UGLJESA, and ALVAZZI DEL FRATE, ANNA. *Criminal Victimisation in the Developing World*. Rome: United Nations Interregional Crime and Justice Research Institute, 1995.

DEVIANCE

The term "deviance" usually refers to some behavior that is inconsistent with standards of acceptable conduct prevailing in a given social group, although the term has also been used to designate personal conditions, ideas, or statuses that are stigmatized or disreputable. Social scientists disagree about a precise definition of deviance because they use different approaches in trying to determine exactly what the standards of conduct or the acceptable statuses and conditions are in a given group (Gibbs, 1981). At least five ways of conceptualizing deviance are used.

Conceptualizations of deviance

The statistical approach. One way of defining standards of conduct and deviance from them is to observe how people in a particular group actually behave (Wilkins, 1964). Accordingly, if a large proportion of people in a group smoke cigarettes, smoking is "normal" while failure to smoke would be atypical, or deviant. With a "statistical" perspective, sky diving, eating snails, and murder are all deviant in the United States since they are all unusual. On the other hand, highway speeding, "fudging" on one's income tax, and pilfering small items from employers are all conforming behaviors since they are currently committed by a fairly large proportion, if not a majority, of the population.

A statistical approach rests on a common observation: many people assume that something that "everybody does" cannot be in violation of conduct standards. Indeed, a frequent justification (or rationalization) for conduct that is being threatened with sanctions is to claim that everybody else or at least most others do it. And, many people decide what is appropriate by watching what others do.

Even though a statistical approach appears to correspond with the everyday thinking of many laypersons, it is not widely used by social scientists. Scholars have found that statistical patterns only superficially reflect how social groups formulate standards of conduct. Most people in the United States, for example, would feel uncomfortable classifying behaviors like church tithing, abstinence from all alcohol use, and maintenance of premarital sexual virginity (all atypical behaviors) as "deviant." There is an underlying agreement that even though they are unusual, these behaviors are somehow "good," acceptable, even desirable, and that they are to be encouraged as ways of behaving. Similarly, most people feel discomfort in thinking of adultery, lying to one's spouse or sweetheart, or pilfering from an employer as appropriate, even though they are frequently committed by a large proportion of the populace. Yet, most can easily endorse the inappropriateness of acts that are atypical in a negative way—more evil, unacceptable, or undesirable than the average. Therefore, most students of deviance contend that despite some tendency for people to refer to statistical guidelines, normative standards mainly revolve around notions of rightness and wrongness or with what people think others "ought" to do.

The absolutist approach. A second approach applies ideal conduct standards set down by a social scientist (or group of social scientists) to all groups and individuals under study. A social scientist decides what is good, useful, or just, and then measures deviations from those evaluative criteria. For example, some theorists (functionalists) view societies as interdependent mechanisms; all parts that work together for maintenance of the society are regarded as essential and in that sense "good" or nondeviant. But a society may contain dysfunctional (dangerous or destructive) elements (see Gross), which are regarded as deviant. Most who use this approach assume that societies will usually condone inherently good behaviors and condemn those that are inherently bad. Indeed, it has been argued that contemporary societies exist because throughout evolutionary history they practiced and condoned useful behavior while avoiding and condemning dangerous behavior. Presumably, social groups that failed to do this did not survive the ravages of time (Parsons).

Functionalists assume that an investigator can, through logic and research, actually determine what is good for a society. For example, incest is thought to be dysfunctional (Davis; Murphy) because if widely practiced, it could lead to biological deterioration of the population, destruction of orderly social relations, and disruption of the mechanisms for efficient child rearing. According to some, therefore, incest is inherently and obviously deviant because it is socially dangerous. Most members of any existing society presumably will disapprove of incest and will refrain from practicing it because only those societies that in the past developed and enforced social rules prohibiting incest would have survived to be represented in the contemporary world. Similar arguments can be made for murder, rape, assault, homosexuality, child abuse, mental illness, and other behaviors.

Other absolutist thinkers employ a different rationale. Radical, Marxist, and humanist scholars often maintain that a sensitive informed researcher can apply absolute moral standards to behavior in any given society or specific situation to decide whether various activities are unjust or evil (deviant) (Schwendinger and Schwendinger). Some believe that any exploitation of one person or a category of persons for the benefit of another, or any conduct that threatens the dignity and quality of life for specific people or humanity as a whole, is inherently evil, and thereby deviant (Simon). Others contend that any behavior causing people to suffer or violating any person's right to self-actualization and freedom is inherently immoral, or deviant (Platt). Marxist scholars, for instance, point up the exploitative nature of economic relations in capitalistic societies and regard this inherent exploitation, along with the selfish and insensitive acts it breeds, as deviant or "criminal" because it corrupts human qualities (Bonger; Quinney, 1970, 1980). Similarly, humanists regard racial discrimination as deviant because it deprives a whole group of people of equal rights and human dignity.

Absolutist approaches to deviance are not widely used because of their subjectivity. Trained (sensitized), careful observers disagree about what is good or bad for society, what is contrary to human dignity, and what is fair or unfair. And what one observer believes to be functional for a society another may find dysfunctional. It has even been argued that a certain amount of deviance itself may benefit society. Dealing with deviance may help a group differentiate its members, crystalize the norms so group members will know how to behave, provide a means for tension to be reduced, keep the mechanisms of social control in good working order so that they will be efficient in true emergencies, and generate cohesion as the members of a group unite in opposition to deviance (Cohen, 1966; Dentler and Erikson). Since there is no reason to believe that the values or insights of social scientists are in any way superior, more desirable, or defensible than those of anyone else, or that the values of any particular social scientist are any more justifiable than those of another social scientist, an absolutist approach in the study of deviance cannot be used in a consistent and meaningful way.

The legalistic approach. A third way of identifying conduct standards and deviant behavior is to simply use illegality as the criterion of whether a given activity is in violation of behavioral norms. Accordingly, if the law prohibits an act, it is deviant; and if the law requires an act, failure to perform it is deviant. If the law is silent about, or permits, an act, then that act is considered consistent with conduct standards, or conforming.

The rationale for a legal criterion of deviance differs depending on how the law is viewed. Some contend that the law expresses collective sentiment indicating that particular activities are dangerous or threatening enough to require efforts at control (see Tittle, 1994). Although recognizing that law making is a political process, which often reflects conflicting interests and the clash of power, some nevertheless believe that, in the main, law reflects popular sentiment as well as efforts to promote the public good.

Others see the law as an instrument by which the powerful maintain their elite positions and protect their privileges, but these scholars accept illegality as the appropriate criterion of behavioral standards because they believe conformity and deviance are inherently whatever people powerful enough to impose their own views say they are. Accordingly, norms (or conduct standards) are "definitions of the situation" imposed upon a social group by power elites (McCaghy; Quinney).

Still others view law as a combination of popular sentiment and elite desires. They contend that some law expresses consensus among the population (such as laws prohibiting assault, murder, child abuse) while other laws reflect the desires of special interests (such as laws prohibiting importation of competitive products, requiring licenses to provide certain services, or denying the right of laborers to strike). For these scholars, whether law is collectively or particularistically oriented is irrelevant; in both instances, law expresses coercive potential—a key element of behavioral norms. Thus, the conduct rules that matter are those that can be enforced. Since the law reflects behavioral rules backed up by power of enforcement, it necessarily encompasses conduct norms—at least those worth social scientists' study.

A legalistic approach is straightforward and usually easily applied (since a scholar need only refer to the codification of laws), and it hinges on an extremely important element of social life—the exercise of political power. Moreover, a related body of inquiry—criminology—almost exclusively uses a legalistic approach to define its subject matter. Yet the legalistic conceptualization is not generally used for the larger study of deviance, of which crime may be a part. For one thing, not all societies have a clearly defined body of written statutes that can be identified as law. Primitive societies, for example, have deviant behavior but no formally written law that defines it as such (Malinowski; Hoebel). Using a legalistic approach in nonliterate societies assumes the resolution of a prior definitional problem—what is law?

In addition, in any society many of the activities that are illegal nevertheless appear to be normatively acceptable. For instance, despite legal prohibitions on the sale of tobacco products to minors, in many places such products are easily available to minors in vending machines and minors are officially allowed to smoke in designated areas by many schools. Moreover, it is rare for the police to arrest anyone for selling tobacco to minors; and most people may not regard such sale as bad, dangerous, or abnormal (although public opinion about this appears to be undergoing a change). Thus, laws are often out of synch with actual behavior and public sentiment, sometimes because society changes without the laws being changed or repealed and sometimes because laws result from political action by interest groups whose agendas may not correspond with views of the general public.

By contrast, many activities that appear to be inconsistent with general conduct standards are not illegal. It is not a crime to lie to one's spouse or sweetheart although evidence suggests that a large proportion of the people disapprove of it (Tittle, 1980). Similarly in some places it is not illegal to operate a topless bar, yet such establishments frequently meet with scorn, protests, and sometimes violent opposition by neighbors. Further, legal statutes rarely prohibit eating human flesh although it is clearly outside the bounds of acceptable conduct in contemporary societies.

Finally, despite the importance of the legal realm, conduct norms are not limited to that realm but instead are ubiquitous at all levels of social life from the interpersonal to the societal. A legalistic approach, therefore, narrowly focuses attention on one tier of a multi-tiered system.

The reactive approach.   A fourth way of defining deviance is by social reaction (what people do about behavior or a condition). According to this approach, when social reaction to some behavior is condemnatory, punitive, or simply disapproving, it indicates that the behavior is in violation of behavioral standards prevailing in that group and is therefore deviant. One variation of the reactive approach emphasizes the "typical" reaction to a class of behaviors. Another stresses social reaction to particular instances of behavior while assuming that this particular reaction implies nothing about the deviance of the entire class of behaviors of which the particular case is an instance. Such basic differences are complicated by questions concerning which part of the social system must react negatively to qualify something as deviant. Some emphasize negative reactions by official agents and functionaries, but others accord more importance to informal reactions by a collective social audience.

Probably the best-known reactive approach to deviance is that embodied in the "labeling perspective" (Tannenbaum; Becker; Schur; Gove). Labeling theorists do not agree about their focus, and they are sometimes ambiguous in presentation. Nevertheless, most scholars agree that the predominant concern of the labeling perspective is legal reaction to specific acts, particularly the reaction of agents of the criminal justice system (such as police) to particular instances of behavior disapproved by power holders, whose interests are embodied in the legal codes (Gove). Accordingly, some labeling proponents recognize no categories or classes of deviant behavior. To them, murder, rape, child abuse, or smoking marijuana are not necessarily deviant. Rather, specific acts of murder, rape, child abuse, or marijuana use may or may not be deviant depending upon whether officials arrest the perpetrator and label him/her as deviant. When labeling occurs, the particular act of murder, rape, child abuse, or marijuana use is deviant; otherwise, it is not.

Some labeling theorists are more restrictive in what they define as deviant. They maintain that an act is not deviant unless and until a collective social audience has accepted the label of deviant for the act and/or the perpetrator. It is said that a label attached by officials must "stick"; that

is, it must be recognized by a social audience and serve as the vehicle through which the group attributes bad character to the actor, or attributes badness to the act (Becker; Kitsuse).

Another variant of the reactionist approach accepts the generally deviant nature of some categories of behavior. Accordingly, if a social collectivity or its chief representatives typically react negatively to some behavior or typically attach a stigma to those who are caught, that kind of behavior is deviant even if a particular perpetrator escapes being labeled. For instance, if a social group usually shows its condemnation of some class of behaviors by punishing specific acts of that class or if it usually attributes bad character to those who commit such acts, then theorists would assume that in that social group those behaviors are deviant. Using this approach, apprehension, punishment, or group attribution of bad character for a specific act may be treated as problematic but such actions are not essential for a given act to be deviant.

Still another variation of the reactive/labeling approach does not limit itself to behavior but includes as deviance, statuses, states of being, or physical conditions (Lemert). According to this approach, "deviance" inheres in disreputable or pejorative statuses, styles of life, or physical attributes; therefore, deviance is a condition not a behavior or set of behaviors. Accordingly, race, gender, poverty, and criminality have all been identified as stigmatized "deviant" statuses while physical handicaps, unattractive appearances, speech impediments, and small statures have been designated as stigmatized conditions qualifying as deviant. Although most approaches to deviance raise issues about how and why particular acts or categories of acts come to be deviant and why individuals come to commit acts that are deviant or that are likely to be regarded as deviant, this particular approach poses different questions—how stigma comes about and how people who are targets of stigma react to, or manage, the deviant identity associated with it.

The reactive approach has been widely used, and during the 1960s and 1970s was the dominant orientation. Even now many people associate the study of deviance exclusively with the reactive approach. This popularity stemmed partly from the key idea that deviant acts or conditions are those disapproved, either by officials or by group members, or in one version of this approach, are considered important enough by key functionaries of the social system to warrant attention. The reactive approach was also popular because of the appeal of the larger labeling argument, from which many of the reactive conceptualizations sprang. The notion that deviant behavior and stigmatized conditions are highly problematic intrigued many. Moreover, the contentions of the labeling school that deviance is a creation of the very forces intending to do something about it and that designating acts as deviant represents unequal power in action, with large consequences for those labeled and for society, meshed with the ideological bent of many social scientists of the time.

In due course, however, numerous problems caused the reactive approach to lose its dominance. Among other concerns, many behaviors that appear to be in violation of conduct standards are not necessarily the focus of negative reactions, especially not official reactions. For instance, adultery in the United States is almost never dealt with by the police or the courts, and it rarely results in a deviant label for the actor. Even when there are citizen complaints, the police normally refuse to make arrests. Yet surveys show that most people believe adultery to be wrong, bad, or inappropriate, and it is thought by many social scientists to have crucial implications for a major social institution—the family.

Furthermore, the police frequently arrest people, and courts sometimes impose severe penalties, for behaviors that are not widely disapproved and do not seem to have much impact on society (such as marijuana use during the 1960s). Third, the narrower reactive definitions created unusual conceptual inconsistencies. If murder is regarded as deviant only when discovered and reacted against by official agents, then it must also be regarded as conformity if the perpetrator escapes punishment—regardless of the number of group members who may disapprove of it, how socially dangerous it might be, or how many people do it. Moreover, according to this kind of reactive definition, deviance can only be studied on a case-by-case basis after the fact, thereby making generalization or consideration and explanation of categories of deviance impossible.

Finally, practical application of some reactive definitions has proven difficult. Empirically ascertaining when labeling has occurred (is an arrest a labeling act, or must one be convicted?) or when a label sticks (how do we know the boundaries of a social audience, how many must accept the label, what constitutes stigma?) renders some versions of the reactive approach almost completely unworkable (see Gove). Furthermore, those reactive definitions that focus on disreputable statuses and conditions raise limited questions leading to repetitious research about the importance of power in the stigmatization process and about the way various stigmatized people manage their identities. In addition, evidence and logical critiques have eroded the luster of labeling theory, which had earlier energized reactive approaches (Gibbs, 1966; Gove; Hagan, 1973; Mankoff; Wellford).

The group evaluation approach. A fifth method of identifying conduct standards and deviance is by the beliefs or opinions of group members. Accordingly, deviant behavior is that regarded as unacceptable, inappropriate, or morally wrong in the opinion of the members of a group. One problem is deciding how many people in a group must believe some behavior to be unacceptable for it to qualify as deviance, although it is generally assumed that a significant consensus exists among group members about rightness or wrongness and about how people ought to behave. If this assumption is correct, social disapproval indicates that some behavior is outside acceptable standards of conduct. And such disapproval would suggest deviance regardless of the typicality or prevalence of the behavior, whether anything is actually done about the offense, or whether the shared concepts about rightness or wrongness grew out of common experiences or out of careful socialization by particular interest groups with an investment in promoting specific ideas.

A group evaluational definition of deviance has never been the dominant approach although it is conceptually clear, has intuitive meaning, permits deviance to be treated meaningfully as a continuous variable expressing the extent to which different behaviors are disapproved, and provokes many sociologically relevant questions—such as why some people do disapproved things, why and how social processes sometimes produce shared opinions of disapproval, why general opinions sometimes change, and why social processes sometimes come to activate collective responses to behavior but not at other times. Perhaps the major reason for under use of the group evaluational approach is its assumption that all group members' opinions are of equal value. Research shows that the opinions of some are more important than the opinions of others because some people can implement their opinions with coercive action, and some are more influential in persuading others to their points of view. In addition, some question the usefulness of a conceptualization of deviance that treats as a violation of conduct standards some acts about which nothing is done and for which no sanctions are brought to bear. Furthermore, efficient application of this approach requires survey data—public opinion information about perceptions of conduct. Such information is rarely available for all the acts that one might want to consider as potentially deviant, and in some societies no survey data about any behavior are available. Finally, this approach assumes that the boundaries of groups are clear enough to permit scholars to ascertain the thoughts of most people within those boundaries about the appropriateness of various behaviors. In reality, however, group boundaries are often ambiguous, particularly in a heterogeneous society with overlapping subcultures and diverse group identities.

The synthetic approach. Some scholars merge different definitions of deviance in an effort to produce more effective, though more complicated, "integrated" approaches. For example one synthetic definition (Tittle and Paternoster) combines the reactive and the group evaluation approaches because they pose especially salient questions about social behavior—do most people believe it is wrong and are there usually negative sanctions associated with the behavior? Deviance is defined as any type of behavior that the majority of a given group regards as unacceptable or that typically evokes a collective response of a negative type. In this definition, "unacceptable" means the behavior is disapproved, or regarded as wrong, inappropriate, bad, or abnormal—in short, behavior that a group evaluates negatively. "Majority" means that over half of the people in a specified, bounded group regard the behavior as unacceptable. Although this is an arbitrary cutoff point, it is used because the main objective is to array behavior on a continuum from very nondeviant (hardly anybody considers it unacceptable) to very deviant (almost everybody in the group considers it unacceptable), with any particular act falling somewhere on the continuum. Collective response of a negative type implies that the majority of the specified group typically does something to express its displeasure, or the officials who possess coercive power over the members of the group typically respond to the behavior in a way that expresses negative evaluation. Whether synthetic, integrated conceptualizations become widely accepted remains to be seen.

The relativity and importance of deviance

Most students of deviance regard it as a socially constructed phenomenon; that is, things regarded as deviant have no inherent pejorative qualities but instead are the objects of social processes in a given context that result in negative attributions. With the exception of those who employ an "absolutist" definition, scholars note that what is deviant behavior varies from group to group, from one time to another, and from one status to another.

Explaining such differences, including differences in legality, has been of prime concern to students of deviance because they believe the processes affecting social attributions of deviance are fundamental to the maintenance and operation of social groups. Émile Durkheim, regarded by many as the father of studies of deviance, called attention to a shifting scale of attribution by which societies adjust their conceptions of unacceptable conduct to the volume of specific behaviors that exist and can be managed. He pointed out that even saints recognize deviant behavior among themselves, although what they regard as deviant is usually quite saintly from the point of view of the outside world. Studies show that groups sometimes shift standards downward, expanding the supply of deviant behavior or enhancing the evilness of acts that were previously regarded as trivial (Erikson). The standards are also sometimes moved upward, reducing the number of things that are regarded as unacceptable or transforming behaviors that were once regarded as bad into acceptable conduct. This general process has been called "the elasticity of evil" (Cohen, 1974) or, when it specifically involves acceptance of things previously thought of as intolerable, "defining deviancy down" (Moynihan). Because transforming deviance into conformity or vice versa is a major means by which social change occurs, students of deviance try to understand the process and the conditions under which conceptions of deviance change.

In addition, Durkheim and his followers believed that the process of identifying and doing something about deviant behavior is normal, even essential for group emergence and maintenance. Much like pain is unpleasant but essential for the human body to protect itself from truly destructive conditions, so is deviance essential for group survival. Although scholars have not been able to demonstrate that identifying and managing deviance is necessary for social organization, they have shown that such processes are ubiquitous so that what is or is not deviant is highly variable, often in predictable ways. As a result, almost all students of deviance reject the idea that deviance is inherent to particular behaviors; rather, they see it as a quality conferred upon some behaviors or individuals by groups as they go about the business of social organization.

Moreover, the fact of being deviant is thought to influence whether people do it or not. For that reason most students of deviance have concluded that one cannot simply explain behavior that happens to be deviant in a given group and expect the explanation to apply to all such behavior in all contexts. Some go even further, arguing that specific forms of deviance in a given social setting, such as addictive drug use, cannot be explained in the same way that other forms of deviance in that context, such as fraud, are explained, nor can acts of crime be explained the same way acts of noncriminal deviance are explained. Such contentions have spawned a controversy concerning the potential value of general theories as opposed to theories aimed explicitly at one or another form of deviance. This controversy also bears on the relationship between criminology and studies of deviance.

Relationship between deviance and crime

To a large extent, criminology and studies of deviance have developed along separate tracks although they show much overlap. Criminologists have typically limited themselves to issues about legality, crime, or crime-related phenomena. Students of deviance, on the other hand, have studied crime as well as a wider range of behaviors or conditions that are deviant by one or another of the definitions reviewed but are not necessarily illegal, such as suicide, alcoholism, homosexuality, mentally disordered behaviors, stuttering, and even such behaviors as public nose picking or flatulence, sectarian religious behaviors, and body mutilation. Hence, it is difficult to distinguish criminology clearly from studies of deviance (Bader et al.).

Many criminologists concede that illegal acts are not fundamentally different from legal but deviant acts, except by the fact of illegality itself, which is largely an arbitrary designation by legal functionaries. At the same time, students of deviance readily acknowledge that many deviant acts are also illegal and they have found data about crime especially useful because it is more systematic than most data concerning legal forms of deviance. Recognizing this overlap is obvious among those deviance scholars who employ a legalistic definition of deviance, but almost every comprehensive treatment of deviant behavior, regardless of the definition used, includes a subsection on criminal acts that are also deviant. Furthermore, both camps have raised similar questions and have come to share a common set of theories for explaining the phenomena in their domains. Among other issues, criminologists as well as students of deviance want to explain why the acts they study are deviant or criminal; they want to describe and explain the distribution, frequency, prevalence, and change in the occurrence of various criminal or deviant acts; they want to explain why and how criminal or deviant acts are committed; they want to explain how social groups manage and respond to crime and deviance and how people who are accused or guilty of crime or deviance respond to being accused or managed; and they want to understand how criminal or deviant phenomena affect and are affected by other aspects of social life.

Because of the overlap between crime and deviance, some scholars now regard distinctions between criminology and deviance studies as false and counterproductive, and they have called for a merger of the subject matters. Since all definitions of deviance, except the legalistic one, portray deviant behavior as a more inclusive concept, merger might imply subsuming criminology under the umbrella of deviance studies. Under that conceptualization, criminal behavior would be treated as a special case of deviant behavior—that which is prohibited in law, thereby meriting the possibility of officially imposed sanctions that legal forms of deviance escape. On the other hand, some contend that criminology has already preempted deviance studies so that deviance as a separate subject matter no longer exists or matters (Sumner), and still others contend that the two fields should clearly differentiate themselves by allocating legally related phenomena exclusively to criminology, leaving other forms of disapproved behavior to deviance studies (Bader et al.).

There are two main intellectual barriers to merging criminology with studies of deviance. First, some criminal behavior in some places (such as gambling) is not deviant, at least by most definitions of deviance, so would be subject to criminological study but not to study by students of deviance. The political processes that produce laws can result in behaviors being declared illegal although the conduct is not deviant by any definition except a legalistic one. How those political processes unfold and how enforcement might fare when illegality does not match social reality are of great importance to some criminologists. In addition, some behaviors are deviant at the time they become illegal but later become non-deviant without the law having been changed. Therefore, those intellectually opposed to merger might note that subsuming criminology under deviance studies would exclude some of the more interesting aspects of criminology.

A second intellectual obstacle to conceiving of crime and deviance as one subject matter hinges on disagreements about the nature of human behavior. Some criminologists and some students of deviance contend that all forms of behavior, including specific acts or types of crime or deviance, are more or less distinct, requiring unique explanations. By observing a plethora of differences, such as whether committed by males or females, blacks or whites, young or old, in some circumstances rather than others, whether legal or not, whether regarded as especially serious or not, whether violent or simply immoral, whether committed with planning or spontaneously, and the like, some conclude that specific behaviors have few similarities that would justify their being explained by the same theories. This orientation has generated a large number of explanations of specific behaviors, such as predatory crime (Braithwaite), common juvenile misdeeds (Hagan, 1989), embezzlement (Cressey), mental illness (Scheff), homicide by females (Ogle et al.), and many others.

Challengers, however, contend that various deviant behaviors are only superficially different because similar underlying causal processes operate in most if not all forms of deviance. They often use the analogy of focusing so closely on individual trees that the forest is overlooked. In addition, those who advocate general theory contend that it is necessary in order to achieve scientific goals of explanation and prediction based on assumptions about unity in nature; and that general theory is more parsimonious because specific accounts already overlap, often in unrecognized ways. The generalist orientation has led to a number of theories that aim to account for wide ranges of deviance in a variety of circumstances. These general accounts usually take one of two forms.

One form of general theorizing assumes a universal causal process that generates different forms of deviance under different conditions. The theories attempt to identify that causal pro-

cess and specify the conditions under which it produces one form of deviance rather than another (some examples are: Akers; Gottfredson and Hirschi; Agnew; Tittle). A second approach to general theory assumes that different causal processes operate at different times and under different conditions. The theories merge several causal processes by specifying when or why one or another will come into play to produce a given form of deviance at a specific point in time or in a given circumstance (some examples are: Braithwaite; Conger and Simons; Elliott et al.; Thornberry).

The generalist orientation clearly implies that crime and deviance are one entity. However, no general theory has yet been generally accepted as better than specific, focused accounts. Therefore, debates concerning the intellectual benefits of general theory and the relative advantages of differentiating criminology and studies of deviance will continue.

The main barriers to conceptualizing deviance and crime as a single entity are not intellectual, however—they are ideological and practical. Criminologists claim a more central role in addressing issues of acute public concern and they position themselves more favorably to receive government funds for research and to offer useful advice for controlling crime. Indeed, criminology has traditionally been identified with practical concerns. In addition, because they regard many forms of deviant behavior that are not illegal as unworthy of serious attention, some criminologists resist identity as students of deviance. Finally, by focusing on illegal conduct and limiting themselves to modern, politically, and geographically demarcated societies, criminologists avoid some of the problems encountered by students of deviance who struggle to identify group boundaries, to measure opinions of group members, or to document disapproval of various behaviors. Students of deviance, on the other hand, often resist the idea that they are also criminologists, maintaining that criminological study is too narrowly focused on behaviors arbitrarily designated by simple acts of legislative bodies. By so limiting itself, criminology ignores a large domain of phenomena crucial for understanding human behavior and social organization. Some students of deviance also regard criminology as a handmaiden of government, committed to preventing acts that are contrary to the interests of powerful groups who influence the content and enforcement of the criminal law.

Perhaps the major practical barrier to criminology and studies of deviant behavior becoming one subject matter is the tendency of criminologists to orient themselves concretely while students of deviance are relativistically oriented. Assuming that concepts of serious illegality are largely invariant across time and place (Wellford), most criminologists have focused on explanations of criminal behavior or its distribution, with only a minority showing concern with explaining variations in the law. Students of deviance, however, have traditionally emphasized variations in social attributions of deviance and have mainly tried to understand why something is or is not deviant in a given place and time, with only a minority being concerned with explaining behavior itself.

Summary

Deviance generally implies pejorative departures from social standards of one kind or another. However, there are many conceptualizations of deviance and how it is conceptualized affects what and how deviance is studied. One key unifying theme is the relativity of deviance. Because much deviance is also illegal, there is great overlap between criminology and deviance studies. Some contend that the two areas of study should be regarded as one, but there are intellectual and practical barriers to such a merger. A related issue concerns whether various forms of deviance can be explained with large general theories or requires special ad hoc accounts. Much work remains to be done before the key questions about deviant behavior can be answered.

CHARLES R. TITTLE

See also CRIME CAUSATION: SOCIOLOGICAL THEORIES; CRIMINOLOGY: MODERN CONTROVERSIES; DELINQUENT AND CRIMINAL SUBCULTURES.

BIBLIOGRAPHY

AGNEW, ROBERT. "Foundation for a General Strain Theory of Crime and Delinquency." *Criminology* 30 (1992): 47–87.

AKERS, RONALD L. *Deviant Behavior: A Social Learning Approach.* 3d ed. Belmont, Calif.: Wadsworth, 1985.

BADER, CHRIS; BECKER, PAUL J.; and DESMOND, SCOTT. "Reclaiming Deviance as a Unique Course from Criminology." *Teaching Sociology* 24 (1996): 316–320.

BECKER, HOWARD S. *Outsiders: Studies in the Sociology of Deviance.* New York: Free Press, 1963.

BONGER, WILLIAM ADRIAN. *Criminality and Economic Conditions.* Translated by H. P. Horton. Boston: Little, Brown, and Company, 1916.

BRAITHWAITE, JOHN. *Crime, Shame, and Reintegration.* New York: Cambridge University Press, 1989.

COHEN, ALBERT K. *Deviance and Control.* Englewood Cliffs, N.J.: Prentice-Hall, 1966.

———. "The Elasticity of Evil: Changes in the Social Definition of Deviance." Occasional paper #7, Oxford University Penal Research Unit. Oxford, U.K.: Basil Blackwell, 1974.

CONGER, RAND D., and SIMONS, RONALD L. "Life-course Contingencies in the Development of Adolescent Antisocial Behavior: A Matching Law Approach." In *Developmental Theories of Crime and Delinquency.* Edited by T. P. Thornberry. New Brunswick, N.J.: Transaction, 1997. Pages 55–57.

CRESSEY, DONALD R. *Other People's Money.* New York: Free Press, 1953.

DAVIS, KINGSLEY. *Human Society.* New York: Macmillan, 1950.

DENTLER, ROBERT A., and ERIKSON, KAI T. "The Functions of Deviance in Groups." *Social Problems* 7 (1959): 98–107.

DURKHEIM, ÉMILE. *The Rules of Sociological Method, 1895.* New York: The Free Press, 1938.

ELLIOTT, DELBERT S.; HUIZINGA, DAVID; and AGETON, SUZANNE S. *Explaining Delinquency and Drug Use.* Newbury Park, Calif.: Sage, 1985.

ERIKSON, KAI T. *Wayward Puritans: A Study in the Sociology of Deviance.* New York: Wiley, 1966.

GIBBS, JACK P. "Conceptions of Deviant Behavior: The Old and the New." *Pacific Sociological Review* 9 (1966): 9–14.

———. *Norms, Deviance, and Social Control: Conceptual Matters.* New York: Elsevier, 1981.

GOTTFREDSON, MICHAEL R., and HIRSCHI, TRAVIS. *A General Theory of Crime.* Stanford, Calif.: Stanford University, 1990.

GOVE, WALTER R., ed. *The Labelling of Deviance: Evaluating a Perspective.* 2d ed. Beverly Hills, Calif.: Sage, 1980.

GROSS, LLEWELLYN, ed. *Symposium on Sociological Theory.* White Plains, N.Y.: Row-Peterson, 1959.

HAGAN, JOHN. "Labelling and Deviance: A Case Study in the 'Sociology of the Interesting.'" *Social Problems* 20 (1973): 447–458.

———. "A Power-Control Theory of Gender and Delinquency." In *Structural Criminology.* Edited by J. Hagan. New Brunswick, N.J.:Rutgers University Press, 1989. Pages 145–162.

HOEBEL. E. ADAMSON. *The Law of Primitive Man.* New York: Atheneum, 1968.

KITSUSE, JOHN I. "Societal Reactions to Deviant Behavior: Problems of Theory and Method." *Social Problems* 9 (1962): 247–257.

LEMERT, EDWIN M. *Social Pathology.* New York: McGraw-Hill, 1951.

MALINOWSKI, BRONISLAW. *Crime and Custom in Savage Society.* London: Routledge and Kegan Paul, 1926.

MANKOFF, MILTON. "Societal Reaction and Career Deviance: A Critical Analysis." *The Sociological Quarterly* 12 (1971): 204–218.

MCCAGHY, CHARLES H. *Deviant Behavior: Crime, Conflict, and Interest Groups.* New York: Macmillan, 1976.

MOYNIHAN, DANIEL PATRICK. "Defining Deviancy Down." *The American Scholar* 61 (1993): 17–30.

MURPHY, ROBERT F. *The Dialectics of Social Life: Alarms and Excursions in Anthropological Theory.* New York: Columbia University Press, 1980.

OGLE, ROBBIN; MAIER-KATKIN, DANIEL; and BERNARD, THOMAS S. "A Theory of Homicidal Behavior among Women." *Criminology* 33 (1995): 173–193.

PARSONS, TALCOTT. *The Social System.* New York: Free Press, 1951.

PLATT, ANTHONY. "Thinking and Unthinking 'Social Control.'" In *Inequality, Crime, and Social Control.* Edited by G. S. Bridges and M. A. Myers. Boulder, Colo.: Westview, 1994. Pages 72–79.

QUINNEY, RICHARD. *The Social Reality of Crime.* Boston: Little, Brown, 1970.

———. *Class, State, and Crime.* 2d ed. New York: Longman, 1980.

SCHEFF, THOMAS J. *Being Mentally Ill: A Sociological Theory.* 2d ed. New York: Aldine de Gruyter, 1984.

SCHUR, EDWIN M. *Labeling Deviant Behavior: Its Sociological Implications.* New York: Harper and Row, 1971.

SCHWENDINGER, HERMAN, and SCHWENDINGER, JULIA. *Rape and Inequality.* Beverly Hills, Calif.: Sage, 1983.

SIMON, DAVID R. *Elite Deviance.* 6th ed. Boston: Allyn and Bacon, 1999.

SUMNER, COLIN. *The Sociology of Deviance: An Obituary.* New York: Continuum, 1994.

TANNENBAUM, FRANK. *Crime and the Community.* Boston: Ginn, 1938.

THORNBERRY, TERENCE P. "Toward an Interactional Theory of Delinquency." *Criminology* 25 (1987): 863–892.

TITTLE, CHARLES R. *Sanctions and Social Deviance: The Question of Deterrence.* New York: Praeger, 1980.

———. "The Theoretical Bases for Inequality in Formal Social Control." In *Inequality, Crime, and Social Control.* Edited by G. S. Bridges and M. A. Myers. Boulder, Colo.: Westview, 1994. Pages 221–252.

———. *Control Balance: Toward a General Theory of Deviance.* Boulder, Colo.: Westview, 1995.

TITTLE, CHARLES R., and PATERNOSTER, RAYMOND. *Social Deviance and Crime: An Organizational and Theoretical Approach.* Los Angeles, Calif.: Roxbury, 2000.

WELLFORD, CHARLES F. "Labeling Theory and Criminology: An Assessment." *Social Problems* 22 (1975): 335–347.

WILKINS, LESLIE T. *Social Deviance, Social Policy, Action, and Research.* Englewood Cliffs, N.J.: Prentice-Hall, 1964.

DIMINISHED CAPACITY

Legal guilt or culpability for the commission of a crime requires both that the prosecution must prove beyond a reasonable doubt all the definitional elements of the crime charged, including the mental state—the mens rea required by the crime's definition—and that an affirmative defense, such as the excuse of legal insanity or duress, is not established.

Diminished capacity refers to two distinct doctrines: the use of evidence of mental abnormality to negate a mens rea required by the definition of the crime charged (the *mens rea variant*) and the use of mental abnormality evidence to establish some type of partial affirmative defense of excuse (*the partial excuse variant*). Courts have used various other terms, such as diminished responsibility, to refer to one or both of these distinct doctrines, but the term used is unimportant. Confusion arises, however, when the two types of doctrine are not clearly distinguished. Neither entails the other and distinct legal and policy concerns apply to each. After a brief description of the reasons these doctrines developed, this essay will address both variants.

Historical background

Prior to the development of either variant of diminished capacity, a defendant suffering from mental abnormality had limited ability to use such abnormality to avoid conviction either by negating the prosecution's prima facie case or by establishing an affirmative defense.

Mens rea variant. Mental abnormality can potentially negate mens rea primarily in cases in which the abnormality is quite severe and produces a cognitive mistake. For example, the commentary to the Model Penal Code uses the example of a hallucinating defendant who strangles a victim believing that he or she is squeezing a lemon rather than a person's throat. This is a famous but silly example because such a hallucination is extremely improbable, but if it were true, the defendant did not form in fact the mental state, the *intent to kill another*, required by the definition of intentional homicide.

Historically, the difficulty for negating mens rea was that traditional doctrine required that mistakes had to be objectively reasonable, and a mistake mental abnormality produces is definitionally unreasonable, even if subjectively mens rea does not exist. Thus, evidence of such mistakes was excluded, even though it is logically relevant to whether a requisite mens rea was in fact present. This result seemed unfair to many courts because a defendant subjectively lacking the requisite mens rea for reasons not the agent's fault does not appear culpable for the crime charged. Consequently, many courts began to permit the admission of mental abnormality evidence to negate mens rea, although for reasons to be explored below, they usually substantially restricted such use of abnormality evidence. But there is a constant and continuing tension in criminal law between objective and subjective approaches to culpability, and many courts continued to exclude such evidence, often because they confused the use of such evidence to negate the prosecution's prima facie case with the entirely distinct, full excuse of legal insanity or because they distrusted mental abnormality evidence altogether.

Partial excuse variant.   The affirmative defense of legal insanity, which was traditionally doctrinally limited and distrusted or feared by juries and judges alike, provided the only means to introduce mental abnormality evidence and few defendants could expect to succeed with this defense, even if the mental disorder was obvious and severe. Some criminal defendants patently suffered from a mental abnormality insufficient to support a successful insanity defense, but that substantially compromised their capacity for rationality. Such defendants might have the mens rea required by the definition of the crime and might be criminally responsible, but they seemed less criminally responsible than defendants without abnormality who were charged with the same crime. Nonetheless, with the very limited exception of the provocation/passion doctrine that re-

duced an intentional killing from murder to the lesser crime of voluntary manslaughter and that, anyway, was not understood as a mental abnormality doctrine, no doctrine provided a partial excuse to legally responsible defendants whose responsibility was diminished by mental abnormality. For example, a mentally abnormal defendant who killed intentionally and with premeditation had no doctrinal tool to avoid conviction and punishment for the most culpable degree of crime—first-degree murder—even if the killing was the highly irrational product of substantial mental abnormality.

Failure to consider partially excusing mental abnormality evidence also seemed unfair and some courts and legislatures tried to create means to permit partial excusing claims. But the tension between subjective and objective guilt applied in the context of partial excuse much as it did in the context of mens rea negation. Consequently, both courts and legislatures feared creating a subjective, generic partial excuse, again, in part, because they lacked confidence in the reliability of evidence of mental abnormality. Furthermore, courts were hindered because creating a genuine partial excuse appears to be a "legislative act" that goes beyond a court's prerogative. In a few jurisdictions, courts tried to develop a partial excuse in the guise of adopting the mens rea variant, but these attempts used extremely problematic mens rea concepts and were confusing. As will be discussed below, legislatures and courts permitted some partial excusing claims, but no generic partial excuse for mental abnormality exists in any jurisdiction in the United States or in English law.

The mens rea variant

The logic of the mens rea variant is impeccable. Crimes are defined by their elements and the prosecution must prove all these elements beyond a reasonable doubt to secure a conviction. If the prosecution is unable to prove an element, either because its case is weak or because the defendant has sufficient evidence to cast reasonable doubt on the presence of an element of the prosecution's case, then the defendant should be acquitted of a crime requiring that element. The defendant using the mens rea variant of diminished capacity seeks simply to use evidence of mental abnormality to cast reasonable doubt on the presence of a mental state element that is part of the definition of the crime charged. Such use of mental abnormality evidence is not a full or partial affirmative defense. Use of mental abnormality evidence to deny the prosecution's prima facie case is functionally and doctrinally indistinguishable from the use of any other kind of evidence for the same purpose, and it thus does not warrant a special name, as if it were a unique doctrine. The general question of whether defendants ought to be allowed to negate mens rea using probative evidence is different from the specific evidentiary question of whether mental abnormality evidence is more or less reliable than other evidence used to negate mens rea.

Justice or fairness seems to require permitting a criminal defendant to use relevant evidence to cast reasonable doubt on the prosecution's case when criminal punishment and stigma are at stake. Indeed, it would be unconstitutional as a denial of various rights, such as the confrontation clause, completely to prohibit introduction of all such evidence. Nonetheless, a criminal defendant's right to introduce relevant evidence may be denied for good reason and the U.S. Supreme Court has never held that the Constitution requires the admission of mental abnormality evidence to negate mens rea. About half the American jurisdictions exclude mental abnormality evidence altogether when it is offered to negate mens rea and the other half permit introduction but typically place substantial restrictions on the use of the evidence.

Total exclusion of mental abnormality evidence. The most common reasons used to justify total exclusion of mental abnormality evidence to negate mens rea are that the use of evidence to negate mens rea is mistakenly understood as an affirmative defense, that mental abnormality evidence is considered particularly unreliable in general or for this purpose, and that permitting the use of such evidence would compromise public safety unduly. If mens rea negation is wrongly thought to be an affirmative defense, it may appear redundant with the defense of legal insanity, or a court might believe that creating a new affirmative defense is the legislature's prerogative. These might be good reasons to reject admission of mental abnormality evidence, if mens rea negation were an affirmative defense. But these reasons are unpersuasive because they rest on an entirely confused doctrinal foundation.

The unreliability rationale for total exclusion is stronger in principle because courts are always free to reject arguably relevant evidence if it is unreliable or confusing. The difficulty with this rationale for total exclusion is that mental abnormality evidence is routinely considered sufficiently reliable and probative to be admitted in an enormous array of criminal and civil law contexts, including competence to stand trial, legal insanity, competence to contract, and others. Exclusion of such evidence offered to defeat the prosecution's case in a criminal case appears unfair. Because the defendant's liberty and reputation are threatened by the power of the state, criminal defendants are afforded special protections in our adversary system, such as the right to have the prosecution prove its case by the rigorous beyond-a-reasonable-doubt standard. For the same reason, there is also powerful reason to provide defendants special latitude to admit potentially exculpatory evidence, especially when it is admitted in other contexts where much less is at stake. It seems especially unfair to exclude evidence of mental abnormality, which is rarely if ever the defendant's fault, when most jurisdictions routinely admit evidence of voluntary intoxication, which is typically the defendant's fault, to negate some mens rea.

The public safety rationale is also sound in principle. Opponents of admission fear that if a mentally abnormal and dangerous defendant uses abnormality evidence successfully to negate all mens rea, outright acquittal and release of a dangerous agent will result. Virtually automatic involuntary civil commitment follows a successful affirmative defense of legal insanity, but the state has less effective means to preventively confine dangerous defendants acquitted outright.

The problem with the public safety rationale is practical rather than theoretical. Mental disorders, including those that are most severe and compromise contact with reality, may cause agents to have crazy reasons to do what they do, but they seldom prevent people from forming intentions to act, from having the narrow types of knowledge required by legal mens rea, and the like. Consequently, very few defendants with mental disorder will be able to gain outright acquittal by negating all mens rea or even to reduce their conviction by negating some mens rea. Moreover, the mens rea termed "negligence"—failure to be aware of a risk that one has created and should be aware of—cannot be negated by mental abnormality because such failure is per se objectively unreasonable.

The only possible exception to the observation that mental abnormality seldom negates mens rea is the mental state of premeditation required by many jurisdictions for conviction for intentional murder in the first degree. On occasion, a person with a disorder may kill on the spur of the moment motivated by a command hallucination or a delusional belief. Such people are capable of premeditating, but the mental abnormality evidence simply tends to show that they did not premeditate in fact on this occasion. Mental disorder thus rarely negates mens rea and permitting defendants to introduce such evidence in the small number of cases in which it might do so would not substantially compromise public safety.

In sum, all the rationales for total exclusion of mental abnormality evidence proffered to negate mens rea are flawed and the criminal defendant's interest in admission of such evidence is strong.

Limited admission of mental abnormality evidence. Many courts have recognized the fairness rationale for admission of mental abnormality evidence to negate mens rea, including awareness of the analogy to the admission of voluntary intoxication evidence. As a logical matter, the evidence should be admitted to negate any mens rea that might have been negated in fact and, indeed, this is the Model Penal Code position. Nonetheless, virtually all jurisdictions that have permitted using mental abnormality evidence to negate mens rea have placed substantial limitations on doing so, largely because they fear the outright acquittal that in principle could result from following the pure logical relevance standard for admission. The logic of limited admission is thus the logic of a policy compromise between considerations of fairness and public safety: A defendant is able to negate some but not all mens rea, which typically results in conviction for a lesser offense than the crime charged. The effect of mental abnormality on culpability is thus considered, albeit partially, and a potentially dangerous defendant does not go free entirely, albeit the sentence is abbreviated.

Courts have tried to justify the particular limitations they place on the admission of mental abnormality evidence to negate mens rea, but other than the consequence of avoiding outright acquittal, there is no particular logic to the various limitations. Some jurisdictions permit only the negation of premeditation, although other mens reas may be negated in fact; others draw the confusing, technical distinction between specific and general intent and permit negation only of the former, even if the latter is in fact negated. Nonetheless, even restricted admissibility provides defendants with some opportunity to mitigate punishment and stigma.

The partial excuse variant

The logic of the partial responsibility variant is also impeccable. In general, the capacity for rationality, the capacity to grasp and be guided by reason, is the touchstone of moral and legal responsibility for one's actions. Mental abnormality potentially compromises moral and legal responsibility because in some cases it renders the defendant so irrational that the defendant is not a responsible agent. In the case of legal insanity, for example, mental disorder must be present as a cause of sufficient irrationality, but it is the irrationality and not the disorder per se that is the genuine basis of the excuse. The capacity for rationality, which is the basis of responsibility, is a continuum, however, and in principle responsibility should also be a continuum. The complete excuse of legal insanity does not contain degrees, but many mentally abnormal defendants who do not meet the test for legal insanity may nonetheless suffer from serious rationality impairments that compromise their responsibility and that thus appear to require a partial excuse.

Notwithstanding the logic, no generic partial excuse variant of diminished capacity that would apply to all crimes exists in any jurisdiction in the United States or in England. Courts are unwilling to create a generic excuse for many reasons, including the belief that they do not have the power to create new excuses, the fear that they will be inundated with potentially confusing or unjustified claims, and the fear that dangerous defendants might go free earlier than concerns for public safety require. Legislatures appear unwilling to enact a generic partial excuse because, in general, legislatures are not responsive to claims that are to the advantage of wrongdoers.

Partial excusing doctrines and practices. Despite reluctance to adopt a partial excuse, courts and legislatures have adopted various doctrines or practices that are in fact forms of partial excuse. Most prominent are (1) the Model Penal Code's "extreme emotional disturbance" doctrine (sec. 210.3.1(b)) and English "diminished responsibility," both of which reduce a conviction of murder to the lesser crime of manslaughter; (2) the use of mental abnormality evidence as a mitigating factor at sentencing hearings; and, (3) one interpretation of the common law provocation/passion doctrine, which reduces an intentional killing from murder to voluntary manslaughter.

The extreme emotional disturbance doctrine, promulgated by the Model Penal Code and adopted in a small minority of American states, reduces murder to manslaughter if the killing occurred when the defendant was in a state of extreme mental or emotional disturbance for which there was reasonable explanation or excuse. Mental abnormality evidence is admissible in most jurisdictions to establish that such disturbance existed. English diminished responsibility permits the reduction to manslaughter if the defendant killed in a state of substantially impaired mental responsibility arising from mental abnormality. Neither doctrine negates the lack of intent or conscious awareness of a very great risk of death that is required for the prosecution to prove murder. Both simply reduce the degree of conviction and thus punishment and stigma because mental abnormality diminishes culpability.

The language of these doctrines is sufficiently general to apply to any crime as an affirmative defense, but this is not the law. Both doctrines exist only within the law of homicide, but in principle both operate and could be formally treated as generic affirmative defenses of partial excuse because nothing in the language of either doctrine entails that it applies only to homicide. Indeed, in some jurisdictions, the extreme emotional disturbance doctrine is explicitly treated as an affirmative defense, but only to homicide, and the defendant bears the burden of persuasion to establish the defense.

Many jurisdictions in the United States and English law also contain the provocation/passion doctrine, which reduces a murder to manslaughter if the defendant killed subjectively in the "heat of passion" in immediate response to a "legally adequate" or "objective" provocation, that is, a provoking event, such as finding one's spouse in the act of adultery, that would create an inflamed psychological state in a reasonable person. The defendant kills intentionally and is criminally responsible, but the provocation/passion doctrine reduces the degree of blame and punishment. The rationale supporting this mitigating doctrine is controversial, but one interpretation is that psychological states such as "heat of passion" diminish rationality and responsibility and the defendant is not fully at fault for being in such a diminished condition because the provocation was sufficient to put even a reasonable person in such a state. On this interpretation, the provocation/passion doctrine is a form of partial excuse related to but narrower than extreme emotional disturbance and diminished responsibility. Indeed, the extreme emotional disturbance doctrine was created to respond to the same moral concerns about responsibility as provocation/passion, but also to expand the class of defendants to whom these moral concerns apply and to whom the benefit of a partial mitigating condition should be provided.

In jurisdictions that give judges unguided or guided sentencing discretion, mental abnormality is a factor traditionally used to argue for a reduced sentence. Many capital sentencing statutes explicitly mention mental abnormality as a mitigating condition and some even use the language of the insanity defense or the extreme emotional disturbance doctrine as the mitigation standard. The partial excuse logic of such sentencing practices is conceded and straightforward. A criminally responsible defendant whose behavior satisfied all the elements of the offense charged, including the mens rea, and who has no affirmative defense, may nonetheless be less responsible because mental abnormality substantially impaired the defendant's rationality.

Confusion with the mens rea variant. A small number of courts have implicitly adopted a form of partial excuse by re-interpreting mens rea elements. For example, the influential California Supreme Court interpreted the elements of murder highly atypically to include not only the intent to kill, but also the requirement that the defendant comprehend his or her duty to govern actions in accord with the law. A defendant lacking such comprehension as a result of mental abnormality could not be guilty of murder, even if the defendant killed intentionally and there was no provocation. It was this interpretation of the elements of homicide that allowed a jury to find that the killer in the famous "Twinkies" case, Dan White, could be guilty only of manslaughter because ingestion of junk food allegedly affected his mental state and in part contributed to depriving him of the necessary comprehension for murder. It is apparent that such "comprehension" is in fact a partial excuse doctrine, rather than a traditional mental state element requirement for murder. Indeed, it seems conceptually and operationally indistinguishable from the extreme mental or emotional disturbance doctrine or from the language of some insanity defense tests. Such indirect and confusing means to establish partial excusing doctrines met with intense criticism and have been abolished in virtually all jurisdictions, including California.

A generic partial excuse?

Although no jurisdiction in the United States and English law contains a formal, generic partial excuse, the theoretical and moral case for such an excuse is strong. Indeed, the moral logic of the excuse is conceded by sentencing practices that reduce sentences because the offender suffered from substantial mental abnormality. Mental abnormality can substantially compromise rationality and responsibility among offenders who are not legally insane, including many who suffer from newly discovered syndromes, but such offenders now have only limited and often entirely discretionary means to make such claims. Consequently, many offenders may be blamed and punished more than they deserve. Creating a partial excuse would create many practical problems, including establishing the standard, insuring that the courts are not inundated with unmeritorious claims, and devising appropriate dispositions for offenders who are partially excused. But if the case for a partial excuse is sufficiently strong, as it seems to be, justice requires that our criminal law should try to develop such a formal doctrine and should not treat such questions in an unduly limited or discretionary manner.

STEPHEN J. MORSE

See also EXCUSE: THEORY; EXCUSE: INSANITY; EXCUSE: INTOXICATION; MENS REA; MENTALLY DISORDERED OFFENDERS.

BIBLIOGRAPHY

American Law Institute. *Model Penal Code.* Philadelphia: American Law Institute, 1962.
ARENELLA, PETER. "The Diminished Capacity and Diminished Responsibility Defenses: Two Children of a Doomed Marriage." *Columbia Law Review* 77 (1977): 827–865.
DRESSLER, JOSHUA. "Reaffirming the Moral Legitimacy of the Doctrine of Diminished Capacity: A Brief Reply to Professor Morse." *Journal of Criminal Law and Criminology* 75 (1984): 953–962.
FINGARETTE, HERBERT, and HASSE, ANN FINGARETTE. *Mental Disabilities and Criminal Responsibility.* Berkeley, Calif.: University of California Press, 1979.
HORDER, JEREMY. *Provocation and Responsibility.* Oxford, U.K.: Clarendon Press, 1992.
MACKAY, R. D. *Mental Condition Defenses in the Criminal Law.* Oxford, U.K.: Clarendon Press, 1995.
MORSE, STEPHEN J. "Diminished Capacity: A Moral and Legal Conundrum." *International Journal of Law and Psychiatry* 2 (1979): 271–298.
———. "Undiminished Confusion in Diminished Capacity." *The Journal of Criminal Law and Criminology* 75 (1984): 1–55.
———. "Diminished Capacity." In *Action and Value in Criminal Law.* Edited by Stephen Shute, John Gardner, and Jeremy Horder. Oxford, U.K.: Clarendon Press, 1993. Pages 239–278.
———. "Excusing and the New Excuse Defenses: A Legal and Conceptual Review." In *Crime and Justice: A Review of Research, Volume 23.* Edited by Michael Tonry. Chicago: University of Chicago Press, 1998. Pages 329–406.
SMITH, JOHN C. *Smith & Hogan: Criminal Law,* 9th ed. London: Butterworths, 1999.
YEO, STANLEY M. H., ed. *Partial Excuses to Murder.* Sydney, Australia: The Federation Press, 1990.
WALKER, NIGEL. *Crime and Insanity in England: One: The Historical Perspective.* Edinburgh: Edinburgh University Press, 1968.

CASES

People v. White, 172 Cal. Rptr. 612 (App. 1981).

DISCOVERY

Each party initially learns the facts of the case through its personal knowledge and investigation. As the trial approaches, a set of procedures, commonly called discovery, permit each side to require disclosure of certain aspects of the opponent's evidence. Whether in civil or criminal cases, the purposes of pretrial discovery are generally the same. Discovery of the opponent's case is thought to further the truth-seeking function of trials by avoiding surprise, sometimes colorfully called "trial by ambush." In addition, early disclosure of the strengths and weaknesses of the case facilitates negotiated settlement and, where appropriate, dismissal of baseless charges. Because discovery facilitates efficiency in litigation, it is believed to save resources.

Discovery in American courts is much less extensive in criminal cases than in civil, and it is somewhat asymmetrical in that greater discovery is provided for the defense than for the prosecution. These features are likely related to each other and each is in part a consequence of the constitutional rights protecting the criminal accused. Criminal discovery has, nevertheless, greatly expanded in the last third of the century. Expansion first concerned principally defense discovery from the prosecution, but in the last several decades, discovery from the defense has grown dramatically. The development and expansion of what is called *reciprocal discovery*—discovery provided to both defense and prosecution—is central to the considerable growth of discovery in criminal cases.

Interestingly, the federal system is not at the cutting edge of developments in criminal discovery. Instead, the movement has been led by the states, and it is perhaps the difficulty of tracking developments that occur in so many different jurisdictions that has resulted in relatively little attention being paid to the reasonably major changes in this field of criminal procedure.

Judicial and legislative authority

Early in our judicial history, courts took the view that they lacked authority to order discovery in criminal cases. That view generally persisted into this century, but it both changed and became less relevant after the 1930s as legislatures created discovery rights directly. That courts have inherent authority to order discovery is now widely accepted, but it has been rendered relatively unimportant as the result of enactment in most jurisdictions of comprehensive discovery legislation. Judicial discretion and inherent judicial authority are often significant but typically as supplementary and interstitial to a basic legislatively defined discovery system.

Special pressures in criminal discovery

Discovery in criminal cases is affected by the constitutional rights that protect the accused. Among the rights that play a role are the Fifth Amendment *rights against compulsory self-incrimination* and to *due process* and the Sixth Amendment *right to effective assistance of counsel*, all made applicable to the states through the Fourteenth Amendment. The right against compulsory self-incrimination means that discovery against the accused will at some point be restricted, which in turn means that criminal discovery cannot be fully a "two-way street." As interpreted by the Supreme Court during the last half of the century, the due process right means that the prosecution is constitutionally obligated to pro-

vide exculpatory information to the defense and to avoid use of false and perjured testimony. Effective assistance of counsel guarantees defendants critical aid in investigating and preparing a defense and occasionally provides arguments against usurpation of the defense counsels' preparation and obtaining defendants' communications.

The background for the debate about discovery in criminal cases is also affected by notions of the proper adversarial "balance," assessments of the state of that balance in the overall system, and predictions of the impact of discovery on it. Other important background factors are the presumption of innocence, the requirement of proof beyond a reasonable doubt, and the proposition that erroneous acquittals are more acceptable than are convictions of the innocent. Many of these propositions suggest that the discovery system should favor disclosure to the defense in service of *protecting the innocent* and in recognition of the prosecution's obligation to shoulder the entire burden of establishing guilt.

Supporting this asymmetry is the complementary argument that many aspects of the system tend to favor the prosecution. The prosecution typically has greater resources and can command an extensive investigative force in the form of police departments and other law enforcement resources. Evidence is usually gathered initially by the police, who have the power to search for and seize evidence under judicial authority and the ability to interrogate witnesses and the accused. The typically less adequately equipped defense attorney usually enters the case much later. Moreover, in some jurisdictions, the grand jury is an important investigatory tool that can compel testimony from witnesses and subpoena evidence.

The above characteristics often put the bulk of the evidence initially in the hands of the prosecution and suggest greater need by the defense to have access to prosecution-held information. In the initial stages of discovery reform, these features supported arguments to provide greater discovery to the defense. Justice William Brennan, one of the most effective advocates of this era, argued in an influential law review article in 1963 that defense discovery should be expanded to help turn the criminal trial from a sporting contest into a search for the truth. Such arguments were accepted for a time and to an extent. Thus, the initial expansion of discovery favored the defense almost entirely. Such discovery was designed to give the accused the basic facts to facilitate the rudiments of a defense. Ultimately, however, that one-sided argument could carry discovery only so far. It quickly encountered several counterarguments about peculiarities of criminal litigation that made unilaterally giving information to the defense highly problematic.

Critics often argued that because the stakes in criminal litigation for the accused are enormous and because many of those charged with crime are guilty and of questionable character, special dangers existed that the information disclosed would be misused. They contended that providing information to the defendant about the details of the prosecution case and its witnesses would likely lead to increased and more effective perjury and to intimidation of witnesses. Rejoinders can be made to many of the critics' arguments. However, at their base, most have some merit, and these concerns helped limit the further expansion of defense-oriented discovery. In addition, those opposing expanded defense discovery noted that in many jurisdictions the preliminary hearing allows the defense an extensive preview of the prosecution's case, although using this proceeding for discovery is sometimes considered an abuse. They also observed that the prosecution does not always enjoy a decided information advantage. Where defense counsel is expert and has adequate resources, independent investigation, aided by the defendant's knowledge of the facts, reduces or eliminates the prosecution's advantage, although most would acknowledge that only a relatively small group of defendants find themselves in this favorable situation.

The central demand for reciprocity

The initial wave of discovery reform generally provided an important set of basic information to the defense to help assure accuracy in outcomes. However, it became increasingly clear that even the powerful argument that potentially innocent defendants needed special protection would not carry reform further if discovery continued to benefit only the defense. The prospects for continued expansion of criminal discovery were likely limited absent more evenhanded treatment of the prosecution and the defense.

Two decisions of the U.S. Supreme Court in the early 1970s—*Williams v. Florida* and *Wardius v. Oregon*—approved basic reciprocity requirements in discovery and opened the possibilities of future expansion. Williams, the first and most important of these cases, eliminated the argu-

ment that the defendant's privilege against compulsory self-incrimination stood as a general bar to prosecutorial discovery. In that case, the defendant challenged the constitutionality of the state's alibi demand rule, which allowed the prosecution to require the defendant to give notice of an intent to rely upon an alibi defense and provide information on where he or she claimed to have been at the time of the crime, and to name and provide addresses of supporting witnesses. The Court ruled that the notice of alibi defense did not violate the privilege because the rule does not compel the disclosure. The forces at trial that cause a defendant to disclose and present a defense do not constitute compulsion, and the Court concluded that the alibi demand rule only accelerated the timing of that disclosure.

Williams noted that, upon defense compliance with the alibi demand rule, the Florida rule required the state to provide the defense with information about the witnesses whom it would offer to negate the alibi. In *Wardius v. Oregon*, decided a few years later, the Court held that such reciprocal disclosures by the prosecution were required and concluded that Oregon's rule violated due process because it contained no such requirements.

Further impetus to expand discovery generally and prosecutorial discovery in particular came from the Discovery Standards published by the American Bar Association (ABA) in 1970. In one important area, the standards proposed disclosure by the prosecution of names and addresses of the witnesses it intended to call together with witness statements. Reading *Williams* as broadly authorizing discovery from the defense as long as the prosecution provided the defense with the same type of information, the Standards adopted a requirement that the defense give the prosecution notice of all defenses it intended to raise and the names and addresses of supporting witnesses. Significantly, under this version of reciprocity, the prosecution's right to discovery is independent of any defense request for similar disclosures.

Williams and the ABA Standards had a very substantial impact. Nearly half the states adopted related provisions, in some instances more expansive and in others more limited, but sharing the new theory that defense disclosures were constitutional and appropriate.

Another major force in the expansion of discovery, albeit a more moderate expansion and one based on a somewhat different theory of reciprocity, was the 1975 revision of discovery in the

Federal Rules of Criminal Procedure. In particular, these rules did not then, and do not in the early twenty-first century, authorize the general discovery of witness names. The federal discovery rules are also premised on a somewhat different theory of reciprocity. Discovery against the defense depends upon a defense request for disclosure of a related category of evidence (and compliance with the request).

Under the federal rules model of conditional discovery, the validity of discovery against the defense rests on the theory of waiver of constitutional rights as opposed to the theory of advancement of the timing of disclosure articulated in *Williams*. Thus, by requesting discovery from the prosecution under a system conditioned on reciprocal obligations, the defense waives its right to object to the requirement that it provide discovery to the prosecution. The validity of this theory of waiver depends upon the defense having no independent right to the discovery requested and upon a determination that the pressures motivating the defendant to request discovery do not compel the request. It is debatable whether, in the absence of *Williams*, the waiver theory of conditional discovery would be sufficient to satisfy the Constitution or instead is constitutionally superfluous. Those jurisdictions that continue to use conditional discovery likely do so largely because it adds a degree of defense control and apparent fairness to requiring defense disclosure of potentially damaging information.

While questions remain regarding the validity of some uses of prosecutorial discovery, its basic constitutionality is relatively clear when coupled with reciprocal duties. The trend in each revision of the federal rules of criminal procedure—the third edition of the ABA Discovery Standards published in 1996, and new state discovery rules, such as Michigan's rule adopted in 1995—is discovery that is largely a "two-way street." Indeed, the authors of the third edition of the ABA Standards were explicit in their conclusion that efforts to limit prosecutorial discovery in the second edition of the Standard had resulted in that edition having very limited influence on legislative developments.

Although some debate over reciprocal discovery will continue, future expansion of criminal discovery is likely to depend on additional discovery being made available against the defense. Discovery against the defense is supported by a number of interests. First, some reformers believe that greater discovery from both sides is preferable because it likely leads to more accurate outcomes. A second group, which supports effective prosecution, argues that allowing the defense to "hide its hand" while requiring disclosure of the prosecution's case creates an unfair imbalance. Third, many defense advocates believe that on the whole greater defense disclosures will ultimately benefit the defense as a necessary precondition to relatively free and complete access to the prosecution's file. They note that typically the defense badly needs access to full information about the prosecution's case and it rarely has much evidence of its own that would be discoverable.

Some defense supporters dissent from embracing broad discovery against the defense. They argue that in some cases the defense conducts its own investigation and develops a significant defense case, and in those situations, discovery requirements can produce a state of affairs unfavorable to the defendant. This debate within the defense community pits the interests of the unusual defendant with resources and/or an affirmative defense case against the general group of defendants who are typically indigent and represented by overworked and underpaid counsel merely testing the adequacy of the prosecution's case.

Discovery distinctions

Those familiar with civil discovery will immediately notice that several of its most important discovery devices—interrogatories, depositions, and demands for admission—are either completely absent from criminal discovery or are available in only a handful of jurisdictions. The pattern in criminal discovery is for the rules or statutes to require the disclosure of specific types of information, rather than to authorize the use of broad discovery devices that would likely produce such information and much more. In the areas of alibi (noted above) and insanity (discussed below) discovery rules specifically applicable to these defenses are the norm. One of the major reasons for general difference between civil and criminal discovery is the existence of the defendant's constitutional privilege against compulsory self-incrimination.

While *Williams* decided that the state could discover from defendants information that they would ultimately provide as a defense, adversarial interrogation of defendants under threat of sanctions and any requirement that defendants admit parts of the prosecution's case are not compatible with the Fifth Amendment. As a result, depositions, interrogatories, and demands for admission directed at the defendant are not available tools. Depositions of other witnesses do not directly offend the Constitution, however.

While used as a discovery device in a handful of states, depositions are used principally to preserve testimony of witnesses who are expected to be unavailable at trial. One reason depositions are not generally available is that most criminal defendants are indigent, and as a result, the cost to the party of taking depositions does not act as a check on excessive use as it does in civil cases. Concern about imposing additional obligations on witnesses, who are often already reticent to become involved in criminal cases and particularly to have contact with the defendant, militates against expanded use of depositions. This concern, highlighted by the victims' rights movement, is particularly acute when a victim is also a witness in the case. Nevertheless, discovery depositions of witnesses other than the defendant (and sometimes victims) are used in a handful of states in criminal cases.

Particular Fifth Amendment restrictions

The Fifth Amendment right against compulsory self-incrimination is clearly implicated by the requirement that the defendant provide a statement to the prosecution. Discovery rules generally steer clear of such requirements, but defense communication is required in connection with discovery for the insanity defense and related defenses where the defendant intends to introduce expert testimony based on direct communications with the defendant. When using such expert testimony, rules in most jurisdictions require the defendant to submit to an examination by another mental health expert or be barred from calling the defense expert. While the precise theory under which this requirement satisfies the privilege against compulsory self-incrimination is unclear, the most appropriate theory is the waiver of the right. By introducing the defense expert's testimony based on communications with the defendant, the defendant effectively waives the right to remain silent. The defendant is allowed to introduce his or her own communications through an expert, and in return, the discovery rules require access to communications from the defendant by other nondefense experts. Rules of this sort have been uniformly upheld.

In addition to the *Williams* analysis that the privilege is not violated by merely advancing the time of disclosing a defense because such is not compelled within the meaning of the Fifth Amendment, the privilege is also not violated if the disclosure is not communicative or if the communication is not otherwise compelled. Communication is involved, of course, when a defendant is required to speak. However, when a defendant has at an earlier time voluntarily written a document, the prosecution's use of that document at trial does not violate the privilege because the defendant was not compelled to make the statement. This is true even though the statement is both incriminating and communicative. As a result, use of statements previously generated does not typically violate the privilege. For related reasons, use of documents containing information that came, not from the defendant, but from others does not violate the defendant's privilege.

In a very limited area, the privilege may be violated by the compelled production of documents, which occurs if the "act of production" itself is communicative. The Fifth Amendment is implicated if producing the document authenticates it, shows the defendant had possession of it, or establishes its existence (*Fisher*). Most discovery avoids these types of problem or involves documents as to which the communicative aspect is already a "foregone conclusion" (*Nobles*), and thus the privilege is not violated.

Open constitutional issues, however, remain in a several isolated areas. Where the defendant is required during discovery to provide information that the prosecution could use to prove guilt as part of its case-in-chief, the discovery requirement may be invalid. The other major open issue involves the use of information to impeach a defendant when the defendant gives notice of a defense in discovery but does not rely on that defense at trial.

Core discovery rights

While typically going further, most modern criminal discovery rules in the United States cover several core types of information, which were generally provided to defendants in the first generation of discovery statutes and rules. This core includes the statements of the defendant, documents, and tangible objects that either the prosecution intends to introduce at trial or were obtained from the defendant, and scientific reports of witnesses that the prosecution intends to call at trial. These items have several characteristics. First, they are often the key elements of the criminal case and defense access is arguably essential to effective testing of the prosecution's case. Second, the evidence often came from the defendant and providing discovery of it seems not only fair but also reveals no prosecution secrets. Third, the evidence provides limited opportunities for effective perjury and even less chance of witness tampering.

One of the most important types of evidence in criminal cases is that of statements made by the defendant. Without exception, the prosecution is required to provide such statements when made by the defendant to individuals then known by the defendant to be law enforcement officials. However, in some jurisdictions, when such statements were made to others, such as undercover agents, they need not be disclosed, and are withheld lest witness identities, not otherwise discoverable, be revealed.

The defendant's criminal record is often added to this core because of its obvious usefulness in trial decisions and the fact that the prosecution has better access to this unalterable type of information. Also typically included is a provision for discovery of evidence material to the preparation of the defense. Obtaining discovery of this latter type requires a showing by the defendant that the evidence is important under the facts of the particular case to adequate preparation of a defense. The effectiveness of this provision depends on the defense having knowledge of the case which, given limited discovery, may not be available, and rests ultimately on the relative liberality of prosecutors and judges, who exercise substantial discretion over this class of discovery.

In addition to the defendant's own statements, some jurisdictions provide those of codefendants. This is the point where systems begin to differentiate themselves as far as their attitude toward discovery. In a number, the information is seen as presenting opportunities for effective fabrication of testimony, and disclosure is not provided unless it can be shown to be material to the preparation of a defense, such as showing a need to have separate trials.

Providing discovery in these core areas to the defense often comes today with basic obligations of reciprocity. Whether conditional upon defense requests for, and prosecution delivery of, similar information from the prosecution or an independent right of the prosecution, a general feature of modern criminal discovery is that the defendant must provide the prosecution with documents and tangible objects that it intends to introduce and with relevant reports of expert witnesses it intends to call.

Controversial areas of discovery

The availability of defense discovery of witness names and their statements is a feature that distinguishes discovery systems. Neither type of information is provided in discovery in federal courts, illustrating the fact that the federal system is not at the forefront of expansive criminal discovery, but many states provide both categories of discovery to defendants. States often also require that the defense provide similar information to the prosecution.

Resistance to disclosure in federal cases of witness names and statements may be explained by more frequent federal prosecution of cases involving organized crime and large criminal enterprises where the prospect of witness tampering is predictably greater. Federal authorities have never accepted that protective orders, which allow courts upon a showing of special need to impose limits on discovery, would be a sufficient protection. The concern is that even though dangers of tampering exist, prosecutors may be unable to support their request for a protective order with sufficient objective evidence of this danger.

The 1970 ABA Discovery Standards supported the disclosure to the defense of witness names and statements. As noted earlier, it also supported a right of the prosecution to obtain a list of defense witnesses as well as a specification of all defenses supported by such witnesses. A substantial number of states adopted some part of this expansive discovery system, and many of these require the defense to provide the prosecution with statements of defense witnesses as well. To facilitate disclosure, many of these states also remove the protection against disclosure of witness statements that is frequently found in the work product doctrine. By contrast, the federal system continues to prohibit discovery of witness statements through longstanding legislation, commonly called the "Jencks Act," which prohibits required pretrial discovery of such statements but mandates their production for defense use in cross-examination and impeachment at the conclusion of the witness' direct examination.

One growing trend in criminal discovery is to require the preparation of a summary of a witness' testimony to be produced during discovery if a statement by the witness does not already exist. This requirement may be imposed on the defense and the prosecution alike. Preparation of such statements is required for all witnesses in some states, and it has been adopted, even in the federal courts, for expert witnesses. For expert witnesses in federal cases, both parties are required to provide their adversary with a written summary of the testimony of expert witnesses, which includes a description of the opinion, its basis, and the expert's qualifications.

Sanctions for discovery violations

Discovery systems commonly list three major remedies for failure to comply with discovery rules: an order to comply, a continuance, and a prohibition against introducing the evidence or calling the witness not properly disclosed. In addition, other remedies are either explicitly authorized by the discovery provisions in some jurisdictions or recognized as an aspect of judicial discretion to control discovery. These other remedies include instructions to the jury regarding adverse inferences it may draw based on discovery violations, contempt sanctions, and, in rare instances, dismissal of the prosecution.

In *Illinois v. Taylor*, the U.S. Supreme Court answered whether it was constitutional to preclude a defense witness from testifying because of a defense failure to comply with a discovery rule. The Court held that preclusion was a proper remedy in some circumstances and ruled that it did not violate the defendant's constitutional right to present defense evidence. Excluding the testimony of witnesses is not a preferred remedy, but the Court ruled it available for a willful discovery violation calculated to gain a tactical advantage in a situation where compliance with the discovery obligation was simple.

Generally, the defendant's own testimony cannot constitutionally be excluded as a sanction for a discovery violation, but potentially all supporting testimony from other witnesses can be. As noted earlier, whether it is constitutional to use a withdrawn discovery notice, such as a notice of a particular alibi, against the defense to impeach another defense offered at trial remains a matter of debate. Many discovery rules prohibit such use of withdrawn defense notices, but others do not, and some courts have found that use of the withdrawn notice to impeach is proper.

Constitutionally mandated discovery

In *Weatherford v. Bursey*, the U.S. Supreme Court stated that the defendant in a criminal case has no federal constitutional right to general discovery. However, in one particular area, the due process clause produces a limited constitutional right to discovery. The Supreme Court began the development of the constitutional right of the defense to disclosure in *Mooney v. Holohan* with a rule that the prosecution could obtain a conviction through deliberate deception by presentation of testimony that was known to be perjured. It expanded this concept substantially in *Brady v. Maryland* by holding that the prosecution violates due process where it fails to disclose to the defense evidence favorable to the accused that is material either to guilt or punishment. The Brady doctrine, as it is called, has been refined by a number of subsequent cases that limit its application to evidence that is "material" in that the evidence would have made a different result in the trial "reasonably probable" had it been disclosed.

Brady did not explicitly require any pretrial disclosure of the evidence. However, the general position adopted by most courts and commentators is that pretrial disclosure is required if advance disclosure is necessary for the evidence to be used effectively. Thus, if the exculpatory material requires defense development before it can be introduced, a constitutionally based discovery requirement is thereby created. The right of defendants under most rules to obtain discovery of information material to the preparation of the defense involves a statutory right to discovery of evidence that is substantially broader than the constitutional right.

Conclusion

Discovery in criminal case will never rival the extensive system in civil litigation. However, its progress in the last three decades of the twentieth century was considerable. While some expansion of discovery can be expected, its rough outer limits have likely been defined. The remaining goal of reformers is to achieve in most jurisdictions a statutory entitlement to what is often called "open file discovery" from the prosecution, which will almost certainly entail further defense disclosures.

ROBERT P. MOSTELLER

See also ADVERSARY SYSTEM; CIVIL AND CRIMINAL DI-
VIDE; COUNSEL: ROLE OF COUNSEL; CRIMINAL PROCE-
DURE: CONSTITUTIONAL ASPECTS; GRAND JURY;
PRELIMINARY HEARING.

BIBLIOGRAPHY

American Bar Association. *Standards Relating to Discovery and Procedure before Trial.* Washington, D.C.: American Bar Association, 1969.

————. *Standards Relating to Discovery and Procedure before Trial, Supplement.* Washington, D.C.: American Bar Association, 1970.

————. "Discovery and Procedure before Trial." In *Standards Relating to the Administration of Justice*, vol. 2, 11–1 to 11–94. 2d ed., Boston: Little, Brown, 1980.

————. *Standards for Criminal Justice: Discovery and Trial by Jury*, 3d ed. Washington, D.C.: American Bar Association, 1996.

BRENNAN, WILLIAM J., JR. "The Criminal Prosecution: Sporting Event or Quest for Truth?" *Washington University Law Quarterly* no. 3 (June 1963): 279–295.

IMWINKELRIED, EDWARD J. "The Applicability of the Attorney-Client Privilege to Non-Testifying Experts: Reestablishing the Boundaries between the Attorney-Client Privilege and the Work Product Protection." *Washington University Law Quarterly* 68 (1990): 19–50.

LAFAVE, WAYNE R., and ISRAEL, JEROLD H. *Criminal Procedure*, 2d ed. St. Paul, Minn.: West Publishing Co, 1992.

LOUISELL, DAVID W. "Criminal Discovery and Self-Incrimination: Roger Traynor Confronts the Dilemma." *California Law Review* 53 (1965): 89–102.

MOSTELLER, ROBERT P. "Discovery against the Defense: Tilting the Adversarial Balance." *California Law Review* 74 (1986): 1567–1685.

TRAYNOR, ROGER J. "Ground Lost and Found in Criminal Discovery." *New York University Law Review* 39 (1964): 228–250.

VAN KESSEL, GORDON. "Prosecutorial Discovery and the Privilege against Self-Incrimination: Accommodation or Capitulation." *Hastings Constitutional Law Quarterly* 4, no. 4 (Fall 1977): 855–900.

CASES

Brady v. Maryland, 373 U.S. 83 (1963).
Fisher v. United States, 425 U.S. 391 (1976).
Kyles v. Whitley, 514 U.S. 419 (1995).
Mooney v. Holohan, 294 U.S. 103 (1935).
Nobles v. United States, 422 U.S. 225 (1975).
Wardius v. Oregon, 412 U.S. 470 (1973).
Taylor v. Illinois, 419 U.S. 522 (1988).
Weatherford v. Bursey, 429 U.S. 545 (1977).

Williams v. Florida, 399 U.S. 78 (1970).

DISPUTE RESOLUTION PROGRAMS

One night in 1974, two young men in Elmira, Ontario, Canada, vandalized the property of twenty-two people: they broke windows, slashed tires, and damaged churches, stores, and cars. They pled guilty to twenty-two charges. The offenders did not pay restitution to the court clerk's office, however. Instead, in an experiment jointly administered by the probation department's volunteer program and the Mennonite Central Committee, the two young offenders met with each of their victims. It was hoped that meeting with the victims would help the offenders to see restitution payments less as fines and more as compensation to real people for real losses. Within six months, the young men had fulfilled their restitution obligations in full. Many see this case as the birth of victim-offender mediation, the principal form of dispute resolution in criminal cases. The success of this experiment encouraged others to develop similar programs.

History

In the mid-1970s, dispute resolution programs began to grow in the United States. The Minneapolis Restitution Center, for example, offered criminal offenders the opportunity to live and work outside the prison setting in order to make restitution payments to the victims of their crimes. As part of the program, offenders would meet with their victims in the presence of a program counselor to discuss the terms of restitution payment. A comparable program in the state of Oklahoma required juvenile offenders to make contact (in person or by letter) with the victims to whom they owed restitution.

Victim-offender mediation programs multiplied dramatically in the 1980s and 1990s. A study in 1998 found more than 289 victim-offender mediation programs in the United States. In 1994, researchers documented 20 projects in England, 26 in Canada, 54 in Norway, 40 in France, 293 in Germany, 130 in Finland, 8 in Belgium, and 1 in Scotland (Umbreit, 1994). The growth of victim-offender mediation has paralleled an increased interest in restitution for victims of crime. Mediation is seen as a cheap, informal way to determine the amount of restitution to be paid, while at the same time allowing for some interaction between victim and offender.

Variety in program structures and protocols

The expectations for interaction vary highly from one program to another. Most victim-offender mediation programs involve face-to-face meetings between crime victims and offenders in the presence of trained mediators. Beyond this basic description, victim-offender mediation programs defy generalization. While many programs concern themselves primarily with hammering out restitution agreements, others also seek to address emotional issues surrounding the crime. Offenders are held more accountable as they face the consequences of their crime for the victim; some take the opportunity, for the first time, to apologize directly to the victim. Victims gain a sense of empowerment and closure by facing their offenders and explaining the impact of the crime. Some victim-offender mediation programs strive not just to establish restitution agreements, but actually to effect some "reconciliation" between the victim and the offender, resolving conflict that the crime has created. These more ambitious goals are frequently found in mediation programs that are called "Victim-Offender Reconciliation Programs."

Some programs focus on cases involving misdemeanors—mostly nonviolent property crimes. Other programs limit their cases to felonies. Most programs mediate some combination of misdemeanors and felonies. Some programs occasionally mediate cases involving severely violent crimes, such as assault with a deadly weapon, sexual assault, negligent homicide, attempted murder, and murder.

The diverse goals of victim-offender mediation programs are reflected in their relative entanglement in the criminal justice system. Most victim-offender mediation programs are distinguishable from standard community mediation programs (even though community mediation programs may also handle cases involving technically criminal conduct) because the victim-offender programs mediate cases in which the participants' roles as victim and wrongdoer are more clearly defined. Indeed, community mediation programs receive referrals primarily from civil, rather than criminal, courts; they also provide an alternative to the adversary system altogether, diverting cases before they enter the criminal justice system. Referrals to victim-offender mediation programs, in contrast, are usually made by law enforcement or criminal court personnel after an offender has entered the criminal justice system. Victim-offender mediation programs catch cases at various points in the criminal justice process: on the early side, mediation occurs after arrest and before any charges are filed; on the late side, mediation may follow an offender's conviction and sentencing. Sometimes the mediation occurs while the offender is serving time in prison.

While some mediation programs are restricted to juvenile offenders, others take exclusively adults. This is an important area of difference, because American courts have treated juvenile offenders differently from adults for the better part of the twentieth century. This difference in treatment is epitomized, of course, by the existence of separate juvenile courts, which have emphasized rehabilitation of offenders and restitution of victims more than adult courts. With respect to adult offenders, the emphasis has shifted to deterrence and incapacitation. Arguably, therefore, mediation involving adult offenders marks a more radical departure (than mediation in juvenile cases does) from the system and its traditional goals.

In most programs, once a case is referred, it is assigned to a mediator—usually a volunteer from the community—who contacts the victim and offender individually. If the parties agree to mediate, the mediator sets a time and place for the mediation to be held and conducts the mediation. If the parties reach agreement, they enter into a written contract outlining the provisions of their agreement, both monetary and nonmonetary (e.g., service to the community or the victim; an apology; or a special project by the offender involving a third party). The mediator returns a written report of the mediation and a copy of the contract to the program office. Generally, the report is a summary of the mediation, including preliminary contacts, the meeting between the parties, and the restitution contract. The administrator of the program forwards the contract (often with a copy of the report as well) to the referring agency. In most victim-offender mediation programs, staff monitor performance of the contract; in some systems, the probation office will also check to insure that restitution is paid if it is a condition of probation.

If one of the parties refuses to mediate or the parties cannot resolve the case in mediation, the case is returned to the referring agency—the prosecutor's office, the court, or the probation office. There, the offender will be subject to the ordinary course of state prosecution and sentencing. Sometimes the mediator will report back to the referring agency about the case. If the offender was somehow responsible for the failure to resolve the case (by refusing to mediate or agree to the victim's demands), the judge may take the failed mediation into account when sentencing the offender. Similarly, if the victim's uncooperative attitude prevented the parties from mediating or reaching agreement, a judge subsequently setting a restitution amount could also be made aware of the victim's actions.

Critique

Victim-offender mediation transforms the criminal justice paradigm by placing victims at the center, rather than on the periphery, of the criminal process. Generally this is viewed as a positive development—one that increases the efficiency of the system and the quality of outcomes for both victims and offenders. Mediation programs are nonetheless controversial because they can transfer the power to resolve all or part of a criminal case from the state to a private party— the victim. Placing such control in the hands of the victim is problematic. Critics of such programs argue that without careful monitoring and administration, victim-offender mediation programs could disserve the interests of victims, offenders, and the state.

Victims could suffer in mediation if the programs place undue stress on forgiveness and reconciliation before victims have the vindication of a public finding that the offender is guilty. If mediators too easily assume that victims' outrage and loss can be expressed and resolved in the course of a few hours with their offenders, mediation might impede, rather than facilitate, victims' healing. This would undercut one of the central goals of such programs.

Victim-offender mediation could disserve offenders in three ways: by using screening criteria that are not clearly related to the goals of the program (thus permitting articulate offenders to participate rather than those who are sincerely remorseful); by eliminating procedural protections such as the right to counsel or rules of evidence; and by using the leverage of pending criminal process to gain advantages for the victim, a private party. If offenders believe that they will be worse off in the ordinary criminal justice system should they fail to reach a mediated agreement satisfactory to their victims, the of-

fenders may have an unduly strong incentive to mediate and reach agreement, no matter what the psychic or monetary cost.

An underlying assumption in many victim-offender mediation programs is that crimes are private disputes that fracture relationships between individuals; the state's interest in these disputes is minimal. The structure of many victim-offender mediation programs belies this assumption, however, because the mediation occurs before a backdrop of state involvement and coercion. Victims of crime negotiate not only with their own individual bargaining strength, but also with the threat of enhanced state punishment should the parties fail to reach agreement. The victim can appropriate some of the state's leverage over the offender if the victim and the offender know that the offender is more likely to be prosecuted or incarcerated if the victim is not satisfied with the mediation.

Moreover, despite proponents' claims that victim-offender mediation can resolve criminal cases according to the substantive standards of the "community" in which the crime occurred, such a community may be difficult to identify, apart from the state itself. When centralized rules of criminal law are rejected in the name of a "community" that may not even exist, any standard may fill the vacuum to resolve individual cases. Often, success is measured by the victim's satisfaction with the outcome rather than consistency with substantive legal rules. Focusing on the end to be obtained (the parties' ability to reach agreement), victim-offender mediation programs may lose sight of important procedural norms, resulting in a lack of counsel for the offender, or coercion prior to and during the mediation.

To maintain the integrity of the criminal justice system as well as the mediation process, some critics have called for a decoupling of mediation from the court system: the success or failure of the mediation should have no impact on the offender's prosecution or punishment. This recommendation turns, to some degree, on empiricism about the deterrent and rehabilitative effects of victim-offender mediation. To the extent that mediation is shown to reduce criminal activity generally or among offender participants, a stronger case can be made that these programs are consistent with, and actually promote, the traditional goals of the criminal justice system. In that case, conditioning prosecution on mediation and its results would be appropriate.

JENNIFER GERARDA BROWN

See also FAMILY RELATIONSHIPS AND CRIME; INFORMAL DISPOSITION; PRETRIAL DIVERSION; PREVENTION: COMMUNITY PROGRAMS; PROSECUTION: COMPARATIVE ASPECTS; RESTORATIVE JUSTICE; VICTIMS; VICTIMS' RIGHTS.

BIBLIOGRAPHY

BRAITHWAITE, JOHN. *Crime, Shame, and Reintegration.* Cambridge University Press, 1989.

———. "Restorative Justice: Assessing Optimistic and Pessimistic Accounts." *Crime and Justice: A Review of Research*, vol. 25. (ed. M. Tonry), 1999, pp. 1–127.

BROWN, JENNIFER GERARDA. "The Use of Mediation to Resolve Criminal Cases: A Procedural Critique." *Emory Law Journal* 43 (1994): 1247–1309.

DANZIG, RICHARD. "Toward the Creation of a Complementary, Decentralized System of Criminal Justice." *Stanford Law Review* 26 (1973): 1–54.

FELSTINER, WILLIAM, and WILLIAMS, LYNNE. "Mediation as an Alternative to Criminal Prosecution: Ideology and Limitations." *Law and Human Behavior* 2 (1978): 223–244.

GALAWAY, BURT, and HUDSON, JOE, eds. *Criminal Justice, Restitution, and Reconciliation.* Monsey, N.Y.: Criminal Justice Press, 1990.

RICE, PAUL. "Mediation and Arbitration as a Civil Alternative to the Criminal Justice System— An Overview and Legal Analysis." *American University Law Review* 29 (1979): 17–81.

UMBREIT, MARK S. *Crime and Reconciliation: Creative Options for Victims and Offenders.* Nashville, Tenn.: Abingdon Press, 1985.

———. *Victim Meets Offender: The Impact of Restorative Justice and Mediation.* Monsey, N.Y.: Criminal Justice Press, 1994.

WRIGHT, MARTIN, and GALAWAY, BURT. *Mediation and Criminal Justice.* London: SAGE, 1989.

ZEHR, HOWARD. *Changing Lenses.* Scottsdale, Penn: Herald Press, 1990.

DOMESTIC VIOLENCE

All states made "wife beating" illegal by 1920. However, only since the 1970s has the criminal justice system begun to treat domestic violence as a serious crime, not as a private family matter. Domestic violence is any physical, sexual, or psychological abuse that people use against a former or current intimate partner. It refers to a number of criminal behaviors: assault and battery; sexual assault; stalking; harassment; violation of a civil restraining order; homicide; and other offenses that occur in the course of a domestic violence incident, such as arson, robbery, malicious destruction of property, and endangering a minor. No person can validly consent to a breach of the peace or a battery that may result in serious injury or death. Furthermore, most states have abolished the marital rape exemption in toto; this exemption precluded husbands from being prosecuted for raping their wives. Thus, in general, there is no legal distinction between crimes committed against intimate partners and those committed against strangers.

Police, prosecutors, and judges are routinely trained in domestic violence, and aggressive interventions are continually implemented. Individuals across the political spectrum have generally supported these changes, although there is ongoing debate as to which interventions work best. Furthermore, some fear that the pendulum has swung too far, and that those who are accused of domestic violence, particularly men, are presumed guilty rather than innocent. Advocates are concerned that the needs of victims are being sacrificed for higher conviction rates. Indeed, the ongoing challenge for the criminal justice system is to protect the rights of both defendants and victims while at the same time treating domestic violence as a serious social problem. Even though the criminal justice system has come a long way since 1920, it still has a long way to go.

Who are the abusers? Who are the victims?

The majority of those arrested for domestic violence are heterosexual men. However, between 5 and 15 percent of those arrested for battering are women. Many of these cases involve self-defending women who have been mistakenly arrested. While women can be the initial aggressor, female abusers are rarely identified or studied. Thus, most theoretical and practical work on domestic violence, as well as the policies and controversies that are discussed in this entry, assume the male batterer/female victim paradigm.

Gay men and lesbians constitute only a small percentage of those arrested for domestic violence. As with female abusers, we know surprisingly little about domestic violence in same-sex relationships. Same-sex victims receive fewer protections and face many more social consequences when reporting domestic violence to the authorities than heterosexual victims. For example, many states define domestic violence in a way that excludes same-sex victims, and some states with sodomy laws also require victims to acknowledge that they are in a domestic relationship, forcing victims to admit to a crime before receiving legal protection.

How many people are victims of domestic violence? The honest answer is that we just do not know. The federal government and a majority of the states collect statistics on domestic violence, but there are wide variations in how each jurisdiction defines offenses, determines what is counted, and measures or reports incidents. Statistics on the incidence and prevalence of domestic violence vary greatly. Thus, it is imperative that when evaluating data one considers the source and the methodology. It is vital to have an accurate picture of domestic violence in order to formulate appropriate policies and maintain intellectual integrity.

There are two official federal measures of crime, the National Crime Victimization Survey (NCVS) and the Uniform Crime Reporting Program (UCR) of the F.B.I. The NCVS gathers information about crime and its consequences from a nationally representative sample of U.S. residents. It surveys respondents about any crimes experienced, including their relationship to the perpetrator. However, there is no way to independently verify this information or to determine how many incidents go unreported to authorities. In fact, it is estimated that about one-half of the incidents of intimate violence experienced by women are never reported to the police. This percentage is likely higher for both straight and gay men and lesbians given that the traditional definition of domestic violence is "wife beating."

The UCR tracks crimes reported to law enforcement. However, it does not require local law enforcement to maintain data on the relationship between victim and offender except in the case of murder. The National Incident-Based Reporting System (NIBRS), authorized by Congress in 1995, will include and standardize data collection on domestic violence. However, NIBRS has not yet been implemented nationally.

Data compiled in 1996 by the Bureau of Justice Statistics yielded the estimate that women experienced 840,000 rape, sexual assault, robbery, and aggravated and simple assault victimizations at the hands of an intimate, down from 1.1 million in 1993. Men experienced about 150,000 such victimizations, with little variation between 1992 and 1996. In 1996, just over 1,800 murders were attributable to intimates, and in almost three out of four of these killings, the victim was a woman. By comparison, in 1976, there were nearly 3,000 victims of intimate murder (Greenfeld). Other studies have suggested that as many as four million women are battered each year, and that 14 percent of women report having been violently abused by a spouse or boyfriend at some time in their lives. (Healy, Smith, and O'Sullivan).

Most intimate relationships are established between people of the same racial and economic background. Domestic violence occurs across all demographic groups. However, official rates of nonlethal, intimate violence are highest among women aged sixteen to twenty-four, women in households in the lowest income categories, and women residing in urban areas (Greenfeld). Couples who cohabitate experience more violence than those who are married (Holzworth-Munroe). Other studies have found that abused women are more likely to live in communities with the highest rates of stranger violence (Fagan). African American women comprise the largest group of victims, although they are also more likely to report intimate victimizations to the police than any other group. However, ethnicity and race are *not* significant correlates with domestic violence when controlling for other socio-demographic variables, such as income, employment status, and age.

Official statistics may be overinclusive of the poor and minorities. Women with higher incomes often have the resources to deal with domestic violence privately without involving the criminal justice system. Furthermore, the police may be more likely to arrest people in poor and middle-class neighborhoods than in upper-class neighborhoods. However, those with fewer resources also face more stressors, and while stress itself does not lead directly to violence, it can exacerbate the risk of violence (Holzworth-Munroe).

The causes of domestic violence

There are many theories as to the causes of domestic violence. Feminist-inspired theories look to the institution of patriarchy and argue that battering mirrors male power and control over females. Family-based theories examine the level of family conflict and the indirect lessons children learn about the relationship between violence and love. Individual-based theories attribute domestic violence to personality disorders or biomedical factors, such as head injuries or mental illness. Evolutionary theorists have suggested that male violence against females, both in primates and cross-culturally, is a strategy used to control the female's reproduction and, in humans, is often precipitated by male sexual jealousy (Daly and Wilson).

Furthermore, domestic violence researchers are exploring how race, class, religion, and culture, as well as psychological variables such as low self-esteem and abusive childhoods, affect one's experiences with violence. As a result, we are beginning to understand how the battering experience is both common and unique among abusers and victims.

No single causal model can explain why people hurt those they claim to love. As research becomes more interdisciplinary, and policies are driven as much by empirical data as by politics, theories will have to account for the complicated interplay of biological, social, economic, cultural, and individual factors that lead to domestic violence.

Federal approaches to domestic violence

Local and state governments are responsible for enforcing most domestic violence crimes. However, in 1994, Congress passed the Violence Against Women Act (VAWA). Among its many provisions, VAWA makes certain offenses federal crimes, such as interstate stalking and violation of a protection order. In addition, the 1996 Lautenberg Amendment to the Gun Control Act of 1968 prohibits the transfer, possession, or receipt of both firearms and ammunition by anyone convicted of a misdemeanor domestic violence offense. These laws reflect a larger trend to federalize the criminal law, and they are controversial. Advocates applaud them as providing for a fundamental change in the criminal justice system's response to domestic violence. Opponents argue that they are overreaching, ineffective, and grant excessive power to the federal government, and insist that combating domestic violence is best left to local, not federal, law enforcement. It is too early to access VAWA's impact on curbing domestic violence.

Arrest policies

Prior to 1984, most police could not legally make a warrantless arrest unless a misdemeanor occurred in the officer's presence, or the officer had probable cause to believe that a felony had taken place. Since most domestic violence cases involve simple assault and battery—a misdemeanor—the police could not make an arrest at the scene. Advising the husband or boyfriend to "take a walk around the block" was often the extent of police intervention.

In 1984, the U.S. Attorney General recommended arrest as the standard police response to domestic violence. This recommendation resulted from a landmark Minneapolis controlled experimental study that compared the deterrent effects of arresting the suspect, mediating the dispute, and requiring the batterer to leave the house for eight hours. The study found that arrest more effectively deterred subsequent violence than did the other courses of action. The results were widely publicized.

That same year, Tracy Thurman received a $1.9 million settlement from the Torrington, Connecticut, Police Department for its policy of nonintervention and nonarrest in domestic violence cases. After the Thurman case, police departments concerned about similar lawsuits began to rethink their policies. All fifty states now provide for warrantless arrests in domestic violence cases.

Since arrest statutes have been broadened, many jurisdictions have adopted mandatory or pro-arrest policies. Under these policies, an arrest is either required or preferred if the police officer has probable cause to believe that a domestic battery has taken place, regardless of the victim's wishes. These policies have received mixed reviews. Some advocates maintain that mandatory arrest not only substantially reduces domestic assaults and murders, especially when prosecution follows, but also provides police officers with clear guidelines on how to proceed, correcting the "take a walk around the block" mentality. Opponents argue that these policies fail to account for the criminal justice system's historic mistreatment of minorities. Furthermore, when officers are either unable or unwilling to discern who was the initial aggressor, mandatory arrest policies can result in both parties being arrested. Thus, these pro-arrest policies have the unintended consequence of penalizing rather than protecting victims. Others argue that police ought to have more discretion to handle domestic violence situations on a case-by-case basis.

Does arrest work? The research is inconclusive. For example, when the Minneapolis study was replicated in other jurisdictions, the results differed significantly. Specifically, arrest consistently deterred employed batterers, but increased repeat violence among unemployed batterers. Yet, these findings were largely ignored. Furthermore, between 1992 and 1996, while the police responded to 90 percent of calls for assistance, in only 20 percent of the cases was the alleged abuser arrested immediately (Greenfeld). These findings raise questions as to how effective arrest policies have been in reducing recidivism or changing police practices.

Prosecution and sentencing policies

Prosecutors routinely fail to initiate cases and follow through with prosecution. Victim noncooperation is often cited as the major reason for dismissing a domestic violence case. Thus, once police began to arrest alleged batterers, advocates began to focus reform efforts on prosecution practices. As a result, prosecutors are undertaking new initiatives. Many have established specialized domestic violence units. A few units specialize in same-sex battering, while others target teenagers in dating relationships, where experimentation with violence often begins. Vertical prosecution, in which one prosecutor is assigned to handle the case from arraignment to completion, thus providing the victim with ongoing support, is becoming common. Increasingly, jurisdictions are employing social workers to counsel victims and their families. Some courts expedite, or *rocket docket*, domestic violence cases. Others divert first-time offenders into batterer treatment prior to trial.

Most controversial, many jurisdictions are implementing *no-drop* policies. Under such policies, prosecutors cannot routinely dismiss charges at the victim's request, but are required to pursue a case if enough evidence exists to substantiate the charge. Moreover, the prosecutor usually signs the charge, relieving the victim of responsibility. At least four states have adopted legislation encouraging the use of no-drop policies, and VAWA has authorized grants to local law enforcement agencies that adopt aggressive prosecution policies.

Pro-prosecution policies are often characterized as either *hard* or *soft* no-drop policies. Under hard policies, cases proceed regardless of the victim's wishes when there is enough evidence to go forward. This can include subpoenaing the victim to testify and requesting that the judge issue an order of contempt if the victim refuses to cooperate. Most states recognize an exemption to marital privilege laws in cases in which one spouse is charged with a crime against the other and, thus, the vast majority of victims can be compelled to testify as a witness for the state and incarcerated for refusing to do so. Some jurisdictions go forward without the victim's testimony, just as if it were a homicide case, by introducing other evidence, such as 911 tapes, photographs, medical records, and testimonies of police officers and expert witnesses.

Under soft policies, victims are provided with support services and encouraged to proceed, but are never mandated to participate. The state will not proceed if the victim insists that the case be dropped.

Those supportive of aggressive prosecution argue that no-drop policies take the burden off the victim by removing her as the "plaintiff." They contend that the batterer has less incentive to try to harm or intimidate his victim once he realizes that she no longer controls the process. Furthermore, aggressive prosecution sends a strong message that domestic violence is a crime against the state as well as the individual. However, many advocates for battered women argue that the use of hard policies has the unintended effect of punishing or revictimizing the victim for the actions of the abuser. It also fails to take into account the effect that prosecution will have on family income or children. The state should neither force the victim into a process over which she has no control, nor undermine her autonomy or decision-making.

Do aggressive prosecution policies work? It is difficult to measure the difference between policies as written and policies as practiced. While early data indicate that aggressive policies can reduce domestic homicides, lower recidivism rates, and change attitudes within the criminal justice system, more research is needed to verify these findings (Hanna, 1996).

Despite these reforms, most domestic violence cases still end in arrest. Of those cases that are prosecuted, many are charged or plead down to misdemeanors even though the conduct constituted a felony. When prosecutors do go forward, the final disposition is most often a period of probation. A growing number of defendants must also complete a batterer's treatment program as a condition of probation. Only a small percentage of domestic violence offenders are sentenced to incarceration (Hanna, 1998).

How do domestic violence cases compare to nondomestic violence cases? As of 1999, no empirical evidence supported the assertion that the criminal justice system treats domestic violence offenses less seriously than other violent crimes. One study in the mid-1980s found that offenders closely related by blood or sexual ties to their victims were usually given probation or had their cases dismissed, but so too were offenders unrelated to their victims (Ferraro and Boychuck). According to a 1998 study of all inmates incarcerated in state prisons, the median sentence for assault was four years *longer* if the victim was the offender's spouse rather than a stranger (Greenfeld). Given the changes in arrest and prosecution policies, as well as increased public pressure on law enforcement to treat domestic violence as a serious crime, it is likely that domestic cases are being treated more seriously than nondomestic cases.

Batterer treatment programs

In 1984, the Attorney General's Task Force on Family Violence concluded that treatment for domestic violence is most successful when the criminal justice system mandates it. Although the Task Force report recommended incarceration for serious offenses, it encouraged the use of batterer treatment programs in cases where the injury to the victim was not serious. Since then, the criminal justice system has adopted faith in treatment as a matter of policy. Some states require courts to order attendance into a batterer treatment program as a condition of probation. Others have pretrial diversion programs in which first-time offenders can avoid conviction by completing a batterer treatment program. VAWA also endorses batterer treatment for violations of its criminal provisions.

Many states mandate the length and content of treatment programs that can be court ordered, although there is no convincing evidence that either the length or model of the treatment determines its effectiveness. Most court-ordered programs are six months to a year long. Program content varies greatly. Early programs were based on the premise that poor conflict management skills within the relationship caused violence and, therefore, treated both parties. Most court-ordered programs today, however, reject couple's therapy and treat the batterer only. While some programs focus on anger control

and the individual's history with violence, increasingly, the majority of court-ordered programs adopt the premise that battering is an outgrowth of patriarchy and focus on the use of violence by the batterer to establish power and control over his victim. Most of these programs will not accept batterers who have substance abuse problems, although more than half of those incarcerated for domestic violence had been using drugs or alcohol at the time of the incident for which they were incarcerated, suggesting that many abusers are in need of multiple interventions (Greenfeld).

Does batterer treatment work? Some available data suggest that court-ordered treatment correlates with a reduction in physical violence, although treatment neither terminates violence in many cases nor curbs the more subtle forms of abuse. However, whether treatment, or simply individual motivation brought on by legal intervention, *causes* the reduction of violence is unclear. In fact, some studies have found that men arrested and treated resume violent behaviors as frequently as do men arrested and not referred to treatment, and that there is no significant difference between men who complete batterer's treatment and men who drop out of the program (Rosenfeld). The available research on batterer treatment is hampered by the lack of a control group. As of 1999, no study has randomly assigned abusers to incarceration, treatment, or unsupervised probation. A control group would give researchers confidence that treatment, and not some other variable, such as threat of incarceration, individual motivation, support from one's partner, social stigma, or other factors, are influencing a change in behavior. Additionally, many studies are methodologically unsound. Sample sizes are often too small to draw valid conclusions and drop-out rates are high. Even more troubling is that most studies that report treatment successes include only subjects who have no substance abuse problems, no psychiatric difficulty, and high motivation. Thus, the complex question of which programs work best for whom, and under what circumstances, remains largely unanswered.

Finally, some jurisdictions have established specialized probation units. Probation officers trained in domestic violence intensively supervise abusers, following their progress in treatment and at home. This is considered to be the last loophole that the criminal justice system needs to close in order to hold abusers accountable for their crimes.

Future of the system's response to domestic violence

One of the most promising developments in the prevention and treatment of domestic violence is research on batterer typologies. Despite popular misconceptions, all abusers are not equally dangerous, nor are they all alike. It is estimated that only two percent of the total male population is repeatedly severely abusive to women in any given year (Dutton). Most men arrested for domestic violence are low-risk offenders, and are violent only with family members. Those who pose the greatest risk often have extensive criminal histories, including property crimes, drug or alcohol offenses, and violent offenses against nonfamily victims (Dutton). This research will help law enforcement to better screen cases and develop interventions that account for the differences among abusers. In addition, research on the relationship between violence and biomedical conditions is likely to lead to treatments for abusers that involve both medical and behavioral therapy.

The criminal justice system also needs to expand its understanding of domestic violence beyond the male abuser/female victim model and to provide adequate protections for all victims regardless of gender or sexual orientation. Further research into why most men do not engage in intimate violence is imperative to understand what role gender does play in domestic violence.

Only time and solid research will tell if the criminal justice system can successfully reduce domestic violence. None of the initiatives described above will work in isolation. The best research suggests that a coordinated community response, which involves police, prosecutors, defense attorneys, judges, probation officers, victims' advocates, treatment providers, and medical professionals, is essential. And, while both lethal and nonlethal intimate violence declined in the 1990s, so too has nondomestic violence. Thus, we must be cautious before attributing progress solely to more aggressive criminal intervention. Nevertheless, many remain optimistic that treating domestic violence as a serious public crime and not a trivial family matter will make for a safer society.

CHERYL HANNA

See also FAMILY ABUSE AND CRIME; HOMICIDE: BEHAVIORAL ASPECTS; JUSTIFICATION: SELF-DEFENSE; SCIENTIFIC EVIDENCE; STALKING; VICTIMS; VIOLENCE.

BIBLIOGRAPHY

ASMUS, MARY; RITMEESTER, TINEKE; and PENCE, ELLEN. "Prosecuting Domestic Abuse Cases in Duluth: Developing Effective Prosecution Strategies from Understanding the Dynamics of Abusive Relationships." *Hamline Law Review* 15 (1991): 115–158.

Attorney General's Task Force on Family Violence. Final Report, U.S. Department of Justice.

BACHMAN, RONET, and SALZMAN, LINDA E. "Violence against Women: Estimates from the Redesigned Survey (NCJ-154348)." Washington, D.C.: U.S. Department of Justice, 1995.

BINDER, ARNOLD, and MEEKER, JAMES W. "Implications of the Failure to Replicate the Minneapolis Experiment Findings." *American Sociological Review* 57 (1993): 698–708.

BUZAWA, EVE S., and BUZAWA, CARL G. *Domestic Violence: The Changing Criminal Justice Response.* Beverly Hills, Calif.: Sage, 1992.

———. *Domestic Violence: The Criminal Justice System Response.* Beverly Hills, Calif.: Sage, 1996.

———. *Do Arrests and Restraining Orders Work?* Beverly Hills, Calif.: Sage, 1992.

DALY, MARTIN, and WILSON, MARGO. *Homicide.* Aldine de Gruyter, 1988.

DUTTON, DONALD G., with GOLANT, SUSAN K. *The Batterer: A Psychological Profile.* New York: Basic Books, 1995.

EDELSON, JEFFREY L. *Intervention for Men Who Batter: An Ecological Approach.* Beverly Hills, Calif.: Sage, 1992.

FAGAN, JEFFREY. "The Criminalization of Domestic Violence: Promises and Limits." Washington, D.C.: U.S. Department of Justice, 1996.

FERRARO, KATHLEEN J., and BOYCHUCK, TASCHA. "The Court's Response to Interpersonal Violence: A Comparison of Intimate and Nonintimate Assault." In *Domestic Violence: The Changing Criminal Justice Response.* Edited by Eve S. Buzawa and Carl G. Buzawa. Beverly Hills, Calif.: Sage, 1992. Pages 209ff.

FINEMAN, MARTHA, and MYKITIUK, ROXANNE, eds. *The Public Nature of Private Violence.* New York: Routledge, 1994.

GELLES, RICHARD, and LOSEKE, DONILEEN R., eds. *Current Controversies on Family Violence.* Beverly Hills, Calif.: Sage, 1992.

GOLDFARB, SALLY. "Describing Without Circumscribing: Questioning the Construct of Gender in the Discourse of Intimate Violence." *George Washington Law Review* U.S. Department of Justice. 64 (1996): 582–631.

GONDOLF, EDWARD W. "Who Are Those Guys? Toward a Behavioral Typology of Batterers." *Violence & Victims* 3 (1980): 187.

———. "An Exploratory Survey of Court-Mandated Batterer Programs, Responses to Victimization." *Women & Children* 13 (1990): 7.

GREENFELD, LAWRENCE, et al. "Violence By Intimates: Analysis of Data on Crimes By Current or Former Spouses, Boyfriends, and Girlfriends." Washington, D.C.: U.S. Department of Justice, Bureau of Justice Statistics, 1998.

HANNA, CHERYL. "No Right to Choose: Mandated Victim Participation in Domestic Violence Prosecutions." *Harvard Law Review* 109 (1996): 1849–1910.

———. "The Paradox of Hope: The Crime and Punishment of Domestic Violence." *William & Mary Law Review* 39 (1998): 1505–1584.

HEALY, KERRY; SMITH, KRISTEN; and O'SULLIVAN, CHRIS. *Batterer Intervention: Program Approaches and Criminal Justice Strategies* (NCJ 168638). Washington, D.C.: U.S. Department of Justice, 1998.

HILTON, N. ZOE, ed. *Legal Responses to Wife Assault.* Beverly Hills, Calif.: Sage, 1993.

HOLZWORTH-MUNROE, AMY, and STUART, GREGORY L. "Typology of Male Batterers: Three Subtypes and the Differences Among Them." *Psychological Bulletin* 116 (1994): 476–497.

Justice Research and Statistics Association. *Domestic and Sexual Violence Data Collection: A Report to Congress Under the Violence Against Woman Act* (NCJ 161405). Washington, D.C.: National Institute of Justice, 1996.

KNUDSEN, DEAN D., and MILLER, JOANN L., eds. *Abused and Battered.* New York: A. de Gruyter, 1991.

MILLER, NEAL. "Domestic Violence Legislation Affecting Police and Prosecutor Responsibilities in the United States: Inferences from a 50-State Review of State Statutory Codes." Presentation to the 5th International Family Violence Consequence, University of New Hampshire, http://www.ilj.org/dv/dvvaw.html (1998).

PENCE, ELLEN, and PAYMAR, MICHAEL. *Education Groups for Men Who Batter: The Duluth Model.* New York: Springer, 1993.

ROSENFELD, BARRY D. "Court Ordered Treatment of Spouse Abuse." *Clinical Psychology Review* vol. 12 (1992): 205–226.

SCHNEIDER, ELIZABETH M. "Particularity & Generality: Challenges of Feminist Theory and Practice in Work on Woman Abuse." *New York University Law Review* 67(1992): 520–568.

SHERMAN, LAWRENCE. *Policing Domestic Violence: Experiments and Dilemmas.* New York: Free Press, 1992.

SMUTS, BARBARA. "Male Aggression Against Women: An Evolutionary Perspective." In *Sex, Power, Conflict.* Edited by David M. Buss and Neil Malamuth. New York: Oxford University Press, 1996. Pages 231–268.

STEINMAN, MICHAEL, ed. *Woman Battering: Policy Responses.* Highland Heights, Ky.: Academy of Criminal Justice Sciences, Northern Kentucky University, 1991.

STRAUS, MURRAY, and GELLES, RICHARD, eds. *Physical Violence in American Families: Risk Factors and Adaptations to Violence in 8,145 Families.* New Brunswick, N.J.: Transaction, 1990.

WEST, ANGELA. "Prosecutorial Activism: Confronting Heterosexism in a Lesbian Battering Case." *Harvard Women's Law Journal* 15 (1992): 249–271.

YLLO, KERTI, A., and BOGRAD, MICHELE, eds. *Feminist Perspectives on Wife Abuse.* Beverly Hills, Calif.: Sage, 1988.

ZORZA, JOAN. "Must We Stop Arresting Batterers? Analysis and Policy Implications of New Police Domestic Violence Studies." *New England Law Review* 28 (1994): 929–990.

DOUBLE JEOPARDY

Ancient civilizations relied on the blood feud to provide justice when one person killed another—the relatives of a slain person had a duty to avenge the death. While the blood feud manifested a rough "eye-for-an-eye" retributive justice, it could, in theory, lead to an endless series of killings as each death was avenged. The Greek playwright Aeschylus dramatized a cycle of blood feud revenge in *The Oresteian Trilogy*, which ended with the Greek gods deciding that a trial is a better way to achieve justice. Part of the reason to replace the blood feud with a trial is to permit the cycle of revenge to end, to provide a final outcome to a dispute, and to create repose in the litigants. But to protect the finality of outcomes, there must exist a principle forbidding a retrial of the same case or the same issue.

A double jeopardy principle has been part of Western legal systems for thousands of years. The Code of Hammurabi, for example, in the nineteenth century B.C.E. sought to prohibit judges from changing judgments (law 15). The Greek philosopher Demosthenes said in 355 B.C.E. that the "laws forbid the same man to be tried twice on the same issue." In the Roman Republic, an acquittal could not be appealed. St. Jerome in A.D. 391 interpreted a passage from the Old Testament to mean that not even God judges twice for the same act.

The English common law principle that there should be one punishment for one crime first manifested itself during the confrontation between King Henry II and St. Thomas Becket that occurred between 1164 and 1170. Henry, the great-grandson of William the Conqueror, enacted a law that required punishment in the king's court of clergy who had already been punished in the church courts. In opposing this law, Becket relied on St. Jerome's principle forbidding more than one judgment for the same act. After four of Henry's knights killed Becket, the pope condemned Henry's provisions permitting the double punishment of clergy. Henry relented and today, over eight hundred years later, courts still condemn double punishment.

The evolution of double jeopardy law from the twelfth century to today cannot be easily summarized, but the great English commentator Sir William Blackstone could state confidently in 1765 that there was a "universal maxim of the common law of England, that no man is to be brought into jeopardy of his life more than once for the same offence." This "universal maxim" led directly to the Fifth Amendment double jeopardy clause, which is strikingly similar to Blackstone's statement of the common law maxim. The Fifth Amendment provides: "nor shall any person be subject for the same offence to be twice put in jeopardy of life or limb."

There are two difficult concepts embedded in the arcane language of the double jeopardy clause—"same offense" and "twice in jeopardy." "Same offense" could be read literally to be the very same statutory offense—for example, the premeditated murder of V is the same offense as the premeditated murder of V but would not be the same offense as manslaughter of V even though manslaughter is a lesser form of homicide. From at least the seventeenth century, however, courts and commentators understood "same offense" in a broader way. Unfortunately, the precise outlines of this broader meaning have long been elusive. In part this is because "same offense" issues were not very troubling in Blackstone's day. The common law recognized a relatively small number of criminal offenses and, aside from homicide, the offense definitions rarely overlapped.

The "twice in jeopardy" issue was also easy in the eighteenth century. If a defendant was acquitted or convicted of murder, he could not again be tried for that murder. Unlike the eighteenth-century English system, modern criminal procedure permits the judge sometimes to dismiss cases before a verdict is rendered—the jury might not reach the required vote (almost all jurisdictions require unanimous verdicts in criminal cases), or the case might be dismissed during the trial for some reason. Errors that could justify dismissing the case after trial begins include the failure of the prosecution's key witness to appear, a remark made by the prosecutor or defense counsel that prejudices the jury, and a mistake made in the indictment that cannot be corrected. Most dismissals during a trial are called "mistrials."

Mistrials

In Blackstone's day, a verdict was required for the double jeopardy principle to operate, but this was probably because outcomes short of a verdict were virtually unknown. The current standard for deciding when a mistrial is equivalent to a verdict, drawn from the 1824 case of *United States v. Perez*, is whether the first trial ended because of "manifest necessity." If so, the first trial does not erect a double jeopardy bar to a second trial. If there was no "manifest necessity" to end the first trial, then a second one is a forbidden second jeopardy.

Three general principles can be drawn from the "manifest necessity" cases. First, if the defendant requests the mistrial and the judge grants it, this will almost always constitute manifest necessity for ending the first trial. This defendant can be retried. Second, if the judge decides that the jurors have been unfairly prejudiced—for example, by hearing something they should not have heard—the judge's decision to terminate the trial will almost always constitute manifest necessity. This defendant, too, can be retried. Third, if the first trial ends because the jury might have acquitted—such as when the prosecution's chief witness did not appear—there is no manifest necessity. If the state fails to produce enough evidence at trial, the defendant is entitled to an acquittal. This defendant cannot be retried.

Other kinds of reasons can lead to a mistrial—for example, one judge granted a mistrial because his mother-in-law died unexpectedly. In these miscellaneous cases, courts balance the reason for the mistrial, including how carefully the judge considered other alternatives, against the unfairness of asking a defendant once again to defend the criminal charge. In the case where the trial judge's mother-in-law died suddenly, the appeals court held that there was no manifest necessity for the mistrial, in part because the judge did not consider asking another judge to take his place. The double jeopardy clause thus barred a second trial.

Multiple punishment

There is another "twice in jeopardy" issue, one that may sound odd to the ear. Is a defendant placed twice in jeopardy if he is tried only once but convicted of two offenses that are the same offense? Courts have long assumed that it is double jeopardy to convict a defendant twice of the same offense whether the convictions occur in one trial or two. If the rule were otherwise, the prosecutor could often circumvent the double jeopardy clause by trying both offenses in a single trial (a procedure that would not have been available to prosecutors in the eighteenth century).

The linguistic oddness of finding that a single trial can be double jeopardy may explain why courts have developed the terminology "multiple punishment" to explain what the double jeopardy clause forbids in a single trial. As the U.S. Supreme Court has stated on numerous occasions, the clause offers three protections in addition to the "manifest necessity" principle—it "protects against a second prosecution for the same offense after acquittal. It protects against a second prosecution for the same offense after conviction. And it protects against multiple punishments for the same offense" (*Brown v. Ohio*).

Using this three-part description of double jeopardy protection, one way to understand the double jeopardy clause is that it constrains judges and prosecutors. If the prosecutor brings more than one charge for the same offense in a single trial, the judge can enter but one conviction. If the prosecutor follows a conviction or acquittal with another charge for the same offense, the judge is obligated to dismiss the second charge. The Supreme Court put the matter this way in *Brown v. Ohio*, one of its most important double jeopardy cases:

[T]he Fifth Amendment double jeopardy guarantee serves principally as a restraint on courts and prosecutors. The legislature remains free under the Double Jeopardy Clause to define crimes and fix punishments; but once the legislature has acted courts may

not impose more than one punishment for the same offense and prosecutors ordinarily may not attempt to secure that punishment in more than one trial.

The multiple punishment issue sometimes arises when the legislature has ordered consecutive sentences for violations of more than one criminal statute. For example, a Missouri statute created an offense of "armed criminal action" to punish the use of a dangerous weapon to commit a felony. This statute stated that any sentence imposed under it "shall be in addition" to the punishment for the felony that was committed using the dangerous weapon. Is this explicit indication of legislative intent significant in deciding whether the consecutive sentences are multiple punishment? Yes, the Court held in *Missouri v. Hunter*. The presence of clear legislative intent to punish offenses consecutively means that consecutive sentences are not multiple punishments within the meaning of the double jeopardy clause regardless of how much the offense definitions overlap.

Second prosecution after conviction

The prosecutor can bring a second prosecution after a conviction unless the charges are for the "same" double jeopardy offense. Same offense issues arise when multiple criminal violations occur during a single criminal "transaction." For example, *R* uses a knife to rob *V*. When another person, *V*2, attempts to prevent the robbery, *R* pulls a gun and threatens *V*2 with the gun, then also robs him. This defendant might have committed four criminal offenses—robbery of *V*1, robbery of *V*2, assault on *V*2 (based on the threat with the gun), and the offense of carrying a gun without a license. A prosecutor who wanted to charge all four offenses must know whether any of them are the same offense for purposes of double jeopardy.

This issue has caused the Supreme Court considerable trouble and is still at least partly unresolved. Since the time of Blackstone, it has been accepted wisdom that two different offenses are the "same" if one is necessarily included in the other—if proving the greater always proves the lesser. To use Blackstone's example, a conviction of manslaughter bars a later trial for murder because manslaughter is a necessarily included offense of murder. Applying this principle, the Supreme Court held in *Brown v. Ohio* that auto theft is the same offense as joyriding because proving auto theft (taking a car without permission and with intent to steal) always proves joy-riding (taking a car without permission). The theory here is that a lesser included offense is simply a species of the greater offense.

Some commentators have criticized this principle on the ground that the defendant who is first prosecuted for the lesser offense is never in jeopardy for the additional culpability manifested in the greater offense (the intent to steal, for example, required for auto theft but not for joyriding). The Court's rationale seems to be that the prosecutor can choose to try the greater offense first. If, instead, the prosecutor chooses to try the lesser, the state is stuck with that choice.

Blackstone's lesser-included offense understanding of "same offense" worked well for two hundred years. In 1889, the Supreme Court applied a version of Blackstone's test in *In re Nielsen* and first clearly relied on the lesser-offense test in the 1932 case of *Blockburger v. United States*. The test is known today as the *Blockburger* test and is usually stated as follows: when the same criminal conduct violates more than one statute, offenses are different if each requires proof of an element that the other does not. If each requires proof of an element the other does not, then neither can be included within the other.

The *Blockburger* test answers the earlier robbery example. Robbery of *V*1 is not the same offense as robbery of *V*2 because the two robberies are based on different conduct. *R* could have stopped after robbing *V*1; when *R* does not stop, he has committed two robberies. On the facts of the hypothetical case, robbery is based on the same conduct as carrying a gun without a license, but these offenses are not the same offense because robbery does not require the use of a gun. But the threat of the gun that constituted assault on *V*2 is the same offense as robbery of *V*2 because robbery does require proof of force or threat of force.

Although the test is both relatively easy to apply and grounded in Blackstone's wisdom, changes in U.S. criminal law have created difficulties for the *Blockburger* test. Today there are many overlapping, complex criminal offenses, and the same conduct will often violate two, three, four, or more criminal statutes. Modern statutes tend to be complex, and many require distinct elements. As early as 1958, well before the various "wars" on drugs, a single sale of narcotics violated nine different federal statues, each of which required an element that the others did not—for example, sale not in the original package, sale without a prescription, and sale knowl-

ing of unlawful importation. In *Gore v. United States,* the Court held that these three narcotics offenses could be *punished* consecutively. What remained unclear after *Gore* was whether separate *trials* could be based on a single sale of narcotics.

Reacting against the unfairness of multiple trials based on the same conduct, the Supreme Court in the 1970s began to suggest that there might be a greater protection against successive prosecutions than against multiple punishment in a single trial. The *Blockburger* test, the Court seemed to say, told us how many punishments were permitted but not how many trials. In 1990 in *Grady v. Corbin,* the Court held that successive prosecutions required a "same conduct" understanding of "same offense." In addition to the *Blockburger* inquiry that focused on offense definitions, *Grady* read the double jeopardy clause to forbid a trial for any criminal charge that required proof of "conduct that constitutes an offense" of which the defendant had already been convicted. For example, manslaughter by auto would be the same offense as drunk driving if the defendant had already been convicted of drunk driving and the manslaughter required proof of the same drunk driving.

The rule proved difficult to apply and, perhaps more importantly, was difficult to justify. As Justice Antonin Scalia sarcastically asked in his dissent in *Grady,* how could the double jeopardy clause words "same offense" mean one thing when there was a single trial and something very different when successive prosecutions were involved? The Court abandoned the "same conduct" definition of same offense in *United States v. Dixon,* decided only three years after *Grady.* In *Dixon,* the Court held that there is only one definition of same offense—the *Blockburger* lesser-included offense definition. If the criminal statutes themselves do not define the same offense when the elements are compared, it does not matter how often the same conduct is reprosecuted. Drunk driving would *not* be the same offense as manslaughter by auto if the latter offense could be proved by other kinds of reckless behavior even if drunk driving was the reckless conduct that killed the victim in the case being prosecuted.

Dixon did not solve all the same offense problems, however. For one thing, the five Justices who voted to overrule *Grady* disagreed among themselves about how to apply *Blockburger* to the complex statutes in *Dixon.* For another, there might still be a "same offense" difference between multiple punishments in a single trial and a second trial after conviction. Recall the *Missouri v. Hunter* rule that a specific legislative requirement of consecutive sentences made the punishments not multiple. But this does not necessarily solve the problem of multiple trials. One way to frame the question is whether the legislature can, by simply stating its intent to create separate offenses, make offenses not the "same" for purposes of successive prosecutions as well as for the multiple punishment doctrine. If, as the Court suggested in *Brown*, the legislature is free to "define crimes and fix punishments," perhaps the legislature can create separate offenses under the double jeopardy clause by simply stating its intent to do so.

But the Court has never suggested that the multiple punishment principle from *Missouri v. Hunter* would extend into the successive prosecution context. Indeed, one member of the current Court, Justice Scalia, has argued just the opposite—that the multiple punishment doctrine is analytically separate from the successive prosecution doctrine. In the single trial context, the argument goes, the legislature can rebut the result of the *Blockburger* test because the rebuttal merely makes clear how many penalties the legislature intended to authorize, but the double jeopardy clause forbids the legislature to authorize more than one trial for the same offense as defined by the *Blockburger* test. This issue remains unresolved.

Second prosecution after acquittal

When the first trial ends in an acquittal, there can be no second prosecution for the same offense. In this way, acquittal and conviction provide the same double jeopardy bar. But the Court has expanded the role of the double jeopardy clause to protect acquittals even when the offenses are not the same offense. In *Ashe v. Swenson*, masked men robbed five poker players. When the prosecutor tried Ashe for robbing one of the players, the evidence that Ashe was one of the robbers was weak, and the jury found Ashe not guilty of that robbery. The prosecutor then tried Ashe for robbing another player. This time the eyewitnesses seemed more certain that one of the masked men was Ashe; the eyewitness who was least certain at the first trial was not called to testify. Ashe was convicted of this robbery.

The same offense rule is that different conduct gives rise to different offenses. Robbery of one victim is never the same offense as robbery

of a second. Thus, Ashe could get no help from the same offense doctrine. If he had been convicted of robbing the first poker player, he could have been tried later for robbing the second one.

But the acquittal provided a broader ban against a second trial. The Court noted that the only issue in the first trial was whether Ashe was one of the masked men, which the first jury determined in Ashe's favor. The Court held that the state could not force Ashe to defend that issue again. To permit the state to bring a prosecution for a different victim would, in effect, permit the second jury to overrule the first. It would also encourage prosecutors to structure later cases to hide evidence that turned out to be favorable to the defendant in the first trial. Forcing a defendant repeatedly to defend the same basic issue, while the state's case gets better and better, can only increase the likelihood that innocent defendants will be convicted.

Appeals

Just as was true in the Roman Republic, a conviction today can be appealed and reversed, but an acquittal is final and cannot be appealed. As with the *Ashe* principle discussed in the last section, one justification is that appeal of an acquittal creates too much risk that an innocent defendant will be worn down by the superior resources of the state. A justification from outside the double jeopardy clause is that permitting an appellate court to reverse a jury's acquittal would violate the Sixth Amendment right to trial by jury (this justification does not explain why acquittals by judges are also non-appealable).

While the jury should have the final say in deciding the facts that underlie an acquittal, the bar of prosecution appeal seems less persuasive when the trial judge has made an error that keeps some important fact from the jury. Suppose the trial judge suppressed a confession that was clearly admissible. The jury's acquittal in this situation is based on incomplete information. In 1937 the Supreme Court in *Palko v. Connecticut* upheld the constitutionality of a state process that permitted the prosecution to obtain a new trial by appealing an acquittal infected by legal errors. The doctrinal framework of *Palko* was rejected in 1969 in *Benton v. Maryland*, however, and most commentators believe that the double jeopardy clause does not permit a prosecution appeal even on the ground of legal error.

Appeals are therefore tilted in favor of the defendant. A guilty verdict can be appealed and reversed, but an acquittal, even if clearly wrong, can never be reversed on factual grounds and probably not on any other ground. This is perhaps a fair price to pay to ensure that innocent defendants are not convicted after repeated trials and appeals.

Lower courts

Thousands of lower court cases have applied the *Blockburger* lesser-included offense test to federal offenses and to offenses from all fifty states. Assault with intent to murder, for example, is a different offense from assault with a dangerous weapon (each requires proof of an element that the other does not). Burglary, which requires entry into a structure, is a different offense from larceny committed inside the structure (one can commit burglary without committing larceny and vice versa). But larceny is the same offense as grand larceny (larceny of property over a certain value), and assault is the same offense as assault with intent to rape or assault with intent to murder.

Lower courts generally recognize that *Blockburger* is just a presumption when applied to multiple punishment in a single trial. For example, *Blockburger* often pronounces different kinds of homicide offenses to be different double jeopardy offenses. The offense of homicide by auto is not the same *Blockburger* offense as intentional murder. The latter requires proof of intent to kill while the former requires proof that the killing was done by auto. *Blockburger* thus permits two homicide convictions for one killing (an intentional killing by means of an auto). Perhaps, however, the number of homicide offenses is better correlated with the number of victims than the number of superficially distinct statutes.

Dozens of lower courts have wrestled with this issue. Most have concluded, by one means or another, that the legislature did not intend to authorize two homicide convictions for killing a single victim. These courts thus use actual legislative intent to rebut the presumption about intent that is created by *Blockburger*.

Dual sovereignty

Although "dual sovereignty" is really a variation of the same offense issue, it is usually treated separately. Suppose the federal Congress and a state legislature have identical criminal statutes. Can a defendant be charged and convicted (or acquitted) of an offense in federal court and then

tried in state court? What if the defendant is first tried in state court? This issue is called "dual sovereignty" because the original thirteen states were separate political entities until they joined the federal union and gave up some of their sovereignty to the federal government. The states did not give up their right to define and punish crimes.

This issue, and its dual sovereignty implication, was recognized by the Supreme Court in the 1820 case of *Houston v. Moore*, but it has only been in the last few decades that the issue affected very many defendants. Congress initially did not create many criminal offenses and there was little overlap between federal and state criminal law. But there has been an explosion of federal criminal law in the last twenty years, and many defendants now potentially face successive state and federal prosecutions.

When the issue was first noted in *Houston*, the various opinions of the Supreme Court laid out the two basic approaches to the problem. Justice Joseph Story argued that it would violate double jeopardy for both sovereigns to prosecute the same offense, which he took to mean the same criminal conduct. Justice William Johnson saw the matter differently—it was not a question of prosecuting the same conduct but the *same offense*. Because each U.S. citizen owes allegiance to two sovereigns, the same conduct that violates state and federal criminal law was *two* offenses, in Johnson's view, not one.

Johnson's view ultimately prevailed. It is not double jeopardy for a defendant to be acquitted of federal bank robbery charges and then tried and convicted in state court for the same bank robbery. Nor is it double jeopardy for a defendant to be convicted in state court and then convicted in federal court. These cases drew a stinging dissent in *Bartkus v. Illinois* from Justice Hugo Black, who wrote: "If double punishment is what is feared, it hurts just as much for two 'Sovereigns' to inflict it than for one. If danger to the innocent is emphasized, that danger is surely no less" when the successive trials are brought by different sovereigns.

The dual sovereignty doctrine is controversial, but there are not very many instances of successive state and federal prosecutions. Both the federal and state governments have imposed limits on their ability to re-prosecute the same conduct. The federal limit is found in a Department of Justice policy that generally forbids prosecuting conduct that has already been prosecuted. There are exceptions for cases in which justice was not done in the prior prosecution—for example, the judge or prosecutor was corrupt or the jury entered an acquittal that was clearly against the evidence. More than half the states have enacted statutes that generally forbid a state prosecution to be based on the same conduct as an earlier federal prosecution. Although there is much to commend in Justice Black's rejection of the dual sovereignty doctrine, the federal and state systems have adjusted to minimize the potential harm.

GEORGE C. THOMAS, III

See also ADVERSARY SYSTEM; APPEAL; CRIMINAL PROCEDURE: CONSTITUTIONAL ASPECTS; TRIAL, CRIMINAL.

BIBLIOGRAPHY

AMAR, AKIL REED. "Double Jeopardy Law Made Simple." *Yale Law Journal* 106 (April 1997): 1807–1848.

BLACKSTONE, WILLIAM. *Commentaries on the Laws of England* (1765), vol. 4. Chicago: University of Chicago Press, 1979.

CASSELL, PAUL G. "The Rodney King Trial and the Double Jeopardy Clause: Some Observations on Original Meaning and the ACLU's Schizophrenic Views of the Dual Sovereignty Doctrine." *UCLA Law Review* 41 (February 1994): 693–720.

FRIEDLAND, MARTIN L. *Double Jeopardy.* Oxford, U.K.: Clarendon Press, 1969.

GUERRA, SANDRA. "The Myth of Dual Sovereignty: Multijurisdictional Drug Law Enforcement and Double Jeopardy." *North Carolina Law Review* 73 (March 1995): 1159–1210.

HERMAN, SUSAN N. "Double Jeopardy All Over Again: Dual Sovereignty, Rodney King, and the ACLU." *UCLA Law Review* 41 (February 1994): 609–647.

KING, NANCY J. "Portioning Punishment: Constitutional Limits on Successive and Excessive Penalties." *University of Pennsylvania Law Review* 144 (November 1995): 101–196.

KIRCHHEIMER, OTTO. "The Act, the Offense and Double Jeopardy." *Yale Law Journal* 58 (March 1949): 513–544.

MOORE, MICHAEL S. *Act and Crime.* Oxford, U.K.: Clarendon Press, 1993.

POULIN, ANNE BOWEN. "Collateral Estoppel in Criminal Cases: Reuse of Evidence after Acquittal." *University of Cincinnati Law Review* 58, no. 1 (1989): 1–57.

———. "Double Jeopardy: *Grady* and *Dowling* Stir the Muddy Waters." *Rutgers Law Review* 43 (summer 1991): 889–931.

RUDSTEIN, DAVID S. "Double Jeopardy and the Fraudulently-Obtained Acquittal." *Missouri Law Review* 60 (summer 1995): 607–651.

SCHULHOFER, STEPHEN J. "Jeopardy and Mistrials." *University of Pennsylvania Law Review* 125 (January 1977): 449–539.

SIGLER, JAY A. *Double Jeopardy: The Development of a Legal and Social Policy.* Ithaca, N.Y.: Cornell University Press, 1969.

SHELLENBERGER, JAMES A., and STRAZZELLA, JAMES A. "The Lesser-Included Offense Doctrine and the Constitution: The Development of Due Process and Double Jeopardy Remedies." *Marquette Law Review* 79 (fall 1995): 1–193.

STRAZZELLA, JAMES A. "The Relationship of Double Jeopardy to Prosecution Appeals." *Notre Dame Law Review* 73 (November 1997): 1–30.

THOMAS, GEORGE C., III. "Sentencing Problems Under the Multiple Punishment Doctrine." *Villanova Law Review* 31 (September 1986): 1351–1428.

———. *Double Jeopardy: The History, the Law.* New York: New York University Press, 1998.

"Twice in Jeopardy." *Yale Law Journal* 75 (December 1965): 262–321.

WESTEN, PETER. "The Three Faces of Double Jeopardy: Reflections on Government Appeals of Criminal Sentences." *Michigan Law Review* 78 (June 1980): 1001–1065.

WESTEN, PETER, and DRUBEL, RICHARD. "Toward a General Theory of Double Jeopardy." *Supreme Court Review* (1978): 81–169.

CASES

Ashe v. Swenson, 397 U.S. 436 (1970).
Bartkus v. Illinois, 359 U.S. 121 (1959).
Benton v. Maryland, 395 U.S. 784 (1969).
Blockburger v. United States, 284 U.S. 299 (1932).
Brown v. Ohio, 432 U.S. 161 (1977).
Gore v. United States, 357 U.S. 386 (1958).
Grady v. Corbin, 495 U.S. 508 (1990).
Houston v. Moore, 5 Wheat. 1 (1820).
In re Nielsen, 131 U.S. 176 (1889).
Missouri v. Hunter, 459 U.S. 359 (1983).
Palko v. Connecticut, 302 U.S. 319 (1937).
United States v. Dixon, 509 U.S. 688 (1993).
United States v. Perez, 22 U.S. 579 (1824).

DRINKING AND DRIVING

The automobile age brought with it unprecedented prosperity and freedom of movement, but motor vehicles have also caused the deaths and injuries of millions of people. From the beginning the abuse of alcohol has been universally viewed as one of the major causes of vehicular carnage, with severe punishments being deemed the best way of dealing with the self-indulgent reprobates responsible.

According to the sociologist Joseph Gusfield, noted for his work on alcohol in American society, behind all legislation aimed at curtailing drinking and driving is the image of "the killer drunk," the morally flawed character who has committed more than an ordinary traffic violation. Unlike the social drinker, who knows his limits and respects the law, the drinking driver is a villain who threatens the lives of the innocent through indulgence in his own pleasure. In this legislation, unlike other kinds of traffic law, it is the behavior itself, the hostile, antisocial menace, which is singled out for special disapproval. From this perspective, the enforcement of drinking-driving legislation is as much a matter of public morality as it is of public convenience and safety (Gusfield).

The specter of the killer drunk is the key image that animates "the dominant paradigm," to use the term coined by H. Laurence Ross, another American sociologist who has done more than any other scholar to elucidate, from an international perspective, the causes and prevention of drinking and driving (Ross, 1982, 1992). The dominant paradigm understands that there is a safe drinking level for the great mass of responsible drivers, differentiated from the levels regularly achieved by the small minority of reckless "drunken drivers." The problem, in fact, is not "drinking and driving" at all, but "drunken driving." The dominance of this paradigm in the United States is one reason why the term *drunken driving* is used so often there, in contrast to most European nations and Australia, where "drinking and driving" or "drink-driving" are the more popular terms.

How one defines the problem is fundamentally important in determining how one thinks about responses. The dominant paradigm calls for severe punishments administered through the criminal justice system. Not only are such punishments fitting, they are capable of deterring further offending, especially if they are backed by rigorous police enforcement. To the extent that the problem is construed in terms of the pathetic drunk rather than the cold-blooded killer, proponents of the dominant paradigm are also comfortable with offering treatment to offenders, provided such programs are not used to evade punishment.

Another way of viewing the problem is through what Laurence Ross calls "the challeng-ing paradigm." Those who think within this framework are uncomfortable about drawing a rigid line between dangerous drunks and social drinkers, although they recognize that heavy drinkers are a critical part of the problem. Their inspiration is the public health perspective, which is not primarily concerned with righting the moral balance of the world but with minimizing alcohol-related harms. Adherents of the challenging paradigm view alcohol-related accidents as the product of the conjunction of the social institutions of transportation and recreation, rather than as a manifestation of moral dereliction. All developed societies rely, to an increasing extent, on private vehicles for all daily functions including recreation, while the consumption of alcohol is accorded an honored place in after-work camaraderie, weekend leisure, and business lunches. Large taverns with even larger car parks are built in the suburbs, and drinking to intoxication remains a core recreational activity for large numbers of people.

If the problem is institutions, perhaps the solutions lie in modifying the way these institutions operate. The challenging paradigm has a place for the criminal justice system, especially if the emphasis is on the general deterrence of the whole driving population. However, they also look beyond the criminal justice system to alcohol and transportation policy, exploring the utility of such measures as reducing alcohol availability or making vehicles or roadside hazards more "forgiving" of the errors of the drinking driver.

In the remainder of this discussion we explore many of the issues raised by the dominant and challenging paradigms, and assess the scientific evidence for the claims made.

The role of alcohol in road accidents

Around the middle of the twentieth century the technical means became available to measure the quantity of alcohol in a person's blood (the blood alcohol concentration, or BAC, usually measured in terms of grams of alcohol per milliliter of blood). Laboratory research using this technology showed that at BAC levels much lower than those normally associated with intoxication, tasks related to driving performance (such as divided attention tasks) were noticeably affected. Although the effects of BAC depend on such factors as an individual's weight, rate of drinking, and presence of food in the stomach, deterioration in performance becomes quite marked between BACs of .05 and .08. As a guide, the average man would attain a BAC of .05 or higher if he drank three "standard drinks" (e.g., three mid-size glasses of mid-strength beer) within one hour, without eating.

The alcohol-crash link was confirmed in a series of case-control studies that compared the BACs of drivers experiencing crashes with those of matched non-crash-involved drivers. These studies found that relative crash risks increase exponentially with BAC: at .05 the risk is double that for a zero-BAC driver, at .08 the risk is multiplied by ten, while at .15 or higher (the levels typically attained by drivers arrested for drinking and driving) the relative risk is in the hundreds. The curve is even steeper for serious and fatal crashes, for single-vehicle crashes, and for young people.

While it is likely that factors other than alcohol, such as a propensity to take risks, contribute both to the levels of drinking and to crash involvement, there is a near universal consensus that there is a direct and causal link between alcohol consumption and crashes, especially serious crashes. For example, eliminating alcohol would probably have prevented about 47 percent of fatal crashes in the United States in 1987 (Evans).

Prevalence and patterns of drinking and driving

The most direct way of measuring the prevalence of drinking and driving is to take breath tests from a random sample of motorists. A number of countries carry out these surveys periodically, usually at nights and at weekends when drinking drivers are more numerous. Two groups of nations emerge in these studies. One group includes Scandinavia and Australia, where there are relatively few drinking drivers on the roads. Moderate to high BACs are found among less than 1 percent of drivers in these countries, even at peak leisure times. The second group includes the United States, Canada, France, and the Netherlands, where between 5 and 10 percent of drivers during nighttime leisure hours have moderate to high BACs. These patterns are broadly consistent with overall road fatality rates for different countries, and also with analyses of the BACs of drivers killed. However, in these latter studies even the Scandinavian countries have found that more than a quarter of drivers have positive BACs, despite the low numbers overall of drinking drivers on the road.

A second main way of estimating the prevalence of drinking and driving is to ask random samples of drivers about their behaviors in the recent past. For example, a 1988 study comparing Norwegian, Australian, and American drivers found that 28 percent of Australians, 24 percent of Americans, but only 2 percent of Norwegians admitted to driving in the past year after four or more drinks (Berger et al.). Despite their poor behaviors, 78 percent of the Australians agreed that it was morally wrong to drive after so many drinks, a higher figure than in the United States, but (again) lower than for the Norwegians, who scored a very high 98 percent. Overall, "general prevention," defined as the influence of moral inhibitions and of social pressures, had taken greater hold in Norway than in the English-speaking countries, but general deterrence (behavior change in response to fear of the threat of legal sanctions) was a more potent force in Australia than in the other countries.

Using intoxication among drivers in fatal crashes as an indicator, dramatic reductions in drinking and driving were experienced in most developed countries in the 1980s. However, the indicators reversed direction in the early 1990s, but then continued in modest decline in the second half of the decade. Formal and informal controls on drinking and driving differ markedly from country to country, but nevertheless there appear to be some common influences. Levels of police enforcement (not the severity of penalties) stand out in all countries as an influence, together with a reduction in per capita alcohol consumption. Attention paid to the problem by political leaders, and the visibility of drinking and driving in the press, appear to be critical factors.

Deterrence

The deterrence of drinking and driving depends primarily on increasing the perceived probability of apprehension in the target population. One way of accomplishing this is to introduce laws that replace the vague offense of "driving under the influence" with the offence of driving with a BAC above a prescribed level (usually .08 or .05). Another way is to initiate a police crackdown on drinking and driving for a period of time. The experience of the United Kingdom in 1967, when it introduced for the first time a .08 BAC limit, illustrates well the usual impact of such interventions. The law was extremely controversial at the time, with the result that most drivers were aware of it and believed they would be caught if they drove after drinking. There was a marked decline in serious accidents at nights and weekends, but not at times when drinking and driving would not be expected. However, the deterrent impact wore off within a few years as drivers gradually became used to the new law, and realized that their chances of detection were in fact not very high.

This pattern of a sharp decline in drinking and driving coincident with a new law or with intensified police enforcement, followed by a gradual decline to pre-intervention levels, is commonly found. Deterrence is an unstable psychological process dependent on continuous publicity and on the perception of a credible police threat. However, random breath testing (RBT) is a major exception to the rule that enforcement effects are invariably temporary.

Under RBT as it is practiced in Australia and some Scandinavian countries, large numbers of motorists are pulled over at random by police and required to take a preliminary breath test, even if they are in no way suspected of having committed an offense or been involved in an accident. Thus RBT should be sharply distinguished from the U.S. practice of sobriety checkpoints, in which police must have reasonable suspicion of alcohol consumption before they can require a test. The RBT law has been very extensively advertised and vigorously enforced in Australia, with the result that 82 percent of motorists reported in 1999 having been stopped at some time (compared with 16 percent in the United Kingdom and 29 percent in the United States).

Time series analyses of accidents show that in Australia RBT had an immediate, substantial, and permanent impact, with every extra one thousand tests conducted each day by police resulting in a 6 percent decline in daily serious accidents (Henstridge et al.). The direct deterrent impact was enhanced by the fact that RBT gave heavy drinkers a legitimate excuse to drink less when drinking with friends. This is a good example of how formal sanctions can reinforce informal sanctions.

The same time series analyses show that a reduction in the legal BAC in some states from .08 to .05 resulted in an average 10 percent decline in serious accidents. This is consistent with experience in other countries where the BAC level has been reduced.

RBT and lower BAC levels concern certainty of detection. Administrative license revocation, the practice in some U.S. states where drivers who drink have their licenses revoked almost as soon as they fail a breath test, concerns swiftness of punishment. Research supports the potential of this procedure to reduce the recidivism of sanctioned drivers and to deter others. As a general rule, the only sanction applied to drivers who drink that reduces recidivism is loss of license. Although many drivers continue to drive while unlicensed, they tend to be more cautious and hence safer. Thus it seems that license loss has (to some extent) a physically incapacitating effect.

Other countermeasures

License loss is effective for both alcohol-related and non-alcohol-related accidents, but its impact on drinking and driving can be enhanced if combined with alcohol treatment. While treatment without license suspension is generally ineffective, suspension plus education, psychotherapy counseling, or follow-up contact probation (preferably in combination) produce an additional 7 to 9 percent reduction in recidivism and accidents (Wells-Parker et al.). Ignition interlock devices, which prevent a vehicle being started until the driver passes a breath test, have been shown to be very effective for many high-risk offenders. However, the effects tend to be limited to the period of the court order unless combined with treatment within a case management framework to deal with the underlying problems.

The problem with all countermeasures focused on apprehended offenders is that most serious alcohol-related crashes involve drivers with no prior drinking and driving convictions. Hard-core drivers who drink comprise about 1 percent of drivers on the road, but more than a quarter of drivers killed. Many of these drivers have a history of violence and serious antisocial behavior including crime, with alcohol abuse simply one facet of their deviant careers. It is likely that for this group a radically different approach is needed, involving early childhood interventions (Farrington).

Most accidents do not involve hard-core offenders, and there is therefore a continuing need for countermeasures directed at the general population. Promising measures include promotion of responsible beverage service for bar staff and managers of on-premise alcohol outlets combined with deterrence of drinking and driving through local enforcement; reduction in retail availability of alcohol to minors; and reductions in the number and density of alcohol outlets to limit general access to alcohol. Any measure that reduces per capita alcohol consumption, such as increases in price through taxation, will reduce alcohol-related accidents.

Reducing dependence on driving has similar promise. Successful measures include designated driver programs (someone in a group stays sober so that that person can drive home), safe rides programs, and increasing the age of driver licensing or restricting licenses to daytime use for young drivers. Promoting public transport would certainly be effective if it were ever evaluated for its impact on drinking and driving. Contrary to expectations, there is no evidence that driver education for young people reduces crash involvement. Indeed, the evidence suggests the reverse: by encouraging young people to gain their license at an earlier age, such training increases exposure to risk, and hence accidents.

Finally, making the vehicle and roadside environment more forgiving of the errors of drinking drivers will reduce deaths and injuries. Frangible poles that minimize damage to vehicles; improved response times and skills of emergency medical teams; more use of seatbelts and airbags; and brighter reflective road signs (so impaired drivers notice them) are but a few examples of effective environmental interventions.

Conclusion

Overall, the picture is one of steady progress, with some setbacks. The challenging paradigm, based on the principles of population health, continues to score successes through such strategies as reducing the legal blood alcohol concentration. General deterrence, especially utilizing random enforcement methods, has achieved permanent reductions in alcohol-related crashes, as has administrative license revocation. Treatment combined with license suspension and ignition interlocks reduce recidivism and accidents. Tougher penalties, the major emphasis of the dominant paradigm, show no promise at all.

The challenges include maintaining the deterrent impact of random enforcement; finding long-term ways of dealing with hard-core offenders; optimizing the use of alcohol and driving controls in politically acceptable ways; and maintaining political and media interest in the drinking and driving problem in the face of stiff competition from other social issues. The fact that drinking and driving declined in most countries in the latter part of the twentieth century, despite wide variations in prevention strategies, suggests that within the challenging paradigm there are many pathways to a safer motoring environment.

ROSS HOMEL

See also ALCOHOL AND CRIME: BEHAVIORAL ASPECTS; ALCOHOL AND CRIME: THE PROHIBITION EXPERIMENT; ALCOHOL AND CRIME: TREATMENT AND REHABILITATION; POLICE: POLICING COMPLAINANTLESS CRIMES.

BIBLIOGRAPHY

BERGER, DALE E.; SNORTUM, JOHN R.; HOMEL, ROSS J.; HAUGE, RAGNAR; and LOXLEY, WENDY. "Deterrence and Prevention of Alcohol-Impaired Driving in Australia, the United States and Norway." Justice Quarterly 7 (3) (1990): 453–465.

EVANS, LEONARD. Traffic Safety and the Driver. New York: Van Nostrand Reinhold, 1991.

FARRINGTON, DAVID. "Early Developmental Prevention of Juvenile Delinquency." Criminal Behavior and Mental Health 4 (3) (1994): 209–227.

GUSFIELD, JOSEPH R. The Culture of Public Problems: Drinking-Driving and the Symbolic Order. Chicago, Ill.: The University of Chicago Press, 1981.

HAUGE, R., ed. Scandinavian Studies in Criminology. Vol. 6, Drinking and Driving in Scandinavia. Oslo, Norway: Universitetsforlaget, 1978.

HENSTRIDGE, JOHN; HOMEL, ROSS; and MACKAY, PETA. The Long-Term Effects of Random Breath Testing in Four Australian States: A Time Series Analysis. Canberra, Australia: Federal Office of Road Safety, 1997.

HINGSON, RALPH. "Prevention of Drinking and Driving." Alcohol Health and Research World 20, no. 4 (1996): 219–226.

HOMEL, ROSS. Policing and Punishing the Drinking Driver: A Study of General and Specific Deterrence. New York: Springer-Verlag, 1988.

———. "Drivers Who Drink and Rational Choice: Random Breath Testing and the Process of Deterrence." In Routine Activity and Rational Choice. Edited by Ronald V. Clarke and Marcus Felson. Vol. 5 Advances in Criminological Theory. New Brunswick, N.J.: Transaction Publishers, 1993. Pages 59–84.

LAURENCE, MICHAEL D.; SNORTUM, JOHN R.; and ZIMRING, FRANKLIN E., eds. Social Control of the Drinking Driver. Chicago, Ill.: The University of Chicago Press, 1988.

McCord, Joan. "Drunken Drivers in Longitudinal Perspective." *Journal of Studies on Alcohol* 45 (1984): 316–320.

Ross, H. Laurence. *Deterring the Drinking Driver: Legal Policy and Social Control.* Rev. and updated ed. Lexington, Mass.: Lexington Books, 1984.

———. *Confronting Drunk Driving: Social Policy for Saving Lives.* New Haven, Conn.: Yale University Press, 1992.

———. "Prevalence of Alcohol-Impaired Driving: An International Comparison." *Accident Analysis and Prevention* 25(6) (1993): 777–779.

Wells-Parker, Elizabeth; Bangert-Drowns, Robert; McMillen, Robert; and Williams, Marsha. "Research Report: Final Results From a Meta-Analysis of Remedial Interventions with Drink/Drive Offenders." *Addiction* 90 (7) (1995) 907–926.

Wilson, R. Jean, and Mann, Robert E., eds. *Drinking and Driving: Advances in Research and Prevention.* New York: The Guilford Press, 1990.

DRUGS AND CRIME: BEHAVIORAL ASPECTS

For more than a century, there have been differences of opinion regarding the relationship between the use of illegal drugs (specifically narcotics and cocaine) and criminal behavior. While representatives of the criminal justice system, the medical profession, and academia have reflected numerous points of view and have espoused widely differing reasons for their interest in the topic, a detailed and focused analysis of the issues and the literature suggests that a variety of questions need to be addressed. For example, is criminal behavior, first of all, antecedent to addiction; or is the former a phenomenon that appears subsequent to the onset of addiction? More specifically, is crime the result of or response to a special set of life circumstances brought about by the addiction to illegal drugs, or is addiction per se a deviant tendency characteristic of individuals already prone to committing predatory crimes? Secondly, and assuming that criminality may indeed be a pre-addiction phenomenon, does the onset of the chronic use of narcotics, cocaine, and other illicit drugs bring about a change in the intensity and frequency of illegal acts? Does criminal involvement tend to increase or decrease subsequent to addiction? Finally, what kinds of criminal offenses do addicts engage in? Do they tend toward violent acts of aggression; or are

their crimes more profit-oriented and limited to thefts and drug sales; or both? One might also ask, Is there any relationship at all between the two phenomena? Whatever the studies may have concluded, can the derived relationships be attributed to differential police behavior, to defects in survey designs, to purposeful or unintended bias, to the structure and functional application of laws circumscribing statuses characteristic of drug-using behaviors, or to a spectrum of changes that have occurred through time? Is our present state of knowledge no more than myth, or too fragmented for a composite picture?

Given these questions, the purpose of this entry is to review and analyze a number of the major research efforts in these areas of inquiry, and to provide a framework for their interpretation. Furthermore, commentary is offered relative to some basic issues that must be addressed when studying drug-taking and drug-seeking behaviors as they may relate to criminal activity.

The criminal model of drug abuse

Although the questions and issues surrounding the professed relationships between drug use and crime did not fully become a public debate until after the passage of the Harrison Act in 1914, a body of attitudes regarding users of narcotics had already evolved many decades prior to the twentieth century.

Opium had been utilized as a general remedy in the United States as early as the settlement of colonial America, but the drug's availability on a large scale did not occur until its inclusion in numerous patent medicines during the nineteenth century. Opium and its derivatives had then become accessible to all levels of society and could be purchased over the counter in drug and grocery stores as well as through the mails. Remedies of this type were consumed for ailments of almost every type, from coughs to diarrhea, and had special favorability for the treatment of "female troubles."

Public concern regarding the "evil effects" attributed to opium contributed to the definition of its chronic use as a social problem. In 1856, for example, Dr. G. B. Wood dramatized the condition of chronic opium intoxication as being "evil," and suggested that indulgence in the use of the drug led to a loss of self-respect, that such usage represented the yielding of an individual to seductive pleasure, and that it was, in fact, a "vice." Other physicians further reiterated this point and estimated that perhaps hundreds of thousands of Americans were exposed to the "evil affects" of opium. In other cases, the affliction described was often viewed in contrast as a "disease." The vast numbers of Civil War veterans, for example, who had become addicted to morphine through its extensive intravenous administration for the relief of pain, were considered as suffering from "army disease." The majority of such individuals were deemed "sick" rather than "deviant" or "criminal," and treatment in the form of medically supervised withdrawal was readily available in the office of one's family doctor.

By the close of the 1880s, however, the notion that addiction was evil seemed to be increasing, even among members of the medical profession. Dr. C. W. Earle, for example, expressed in the *Chicago Medical Review* the opinion that the opium habit, like the use of alcohol or gluttony, constituted a vice; and similarly, John Shoemaker's 1908 edition of *Materia Medica and Therapeutics* reflected on "opium-eating" as a moral rather than a medical problem. Medical practitioners who supported the opinion that the user of opium was to be pitied rather than degraded, on the other hand, nevertheless contributed to an encompassing definition of the addict as someone quite divergent from the more "normal" members of society. In 1894, for example, physician Paul Sollier indicated that a neuropathic or psychopathic condition predisposed opiate addiction; and, Wilson and Eshner's *American Textbook of Applied Therapeutics* (published in 1896) investigated the phenomenon in terms of a disease of both the body and the mind.

In addition to drug dependence instigated through exposure to opium in patent medicines or by injectable morphine, public concern was also mounting relative to the opium-smoking parlors. Although the use of opium was not a crime during this period, the operation of the opium parlors was illegal in New York City and elsewhere, and police closings of these establishments were widely publicized. Furthermore, descriptions of the opium habit and its consequences were dramatized as "evil" in police literature and the behavior under observation was associated with criminality. And finally, by 1896, the term "dope fiend" had made its way into popular slang usage, implying that drug-taking was, or at least resulted in, an evil obsession. By the end of the nineteenth century, cocaine and heroin had been added to the over-the-counter pharmacopeia, creating ever greater concerns about drug "abuse."

The Harrison Act of 1914

It would appear that American drug policy originated from two competing models of addiction. As noted above, the "criminal model" viewed addiction as one more of the many antisocial behaviors manifested by the growing classes of predatory and dangerous criminals. But there also was the "medical model," in which addiction was considered to be a chronic and relapsing disease that should be addressed in the manner of other physical disorders—by the medical and other healing professions.

Many commentators have viewed the Harrison Act of 1914 as the ultimate triumph of the criminal model over the medical view, and as such that single piece of legislation served to shape the direction of drug policy for years to come and generations yet unborn. However, history suggests a somewhat alternative story. Briefly, the Harrison Act required all people who imported, manufactured, produced, compounded, sold, dispensed, or otherwise distributed cocaine and opiate drugs to register with the Treasury Department, pay special taxes, and keep records of all transactions. As such, it was a revenue code designed to exercise some measure of public control over narcotics and other drugs. Certain provisions of the Harrison Act permitted physicians to prescribe, dispense, or administer narcotics to their patients for "legitimate medical purposes" and "in the course of professional practice." But how these two phrases were to be interpreted was another matter entirely.

On the one hand, the medical establishment held that addiction was a disease and that addicts were patients to whom drugs could be prescribed to alleviate the distress of withdrawal. On the other hand, the Treasury Department interpreted the Harrison Act to mean that a doctor's prescription for an addict was unlawful. The United States Supreme Court quickly laid the controversy to rest. In *Webb v. U.S.*, 249 U.S. 96 (1919), the Court held that it was not legal for a physician to prescribe narcotic drugs to an addict-patient for the purpose of maintaining his or her use and comfort. *U.S. v. Behrman*, 258 U.S. 280 (1922), went one step further by declaring that a narcotic prescription for an addict was unlawful, even if the drugs were prescribed as part of a "cure program." The impact of these decisions combined to make it almost impossible for addicts to obtain drugs legally. In 1925 the Supreme Court emphatically reversed itself in *Linder v. U.S.*, 268 U.S. 5 (1925), disavowing the *Behrman* opinion and holding that addicts were entitled to medical care like other patients, but the ruling had almost no effect. By that time, physicians were unwilling to treat addicts under any circumstances, and well-developed illegal drug markets were catering to the needs of the addict population.

In retrospect, numerous commentators on the history of drug use in the United States have argued that the Harrison Act snatched addicts from legitimate society and forced them into the underworld. As attorney Rufus King, a well-known chronicler of American narcotics legislation, once described it, "Exit the addict-patient, enter the addict-criminal" (p. 22). However, the Harrison Act did not instantly create a criminal class. Without question, at the beginning of the twentieth century, most users of narcotics were members of legitimate society. In fact, the majority had first encountered the effects of narcotics through their family physician or local pharmacist or grocer. Over-the-counter patent medicines and "home remedies" containing opium, morphine, and even heroin and cocaine had been available for years, and some even for decades. Yet long before the Harrison Act had been passed, or had even been conceived, there were indications that this population of users had begun to shrink. Agitation had existed in both the medical and religious communities against the haphazard use of narcotics, defining much of it as a moral disease. For many, the sheer force of social stigma and pressure served to alter their use of drugs. Similarly, the decline of the patent-medicine industry after the passage of the Pure Food and Drug Act in 1906 was believed to have substantially reduced the number of narcotics and cocaine users. Moreover, by 1912, most state governments had enacted legislative controls over the dispensing and sales of narcotics. Thus, it is plausible to assert that the size of the drug-using population had started to decline years before the Harrison Act had become the subject of Supreme Court interpretation. In addition, there is considerable evidence that the Harrison Act was the culmination of a broad, popularly and professionally based social reform movement. It was not governmental intrusion on an unwilling citizenry, but rather a reflection of then-current progressive social reform.

In addition, there is historical evidence that a well-developed subculture of criminal addicts had emerged many years before the passage of the Harrison Act. The opium den, "dive," or "joint," for example, was not only a place for smoking, but a meeting place, a sanctuary. For members of the underworld it was a place to gather in relative safety, to enjoy a smoke (of opium, hashish, or tobacco) with friends and associates. The autobiographies of pickpockets and other professional thieves from generations ago note that by the turn of the twentieth century, opium, morphine, heroin, and cocaine were in widespread use by criminals of all manner. And it might also be pointed out that the first jail-based program for the treatment of heroin addiction was established in the infamous New York Tombs (Manhattan City Prison), two years before the Harrison Act went into effect. At the time, it was estimated that some 5 percent of the city's arrestees were addicted to narcotics.

Thus, while the Harrison Act contributed to the criminalization of addiction, subcultures of criminal addicts had been accumulating for decades before its passage. Nevertheless, the Harrison Act was the first piece of federal antidrug legislation, and it carried with it the potential for applying the criminal label to addiction in a broader sense. Not only was the possession of the narcotic drugs interpreted as a criminal offense, but the risk of arrest was also expanded in that the drugs became available only through nonlegal sources. During the period shortly after the new drug law was enacted, it was widely held that 25 percent or all crimes were committed by addicts, and that such offenses were due to the alleged "maddening" effects of drugs.

Early research initiatives

Perhaps the first empirical effort in behalf of the drugs/crime linkage was undertaken by C. E. Sandoz, which examined the drug-seeking behaviors of some ninety-seven male and thirty-three female morphinists who passed through the Municipal Court of Boston in 1920. His conclusions suggested that the majority of the subjects studied had become criminal as a result of their addiction, but at the same time, there were others who were criminals first. Less than a half decade later, Dr. Wilson Kolb's analysis of 181 cases suggested that those addicts who were also habitual law violators tended to have been either actual or potential offenders prior to their addiction, and among a quantity of others, the offenses committed were principally for violations of the narcotic laws. Furthermore, an absence of aggressive crimes was generally characteristic of the criminal records of both groups studied.

The analyses of Sandoz and Kolb were the first to offer conclusions based upon concrete data, and in differentiating between the two sets of narcotic addicts with their corresponding patterns of criminality, the authors provided a foundation upon which the crucial issues of the drugs and crime controversy were to evolve. Essentially, these issues involved four general ideologies:

1. that addicts ought to be the object of vigorous police activity since the majority are members of a criminal element and drug addiction is simply one of the later phases in their criminal careers;
2. that addicts prey upon legitimate society and the effects of their drugs do indeed predispose them to serious criminal transgressions;
3. that addicts are essentially law-abiding citizens who are forced to steal in order to adequately support their drug habits; and,
4. that addicts are not necessarily criminals, but they are forced to associate with an underworld element that tends to maintain control over the distribution of illicit drugs.

The notion that addicts ought to be the objects of vigorous police activity was a posture that was actively and relentlessly taken by the Federal Bureau of Narcotics and other law enforcement groups. Their argument was fixed on a notion of criminality, since their own observations suggested that the majority of the addicts encountered were members of the underworld and addiction was simply a component of their criminal careers. In support of this view, an early report of the Bureau of Narcotics (1940) highlighted that the overwhelming majority of narcotics users indeed had criminal histories that preceded their careers in addiction by as much as eight to ten years. Furthermore, the records of 119 trafficker-addicts were cited, indicating that 83 percent of the cases had criminal records prior to addiction. The position taken by the bureau was firm and unconditional. Addicts, it emphasized, represented a destructive force confronting the people of America, and whatever the sources of their addiction might be, they were members of a highly subversive and antisocial group in the nation. And the approach of the bureau had some basis in reality. Having been charged with the enforcement of a law that prohibited the possession, sale, and distribution of a commodity that was sought by perhaps millions of the population, the bureau's agents were confronted by addicts only under the most dangerous of circumstances. It was not uncommon for officers to be killed or wounded in an arrest situation,

and analyses of the criminal careers of many of the addicts apprehended suggested that the underworld was well represented among them.

While the Bureau of Narcotics (and now the Drug Enforcement Administration) remained silent on this issue in subsequent years, other police agencies continued to stress criminality in addiction. Joseph Coyle, a former commanding officer of the Narcotics Bureau of the New York City Police Department, demonstrated that of the 3,386 narcotic violators arrested in New York City during 1957, 84 percent had arrests for non-narcotic violations prior to their first narcotic arrest.

In a contrasting perspective, researchers and clinicians offered data suggesting that in the majority of cases, criminal involvement occurs subsequent to the onset of addiction and that offense behavior represents the avenue of supporting one's addiction to drugs. During the 1930s, Bingham Dai found that as many as 81 percent of 1,047 Chicago arrestees became criminal subsequent to addiction, and in the following decade, a study of 1,036 patients at the U.S. Public Health Service Hospital in Lexington, Kentucky, found that 75 percent of the cases were addicts first.

Contemporary drugs and crime research

Among the difficulties reflected in the research from the 1920s through the 1960s was the static frame of reference in which addiction has been repeatedly perceived. For although different types within addict populations were observed as early as the 1920s, a major portion of later efforts failed to adequately address this phenomenon. Sample bias was a major issue, particularly with police agencies that limited their analyses to arrestees. Similar contamination often emerged from data generated by serious researchers as well. Initially, addicts receiving inpatient care—arrestees, probationers, parolees, or inmates—typically represent the more dysfunctional members of the drug-using community in that their involvement is sufficient enough to bring them to official attention. In addition, many samples were exceedingly small, and differences with respect to even the more common variables of age, sex, and ethnicity were not always factored. Furthermore, since the unreliability of official criminal statistics as a measure of the prevalence and incidence of offense behavior has been long since documented, interpretations grounded in arrest data are highly suspect. In an alternative direction, populations have been drawn for study from treatment settings with little account taken for the possibility of changing styles in addiction over time.

To recap, from the 1920s through the close of the 1960s, hundreds of studies of the relationship between crime and addiction were conducted. Invariably, when one analysis would support the medical model, the next would affirm the view that addicts were criminals first, and that their drug use was but one more manifestation of their deviant lifestyles. In retrospect, the difficulty lay in the way the studies had been conducted, with biases and deficiencies in research designs that rendered their findings to be of little value.

Research since the middle of the 1970s with active drug users in the streets of New York, Miami, Baltimore, and elsewhere has demonstrated that, at least with those drug users active in street subcultures, the medical model has little basis in reality. All of these studies of the criminal careers of heroin and other drug users have convincingly documented that while drug use tends to intensify and perpetuate criminal behavior, it usually does not initiate criminal careers. In fact, the evidence suggests that among the majority of street drug users who are involved in crime, their criminal careers were well established prior to the onset of either narcotics or cocaine use. As such, it would appear that the inference of causality, that the high price of drugs on the black market per se causes crime, is simply not supported. On the other hand, these same studies suggest that drugs drive crime in that illicit drug use tends to intensify and perpetuate criminal careers.

The drugs-violence connection

It has been a recurring theme over the years that drugs instigate users to acts of wanton violence. This has especially been the case since the mid-1980s with arguments about cocaine and crack. In early studies of drug users, however, it was clear that most addict criminals were nonviolent, with their offenses focusing primarily on income-generating crimes. Beginning in the 1970s, however, this tendency appeared to be changing. Based on the growing number of studies of "poly-drug abusers"—an emergent cohort of multiple drug users that had evolved from the drug revolution of the 1960s—it became apparent that a new and different breed of heroin user was living on the streets of American cities. They not only used heroin, but other drugs as well. Most importantly, their criminality was "situational" in nature. Rather than repeatedly committing burglaries, they lacked any type of criminal specialization. They engaged in a wide variety of crimes—including assaults, muggings, and armed robberies—selected according to the nuances of situational opportunity.

During the 1980s, Paul J. Goldstein of the University of Illinois conceptualized the whole phenomenon of drugs and violence into a useful theoretical framework encompassing three models of drug-related violence—psychopharmacological, economically compulsive, and systemic. His psychopharmacological model of violence suggests that some individuals, as the result of short-term or long-term ingestion of specific substances, may become excitable, irrational, and exhibit violent behavior. The economically compulsive model of violence holds that some drug users engage in economically oriented violent crime to support costly drug use. The systemic model of violence maintains that violent crime is intrinsic to the very involvement with any illicit substance. As such, systemic violence refers to the traditionally aggressive patterns of interaction within the systems of illegal drug trafficking and distribution.

The early statements attributing violent behavior to drug use generally focused on the psychopharmacological argument. More recently this model has been applied to cocaine, barbiturates, and PCP, with a major focus on the amphetamines, "crank," and crack. In study after study, it was reported that the chronic use of amphetamines produced paranoid thought patterns and delusions that led to homicide and other acts of violence. The same was said about cocaine. The conclusion is a correct one, although it did not apply to every amphetamine and cocaine user. Violence was most typical among the hard-core, chronic users.

Contrary to everything that has been said over the years about the quieting effects of narcotic drugs, recent research has demonstrated that there may be more psychopharmacological violence associated with heroin use than that of any other illegal drug. Goldstein's studies of heroin-using prostitutes in New York City during the 1970s found a link between the effects of the withdrawal syndrome and violent crime. The impatience and irritability caused by withdrawal motivated a number of prostitutes to rob their clients rather than provide them with sexual services. This phenomenon was found to be common in Miami, and not only among prostitutes but with other types of criminals as well. And to these can be added the many incidents of violence precipitated by the irritability and paranoia associated with crack use.

The economically compulsive model of violence best fits the aggressive behavior of contemporary heroin, cocaine, and crack users. Among 573 narcotics users interviewed in Miami, for example, more than a one-third engaged in a total of 5,300 robberies over a one-year period as a source of income. Some of these were "strong-arm" robberies or muggings with the victim attacked from the rear and overpowered, while the majority occurred at gunpoint. In fact, over a one-fourth of the respondents in this study used a firearm in the commission of a crime. A similar phenomenon was found among a cohort of 429 nonnarcotics users in Miami, with weapon use most common among those who were primarily cocaine users.

In the systemic model, acts of drug-related violence can occur for a variety of reasons: territorial disputes between rival drug dealers; assaults and homicides committed within dealing and trafficking hierarchies as means of enforcing normative codes; robberies of drug dealers, often followed by unusually violent retaliations; elimination of informers; punishment for selling adulterated, phony, or otherwise "bad" drugs; retribution for failing to pay one's debts; and general disputes over drugs or drug paraphernalia.

Most street drug users report having been either the perpetrator or victim of drug-related violence, and many women drug users reported over the years that they were the victims of rape at the hands of drug dealers.

Violence associated with disputes over drugs has been common to the drug scene probably since its inception. Two friends come to blows because one refuses to give the other a "taste." A husband beats his wife because she raided his "stash." A woman stabs her boyfriend because he did not "cop" enough drugs for her too. A cocaine injector kills another for stealing his only set of "works." In short, systemic violence seems to be endemic to the parallel worlds of drug dealing, drug taking, and drug seeking.

Comment

Researchers in the drug field have maintained that narcotics addicts are responsible for tens of millions of crimes each year in the United States. In addition, an unknown and perhaps a greater level of crime is committed by cocaine, crack, and other drug users. Contemporary data and analyses tend to support such contentions. Significant in this behalf are the findings of the Arrestee Drug Abuse Monitoring Program (ADAM).

The Arrestee Drug Abuse Monitoring Program (formerly known as the Drug Use Forecasting program or DUF) was established by the National Institute of Justice to measure the prevalence of drug use among those arrested for serious crimes. Since 1986, the ADAM program has used urinalysis to test a sample of arrestees in selected major cities across the United States to determine recent drug use. Urine specimens are collected from arrestees anonymously and voluntarily, and tested so as to detect the use of ten different drugs, including cocaine, marijuana, PCP, methamphetamine, and heroin. What the ADAM data have consistently demonstrated is that drug use is pervasive among those coming to the attention of the criminal justice system.

In the final analysis, then, are drug users—and particularly cocaine, crack, heroin, and other narcotics users—driven to crime, driven by their enslavement to expensive drugs that can be afforded only through continuous predatory activities? Or is it that drugs drive crime, that careers in drugs intensify already existing criminal careers? Contemporary data tend to support the latter position more than any other explanation.

JAMES A. INCIARDI

See also ALCOHOL AND CRIME: BEHAVIORAL ASPECTS; CRIMINALIZATION AND DECRIMINALIZATION; DRUGS AND CRIME: LEGAL ASPECTS.

BIBLIOGRAPHY

ANDERSON, ELIJAH. *Code of the Street: Decency, Violence, and the Moral Life of the Inner City.* New York: W.W. Norton, 1999.

AUSTIN, GREGORY A., and LETTIERI, DAN J. *Drugs and Crime: The Relationship of Drug Use and Concomitant Criminal Behavior.* Rockville, Md.: National Institute on Drug Abuse, 1976.

Bureau of Narcotics, U.S. Treasury Department. *Traffic in Opium and Dangerous Drugs for the Year Ended December 31, 1939.* Washington, D.C.: U.S. Government Printing Office, 1940.

COURTWRIGHT, DAVID. *Dark Paradise: Opiate Addiction in America before 1940.* Cambridge, Mass.: Harvard University Press, 1982.

DAI, BINGHAM. *Opium Addiction in Chicago.* Shanghai: The Commercial Press, 1937.

GOLDSTEIN, PAUL J. "The Drug/Violence Nexus: A Tripartite Conceptual Framework." *Journal of Drug Issues.* Vol. 15, no. 4 (fall 1985): 493–506.

GREENBERG, STEPHANIE, and ADLER, FREDA. "Crime and Addiction: An Empirical Analysis of the Literature 1920–1973." *Contemporary Drug Problems* 3, no. 2 (1974): 221–270.

INCIARDI, JAMES. *The War on Drugs II: The Continuing Epic of Heroin, Cocaine, Crack, Crime, AIDS, and Public Policy.* Mountain View, Calif.: Mayfield, 1992.

INCIARDI, JAMES, and POTTIEGER, ANNE. "Drug Use and Street Crime in Miami: An Almost Twenty-Year Retrospective." *Substance Use and Misuse* 33, no. 9 (1998): 1839–1870.

KING, RUFUS. "The American System: Legal Sanctions to Repress Drug Abuse." In *Drugs and the Criminal Justice System.* Edited by J. A. Inciardi and C. D. Chambers. Beverly Hills, Calif.: Sage, 1974.

LINDESMITH, ALFRED. *The Addict and the Law.* Bloomington, Ind.: Indiana University Press, 1965.

President's Commission on Law Enforcement and Administration of Justice. *Task Force Report: Narcotics and Drug Abuse.* Washington, D.C.: U.S. Government Printing Office, 1967.

TERRY, CHARLES, and PELLENS, MILDRED. *The Opium Problem.* New York: Bureau of Social Hygiene, 1928.

CASES

Linder v. U.S., 268 U.S. 5 (1925).
U.S. v. Behrman, 258 U.S. 280 (1922).
Webb v. U.S., 249 U.S. 96 (1919).

DRUGS AND CRIME: LEGAL ASPECTS

A systematic description of drug regulations must begin by identifying the parameters of the inquiry. What exactly is a *drug*? Unfortunately, no standard definition exists; different answers are given for different purposes. The most widely cited legal definition, contained in the Food, Drug, and Cosmetic Act (21 U.S.C. secs. 1–5), basically contains three disjunctive clauses. It identifies drugs as "substances recognized in the official *United States Pharmacopeia*," or "substances intended for use in the diagnosis, cure, mitigation, treatment, or prevention of disease in man or other animals," or "substances (other than food) intended to affect the structure or any function of the body of man or other animals." This definition cannot be thought to be adequate. The second and third clauses make a curious reference to intentions, as though the status of a substance as a drug could depend on the mental states of those who produce or use it. According to these definitions, a placebo (or indeed any substance whatever) would qualify as a drug as long as persons had the appropriate intentions. The second clause is far too broad, including diagnostic tools like stethoscopes. The first clause identifies drugs by deferring to the expertise of persons with the authority to include or delete a substance from the *Pharmacopeia*. No guidance is offered about how these experts should make their decisions. In fact, political rather than pharmacological considerations have influenced their determinations. Tobacco was removed from the *Pharmacopeia* in order to persuade legislators from tobacco-producing states to support passage of the Food and Drug Act.

The most frequently cited medical definition of a drug is "any substance other than food which by its chemical nature affects the structure or function of the living organism." This definition is a modification and slight improvement over that in the third clause of the Food and Drug Act. Still, this medical definition is problematic—for at least three reasons. First, it is doubtful that a substance becomes a drug whenever it produces an effect on the structure or function of the living organism by its chemical nature. A bullet lodged in the brain may cause structural and functional changes through processes that seemingly are chemical. Should this bullet be classified as a drug? Second, the definition presupposes some baseline from which to judge whether structure or function have been affected. Is this baseline statistical, biological, normative, or some combination of the three? For example, is a substance that blocks ultraviolet radiation a drug because it decreases the likelihood that the average user will contract skin cancer? Finally, the definition precludes the possibility that a food can be a drug. What exactly is a food? Some substances, such as herbs, seem to qualify as both foods and drugs. In light of these (and other) difficulties, this definition is inadequate. Unless some better candidate becomes available, it is probably fair to conclude that no satisfactory definition of a drug exists.

Neither of these definitions make any reference to the law; a substance need not be regulated or proscribed in order to qualify as a drug.

For this reason, this definition deviates from how ordinary speakers of English tend to identify drugs. Empirical studies indicate that respondents are far more likely to recognize a substance as a drug when its use is prohibited. Few Americans regard alcohol, tobacco or caffeine as drugs, while nearly everyone recognizes heroin, cocaine, and marijuana as drugs. But these distinctions have no definitional basis. Nothing in the definition of a drug provides any basis for exempting (the active ingredients in) alcohol, tobacco, and caffeine from the scope of a comprehensive set of drug regulations. The failure to distinguish licit from illicit drugs is unquestionably an advantage rather than a shortcoming of the foregoing definitions. Surely the question of whether a given substance is or is not a drug should depend on its pharmacological properties and its effects on persons who use it, rather than on whether or how it is regulated by law. The status of a substance as a drug should not fluctuate as legal regulations are adopted and repealed. Moreover, many knowledgeable people have questioned whether our drug policy is sensible. If thoughts about our policy could not be applied to licit substances because they are not defined as drugs, the insights of reformers would be deprived of their full critical potential, and hard questions would be resolved by definitional fiat.

Without an adequate definition, and in light of the enormous scope of the definitions that exist, it is difficult to say whether the United States has something that could be called a "drug policy"—or whether it would be desirable to have such a policy. Clearly, very different regulations are applied to very different kinds of drugs. Many drugs are used almost entirely for medical purposes. Some of these drugs are available only by prescription; others can be bought and sold at convenience stores. A handful of drugs are widely used for recreational purposes. They have psychoactive effects that many users find to be pleasurable. These drugs are also subject to very different kinds of controls. Caffeine is virtually unregulated, and is frequently consumed by children. Tobacco and alcohol are available to adults; devices (largely unsuccessful) to prevent access to adolescents are implemented. Many of these licit substances pose significant risks to public health and are implicated in a wide range of antisocial activity. According to some estimates, the use and abuse of prescription drugs kills as many as 100,000 Americans each year. The use of tobacco is the leading cause of preventable

death in the United States, killing far more people annually (450,000) than all other drugs combined. Many more criminals are under the influence of alcohol than any other illicit drug. Consequently, researchers often call for more stringent regulations of these substances. But almost no one proposes to duplicate a scheme that remotely resembles the prohibitionist regime implemented in the case of illicit drugs. That is, no one proposes that the criminal law should punish all producers, sellers, possessors, or users of alcohol and tobacco.

One might anticipate that this definitional confusion would complicate endeavors to regulate drugs. In fact, current laws that govern illicit substances are largely unaffected by the lack of an adequate definition. The Controlled Substances Act creates the authority to regulate "drugs or controlled substances." "Substance" is undefined, and a substance is "controlled" if the act regulates it. Therefore, anything the statute regulates is a controlled substance (although alcohol and tobacco are explicitly exempted). The question of whether a substance is or is not a drug turns out to be irrelevant to the issue of whether it is subject to regulation under the terms of the act. No definition of drugs is needed.

Despite the fact that many more substances qualify as drugs than popular opinion would indicate, surely the topic of "drugs and crime" should focus on legal regulations of illicit substances. In what follows, "drugs" will be taken to include only those substances that are illicit and widely used for recreational purposes—primarily, the opiates (heroin, morphine, opium), cocaine (powder and crack), psychedelics (LSD and ecstasy), and marijuana.

Drug control regulations in the twentieth century

At the beginning of the twentieth century, the use of (what are now) illicit substances was virtually unregulated. Although several states outlawed the smoking of tobacco and the drinking of alcohol, Americans were free to buy opiates (primarily opium and morphine) and cocaine in a variety of forms. These substances were widely dispensed by doctors, and available for purchase in pharmacies, retail outlets, and even by mail order. Many popular patent medicines contained mixtures of opiates and cocaine. Although millions of Americans consumed these substances throughout the nineteenth century, these drugs were rarely linked with deviance, violence, crime, or other social pathologies often associated with illicit drugs today. At the time, the typical opiate addict was a southern, middle-age, middle-class white woman. Relatively few users were addicts. Many of those users who were addicts did not know the contents of the patent medicines that helped to make them feel better.

The first significant federal drug regulation—the Food, Drug and Cosmetic Act of 1906—required manufacturers to list the drugs contained in their products. As a result of better information, the sales of patent medicines containing opiates and cocaine plummeted, and the incidence of illicit drug use and addiction declined. Further steps were advocated by a coalition of religious leaders, health professionals, and xenophobic Americans worried about the behavior of immigrants. The subsequent decade introduced sweeping federal regulations, culminating with the national prohibition of alcohol in 1920. Although local ordinances dating to 1875 forbade modes of drug consumption preferred by immigrants and minorities—such as the smoking of opium—the first prohibitionist measure on the federal level was the Harrison Narcotics Act of 1914. This act did not explicitly prohibit the use or possession of narcotics, but required doctors and chemists to register, pay taxes, and keep records of drug transactions. In 1919, the Supreme Court (in *Webb v. United States*, 249 U.S. 96) construed the act to prohibit physicians from prescribing narcotics to treat the "disease" of addiction. By the 1920s, the United States had reached a consensus that neither opiates nor cocaine had a legitimate use except for a handful of medical purposes. As a result, recreational use and addiction were transformed from medical problems to a concern for the criminal justice system. By this time, the demographic profile of the typical opiate or cocaine user had changed dramatically. The use of opium and cocaine had declined among the middle classes, but had risen among minorities and the poor. Although alcohol prohibition was repealed in 1933, no significant group called for the repeal of prohibitions of opiates or cocaine.

Although marijuana was not included in the Harrison Act, thirty-three states had adopted legislation against the nonmedical distribution of marijuana by 1933. In 1937, Congress effectively added marijuana to the list of illegal substances by passing the Marihuana Tax Act—enacted under the state's taxing power to avoid a constitutional challenge to a law enacted under the

power to regulate interstate commerce. In 1961, through the United Nations Single Convention on Narcotic Drugs, fifty-four nations agreed to prevent illicit traffic in cannabis.

LSD, discovered by a Swiss chemist in 1938, was frequently used in psychotherapy, but prohibited in 1966 when medical opinion turned against its safety and effectiveness. MDMA, or ecstasy, also originally developed as a therapeutic drug, was banned in 1985—despite continuing opposition from a vocal group of psychiatrists.

Regulations in place in 2001

In 1970, Congress supplanted previous statutory schemes for prohibiting drugs by enacting the Comprehensive Drug Abuse Prevention and Control Act, more popularly known as the Controlled Substances Act. This act, amended many times, continues to serve as a model for drug prohibitions by the majority of states—although the details vary from one jurisdiction to another. This act divides "drugs or other substances" onto five "schedules." The placement of a drug on a given schedule affects manufacturing quotas, import restrictions, dispensing limits, and criminal penalties for unlawful trafficking. Drugs without a currently acceptable medical use and with a high potential for abuse are assigned to Schedule I—which includes marijuana, LSD, and heroin. Of course, the determination of whether a substance has or lacks a medical use is enormously controversial. By 2001, initiatives to allow the medical use of marijuana had been approved in each of ten jurisdictions in which they had been placed on the ballot (California, Hawaii, Oregon, Washington, Arizona, Alaska, Maine, Nevada, Colorado, and the District of Columbia). These initiatives remain incompatible with federal law, which continues to proscribe the possession of marijuana for any purpose.

Under federal law, the severity of punishment is derived from the complex interaction of sentencing guidelines with mandatory minimum statutes. Prior to 1986, federal judges retained broad flexibility to tailor sentences for drug offenders to the particular circumstances of the offender. The Anti-Drug Abuse Act of 1986 dramatically transformed the sentencing of drug offenders by imposing mandatory minimum sentences, eliminating the possibility of probation or parole for most offenses, and increasing terms of incarceration. This act mandated a five to forty year sentence, with no possibility of parole, for first offenders convicted of possession with intent to distribute relatively small quantities of designated drugs (e.g., 10 grams of PCP or 1 gram of LSD, even if these drugs are diluted in mixtures). Sentences of ten years to life, with no possibility of parole, were mandated for first offenders convicted of possession with intent to distribute large quantities of drugs. Amendments to the act in 1988 imposed mandatory minimums for simple possession offenses, provided for the eviction of public housing residents if any member or guest of the household was involved in given drug offenses, and established the death penalty for persons engaged in "continuing criminal enterprises" who commit or solicit the commission of murder to further the criminal enterprise. The Violent Crime Control and Law Enforcement Act of 1994 significantly increased mandatory minimums for possession offenses still further, and authorized capital punishment for several new offenses. Mandatory minimums were doubled for defendants with a prior conviction for a drug felony, and were increased if drugs are distributed to a person under twenty-one, to a pregnant woman, or near a school or video arcade facility.

Punishments for the possession of crack are especially harsh. The maximum term of imprisonment for possession of up to 5 grams of crack is one year, but a first offender convicted of possessing more than 5 grams receives a mandatory minimum of five years. Five hundred grams of powder cocaine are needed before defendants receive a mandatory five-year sentence, thus creating the notorious 100–1 sentencing disparity that has given rise to strong allegations of racist sentencing practices. Crack offenders are disproportionately black, whereas powder cocaine offenders are more likely to be white. In 1995, the Sentencing Commission recommended that Congress reevaluate the disparity in punishment between cocaine and crack offenses, but both Houses of Congress rejected the commission's recommendation. Shortly before leaving office, President Clinton recommended that this disparity be reduced.

Under federal law, a defendant may evade the mandatory minimum sentence in only one way. Upon a motion by the prosecution—which remains within his discretion—the sentence may be reduced for a defendant who fully cooperates with the government in the investigation or prosecution of other drug offenders. This exception is unlikely to be available to persons who play relatively minor roles in drug distribution schemes and thus have no useful information to provide.

Far more prevalent are provisions that enhance sentences. Offenders with a prior criminal history, who use a gun, who create a substantial risk of bodily harm to others, or who victimize someone especially vulnerable, all are subject to increased sentences.

Marijuana has been the least harmful and most widely used illicit drug during the last century. As a result, criminal prohibitions are the most controversial, and differ significantly from state to state. In ten states, possession of small amounts of marijuana is punishable only by a fine. In many other states, incarceration is an option that is exercised infrequently. Federal law, however, punishes possession of small amounts of marijuana with a fine of $1,000 to $10,000 and up to one year in prison—the same sentence imposed for possession of small amounts of heroin or crack. Between 1991 and 1995, arrests for the use of marijuana doubled in the United States; by 1999, over 700,000 persons were arrested for marijuana offenses. New York City led the nation in these arrests, 88 percent of which were for simple possession.

New drugs are added or rescheduled from time to time. Highly publicized cases of drugs used to facilitate rape led to the Date-Rape Drug Prohibition Act of 1999, which added penalties for GHB (gamma hydroxybutyric acid).

Dissatisfaction with drug prohibition

A broad consensus has emerged that punishments for nonviolent drug offenses are too severe. Many commentators and citizen groups (such as Families Against Mandatory Minimums) argue that the mandatory minimum sentences for drug offenders should be repealed to restore judicial discretion in sentencing. Among other difficulties, these sentences create "cliffs," and thus are alleged to produce the very inequities they were designed to rectify. The mandatory minimum for an offender who sells 500 grams of cocaine, for example, is double that of an otherwise identical offender who sells 499 grams. In addition, sentences are based on the weight of the drugs seized, rather than on the role of the defendant in the distribution scheme.

Many thoughtful and knowledgeable citizens make more radical criticisms, arguing that contemporary drug policy is fatally flawed and should be drastically revised. They allege that drug prohibition is both ineffective and counterproductive. They point to the fact that the billions of dollars expended on law enforcement over dozens of years has failed to achieve a significant reduction in either the demand or the supply of illicit drugs. A few statistics help to tell the story. In 2000, approximately 460,000 drug offenders were incarcerated—about the same number as the entire prison population in 1980. Nearly one in four prisoners in America is behind bars for a nonviolent drug offense. In each year since 1988, more drug offenders than violent criminals have been incarcerated. Nonetheless, about 80 or 90 million living Americans have experimented with illicit drugs at some time in their lives. Every day, about sixty-four thousand Americans try marijuana for the first time. In 1999, approximately 15 million Americans were regular users of illicit drugs. Although this figure is roughly two-thirds of the peak of illicit drug use in 1979, it is comparable to statistics in preceding years. An ongoing effort often likened to a "war" has had little obvious impact on recent trends in drug use. Totalitarian countries like China may have succeeded in reducing its population of addicts from about 40 million (in the end of the 1930s) to almost zero in the span of a single generation. A free society, however, may lack acceptable means to reduce demand further.

Efforts to curb supply have proven no more successful. In 1999, 90 percent of high school seniors reported that marijuana is fairly easy or very easy to obtain; 44 percent say the same about cocaine, and 32 percent say the same about heroin. The street price of most illicit drugs has fallen since 1980—sometimes dramatically—indicating that quantities remain abundant. Even when eradication programs are successful in some countries (such as Peru, Bolivia, and Afghanistan), other countries (like Mexico) simply increase production to fill the void. Sometimes, production moves to the United States; at the outset of the twenty-first century, much and perhaps most of the marijuana consumed in this country is grown domestically. Economic considerations indicate that effective curbs on production are unrealistic. The value of global drug markets exceeds the GNP of 90 percent of countries in the United Nations. Prohibitionists frequently demand to redouble efforts to curtail supplies when the above statistics are cited. Skeptics ask why they should suppose that success is possible tomorrow, when efforts have failed thus far.

Just as importantly, drug prohibitions are said to be counterproductive in many ways. Drug prohibitions have created enormous profits for organized crime, contributed to widespread corruption in law enforcement, increased hypocrisy and mistrust, decreased the purity and safety of drugs, eroded civil liberties, glamorized drugs through the "forbidden fruit" phenomenon, discouraged the use of illicit drugs for legitimate medical purposes, fostered disrespect for law and legal institutions, distorted foreign policy, and placed a lucrative industry beyond the reaches of taxation.

Three counterproductive effects are especially worrisome. First, drug prohibitions have always been enforced more vigorously against minorities. Although whites and blacks are roughly comparable in their rates of drug use, blacks are arrested, prosecuted, and punished for drug offenses far more frequently and harshly than whites. In 2000, about ten million whites and two million blacks were current users of drugs. Even though white drug users outnumber blacks by a 5-to-1 margin, blacks comprise 62.7 percent and whites 36.7 percent of all drug offenders admitted to state prisons. These racial disparities are significantly higher in some states than in others. In Maryland, blacks constitute 90 percent of all drug admissions. In Illinois, the state with the highest rate of black male drug offender admissions to prison, a black man is fifty-seven times more likely to be sent to prison on drug charges than a white man. Some of these disparities result from controversial practices of "racial profiling"—the police practice of stopping, searching, and questioning criminal suspects solely on the basis of their race.

Second, drug prohibitions have a significant impact on women and their families. Between 1990 and 1997, the number of women serving time in prison for drug offenses nearly doubled, compared to a 48 percent increase in the number of men in prison for drug offenses. Forty-four percent of women incarcerated for drug offenses were convicted of mere possession. The impact of drug prohibitions has fallen disproportionately on black women. Black women constitute 6.3 percent of the national adult population and 7 percent of prison drug admissions; white women constitute 43.2 percent of the national adult population but only 5.4 percent of drug admissions. Punishing women is especially harmful to the welfare of their children, who are more likely to become criminals themselves when their mothers are incarcerated.

Finally, drug prohibitions have had a terrible impact on the lives of tens of millions of Americans whose only crime has been the use of drugs.

Simple possession was the most serious conviction in 28 percent of drug offenders sentenced to state prison. By 1996, the median sentence imposed for mere possession of a controlled substance in state courts rose to twenty-four months. After release, these individuals are less employable, more likely to be rearrested, and ineligible for many public benefits and services.

Those who defend the status quo are understandably disturbed by the foregoing problems. Still, supporters of prohibitionist policies typically counter that a relaxation in punishment would swell the numbers of drug users and the myriad social pathologies associated with drug use. Criminal justice experts are divided on such issues as whether more or less economic crime would result from less punitive policies. Reduced punishments for sellers would probably decrease the cost of drugs, so users might not need to resort to property offenses to obtain the money to buy drugs. On the other hand, reduced punishments would be likely to increase the number of drug users, thereby expanding the size of the population prone to commit economic crimes. Experts also disagree about the extent of psychopharmacological crime caused by the use of various drugs. Public anxiety about drug use is fueled by the perception that people under the influence of drugs often behave violently and irrationally. Evidence suggests, however, that the effects of drugs on aggression are mediated by individual predispositions, social expectations, and cultural differences. Changes in these psychopharmacological effects are impossible to predict in the event that the criminal justice system became more tolerant of the use of various drugs.

Even apart from economic and psychopharmacological crime, many thinkers in criminal justice regard drug control as crime control. Violent crime has fallen precipitously in the United States throughout the 1990s. The enforcement of petty drug offenses (especially in big cities like New York) has been more vigorous over the same period of time. These two phenomena are likely to be related. The kinds of persons arrested and punished for drug offenses (e.g., young, male, black, willing to defy authority) overlap significantly with the kinds of persons who are likely to commit violent crimes. If drug prohibitions were enforced less vigorously, some predict an eventual increase in the crime rate. Others dispute these allegations.

Significantly, public opinion seems not to regard this dispute as pivotal. About two-thirds of the American public say they would oppose the legalization of cocaine and heroin, even if they could be guaranteed that it would lead to less crime. This finding suggests that public support for punitive policies is more about moral values than about many of the tangible harms that drug use is said to cause. William Bennett and Barry McAffrey—the country's two most prominent "drug czars"—have also characterized drug prohibitions as a moral crusade in several publications from the Office of the National Drug Control Policy.

Perhaps the most hotly contested issue between prohibitionists and their critics is how the failure to punish users would affect the incidence of drug use. Estimates vary wildly. What data are helpful in attempts to answer this question? The recent experience in many European countries may be suggestive. By 1999, the use of marijuana had been decriminalized in many parts of Europe (Italy, Spain, Switzerland, Ireland, and parts of Germany and Austria), and is openly tolerated in the Netherlands. Yet rates of illicit drug use (apart from heroin) are never higher, and usually are much lower, than those in the United States.

Models of drug control should not assume that the only or most effective means to discourage the use of illicit drugs is by punishing offenders. The deterrent efficacy of drug prohibition may be marginal. Approximately seven-eights of frequent users of cocaine or heroin are never arrested. Few nonusers of illicit drugs indicate that they would be willing or eager to experiment if they could be confident that they could escape detection. Significant reductions in the use of licit substances such as tobacco and alcohol have been achieved in the last two decades of the twentieth century without the need to resort to criminal punishment. Public advertising campaigns have helped people recognize the health hazards posed by these substances. In addition, many private companies test employees for illicit drug use. States can also implement licensing, prescription controls, time and place restrictions, taxation, zoning ordinances, bans on advertising, and a host of other measures to discourage use.

Even those who are firmly persuaded that our drug policies are fundamentally flawed disagree about what should replace them. "Harm-reduction" has become a popular framework for evaluating alternatives to prohibition. According to this perspective, an ideal drug policy should strive to minimize the sum of harm or disutility caused by drug use and by drug law enforcement. This objective has an obvious plausibility. Experts disagree, however, about which combination of policies is most likely to achieve this goal. Moreover, the supposition that our policies should strive to minimize harm threatens to lose sight of the principles that many believe to be at stake in drug prohibition. The allegation that drug policies are unjust is independent of the foregoing objections, inasmuch as it does not depend on whether drug prohibitions can be made to work, or to produce more good than harm. Of course, arguments of principle are made on both sides of the debate.

Arguments in favor of fundamental change in existing drug policy are difficult to construct in the absence of a detailed argument in support of the status quo to which they can respond. Drug prohibitions have been defended as necessary to protect the young, to reduce crime, to safeguard public health, to prevent moral corruption, and to reverse just about everything that anyone has ever believed to be deficient about contemporary society. There may be no evil that has not been blamed on drugs. A comprehensive argument for radical change must rebut each of these arguments for criminalization.

Little about drug policy seems to be settled at the beginning of the twenty-first century. The waning of the "crack epidemic" of the late 1980s—and the public hysteria that surrounded it—may help to make the political climate more receptive to change. The inevitable development of new drugs—such as those used to increase sexual potency and pleasure—threaten to create problems for existing regulatory schemes. One thing is clear. Ambitious calls to achieve a "drug-free" society are doomed to failure. The use of psychoactive substances to alter consciousness and produce euphoria is pervasive in human history. No known societies (except perhaps that of the Eskimos) have been "drug-free." Some researchers have speculated that the desire to alter consciousness may be an innate, biological characteristic of our species.

DOUGLAS HUSAK

See also ALCOHOL AND CRIME: LEGAL ASPECTS; CRIMINALIZATION AND DECRIMINALIZATION; DRUGS AND CRIME: BEHAVIORAL ASPECTS; EXCUSE: INTOXICATION; POLICE: POLICING COMPLAINANTLESS CRIMES; VICTIMLESS CRIMES.

BIBLIOGRAPHY

American Pharmaceutical Association. *United States Pharmacopeia* 20th revision. Rockville, Md.: U.S. Pharmacopeial Convention, 1979.

FELLNER, JAMIE. "Punishment and Prejudice: Racial Disparities in the War on Drugs." *Human Rights Watch* 12, no. 2 (2000): 1–28.

HUSAK, DOUGLAS. *Drugs and Rights.* Cambridge, U.K.: Cambridge University Press, 1992.

INCIARDI, JAMES, and MACELRATH, JAMES, eds. *The American Drug Scene,* 3d ed. Los Angeles: Roxbury Publishing Co., 2001.

MUSTO, DAVID. *The American Disease: Origins of Narcotic Control,* 3d ed. New York: Oxford University Press, 1999.

NADELMANN, ETHAN. "Drug Prohibition in the United States: Costs, Consequences, and Alternatives." *Science* 245 (1989): 939–947.

Office of the National Drug Control Policy. *National Drug Control Strategy* 7–12 (1995–2000).

TONRY, MICHAEL. *Malign Neglect: Race, Crime, and Punishment in America.* New York: Oxford University Press, 1995.

U.S. Department of Justice, Bureau of Justice Statistics. *Sourcebook of Criminal Justice Statistics.* Washington, D.C.: U.S. Justice Department, 2000.

WILSON, JAMES Q. "Against the Legalization of Drugs." *Commentary* (1990): 21–28.

ZIMMER, LYNN, and MORGAN, JOHN. *Marijuana Myths, Marijuana Facts.* New York: Lindesmith Center, 1997.

STATUTES AND CASES

Anti-Drug Abuse Act of 1986 (21 U.S.C. secs. 841–969).

Comprehensive Drug Abuse Prevention and Control Act of 1970 (21 U.S.C. secs. 801).

Date-Rape Prohibition Act of 1999 (21 U.S.C. sec. 812).

Food, Drug, and Cosmetic Act of 1906 (21 U.S.C. secs. 1–5).

Violent Crime Control and Law Enforcement Act of 1994 (42 U.S.C. secs. 13701–14223).

Webb v. United States, 249 U.S. 96 (1919).

E

ECOLOGY OF CRIME

Ecological variation in crime, delinquency, and fear of crime are examined in this entry. The discussion examines macro-level variations at the regional and city-levels, this considers community level variations.

City and regional and city differences

Documented variations in local crime or arrest or offender rates date to the mid-nineteenth century. In France, for example, officials and researchers were particularly interested in seeing the effects of their new criminal laws. They looked at how many people were being arrested, imprisoned, flogged, or hung in different parts of the country. Researchers like Guerry and Quetelet found *spatial variation* in the rate at which people were being arrested for crime in different parts of the country (Brantingham and Brantingham).

The specifics of the patterns observed by these researchers still hold true when looking at spatial differences in crime rates today. In France, a few administrative subdivisions had very high rates, a few had very low rates, and many places were in between. Differences between regions were stable over time. In the United States, the South has been the highest violence region for quite some time K. Harris). Nevertheless, rates have varied widely in a range of locations. For example, the rate for people accused of crimes against persons for the period 1826–1830 ranged from 1 in 2,199 on the Mediterranean island of Corsica to 1 in 37,014 in Creuse in central France. In the United States reported violent crime rates at the state level in 1998 varied from 1,023 per 100,000 in Florida to 87 per 100,000 in North Dakota (Maguire and Pastore, eds. Table 3.118).

Patterns for violent and property crimes differ. Violent crimes were highest in rural areas of the U.S. South; in France during the 1990s property rates were highest in the industrialized, northern urban departments. During the same period in the United States, states with high rates of property crime were found not only in the South (Florida), but also in the far West (particularly in Arizona, Nevada, and New Mexico) (Maguire and Pastore, eds., Table 3.116). In short, such patterns of local crime rates have proven durable in research over the past one hundred fifty years. Researchers in Britain during the mid-nineteenth century found comparable patterns at the county and local level (Glyde).

By the end of the nineteenth century, environmental criminologists had discovered the following fundamental features about spatial and temporal distributions of crime:

1. There is spatial variation in rates of reported crime, and that variation shows up no matter the level of detail. The variation is higher in some places than in others, regardless of whether one looks at the large-scale units, such as counties, or at areas within counties, like different towns or different cities, or different sections of a city (Brantingham et al.).
2. The spatial variation was persistent. Areas that were high on offense or offender or delinquency rates might stay high for a decade, or even generations, regardless of the physical changes made in or the population changes occurring in the locale.

3. Sometimes the spatial patterns are not what one might expect. High violence in rural areas represents one case in point. In 1980, seventy-one out of the one hundred highest homicide rate counties in the United States were rural counties (Kposowa et al.).

American criminologists have worked hard to explain the higher rates of violence in the South. Some have suggested that historically rooted and racially linked subcultural variations are linked to higher violence (e.g., Messner and Rosenfeld). Studies since the early 1990s, however, focus not on race but on a culture of honor originating in historical patterns of independent pig farming in the Deep South (Cohen and Nisbett). The famous Hatfield-McCoy feud, for example, started over a pig.

A more micro-scale view on subcultural differences has emerged since the mid-1970s. This view builds on Louis Wirth's theory of urbanism (1938), which sought to explain differences in how people acted in cities as compared to nonurban locations. City size, density, and heterogeneity of populations were expected to affect residents' social networks, mood, and community involvement.

The subcultural theory of urbanism does not address crime per se, but rather unconventional behavior that deviates from broader societal norms. Both criminal behavior and delinquency could presumably be considered unconventional behaviors. The theory contains four propositions:

1. Larger places develop more and more specialized subcultures than do less populous ones, and are therefore more culturally heterogeneous.
2. More populous places develop not only more distinct subcultures but also more intense subcultures than less populous places.
3. Between-group contact leads to mutual influence. Diffusion from more unusual to more typical groups is likelier the larger the atypical subculture and is therefore more likely in urban places.
4. The more urban the place, the higher the rates of unconventionality relative to the wider society, because a) larger places generate more diverse and more specialized subcultures; and b) critical mass and intergroup friction are likelier in larger places (Fischer, 1995, pp. 545–546).

Subcultural theory is an ecological theory because it is about impacts of places, usually cities. This model could explain differences in crime and delinquency linked to city size, as well as urban versus suburban versus rural differences in offending rates and delinquency rates.

Researchers have tried to explain the causes of city-to-city (or metro area-to-metro area) differences in crime rates, the net of regional differences, concentrating largely either on economic or racial differences. A range of theorists link crime and related outcomes to structural inequality. Models differ in the aspects of inequality addressed, forces giving rise to inequality, outcomes of interest, or the different processes whereby inequality leads to crime or related outcomes. All these models presume a conflict perspective.

From the mid-1850s to the 1950s large U.S. cities witnessed increases in industrial manufacturing, and increasing needs for disciplined, cooperative workers. These shifts resulted in increasing orderliness and routine in white and ethnic urban neighborhoods, the improvements in the latter neighborhoods taking place as immigrants became assimilated into the workforce. African Americans, in response to strong demand during World War II, and decreased segregation at least in some cities in the 1960s, also joined these occupational groups, with concomitant shifts in their neighborhoods. This was followed, from about 1965 onward, by deindustrialization and the economic deconcentration of manufacturing jobs from central city locations. Particularly hard hit were African American communities because those workers were the last group permitted entry to the industrial jobs, and the group whose ability to move to the new jobs was lowest.

Inequality theorists describe how in the last thirty years industrial restructuring and the shift to post-industrial economies have further accelerated processes leading to increased inequality across urban communities (e.g., Hagan and Peterson). These shifts have markedly affected urbanites' mood (Fisher, 1982) and their economic well-being. More specifically, since the 1960s poverty has increased rapidly in urban centers, with African Americans being heavily represented among the urban poor. These rapidly increasing concentrations of poverty have transformed low-income, urban communities. In many communities welfare-dependent, female-headed households have become the norm.

Concentration effects linked to high poverty levels may explain between-city differences in crime rates as well as between-community differences. In extremely poor, predominantly African American urban communities, fundamental transformations take place in neighborhood life when poverty rates climb past 39 percent following class-selective out-migration by lower-middle to middle income African American households (Wilson). The broader commitment to the formal economy falters, as does commitment to mainstream values. Neighborhood institutions disappear, their customer base severely eroded. The joblessness itself triggers a range of social problems, including more disorderly street life, drug use, and crime. Concentration effects are economic in origin, and can operate in the context of a stratified labor market.

As neighborhoods become increasingly disorderly and socially isolated, outsiders avoid them and outside employers become more wary of hiring residents from these stigmatized locations; those remaining become increasingly socially isolated, making it even more difficult to network and get back into the mainstream economy. These represent concentration effects emerging from the extremely high density of unemployment, problems and disadvantage in these locations, not from the racial composition of the locales themselves. Recent ethnographies confirm such isolation in predominantly African American and some predominantly Hispanic communities (e.g., Bourgois).

As neighborhoods become increasingly disadvantaged one might expect crime to go up for any number of reasons. Four possible functional dynamics have been proposed at the city level, focusing on racial inequality, that could be driven by the concentration effects described by W. J. Wilson (Messner and Golden). One path expects more widespread "social disorganization/anomie" and thus more violence as racial inequality increases. Ties across communities will be poorer, and commitment to norms will weaken. Wilson would say that commitment to the formal economy and associated values would weaken. A second pathway ("relative deprivation/frustration-aggression") expects that increasing racial inequality makes the disadvantaged groups experience more relative deprivation; these sentiments increase offending rates among members of those disadvantaged groups. So violence rates just among the deprived groups should increase. A third pathway ("relative gratification/reduced aggression") looks at the reverse; as racial inequality increases those in the better-off contingent, that is, whites,

should have lower offending rates because they are less deprived and more advantaged. Finally, an "opportunity effect" model suggests that as concentrations of extremely poor and often African American groups increases in cities, and chances for meaningful contacts between various racial groups decrease, interracial violence rates should drop. Blacks and whites simply have fewer chances of interacting with each other as racial inequality and isolation increase.

In addition to crime being an outcome influenced by inequality, if it increases as disadvantage increases, it can spur further concentration effects, including neighborhood depopulation, as selective out-migration increases.

An alternate view on racial inequality and crime emerges from D. Massey's work on segregation (Massey and Denton). His historical perspective suggests that virtually all ethnic groups except African Americans have moved out of segregated, inner-city, impoverished locations, and successfully assimilated. His work also highlights the constraints on African Americans migrating out of severely distressed neighborhoods. Crime's ability to cause neighborhood depopulation may be limited by poor African Americans continuing to move in, and limitations on the African Americans attempting to leave the distressed neighborhoods. For Massey, concentration effects emerge from long-standing racial attitudes and practices, not economic shifts.

Many researchers addressing city and metropolitan area changes work within a "new urban sociology" perspective, and the processes they highlight may help explain increasing crime rates from the late 1960s through the early 1990s in many large cities, and differences in crime rates between cities and suburban locations (Gottdiener, *The New Urban Sociology*). These analysts point out:

1. The international political economy has significant effects on urban, suburban, and rural life.
2. A fundamental transformation of metropolitan structures took place in the last thirty to forty years as hierarchically arranged, central-city-dominated metro areas serving outlying suburbs and rural areas were transformed into highly differentiated, economically deconcentrated polynucleated metropolitan structures.
3. The transformation has produced highly uneven development, as capitalist growth always does, resulting in more radical spatial

separations of different races and classes, reflected, for example, in increasing numbers of gated communities, hypersegregated "excluded ghettos," and "totalizing suburbs" where all residents' needs can be met in a small area (Marcuse); there is increasing economic, social, and political separation not only within the cities but also in the broader metropolitan areas.

4. As homogeneity in many city neighborhoods has decreased, so too have shared local ties. These shifts make for weaker local political cultures. In the language of systemic control theory, the increased heterogeneity and decreased local ties weaken informal local ties or parochial control, and the strength of public control as well. In the language of routine activity theory, fewer committed informal place managers may be present, or it may be harder to place managers to decide who belongs where.

The recent crime drop seen in many larger cities starting around 1990 or 1992, and continuing into the mid or even late 1990s has drawn considerable attention. Some have suggested the decline is due to better, "smarter" policing (e.g., Bratton), others have suggested it was due to declining gun use among juveniles, which may have linked to declining activity of crack cocaine-drug dealing activities, but the causes may vary from city to city (Fagan et al.).

Variation at the community and streetblock levels

Within cities, there are safe neighborhoods and crime-ridden ones; even within crime-ridden neighborhoods, there are safe streetblocks—the two sides of the street bounded by the two cross streets—and dangerous ones. What do these patterns look like, and how are they to be explained? Most of the work in this area has examined neighborhood-to-neighborhood variations, although some have considered block-to-block differences (Taylor et al., 1984). Further, the bulk of the work has focused on social, economic, and cultural factors, although physical design features including landuse mix and design features linked to territorial functioning are relevant as well.

Many of the explanatory models used here have relied on a family of loosely associated perspectives on attributes of community including social problems, called *human ecology* (Hawley,

1981). These views seek to explain geographic variation in those attributes by concentrating on features of the immediate surround, whether that be streetblock, neighborhood, or city sector, and the connections between that surround and the broader geographic arena. Three fundamental premises of this family of perspectives are that place-to-place differences in racial and ethnic composition, socioeconomic status, and stability and family structure arise from broader dynamics at work in the larger spatial context; that those place-to-place differences in turn simultaneously instigate and reflect local, face-to-face and small group social dynamics; and that those local dynamics link to a wide range of crime-related outcomes such as delinquency rates, local crime rates, and fear of crime and related reactions to crime.

In 1925 Sir Cyril Burt, a British psychologist, published *The Young Delinquent*. He looked up the addresses of boys and girls reported as "industrial school cases" in London. Then he looked up where they lived, and made up a *delinquency rate*. Delinquency rates were highest in the areas right near the central business district (CBD), and declined as one moved outward. In addition, the areas of highest delinquency were also the areas of highest poverty. Burt concluded a relationship existed between social class and delinquency. Furthermore, even though his data were cross-sectional, he concluded that the relationship was causal. Later research of individuals continues to find connections between delinquency and social class (e.g., Hindelang et al.). But this does not mean the relationship holds at the individual level—to presume so is to commit the *ecological fallacy*.

Sociologists at the University of Chicago in the first half of this century investigated a wide array of urban social problems: delinquency, petty theft, dance halls, gambling, and immigrants' "culture shock," to name a few.

Two of these sociologists, Clifford Shaw and Henry McKay, investigated delinquency. They collected data not only from Chicago, but from other cities as well: Philadelphia, Richmond, Cleveland, Birmingham, Denver, and Seattle. Shaw and McKay went to juvenile courts and collected data about the number of juveniles who had been adjudicated delinquent. They were able to construct delinquency rates by posing the question, for every one thousand youths living in the community between the ages of nine and fifteen, how many had officially been adjudicated delinquent by the court? They also constructed rates using other spatial units, such as one square mile areas.

As had Burt, Shaw and McKay found higher delinquency rates closer to the center of the city, the central business district (CBD), than they did further away from the center city. Indeed, they observed that the further away a community was from the center city, the lower its delinquency rate. This pattern appeared not just in Chicago, but in each of the other cities they examined as well.

As is often time in cities, spatial differences link to social and economic differences. At the time Shaw and McKay were writing, populations were increasing in older cities. This "engine" of city growth led to economic differences across communities at varying distances from the city center. More specifically, because of city growth the CBD was expanding to keep up and "serve" the growth in the broader city. This, of course, had happened in the past as well. Given this historical and ongoing pattern, more desirable locations were always at the outer edge of the expanding city. Land use closer to the city center was often converted to nonresidential land uses such as large industries, stockyards (in the case of both Chicago and Baltimore), and large commercial concerns.

Not only were more central locations less desirable per se, they also were the sites of older housing. For the most part, older housing is also more worn-out housing. Given these less desirable locations, and the more dilapidated housing stock, housing in these areas tended to be cheaper. As prices shifted so too did the types of households living there. Poorer households were more likely to locate close to the city center, where housing was cheapest. Further away one would find housing occupied by low wage or blue-collar workers. More distant, one would find middle-income households. And finally, even further away, in an outer-city or perhaps in a more distant suburban location, one would find the highest income households.

These economic differences in house values and rents were exacerbated by the threat of invasion from the expanding CBD. People were constantly trying to "trade up" in their housing anyway, and move to a slightly better location. But since the CBD was growing at the time, residents from each inner zone would be "invading" the zones just beyond. In the innermost zone, the residential areas were in transition, converting from residential to commercial or industrial. This zone was thus labeled the *transition zone*.

These impending changes led those residents who could get out to do so, those who owned properties there to stop maintaining them, and to maximize their return by converting these units to apartments. Left living in these sites were low-income individuals and households that could not afford housing anywhere else. The residential environment there was rather chaotic.

Linked to the economic differences were ethnic ones. It is generally true, with some exceptions (Massey and Denton), that the newest immigrants to a city make up predominantly lower-income households. This is still true today in large U.S. cities even though the immigrant groups in question are different now than they were then. Consequently, many members of these immigrant groups, when they first arrived in U.S. cities, were limited to central-city, low-income neighborhoods where housing was cheap.

In short, Shaw and McKay's basic model was an economic one; location-based dynamics were set in motion based on the socioeconomic status of the group in question. The physical dilapidation of an area matched the segregation of the population on an economic basis. Given the ethnic heterogeneity in these more dilapidated areas, and shorter tenures, supervision of juveniles was more lax, willingness to reprimand others' children was weaker, and delinquency was higher (Maccoby et al.).

The spatial pattern described above has shifted markedly in large cities in the post–World War II era:

1. Centralized city planning increased in the years following World War II. Urban renewal initiatives destroyed vast tracts of older, worn-out housing in older cities, and replaced them with large numbers of public-housing communities. Many of those displaced from older "slum" locations lost many friends in the process (Frey; Gans). The siting of these communities influenced the surrounding locations, sometimes destabilizing them.

2. Suburbanization increased as federal highway initiatives, especially under President Dwight D. Eisenhower, provided drastically improved road access to cities.

3. But for a number of reasons, the suburbanization of African American households proceeded more slowly than the suburbanization of white households (Massey et al.). Consequently, the larger, older cities them-

selves became increasingly African American in composition.

4. Passage of various fair housing laws, and related court cases in the 1950s and 1960s increased African Americans' access to housing. In cities where African Americans had historically been limited to specific sections of the city, pent-up demand resulted in rapid racial turnover in large numbers of neighborhoods.

Since about 1970 additional changes in cities have further modified the spatial pattern described above. Most importantly, large numbers of manufacturing jobs have left, migrating from central city locations first to southern locations, then abroad, making it increasingly difficult for those with relatively low education levels to secure employment. Receiving more media attention than has perhaps been warranted given the relatively small number of locations where it has occurred, central city neighborhoods in many urban locations have become partially gentrified. Lower-income households were partially replaced by middle or upper income households that moved in and improved the housing stock.

Given these shifts in cities since around 1950, one would not necessarily expect to see the same spatial pattern for delinquency rates, or crime rates, as were reported for the years prior to World War II. Nonetheless, one still might expect community characteristics to link to these outcomes in a similar way.

At the heart of the human ecological model of offense and delinquency rates is a constellation of processes: *social disorganization*. Its opposite is *collective efficacy*. A locale is socially disorganized if several things are true: residents do not get along with one another; residents do not belong to local organizations geared to bettering the community and thus cannot work together effectively to address common problems; residents hold different values about what is and what is not acceptable behavior on the street; and residents are unlikely to interfere when they see other youths or adults engaged in wrongdoing (Bursik, 1988).

By contrast, if collective efficacy is high in a locale, residents will work together on common, neighborhood-wide issues, will get along somewhat with one another, and will take steps to supervise activities of youth or teens taking place in the immediate locale. These outcomes link to organizational participation ("Do you belong to the local improvement association? Does your neigh-

bor?"); informal social control ("If your neighbor saw a young teen spray painting the side of a building about midnight, would he do something about it?"); and local social ties based on propinquity ("How many of the people living on your block do you know by name? How many can you recognize when you see them? If you needed to borrow a tool, could you do so from a close neighbor?").

Researchers have suggested that three levels of resident-based control shape the level of social disorganization versus collective efficacy in a locale (e.g., Bursik and Grasmick). *Private control* refers to dynamics within families and between close friends. If Junioretta extorts school lunch money from two other neighbors while walking to school, and her parents find out about it, will they punish her appropriately? *Parochial control* refers to supervisory efforts made by neighbors and acquaintances. If a neighbor while gardening out back sees Junioretta walking down the alley threatening two other children and demanding their lunch funds, will she grab Junioretta by the ear and walk her home to her dad, or will she, the neighbor, just shrug her shoulders and go about planting her tomatoes? How much parochial control is exercised varies from block to block in a neighborhood. *Public control* refers to the neighborhood leadership's ability to garner resources from public and private agencies outside the neighborhood. Can the community association's leaders effectively lobby city hall for resources for neighborhood improvements and programs? For example, can they obtain funding for more school crossing guards on well-traveled routes leading to and from the local school? Can they work collaboratively with other neighborhood organizations on issues affecting their part of town?

High delinquency rates occurred in low income, ethnically heterogeneous, unstable locations because those ecological characteristics made social disorganization more likely. In lower income locales residents' concerns are more spatially circumscribed than in higher income locales (Taylor, 1988). In some low-income neighborhoods residents only feel safe within their own dwelling. As ethnic heterogeneity increases, it becomes increasingly difficult for residents to "decode" what other residents are doing. Increasing intercultural distance and perhaps language barriers make it harder to figure out what is going on. As instability increases, residents have less time to get to know their neighbors; it is harder to figure out who "belongs" on the block and who does not belong.

In other words, these structural attributes of the community either increase or decrease the chances that residents would exert some control over what took place in their community; these dynamics in turn would influence outcomes like delinquency, the local offending rate, and local victimization rates. Note that social disorganization mediates the impacts of community structure on the outcomes. It represents a crucial link connecting community fabric with the outcomes. It does appear, however, that community fabric; although it affects social disorganization, continues to exert an independent influence on outcomes like delinquency, victimization, and offending (Veysey and Messner). In short there are structural causes of these community-level differences beyond differences in social disorganization or collective efficacy.

Social disorganization is likely to be strongest, and collective efficacy weakest, when a community is in the midst of an *invasion-succession* cycle. In such a cycle, a neighborhood "turns over," with one type of resident replacing another. In the midst of such a cycle residents are unlikely to know their neighbors, and the local population will be quite heterogeneous in makeup.

Neighborhood residents are always changing: people move in and people move out. But if the two rates are roughly matched, and if the volume is relatively modest, and if those moving in are sociodemographically similar to those moving out, then the neighborhood is stable (Ahlbrandt and Cunningham). But if the volume of in-movers increases beyond a relatively low rate, and if the in-movers are sociodemographically dissimilar from the current residents, then over time the population in the locale would change. There would be an "invasion" of a new type of resident, and eventually that new type of resident would "succeed" the older type of resident.

Such cycles could be seen most clearly in the 1960s and 1970s in urban neighborhoods where racial succession took place, and white populations were replaced in relatively short order by African American households. Many expected that gentrified neighborhoods would follow the same cycle; but they have not. Even in some of the most reclaimed neighborhoods, higher-income, recent in-migrant owners mingle on the street with lower-income, longer-term, renters (Lee and Mergenhagen). The invasion-succession cycle can "stall" before completion. In these partially gentrified locations violent and property crime rates can be higher (Covington and Taylor).

Shaw and McKay's initial cross-sectional findings have been supported again and again (e.g., Baldwin, 1975). Studies routinely find the following.

Delinquency and offense and offender rates are higher closer to the city center than farther away, although there are exceptions, and although each of these outcomes maps differently onto spatial structure (Baldwin and Bottoms). Delinquency and offense and offender rates are higher in lower income, and/or less stable, and/or more predominantly African American communities (K. D. Harries, 1980), although differences have arisen regarding the relative contribution of each attribute, and the appropriate labels to apply to some of the dimensions of urban community structure examined (Sampson and Lauritsen). For example, some have argued that relative socioeconomic status in a locale—how poor the residents are, or how poor they are relative to those residents in adjoining neighborhoods—is the most important community correlate of high violent crime rates (Land et al.). Others argue that family disruption, and/or family structures that are less stable or provide less supervision of the locale are the most important (Sampson and Lauritsen). This debate is not about to end anytime soon.

In essence, the human ecological theory focuses on a community's position in the larger urban fabric, and how that position changes over time. It is its relative status, stability, and racial composition, and the changes in those features, that determine changes in offense, offender, and delinquency rates.

In a series of studies using Shaw and McKay's data on delinquency and census characteristics in Chicago, from the 1930s through the 1960s, more rapid community shifts connected with more rapid changes in the delinquency rate (e.g., Bursik, 1986). The ways in which neighborhoods changed varied across each decade, as did the relative contribution of different types of neighborhood changes to changes in delinquency. What was happening each decade was conditioned by the historical context. But despite these variations in each decade, community changes linked to delinquency changes in the expected ways. For example, increasing unemployment and increasing nonwhite racial composition were both tied to increasing delinquency rates.

Changes in neighborhood fabric are linked not only to changes in delinquency but also to changes in violence. A Baltimore study of changes in the 1970s found that neighborhoods shifting more dramatically on stability or status experienced more sizable shifts in violence as well (Taylor and Covington, 1988). Which particular feature of neighborhood fabric proved important depended on the type of violent crime examined.

Briefly put, one of the major extensions of social disorganization theory in the last two decades has been the application of the model to ecological changes over time. As the theory predicts, neighborhoods whose composition is changing more rapidly, relative to the other neighborhoods in the city, are more likely to experience increasing delinquency or crime problems. Even if the rapid change is in a "positive" direction, such as gentrification, increasing crime may accompany the shift (Covington and Taylor, 1989).

The features of neighborhood structure only predispose a neighborhood to have more or less social disorganization. Key studies, in Britain and in the United States, highlight the central importance of social disorganization versus collective efficacy processes (e.g., Sampson et al.). These processes mediate the impacts of structure on outcomes like offending and victimization, but structural impacts like differences in status and stability continue to exert some impacts on the outcomes separate from these processes (Versey and Messner).

Responses to crime like fear of crime are also ecologically patterned and social disorganization versus collective efficacy processes likewise appear to mediate the impacts of structure—status, race, stability—on the outcomes (Taylor, 1996). Similarly, rapid structural change affects these processes that in turn affect fear of crime (Taylor and Covington, 1993). Generally these studies show that although there are differences from study to study, neighborhood structure—especially status and stability—affects these outcomes in ways anticipated by the human ecological model, and that indicators of social disorganization versus social efficacy at least partially mediate the relationship.

In the last few years a related set of models concentrating on social and physical aspects of disorder in neighborhoods has emerged. The model terms these features *incivilities*. Physical incivilities include abandoned cars, weed-filled lots, vacant houses, and unkempt properties and yards. Social incivilities, although viewed by some as just misdemeanor crimes, include vandalism, rowdy groups of unsupervised teens, fighting neighbors, public drug use or drug sales, and the like. These models come in different forms, but the version drawing the most attention has suggested that incivilities can contribute independently, over time, to increasing neighborhood crime, neighborhood structural decline, and increased neighborhood fear (Skogan). Longitudinal analyses, however, show that incivilities do not change uniformly in locations (suggesting they are indicative of separate and somewhat unrelated problems) and the independent impacts of incivilities on neighborhood level outcomes are far weaker than the theory anticipates, although some predicted impacts do emerge (Taylor, 2001).

Policy impacts of work on the ecology of crime have been several. Since the early 1900s, city programs have targeted some of the areas where youths are at greatest risk of delinquency. More recently more refined geographic analyses of crime have concentrated enforcement efforts on crime "hot spots"—locations where police are called repeatedly to deal with crimes or disturbances. These targeted interventions can under some conditions have some deterrent or preventive impacts. Concern about incivilities has led to community policing initiatives targeted at these problems in the beliefs that reducing these problems will reduce crime. One recent longitudinal work suggests this enthusiasm may be misplaced (Taylor, 2001).

Interest in this work in the future will increase due in large part to increased availability of mapping software for locating crime and community data geographically, and allowing sophisticated spatial analyses (Weisburd and McEwen). Increasing availability of multilevel models also facilitate work in this area (Bryk and Raudenbush). In addition, after having fallen out of favor in the 1960s and 1970s, interest in the ecology of crime has increased in recent years and sociologists generally are discovering "neighborhood effects" in a range of topic areas. Nonetheless, one of the biggest factors holding work in this area back is the lack of routinely updated data that includes community characteristics, police calls for service and crime data, and social disorganization versus collective efficacy indicators for a number of neighborhoods in a number of cities. Hopefully future efforts of an inter-university consortium will work on such an effort.

RALPH B. TAYLOR

See also CRIME CAUSATION: SOCIOLOGICAL THEORIES; PREVENTION: ENVIRONMENTAL AND TECHNOLOGICAL STRATEGIES; RURAL CRIME; URBAN CRIME.

BIBLIOGRAPHY

AHLBRANDT, ROGER, and CUNNINGHAM, JAMES. *A New Public Policy for Neighborhood Preservation.* New York: Praeger, 1979.

BALDWIN, JOHN. "British Areal Studies of Crime: An Assessment." *British Journal of Criminology* 15 (1975): 211–227.

BALDWIN, JOHN, and BOTTOMS, ANTHONY E. *The Urban Criminal.* London: Tavistock, 1976.

BOURGOIS, PHILIPPE. *In Search of Respect.* Cambridge, U.K.: Cambridge University Press, 1996.

BRANTINGHAM, PAUL J., and BRANTINGHAM, PATRICIA L. "Introduction: The Dimension of Crime." In *Environmental Criminology.* 2d ed. Edited by P. J. Brantingham and P. L. Brantingham. Prospect Heights, Ill.: Waveland Press, 1996. Pages 7–26.

BRANTINGHAM, PAUL; DYRESON, DELMAR A.; and BRANTINGHAM, PATRICIA. "Crime Seen Through a Cone of Resolution." *American Behavioral Scientist* 20 (1976): 261–274.

BRATTON, WILLIAM. *Turnaround.* New York: Random House, 1998.

BRYK, ANTHONY S., and RAUDENBUSH, STEPHEN W. *Hierarchical Linear Models: Applications and Data Analysis Methods.* Newbury Park, Calif.: Sage, 1992.

BURSIK, ROBERT J. "Urban Dynamics and Ecological Studies of Delinquency." *Social Forces* 63 (1984): 393–413.

———. "Ecological Stability and the Dynamics of Delinquency." In *Communities and Crime.* Edited by A. J. Reiss and M. Tonry. Chicago: University of Chicago Press, 1986. Pages 35–66.

———. "Social Disorganization and Theories of Crime and Delinquency." *Criminology* 26 (1988): 519–551.

BURSIK, ROBERT J., and GRASMICK, HAROLD G. "The Multiple Layers of Social Disorganization." Paper at the American Society of Criminology in New Orleans. November, n.d.

BURT, CYRIL. *The Young Delinquent.* London: University of London Press, 1925.

COHEN, DON, and NISBETT, RICHARD E. "Self-Protection and the Culture of Honor: Explaining Southern Violence." *Personality and Social Psychology Bulletin* 20 (1994): 551–567.

COVINGTON, JEANETTE C., and TAYLOR, RALPH B. "Gentrification and Crime: Robbery and Larceny Changes in Appreciating Baltimore Neighborhoods in the 1970s." *Urban Affairs Quarterly* 25 (1989): 142–172.

FAGAN, JEFFREY; ZIMRING, FRANKLIN E.; and KIM, JUNE. "Declining Homicide in New York City: A Tale of Two Trends." *Journal of Criminal Law and Criminology* 88 (1998): 1277–1323.

FISCHER, CLAUDE S. *To Dwell Among Friends: Personal Networks in Town and City.* Chicago: University of Chicago Press, 1982.

———. "The Subcultural Theory of Urbanism: A Twentieth-year Assessment." *American Journal of Sociology* 101 (1995): 543–577.

FREY, WILLIAM H. "Lifecourse Migration of Metropolitan Whites and Blacks and the Structure of Demographic Change in Large Central Cities." *American Sociological Review* 49 (1984): 803–827.

GLYDE, JOHN. "Localities of Crime in Suffolk." *Journal of Statistical Society of London* 19 (1856): 102–106.

GOTTDIENER, MARK. *The New Urban Sociology.* New York: McGraw Hill, 1994.

HAGAN, JOHN, and PETERSEN, RUTH D., eds. *Crime and Inequality.* Stanford, Calif.: Stanford University Press, 1995.

HARRIES, KEITH. *The Geography of Crime and Justice.* New York: McGraw-Hill, 1974.

———. *Crime and the Environment.* Springfield, Mass.: Charles C. Thomas, 1980.

HAWLEY, AMOS H. "Human Ecology." *American Behavioral Scientist* 24 (1981): 423–444.

HINDELANG, MICHAEL J.; HIRSCHI, TRAVIS; and WEIS, JOSEPH G. *Measuring Delinquency.* Beverly Hills, Calif.: Sage, 1981.

KPOSOWA, AUGUSTINE J.; BREAULT, KEVIN D.; and HARRISON, BEATRICE M. "Reassessing the Structural Covariates of Violent and Property Crimes in the USA: A Country Level Analysis." *British Journal of Sociology* 46 (1995): 79–105.

LAND, KENNETH C.; MCCALL, PATTY; and COHEN, LAWRENCE C. "Structural Covariates of Homicide Rates: Are There Any Invariances Across Time and Space?" *American Journal of Sociology* 95 (1990): 922–963.

LEE BARRY A., and MERGENHAGEN, PAULA M. "Is Revitalization Detectable? Evidence from Five Nashville Neighborhoods." *Urban Affairs Quarterly* 19 (1994): 511–538.

MACCOBY, ELEANOR E.; JOHNSON, JOHN P.; and CHURCH, RICHARD M. "Community Integration and the Social Control of Juvenile Delinquency." *Journal of Social Issues* 14 (1958): 38–51.

MAGUIRE, KATHLEEN, and PASTORE, ANNE L., eds. *Sourcebook of Criminal Justice Statistics 1998.* Washington, D.C.: United States GPO, 1999.

MARCUSE, PETER. "The Ghett of Exclusion and the Fortified Enclave: New Patterns in the United States." *American Behavioral Scientist* 41 (1997): 311–327.

MASSEY, DOUGLASS, and DENTON, NANCY. *American Apartheid: Segregation and the Making of the Underclass.* Cambridge, Mass.: Harvard University Press, 1993.

MASSEY, DOUGLAS; GROSS, ANDREW B.; and SHIBUYA, KUMIKO. "Migration, Segregation, and the Geographic Concentration of Poverty." *American Sociological Review* 59 (1994): 425–445.

MESSNER, STEVEN F., and GOLDEN, REID M. "Racial Inequality and Racially Disaggregated Homicide Rates: An Assessment of Alternative Theoretical Explanations." *Criminology* 30 (1992): 421–445.

MESSNER, STEVEN F., and ROSENFELD, RICHARD. *Crime and the American Dream.* Monterey, Calif.: Wadsworth, 1994.

SAMPSON, ROBERT J., and LAURITSEN, JANET L. "Violent Victimization and Offending: Individual, Situational- and Community-Level Risk Factors." In *Understanding and Preventing Violence.* Vol. 3: *Social Influences.* Edited by A. J. Reiss and J. A. Roth. Washington, D.C.: National Academy Press, 1994. Pages 1–114.

SAMPSON, ROBERT J.; RAUDENBUSH, STEPHEN W.; and EARLS, FELTON. "Neighborhoods and Violent Crime: A Multi-level Study of Collective Efficacy." *Science* 277 (1997): 918–924.

SHAW, CLIFFORD R., and MCKAY, HENRY D. *Juvenile Delinquency and Urban Areas,* 2d ed. Chicago: University of Chicago Press, 1969 [1942].

SKOGAN, WESLEY. *Disorder and Decline: Crime and the Spiral of Decay in American Cities.* New York: Free Press, 1990.

TAYLOR, RALPH B. *Human Territorial Functioning.* Cambridge, U.K.: Cambridge University Press, 1988.

———. "Neighborhood Responses to Disorder and Local Attachments: The Systemic Model of Attachment, and Neighborhood Use Value." *Sociological Forum* 11 (1996): 41–74.

———. *Breaking Away from Broken Windows: Evidence from Baltimore Neighborhoods and the Nationwide Fight Against Crime, Grime, Fear, and Decline.* New York: Westview Press, 2001.

TAYLOR, R. B., and COVINGTON, JEANETTE. "Neighborhood Changes in Ecology and Violence." *Criminology* 26 (1988): 553–589.

———. "Community Structural Change and Fear of Crime." *Social Problems* 40 (1993): 374–397.

TAYLOR, RALPH B.; GOTTFREDSON, STEPHEN D.; and BROWER, SIDNEY. "Understanding Block Crime and Fear." *Journal of Research in Crime and Delinquency* 21 (1984): 303–331.

VEYSEY, BONITA M., and MESSNER, STEPHEN E. "Further Testing of Social Disorganization Theory: An Elaboration of Sampson and Grove's 'Community Structure and Crime'." *Journal of Research in Crime and Delinquency* 36 (1999): 156–174.

WEISBURD, DAVID, and MCEWEN, JOHN T. *Crime Mapping and Crime Prevention.* Greenwich, Conn.: Criminal Justice Press, 1997.

WILSON, WILLIAM J. *When Work Disappears: The World of the New Urban Poor.* New York: Knopf, 1996.

WIRTH, LOUIS. "Urbanism as a Way of Life." *American Journal of Sociology* 44 (1938): 1–23.

ECONOMIC CRIME: THEORY

There is no widely accepted definition of economic crime, and it is impossible to enumerate briefly the various definitions, theories, and offenses included in this category. We focus on the theoretical work that explores three aspects of economic crime: *offender motivations, economic outcomes,* and *economic processes.*

The first tradition refers to economic crimes as illegal acts in which offenders' principal motivation appears to be economic gain (e.g., Freeman). Here, an economic crime is conceived of as any offense in which individuals or collectivities of people *purposively* act in an illegal manner in order to gain financial returns (e.g., robbery, drug selling, tax evasion, computer crime, and abuses of economic aid). Although conceptually appealing, this tradition has several drawbacks. For example, it assumes that offenders' motivations are readily observable or knowable from the criminal act itself. Although the motive behind robberies may appear to be the desire for property, perpetrators' primary motivation may be different (e.g., thrill seeking or racial hatred). Some crimes have multiple motives and economic gain may be a secondary goal. Furthermore, offenders themselves are not always conscious of their motives and they may be unable to distinguish between the reasons that precipitated their actions and the rationalizations or justifications that follow them.

A second tradition avoids difficulties associated with trying to infer motives and focuses on illegal acts that successfully provide offenders with an economic return (e.g., Chamlin and Kennedy). However, excluding attempted crimes from analysis limits our understanding; successfully completed offenses may differ in important ways from those that are failures. A variation of this tradition defines economic crime as offenses for which victims incur an economic cost (e.g., Salvesberg; Reuvid). Typical victims include individuals, groups, or organizations against which the act was directed; however, a much wider group of victims may have been indirectly affected by such crimes. This occurs in cases in which a criminal act subverts or undermines the commercial effectiveness of normative business practices and the negative consequences extend beyond those at whom the specific immediate harm was intended (e.g., computer hacking, insider trading in stock market transactions). This definition addresses a common oversight in criminology—ignoring or under-representing victim issues—nonetheless, it is too narrow in some respects and too broad in others. For example, it excludes "victimless" crimes that have economic implications (e.g., prostitution) and includes any offense for which victims experience a cost (e.g., an assault that results in medical expenses or loss of wages).

A third tradition contends that the processes that lead to criminal behavior are the same as those that guide consumer behavior in the marketplace. This approach informs most theoretical work on crime offered by economists since the late 1960s. Its most cogent statement is found in Gary Becker's neoclassical or "economic" approach to explaining crime (1968; repr. 1974). The remainder of this entry describes this approach and discusses its advantages and weaknesses; reviews other social science perspectives that address some of the shortcomings of the neoclassical approach; and summarizes recent directions in the study of economic crime.

Classical approach to crime

The classical approach to crime originated in the Enlightenment and is evident in the writings of Thomas Hobbes, John Locke, Jean Jaques Rousseau, and others. According to this perspective, intelligence and rational thought are fundamental characteristics of people and the principal basis for their behavior. In other words, people have free will, make choices and pursue their own interests. In the late 1700s, philosophers Cesare Beccaria and Jeremy Bentham ap-

plied these ideas to crime, arguing that people freely chose to offend. According to Beccaria and Bentham, people's decisions to offend are guided by calculations that weigh the pleasure they hope to obtain from criminal acts against the potential pain they would receive if they were caught and punished for their crimes. This perspective, known as the classical school of criminology, maintains that people's calculations involve their knowledge of the law and their perceptions of the likelihood of punishment (based on their experiences and knowledge of the experiences of others). It proposes that crime can be most effectively deterred by punishments that are certain, swift, and proportional to the harm caused. Punishments that met these criteria would discourage offenders from re-offending and would encourage others to be law-abiding. This "deterrence" philosophy was the preeminent explanation of crime for over a hundred years; yet, by the start of the twentieth century its popularity was eclipsed by positivist explanations arguing that offenders differ from nonoffenders in important ways (e.g., socialization).

Neoclassical or economic approach

In the late 1960s the economist Gary Becker questioned positivist approaches to crime, arguing that: "[a] useful theory of criminal behavior can dispense with special theories of anomie, psychological inadequacies, or inheritance of special traits, and simply extend the economist's usual analysis of choice" (repr. 1974, p. 2). Characterizing his approach as an effort of "resurrection, modernization, and . . . improvement" (p. 45) of the rational approach of Beccaria and Bentham, Becker argued that criminals were not biologically, psychologically, or sociologically different from noncriminals; and that the decision to offend did not originate in a unique set of motives but was influenced by the same factors that motivate all purposive behaviors. Becker and others developed these ideas in what is now called the *neoclassical* or *economic approach* to crime. According to this perspective, people choose criminal over noncriminal alternatives in the same way that they choose particular strategies when they act as consumers in the marketplace. This theoretical explanation (Becker, 1976) is based on the following assumptions:

1. People's actions can be understood as rational; that is, people are naturally motivated to pursue their own interests and their behav-

iors can be examined as attempts to meet these desires. This does not preclude people from acting irrationally, as for example when they choose something on the basis of its availability rather than its ability to meet a desire, nor does it mean that people are necessarily conscious of their attempts to maximize their self-interests. Instead, the economic approach simply assumes that most actions can be understood as rational.

2. Material gain is a common interest, but it is not the only, nor necessarily the primary influence in people's decisions. People have a much richer set of interests, and the actions they undertake reflect their attempts to maximize these. Unfortunately, it is all but impossible for people to meet or accommodate completely their interests: people's desires are unlimited, whereas wealth, income, opportunities, and other resources are finite.

3. Because they are rational and must make choices, people can always express preferences between outcomes and the things they desire (commodities). Their preference rankings reflect their expectations of how much satisfaction (utility) an outcome or commodity will provide (utility function) and how much it will cost (opportunity cost). When given a choice, rational economic actors choose actions that will provide an outcome or commodity that they believe will maximize utility (satisfaction, not necessarily pleasure) and minimize costs. People's preferences are stable over time and at any point can be hierarchically ordered from most to least valued.

4. Rationally economic actors prefer more of a desired outcome or commodity to less, and prefer a lower cost to a higher one; however, the more people have of an outcome or commodity, the less likely it is that further increases will contribute to their satisfaction (diminishing marginal utility). Thus people who have an abundance of something are willing to give up a lot for relatively little in return (money may be the one significant exception because, in essence, it can become any commodity).

5. People base their rational decisions on information they collect. They endeavor to know as much as is optimally possible about each potential outcome's and commodity's utility, availability, and costs; however, they recognize that gathering information is itself a cost (e.g., see the theory of optimal or rational ac-

cumulation of costly information). Thus, although rationally economic actors endeavor to use all available information in making decisions, many decisions will be made on incomplete information and may not serve to maximize utility.

6. People have imperfect memories and often miscalculate; these attributes can further compromise their ability to maximize utility.

7. The future is not completely predictable. All decisions are based on expected utilities and have an element of risk or uncertainty. Thus, people's attitudes toward uncertainty and risk affect their assessment of the satisfaction associated with various outcomes or commodities. As a result, people may agree about a commodity's or outcome's utility but vary widely in their comfort with the gambles involved in acquiring one of these; thus they will assign different utilities to the commodity or outcome. A person who generally refuses to accept what is calculated to be a "fair gamble" is said to be *risk averse*. Those who generally have a preference for taking fair gambles are referred to as *risk seekers*. Finally, between the extremes of risk seekers and those who are risk averse, there are those that are *risk neutral*; those who are generally indifferent to accepting or refusing a fair gamble.

Although these assumptions are usually used to describe legal business decisions and actions, Becker (1974) and other neoclassical theorists argue that they can be extended to include criminal behavioral choices. Thus:

1. People choose to offend using the same cost-benefit analysis they use when choosing legal behaviors: a decision to offend reflects a normal, rational, calculation. Thus, this explanation of crime does not need to introduce personality characteristics, background experiences, or situational contingencies.

2. The decision to offend involves calculations based on estimates of a legal opportunity's availability, costs, and ability to provide a desired end (i.e., expected utility), versus an illegal opportunity's availability, costs, and ability to provide the same or comparable end. Both legal and illegal behaviors can provide an array of benefits that include material gain, approval or prestige, "psychic" or emotional returns (e.g., thrill, honor, revenge, a sense of equity), and other nonpe-

cuniary returns. The potential costs of these behaviors include time, transaction, and "psychic" costs (e.g., anxiety). Crime, however, introduces a unique set of reputational (e.g., loss of respect), psychological (e.g., guilt, shame, anxiety) and punishment costs (e.g., fines and incarceration).

3. The decision to offend is also influenced by a person's tolerance or enjoyment of taking risks. Thus, all things equal, those who commit crime at relatively high rates are comparatively more risk seeking or risk tolerant, those who offend at moderate rates are relatively more risk neutral, and those who seldom, if ever, violate criminal laws are relatively more risk averse.

4. The most effective way to reduce crime is to increase people's perceptions that costs of offending will exceed its rewards, and that the benefits of legal behavior surpass its costs.

Advantages of the neoclassical approach

The neoclassical approach offers several challenges to alternative theories of crime. First, it simplifies the search for motives by assuming that self-interest guides all behaviors, criminal and otherwise. Second, it removes distinctions between offenders and nonoffenders, and reminds us that when we examine economic crime we must remember that "the greatest exponents of criminality in business are [often] business people" (Reuvid, p. 561). Third, it is generalizable: although most researchers used the theory to study crimes that provided a material return, the theory did not distinguish crimes by types and is as applicable to murder as it is to theft (Becker, 1976). Fourth, it unifies a group of materially based crimes that are often treated as distinct (e.g., common "street crimes" such as prostitution and breaking and entering, and white-collar offenses such as stock fraud and money laundering). Fifth, it introduces an array of economic concepts and approaches that enhance the study of crime. Several scholars study the extent to which decisions to offend resemble legal employment decisions, as well as the interconnections between illegal and legal "work" (Ehrlich; Fagan and Freeman). Others use ideas about market forces to examine how internal and external market conditions influence crime (see Fagan and Freeman). And some writers add economic concepts to more sociological or psychological oriented theories. For example, Hagan, Gillis, and Simpson introduce propensity for risk-taking in their power-control theory of crime; Sampson and Laub address the consequences of conventional human and social capital in their life-course theory of offending; and Hagan and McCarthy focus on the effects of criminal capital in their capital theory of crime.

Problems with the neoclassical approach

A number of psychological, sociological, and criminal decision theorists and researchers have challenged the theoretical accuracy and empirical validity of the neoclassical approach (e.g., see Cornish and Clarke; Gottfredson and Hirschi). The most prominent critics argue that a theory grounded too deeply in instrumental rationality misrepresents people's basic nature. Some commentators argue that rationality is simpler than suggested by the neoclassical approach. They maintain that it is "bounded" or limited in ways unrecognized by neoclassical theory (e.g., by cognitive dissonance) and that people typically select from a few alternatives rather than considering a larger set of options (i.e., they use a "satisficing" rather than optimizing approach). Others argue that rationality is more complex and involves morals, norms, and forms of rationality other than the purely instrumental type. Critics also note that the neoclassical approach mistakenly portrays people as making decisions as individuals, independent of the influence of others.

Neoclassical theorists respond by reminding commentators that they do not assume that people necessarily always make explicit, rational cost-benefit calculations. Rather, they contend that one can make useful predictions by assuming that people act "as if" they made such calculations. For example, Milton Friedman argues that neoclassical theory should not be judged on the accuracy of its central assumptions of how cost-benefit calculations are made but on how well it predicts behavior. By this criterion, Friedman concludes that it performs quite well indeed. He maintains that we gain valuable and accurate insights into human behavior by assuming that actions, in general, occur "as if" they were governed by the rules of rational decision-making. By trial and error, people generally internalize such rules in the same manner that pool players eventually learn to play the game as if they understood the laws of physics.

Notwithstanding Friedman's optimism, the available evidence on the neoclassical or economic approach to crime is inconclusive. For example, Gary Lafree notes that longitudinal studies of postwar crime rates in the United States generally confirm that high levels of punishment reduce crime rates, as do some programs that increase the rewards of noncriminal behavior (also see Zhang); however, the effects on crime are not as large as predicted by the neoclassical approach, nor do they apply equally to all groups (e.g., members of racial minorities). Moreover, although the neoclassical approach is consistent with analysis of data in some other countries it does not explain criminal behavior equally well in others. For example, Tsushima's analysis of Japanese data is fairly consistent with the neoclassical perspective, whereas Reilly and Witt's analysis of data from England, and Scorcu and Cellini's (1998) study of Italian data, reveal several inconsistencies between the data and neoclassical predictions. The limits to the neoclassical approach are also evident in an analysis of aggregate data from several countries for the years 1979–1995 (Gould, Weinnberg, and Mustard in Fagan and Freeman). Consistent with the neoclassical approach, increasing wages and lowering unemployment reduced both property and violent crime rates; but in contrast to neoclassical predictions the effect was larger for property crime, specific to young and unskilled men, and varied considerably over time.

Researchers have also identified a variety of "anomalies" in which a significant proportion of subjects make decisions that appear to contradict the basic assumptions and predictions of neoclassical theory. For example, many decisions to offend appear to be made on impulse without any apparent rational calculations (Cornish and Clarke; Shover). In other settings, offenders' decisions appear to be based on limited knowledge and little or no effort is made to gather additional information. Research also suggests that most offenders have only the vaguest notions of the likelihood of being apprehended or of the probabilities of receiving different penalties if convicted. As well, many decisions are inconsistent with the notion of simple self-interest and for all intents and purposes appear to be irrational (i.e., inconsistent with the decision-maker's preferences), as for example when people make contradictory choices.

Several sociologically oriented criminologists sympathetic to some aspects of the neoclassical approach have suggested modifications to the economic perspective. In the following we review several of these advancements.

Ecological theory of illegal expropriation

In a series of papers, Lawrence Cohen and colleagues (see Cohen and Machalek) offer an *ecological theory of illegal expropriation*. This theory is consistent with the neoclassical assumption that the frequency of a behavior, including an illegal one, typically reflects its ability to satisfy people's preferences; however, an ecological approach to crime differs from the neoclassical perspective in two key ways. First, it does not assume that people necessarily know the benefits of behaviors before they act. Instead, it assumes that actions can have unintended positive results, consequences that encourage people to repeat their actions. Thus, people's behavioral choices do not necessarily reflect rational calculations based on complete information, nor are their behaviors always directed toward their most valued preference. Second, Cohen and Machalek's theory differs from the neoclassical approach in that it explicitly treats behaviors as strategies that are influenced by the actions of others. A strategy is simply a set of behaviors that yield benefits, whether the benefits were intended or not; the greater the benefits a strategy provides, the more likely that it will be repeated and proliferate within and across populations.

Drawing on behavioral biology and earlier work on routine activity theory (Cohen and Felson), Cohen and Machalek argue that expropriation is just one of many strategies that people can follow. They define illegal expropriation as a process whereby individuals or groups use coercion, deception, or stealth to usurp material resources or services from others. People may use an illegal expropriation strategy for a variety of reasons; however, they are most likely to continue to employ such a strategy because of its success. Likewise, others are most likely to adopt or copy an illegal expropriation strategy when they observe, or acquire knowledge about, its success. Note, however, that people often choose strategies impulsively, and can select one that is suboptimal. Thus, choosing an expropriative crime strategy may be inconsistent with a person's best interests.

The success of an expropriative strategy has two dimensions: the extent to which it provides valued returns for those who use it and the extent to which it proliferates in a group or population. Several characteristics influence a strategy's success: how it is executed, how it responds to the defensive counter-strategies of victims, and the manner in which it spreads. A strategy is most likely to succeed when it is (1) cryptic, (2) deceptive, (3) bold, (4) surprising, (5) evasive, (6) resistant, (7) mobile, (8) mutable, and/or (9) stimulating. A cryptic strategy is not detected by the victim until after the expropriation occurs (e.g., embezzlement). A deceptive strategy is one that is detected, but the victim interprets the strategy as benevolent or innocuous (e.g., a confidence game). In other contexts, a strategy may be more effective when it is bold; that is, it overpowers the victim (e.g., robbery). A bold strategy is often more efficient if it involves the element of surprise (e.g., highjacking). A strategy that is evasive moves easily from location to location, thereby avoiding or neutralizing victim recognition or retaliation (e.g., con games and telephone sales frauds) whereas a resistant strategy is impervious to victim retaliations (e.g., extortion or gang crime). A mobile strategy spreads easily: it can be transmitted from one person to another and can migrate from one group or population to another (e.g., computer crimes). A strategy that is mutable adapts to accommodate changing victim counter strategies, as well as to cultural and social transformations (e.g., the addition of alarm deactivation skills to a car theft strategy). Finally, a strategy that is stimulating or exciting may also proliferate because of the pleasure it provides (e.g., the thrill of shoplifting).

Several factors external to a strategy also effect its likelihood of success. For example, expropriative strategies may become ineffective in situations where the number of expropriators exceeds the number of producers, or when past victimizations educate people against further victimizations. Thus, the extent to which an expropriative strategy is used and is successful is the result of a dynamic process that involves the past and current experiences of exploiters and producers, and the nature of the social, cultural, and material world in which they live.

Game theory

A related extension of the neoclassical approach involves integrating it with ideas first developed by John von Neumann and Oscar Morgenstern (1944) in their work on game theory. The neoclassical approach suggests a world in which individual people gather information and make choices and decisions independently of others; yet, von Neumann and Morgenstern argue that people's choices are influenced by the decisions of others and that people consider these influences when they make their decisions.

In other words, people's choices are interdependent, not independent. Von Neumann and Morgenstern's work on game theory, and subsequent research in this tradition, has developed this insight, revealing that people use various strategies when making decisions and that part of a strategy is anticipating the decisions of others.

Game theory research has several implications for crime. Bruce Bueno de Mesquita and Lawrence Cohen use game theory to explore how the decision to offend is part of a sequential process that involves various government decisions on the allocation of resources. Game theory logic suggests that governments that support economic inequality can sometimes encourage the poor to commit economic crimes even when the poor and the rich have the same preferences for legal behavior. Exploitative or unfair governments can also turn nonoffenders into criminals by destroying their confidence that the government will treat them fairly. Moreover, government policies that increase punishment and short-term transfer payments (e.g., welfare) will often have little effect on reducing economic crime among the poor. In contrast, policies that raise people's standard of living and their belief in a system's fairness will more often discourage them from choosing crime. Importantly, Bueno de Mesquita and Cohen note that game theory logic predicts that if people are abysmally poor, no increase in their trust in society's fairness will be sufficient incentive for them to choose legal over illegal behavior.

Criminal cooperation

Other scholars have used game theory research to understand a characteristic common to many economic crimes: the presence of co-offenders. For example, Bill McCarthy, John Hagan, and Lawrence Cohen argue that like other economic activities, co-offending requires people who recognize that, in some cases, the probability of attaining a desired outcome rises with a cooperative effort. Yet, working cooperatively with others typically involves uncertainty: there are often few if any ways to enforce people's pledges to cooperate, people may benefit from the actions of others and then fail to fulfill their commitments (i.e., they may cheat), and people may take advantage of the actions of others without providing any reciprocity (i.e., they may "free-ride").

Critics note that the neoclassical model offers little insight into the cooperative process. Criminal cooperation is typically more unpredictable than offending alone, and the neoclassical model offers few insights into the process by which people choose actions that have uncertain outcomes. As well, the assumption of instrumental rationality suggests an individual who makes decisions based solely on his or her preferences and is oblivious to those of others; such an individual is an unlikely cooperator. Social dilemma theorists resolve these problems, suggesting that people have both instrumental and "collective rationality." Like instrumental rationality, collective rationality involves cost-benefit analyses aimed at maximizing one's preferences; however, it includes the recognition that in some situations, one's interests may be best met as a result of the decisions and actions of others. Cooperation further requires that people, including offenders, "trust" others to fulfill their obligations.

Experimental research suggests that several conditions promote collective rationality, trust, and cooperation in economic activities. These include the type, history, and strength of the relationship between people; people's fear of reprisals for noncooperation; their beliefs about each other's honesty and cooperativeness; their knowledge other's past cooperation; and their tolerance for risk. Nonexperimental research also suggests that cooperation may be encouraged by mutual need. Consistent with some of these findings, McCarthy et al.'s research on theft among Canadian street youth indicates that need, associations with other offenders, and a willingness to take risks all increase criminal cooperation. Furthermore, offenders who cooperate steal more frequently than do those who steal alone.

Returns versus costs

A further extension of the neoclassical approach is critical of the tendency to focus on calculations that involve the costs associated with offending. Several scholars disagree with the suggestion that calculations of the probabilities and consequences of detection are based solely on the amount of information gathered; instead, they argue that calculations can be influenced by a number of demographic characteristics (e.g., Cornish and Clarke). For example, young people may have a greater tendency to disregard information about detection probabilities because they are more likely to believe that they are immune to negative consequences. Compared to

adults, youth may be more likely to believe that they are the ones who will "get away with it."

Several writers also argue that, like the assessment of other economic options, the decision to offend is more profoundly influenced by beliefs about the possible gains rather than potential costs (e.g., Ehrlich). Thus, the decision to offend focuses on a crime's capacity to provide one or more valued resources including an emotional thrill, a means to impress others, and financial resources (e.g., Katz; Shover; Fagan and Freeman). This approach further suggests that people make offending decisions in ways that resemble their decisions made about noncriminal activities. For example, several studies of drug sellers and property offenders indicate that they increase their incomes by combining illegal work with work in the legal economy (see Fagan and Freeman). Offenders who are adept at making use of their resources are also more likely to succeed (Grogger). For example, success in noncriminal economic activities is influenced by a person's ability to make the most effective use of their human (e.g., knowledge and specialized skills), social (e.g., connections with others), personal (e.g., competency, entrepreneurial skills, or business acumen), and financial (e.g., wealth) capital. Research also suggests that people who effectively utilize these resources profit the most from their decisions to offend: thus, the most successful offenders learn from previous experiences. They specialize, use their associations as a source of information, are willing to work with others, and are competent entrepreneurs (e.g., see Matsueda, Gartner, Piliavin, and Polakowski).

Conclusions

The study of economic crime has had an uneven history. Over the last few centuries, writers have offered a variety of definitions of economic offenses and theories that use an economic approach to crime. Throughout this period, interest in economic crime and the economic approach to offending has ebbed and flowed. Its most recent revival begin at the end of the 1960s with Gary Becker's seminal work on a neoclassical approach to crime and more than thirty years later, economists, sociologists, and criminologists continue to use, revise, and argue about this perspective.

The debate over the economic approach to crime will undoubtedly continue as we learn more about the ways in which people interpret the costs and benefits of crime and how they use this information when choosing criminal behaviors over noncriminal ones. The relationships between crime rates, punishment patterns, and economic changes in the United States in the 1990s offer one example of this debate's longevity. From the mid-1970s until the early 1990s imprisonment rates expanded while the income disparity between rich and poor widened. Neoclassical theory suggests that these two trends would have opposite effects, with increasing imprisonment discouraging crime and increasing income inequality encouraging it. The latter effect may have been greater, as crime rates rose throughout much of this period. Moreover, some criminologists (see Fagan and Freeman) argue that the increase in imprisonment actually contributed to the increasing crime rate by diminishing its subjective costs (e.g., its perceived reputational and loss of income costs) even though its objective cost increased (e.g., actual certainty and severity of imprisonment rates). However, in the early 1990s crime in the United States began a long decline, a trend that began in an economic recession. To further complicate matters, the U.S. economic recovery of the mid- and late 1990s occurred in a period of continually expanding punishment. Only time will tell if the crime trends of ensuing decades support or refute the economic approach to offending.

BILL MCCARTHY
LAWRENCE E. COHEN

See also CORPORATE CRIMINAL RESPONSIBILITY; CRIME CAUSATION: ECONOMIC THEORIES; CRIMINALIZATION AND DECRIMINALIZATION; ECONOMIC CRIME: ANTITRUST OFFENSES; ECONOMIC CRIME: TAX OFFENSES; ORGANIZED CRIME; STRICT LIABILITY; VICARIOUS LIABILITY; WHITE-COLLAR CRIME: HISTORY OF AN IDEA.

BIBLIOGRAPHY

BECKER, GARY S. "Crime and Punishment: An Economic Approach." In *Essays in the Economics of Crime and Punishment*. Edited by Gary S. Becker and William M. Landes. New York: Columbia University Press, 1968; repr. 1974. Pages 1–54.

———. *The Economic Approach to Human Behavior*. Chicago: University of Chicago Press, 1976.

BUENO DE MESQUITA, BRUCE, and COHEN, LAWRENCE E. "Self-Interest, Equity and Crime Control: A Game-Theoretic Analysis of Criminal Decisions." *Criminology* 33 (4) (1995): 483–517.

CHAMLIN, MITCHELL B., and KENNEDY, MARY BALDWIN. "The Impact of the Wilson Administration on Economic Crime Rates." *Journal of Quantitative Criminology* 7(4) (1991): 357–372.

COHEN, LAWRENCE E., and FELSON, MARCUS. "Social Change and Crime Rate Trends: A Routine Activity Approach." *American Sociological Review* 44(4) (1979): 588–608.

COHEN, LAWRENCE E., and MACHALEK, RICHARD. In *Crime and Public Policy: Putting Theory to Work*. Edited by Hugh D. Barlow. Boulder, Colo.: Westview Press, 1995. Pages 157–178.

CORNISH, DEREK B., and CLARKE, RONALD V. *The Reasoning Criminal*. New York: Springer-Verlag, 1986.

EHRLICH, ISSAC. "Participation in Illegitimate Activities: An Economic Analysis." In *Essays in the Economics of Crime and Punishment*. Edited by Gary S. Becker and William M. Landes. New York: Columbia University Press, 1974.

FAGAN, JEFFREY, and FREEMAN, RICHARD B. "Crime and Work." In *Crime and Justice: A Review of Research*, Vol. 25. Edited by Michael Tonry. Chicago: University of Chicago Press, 1999.

FREEMAN, RICHARD B. "Why Do So Many Young American Men Commit Crimes and What Might We Do About It?" *Journal of Economic Perspectives* 10(1) (1996): 25–42.

FRIEDMAN, MILTON. *Essays in Positive Economics*. Chicago: University of Chicago Press, 1953.

GOTTFREDSON, MICHAEL R., and HIRSCHI, TRAVIS. *A General Theory of Crime*. Stanford, Calif.: Stanford University Press, 1990.

GROGGER, JEFF. "Market Wages and Youth Crime." *Journal of Labor Economics* 16(4) (1998): 756–791.

HAGAN, JOHN; GILLIS, A. R.; and SIMPSON, JOHN. "Clarifying and Extending a Power-Control Theory of Gender and Delinquency." *American Journal of Sociology* 95(4) (1990): 1024–1037.

HAGAN, JOHN, and MCCARTHY, BILL. *Mean Streets: Youth Crime and Homelessness*. New York: Cambridge University Press, 1997.

KATZ, JACK. *Seductions of Crime: Moral and Sensual Attractions in Doing Evil*. New York: Basic Books, 1988.

LAFREE, GARY. *Losing Legitimacy: Street Crime and the Decline of Social Institutions in America*. Boulder, Colo.: Westview Press, 1998.

MATSUEDA, ROSS L.; GARTNER, ROSEMARY; PILIAVIN, IRVING; and POLAKOWSKI, MICHAEL. "The Prestige of Criminal and Conventional Occupations: A Subcultural Model of Criminal Activity." *American Sociological Review* 57(6) (1992): 752–770.

McCARTHY, BILL; HAGAN, JOHN; and COHEN, LAWRENCE E. "Uncertainty, Cooperation and Crime: Understanding the Decision to Co-Offend." *Social Forces* 77(1) (1998): 155–184.

REILLY, BARRY, and WITT, ROBERT. "Crime, Deterrence and Unemployment in England and Wales: An Empirical Analysis." *Bulletin-of-Economic-Research* 48(2) (1996): 137–159.

REUVID, JONATHAN. *The Regulation and Prevention of Economic Crime Internationally.* London: Kogan Page, 1995.

SAVELSBERG, JOACHIM. "The Making of Criminal Law Norms in Welfare States: Economic Crime in West Germany." *Law and Society Review* 21(4) (1987): 529–561.

SAMPSON, ROBERT, and LAUB, JOHN. *Crime in the Making: Pathways and Turning Points Through Life.* Cambridge: Harvard University Press, 1993.

SCORCU, ANTONELLO E., and CELLINI, ROBERTO. "Economic Activity and Crime in the Long Run: An Empirical Investigation on Aggregate Data from Italy, 1951–1994." *International Review of Law and Economics* 18(3) (1998): 279–292.

SHOVER, NEAL. *Great Pretenders: Pursuits and Careers of Persistent Thieves.* Boulder, Colo.: Westview Press, 1996.

TSUSHIMA, MASAHIRO. "Economic Structure and Crime: The Case of Japan." *Journal of Socio-Economics* 25(4) (1996): 497–515.

VON NEUMANN, JOHN, and MORGENSTERN, OSCAR. *Theory of Games and Economic Behavior.* Princeton: Princeton University Press, 1944.

VISCUSI, W. KIP. "Market Incentives for Criminal Behavior." *Inner-City Black Youth Unemployment.* Edited by R. Freeman and H. Holzer. Chicago: University of Chicago Press, 1986.

ZHANG, JUNSEN. "The Effect of Welfare Programs on Criminal Behavior: A Theoretical and Empirical Analysis." *Economic Inquiry* 35(1) (1997): 120–137.

ECONOMIC CRIME: ANTITRUST OFFENSES

Corporate executives at the close of the twentieth century committed and concealed a remarkable amount of antitrust crime. The discovery of these crimes underlined a criminal offense that has existed in the United States since 1890 but that nonetheless has remained a peripheral and exotic species within the general criminal law.

American antitrust law begins with the Sherman Act of 1890 (15 U.S.C. §1, et seq.). This landmark statute has but two main sections: Section 1's prohibition of agreements "in restraint of trade" and Section 2's ban on "monopolizing." Congress delegated considerable policy power to the federal courts by declining to define these two pregnant but vague phrases, and it upped the ante by making the rules criminal as well as civil in character. Congress later added the Clayton Act, the Federal Trade Commission Act, and the Robinson-Patman Act, but violations of these laws are not crimes. (The exception to this statement is the price discrimination provision of §3 of the Robinson-Patman Act, 15 U.S.C. §13a, which provides for imprisonment of not more than a year and a fine of not more than $5,000 or both. This law is virtually never invoked.)

Four types of litigants enforce the Sherman Act:

private plaintiffs, for whom section 4 for the Clayton Act authorizes civil suits for treble damages, costs, and attorneys fees;

state attorneys general, who may sue on behalf of an injured state itself and as parens patriae on behalf of injured citizens;

the Federal Trade Commission, which in effect can enforce the Sherman Act by enforcing the FTC Act; and

the Antitrust Division of the U.S. Department of Justice, which has the power to bring civil equitable actions to restrain antitrust violations.

Of these four groups, only the Antitrust Division also has the power to enforce the criminal provisions of the federal antitrust laws.

The Antitrust Division has made varied use of the criminal antitrust sanction over time. Before 1938, the government hardly used the tool at all. During Thurman Arnold's tenure at the Antitrust Division from 1938 to 1943, however, 220 of the 330 cases he brought under Section 1 included criminal charges (Russell, p. 680; see also Posner (1970) and Gallo et al. (1994 and 2000)). Later in the twentieth century, the government made its criminal prosecution policy far more selective and restrictive, confining criminal investigation and prosecution to "cases involving horizontal, per se unlawful agreements such as price fixing, bid rigging and horizontal customer and territorial allocations." Even in these cases, moreover, the government may decide criminal prosecution is inappropriate where there is "confusion in the law" or where people "were not aware of, or did not appreciate, the conse-

Table 1

Changing criminal antitrust penalites

1890	Passage of Sherman Act. Violation is a misdemeanor, subject to up to one year in jail and a $5,000 fine for individuals and corporations.
1955	Maximum fine increased to $50,000.
1974	• Violations increased from misdemeanor to felony status. • Maximum prison term increased from one to three years. • Maximum fine increased from $50,000 to $100,000 (individuals) and $1 million (corporations).
1977	Department of Justice: • advocates an 18-month "base period" sentence for Sherman Act convictions. • argues that fines are "usually poor alternatives to prison sentences."
1984	• Fine increased to $250,000 for individuals. • Fine may be the greater of $250,000 or twice the defendant's gross gain or the victims' loss (for individuals and entities) (see 18 U.S.C. §3571(d)).
1987	Sentencing guidelines take effect and provide for further increases in possible penalties.
1990	Maximum fine increased to: • $10 million for entities. • $350,000 for individuals.
1991	Corporate sentencing guidelines take effect and provide that fine can be twice the gross pecuniary gain from the crime or twice the victims' gross pecuniary loss (18 U.S.C. §3571(d)).
2000	Proposed increase from $10 million to $100 million in maximum corporate fine (Senate bill 2783, §5036 (introduced 26 June 2000); see Spratling (1998) p.14 explaining DOJ support for this proposal).

SOURCE: Updated and modified from Calkins (1997) p. 131

quences of their action" (*Antitrust Division Manual*, Chapter III.C.5.).

In the latter half of the twentieth century, the government periodically stiffened the criminal penalties for Sherman Act violations. Despite these increases, Gallo and others (1994) and Craycraft (1997) found that actual statutory fines are less than one percent of the optimal fines needed to deter cartelization attempts.

The rationale for criminal antitrust enforcement

Among the actions that antitrust law suppresses, none is so definitely harmful and so plainly illegal as express cartel agreements to raise prices or to reduce output. Cartel pricing is the effort by a group of erstwhile competitors cooperatively to mimic the high price and restricted output that a single monopolist would establish in that market. Price theory provides useful background.

Competitive pricing differs fundamentally from monopoly pricing. To simplify, competitive prices are based on producer costs because consumers have choices under perfect competition and can simply go elsewhere if one producer raises prices above its costs (counting a normal return to capital as a producer cost). A monopoly price is not based only on costs, however, but also on what the traffic will bear. Consumers have no choice when facing a monopolist, so the monopolist can raise price to the level of consumers' willingness to pay. What consumers are willing to pay can be far greater than a competitive cost-based price. That difference—*consumer surplus*—is the most definite benefit that competition delivers to consumers. It is the rationale for the Sherman Act's insistence on competition. Scholars debate the proper way precisely to define this rationale in the abstract, but this debate is of little practical consequence to the topic of criminal antitrust enforcement.

Cartelists can pursue their cooperative goal of high pricing in several ways. The simplest is the old-fashioned price fix. An immortal attempt was the telephone call between Howard Putnam, president of Braniff Airlines and Robert Crandall, president of competitor American Airlines:

PUTNAM: Do you have a suggestion for me? CRANDALL: Yes. I have a suggestion for you. Raise your goddamn fares twenty percent. I'll raise mine the next morning. PUTNAM: Robert, we—CRANDALL: You'll make more money and I will too. PUTNAM: We can't talk about pricing. CRANDALL: Oh bull—Howard. We can talk about any goddamn thing we want to talk about.

Putnam did not raise Braniff's fares in response to Crandall's proposal; instead he presented the government with a tape recording of the conversation. (*United States v. American Airlines, Inc.*, 743 F.2d 1114, 1116 (5th Cir. 1984), *cert. dismissed*, 474 U.S. 1001 (1985).)

Besides simple price fixing, other cartel techniques include market division (splitting territories between sellers), output quotas (setting production limits for each cartel member to reduce output and drive up price), customer allocation (assigning particular buyers to particular sellers) and bid rigging. Cartels may use some or all of these methods (U.S. Department of Justice (2001); International Competition Policy Advisory Committee [ICPAC], pp. 171–174; *United States v. Andreas and Wilson*, pp. 666–668).

The role of criminal sanction

When considering the proper role for criminal enforcement of antitrust policy, it matters that the antitrust field generally has been riven by normative controversy. Litigants have brought cases about business practices faster than economists have developed theories to comprehend the true nature of those practices. Some practices that initially seemed suspiciously anticompetitive have turned out in reality to have neutral or pro-consumer effects. Violating the antitrust laws, then, is not like robbing a bank. Everyone agrees that bank robbery is morally wrong and socially harmful. Over time, however, antitrust law has learned not to be nearly so sure of itself. Facing this complex and evolving understanding, one fairly can question exactly what role—if any—the mighty force of criminal law should play.

Criminal enforcement of antitrust law has been controversial on grounds of both efficiency and fairness. Beginning with the efficiency perspective, there was past concern that excessive enforcement would deter efficient business conduct, but the government's prosecutorial restraint towards the end of the 20th century largely has removed this debate from the criminal sphere. A different issue addresses the proper relationship of criminal to civil enforcement. Some utilitarians favor prison over civil liability as a superior deterrent (Baker and Reeves; Werden and Simon; Blair; Dau-Schmidt). Other utilitarians, however, recommend using civil sanctions to the maximum possible extent before turning to criminal penalties. Posner (1980), Polinsky and Shavell, Shavell (1985, 1987), and

Kaplow and Shavell (1994, 1999) develop this literature, which originates in the eighteenth-century work of Jeremy Bentham. The core idea is that the civil process and civil fines are both cheaper than, and thus preferable to, criminal litigation and incarceration—so long as the civil process adequately deters the proscribed conduct. These influential utilitarians then emphasize the muscular power of the treble damage deterrent as well as the calculating character and financial motivation of business conduct, and wonder why there is any need for criminal antitrust enforcement at all.

Yet a central problem for competition policy is to discover and to gather evidence against cartelists at work. This task is hard because this evidence is so elusive. Cartelists have perhaps more management training and corporate resources than any other sort of villain. Before the 1990s, it appears many cartels escaped detection. During that decade, however, some proved newly vulnerable to credible governmental threats of prison, to the promise of leniency for the first to cooperate with the government, and to special powers that criminal investigators wield. This policy combination created incentives for cartel defection that led to impressive government successes.

One important incentive dates from August 1993, when the Antitrust Division changed its corporate leniency program to marked effect. The old policy was that leniency was always discretionary and never automatic, and was never available once an investigation was underway. The new policy made amnesty automatic if there was no existing investigation, and made amnesty possible even after an investigation had been started. The new policy also promised amnesty from criminal prosecution to all corporate officials who cooperated with the government. Division officials reported striking results. During 1999, they received about two leniency applications per month—more than a twenty-fold increase over the old application rate. (Spratling 1999).

As Figure 1 illustrates, in the late 1990s the government reported a spectacular increase in criminal fines from corporations convicted of criminal antitrust charges. Time will tell whether this increase will prove an isolated spike or will achieve a new and stable future plateau. One source stated that, "[a]necdotally, U.S. antitrust authorities report [in 1999] that those cartels prosecuted over the past several years represent just the tip of the iceberg" (ICPAC, p. 168). Gov-

Figure 1

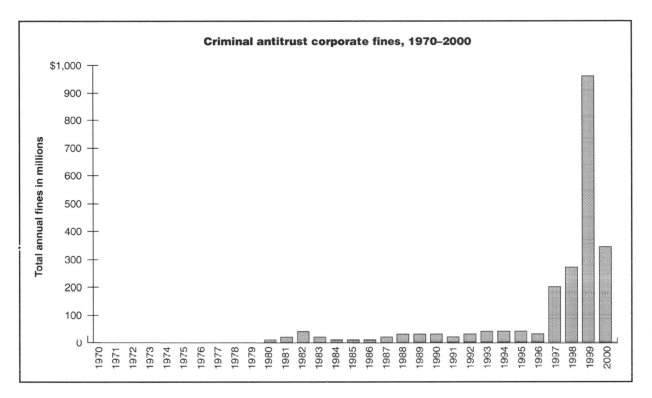

SOURCE. U.S. Department of Justice, Antitrust Division, Workload Statistics.

ernment enforcers say their leniency policy has been important to the detection and prosecution of conspiracies that otherwise would have remained hidden (ICPAC, pp. 172–174, 177–180; Klein (1997, 1999); Spratling (1998, 2000)).

Three aspects of these cartel prosecutions in the 1990s are notable. First, not all of the successful cartel prosecutions of the late 1990s originated with this corporate leniency policy change. A highly-publicized prosecution of a cartel in the lysine industry began with information that predated this policy change, as Eichenwald (pp. 48–53, 536–538) and the *Andreas* decision (p. 655) report. It was a bizarre and lucky break and not a change in enforcement policy that triggered at least one major Antitrust Division success in the late 1990s.

Second, the cartel investigations of the 1990s improved our understanding of the world. These investigations painted a new and remarkable picture of illegal activity that previously had been extremely difficult even to detect, let alone to study. The picture included, for instance, undercover recordings of secret cartel meetings at which the cartelists joked about being watched by

the F.B.I., while the F.B.I. in fact was watching— and videotaping (Eichenwald pp. 265–266; see also Barboza, Connor (1997, 2001a, 2001b); Griffin; ICPAC, pp. 171–176; Lieber; White). This new information revealed that, according to cartelists' own words and actions, the cartel threat is a very serious one, arising in large and diverse international markets. Economists long have debated the seriousness of the cartel threat. Centuries ago Adam Smith in his *Wealth of Nations* (p. 135–136) wrote that "[p]eople of the same trade seldom meet together, even for merriment and diversion, but the conversation ends in a conspiracy against the public, or in some contrivance to raise prices." Later and more skeptical economists tempered Smith's view, however, by noting that cartels face a persistent cheating incentive that can make large and effective cartels difficult to organize and maintain. Another source of skepticism was that expressed by respected authority William Baxter in 1995: "The larger companies are well-counseled and don't get into the kind of trouble that the antitrust division is looking for." (Labaton 1995). The prosecutions of the late 1990s showed that

Figure 2

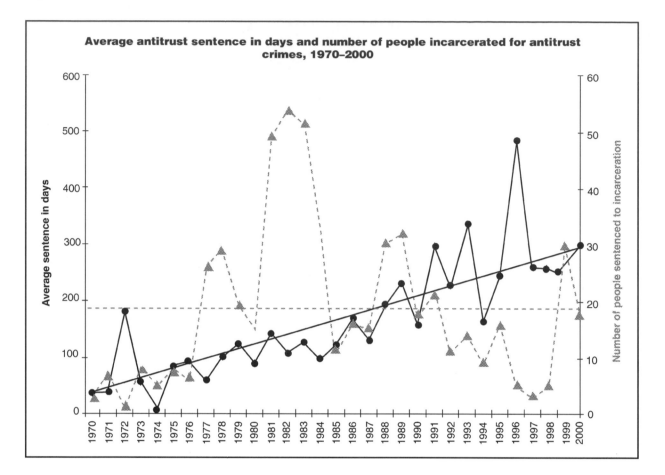

SOURCE: U.S. Department of Justice Antitrust Division, Workload Statistics.

cartel attempts were more common and more dangerous than skeptics had suspected. Civil enforcement alone had failed to detect the magnitude of the cartel threat from larger companies. We still remain unsure, however, of whether more cartels or an improved detection rate propelled the fine increase of the 1990s.

Third, using a criminal leniency policy to create the incentive for cartelists to break ranks seems appealingly efficient and comparatively cheap. The total number of cases and the average sentences are relatively small. Given that some cartels targeted worldwide markets for important commodities, it apparently required only rather small expenditures on criminal remedies to create a sentencing threat of superior effectiveness.

Figure 2, which shows average sentences and the number of people incarcerated, is consistent with this picture. For decades, the average num-

ber of convicts and their average sentences have remained noticeably modest: annually, for the entire country U.S. courts sentence only about 20 antitrust violators to an average sentence of less than a year each. Average sentence duration has steadily increased since 1970 but has remained relatively short, while the average number of defendants incarcerated annually has remained generally constant (with pronounced variance around the mean). Strictly in terms of efficiency, then, this cost of criminal antitrust enforcement seems relatively slight compared, for instance, to the resources we devote to incarcerating other types of federal criminals. Comparing Figures 1 and 2 also suggests that enforcement changes in the late 1990s were generally consistent with the utilitarian prescription of emphasizing fines more than incarceration. If one accepts that cartelists pose a significant threat to consumers, at an impressionistic level this enforcement deal for the public seems a very good one.

Moving from the perspective of efficiency to that of fairness, retributivists have shared doubts about criminal antitrust enforcement. Those who believe in reserving the singular stain of the criminal law to morally blameworthy conduct worry about overcriminalizing mere economic regulation (e.g., Hart, pp. 422–425). One crucial concern is the injustice of imprisoning morally blameless people under laws that are exceedingly complex and uncertain. Every retributivist should be satisfied, however, if prosecutors prove that defendants acted with the blameworthy awareness that their conduct was wrongful or illegal (Hart, pp. 415, 418; Green, pp. 1577–1578).

In sum, criminal antitrust enforcement can be efficient as well as fair. It can be efficient if the threat of criminal prosecution powers an effective leniency program that induces cartel defection, discovery, and prosecution. It can be fair if the law requires proof of blameworthy awareness of wrongdoing or illegality as an element of the criminal offense.

Confining criminal liability to culpable conduct

Congress effectively delegated the formulation of antitrust policy—including criminal antitrust policy—to federal judges. Have they interpreted the Sherman Act to confine its criminal reach only to people who indeed are morally blameworthy? The Supreme Court has delivered mixed results on this score.

Before turning to the cases, however, one must confront an initial question: should not this culpability issue be a concern for prosecutors during case selection, and not one for judges during statutory interpretation? Supreme Court justices could and indeed once did consign concerns about the culpability of defendants entirely to prosecutorial discretion, but in practice they no longer do so (Wiley, 1999, pp. 1058–1068, 1160–1161). Since 1985, the Supreme Court has interpreted federal criminal statutes on the apparent premise that Congress means to permit federal prosecutors to prosecute only morally blameworthy people (Wiley, 1999, pp. 1026–1056).

The Supreme Court's jurisprudence about criminal antitrust predates this interpretive shift. There are two main cases: *Nash v. United States*, 229 U.S. 373, 377–378 (1913) and *United States v.*

U.S. Gypsum Co., 438 U.S. 422 (1978). *Nash* ruled that criminal application of the Sherman Act was not unconstitutionally vague, but the decision did not set forth the elements prosecutors must prove in a criminal antitrust action. The *Gypsum* decision tackled just this task. *Gypsum* involved three pertinent holdings, which respectively seem (1) attractive; (2) questionable; and (3) unpersuasive and troubling.

The first holding—the attractive one—was the Court's conclusion that "[w]e are unwilling to construe the Sherman Act as mandating a regime of strict-liability criminal offenses" and therefore that "the criminal offenses defined by the Sherman Act should be construed as including intent as an element" (pp. 436, 443). This holding is attractive because criminal violation of the Sherman Act exposes a person to a potential three-year prison sentence. Without a showing of bad intent, there would be no guarantee that this person is morally blameworthy. To imprison a blameless person would be unjust.

The Court's second holding—the questionable one—was its decision (at 448 n.23 and 444) that "*knowledge* of the probable consequences of conduct [is] the requisite mental state in a criminal prosecution like the instant one where an effect on prices is also alleged." The Court summarily dismissed other levels of culpability with the opaque statement that, "[i]n dealing with the kinds of business decisions upon which the antitrust laws focus, the concepts of recklessness and negligence have no place." This second holding is mystifying and unjustified because the Court did not say why the concepts of recklessness and negligence have no place in dealing with business decisions. In contrast, the Model Penal Code recommends "recklessness" and not "knowledge" as the correct culpability default because recklessness is "the basic norm [that] usually is regarded as the common law position" (Model Penal Code §2.02(3) cmt. 5 (1985)). Jeffries and Stephan likewise observe that "the minimum culpability most widely found in the penal law is recklessness" (p. 1372). The *Gypsum* Court's preference for culpability at the level of knowledge rather than recklessness remains questionable (see Wiley, 1999, pp. 1111–1128). Procedurally this issue now seems fixed in concrete, however, because it seems extremely unlikely that any prosecutor would seek jury instructions that violate this rule simply on a remote prospect of eventual review in the Supreme Court, which is the only court with power to revise this *Gypsum* holding. Without any apparent prospect of Supreme Court review or congressional revision, this point seems of purely academic interest.

The Court's third holding—the unpersuasive one—is about the type of criminal intent the government must prove. The *Gypsum* decision failed to require the government to prove that the defendants were aware that they were acting *wrongfully* or *illegally*, which seems a logical state of mind to require if a court seeks (as the *Gypsum* decision sought, see 438 U.S. at 442) to guarantee that defendants are morally culpable. A standard of this sort is what the government must prove, for instance, in drug and tax prosecutions. The typical Ninth Circuit jury instruction for drug cases (No. 9.13) requires the government to prove that defendants knew that they possessed "some kind of a *prohibited* drug," while in tax evasion prosecutions the government must prove defendants knew of the duty imposed by law and intentionally violated that duty (*Cheek v. United States*, 498 U.S. 192, 201 (1991)). At least one district court has imposed a standard of this kind in a criminal antitrust case by requiring the jury to find both that "the defendants knowingly joined a conspiracy whose purpose was illegal and that they understood the illegality of that purpose" (*United States v. Brown*, 936 F.2d 1042, 1046 n.3 (9th Cir. 1991)). Proof of this kind of culpability has been readily available in recent cartel prosecutions, where defendants have shown their consciousness of guilt by using elaborate concealment precautions, false names, and the other standard tools of people with something to hide. If prosecutors in a particular case find it difficult to prove that defendants were aware of the illegal or wrongful nature of their conduct, this difficulty is a good reason for prosecutors to reexamine their decision to prosecute that case as a criminal matter.

Rather than require awareness of wrongful or illegal conduct, however, the *Gypsum* Court apparently held the government must prove an entirely different intent: awareness of the probable consequences of conduct. The decision phrased this requirement in slightly different ways: "knowledge of the probable consequences of conduct" (438 U.S. at p. 448 n.23); "action undertaken with the knowledge of its probable consequences" (id. p. 444); and "the perpetrator's knowledge of the anticipated consequences" (id. p. 446). The Court did not elaborate upon this point, but it appears that all of these formulations fail to guarantee that convicted persons are morally culpable. Take *United States v. Topco*, for instance. This oft-cited 1972 antitrust decision involved independent grocers from different regions who formed a buying cooperative and a private label brand called Topco. Each participating grocer owned an equal share in Topco, and each received an exclusive territory in which to market the new Topco brand. These grocers were the small firms in their regions; each one held only six percent of the market on average. Scholars have demonstrated convincingly that the grocers' conduct was beneficial to consumers and society (Baxter and Kessler, pp. 628–629; Bork, pp. 274–279; Hovenkamp, pp. 205–206). Yet the Supreme Court ruled that these defendants had committed a per se violation of the Sherman Act. Had the government opted to proceed criminally instead of civilly against the *Topco* defendants, it apparently could have obtained a conviction against them under the *Gypsum* standard because it seems clear that these defendants had knowledge of at least very many of the probable consequences of their group conduct. As far as one can tell, however, the *Topco* defendants were morally blameless people whose only sin was a good-hearted attempt to compete against the much larger grocery chains of A&P, Safeway, and Kroger—the three firms that the Court's decision identified as the market leaders. To imprison the *Topco* defendants would have been unjust, yet the *Gypsum* interpretation of the Sherman Act would have permitted it. *Topco* is not a fluke; a similar analysis could be performed with *Sealy, Associated Press*, and other cases. *Gypsum*'s third holding thus is unpersuasive and troubling.

Supreme Court developments since 1985 may have cast doubt on the soundness of *Gypsum*'s interpretation of the Sherman Act. (For the moment, put aside the mental state debate about knowledge versus recklessness and accept *Gypsum*'s holding that knowledge is the right level of awareness.) On the matter of *Gypsum*'s third holding, a better formulation would require the government to prove that the defendant in a price fixing case (1) agreed with a competitor (2) about price (3) knowing that this conduct was illegal or wrongful. This formulation goes beyond *Gypsum* and is at odds with some lower court case law (see, e.g., *United States v. W.F. Brinkley & Son Construction Co.*, 783 F.2d 1157, 1162 (4th Cir. 1986)), but it would accord with the thrust of the Supreme Court's general criminal interpretive jurisprudence since 1985. It would assure that federal antitrust prosecutions can imprison only people who are morally culpable.

One might hope that the Department of Justice would adopt this formulation as a matter of self-restraint, and would propose it in the jury instructions the Antitrust Division offers to district courts in criminal cartel cases. Should the Antitrust Division decline this measured self-restraint, it will open itself to challenges from defense counsel seeking jury instructions that require proof that defendants knew their conduct was illegal or wrongful. There are two risks for the government in this course. The first is that the district court may agree with the government but that an appellate court may not. The government then would face the need for a costly retrial of a case, and the passage of time never improves a case-in-chief. The second risk is that the appellate court may formulate jury instructions differently than would the government, and these instructions then would be chiseled in appellate stone. Self-imposed matters of discretion retain more flexibility than do judicial dictates. Arguments of tactical prudence as well as of principle thus support the case for prosecutorial self-restraint in antitrust cases.

Conclusion

Criminal antitrust enforcement led to government success in discovering cartels in the 1990s. By combining the threat of prison with a policy of increased leniency for cartelists who defect to cooperate with the government, prosecutors dramatically increased the effectiveness of antitrust enforcement policy. The Department of Justice could improve its policy still further by using jury instructions in criminal cases that guarantee that only morally culpable people can be convicted of antitrust crimes.

JOHN SHEPARD WILEY, JR.

See also CORPORATE CRIMINAL RESPONSIBILITY; ECONOMIC CRIME: THEORY; FEDERAL CRIMINAL LAW ENFORCEMENT; WHITE-COLLAR CRIME: HISTORY OF AN IDEA.

BIBLIOGRAPHY

ARNOLD, THURMAN. "Antitrust Law Enforcement, Past and Future." Law and Contemporary Problems 7 (1940): 5–23.
ASCH, PETER, and SENECA, JOSEPH J. "Is Collusion Profitable?" Review of Economics and Statistics 58 (1976): 1–11.
BAKER, DONALD I. "To Indict or Not to Indict: Prosecutorial Discretion in Sherman Act Enforcement." Cornell Law Review 63 (1978): 405–418.
BAKER, DONALD I., and REEVES, BARBARA A. "The Paper Label Sentences: Critiques." Yale Law Journal 86 (1977): 619–625.
BALL, HARRY V., and FRIEDMAN, LAWRENCE M. "The Use of Criminal Sanctions in the Enforcement of Economic Legislation: A Sociological View." Stanford Law Review 17 (1965): 197–223.
BARBOZA, DAVID. "Tearing Down The Facade of 'Vitamins Inc.'" The New York Times, 10 October 1999. Section 3.
BAXTER, WILLIAM F., and KESSLER, DANIEL P. "Toward a Consistent Theory of the Welfare Analysis of Agreements." Stanford Law Review 47 (1995): 615–631.
BLAIR, ROGER D. "A Suggestion for Improving Antitrust Enforcement." Antitrust Bulletin 30 (1985): 433–456.
BORK, ROBERT H. "Legislative Intent and the Sherman Act." Journal of Law & Economics 9 (1966): 7–48.
———. The Antitrust Paradox: A Policy At War With Itself. New York: Basic Books, 1993. Reprint with a new introduction and a new epilogue.
CALKINS, STEPHEN. "Corporate Compliance and the Antitrust Agencies' Bi-Modal Penalties." Law and Contemporary Problems 60 (1997): 127–167.
CONNOR, JOHN M. "The Global Lysine Price-Fixing Conspiracy of 1992–1995." Review of Agricultural Economics 19 (1997): 412–427.
———. "'Our Customers Are Our Enemies': The Lysine Cartel of 1992–1995." Review of Industrial Organization 18 (2001a): 5–21.
———. Global Price-Fixing: "Our Customers Are The Enemy." Norwell, Massachusetts: Kluwer Academic Publishers, 2001b.
CRAYCRAFT, CATHERINE; CRAYCRAFT, JOSEPH L.; and GALLO, JOSEPH C. "Antitrust Sanctions and a Firm's Ability to Pay." Review of Industrial Organization 12 (1997): 171–183.
DAU-SCHMIDT, KENNETH G. "An Economic Analysis of the Criminal Law as a Preference-Shaping Policy." Duke Law Journal 1990 (1990): 1–38.
EICHENWALD, KURT. The Informant. New York: Broadway Books, 2000.
ELZINGA, KENNETH G., and BREIT, WILLIAM. The Antitrust Penalties: A Study in Law and Economics. New Haven: Yale University Press, 1976.
FRAAS, ARTHUR G., and GREER, DOUGLAS F. "Market Structure and Price Collusion: An Empirical Analysis." Journal of Law and Economics 26 (1977): 21–44.

GALLO, JOSEPH C.; DAU-SCHMIDT, KENNETH G.; CRAYCRAFT, JOSEPH L.; and PARKER, CHARLES J. "Criminal Penalties Under the Sherman Act: A Study of Law and Economics." *Research in Law and Economics* 16 (1994): 25–71.

———. "Department of Justice Antitrust Enforcement 1995–1997: An Empirical Study." *Review of Industrial Organization* 17 (2000): 75–133. Updated version is available on the Internet: http://academic.wsc.edu/socialsci/parker_c/doj.htm.

GREEN, STUART P. "Why It's Illegal to Tear the Tag Off a Mattress: Overcriminalization and the Moral Content of Regulatory Offenses." *Emory Law Journal* 46 (1997): 1533–1615.

GRIFFIN, JAMES M. "An Inside Look at A Cartel at Work: Common Characteristics of International Cartels." Address to the American Bar Association Section of Antitrust Law, 6 April 2000. On the Internet: http://www.usdoj.gov/atr/public/speeches/4489.htm.

HART, HENRY M., JR. "The Aims of the Criminal Law." *Law & Contemporary Problems* 23 (1958): 401–441.

HAY, GEORGE A., and KELLY, DANIEL. "An Empirical Study of Price Fixing Conspiracies." *Journal of Law and Economics* 17 (1974): 13–38.

HOVENKAMP, HERBERT. *Federal Antitrust Policy: The Law of Competition and Its Practice*, 2d ed. St. Paul, Minn.: West Group, 1999.

International Competition Policy Advisory Committee. Final Report to the Attorney General and Assistant Attorney General for Antitrust, 2000. http://www.usdoj.gov/atr/icpac/finalreport.htm.

JEFFRIES, JOHN CALVIN, JR., and STEPHAN, PAUL B. "Defenses, Presumptions, and Burden of Proof in the Criminal Law." *Yale Law Journal* 88 (1979): 1325–1407.

KADISH, SANFORD H. "Some Observations on the Use of Criminal Sanctions in Enforcing Economic Regulations." *University of Chicago Law Review* 30 (1963): 423–449.

KAPLOW, LOUIS, and SHAVELL, STEVEN M. "Optimal Law Enforcement with Self-Reporting of Behavior." *Journal of Political Economy* 102 (1994): 582–606.

———. "Economic Analysis of Law." Olin Working Paper No. 251. http://www.law.harvard.edu/programs/olin_center/. Forthcoming in *Handbook of Public Economics*. Edited by A. J. Auerbach and M. Feldstein. New York: Elsevier Science, 2002.

KLEIN, JOEL I. "The War Against International Cartels: Lessons From the Battlefront." Speech to Fordham Corporate Law Institute Conferences on International Antitrust Law and Policy, 14 October 1999. http://www.usdoj.gov/atr/public/speeches/3747.htm.

———. "A Practical Approach to Criminal Investigations: Criminal Enforcement in a Globalized Economy." Address at the Advanced Criminal Antitrust Workshop, 20 February 1997. http://www.usdoj.gov/atr/public/speeches/jik97220.htm.

LABATON, STEPHEN. "At Justice, The Taming of A Whirlwind." *New York Times*, 22 October 1995. Section 3, p. 1.

LIEBER, JAMES B. *Rats in the Grain: The Dirty Tricks and Trials of Archer Daniels Midland*. New York: Four Walls Eight Windows, 2000.

Ninth Circuit Model Criminal Jury Instruction 9.13, Controlled Substance—Possession With Intent To Distribute. http://www.ce9.uscourts.gov/web/sdocuments.nsf/crim.

POLINSKY, A. MITCHELL, and SHAVELL, STEVEN M. "The Optimal Use of Fines and Imprisonment." *Journal of Public Economics* 24 (1984): 89–99.

POSNER, RICHARD A. "A Statistical Study of Antitrust Enforcement." *Journal of Law & Economics* 13 (1970): 365–419.

———. "Optimal Sentences for White Collar Crime." *American Criminal Law Review* 17 (1980): 409–418.

———. *Antitrust Law*. 2nd edition. Chicago: University of Chicago Press, 2001.

———. *Economic Analysis of Law*. 5th edition. New York: Aspen Law & Business, 1998.

RUSSELL, KEVIN A. "Economic Crime: Antitrust Offenses." In *Encyclopedia of Crime and Justice*. Edited by Sanford H. Kadish. New York: The Free Press, 1983. Pages 679–683.

SHAVELL, STEVEN M. "Criminal Law and the Optimal Use of Nonmonetary Sanctions as a Deterrent." *Columbia Law Review* 85 (1985): 1232–1262.

———. "The Optimal Use of Nonmonetary Sanctions as a Deterrent." *American Economic Review* 77 (1987): 584–592.

SMITH, ADAM. *An Inquiry Into The Nature and Causes of the Wealth of Nations* (1776). Edited by Rogers, James E. Thorold. Oxford: Clarendon Press, 1880.

SPRATLING, GARY R. "Are the Recent Titanic Fines in Antitrust Cases Just the Tip of the Iceberg?" Remarks Before the 12th Annual National Institute on White Collar Crime, 6 March 1998. http://www.usdoj.gov/atr/public/speeches/1583.htm.

———. "Making Companies An Offer They Shouldn't Refuse—The Antitrust Division's Corporate Leniency Policy—An Update."

Presented at The Bar Association of the District of Columbia's 35th Annual Symposium on Associations and Antitrust, 16 February 1999. http://www.usdoj.gov/atr/public/speeches/2247.htm.

———. "The Race for Amnesty in International Antitrust—If You Don't Come in First, The Rewards For Second Place Are No Small Consolation." Speech to American Bar Association's 14th Annual Institute on White Collar Crime, 2 March 2000.

Sproul, Michael F. "Antitrust and Prices." *Journal of Political Economy* 101 (1993): 741–754.

United States Department of Justice Antitrust Division. *Antitrust Division Manual*, 3rd edition. 1998. http://www.usdoj.gov/atr/foia/divisionmanual/table_of_contents.htm.

———. *Corporate Leniency Policy.* 10 August 1993. http://www.usdoj.gov/atr/public/guidelines/lencorp.htm.

———. "Price Fixing & Bid Rigging, They Happen: What They Are and What to Look For." 2 January 2001. http://www.usdoj.gov/atr/public/guidelines/guidelin.htm.

———. "10-Year Workload Statistics Report, FY 1991–2000." http://www.usdoj.gov/atr/public/4504.htm.

Werden, Gregory J., and Simon, Marylin J. "Why Price Fixers Should Go To Prison." *Antitrust Bulletin* 32 (1987): 917–937.

White, Lawrence J. "Lysine and Price Fixing: How Long? How Severe?" *Review of Industrial Organization* (forthcoming). http://papers.ssrn.com/paper.taf?abstract_id=164868.

Wiley, John Shepard, Jr. "Reciprocal Altruism as a Felony: Antitrust and the Prisoner's Dilemma." *Michigan Law Review* 86 (1988): 1906–1928.

———. "Not Guilty By Reason of Blamelessness: Culpability In Federal Criminal Interpretation." *Virginia Law Review* 85 (1999): 1021–1162.

CASES

Associated Press v. United States, 326 U.S. 1 (1945).

Cheek v. United States, 498 U.S. 192 (1991).

Nash v. United States, 229 U.S. 373 (1913).

United States v. American Airlines, Inc., 743 F.2d 1114 (5th Cir. 1984), *cert. dismissed,* 474 U.S. 1001 (1985).

United States v. Andreas and Wilson, 216 F.3d 645 (7th Cir.), *cert. denied,* 121 S.Ct. 573 (2000).

United States v. Brown, 936 F.2d 1042 (9th Cir. 1991).

United States v. Sealy Corp., 388 U.S. 350 (1967).

United States v. Topco Associates, 405 U.S. 596 (1972).

United States v. U.S. Gypsum Co., 438 U.S. 422 (1978).

United States v. W. F. Brinkley & Son Construction Co., 783 F.2d 1157 (4th Cir. 1986).

ECONOMIC CRIME: TAX OFFENSES

A traditional view holds that criminal tax offenses exist to combat tax evasion. Tax evasion is indeed a widespread, serious, and persistent problem in the United States and elsewhere. In the last part of the twentieth century, however, the United States government broadened its criminal enforcement focus from the suppression of classical tax evasion to a more general attack on crime, including drug dealing and financial crimes. The federal government still prosecutes tax cheats, but at the turn of the century "criminal tax enforcement" more accurately represents a particular style of investigation than a single-minded effort to secure the federal fisc.

Tax noncompliance

Tax compliance typically relies on voluntary self-assessment, which requires taxpayers to calculate their own tax liability and voluntarily to pay the amount due. For income taxes, there are three kinds of noncompliance: failure to file tax returns; underreporting of taxable income (either through underreporting income or overstating deductions); and failure to pay established liabilities. Tax scholars often distinguish between tax minimization, tax avoidance, and tax evasion, but no precise lines divide this continuum of conduct.

Tax noncompliance is socially harmful. Most obviously, tax noncompliance reduces tax revenues, which is a bad thing if one believes that legitimately elected governments should be able to carry out their policies as they choose. Tax noncompliance also can distort labor markets, as when people select jobs to dodge taxes. Efforts to avoid taxes (like efforts to increase compliance) are deadweight losses to society. Tax evasion can create unfairness and can fuel perceptions of rampant cheating that undermine respect for government. Left unchecked over time, these perceptions would tend to snowball as more people conclude that cheating is common, normal, and inviting.

The tax noncompliance problem in the United States is large and growing. The tax gap (the difference between what taxpayers owe and pay) was an estimated $195 billion/year in 1998, or about $1600 per year for every tax return filed by compliant taxpayers (Rossotti). Estimates are that American taxpayers voluntarily pay 83 percent of the taxes they owe. The compliance rate in other countries is often much lower (IRS, Sept. 1997; Graetz and Wilde). The dollar cost of noncompliance has risen sharply since about 1980 even as the rate of tax noncompliance has remained fairly stable (IRS, Sept. 1997). Most academic focus has been on evasion of income taxes, but noncompliance problems also exist for other taxes (e.g., employment taxes, excise taxes, retail sales taxes, estate and gift taxes).

Who is not paying? Three-quarters of the problem has been the fault of individuals rather than corporations, according to data that Slemrod and Bakija report. The bulk of noncompliance seems to come from the underreporting of personal income, which accounted for 47.5 percent of the tax gap in 1992. Corporations, however, may be closing the gap. In the late twentieth century there has been a dramatic increase in the number of corporate tax shelters that corporate taxpayers use to reduce tax liability by entering into transactions that purportedly lack economic substance apart from tax benefits. Bankman estimates that the lost corporate tax revenues may amount to billions of dollars. It is difficult to generalize about the types of transactions deemed corporate tax shelters. They do share some common elements: (i) they seek to obtain a tax benefit not clearly contemplated by the applicable tax provision; (ii) they lack economic substance, in that the reasonable expected pre-tax economic profit is insignificant relative to the reasonably expected net tax benefits; (iii) they result in inconsistent financial accounting and tax treatment; and (iv) they use tax-indifferent parties (generally foreign and tax-exempt entities) to absorb or deflect taxable income (Department of Treasury 1999, 2000).

Compliance also varies greatly by types of income. For example, the compliance rates for wages and salaries (99.5%), pensions and annuities (98.4%), interest and dividends (94.6%), and income from capital gains (88.3%) are relatively high, while the compliance rates for partnerships and S corporations (42.1%) and self-employment income (41.4%) are quite low (in all cases estimated for reported net income as a percentage of

Figure 1

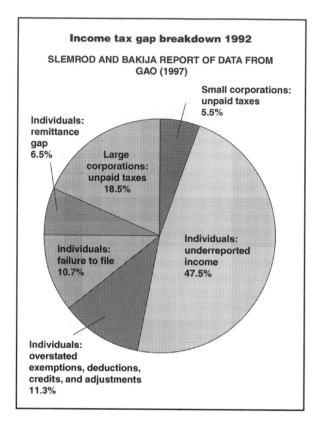

Income tax gap breakdown 1992

SLEMROD AND BAKIJA REPORT OF DATA FROM GAO (1997)

- Small corporations: unpaid taxes 5.5%
- Individuals: remittance gap 6.5%
- Large corporations: unpaid taxes 18.5%
- Individuals: failure to file 10.7%
- Individuals: underreported income 47.5%
- Individuals: overstated exemptions, deductions, credits, and adjustments 11.3%

true net income for filers only) (Slemrod and Bakija).

To spur tax compliance, two techniques are *coercive incentives* and *structural components*. Coercive incentives seek to induce tax compliance, primarily through a program of audits, civil penalties, and, rarely, criminal prosecutions. Structural components aim to get the owed money (or the information that leads to the money) before taxpayers can hide it, mainly by means of increased withholding and information reporting.

The IRS has changed its enforcement approach by relying more on structural components and less on coercive incentives. This shift has changed the types of noncompliance detected and prosecuted, and may have reduced the deterrent effect that tax cheats face. The shift also has reduced reliance on the ultimate deterrent: criminal prosecution of traditional tax crimes.

The coercive incentive approach begins with auditing, and the decline in IRS auditing has been marked. In the mid-1960s, the audit rate was about 6 percent for individuals (Dubin, Graetz, and Wilde), but this rate fell to less than one half of one percent by the century's end. Audits of individual taxpayers thus were twelve times less common in the late 1990s than in the mid 1960s.

The rate of corporate auditing likewise fell at the end of the twentieth century. For the largest corporations (those with assets over $250 million) the audit probability fell from 54 percent to 37 percent from 1992 to 1998. Over the same time period, the audit rates for small corporations (those with less than $250,000 of assets) fell from 1.18 percent to .75 percent. In contrast, there has been a dramatic increase in the use of structural components in the last thirty-five years. The IRS has been quite successful in requiring information reporting on certain transaction and matching that information to income tax returns. In 1965, the IRS received about 340 million information documents; by the 1990s the annual number had increased to over 1 billion documents. The IRS estimates that over 75 percent of all income that should be reported on income tax returns is subject to information reporting requirements (Andreoni, Erard, and Feinstein).

Economics of tax evasion

Economists have made important strides in trying to understand tax evasion. Gary Becker's classic article on the economics of crime used economic theory to tackle normative questions such as how many resources should be spent on law enforcement of laws and what penalties the government should impose. Becker's theory about criminal behavior assumed that individuals evaluate the benefits and costs of various activities (including criminal activities like tax evasion) and choose those activities that provide the highest income (or expected utility), after taking into account the associated net costs.

Allingham and Sandmo apply Becker's general approach to issues of tax avoidance and evasion. Using similar assumptions about the rational maximizing behavior of individuals, Allingham and Sandmo posit a simple situation where individuals must decide whether to declare all of their income on a tax return or deliberately underreport the income to tax authorities. The rational individual evaluates the expected gains or losses associated with the decision and seeks to maximize the expected utility or income. The gain derived from underreporting is the expected value of the reduced taxes. The cost or loss associated with tax evasion is a

function of the probability of detection and conviction and the penalties imposed.

This model of tax compliance is consistent with two intuitions. First, taxpayers will cheat if they think they can get away with it. Second, taxpayers voluntarily will improve their compliance when penalties increase or when the probability of getting caught goes up.

Allingham and Sandmo and others have attempted to estimate the impact of several factors on voluntary tax compliance. For example, commentators have examined the relationship of demographics and social factors to levels of noncompliance, the effectiveness of different penalty structures on increasing deterrence, and the deterrent effect of past audits on future compliance (Andreoni, Erard, and Feinstein).

Simple economic models cannot adequately capture the dynamics of tax evasion. Andreoni, Erard, and Feinstein offer three factors that may influence taxpayers' compliance decisions. These factors also explain why the level of tax compliance, at least in the United States, is higher than the economic models would predict. First is the role of guilt and shame. It is difficult to model these factors, but it is clear that many taxpayers will feel guilt about evading taxes and shame upon apprehension. Second, taxpayers' perception of fairness of their tax burden will influence compliance. There is substantial evidence that the existence, real or perceived, of an unfair tax system will allow taxpayers to rationalize cheating on their own tax returns. Finally, the degree of taxpayers' satisfaction with the performance of government will influence tax compliance. Taxpayers are more willing to comply with tax laws if they believe that their tax money is being well spent. All these factor play an important role in the level of tax compliance in the United States. These factors also help explain the high level of tax evasion in countries in Eastern Europe and the former Soviet Union.

The role of criminal sanctions

The most serious federal tax crime is willful tax evasion, which carries a five-year maximum prison sentence and a maximum fine of $250,000 ($500,000 in the case of a corporation) plus costs of prosecution (26 U.S.C. § 7201 18 U.S.C. § 3571). As decisions in *Spies v. United States,* 317 U.S. 492 (1943), and *United States v. Carlson* (2000) clarify, this felony requires the government to prove three elements: (1) the existence of a tax deficiency; (2) willfulness; and (3) an affirmative act of evasion or affirmative attempt to evade. The "affirmative act" or "affirmative attempt" requirement distinguishes felony tax evasion from the misdemeanor offenses proscribed by 26 U.S.C. § 7203. Conduct like keeping double books or destroying records satisfies this affirmative act requirement. "Willful but passive neglect of the statutory duty may constitute the lesser offense, but to combine with it a willful and positive attempt to evade tax in any manner or to defeat it by any means lifts the offense to the degree of felony" (*Spies*, p. 499).

Less severe tax felonies cover other misconduct: willfully making false statements under penalty of perjury, 26 U.S.C. § 7206(1) (maximum three-year imprisonment, same maximum fines); willfully aiding or assisting the preparation of false tax documents, 26 U.S.C. § 7206(2) (same); and interfering with or offering bribes to federal tax officials, 26 U.S.C. § 7212(a) (same). Willful tax evasion is a felony, but willful failure to file a tax return is a misdemeanor only, as is the willful delivery of false statements (See 26 U.S.C. §§ 7203 and 7207).

The provisions of 26 U.S.C. § 3571 raise the maximum fine for all of these crimes, including possibly to twice the "gross gain" to the defendant (or twice the "gross loss" to the government, whichever is greater). Why the *criminal* sanction? Tax noncompliance differs from conduct that more typically is the target of the criminal law. These differences raise questions about the appropriate role for criminal tax enforcement.

One utilitarian perspective questions why, as a general matter, *any* criminal tax enforcement is appropriate. The focus here is on how best to achieve efficient deterrence. Tax noncompliance seems like the kind of conduct that appropriately severe civil penalties generally can deter. Tax evaders should respond to the prospect of harsh but purely financial penalties, because the point of tax noncompliance is financial gain, and because tax evaders at some point must have had enough financial resources to incur a tax problem in the first place. Tax evasion, moreover, is not the sort of impulsively sudden or passionate conduct that some skeptics doubt can be deterred. Under these conditions, some utilitarians advise government enforcers to use civil enforcement machinery, because the civil enforcement process and civil penalties both are cheaper to administer than are their criminal counterparts. The main conclusion here, which Kaplow and Shavell trace back to Bentham (p. 183), is that financial penalties should be imposed to the maxi-

mum extent feasible before turning to the criminal penalty of incarceration. (See also Polinsky and Shavell; Shavell, 1985, 1987.) This perspective is controversial, politically and otherwise, in its possible implication that the justice system should be more willing to imprison the poor than the wealthy. Calkins comments that "[a]ny suggestion that prison should be reserved for those who lack sufficient assets is a political non-starter that does not deserve serious discussion except as an interesting academic exercise" (p. 143, n.63). Utilitarians would agree that their analysis has limited relevance when federal law holds financial penalties to ineffectively low levels, as is true when fines cannot be set at more than double the actual gain from evasion and when the risk of prosecution is far less than 50 percent. In this situation—and especially when audits are uncommon—the threat of incarceration can be an important tax compliance incentive.

Retributivists begin with moral analysis rather than a utilitarian calculus, but here again the tax context has notable features. Social norms in support of paying taxes are weaker than the norms supporting many more traditional crimes. Tax sanctions compel nearly the entire adult population to undertake affirmative conduct that often is annoying, expensive, and popularly reviled. Conventional wisdom rates paying taxes with death. Even judges, the federal officials who ultimately enforce the tax code, sometime disparage the moral basis for tax obligations. The revered Judge Learned Hand, for instance, wrote in *Newman v. Commissioner of Internal Revenue* (159 F.2d 848 (2d Cir. 1947), cert. denied 331 U.S. 859 (1947)): "Over and over again courts have said that there is nothing sinister in so arranging one's affairs as to keep taxes as low as possible. Everybody does so, rich or poor; and all do right, for nobody owes any public duty to pay more than the law demands: taxes are enforced exactions, not voluntary contributions. To demand more in the name of morals is mere cant" (pp. 850–851). In the nation that venerates the Boston Tea Party, criminalizing the failure to pay taxes creates offenses that must get their moral core, not from the accepted badness of the failure itself, but rather from a condemnation of deliberate cheating on rules that govern everyone. From this perspective, the conventional wisdom about death and taxes reveals that most people accept taxes as something inevitable—something that most people dislike, true, but something that most people plan to pay. Retributivists focus on this mutual obligation and would tend to limit criminal prosecutions to cases where people shirk it with a blameworthy sense of wrongdoing. As with any sort of cheating, cases of tax evasion that are flagrant and outrageous provoke strong retributive reactions.

These utilitarian and retributive perspectives do fit with some aspects of U.S. criminal tax enforcement. Beginning with the utilitarian view, it is significant that U.S. criminal tax prosecutions are quite rare. During 1994–1998, for instance, the federal government prosecuted before district court judges on average only 846 people per year on tax law violations (DOJ, 1999, p. 24, Table A.3). (There seem to be many differing definitions of "tax law" and "prosecutions," so statistics of this sort must be treated with care and are most safely used only for general points of illustration.) Officials resort to criminal actions so rarely in part because they have a wide array of powerful civil enforcement remedies, including fines, interest, and property seizures.

Turning to the retributive perspective, a second striking feature of federal criminal tax policy is its demand for an unusually high level of culpability. Most federal tax crimes require proof that a defendant acted "willfully," which is a word of notorious ambiguity. (See generally Model Penal Code § 2.02 cmt. 10 n.47 (1985).) A recent Supreme Court attempt to define what "willfully" means in tax evasion cases is the decision in *Cheek v. United States*. Phrasing the matter in Model Penal Code terms (as the *Cheek* Court did not), the *Cheek* decision in essence held that "willfulness" requires knowledge by defendants that their actions violate the law. It is not enough to prove that these defendants acted recklessly in taking a risk that their actions might be illegal. Under *Cheek*'s knowledge standard, a jury must acquit defendants who convince that jury that their beliefs about the tax laws are sincere—no matter how nutty or risky those beliefs might be. For tax crimes requiring "willful" conduct, then, the *Cheek* case established that ignorance of the law indeed is an excuse—even when that ignorance is objectively unreasonable. This high requirement of *knowing* culpability does contrast with the lower and more usual criminal law requirement of *reckless* culpability. (See Model Penal Code § 2.02(3); Wiley.) By judicial interpretation, then, tax crimes require the government to prove an unusually high level of culpability—more culpability than retributivists generally require for criminal liability.

Criminal tax prosecutions have declined in number and shifted in focus. The decline began in 1987 (see Syracuse University) and has been marked as a percentage of filed tax returns. The shift in enforcement focus stems in part from the decisions in the past two decades to enlarge the jurisdiction of the Criminal Investigation Division (CI) of the IRS. The Criminal Investigation Division has moved from investigating mainly pure tax crimes to participating in investigating other criminal violations in which tax components are related conduct: for example, money laundering, currency reporting, narcotics trafficking, and various frauds (including frauds in bankruptcy, gaming, health care, insurance, and telemarketing) (IRS, CI FY1999 Annual Report; see also Abrams). The general decline in the number of federal tax prosecutions thus is even sharper for traditional tax crimes like tax evasion. In 1998, for example, there were only 771 tax fraud prosecutions in the U.S., half the number from 1981 (TRAC at http://trac.syr.edu/tracirs/findings/aboutIRS/keyFindings.html).

A 1999 review of the Criminal Investigation Division by former judge and F.B.I. Director William H. Webster criticized this trend and recommended that the Criminal Investigation Division should focus its caseload more specifically on cases promoting voluntary compliance with the tax law—the historic and stated mission of the Criminal Investigation Division (Webster, 14). In the wake of the Webster Report's criticism, the IRS has defended its policies in documents entitled "Why Is IRS Criminal Investigation Involved in Narcotics Investigations?" and "Why Is IRS Criminal Investigation Involved in Financial Crimes?" The latter document explained that:

IRS is involved because IRS CI special agents conduct full, in-depth financial investigations which are intensely revealing about life style, habits, business transactions and business associates. Such complex financial investigations often lead right to the door of the drug kingpin, the fraudulent telemarketer, or corrupt individuals such as health care executives, political leaders, return preparers or even the local grocery store operator. (p. 1)

This rationale suggests that the Criminal Investigation Division will continue its past policies. It likewise suggests that federal "tax prosecution" may denote more a set of investigative techniques than a particular kind of crime that the Treasury Department has targeted.

The advent of the Federal Sentencing Guidelines in 1987 had a dramatic impact on

Figure 2

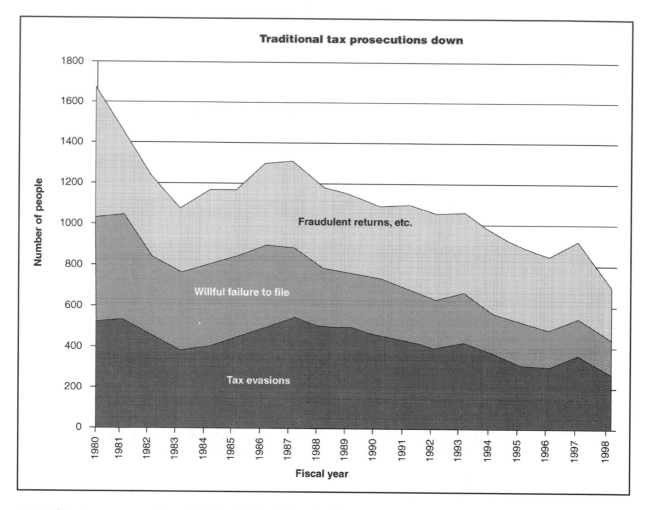

SOURCE: http://www.trac.syr.edu/tracirs/findings/national/crimrefgph.html.

sentencing for all federal crimes, including tax crimes. The guidelines set out a mandatory approach that greatly reduced the judicial discretion that previously had characterized federal sentencing. Under the cookbook approach of the guidelines, the crucial factor driving sentencing is the size of "tax loss"—the revenue loss that would have resulted had the offense been successfully completed, or the sum that the taxpayer owed but did not pay. (Tax payments after the crime has been committed do not reduce tax loss.) A graded table of tax losses sorts cases into twenty different categories. The most lenient category applies if the tax loss is less than $1700, for instance, in which case the guidelines dictate a prison sentence in the range of 0–6 months and permit probation instead of custody. In contrast, a tax loss of $80 million or more triggers the most

severe treatment, which requires a mandatory prison sentence in the range of 63–78 months. The guidelines also adjust prison time for a range of related culpability factors. "Sophisticated concealment" or a previous criminal history, for instance, increase the prescribed sentencing ranges, while "acceptance of responsibility" leads to a shorter prison terms (U.S. Sentencing Guidelines Manual).

The U.S. Attorney's Manual section 6–4.340 states that "the Tax Division prefers that government counsel request the imposition of a jail sentence" in tax cases, but there are provisions for exceptions in "unusual and exceptional circumstances." In recent years, slightly more than half of those convicted of tax crimes actually do go to prison. At the same time, average federal tax crime penalties have remained roughly constant,

Figure 3

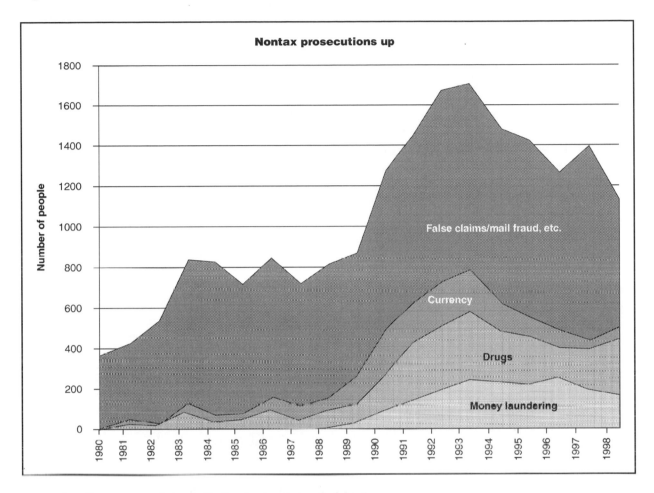

Nontax prosecutions up

SOURCE: http://www.trac.syr.edu/tracirs/findings/national/crimrefgph.html.

at least at an aggregate level. The average jail sentence was twenty-two months in 1994 and 1995, twenty-six months in 1996 and 1997, and twenty-four months in 1998. The average fine was $8119 in 1994, $7140 in 1995, $9461 in 1996, $11,893 in 1997, and $7434 in 1998 (TRAC, at http://trac.syr.edu/tracirs/findings/98/index.html).

Conclusion

Theory and evidence mark tax evasion as a serious and persistent federal problem. Yet the government has responded with only a modest level of criminal prosecution. It is possible for a low level of criminal tax prosecution to be both just and efficient: this policy might appropriately reserve the criminal sanction for cases of exceptional culpability while promoting tax compli-

ance through use of civil sanctions that are effective but more economical than the criminal process. The jury is out on whether current U.S. tax enforcement policy achieves these desirable goals. It is clear that federal criminal tax enforcers in recent years have broadened their criminal tax investigations to narcotics cases and financial crimes, so that "criminal tax enforcement" today may signify more a style of investigation than an effort to suppress a particular type of criminal conduct.

JOHN SHEPARD WILEY, JR.
ERIC M. ZOLT

See also FEDERAL CRIMINAL JURISDICTION; FEDERAL CRIMINAL LAW ENFORCEMENT; MISTAKE; ORGANIZED CRIME; WHITE-COLLAR CRIME: HISTORY OF AN IDEA.

BIBLIOGRAPHY

ABRAMS, NORMAN. "The New Ancillary Offenses." *Criminal Law Forum* 1 (1989).

ANDREONI, JAMES; ERARD, BRIAN; and FEINSTEIN, JONATHAN. "Tax Compliance." *Journal of Economic Literature* 36 (1998): 818–860.

ALLINGHAM, MICHAEL G., and SANDMO, AGNIAN. "Income-Tax Evasion: A Theoretical Analysis." *Journal of Public Economics* 1 (1972): 323–338.

BANKMAN, JOSEPH. "The New Market in Corporate Tax Shelters." *Tax Notes* 83 (1999): 1775.

BECKER, GARY S. "Crime and Punishment: An Economic Approach." *Journal of Political Economy* 76 (1968): 169–217.

BENTHAM, JEREMY. "An Introduction to the Principles of Morals and Legislation." In *The Utilitarians*. Garden City, N.Y.: Anchor Books, 1973.

CALKINS, STEPHEN. "Corporate Compliance and the Antitrust Agencies' Bi-Modal Penalties." *Law and Contemporary Problems* 60 (1997): 127–167.

Department of Treasury. *General Explanations of the Administration's Fiscal Year 2001: Revenue Proposals.* Washington, D.C.: Government Printing Office, 2001.

Department of Treasury. *The Problem of Corporate Tax Shelters: Discussion, Analysis and Legislative Proposals.* Washington, D.C.: Government Printing Office, 1999.

DUBIN, JEFFREY A.; GRAETZ, MICHAEL J.; and WILDE, LOUIS L. "The Effect of Audit Rates on the Federal Individual Income Tax, 1977–1986." *National Tax Journal* 43 (1990): 395–409.

DUBIN, JEFFREY A.; GRAETZ, MICHAEL J.; and WILDE, LOUIS L. "Are We A Nation of Tax Cheaters? New Econometric Evidence on Tax Compliance." *American Economic Review* (AEA Papers and Proceedings) 240 (May 1987).

GRAETZ, MICHAEL J., and WILDE, LOUIS L. "The Economics of Tax Compliance: Fact and Fantasy." *National Tax Journal* 38, no. 3 (1985): 355–363.

Internal Revenue Service. "Criminal Investigation, FY 1999 National Operations' Annual Report." http://www.treas.gov/irs/ci/annual_report/fy99annual_report.pdf.

Internal Revenue Service. "1977 Data Book." Publication 55B, Catalog 215671. Washington, D.C.: Government Printing Office, 1998.

Internal Revenue Service. "News Release, The Individual Income Tax Gap and Accounts Receivable." 1997 WL 585427 (I.R.S.) (September 1997). Washington, D.C.: Internal Revenue Service, 1997.

Internal Revenue Service Criminal Investigation Division. "Three Year Comparison." Washington, D.C.: Internal Revenue Service, 1998. http://www.treas.gov/irs/ci/numbers/docthree.htm.

Internal Revenue Service Criminal Investigation Division. "Why Is IRS Criminal Investigation Involved in Narcotics Investigations?" http://www.treas.gov/irs/ci/docnarcotics.htm.

Internal Revenue Service Criminal Investigation Division. "Why Is IRS Criminal Investigation Involved in Financial Crimes?" http://www.treas.gov/irs/ci/docfinancialcrimes.htm.

KAPLOW, LOUIS, and SHAVELL, STEVEN M. "Economic Analysis of Law." Olin Working Paper no. 251. http://www.law.harvard.edu/programs/olin_center/ (February 1999). Forthcoming in *Handbook of Public Economics*, edited by A. J. Auerbach and M. Feldstein. New York: Elsevier Science, 2002.

Model Penal Code. (1985).

POLINSKY, A. MITCHELL, and SHAVELL, STEVEN M. "The Optimal Use of Fines and Imprisonment." *Journal of Public Economics* 24 (1984): 89–99.

POSNER, HON. RICHARD A. *Economic Analysis of Law*, 5th ed. New York: Aspen Law and Business, 1998.

ROSSOTTI, CHARLES O. Prepared Statement of Charles O. Rossotti, Commissioner, Internal Revenue Service, 1 May 1998. *IRS Oversight: Hearings before the Senate Comm. on Finance*, 105th Cong. 276, 276 (1998).

SHAVELL, STEVEN M. "Criminal Law and the Optimal Use of Nonmonetary Sanctions as a Deterrent." *Columbia Law Review* 85 (1985): 1232–1262.

———. "The Optimal Use of Nonmonetary Sanctions as a Deterrent." *American Economic Review* 77 (1987): 584–592.

SLEMROD, JOEL, and BAKIJA, JON. *Taxing Ourselves: A Citizen's Guide to the Great Debate over Tax Reform*, 2d ed. Cambridge, Mass.: MIT Press, 2000.

Syracuse University, Transactional Records Access Clearinghouse (TRAC). http://trac.syr.edu/tracirs/index.html.

U.S. Attorney's Manual § 6–4.340 B and C (1999).

United States Department of Justice, Office of Justice Programs, Bureau of Justice Statistics. "Federal Criminal Case Processing, 1998, With trends 1982–98, Federal Justice Statistics: Reconciled Data (August 1999, NCJ 169277)." http://www.ojp.usdoj.gov/bjs/abstract/fccp98.htm.

U.S. Sentencing Guidelines Manual §§ 2T1.1, 2T4.1 and 3E1.1 (2000).

WEBSTER, WILLIAM H. HON. "Review of the Internal Revenue Service's Criminal Investigation Division." IRS Publication 3388 (4-1999) catalog number 27623P (April 1999) (Webster Report). http://www.treas.gov/irs/ci/ci_structure/webster_report.pdf.
WILEY, JOHN SHEPARD, JR. "Not Guilty by Reason of Blamelessness: Culpability in Federal Criminal Interpretation." *Virginia Law Review* 85 (1999): 1021.

CASES

Cheek v. United States, 498 U.S. 192 (1991).
Newman v. Commissioner of Internal Revenue, 159 F.2d 848, 850, 851 (2d Cir. 1947), cert. denied 331 U.S. 859 (1947).
Spies v. United States, 317 U.S. 492 (1943).
United States v. Carlson, 235 F.3d 466, 2000 WL 1847536 (No. 99-10525 9th Cir. 12/19/2000).

EDUCATION AND CRIME

In modern societies, an individual's life trajectory—including an individual's involvement in criminal activity—has become increasingly determined by his or her educational experiences. Over the past few centuries, schools have in many ways come to challenge families as the primary site for childhood socialization. The expanding role of formal education in the lives of youth has many causes. Economic production has become more dependent on cognitive skills taught in schools. Work has become typically set off from home life, limiting parents' ability to monitor and train children informally. Increasing female labor participation rates in recent decades have accelerated this trend, with over two-thirds of mothers with children under age eighteen now currently employed. At the same time that work responsibilities have increasingly separated parents from their children, public education has been expanded to command greater portions of a youth's time. At the beginning of the nineteenth century only about ten percent of U.S. individuals age fourteen to seventeen attended high school; by the end of the century, only about ten percent of young adults failed to complete high school. As recently as in the 1940s, less than ten percent of individuals attained a bachelor's degree; by the end of the century, almost one-third of young adults were expected to attain such degrees. Not only have the number of years an individual is involved in a formal education system increased, but the amount of time

per year has also dramatically expanded. The length of the school day has grown and the days in an academic school year have roughly doubled over the past century.

Research has clearly demonstrated how an individual's educational outcomes structure a wide range of adult life-course outcomes. Given the prominent role of education in an individual's life, educational experience has both significant direct and indirect effects on criminality. Over the past decade, educational experience has come to mediate the influence of social background on occupational destinations. By the end of the twentieth century, educational attainment had come to replace social origins as the primary determinant of occupational status, earnings, and even one's choice of marital partners. It is not surprising, therefore, that educational attainment plays a prominent role in explaining who is likely to commit criminal acts or subsequently to become incarcerated. Individuals who are incarcerated are less likely to have had previous success either in labor or marriage markets: about half of jail and prison inmates have never been married, close to half were unemployed prior to incarceration, and more than half had been living in poverty. More direct effects of educational experience are apparent when one examines the educational characteristics of those who are incarcerated. Only about 28 percent of incarcerated individuals in state and federal prisons have successfully graduated from high school (U.S. Department of Justice).

Schools play such a critical role in adult life-course outcomes because they affect individuals through several important social mechanisms. Schools are responsible for the socialization of youth. Schools work to train individuals for different roles in society and thus determine the selection of individuals for the allocation of scarce resources. Schools also structure an individual's interpersonal interactions and associations. The criminological significance of these distinct educational functions will first be explored and then connected to the relationship between crime and variation in educational performance and the structure of schooling. Lastly, conclusions and implications about the relationship between education and crime will be identified.

Mechanisms producing education-crime associations

As youth increasingly spend time in educational (rather than family) settings, the role of schools in the socialization of children and adolescents increases. Schools provide the context where much of the drama of the maturation process now unfolds. Children and particularly adolescents struggle—often in interaction with school authority—to define themselves as individuals with distinct identities. Identity formation involves challenges in many social psychological domains, including moral development. Educational psychologists have long argued that a critical stage in the process of moral development occurs during adolescence. Youths struggle to create their own definitions of right and wrong, as well as their own place in such a moral order (see Gilligan; Kohlberg).

Émile Durkheim, one of the founding influences on modern sociology, devoted a significant portion of his writings to how schools contribute to this socialization process. In *Moral Education: A Study in the Theory and Application of the Sociology of Education* (1903), Durkheim argued that schools confront individual students as the embodiment of society's moral authority. Youths learn in schools to respect society's moral authority if the rules they confront do not appear arbitrary, unenforceable, or unjust. Durkheim argued that discipline is needed in education "to teach the child to rein in his desires, to set limits on his appetites of all kinds, to limit and, through limitation, to define the goals of his activity" (p. 43). Essential to Durkheim's conception of the role of school discipline in the socialization of youth is his attention to the Hobbesian problem of order. The philosopher Thomas Hobbes argued that since individuals are governed by passions and desires, the threat of sanctions from a greater authority was necessary to constrain individual actions and promote social order. Durkheim countered that the strength of external sanctions was ultimately dependent on individuals internalizing these restrictions as normative rules. Durkheim argued that schools provide social settings whereby individuals are able to develop attachments to and integration with a larger societal moral order.

Durkheim's insights were most effectively introduced into contemporary criminological research by Travis Hirschi. Following Durkheim's insights, Hirschi was instrumental in developing criminological *control theory*, which has argued that individuals are subject to greater likelihood of criminal involvement when they have less attachment and integration with conventional authority. Since control theory owes its intellectual origins to earlier explorations of the role of

schools in moral development, it is not surprising that—given the dramatic expansion of the role of schools in the lives of youth—much of the contemporary research from this perspective has emphasized the relationship between educational experience and criminality. Hirschi in later work with Michael Gottfredson argued that schools in fact were in many respects better situated than families to control and properly socialize youth. School personnel were argued to have a greater ability than family members to monitor, assess, and sanction youth misbehavior. School personnel were also claimed to have a greater incentive and need to control youthful behavior because of the large concentration of children and adolescents in close proximity to each other. Regardless of whether it has in any way replaced family-based socialization, involvement in schooling also serves an important role in the socialization of individuals. Schools provide youth with forms of attachment to conventional activities and thus increase an individual's ability to resist the temptations of criminal behavior.

While socialization of youth is one of the primary mechanisms whereby a causal relationship develops between educational experience and crime, the role of the education system in training, selection, and allocation is also critical. Sociologists Max Weber and Pitrim Sorokin, writing in the first third of the twentieth century, highlighted the fact that schools not only were responsible for training individuals for specific occupational tasks, but more importantly schools also served as closure mechanisms preventing individuals from gaining access to lucrative subsequent occupational positions. A second primary function of schools is thus "to sort and sieve" students for either success or failure. Schools directly determine through grades and promotions which students will have access to privileged advanced training leading to coveted occupational positions in a society and which will instead face the greatest risk of economic hardship.

Criminologists have argued that since schools are involved in selection and the allocation of scarce resources, they are sites where individuals confront obstacles to their aspirations for upward social mobility. Social scientists such as Richard Cloward, Lloyd Ohlin, and Arthur Stinchombe have developed *strain theories* of delinquency that link criminal behavior to blocked and frustrated status attainment. To the extent that schools produce resistance and misbehavior associated with institutional barriers to adult occupational success, a second mechanism underlying an association between crime and education is identified.

In addition to socialization and selection, schools also function to structure patterns of individual interpersonal interactions and associations. Social scientists, such as George Simmel and George Herbert Mead, argued early in the twentieth century that interpersonal interactions and associations were critical dimensions of how individuals came to understand and act in society. Criminologists have applied these insights by focusing on two processes. First, researchers such as Edwin Sutherland argued that delinquency could result from patterns of *differential association*. Since schools can structure youth interaction through a variety of mechanisms, the likelihood of youth misbehavior could be increased or dampened through such a structuring process. Second, schools provide settings where individual interactions occur. Researchers have argued that personnel within formal institutions often engage in a *labeling process*. Students are argued to have negative labels applied to them, which carry social stigmas. Since this research tradition assumes that individual meanings are the product of the dynamics of social interactions, often students will accept the negative labels assigned to them by authority figures. Rather than labels being easily rejected by students as being erroneous, they instead are argued to often become self-fulfilling prophecies.

Crime and educational performance

Given the multiple mechanisms whereby schools can influence adult life-course outcomes, it is not surprising that researchers repeatedly and consistently have demonstrated that educational performance and commitment are both negatively associated with adolescent delinquency, adult criminality, and incarceration. The more education an individual has the lower the risk of both criminal behavior and penal sanction. The higher the score on standardized cognitive tests, which partially reflect school learning, the lower the risk of criminality. High grade point averages and positive student attitudes toward school also have repeatedly been demonstrated to reduce the likelihood of adolescent delinquency and presumably adult criminality. Youth records of school sanction for student misbehavior, such as expulsion and suspension, are also clearly associated with adult criminality (Laub and Sampson; Gottfredson and Hirschi; Wilson and Herrnstein). These pat-

terns are consistent with various criminological theoretical expectations discussed above. Students who are successful in terms of test score, grade point average, and years of education, are: defined as "bright" and "good" (labeling theory); have generally high degrees of attachment to conventional school activities (control theory); face easier success in pursuit of their ambitions (strain theory); and often are segregated off from students who are disruptive (differential association).

Several important research efforts have documented the relationship between school performance and crime. In 1950, Sheldon and Eleanor Glueck published an influential study of delinquency that documented the early onset of delinquent behaviors. Nearly half the delinquent youth had identifiable behavior problems before entering the fourth grade. Individuals who demonstrate early onset of serious identifiable misbehavior are likely to have entered school predisposed to failure as a result of the absence of early childhood family socialization. Even for these students, however, it is likely that schools can serve to either reinforce or dampen their preexisting tendencies for misbehavior. In 1969, Travis Hirschi published a seminal study of delinquency that focused much greater attention on educational behavior than did the earlier study by the Gluecks. Hirschi surveyed over five thousand junior and senior high school students in the San Francisco Bay area. He found systematic evidence that school performance and attachment (as measured by cognitive test scores, grades, and attitudes toward school) each had significant effects on the number of self-reported delinquent acts. Hirschi attributed this pattern of results to variation in the extent to which students formed positive attachments to school authority and activities. In the early 1990s, criminologists John Laub and Robert Sampson extended Hirschi's work, demonstrating that school attitudes and performance (as measured by grades) affect delinquency rates.

Variation in the structure of schooling and crime

Years of educational attainment, cognitive test score, student grades, and attitudes toward school, however, are only a small part of how schools structure adolescent experience. Educational research demonstrates that other school factors—such as curriculum, resources, and school peer climates—also strongly influence a student's life chances. While numerous studies have examined the overall effect of schooling on deviance and crime, much of the existing criminological research has largely ignored the actual character of schooling. Criminological research has only begun to provide a more pedagogically sensitive examination of an adolescent's involvement with educational institutions. Such an examination requires a more complete elaboration and specification of the high school context that serves to diminish or increase the probability of criminality. Educational research has begun to inform criminological investigation by focusing on the role of vocational education, educational resources, and peer climates in affecting the incidence of delinquency, crime, and incarceration.

Vocational education

Vocational programs were instituted and expanded in high schools based on proponents' claims that occupational course work would reduce unemployment, crime, and deviant behavior in young adults. Criminological research has suggested mixed evidence on whether these programs have actually served to reduce individual propensity for criminal behavior. Because vocational education can function to segregate low-achieving students in particular courses either within a school or actually in a separate school within a larger district, many criminologists are skeptical that any positive effects of the programs can emerge. Setting vocational students off from academic students could lead to detrimental patterns of differential association or the labeling of vocational students as "less able" or as "youthful troublemakers."

It is important to note, however, that such negative effects are conditional on the actual structure of how vocational programs are organized. In many European countries such as Germany, for example, vocational programs and adolescent apprenticeships are an integral part of a socially validated educational system. In these settings, there is neither great stigma nor profound social segregation associated with these programs. In the United States, many schools in recent years have attempted to adopt an academy model for their vocational programs, where vocational education is integrated into both academic course work and the world of work: in these programs significant stigma or segregation is less likely. In 1971, Ahlstrom and Havighurst published what became a prominent skeptical evaluation of the role of vocational education

in reducing the prevalence of delinquency. Ahlstrom and Havighurst investigated a specialized vocational work-study program designed for four hundred inner-city, maladjusted youth. The program was shown to have little effect on crime rates during student teen years.

Vocational education, however, has been demonstrated to have positive effects on student reports of satisfaction with school and positive perceptions of their teachers. Positive adolescent work experience is also related to psychological feelings of mastery, internal control, and self-competence. Given the significance of these factors in predicting criminality, it is likely that under certain circumstances vocational education can significantly discourage criminality. Recent criminological research has demonstrated that vocational education course work significantly reduces the likelihood of adult incarceration, if the course work occurs in an educational setting that does not concentrate and segregate high proportions of economically disadvantaged youth (Arum and Beattie).

Educational resources

Few criminological studies have attempted to estimate the effects of educational resources on individual delinquency and propensity for criminal behavior. One exception is Gary Gottfredson and Denise Gottfredson's *Victimization in Schools* (1985). The Gottfredsons argue that rates of student and teacher victimization in schools are a product of a range of school characteristics, including school resources, peer composition, and vocational curricular emphasis. Educational resources are likely important in that they can allow schools to reduce class size and thus increase a student's opportunities for learning from, and relating to, their teachers—that is, their likelihood of attachment to conventional activities. Educational resources can also be used to ensure greater monitoring of youth.

Educational resources likely affect a school's ability to influence positively an individual's life course, since schools with greater resources are better able to provide more positive enriched educational experiences for adolescents (such as costly vocational education programs). Recent noncriminological research has identified a clear pattern of the effects of educational resources on a range of socioeconomic outcomes including growth in test scores, increased years of educational attainment, and higher lifetime earnings. These socioeconomic outcomes have all been related to individual criminality and incarceration risk. It is therefore not surprising that high school student-teacher ratios have also been demonstrated to affect adult incarceration risk (Arum and Beattie).

Peer climates

Peer climates can affect criminality in a number of ways, including differential association and altering social norms for acceptable behavior. Peer climates emerge in school as a product of both ecological and institutional factors. While peer climates are partly a reflection of peer composition, they are also structured by institutional factors. School practices in general and school disciplinary practices in particular define the parameters in which specific peer climates emerge and flourish. In the United States, significant variation in disciplinary practices exist: many public schools still practice corporal punishment, while in other schools often little is done to control student misbehavior and gang activity.

Peer composition has been demonstrated to be clearly associated with delinquency and subsequent incarceration in a large number of studies. Peer climates characterized by higher dropout rates and students of lower socioeconomic origins provide settings that make conventional school attachment more difficult. Research by James Coleman has emphasized, however, that schools have a role in structuring the manner in which peer climates exist. Work by Émile Durkheim also suggests the importance of school disciplinary practices in the socialization of youth. Punishment is necessary, according to Durkheim, because it unequivocally communicates that a normative rule has been broken.

Challenges to school disciplinary practices, regardless of whether they are from external environmental or internal organizational sources, would be particularly unsettling to the normative order of the school. Conservatives argue that due to administrative and legal challenges to school authority, students no longer view school rules as inviolate (Toby). At a practical level, school discipline works to generate student compliance and academically focused peer cultures. Peer climates have long been associated with student academic performance. In recent work, Coleman and his colleagues have argued that private schools outperform public schools in part because they are able to maintain stricter disciplinary climates with lower rates of student absenteeism, vandalism, drug use, and disobedience. Sociologists have also found that rates of misbehavior during the senior year are lower in schools that have higher rates of disciplining of sophomore students (Diprete et al.). Misbehaving students also have lower levels of educational achievement as measured by change in grades and test scores. Conservatives claim that without proper order and discipline, schools are unable to function properly and effective socialization is impossible.

Progressive educators, however, have countered that as traditional authoritarian disciplinary practices are eliminated from public schools, students will be less alienated from their educational environments, and more likely to remain in school and apply themselves to their studies. Support for this is suggested by the fact that the use of strict disciplinary practices, such as corporal punishment, leads to lower educational achievement and higher rates of delinquency. Researchers also argue that these school practices can lead to the formation of oppositional peer groups that resist formal education.

Conclusions and implications

Criminologists who believe that propensity for adult criminality is established in early childhood attempt to dismiss empirical research that identifies significant school effects on delinquency and crime. These critics argue that selection bias accounts for education-crime associations. That is, some criminologists will argue that both educational and criminal trajectories are set at a very early preschool age. By the time that children enter school, the argument goes, families (or genetics) have already produced "bad kids." Individuals fail in school because they lack social control: failure in school thus reflects individual-level socialization problems that underlie criminal propensity; poor educational performance itself therefore does not produce criminal behavior. While some criminologists might still argue this position, it is fundamentally inconsistent with the larger social scientific research community's understanding of the role of education in life course development. At least since the late 1960s, social scientists have recognized that educational experience has come to mediate the relationship between social origins and adult life-course outcomes. While poorly socialized youth certainly are less likely to do well in terms of educational attainment, schools—if properly structured—can successfully counter these tendencies. Schools are institutions that can serve as "turning points" in individual lives. As the criminologists John Laub and Robert Sampson have argued: "despite the connection between childhood events and experiences in adulthood, turning points can modify life trajectories—they can 'redirect paths.'"

Since schools play a critical role in determining the likelihood of delinquency, crime, and incarceration, policymakers historically have turned to educational reform to address social problems associated with adolescent delinquency and adult criminality. The last two decades of the twentieth century, however, were exceptional in U.S. history in terms of both educational and criminological policy. In unprecedented ways, policymakers have relied on incapacitation by the penal system to address the crime problem in society. Concurrently, educational policy has lost its focus on designing programs to integrate and socialize economically disadvantaged youths to become productive members of society. Instead, educational policymakers have become fixated on the narrow task of improving school performance and efficiency in terms of measurable student gains on cognitive standardized tests. While prison rolls have more than doubled in the last two decades of the twentieth century, high school vocational education enrollments have plummeted as the programs have been dismantled due to their high cost. While the penal system has demanded an increasing portion of local, state, and federal finances, educational budgets have struggled just to keep up with inflation and demographic growth in school age populations. While government officials increasingly threaten to sanction schools for the lack of student progress on cognitive tests, schools as institutions have become legally constrained from applying disciplinary sanctions to maintain peer climates conducive to learning and socialization. How policy reformers reconcile these tensions and contradictions in educational and social policy will determine the character of the education-crime relationship in the future.

RICHARD ARUM

See also CLASS AND CRIME; CRIME CAUSATION: SOCIOLOGICAL THEORIES; FAMILY RELATIONSHIPS AND CRIME; INTELLIGENCE AND CRIME; JUVENILE AND YOUTH GANGS; SCHOOLS AND CRIME.

BIBLIOGRAPHY

AHLSTROM, WINTON, and HAVIGHURST, ROBERT. *400 Losers: Delinquent Boys in High School.* San Francisco: Jossey-Bass Publishers, 1971.

ARUM, RICHARD, and BEATTIE, IRENE. "High School Experience and the Risk of Adult Incarceration." *Criminology* 37, 3 (1999): 515–538.

CLOWARD, RICHARD, and OHLIN, LLOYD. *Delinquency and Opportunity.* New York: Free Press, 1960.

COLEMAN, JAMES, and HOFFER, THOMAS. *Public and Private High Schools: The Impact of Communities.* New York: Basic Books, 1987.

COLEMAN, JAMES; CAMPBELL, ERNEST; HOBSON, CAROL; MCPARTLAND, JAMES; MOOD, ALEXANDER; WEINFELD, FREDERICK D.; and YORK, ROBERT. *Equality of Educational Opportunity.* Washington, D.C.: Department of Health, Education and Welfare, 1966.

DIPRETE, THOMAS; MULLER, CHANDRA; and SHAEFFER, NORA. *Discipline and Order in American High Schools.* Washington, D.C.: Government Printing Office, 1981.

DURKHEIM, ÉMILE. *Moral Education: A Study in the Theory and Application of the Sociology of Education* (1903). New York: Free Press, 1961.

GILLIGAN, CAROL. *In a Different Voice: Psychological Theory and Women's Development.* Cambridge, Mass.: Harvard University Press, 1982.

GLUECK, SHELDON, and GLUECK, ELEANOR. *Five Hundred Criminal Careers.* New York: Knopf, 1930.

GOTTFREDSON, GARY, and GOTTFREDSON, DENISE. *Victimization in Schools.* New York: Plenum Press, 1985.

GOTTFREDSON, MICHAEL, and HIRSCHI, TRAVIS. *A General Theory of Crime.* Stanford, Calif.: Stanford University Press, 1990.

HIRSCHI, TRAVIS. *Causes of Delinquency.* Berkeley: University of California Press, 1969.

KOHLBERG, LAWRENCE. *Essays on Moral Development.* San Francisco: Harper and Row, 1981.

LAUB, JOHN, and SAMPSON, ROBERT. "Turning Points in the Life Course: Why Change Matters to the Study of Crime." *Criminology* 31 (1993): 301–325.

POLK, KENNETH, and SCHAFER, WALTER. *Schools and Delinquency.* Englewood Cliffs, N.J.: Prentice Hall, 1972.

RUTTER, M.; MAUGHAN, B.; MORTIMORE, P.; and OUSTON, J. *Fifteen Thousand Hours: Secondary Schools and Their Effects on Children.* Cambridge, Mass.: Harvard University Press, 1979.

SAMPSON, ROBERT, and LAUB, JOHN. *Crime in the Making: Pathways and Turning Points Through Life.* Cambridge, Mass.: Harvard University Press, 1993.

SOROKIN, PITRIM. *Social and Cultural Mobility.* New York: Free Press, 1927.

STINCHOMBE, ARTHUR. *Rebellion in a High School*. Chicago: Quadrangle Books, 1993.

SUTHERLAND, EDWIN. *Principles of Criminology*. Philadelphia: Lippincott, 1937.

TOBY, JACKSON. "The Schools." In *Crime*. Edited by James Q. Wilson and Joan Petersilia. San Francisco, Calif.: Institute for Contemporary Studies, 1995.

U.S. Department of Justice. *Report to the Nation on Crime and Justice*. Washington D.C.: Bureau of Justice Statistics, 1988.

WEBER, MAX. "The Rationalization of Education and Training." *Max Weber: Essays in Sociology*. New York: Oxford University Press, 1946.

WILSON, JAMES Q., and HERRNSTEIN, RICHARD. *Crime and Human Nature*. New York: Simon and Schuster, 1985.

EMPLOYEE THEFT: BEHAVIORAL ASPECTS

The term employee theft refers to the unauthorized taking, transfer, or use of property of a work organization by an employee during the course of work activity. Straightforward as it seems, the application of the definition to employees' activity is complicated by two essential problems. The first centers on the issue of what is meant by unauthorized taking. If the activity is prohibited by company policy (formal norms) but sanctioned by the work-group and work-culture (informal norms), is it unauthorized taking? Technically and legally it is; operationally it may or may not be dependent on other elements of the work-group norms that prescribe and proscribe the behavior. The second problem in applying the definition to practice centers on the question of what constitutes company property. Not only are there several types of property in an organization—company, personal, and property of uncertain ownership (e.g., items in a wastebasket, unsolicited samples from vendors)—there are also forms of company property that do not ordinarily enter into the traditional calculus of employee theft. The latter might include the use of facilities and equipment for personal use—personal phone calls, typing personal correspondence on company computers, the use of sick leave for personal days off, or the theft of work time through simply "goofing off." In defining employee theft one needs to consider carefully what is meant by unauthorized taking and what property is included in the activity defined as theft (Greenberg; Hollinger and Clark; Horning).

Ancient or modern problem

Many regard and treat theft by employees as a relatively new phenomenon that emerged with the development of large bureaucratic organizations with their impersonal relationships between employers and employees. Employee theft is neither a new problem nor one limited to modern work systems. Reference to employee theft is found in one of the earliest bodies of laws, the Code of Hammurabi, carved on diorite columns during the eighteenth century B.C.E. The code's 288 laws contain at least eight specific references to employer-employee, consigner-consignee relations that apply to what is today called employee theft. For example, the 265th law states, "If a shepherd to whom oxen or sheep have been given to pasture become unfaithful, alter the brand or sell them, they shall convict him and he shall restore tenfold to their owner the oxen and sheep he has stolen" (Luckenbill).

What makes the problem of employee theft appear modern or of recent origin are the significant social changes that modern work systems represent: new organizational structures, new relationships between employers and employees, new configurations of material and products, new victims (including new legal constructs such as corporations), new opportunity structures that give workers access to more goods, facilities and services, new configurations of work norms regulating employee behavior, new systems for preventing or coping with employee theft, and the separation of property ownership from property control in the modern organization. Viewed together, these make the problem appear a modern one or at least one of a different order than earlier employee theft.

Terms used to describe employee theft

A sociolinguistic analysis of the terms used by the employee-perpetrator and the employer-victim to describe acts of employee theft reveal significant differences in the way the act of theft is perceived. All but the high incident/high value perpetrators refer to their acts of taking property in more neutral terms, placing the act within acceptable work-group normative boundaries, by using euphemisms such as *taking, salvaging, evening-up, compensating, borrowing, dipping, scrounging, taking out a loan, doing government work* (especially for use of equipment and facilities), *boss work* (following the boss's example), and *taking stuff for homework*. Employee-perpetrators go to great lengths to avoid the term theft and having to define their behavior as theft. Describing those same acts, the employer-victims use more judgment-laden legal terms such as *pilfering, theft, fraud, stealing, embezzling,* and *poaching.* Although both are referring to the same act, each is revealing a different perception of it. Hence, what is a clear case of employee theft to the employer may be perceived by the perpetrating employee as a compensatory act that makes up for some perceived injustice or as a form of salvaging materials that would otherwise be tossed out. Often employees feel that the appropriation of materials from the work place is a *job right,* a fringe benefit of the job. Although the employer and employee may both agree that the theft of company property is wrong, they often fail to recognize that they may be referring to different classes of acts, categories of materiel, concepts of property, or views of ownership. It is not uncommon for employees to consider employee theft reprehensible while regarding their own taking of property as legitimate. An important element in this process is the division of property in the work system into that which is pilferable (comprising some forms of company property and property of uncertain ownership) and that which is not (some forms of company property and personal property). High incident/high value thieves cannot claim exemption from the designation thief; their acts are not legitimated in the work-group norms (Altheide et al; Greenberg; Hollinger and Clark; Horning; Terris).

Characteristics of the employee thief

Empirical research on employee theft reveals that it is the rare employee who does not pilfer something during the course of a work career. What differs for all but that rare employee, however, is the frequency of theft and the value of the goods taken: some steal often, others almost never steal; some steal goods having considerable value, others confine their behavior to items that have little or no value. Although any given episode of employee theft may involve seemingly insignificant amounts, the cumulative effect over time may be considerable.

Numerous attempts have been made to describe the typical employee thief. Many experts in security management have developed profiles that describe the prototypical employee thief: male, either young or older (competing data support either conclusion), has a financial problem stemming from gambling, drinking, drugs, or other equally costly excesses such as an expensive hobby or poor financial management (e.g., credit card problems). Although these descriptions may apply to those workers who are high incident/high value thieves, they are not particularly useful when one considers that only a few workers (normally less than 5 percent) steal with the intent to convert the goods to money. Most workers take only for personal use (Altheide et al; Greenberg; Hollinger and Clark; Horning; Terris).

Nonwork-related correlates. Many of the standard demographic variables—such as age, sex, race, education, religious affiliation, religiosity, residential mobility, number of dependents, size of community, marital status, marital stability, and home ownership—which play an important role in differentiating behavior in other forms of crime do not appear to have much predictive value in the case of employee theft. The evidence is often contradictory. However, some nonwork-related correlates, such as erratic personal and job history, poor credit ratings resulting from fiscal mismanagement, difficulty in getting along with others, a history of dismissal for employee theft and alcohol and drug abuse, do appear to be strongly associated with a high risk of employee theft. When all of the evidence is considered, one must conclude that in general most nonwork-related factors, taken separately, are not particularly useful in predicting either the incidence of an employee theft or the amount that the employee will steal (Altheide et al.; Baker and Westin; Greenberg; Hollinger and Clark; Horning; Terris).

Work-related correlates. Many factors in the work setting may have a bearing on the frequency and cost of employee theft.

Type of work system. Although all work systems have elements in common, each provides a unique configuration of opportunity and pilferability to its employees. Offices, mines, mills, factories, farms, hospitals, warehouses, retail stores, food processing plants, road construction businesses, and foundries have many elements in common, but more notable are the differences that shape the opportunity for pilfering from each. Some are generally low access/low opportunity systems with few pilferable items (e.g., mines or well-drilling operations), others are high access/high opportunity systems with necessarily minimal goods control (e.g., hospitals that have a high disposability factor for supplies). Compounding this is the great variability that exists within similar work systems (e.g., medical offices) that differ in scale, organizational structure, managerial philosophy, levels of technology, and levels of control and security. Add to these the specific elements of each organization's work subculture, which defines and sets parameters within which employee theft occurs, and one can see why measurement, prediction, and generalization are difficult.

Thus, to fully understand employee theft it is necessary first to acknowledge the importance of variations in work systems, and second, to recognize the role that individual work subcultures play in defining what constitutes theft in a specific organization.

Job classification and job skills. A national survey of internal company theft reported in 1982 that whereas executive level employees committed only 15 percent of the theft they were responsible for 85 percent of the total dollar loss. So, while it is true that most thefts are committed by workers such as clerks, delivery personnel, warehouse and sales personnel, and office and assembly workers, their activities account for only a small portion of the total amount pilfered. Normally, control efforts are directed at these more numerous but aggregately less costly thieves. Those in executive positions are generally considered to occupy positions of trust and less needful of security controls, but they are also the ones whose pilfering leads to substantially greater aggregate loss.

Length of service with the employer. Conventional wisdom argues that length of service can be both a positive and negative factor in employee theft. Research supports both perspectives. Length of service can be a deterrent to employee theft, where loyalty and the cost of job loss enter into the equation. Conversely, the longer one is employed, the greater one's knowledge about work practices, work norms, opportunity structures, and security systems, which can increase the likelihood of theft. The data on the importance of length of service is conflicting.

Level of job satisfaction. Many authorities contend that a satisfied employee is less likely to pilfer than a dissatisfied one. Although this is generally true, there are many types of satisfaction and these seem to have a differential effect. Dissatisfaction with one's supervisor or job does not appear to have a significant effect on employee theft; dissatisfaction with the work organization does. Generally, the greater the satisfaction with the work organization, the lower the level of employee theft (Altheide et al.; Baker and Wes-

tin; Greenberg; Hollinger and Clark; Horning; Terris; Traub).

Modus operandi

Most employee theft is solitary behavior and does not require special equipment, procedures, or accomplices. Pilfered items are generally hidden on the person, carried in a lunch pail, purse, pocket, or briefcase. Theft at the lower end of the pilfering continuum does not call for extraordinary measures for its execution nor is it at a level that one needs an elaborate justifying rationale. At the upper end of the pilfering continuum elaborate schemes are necessary to move quantities of goods or to appropriate large amounts of money or services. Theft at this level requires a higher order justifying rationale and is less amenable to attempts at legitimization through neutralization of the behavior (Baker and Westin; Greenberg; Hollinger and Clark; Horning; Traub; Weiner).

DONALD N. M. HORNING

See also COMPUTER CRIME; EMPLOYEE THEFT: LEGAL ASPECTS; POLICE: PRIVATE POLICE AND INDUSTRIAL SECURITY; PREVENTION: ENVIRONMENTAL AND TECHNOLOGICAL STRATEGIES; THEFT.

BIBLIOGRAPHY

ALTHEIDE, DAVID; ADLER, PATRICIA A.; ADLER, PETER; and ALTHEIDE, DUANE A. "The Social Meanings of Employee Theft." In *Crime at the Top: Deviance in Business and Professions.* Edited by John M. Johnson and Jack D. Douglas. Philadelphia: Lippincott, 1978. Pages 90–124.

BAREFOOT, J. KIRK, *Employee Theft Investigation,* 2d ed. Woburn, Mass.: Butterworth-Heinemann, 1990.

GREEN, GARY S. *Occupational Crime,* 2d ed. Chicago: Nelson-Hall Publisher, 1997.

GREENBERG, JERALD. "The Cognitive Geometry of Employee Theft: Negotiating 'The Line' Between Taking and Stealing." In *Dysfunctional Behavior in Organizations: Violent and Deviant Behavior,* Part B. Edited by Ricky W. Griffin, Ann O'Leary-Kelly, and Judith Collins. Stamford, Conn.: JAI Press, 1998.

HASSETT, JAMES. "But That Would Be Wrong: *Psychology Today*'s Survey Report on Cheating, Lying, and Bending the Rules in Everyday Life." *Psychology Today* 15 (November 1981): 34–50.

HOLLINGER, RICHARD C., and CLARK, JOHN P. *Theft by Employees.* Lexington, Mass.: Lexington Books, 1983.

HORNING, DONALD N. M. "Blue Collar Theft: Conceptions of Property, Attitudes Towards Pilfering, and Work Group Norms in a Modern Industrial Plant." In *Crimes against Bureaucracy.* Edited by Erwin O. Smigel and H. Laurence Ross. New York: Van Nostrand-Reinhold, 1970. Pages 46–64.

LUCKENBILL, DANIEL D., TRANS. "The Code of Hammurabi." In *The Origin and History of Hebrew Law.* Reprint. Edited by John M. Powis Smith. Chicago: University of Chicago Press, 1931.

MURPHY, KEVIN, R. *Honesty in the Workplace.* Pacific Grove, Calif.: Brooks/Cole, 1992.

TERRIS, WILLIAM, ed. *Employee Theft Research, Theory, and Applications.* Park Ridge, Ill.: London House Press, 1985.

TRAUB, STUART H. "Battling Employee Crime: A Review of Corporate Strategies and Programs." *Crime and Delinquency* 42, no. 2 (1996): 244–256.

WEINER, ALFRED N. *How to Reduce Business Losses from Employee Theft and Consumer Fraud.* Rev. ed. Lanham, Md.: Madison Books Inc., 1998.

EMPLOYEE THEFT: LEGAL ASPECTS

Virtually every society, type of economy, enterprise, and occupation has a variant of employee theft. In security-intensive work systems such as banking, pharmaceutical, and electronic microchip plants, employee theft is limited to relatively few items. In security-loose systems, the gray areas of pilferability are more inclusive, covering a wide range of goods and services. There are some work systems such as construction and cargo handling where employee theft is extensive and endemic (Baker and Westin; Ditton; Greenberg; Hollinger and Clark; Horning).

Estimates of cost

Each year millions of workers pilfer billions of dollars worth of goods and services from the places where they work. Approximations of the cost, while expected by the business community and security system providers, are not of much value to the social science community because they are only crude guesses. Consider the range of estimates cited in 1999 on the Internet: The American Management Association reports that

U.S. businesses lose more than $10 billion annually to employee theft and commercial bribery; the U.S. Department of Commerce estimates that employee theft costs about $50 billion annually; the American Society for Industrial Security reports that employee theft currently costs U.S. businesses $100 billion annually; and the Federal Bureau of Investigation estimates that *shrinkage* due to employee theft, error, and shoplifting range from $10 billion to $150 billion. Other estimates are as high as $200 billion annually. Recently, several efforts to provide benchmark data have been initiated, but only for selected industries. Jack Hayes International, a security business, provides an annual retail theft survey representing twenty-two retail companies and ten thousand stores; summaries of these reports are available on the Internet. Richard Hollinger of the Security Research Project at the University of Florida provides an annual report entitled "The National Retail Security Survey." Hollinger's 1998 report indicated that the annual cost of inventory shrinkage in selected segments of the retail industry was $26 billion, an inventory shrinkage of 1.7 percent of total sales. Of that, employee theft represents 43 percent of the total, shoplifting 34 percent, administrative error 18 percent, and vendor fraud 6 percent. The report indicates that retailers lost an average of $212 per shoplifting incident and $1,058 per employee theft incident. Evident in these statistics are many of the problems inherent in studies estimating the costs of employee theft. Note first that the total figures for estimated loss are for all inventory shrinkage, of which employee theft is only a part. Note secondly that the value of the employee theft per incident does not represent the pilfering of most employees, that is, petty theft on an irregular basis. Finally, note that these figures are inventory based and do not include many employee activities that could be included in a more comprehensive definition of theft such as *time theft*, or the unauthorized use of facilities or services. According to the U.S. Department of Commerce approximately one-third of all business failures each year can be traced to employee theft and other employee crimes. It should be noted, however, that an employee does not need to steal large quantities of expensive items to have a significant cumulative effect. If a worker in a supermarket takes a can of soda and a deli sandwich and a small bag of potato chips for lunch every day, at a retail value of $3.50, for one work year (240 days) the cost of that "job benefit" is $840. Most studies of employee theft do not include losses of this type nor do they include other so-called job benefit losses such as the value of employee phone calls to family and friends or the cost of the time used for those calls (e.g., a five-minute call by a $12 an hour employee equals $1 for each call, or $240 per work year).

It can be seen from the above why estimates of the amount of pilfering vary so much. The lower estimates focus primarily on major acts of theft, while those at the upper end are more inclusive of all theft. Like other forms of crime, employee theft can be only crudely estimated; like other forms of crime it too is subject to the *dark figure of crime* concept, that is, that there is a large amount of it that cannot be determined (Hollinger; Hayes).

Legal status of employee theft

Employee theft is a violation of the criminal law, a misdemeanor or felony depending upon the value of the goods taken. However, its legal status is clouded by its being an activity that has achieved legitimation, as a "job right," in its lesser forms. Employee theft has an unusually high immunity from prosecution in that most victims seek solutions other than through legal procedures. The victim's tacit approval of low level pilfering is often an important factor in the decision not to prosecute. Other factors are those of establishing proof, fear of charges of false arrest, and concern that theft will be viewed as a manifestation of poor management. In lieu of criminal prosecution, there are often civil arrangements requiring restitution and sometimes the termination of employment. For most workers, some level of pilfering is viewed as a legitimate or quasi-legitimate (not in the job description or work rule manual) job right. Thus, the workers are spared having to view their pilfering as a crime and having to view themselves as criminal (Greenberg; Hollinger and Clark; Horning; Robin; Shepard and Duston; Snyder).

Conceptions of property

Legally, there are only two types of property in the work system: company property owned by the enterprise, and personal property owned by the employees. Conceptually, workers acknowledge the existence of both of these but add a third type—property of uncertain ownership. The latter has no official status but to those in the work system it is very real. Property of uncertain ownership is a malleable entity, contracting and expanding as ownership is claimed, ignored, or relinquished. It comprises countless items such as paper clips, pencils/pens, tools, samples, post-it note pads, damaged goods, returned goods that cannot be returned to stock, scrap, and much more. This category of property has the following general characteristics: the items comprising it are system-specific, they vary from one work system to another; the items are those used up in the course of one's work or are the by-products of work or are not part of the work system's materials; they are items for which no accounting is thought necessary or possible; they are items the control of which has been relinquished to those who use them in the course of their work.

Most workers agree on a core of items in the category of uncertain ownership; however, as one moves out from the core, agreement diminishes. Viewed through time, the items in this category ebb and flow as ownership is claimed or relinquished. Ultimately, this results in a distribution of property that embraces the full spectrum of property in a work organization. The opposing ends of the spectrum represent property of certain ownership: company property at one end, personal property at the other. Between these, in the malleable middle, is the property of uncertain ownership, which flows from the owned property. Property of uncertain ownership is most amenable to theft, offering the advantage of having no victim and of not requiring that one define one's behavior as theft (Greenberg; Henry and Mars; Hollinger and Clark; Horning; Sykes).

Employee norms and employee theft

In time, every work system develops both formal and informal work-group norms that are unique to it. The formal norms comprise the official policies, rules, and procedures; the informal norms emerge as workers seek to adapt the formal norms to their particular work culture and environment. These adaptions often produce subtle, sometimes significant, divergences from the formal norms, and this process is often particularly apparent in the work-group norms on pilfering. Because the formal norms are legalistic, they ordinarily acknowledge only legal forms of property: company and personal. Informal norms, grounded in workers' experience, reflect the full spectrum of property—company, personal, and property of uncertain ownership. The formal norms generally proscribe any form of employee theft or in some instances define what goods and services can be contractually taken (e.g., unusable tools, damaged goods, limited product, personal phone calls). Some contracts also provide a *purchase at cost policy* to allay workers' desire for the product. The informal norms define what is acceptable behavior as it applies to the taking of property, all types. In general, work-group norms are characterized by the following:

1. The norms relative to employee theft are situationally specific; those found in one work setting may differ significantly from those in another.
2. The norms of pilfering are disseminated in the course of worker socialization at work; precept and folklore are prime elements in the transmission of those norms.
3. Although necessarily vague, the norms delineate the boundaries within which *legitimate employee theft* may occur.
4. *Legitimated employee theft* is bounded by prescriptive and proscriptive definitions of takeable property, modus operandi, the value of pilfered goods, and legitimacy rationales.
5. An important element in the boundary-establishing process is *collusive tolerance* by management wherein management, through enforcement, coveys to workers what is *acceptable taking* and what is not. Workers learn that there is an operational calculus that sets limits to managerial action on pilfering.
6. Those who operate within these customarily accepted boundaries adopt acceptable modes of action (e.g., open vs. concealed taking); coterminously, they adopt *legitimating vocabularies of justification*, standards for assessing and limiting their behavior, and strategies for coping with guilt.
7. Those who operate within the parameters established by the norms receive tacit support of the work group. Those who violate work group norms (e.g., pilfering excessively or openly) are viewed as a threat to the *collusive tolerance* of management (possibly forcing a redefinition of property or the establishment of new limits). They are not supported by the work group, are viewed as a threat to it, and are often pressured to limit their activities. Often the work group will put pressure on extreme pilferers to limit their behavior.
8. Workers who inform on pilferers do so at considerable risk from the work group because snitching is considered unacceptable behavior. Even extreme pilferers are accorded this protection.

Control strategies

It is important to employees that their *taking behavior* be perceived as something other than theft. Among the cognitive strategies they use are minimalization, neutralization, externalization, compartmentalization, rationalization, superordination, and reconceptualization. Historically, efforts to deter employee theft centered on close supervision and controlled access; those are now augmented with a full panoply of physical and psychological control strategies. Physical control includes simple barriers, such as fences, sealed windows, and gates; its more sophisticated forms include electronic surveillance, electronic monitoring, elaborate inventory control schemes, and property branding, to mention only a few. Psychological control includes pre-employment screening, and the posting of company policies and rules regarding theft; often open prosecution of those apprehended is used to deter theft by others. One of the most significant deterrents involves the neutralization of the cognitive strategies that workers use to dissuade others from interpreting their taking behavior as theft (Greenberg; Hollinger and Clark; Shepard and Duston; Snyder; Traub; Victor, Klebe, and Shapiro).

DONALD N. M. HORNING

See also COMPUTER CRIMES; THEFT; WHITE-COLLAR CRIME: HISTORY OF AN IDEA.

BIBLIOGRAPHY

BAKER, MICHAEL, and WESTIN, ALAN. *Employee Perceptions of Workplace Crime.* Washington, D.C.: U.S. Department of Justice, Bureau of Justice Statistics, 1987.

CROPANZANO, RUSSELL, ed. *Justice in the Workplace: Approaching Fairness in Human Resource Management.* Hillsdale, N.J.: Lawrence Erlbaum Associates, 1993.

DITTON, JASON. *Part-time Crime: An Ethnology of Fiddling and Pilferage.* London: Macmillan, 1978.

GREENBERG, JERALD. "The Cognitive Geometry of Employee Theft: Negotiating "The Line"

Between Taking and Stealing." In *Dysfunctional Behavior in Organizations: Violent and Deviant Behavior,* Part B. Edited by Ricky W. Griffin, Ann O'Leary-Kelly, and Judith Collins. Stamford, Conn.: JAI Press, 1998.

HAYES, JACK. "Annual Retail Theft Survey." World Wide Web document, 1998. http://www.hayesinternational.com.

HENRY, STUART, and MARS, GERALD. "Crime at Work: The Social Construction of Amateur Property Theft." *Sociology* 12 (1978): 245–263.

HOLLINGER, RICHARD C., ed. *Crime, Deviance, and the Computer.* Brookfield: Dartmouth, 1998.

HOLLINGER, RICHARD C. "National Retail Security Survey." Annual publication, University of Florida Sociology Department, Gainesville, Fla. Available on the World Wide Web or through direct request.

HORNING, DONALD N. M. "Blue Collar Theft: Conceptions of Property, Attitudes Towards Pilfering, and Work Group Norms in a Modern Industrial Plant." In *Crimes Against Bureaucracy.* Edited by Erwin O. Smigel and H. Laurence Ross. New York: Van Nostrand-Reinhold, 1970. Pages 49–64.

MARS, GERALD. *Cheats at Work: An Anthropology of Workplace Crime.* London: George Allen and Unwin, 1982.

ROBIN, GERALD D. "The Corporate and Judicial Disposition of Employee Thieves." In *Crimes Against Bureaucracy.* Edited by Erwin O. Smigel and H. Laurence Ross. New York: Van Nostrand-Reinhold, 1970. Pages 119–142.

SHEPARD, IRA M., and DUSTON, ROBERT. *Thieves at Work: An Employer's Guide to Combating Workplace Dishonesty.* Rockville, Md.: Bureau of National Affairs, 1988.

SNYDER, NEIL H. *Reducing Employee Theft: A Guide to Financial and Organizational Controls.* Westport, Conn.: Greenwood Publishing Group, 1991.

SYKES, GRESHAM, and MATZA, DAVID. "Techniques of Neutralization: A Theory of Delinquency." *American Journal of Sociology* 22 (1957): 664–670.

TRAUB, STUART H. "Battling Employee Crime: A Review of Corporate Strategies and Programs." *Crime and Delinquency* 42, no. 2 (April 1996): 244–256.

VICTOR, BART; KLEBE, LINDA; and SHAPIRO, DEBRA. "Peer Reporting of Unethical Behavior: The Influence of Justice Evaluations and Social Context Factors." *Journal of Business Ethics* 12 (1993): 253–263.

ENTRAPMENT

The entrapment defense has received wide public attention in many prosecutions ranging from drug sales, to public corruption, to financial crimes. The defense is very significant, for the criminal defendant successfully raising entrapment will have all charges dismissed if a showing is made that the government was improperly involved in the creation of the criminal activity. Entrapment has been controversial in the United States since its inception. Some individuals view the defense as imposing improper judicial or legislative restrictions on effective law enforcement investigative techniques. Others would expand the defense in order to ensure that individuals' rights in the criminal justice system are preserved.

Most of the usual defenses in criminal cases have long traditions, dating back to the early English common law. Claims such as duress, self-defense, and insanity have been litigated for hundreds of years in both England and the United States. The defense of entrapment does not have roots traceable back to English common law. Rather, the entrapment defense developed in the United States in the early part of the twentieth century. Judges were tentative then, but began to offer outlines of the defense in a series of cases involving quite egregious overreaching by law enforcement officers. Perhaps the most important early statement concerning entrapment was made by a famous Justice of the U.S. Supreme Court, Louis Brandeis, when he commented in the case of Casey v. United States:

The Government may set decoys to entrap criminals. But it may not provoke or create a crime and then punish the criminal, its creation . . . this prosecution should be stopped, not because some right of [the defendants] has been denied, but in order to protect the Government. To protect it from illegal conduct of its offices. To preserve the purity of its courts.

By the middle of the century the defense was well established, with the Court issuing several opinions explaining the rationale and procedures for it.

In more recent times, the defense has provoked an intense debate centering on the proper balance in the criminal justice system. That is, some government officers have emphasized the need for strong tools to be given to law enforcement officers in the investigation and prosecution of crime. At the same time, other criminal justice professionals have been concerned with the preservation of individual rights of criminal defendants in the criminal justice system. The entrapment defense brings into sharp focus both points of view, as all have recognized that the infiltration of and participation in criminal endeavors by law enforcement can be an important component in the effort to prosecute widespread conspiracies. The Supreme Court has always indicated that such approaches by the government are "recognized as permissible means of investigation." Especially in combating crimes involving narcotics and white collar offenses, close involvement by law enforcement may well be crucial.

The two approaches to entrapment

A division exists in the United States regarding the manner in which the entrapment defense should be applied. Most state courts, and the federal courts, use the so-called *subjective test*, which looks principally to the state of mind of the individual. These jurisdictions find the entrapment defense is based on a belief that legislators, in identifying criminal behavior in criminal codes, could only have intended to sanction individuals who would have committed a crime without the major inducement of government agents. The point of the subjective test, then, is to make sure that otherwise innocent persons will not be lured into criminal activity by government over-involvement. Because the evidence with respect to the particular individual defendant is the central theme of the entrapment, this form of the defense is viewed as *subjective*.

Other states, including some of the largest, such as California, Texas, and Michigan, use the so-called *objective test*. These jurisdictions reject the position of the subjective test proponents as to the legislative intent. Instead, the theory here is that the entrapment defense was created in order to impose responsible limitations on the actions of government agents in investigating and prosecuting criminal behavior. With this test, the courts scrutinize the level of government involvement in the criminal actions to determine if the officers acted in such a way that they would, in a usual case, affirmatively create crime where none would have existed without their actions. The individual state of mind of the defendant is not material in these states, hence the term *objective* is used.

One might well ask why similarly situated states—and the federal courts—can use such different applications of the entrapment defense.

The answer is that most defenses in criminal cases are not constitutionally based; rather, they result from common law use or legislative enactment. As a consequence, states have been permitted under the U.S. Constitution to adopt whichever versions of criminal justice defenses are perceived as most appropriate. This difference in the adoption of defenses can be seen vividly with distinctive applications of the insanity defense, and even of self-defense. As to entrapment, the federal courts use the subjective approach, which results from judicial—rather than legislative—initiative. In some states, the legislature has enacted specific statutes covering the entrapment defense; in others, the defense has been developed, as in the federal courts, through judicial opinions.

The subjective test.   As noted earlier, in the jurisdictions that utilize the subjective test, the key consideration is the defendant's state of mind. The principal question asks whether this individual was disposed to commit the crime before any involvement by the government. Still, in all jurisdictions following the subjective approach, in order to prevail the defendant must also show that a government agent induced him to commit the offense charged. If the defendant offers sufficient evidence of such inducement, the government must then demonstrate, beyond a reasonable doubt, that he was predisposed to commit the crime prior to the time of the government contact.

The inducement requirement for defendants is not often a major hurdle. Generally, the defendant has to prove more than the fact that an opportunity was offered by the government. It is not enough to show a mere request to buy or sell narcotics or stolen goods. The standard in most courts is that the evidence of inducement is high enough so that an innocent party in response to such government behavior might have engaged in illegal activities. One court wrote that the requirement is satisfied if the inducement creates "a substantial risk that the offense would be committed by a person other than one ready to commit it." Sufficient acts of inducement would include repeated requests by the government agent or a large financial incentive offered to the defendant.

Both in statutory form and in judicial practice, predisposition is the more difficult element. The government has to persuade the trier of fact that, even though it induced the defendant to act, the defendant was inclined to commit this sort of crime prior to such government contact.

The proof problems regarding predisposition can be especially thorny, for the jury is being asked to evaluate an individual's state of mind before any crime was committed. The prosecution is given wide discretion in offering evidence of the defendant's predisposition. Similar crimes committed previously by a defendant are normally not allowed in evidence in a criminal prosecution to prove that person's guilt. The concern here is that the limited probative value of such earlier crimes will be outweighed by the undue weight jurors will attach to such prejudicial evidence. If, however, the defendant raises an entrapment defense, these prior acts generally are admissible. The defendant has challenged the government's proof as to her mental state, so the prior crimes help to indicate that the individual was predisposed to act unlawfully. Such prior crimes may include the purchase or sale of drugs, the ordering of obscene materials, or the commission of financial crimes.

The government may also demonstrate predisposition by offering proof that with a relatively modest inducement, the defendant responded eagerly and quickly to an offer to participate in a criminal action. This evidence, it is argued, shows that the defendant was inclined to act unlawfully, as she did not hesitate in response to the government agent's act of inducement or solicitation. Some judges, however, are less inclined to weigh heavily the ready response of the defendant. Instead, they look to whether the person had sufficient ability and experience on her own such that she not only would have attempted to commit the crime without the government involvement, but that she would likely have been successful in doing so. This debate over the evidence surrounding the defendant's response has not yet been resolved by the Supreme Court.

Questions regarding the subjective test for entrapment are normally argued to the jury. As a general matter, issues as to motive and intent traditionally are given to the jury throughout our criminal justice system. With the subjective approach to entrapment, the ultimate question of predisposition is seen as especially appropriate for jurors. In two instances, however, the matter will be resolved by the judge. The first involves the case in which the evidence of the defendant's state of mind is so certain that no reasonable person could conclude that the defendant lacked predisposition prior to the government contact. Even if the government inducement is heavy, there is no doubt of the defendant's great willingness to commit the offense as charged. In short, the evidence is so clear this person would have committed the crime without the governmental action that the judge should resolve this issue. To be sure, the Supreme Court has applied this doctrine in cases in which agents were active participants in the sale and purchase of illegal drugs, finding no entrapment because of the evidence of predisposition.

The second situation in which jurors will not decide the entrapment claim is quite different. If the judge concludes that no juror could find beyond a reasonable doubt that the defendant was predisposed, entrapment as a matter of law has been found and the prosecution must be terminated. The most famous Supreme Court decision evaluating evidence of entrapment dealt with the latter circumstance of entrapment as a matter of law. In this case, undercover U.S. postal investigators, over a prolonged two-year period, repeatedly wrote to the defendant criticizing the government's obscenity policy, encouraging the defendant to challenge the policy, and urging him to exercise his freedom of speech. Indeed, on numerous occasions, they explored with the defendant his interest in child pornography. When the agents finally made a concrete solicitation to send him pornographic materials through the mail, the defendant—a Nebraska farmer—immediately responded, and placed an order. The agents then mailed him the magazine and he was convicted of receiving illegal, obscene written matter through the federal mail system. The defendant raised an entrapment defense at trial, but the jury rejected it, presumably relying on his ready response to the ultimate solicitation. The Supreme Court, however, held that the case should have been dismissed, as there was insufficient evidence of criminal predisposition prior to the government's protracted and intense contact with the defendant. The defendant had never engaged in prior illegal activity, sexual written materials found in his home were legal when ordered, and it took more than a two-year period of inducement before any particular solicitation was offered. The Justices concluded that a reasonable doubt necessarily existed as to this person's alleged predisposition to commit unlawful acts. In addition, the Court was sharply critical of the postal undercover operation:

When the Government's quest for convictions leads to the apprehension of an otherwise law-abiding citizen who, if left to his own devices, likely would have never run afoul of the law, the Court should intervene.

(Jacobson v. United States, 503 U.S. 540, 553–54 (1992).

The objective test. The states that have adopted the objective test for entrapment do not look to the actions or motivations of the individual offender. Instead, they are far more concerned with the nature of the government's participation in the criminal endeavor. In these states, the entrapment defense is used to determine whether police conduct has fallen below standards for the proper use of law enforcement power. The question here, therefore, does not go to any one person's state of mind at any particular time. Rather, the test used is whether the government action would have caused "a normally law-abiding person to commit the offense." Some states in applying this test allow the judge to make the determination as a matter of law either during a trial, or at a pretrial hearing. Other states ask jurors to consider whether the behavior of the police was appropriate under the circumstances. In almost all states following the objective approach, the burden of proof is on the defendant, not the prosecution; the key question is whether the behavior of the government has demonstrated the need for the application of a strong public policy to deter instigation of crime by the government in order to get a conviction. Cases in which improper government action was found include excessive financial inducements, sexual favors given to the suspect, and exploitation of special emotional problems of the defendant. In such cases, the conclusion has been reached that the government simply has gone too far in creating crime rather than in detecting it.

Due process

The due process clause of the Fourteenth Amendment of the U.S. Constitution sets forth a minimal standard for government behavior in the criminal justice system. The clause has been used in a variety of contexts involving the investigation and prosecution of crime. In the most prominent case, Rochin v. California, the Supreme Court used the due process analysis to invalidate a search and seizure in which police officers required the defendant to undergo a medical stomach-pump procedure. The Court concluded that such a requirement was an affront to even the most rigid supporters of police force. Even though strong evidence of crime was found, the evidence was excluded from trial because of the improper actions of the police.

Many lawyers have argued forcefully that such due process considerations must be used in the entrapment setting as well. If the government involvement is too great or intense, the defendant's conviction would need to be set aside, wholly apart from the application of the entrapment defense. This situation arises where the government action was extreme, but the defendant was also predisposed to commit the crime.

Not all believe that the due process analysis should apply in the entrapment context, where the focus is not on shocking behavior, but rather on over-involvement by law enforcement. Some judges question whether any sort of principled determination could be brought to bear on the numerous fact patterns present in this setting. Most judges, however, believe that the constitutional basis for the due process analysis would require its application in those relatively few cases involving clearly unacceptable government conduct. The Supreme Court has never reached a decision based upon due process considerations in the entrapment area, though several of the Justices have referred to the claim as one that could be raised in the appropriate case.

The leading federal opinion using the due process analysis, United States v. Twigg, involved government agents fully immersed in establishing and operating a drug laboratory; in addition, they strongly encouraged the criminal behavior of the defendants. The federal circuit judges reversed the defendants' drug convictions, noting that such convictions would violate "fundamental fairness" because the government agents had truly been the lead figures in the criminal enterprise. State judges, too, apply the due process analysis, though more often under state—rather than federal—constitutional principles. When a finding of "egregious police conduct" has been made, judges in a number of states have applied their own constitutional standards to invalidate the underlying criminal convictions.

PAUL MARCUS

See also CRIMINAL PROCEDURE: CONSTITUTIONAL ASPECTS; EXCUSE: THEORY; EXCUSE: DURESS; OBSCENITY AND PORNOGRAPHY: BEHAVIORAL ASPECTS; POLICE: POLICE OFFICER BEHAVIOR; POLICE: POLICING COMPLAINTLESS CRIMES; SEX OFFENSES: CONSENSUAL.

BIBLIOGRAPHY

ABRAMSON, LESLIE W., and LINDEMAN, LISA L. "Entrapment and Due Process in the Federal Courts." *American Journal of Criminal Law* 8 (1980): 139–182.

ALLEN, ROBERT J.; LUTTRELL, MELISSA; and KREEGER, ANNE. "Clarifying Entrapment." *Journal of Criminal Law and Criminology* 89 (1999): 407–431.

BENNETT, FRED WARREN. "From *Sorrells* to *Jacobsen*: Reflections on Six Decades of Entrapment Law, and Related Defenses, in Federal Court," *Wake Forest Law Review* 27 (1992): 829–852.

CAMP, DAMON D. "Out of the Quagmire after *Jacobsen v. United States*, toward a More Balanced Entrapment Standard." *Journal of Criminal Law and Criminology* 83 (1993): 1055–1097.

CARLSON, JONATHAN C. "The Act of Requirement and the Foundations of the Entrapment Defense." *Virginia Law Review* 73 (1987): 1011–1046.

DEFEO, MICHAEL A. "Entrapment as a Defense to Criminal Responsibility: Its History, Theory, and Application." *University of San Francisco Law Review* 1 (1967): 243–276.

DONNELLY, RICHARD C. "Judicial Control and Informants, Spies, Stool Pigeons, and Agent Provocateurs." *Yale Law Journal* 60 (1951): 1091–1131.

GROOT, ROGER D. "The Serpent Beguiled Me and I (Without Scienter) Did Eat—Denial of Crime and Entrapment Defense." *University of Illinois Law Forum* (1973): 254–278.

MARCUS, PAUL. "The Development of Entrapment Law." *Wayne Law Review* 33 (1986): 5–37.

——— "Toward an Expanded View of the Due Process Claim in Entrapment Cases." *Georgia State University Law Review* 6 (1989): 73–84.

———. *The Entrapment Defense*, 2d ed. Charlottesville, Va.: Michie, 1995.

———. "Presenting, Back from the [Almost] Dead, the Entrapment Defense." *Florida Law Review* 47 (1996): 205–245.

MASCOLO, EDWARD G. "Due Process, Fundamental Fairness and Conduct That Shocks the Conscience: The Right Not to Be Enticed or Induced to Crime by Government and its Agents." *Western New England Law Review* 7 (1984): 1–54.

MULLOCK, PHILIP. "The Logic of Entrapment." *University of Pittsburgh Law Review* 46 (1985): 739–753.

PARK, ROGER. "The Entrapment Controversy." *Minnesota Law Review* 16 (1976): 163–274.

SEIDMAN, MICHAEL. "The Supreme Court, Entrapment, and Our Criminal Justice Dilemma." *The Supreme Court Review* (1981): 111–155.

CASES

Casey v. United States, 276 U.S. 413 (1928).
Rochin v. California 342 U.S. 165 (1952).
United States v. Twigg, 588 F.2d 373 (3rd Cir. 1978).

EUTHANASIA AND ASSISTED SUICIDE

Euthanasia is translated from Greek as "good death" or "easy death." As originally used, the term referred to painless and peaceful natural deaths in old age that occurred in comfortable and familiar surroundings. That usage is now archaic. As the word is currently understood, euthanasia occurs when one person ends the life of another person for the purpose of ending the killed person's pain or suffering.

Euthanasia is sometimes divided into different categories. "Voluntary euthanasia" is when a person is killed upon that person's request for reasons of ending suffering. "Involuntary or nonvoluntary euthanasia" is the mercy killing of a medically or legally incompetent person, such as a child or a demented elderly patient, at the request of, or by, a caregiver or family member.

Some people also use the term "passive euthanasia" to describe a death that occurs after undesired, life-sustaining medical treatment is withheld or withdrawn. This is a misnomer. Euthanasia, at least as the term is presently utilized, involves intentional killing. That being so, "passive euthanasia" is not euthanasia, since death, when it comes—not everyone who has life-sustaining treatment dies as a result of withheld treatment—is naturally caused by the underlying illness or injury.

Assisted suicide is closely related to euthanasia. An assisted suicide occurs when one person gives another person the instructions, means, or capability to bring about their own demise. In the context of the modern moral and public policy debates, the motive in assisted suicide, as in euthanasia, is to bring about an end to suffering. Suicide per se is not considered to be the same as "assisted suicide" because the former is an individual act while the latter involves a joint enterprise between the suicidal person and a helper to bring about death.

The Hippocratic oath explicitly prohibited doctors from giving their patients poisons to end life and thus, traditionally, euthanasia and assisted suicide have not been considered legitimate medical acts. Legalizing either practice would transform hastening patient deaths from an ethically proscribed and (usually) criminal act into a legitimate medical practice. Thus, widespread legalization would be a profound and dramatic shift in the traditional ethics of medical practice.

Euthanasia is currently illegal and punishable as murder throughout the United States. Assisted suicide is a felony akin to manslaughter in most states, proscribed either by statute or court interpretation of the common law. The federal government has outlawed the use of federal funds in assisted suicide.

Assisted suicide is, however, legal in Oregon, where state law authorizes physicians to write lethal prescriptions at the request of patients who have been diagnosed with a terminal illness reasonably likely to cause death within six months. In order for the assisted suicide to be legal, the prescribing physician must follow regulatory guidelines. These guidelines include: requiring a second opinion to verify the diagnosis; referral of the patient to a mental health professional if the doctor suspects the patient has a psychiatric or psychological condition that causes "impaired judgment"; a fifteen-day waiting period between request and prescription; and, reporting the assisted suicide to the Oregon Department of Health. Most current legalization proposals in the United States follow the format of the Oregon law.

Internationally, both euthanasia and assisted suicide are almost universally outlawed. There are a few exceptions to this general rule. In Colombia euthanasia is legal due to a ruling by that country's supreme court (Republic of Colombia Constitutional Court: Sentence: no. C-239/97: REF. EXPEDIENT no. D-1490. May 20, 1997). As of this writing the Colombia law has not gone into effect pending the creation of legal guidelines to govern the practice. Euthanasia and assisted suicide, while technically illegal, are practiced widely by doctors in the Netherlands. The Netherlands experience will be discussed in detail below. Assisted suicide is not illegal in Switzerland, where assisted suicides committed by physicians and laypersons alike are reportedly not prosecuted if based on alleviating suffering caused by serious illness.

The modern euthanasia movement

A few proposals to legalize euthanasia were made in the United States and Germany during the latter portion of the nineteenth century. However, it was not until after World War I that euthanasia advocacy began in earnest. In 1920, two highly respected German academics, Karl Binding, a law professor, and Alfred Hoche, a physician, wrote *Permission to Destroy Life Unworthy of Life*, which advocated euthanasia as a compassionate "healing treatment." The authors argued that mercy killing should be permitted for three categories of patients upon request of competent patients or the families of the incompetent: the terminally ill or mortally wounded, people who were unconscious, and disabled people—particularly those with cognitive impairments. The book, which may have coined the term "right to die," also promoted euthanasia of cognitively disabled people as a way of saving societal resources.

Binding and Hoche's book generated tremendous interest among Germany's intelligentsia and the public, which quickly came to support legalization of euthanasia. Euthanasia was popular enough in 1933 for Adolph Hitler to attempt to formally legalize the practice. However, strong opposition from the churches caused the German government to drop the proposal.

Euthanasia was also advocated in the United States during the 1930s. In 1938, the *New York Times* announced the formation of a national euthanasia society that eventually became known as the Euthanasia Society of America. In 1939, the group had drafted a proposed law permitting voluntary euthanasia. Dr. Foster Kennedy, the group's president, also called for the legalization of euthanasia for babies born with birth defects. The incipient euthanasia movement in the United States grew quiescent in the aftermath of the Holocaust as the world recoiled in horror to the news that between 1939 and 1945, German doctors killed more than 200,000 disabled people, including infants and the mentally retarded people.

After the war, organized euthanasia groups continued to exist in the United States but made little headway until the early 1980s, when societal changes that began in the 1960s and the resulting weakening of traditional moral values, as well as intellectual support by some within the medical intelligentsia, provided fertile ground for renewed euthanasia advocacy. In a dramatically short period of time, legalized euthanasia went from an "unthinkable" prospect to one of the most contentious and controversial issues debated in the public square.

Pros and Cons

Perhaps the strongest argument made on behalf of legalizing euthanasia or assisted suicide is that it, like abortion, is a "choice" issue. Proponents argue that euthanasia/assisted suicide is "the ultimate civil right," and that to deprive mentally competent, terminally ill people who want to end their suffering of a peaceful "aid in dying" is to fundamentally disrespect their right to personal autonomy. Proponents also argue that legalizing euthanasia/assisted suicide is a necessary "insurance policy" that will ensure that no one dies in painful agony or unremitting suffering. Advocates contend that euthanasia/assisted suicide is little different from pain control since both use strong drugs and patients' deaths are occasionally unintentionally hastened as a side effect of the narcotics used in palliation. They also claim that doctors commonly engage in euthanasia/assisted suicide surreptitiously and promote legalization as a way to protect vulnerable patients from abuses inherent in the current "unregulated" practice. Acknowledging worries about potential abuses, advocates assure that "protective guidelines" would protect the vulnerable from wrongful death while still permitting suffering patients who are eligible for euthanasia/assisted suicide to obtain a desired, peaceful "death with dignity." Proponents also claim that opposition to euthanasia/assisted suicide is based primarily in religion and that laws prohibiting the practice are thus unconstitutional because they violate the division between church and state.

Opponents counter that legalizing euthanasia/assisted suicide would lead society down a dangerous "slippery slope" with legalized killing eventually being permitted for disabled, elderly, and depressed people, as well as for those who are not mentally competent to request to die. Protective guidelines "do not protect," opponents declare, pointing to the Dutch experience with euthanasia as "proof" of both the reality of the slippery slope and the relative meaninglessness of guidelines. Opponents also argue that the economics of modern medicine would promote euthanasia/assisted suicide as a form of health care cost containment, noting that the drugs in an assisted suicide cost only about forty dollars,

while proper care for a dying patient can cost tens of thousands of dollars. They also note that forty-four million Americans do not have health insurance, and that medicine is sometimes practiced in a discriminatory manner against racial and other minorities. Thus, they argue that "the last people to receive medical treatment will be the first to receive assisted suicide." Opponents also deny that there is widespread surreptitious euthanasia practiced in clinical medicine, citing several published studies as proof, and urge that hospice care and proper medical treatment provide the morally acceptable answers to the difficulties that are sometimes associated with the process of dying.

The people vote

There have been several attempts in the United States to legalize euthanasia and assisted suicide through state initiatives. The first attempt came in 1988, when euthanasia supporters attempted to qualify an initiative for the ballot in California, which would have permitted physicians to administer lethal injections for terminally ill patients who asked to have their deaths hastened. The attempt failed to garner enough signatures to qualify for the ballot. However, in 1991, Initiative 119, a similar proposal, was successfully placed on Washington's ballot. After initial polling showed voter support in excess of 70 percent, the initiative lost 54 to 46 percent. The pattern repeated itself in California in 1992, when a virtually identical proposal appeared on the California ballot in November 1992 as Proposition 161. After initial support in excess of 70 percent, the measure also lost by a margin of 54 to 46 percent.

Two years later, in Oregon, Measure 16—the Oregon Death with Dignity Act—qualified for the November 1994 ballot. Unlike the earlier failed initiatives, Measure 16 limited its scope to legalizing physician-assisted suicide. The measure passed narrowly, 51 to 49 percent. The law was soon overturned as a violation of the equal protection clause of the Fourteenth Amendment to the U.S. Constitution. However, this decision was itself overturned by the Ninth Circuit Court of Appeals on procedural grounds (*Lee v. Oregon*). The United States Supreme Court refused to review the Ninth Circuit's opinion. An attempt by opponents to repeal Measure 16 through another ballot initiative, Measure 51, failed in November 1997 by a margin of 60 to 40 percent. The law was in effect as of 1999.

In 1998, supporters of assisted suicide qualified Proposal B for the November ballot in Michigan. Proposal B, like Measure 16, would have restricted legalization to assisted suicide and its terms were very similar to those of the Oregon law. The debate over Proposal B was complicated by two factors: Michigan was the home state of Dr. Jack Kevorkian and Kevorkian's attorney, Geoffrey Fieger, was the Democratic nominee for governor. Whatever the impact of these ancillary issues, when the votes were counted, Proposal B lost by an overwhelming 71 to 29 percent.

Jack Kevorkian

During the 1990s, Jack Kevorkian was undoubtedly the most well known assisted suicide and euthanasia advocate in the world. A retired pathologist from Michigan, Kevorkian made headlines internationally when he undertook a well publicized assisted-suicide campaign between 1990 and 1998 that reportedly ended the lives of approximately one hundred thirty people. Some of those whose deaths Kevorkian facilitated were terminally ill and diagnosed as having less than six months to live, but most were disabled or chronically ill. According to autopsy reports, four of the people whose suicides Kevorkian helped had no discernible organic illness.

Kevorkian's campaign began on 4 June 1990, when he assisted the suicide of Janet Adkins, a woman diagnosed with early Alzheimer's disease. At the time, Michigan had no law against assisted suicide and Kevorkian was not arrested. His next publicly acknowledged assisted suicide was conducted on 23 October 1991, when Kevorkian made headlines for assisting the suicide of two women at the same location, one with multiple sclerosis and another who complained of chronic, severe pelvic pain. Kevorkian was arrested for murder but the case was dismissed. The prosecution appealed and the state legislature hastily cobbled together a poorly worded, temporary criminal statute proscribing assisted suicide intended to "stop Kevorkian."

Kevorkian openly defied the law and was arrested, tried, and acquitted. The temporary prohibition lapsed but the prosecution's earlier appeal succeeded when the Michigan Supreme Court ruled that assisted suicide was a common law felony in Michigan (*People of Michigan v. Jack Kevorkian*). Kevorkian was again arrested and tried. Once again, a jury found him not guilty. A third case against Kevorkian was later declared a mistrial because of the courtroom conduct of Kevorkian's lawyer, and the case was dropped. Kevorkian, it seemed, had a free hand.

In 1998, Kevorkian's actions grew increasingly erratic. In June, after he assisted the suicide of Joseph Tushkowski, a man with quadriplegia, Kevorkian held a press conference in which he claimed to have procured the man's kidneys, and offered them for organ transplant, "first come, first served." There were no takers. In late October, he videotaped himself lethally injecting Thomas Youk, an ALS (Lou Gehrig's disease) patient. Kevorkian then took the tape to CBS-Television's news program *60 Minutes*, which aired it to a nationwide audience, during which Kevorkian dared the authorities to prosecute him. Kevorkian was arrested and convicted of second-degree murder. He is currently in prison for a term of ten to twenty-five years.

Legal challenges

Proponents of legalization mounted a significant effort to have laws against assisted suicide declared unconstitutional, hoping to garner an "assisted suicide" *Roe v. Wade* (410 U.S. 113 (1973)) that would settle the issue nationally, as *Roe* did with abortion. They were unsuccessful. In *Washington v. Glucksburg* (117 S. Ct. 2258 (1997), the Supreme Court justices voted 9–0 that "the asserted 'right' to assistance in committing suicide is not a fundamental liberty interest protected by the Due Process Clause [of the Fourteenth Amendment]." The decision also emphasized that state laws banning assisted suicide were consistent expressions of the individual states' commitment to protecting all human life.

In the closely associated case of *Vacco v. Quill* (117 S. Ct. 2293 (1997)), the Supreme Court ruled against assisted-suicide advocates who had argued that New York's law proscribing assisted suicide violated the equal protection clause of the Fourteenth Amendment. They argued that since it is legal for terminally ill persons to refuse life-sustaining medical treatment and die immediately but illegal for terminally ill people who do not require life support to secure immediate death through physician-assisted suicide, New York violated its constitutional obligation to treat similarly situated people equally. In rejecting the argument, the Supreme Court ruled that the New York law actually treated similarly situated people alike: all patients are permitted to refuse unwanted treatment and none are allowed legal access to assisted suicide. The Court also ruled that there was a significant and rational distinction between refusing life-sustaining treatment and seeking assisted suicide. In the former circumstance, the doctor's intention may be to simply stop performing useless procedures when a patient will not benefit, while in assisted suicide, the doctor must without a doubt intend for the patient's death.

Both sides claimed victory in the Court's two rulings. Opponents were relieved that assisted suicide would not be "imposed" nationally by judicial fiat. Proponents took heart that several concurring opinions muddied the waters and seemed to indicate that the issue could be brought back to the courts for further review if a case of a patient with truly irremediable suffering were presented. Proponents also claimed that the Court's decision freed the states to experiment with laws concerning the end of life, perhaps including assisted suicide, although opponents pointed out that the issue of a state's right to pass a law legalizing assisted suicide had not been before the Court.

There have been at least three attempts to invalidate state laws proscribing assisted suicide based on privacy provisions contained in state constitutions. A lawsuit challenging Alaska's proscription is currently pending in that state's courts (Sampson v. State of Alaska, No. 3 AN–98–11288 CIV). A California Court of Appeals decision refused to permit a terminally ill man to have legal assistance with suicide so that his body could be cryogenically preserved. The most notable case to decide this issue in state courts was *Krischer v. Florida* (697 So.2d, 97 (1997)), in which the Florida Supreme Court ruled that the state's assisted-suicide prohibition did not violate the state constitution's guarantee of privacy.

Euthanasia in the Netherlands

The Netherlands has the most experience with physician-hastened death. Both euthanasia and assisted suicide remain crimes there but doctors who end their patients' lives will not be prosecuted if legal guidelines are followed. Among the guidelines are:

- The request must be made entirely of the patient's own free will.
- The patient must have a long-lasting desire for death.
- The patient must be experiencing unbearable suffering.
- There must be no reasonable alternatives to relieve suffering other than euthanasia.

- The euthanasia or assisted suicide must be reported to the coroner.

These guidelines are similar to those proposed in legalization proposals in the United States, although the Oregon law requires a terminal illness, a limitation not included in the Dutch guidelines. On the other hand, the Oregon guidelines do not require that the patient be experiencing unbearable suffering or that there be no reasonable alternatives to relieve suffering other than assisted suicide.

There have been several professional studies conducted into Dutch euthanasia practice. Most have reported that approximately 2,700 deaths are caused each year in the Netherlands by either euthanasia or assisted suicide—approximately 3 percent of all Dutch deaths. Proponents claim this relatively low figure rebuts opponent's fears that euthanasia will become a relatively routine event. Opponents counter that this figure is horrifying: if the same percentage of Americans died with the direct assistance of doctors, it would amount to approximately sixty-eight thousand annual deaths, more than tripling the U.S. suicide rate.

Opponents also claim that the number of people actually killed by Dutch doctors is significantly understated in these studies. They note that the term "euthanasia" is very narrowly defined by the Dutch government, with the effect if not the design of undercounting the actual number of euthanasia deaths. If a doctor kills a patient with barbiturates and a curare-like poison at the patient's request, the Dutch classify the death as "euthanasia." However, if the patient is killed by an intentional overdose of morphine administered with the primary intention of ending the patient's life, it is not considered euthanasia because morphine is a palliative agent. Yet, intentional morphine overdoses may exceed "euthanasia" deaths. In 1990, according to a Dutch government report, 8,100 patients died through the intentional morphine-overdose method of mercy killing. A latter study found that about 1,500 die annually through the intentional morphine-overdose method of killing. Whatever the actual annual figure, if intentional morphine-overdose deaths are counted as euthanasia, the statistical mercy killing rate in the Netherlands significantly exceeds the published statistics.

Opponents point to the many documented cases of chronically ill people, as well as to terminally ill people, put to death by doctors at the patient's request as further proof of euthanasia's many dangers. A Dutch documentary showed a young woman in remission from anorexia requesting doctor-induced death because she was afraid of resuming food abuse. Her doctor assisted her suicide without legal consequence. Another documented case showed an asymptomatic, HIV-positive patient assisted in suicide because he feared future suffering.

Opponents point with alarm to the Dutch Supreme Court's decision approving euthanasia for cases of severe depression—even in the absence of physical illness (*State v. Chabot,* Supreme Court of the Netherlands, Criminal Chamber, 21 June 1994, nr. 96.972). This decision resulted from the case of a Dutch psychiatrist who assisted the suicide of a woman who wanted to end her life because her children had died. The court supported the psychiatrist's actions, ruling that for purposes of judging the propriety of euthanasia or assisted suicide, suffering is suffering and it does not matter whether the cause is physical or psychological.

Another disturbing statistic that is found consistently in studies into Dutch euthanasia practices demonstrates to opponents the ultimate danger of euthanasia: approximately one thousand Dutch patients are euthanized each year by their doctors "without request or consent," in other words, involuntary or nonvoluntary euthanasia. Since euthanasia is only supposed to be allowed for people who consistently ask to be killed, the fact of involuntary killing demonstrates the unworkability of guidelines. Proponents counter that the number, while too high, has been relatively constant over several years, thus belying fears of the slippery slope.

Pediatric euthanasia has also become a part of Dutch euthanasia practice. Opponents point with alarm to a 1997 study published in the British medical journal *The Lancet* indicating that about 8 percent of all infants who die in the Netherlands are euthanized—approximately 80 per year. Pediatric euthanasia, they claim, is a human rights abuse and a proof that guidelines do not protect vulnerable patients. Proponents counter this criticism with the defense that the infant-euthanasia deaths are only of the most severely impaired babies, most of whom would not live anyway, and note that the parents make the decision based on their judgment of what is best for their children.

Opponents also claim that Dutch euthanasia is "beyond significant control" since approximately 59 percent of euthanasia and assisted-suicide deaths are not reported to the coroner as required by the guidelines. Thus, they claim that the actual number of Dutch patients killed is probably far higher than the statistics seem to show. Proponents admit that unreported euthanasia deaths are a problem but counter that full legalization would remove fear of prosecution thereby increasing compliance with reporting requirements.

In 1999 the Dutch government announced its intention to formally legalize euthanasia. As with anything having to do with euthanasia, the announcement was extremely controversial: the proposed law would permit the euthanasia of children as young as twelve at the request of the child, even if the parents object.

The Oregon experience

Assisted suicide has been legal for too short a time in Oregon to know its actual impact. As of 1999, just one study has been conducted analyzing the Oregon experience. Published in the *New England Journal of Medicine* in 1999, the study reported that fifteen people died legally by assisted suicide in the calendar year 1998. None was in intractable pain. One feared future pain. The primary reason the patients gave for requesting assisted suicide, according to the prescribing doctors who were interviewed for the study, was fear of future dependency.

Proponents of the Oregon law claimed that the study demonstrated that legalized assisted suicide is a rare procedure and that the law's guidelines work to protect vulnerable people. They also stressed that the deaths were apparently peaceful with none of the patients suffering side effects, such as extended coma, about which opponents had warned. Moreover, they noted that financial pressures did not appear to be a factor in any of the cases.

Opponents countered that the law was "sold" to voters as a last resort measure for people in extreme pain, but none of the patients fits that description, thereby demonstrating the existence of the "slippery slope." Disability rights activists argued that once assisted suicide is deemed a proper response to fears of dependency, as was the case in the fifteen Oregon deaths, it cannot be logically limited to terminally ill people since disabled and elderly people also face dependency issues and for far longer periods of time. Opponents also noted with alarm that six of the people who died by assisted suicide consulted with two or more doctors before finding a physician willing to write a lethal prescription. Moreover, some of the patients knew the prescribing doctor for a very short time, indicating, opponents contend, that some of the prescriptions were written for political rather than medical purposes.

Conclusion

The assisted suicide/euthanasia debate is still in its infancy, with the ultimate outcome very much in doubt. Public opinion polls show solid majority support for limited legalization, but the polls also demonstrate that popular support drops significantly when specific details of legislative proposals are examined. Oregon was a major breakthrough for advocates of assisted suicide but five states have outlawed assisted suicide since Oregon's Measure 16 passed in 1994, and one state passed legislation subjecting a person who assists in a suicide to civil liability. One thing is clear: euthanasia/assisted suicide controversy is likely to be a significant source of societal contention and political argument for many years to come.

WESLEY J. SMITH

See also ABORTION; CRIMINALIZATION AND DECRIMINALIZATION; EXCUSE: THEORY; HOMICIDE: LEGAL ASPECTS; JUSTIFICATION; NECESSITY; SUICIDE: LEGAL ASPECTS; VICTIMLESS CRIME.

BIBLIOGRAPHY

BYOCK, IRA. *Dying Well: The Prospect for Growth at the End of Life.* New York: Putnam, 1997.
CHIN, HEDBERG et al. "Legalized Physician-Assisted Suicide in Oregon—The First Year's Experience." *New England Journal of Medicine* 340, no. 7 (February 1999): 577–589.
HENDIN, HERBERT. *Seduced by Death: Doctors, Patients, and the Dutch Cure.* New York: Norton, 1997.
HUMPHRY, DEREK, and CLEMENT, MARY. *Freedom to Die: People, Politics and the Right-to-Die Movement.* New York: St. Martin's, 1998.
KAMISAR, YALE. "Some Non-Religious Views Against Proposed 'Mercy-Killing' Legislation." *Minnesota Law Review* 42 (1958): 969–1042.
———. "Physician-Assisted Suicide: The Problems Presented by the Compelling, Heartwrenching Case." *Journal of Criminal Law and Criminology* 88 (1998): 1121–1146.
KEIZER, BERT. *Dancing with Mister D: Notes on Life and Death.* New York: Doubleday, 1996.
KEOWN, JOHN, ed. *Euthanasia Examined: Ethical, Clinical and Legal Perspectives.* Cambridge, U.K.: Cambridge University Press, 1997.
MARKER, RITA. *Deadly Compassion: The Death of Ann Humphry and the Truth about Euthanasia.* New York: Morrow, 1993.
New York Task Force on Life and the Law. *When Death Is Sought: Assisted Suicide and Euthanasia in the Medical Context.* New York: New York Task Force on Life and the Law, 1994.
PECK, M. SCOTT. *Denial of the Soul: Spiritual and Medical Perspectives on Euthanasia and Mortality.* New York: Harmony Books, 1997.
QUILL, TIMOTHY E. *Death and Dignity: Making Choices and Taking Charge.* New York: Norton, 1993.
SMITH, WESLEY J. *Forced Exit: The Slippery Slope from Assisted Suicide to Legalized Murder.* New York: Times Books, 1997.
UHLMANN, MICHAEL E., ed. *Last Rights: Assisted Suicide and Euthanasia Debated.* Grand Rapids, Mich.: Wm. B. Eerdmans Publishing Company.
VAN DER HEIDE, VAN DER MAAS et al. "Medical End-of-Life Decisions Made for Neonates and Infants in the Netherlands." *The Lancet* 350 (July 1997): 251–253.
WILLIAMS, GLANVILLE. *The Sanctity of Life and the Criminal Law.* London: Faber and Faber, 1958.

EXCLUSIONARY RULE

The exclusionary rule permits a criminal defendant to prevent the prosecution from introducing at trial otherwise admissible evidence that was obtained in violation of the Constitution. In a sense the term "exclusionary rule" is misleading, because there are many exclusionary rules. Some, such as the rule against hearsay, exclude evidence because it is not very reliable. Others, such as a rule prohibiting a witness from testifying if the calling party did not disclose the witness before trial, are sanctions for the failure to comply with a nonconstitutional rule.

While every legal system excludes some evidence deemed irrelevant or untrustworthy, the constitutional exclusionary rule is unusual in rejecting highly probative evidence, often with the consequence of nullifying a meritorious prosecution. It is therefore not surprising that the exclusionary rule has occasioned sustained and sometimes bitter controversy.

A simple example helps to explain both the practical operation, and the controversial nature, of the exclusionary rule. Suppose the police stop a driver for speeding, and in the course of issuing the citation they discover cocaine in the glove compartment of the car. If the defendant did not consent to the search, and if the police did not have probable cause to believe illegal drugs could be found in the glove compartment, the search would be illegal under the Fourth Amendment.

To invoke the exclusionary rule the defendant would move before trial to suppress the drugs as illegally seized. This motion would be decided by a judge sitting without a jury. The defense would have the burden of proving that the defendant's rights were violated. If the facts are disputed (as they usually are), the parties would be allowed to call witnesses. If the accused testifies at the suppression hearing, this testimony is not admissible against him at a later trial.

If the judge decides that the search was illegal, the exclusionary rule comes into play and the evidence will be suppressed in the pending case. In our example, the government has no case without the drugs, and the court would have to dismiss the charge. Note that the defendant who moves to suppress incriminating evidence is usually in fact guilty. Maybe the driver had no idea that someone else had put cocaine in the glove box, or maybe the officer planted it, but the most likely hypothesis is that when there is physical evidence to be suppressed the person seeking suppression is indeed guilty as charged.

Note also that the rule does not automatically result in acquittal. Suppose the police found cocaine in both the glove compartment and the trunk, and the court ruled that the cocaine in the trunk was seized illegally but that the search of the glove compartment was legal. The suppression of the cocaine from the trunk would not protect the defendant from being convicted for possessing the cocaine in the glove compartment.

Note, finally, that the rule does not require returning contraband to the defendant. If the evidence at issue were lawful to possess, such as a diary or a properly registered firearm, the defendant would be entitled to its return at the close of the proceedings. Even when contraband is illegally seized, however, the defendant is entitled only to its exclusion from evidence, not to its return. Were it otherwise the defendant could be arrested on the courthouse steps for possessing the returned contraband.

If the judge grants the motion to suppress, the government would be allowed to appeal before a verdict is entered on the pending charge. Otherwise, the double jeopardy clause would bar appellate review of the trial court's decision to grant the suppression motion. If the judge decides that the evidence was not seized illegally, the motion will be denied and the case will be set for trial. If the defendant is convicted, he will be free to appeal on the ground that the trial court should have granted the motion to suppress.

Why does the law permit the guilty to escape justice because the police violated the Constitution? Would it not make more sense to admit the evidence and punish the police by demotion or suspension, or through civil lawsuits? The standard explanation is that these alternative remedies for constitutional violations have been found, in practice, to be ineffectual. Law enforcement agencies have not shown the willingness to discipline officers whose excesses lead to successful prosecutions. In civil suits against the police, the damages juries might return for illegal searches, together with the good-faith immunity defense available to the police, have blunted the deterrent force of the tort remedy. Freeing the guilty is not very appealing, but doing nothing about violations of the Constitution has seemed even worse.

Origins and development of the rule

The history of the rule reflects this ambivalence. The common law did not allow the exclusion of evidence on account of irregularities in the way in which a party acquired it. Instead, a citizen wronged by an illegal search could sue the wrongdoers for the tort of trespass. Anyone who invaded another's property was guilty of trespass and had to pay damages, unless the intruder had some positive legal authority such as a valid warrant. The framers of the Fourth Amendment included the warrant clause to prevent the new government from cutting off the trespass remedy by issuing general warrants—one of the abuses that had incited the revolution.

A decline in the efficacy of the tort remedy coincided with the development of modern police forces in the mid–nineteenth century. Typically the police did not (and do not) target the rich and powerful for intrusive investigations. The generally poor, generally uneducated, and often minority-race victims of illegal searches were in a poor position to recruit lawyers to bring suits; they certainly could not count on generous jury verdicts against the police.

The Supreme Court recognized the exclusionary rule early in the twentieth century. Although the Fourth Amendment exclusionary rule may have arisen from the then-prevailing view that the Fifth Amendment privilege against self-incrimination shielded individuals from having their own property used against them as evidence, the early cases soon recognized a Fourth Amendment right to suppress illegally seized evidence even when the party invoking the rule had no Fifth Amendment rights (i.e., a corporation) and even when the evidence to be suppressed was illegal to possess at all.

The early cases, however, were limited to federal prosecutions. Criminal law enforcement in the United States is primarily the responsibility of state, rather than federal, officers. Some state courts followed the Supreme Court's lead and adopted the exclusionary rule; others adhered to the common law rule admitting evidence without regard to how it was obtained. Two of the past century's most celebrated American jurists wrote opposing opinions on the issue during this period. A good way to begin thinking about the exclusionary rule is to compare Judge Benjamin Cardozo's opinion for the New York Court of Appeals in *People v. Defore*, 150 N.E. 585 (N.Y. 1926), refusing to adopt the exclusionary rule, with Justice Roger Traynor's opinion for the Supreme Court of California in *People v. Cahan*, 282 P.2d 905 (Cal. 1955), adopting the exclusionary rule.

Not until 1961, in the watershed case of *Mapp v. Ohio*, 367 U.S. 643 (1961), did the Supreme Court hold that the exclusionary rule applies to the states as a matter of Fourteenth Amendment due process. In states that had not followed the exclusionary rule on their own prior to *Mapp*, the *Mapp* decision had a dramatic impact. Warrant use in major cities went from a handful to hundreds per year; search-and-seizure law became the subject of police training programs. These developments would not have occurred if the tort remedy had been an effective deterrent. Had the tort remedy been effective, the police in states without the exclusionary rule would have been using warrants and training their officers in constitutional law all along.

Even the liberal Warren Court, however, was reluctant to free the guilty. As soon as the rule applied to the states, where crimes of violence are typically prosecuted and where the great majority of prosecutions for all types of offenses are brought, the Court began to adopt narrower interpretations of substantive Fourth Amendment rights, and to recognize exceptions to the exclusionary remedy. For example, shortly after *Mapp* the Court excluded undercover operations from any scrutiny whatsoever under the Fourth Amendment; refused to apply *Mapp* to free prisoners previously convicted by illegally obtained evidence; and reaffirmed the rule that only the search victim can invoke the rule, even when the evidence incriminates others.

As the Court grew more conservative during the 1970s (as it has remained ever since), the exceptions to the exclusionary rule have threatened to swallow the rule. Illegally obtained evidence is now admissible in the following situations:

1. in the government's case at trial against any person whose rights were not violated by the illegal search;
2. in the government's case at trial if the officers who committed the illegal search were acting in reasonable, good-faith reliance on a warrant, a statute, or a court record later determined to be unconstitutional or erroneous;
3. in the government's case at trial, if the government can prove that the evidence would have been discovered inevitably in the absence of the illegality;
4. in the government's case at trial, if the illegal police conduct led to the evidence only by an attenuated chain of events;
5. to impeach the defendant's testimony, if he chooses to take the stand at trial;
6. in preliminary and collateral proceedings, such as before the grand jury.

In deciding these cases the Court has regarded deterring future police misconduct as the sole reason for the rule. When weighing the desirability of an exception, the Court has explicitly balanced the likely deterrent benefits against the apparent costs of freeing the guilty. Although this approach has usually favored the prosecution, the Court has at least once found that the balancing test requires a narrower, rather than a broader, interpretation of the exceptions. In that case, the Court held that the impeachment exception did not allow the use of tainted evidence to contradict the testimony of a third-party witness for the defense, as distinct from the testimony of the defendant himself.

In the main, however, the balance has clearly inclined in favor of the government. One dramatic illustration is the good-faith exception recognized for searches conducted pursuant to facially-valid warrants recognized in *United States v. Leon*, 468 U.S. 897 (1984). Because the police enjoy good-faith immunity from tort suits, withholding the exclusionary rule leaves no apparent remedy when the police obtain a warrant without showing probable cause. The Fourth Amendment flatly declares that "no warrants shall issue, but upon probable cause." The good-faith exception means that when warrants do issue without probable cause, neither exclusion of the fruits, nor civil liability, follows from the violation.

As the Court has come to focus exclusively on deterrence in applying the rule, some legal scholars have argued that illegally obtained evidence should be suppressed without regard to deterrence. It is claimed, for instance, that excluding tainted evidence is necessary to preserve judicial integrity, or to vindicate the principle of judicial review. The challenge confronting all such non-deterrent theories of exclusion is to connect the search for, and the use of, the evidence, even when the courts impose a sanction adequate to deter future violations.

This connection is not immediately apparent. Suppose the police discover narcotics at the home of *A* pursuant to a valid warrant, and an identical lot of drugs in the home of *B* but without a warrant. There does not seem to be any normative distinction in favor of *B*. We do not want the police in future cases to search without warrants, so we might exclude the evidence against *B* to prevent searches of completely innocent persons in other cases. But we would not say that *B* has a personal right to exclusion divorced from future consequences.

Suppose instead that the police, without a warrant, search the home of *C* and discover nothing incriminating. If exclusion were thought of as a personal right, the innocent *C* would have less protection against unreasonable searches than the guilty *B*. The Fourth Amendment is not generally regarded as conferring substantive immunity for crimes committed in private. So long as that judgment stands, connecting the search and the use of the evidence will be difficult. Given that innocent search victims possessed no evidence a court could later exclude, exclusion would not seem to be an indispensable remedy. What is indispensable is some effective deterrent against future violations. The Supreme Court has been willing to require the exclusionary rule until such time as Congress or the states establish an effective alternative.

A jurisdiction that adopted and enforced an effective alternative deterrent to police misconduct would have a strong case for abolishing the exclusionary rule. If, for instance, police who engaged in illegal searches were suspended for a year without pay for the first infraction, and ter-

minated for a second, and if this policy were monitored and enforced effectively, there would be few illegal searches and no need for the further deterrent of the exclusionary rule. Note, however, that under such a system, the public would lose the same evidence as the exclusionary rule suppresses, because it would never be discovered in the first place. Note also that under such a regime the exclusionary rule would not be particularly unpopular because it would only rarely come into play, as the administrative disciplinary system would prevent most illegal searches from ever taking place. Perhaps because of these considerations, no jurisdiction in the United States has adopted strict administrative, tort, or criminal sanctions for illegal searches.

Even if deterrence is the key to the rule, it hardly follows that the Court has assessed the costs and benefits of exclusion correctly. For example, preventing persons other than the search victim to invoke the exclusionary rule goes a long way toward undermining the rule's deterrent threat. In some cases the police deliberately target third-party custodians of evidence for illegal searches, knowing that the target of the investigation will not be allowed to challenge the legality of the search. More commonly, law enforcement agents investigating a conspiracy know that many of the conspirators will not have standing to challenge the search or arrest of one of their number. The standing exception seems more like a convenient way to escape the substantive limits of the Fourth Amendment than a reasoned exposition of a deterrent theory of the exclusionary rule.

Moreover, each exception to the exclusionary rule recognized by the Court reduces the sanction imposed on the government for illegal searches and seizures. Standing alone, the impeachment exception or the inevitable discovery exception might do little damage to deterrence. Given all the exceptions together, however, the disincentive to conduct illegal searches has been significantly reduced.

Despite the various exceptions, the exclusionary rule lives on, thirty years after Warren Burger replaced Earl Warren as Chief Justice. Even conservative justices have been unwilling to abolish the rule, just as even liberal judges recognized some exceptions. The exceptions reflect the reluctance to release patently guilty offenders; the persistence of the rule reflects the reluctance to provide no effective remedy for violations of the Constitution.

The policy debate

Is the exclusionary rule justifiable? To put this question in context we must qualify the question by adding another: "Compared to what?" Defenders of the exclusionary rule rely heavily on the inadequacy of other remedies. If the constitution requires some effective remedy for violations, and if tort and administrative remedies have proved inadequate in practice, there is a strong case for requiring exclusion.

Critics have made a variety of objections to the rule. They argue that:

1. exclusion is costly inasmuch as it requires freeing guilty offenders;
2. that the rule does nothing for innocent victims of police misconduct, who have no evidence of crime to be suppressed;
3. that the rule's deterrent benefits are, as an empirical matter, doubtful;
4. that, if the rule does deter, it may overdeter by causing the police not to engage in searches that, although close to the line of illegality, are not over that line;
5. that the tort remedy might be made more effective by plausible reforms;
6. that exclusion causes police perjury, tolerance of police perjury by judges, and narrow interpretations of substantive Fourth Amendment rights by judges reluctant to free the guilty.

With respect to the cost associated with freeing the guilty, defenders of exclusion reply that any effective remedy for Fourth Amendment violations would result in the escape of guilty criminals. If the tort remedy, for example, were made a credible deterrent, fear of tort liability would cause the police to refrain from illegal searches. Since some illegal searches would reveal evidence of crime, alternative remedies would have the same costs as the exclusionary rule, in precise proportion to their effectiveness in deterring police misconduct.

In some cases, however, exclusion does cost the public a conviction that might have been obtained without violating the Constitution. If the police, having probable cause, decline to seek a warrant when one would have been issued, the suppression of the evidence prevents the police from obtaining it lawfully. A large majority of reported offenses, however, are never cleared by the police, so that it seems fair to assume that absent the illegality the police would not have come by the evidence lawfully. Drug cases, which involve offenses that would not be reported by a complaining witness, are even less likely to have been made lawfully. In those cases in which the prosecution can prove that the police would have obtained the evidence lawfully absent the illegality, the inevitable discovery exception allows the admission of the evidence. On the whole it seems fair to say that although the exclusionary rule may abort a few prosecutions the Constitution permits, the "cost" of freeing guilty criminals is for the most part attributable to the substantive constitutional rights that limit police power to search for evidence, rather than to the remedy used to deter future violations of those limits.

Indeed, an effective tort remedy might well overdeter the police, in the sense that officers fearful of personal liability might pass by lawful but borderline searches that might lead to the conviction of the guilty. Imposing tort liability on the police department or the municipality would create similar incentives on the part of police supervisors, who might train their officers to act conservatively out of fear of liability.

Defenders of the exclusionary rule admit that the rule does not provide any direct relief for innocent victims of police misconduct. Proponents of exclusion point out that if the rule deters, it will protect innocent citizens in future cases, although police motivated by sadism or racism rather than the desire to secure convictions will be unimpressed by the threat of exclusion. Because any effective deterrent will benefit guilty and innocent alike in future cases, tort remedies have an advantage over exclusion only to the extent that they compensate innocent victims, which exclusion clearly fails to accomplish. But so long as the tort remedies are ineffective, they fail to compensate the great majority of innocent search victims.

With respect to the empirical issue of the rule's deterrent effect on police behavior, proponents of the rule point to the following evidence. First, all modern studies find that the suppression of evidence is quite rare, involving perhaps 1 percent of felony cases (and in many of these cases the defendant may still be convicted on the force of untainted evidence). If evidence is only rarely suppressed, the argument goes, the police must be complying with constitutional standards. If, however, the rate of suppression is low because of successful police perjury or trial court hostility to freeing the guilty, there is no inconsistency between a low suppression rate and a low compliance rate.

Exclusionary rule proponents also point to the dramatic increase in warrant use that followed *Mapp v. Ohio* in those states whose courts had not adopted the exclusionary rule on their own. The increase is hard to explain except as deterrence in operation, because while other factors might have spurred the police to increase the frequency of searches, there was no practical reason for them to obtain search warrants except for the Supreme Court's decision in *Mapp*. Exclusionary rule proponents also point out that the police now devote considerable time to training officers in constitutional standards, to educating the force about new judicial developments, and to developing tactics that work around constitutional rules announced by the courts. Each of these phenomena is consistent with the hypothesis that the exclusionary rule deters. On the whole it seems fair to say that the exclusionary rule does influence police behavior, but that the extent of that influence is open to reasonable dispute.

Indeed, some commentators have taken the position that the exclusionary rule overdeters, reasoning that because the social cost of illegal searches is modest (the criminal's interest in escaping just punishment is not, on this view, a cost at all), and the loss of good cases is a substantial penalty on the police, that the police will be discouraged from aggressive action. If, however, it is true that the cost of lost convictions is attributable to the Fourth Amendment itself, not to the exclusionary remedy, the imbalance between the social costs and benefits of illegal searches disappears. Optimal deterrence comes from setting the sanction equal to the wrongdoer's expected gain discounted by the probability of escaping the sanction. Because the primary motive for illegal searches is successful prosecution, the rule comes close to setting the sanction equal to the government's anticipated gain. Indeed, from a strictly economic point of view, the rule may underdeter, because even when tainted evidence is suppressed the police still succeed in taking contraband off the street and acquiring information about criminal operations. Police therefore sometimes retain an incentive to search illegally even if they are certain that the fruits will be excluded.

Critics of the exclusionary rule usually admit that existing tort remedies are ineffective. They have proposed various reforms to make the tort remedy a more formidable deterrent. Among the more common suggestions are imposing liability on police departments and municipalities, assessing liquidated or punitive damages, and curtailing or abolishing good-faith immunity defenses. Whether reforms such as these could convert the tort remedy into an effective deterrent is a debated, but probably purely academic, point. Neither courts nor legislatures have embraced the reform proposals, even though they have appeared from prominent quarters in a steady stream for more than fifty years.

There are two major reasons for this failure. First, as a political matter, making it easier to sue the police at the expense of the taxpayer is not an attractive proposition to typical legislators. The beneficiaries of such a proposal are the likely targets of police excess, that is, young men, disproportionately black. The potential losers are those who might be protected from predatory crime by police disregard of constitutional standards. The latter group is more numerous and more influential than the former.

Second, on the merits, there is the standing risk that a tort remedy might set the sanction for Fourth Amendment violations higher than the social costs attending the violation, and thus inhibit justifiable as well as unjustifiable police actions. There is some evidence that officials exaggerate their exposure to liability. The police themselves seem to prefer exclusion to personal liability.

Evaluating the damages for Fourth Amendment violations is quite difficult. Should the victim of an arrest without probable cause recover the value of the lost time (say, thirty dollars an hour for the ten hours between arrest and release?) or ten thousand dollars for the arbitrary and degrading deprivation of personal liberty? Should the homeowner subjected to a warrantless search be awarded the price of new hinges and one visit from a cleaning service, or ten thousand dollars or more for invasion of privacy?

Even if broad agreement existed on the compensatory aspect of tort damages, the deterrent aspect poses further problems. What amount suffices to deter future illegal, but not future legal, arrests and searches? Set too high and damages would discourage legitimate police work; set too low and they would put constitutional rights up for sale at bargain prices. One advantage of the exclusionary rule is that it sets the sanction roughly equal to the government's expected gain, thereby approximating the sanction suggested by optimal deterrence theory.

The question whether alternative remedies might be made effective largely subsumes another issue sometimes raised about the exclusionary rule. Prior to *Mapp v. Ohio* relatively little substantive Fourth Amendment law was established, because many jurisdictions had no exclusionary rule and because few tort suits were brought. Since *Mapp* the Supreme Court alone has decided dozens if not hundreds of Fourth Amendment cases. While uncertainties and confusion still surround some issues, the law has become better defined as a result.

Some defenders of the exclusionary rule point out that without the rule, there would be no procedural vehicle for establishing or changing the substantive law. This is a strong point against simple abolition of the rule. But if an effective tort remedy replaced the exclusionary rule, and if damages were generous enough to encourage suits, the tort system would provide a new procedural forum for shaping substantive Fourth Amendment law.

There is growing recognition that some police officers will commit perjury to avoid the suppression of evidence. The extent of the phenomenon is necessarily conjectural. If the reason why suppression motions rarely succeed is that the police violate the applicable rules and then successfully lie about it later, the exclusionary rule would not have accomplished very much.

Widespread perjury is by no means inconsistent with widespread compliance. Proponents of the rule believe that the training programs and changes in police culture fostered by *Mapp* reduce the occasions in which the police violate the applicable law in the first instance, even if some officers are willing to lie on the stand after it becomes clear that the discovery of the evidence was illegal. Police testimony could be subjected to more searching scrutiny, by such measures as evidentiary presumptions against consent to search or the admissibility of polygraph evidence at suppression hearings. Finally, it is worth noting that tort remedies, which might expose police departments or individual officers to substantial financial liabilities, would be more likely to transfer police perjury from the criminal to the civil courts than to reduce its prevalence.

Other constitutional exclusionary rules

Thus far we have concentrated on the exclusion of evidence obtained in violation of the Fourth Amendment. Sometimes, however, the police obtain evidence in violation of other constitutional provisions. For example, the Fifth Amendment privilege against self-incrimination

can be overcome by a grant of official immunity. When a witness testifies before a grand jury or a legislative committee under an immunity order, the subsequent testimony may not be used at a subsequent criminal prosecution of the witness. Nor can the government use other evidence derived from the immunized testimony. The burden is on the government to prove that the additional evidence was obtained independently of the compelled testimony. If, at a subsequent trial, the previously immunized witness takes the stand and testifies inconsistently with the prior immunized testimony, the immunized testimony may not be admitted even for impeachment.

By contrast, although the famous warnings required by *Miranda v. Arizona* are premised on the Fifth Amendment privilege against self-incrimination, the *Miranda* exclusionary rule operates more like the Fourth than the Fifth Amendment exclusionary rule. Statements obtained in violation of *Miranda v. Arizona* are admissible to impeach, and other evidence derived from such statements is often admitted when the causal connection between the violation and the discovery of the evidence is attenuated. Although the Supreme Court recently reaffirmed the constitutional basis of the *Miranda* rules, the Court stopped short of equating *Miranda* violations with compelled testimony.

Before *Miranda*, the Supreme Court had established a due process test excluding confessions obtained by brutal or coercive police methods. The due process test remains as a supplement to *Miranda*. Because coerced confessions are thought to be both less reliable, and more offensive, than admissions obtained in violation of *Miranda*, a stricter exclusionary rule applies to coerced confessions. When a confession is actually coerced by brutality or other extreme forms of police pressure, the confession is not admissible even if the defendant at trial testifies inconsistently with the coerced admission.

The exclusion of eyewitness identification evidence obtained in violation of the Sixth Amendment right to counsel, or by unfair suggestiveness in violation of due process, differs from both the Fourth and Fifth Amendment context. Evidence of an unconstitutional pretrial lineup or photo identification procedure must be suppressed, but the witness will ordinarily be allowed to testify at the trial that she recognizes the defendant as the offender. The theory is that the witness's memory of the crime is independent of the pretrial lineup. Although highly doubtful in light of modern psychological research on identification, courts frequently allow the in-court identification, provided that the witness testifies that current memory is independent of the prior, tainted lineup or photo array. In this situation defense counsel sometimes introduces proof of the prior suggestive lineup (which counsel worked hard to have suppressed in the first place) as a necessary means to discredit the in-court identification.

Whether the exclusionary rule is an appropriate remedy for violations of the equal protection clause is an open question. If the police have probable cause to search or arrest a suspect, but the suspect can prove that the police were motivated by racial animus, there is a violation of the equal protection clause but not a violation of the Fourth Amendment. Some lower courts have considered whether such a suspect may suppress the fruits of the equal protection violation or if a damage action provides the exclusive remedy. It seems likely that the issue eventually will present itself to the Supreme Court.

Proposals for reform

Forty years have passed since *Mapp v. Ohio*. Outright abolition of the exclusionary rule has not yet occurred and seems extremely unlikely absent legislative creation of innovative alternative remedies. Since legislative reforms seem unlikely as well, the exclusionary rule appears to be with us for some time to come. While the argument has been made that abolition would force legislatures to adopt effective alternatives, the state experience prior to *Mapp* offers evidence to the contrary. Modifications of the rule's current operation, however, might be somewhat more likely.

By now the Supreme Court has embraced most pro-prosecution reforms of the exclusionary rule. Two that have not yet been recognized are a general good-faith exception and a comparative-reprehensibility rule. Thus far the Supreme Court has recognized a good-faith exception only when the police reasonably have relied on a warrant issued by a judge, on a statute passed by a legislature, or on a judicial record maintained by a clerk of the court. At least one circuit court of appeals has gone further, and held that even without statutory or judicial authorization, the exclusionary rule does not apply when illegal police conduct is the product of a reasonable good-faith mistake. Defenders of such a rule argue that police cannot be deterred from conduct they think is legal. Critics respond

that the Fourth Amendment itself permits "reasonable" searches and seizures, and that incentives favoring prudence can deter negligence by police, just as negligence by doctors or drivers can be deterred.

The comparative-reprehensibility theory calls for considering the seriousness of the defendant's crimes and the officer's misconduct before excluding evidence. A turn to such a discretionary exclusionary rule has been criticized as inviting trial judges—often elected—to give the police a free hand in serious cases. The comparative-reprehensibility approach does not seem to have as much support as the general good-faith exception. As a matter of legal realism the seriousness of the offense and the extent of police wrongdoing will factor into the decision to some degree even without doctrinal authorization.

Commentators and dissenting justices have put forward a variety of pro-defense proposals. These include:

1. target standing, permitting a third party to invoke the exclusionary rule when the third party was the target of the investigators who illegally searched the victim;
2. a bad-faith exception to the other exceptions, so that when the police knew or should have known that their actions were illegal, the other exceptions would no longer apply;
3. replacing all current exceptions with a single inevitable-lawful-discovery exception, such that if the government failed to prove that the evidence would have been discovered consistently with the Constitution no other exceptions would apply.

All of these reforms have strong support in the deterrence theory. Current Supreme Court precedent, however, rejects each of these approaches.

Conclusion

The exclusionary rule persists because there is no credible alternative. Freeing the guilty is unpalatable, and on many occasions the courts have sought to avoid that result by narrowing the substantive Fourth Amendment law or by recognizing exceptions to the exclusionary rule. But absent some other meaningful remedy, outright abolition of the exclusionary rule would, in the words of Justice Holmes, "reduce the Fourth

Amendment to a form of words." The Supreme Court has not been willing to go that far.

DONALD DRIPPS

See also CONFESSIONS; COUNSEL: RIGHT TO COUNSEL; CRIMINAL PROCEDURE: CONSTITUTIONAL ASPECTS; SEARCH AND SEIZURE; WIRETAPPING AND EAVESDROPPING.

BIBLIOGRAPHY

DAVIES, THOMAS Y. "A Hard Look at What We Know (and Still Need to Learn) about the Exclusionary Rule: The NIJ Study and Other Studies of 'Lost' Arrests." *American Bar Foundation Research Journal* (1983): 611.

DRIPPS, DONALD A. "Living With *Leon*." *Yale Law Journal* 95 (1986): 906.

FOOTE, CALEB. "Tort Remedies for Police Violations of Individual Rights." *Minnesota Law Review* 39 (1955): 493.

HALL, CONNOR. "Letters of Interest to the Profession, Evidence and the Fourth Amendment." *American Bar Association Journal* 8 (1922): 646.

KAMISAR, YALE. "Does (Did) (Should) the Exclusionary Rule Rest on a 'Principled Basis' Rather Than on an 'Empirical Proposition'?" *Creighton Law Review* 16 (1983): 565.

LAFAVE, WAYNE R. *Search and Seizure*, 3rd edition. St. Paul, Minn.: West Publishing Co., 1996.

ORFIELD, MYRON W., JR. "Deterrence, Perjury, and the Heater Factor: An Exclusionary Rule in the Chicago Criminal Courts." *University of Colorado Law Review* 63 (1992): 75.

SCHLESINGER, STEPHEN R. *Exclusionary Injustice*. New York: M. Dekker, 1977.

SLOBOGIN, CHRISTOPHER. "Why Liberals Should Chuck the Exclusionary Rule." *University of Illinois Law Review* (1999): 363.

STEWART, POTTER. "The Road to *Mapp v. Ohio* and Beyond: The Origins, Development and Future of the Exclusionary Rule in Search and Seizure Cases." *Columbia Law Review* 83 (1983): 1365.

STUNTZ, WILLIAM J. "The Virtue and Vices of the Exclusionary Rule." *Harvard Journal of Law and Public Policy* 20 (1997): 443.

THOMAS, GEORGE C., and POLLACK, BARRY S. "Balancing the Fourth Amendment Scales: The Bad-Faith Exception to Exclusionary Rule Limitations." *Hastings Law Journal* 45 (1993): 21.

WIGMORE, JOHN HENRY. "Using Evidence Obtained by Illegal Search and Seizure." *American Bar Association Journal* 8 (1922): 479.

CASES

Mapp v. Ohio, 367 U.S. 643 (1961).
Miranda v. Arizona, 384 U.S. 436 (1966).
People v. Cahan, 282 P.2d 905 (Cal. 1955).
People v. Defore, 150 N.E. 585 (N.Y. 1926).
United States v. Leon, 468 U.S. 897 (1984).

EXCUSE: THEORY

To approach the theory of excuse, one needs first to understand how excuses relate to other components of punishable, criminal conduct. Excuses become relevant only after proof that the actor has committed an unjustified act in violation of a criminal statute. Acts that fall outside the scope of the criminal law require no excuse; nor do nominal but justified violations of the law. If the actor has committed a criminal wrong (an unjustified violation of the statute), excuses speak to the question whether the actor is personally accountable for the wrongful act. This factor of personal accountability goes by many different names, including *culpability, blameworthiness, fault,* and *mens rea*. These overlapping terms have in common their logical incompatibility with excuses. A valid excuse implies that the actor is not to blame (not culpable, not at fault, without mens rea in the normative sense) for the wrongful act.

The range of excuses

Western legal systems have recognized, in varying degrees, a range of possible excusing circumstances. The paradigmatic excuse is that of insanity. Although definitions of *insanity* differ, all Western legal systems recognize that actors who, because of psychological incapacity, either do not realize they are doing wrong or cannot prevent themselves from doing wrong cannot be blamed for their wrongful violations of the law.

The claim of involuntary intoxication invites an analogy with insanity. If the intoxication is sufficiently acute and if it arises without the actor's voluntary choice, then the circumstances of the actor's incapacity closely resemble insanity. Indeed, West German law integrates acute intoxication into the framework of insanity (German (Federal Republic) Penal Code § 20). American law recognizes involuntary intoxication as a distinct excuse.

The claim of duress arises if another person threatens the actor with death or other serious harm if the actor does not commit a specific criminal act. Surrendering to the threat generates a possible excuse for the criminal act. As compared with insanity, however, claims of duress receive highly differential treatment. First, some legal systems, such as the Soviet system, do not recognize duress based on threats as an excuse, although some cases might fall under the justification of lesser evils. Second, even in systems recognizing duress as an excuse, considerable controversy attends the range of crimes that may be excused. German law recognizes the availability of duress in homicide cases. In English and American law, however, there is considerable resistance to recognizing duress as an excuse in homicide cases. Third, in legal systems recognizing duress as a distinct defense to at least some offenses, some scholars argue that the defense is grounded in a theory of justification rather than excuse (LaFave and Scott, pp. 378–379). The argument for this view is that the threat to the actor creates a conflict of interests: if the threat is sufficiently great and outweighs the interest sacrificed in committing the crime, the actor's submission to the threats will be justified on grounds of lesser evils. The more common interpretation of duress is that the threats do not justify the crime, but merely excuse the actor's having surrendered to the intimidating threats.

Even more controversial than the status of duress is the analogous situation of the actor committing an offense in response to the pressure of natural circumstances. The typical cases are those of stealing to avoid starvation or, as the issue was posed in *Regina v. Dudley and Stephens*, 14 Q.B.D. 273 (1884), killing and committing cannibalism in order to fend off starvation on the high seas. This case held that natural circumstances could neither excuse nor justify homicide, and the influential opinion even ruled out starvation as an excuse for theft. Although this case still influences the course of English and American law, both French and German law would endorse starvation and other natural circumstances as excuses even for homicide (French Penal Code art. 64; German (Federal Republic) Penal Code sect. 35). Hereafter, this article will refer to this possible excuse as "personal necessity."

An important middle ground between duress and personal necessity arises in cases of prison escapes to avoid threatened violence. The situation resembles duress in that the actor responds to a human threat. Yet, in his response, the actor seeks to avoid the threat rather than to comply with it. American courts have responded

to this problem on the assumption that avoiding threatened violence falls outside the scope of duress. With personal necessity not recognized as an excuse in American law, the courts have had considerable difficulty recognizing a defense based on intolerable prison conditions. Since 1974, however, a number of courts have moved in that direction (*People v. Lovercamp*, 43 Cal. App. 3d 823, 118 Cal. Rptr. 110 (1974); *People v. Harmon*, 53 Mich. App. 482, 220 N.W.2d 212 (1974)). Although the rationale for this new defense remains uncertain, the argument seems to be one of excuse rather than of justification.

The prison-break situation illustrates why it is important to distinguish between claims of excuse and of justification. The distinction bears upon the question whether prison guards, fully aware of the reasons for the attempted escape, may use force to thwart the attempt. One should think of the guards' use of force as potentially privileged law enforcement. The guards may use reasonable and necessary force to uphold the order of the prison, but only against unlawful or wrongful challenges to that order. They could not, for example, use force against a lawful order to transfer specific prisoners to another facility. The question, then, is whether the attempted escape poses a lawful or unlawful challenge to the order of the prison.

If the escape were deemed justified, one would be inclined to think of the attempted escape as lawful (or, at least, not unlawful). After all, a valid claim of justification renders conduct right and proper. If the escape is not unlawful, the guards have no right to resist. Not so with an excuse: an excuse does nor challenge the wrongfulness or unlawfulness of the conduct, but merely denies the personal accountability of the actor for the wrongful act. The guards retain the right to resist escapes excused on grounds of insanity, voluntary intoxication, duress, or personal necessity.

Some theorists might wish to argue that under certain circumstances—say when a fire threatens the lives of the inmates—the guards should not have the right to resist attempted escapes. In most cases of escape, however, the consensus would probably be that the guards have not only the right, but the duty, to protect society by resisting prisoners seeking to escape even from dire conditions. If this is the normative judgment, logic requires that conditions prompting escape be treated as a basis for excuse rather than justification.

In the period of the early common law, the courts clearly recognized an excuse of personal necessity in homicide cases. The excuse, called *se defendendo*, was limited to cases of self-preservation against a combatant. When the actor had no choice but to kill or be killed, he could excuse killing his opponent on the ground of *se defendendo*. The courts refused to expand this excuse to encompass cases such as *Dudley and Stephens*. Eventually, the statutory justification of self-defense supplanted *se defendendo* and became the standard for assessing liability in cases of killing aggressors or other combatants.

It is difficult to distinguish, in principle, between duress and personal necessity. Since the enactment of its first criminal code in 1871, German law has clearly recognized both excuses. Indeed, the 1975 code unites duress and personal necessity in one overarching provision (§ 35). It follows that in *Dudley and Stephens*, German courts would have considered the possibility of excusing the homicide. Despite some signs to the contrary (namely, in the prison-break cases), Anglo-American courts persist in distinguishing between duress, which they recognize, and personal necessity, which they have yet to recognize as an excuse.

Anglo-American ambivalence about personal necessity as an excuse corresponds to skepticism about another excuse well-recognized in German law: mistake of law. This claim arises if the actor violates the law without knowing it and under circumstances where it would have been unfair to expect him to have better informed himself of his legal obligations—for example, because the law is vague or imposes an obligation that bears no relation to conventional moral sentiments. Section 2.04(2) of the Model Penal Code recognizes a defense in cases in which the actor relies on an authoritative statement of the law that proves to be false. This limited defense is of no avail in cases in which the actor simply has no knowledge, and no basis for suspecting, that his conduct runs afoul of a prohibition in the criminal code. In *Lambert v. California*, 355 U.S. 225 (1957), Lambert was convicted for violating an ordinance requiring her, as a convicted felon, to register with the Los Angeles police within five days of entering the city. Her failure to register derived from understandable, potentially excusable ignorance of the ordinance. It is widely believed that her conviction under these circumstances was unjust. Yet the Model Penal Code's recommendation would have provided no relief, for Lambert had not relied on an authoritative statement of the law. Although the United States Supreme Court did not address the problem explicitly as an excusable mistake of law, it declared the conviction unconstitutional, holding that the government violated the due process clause by failing to provide sufficient notice of the obligation to register.

The rationale of excuses

The range of excuses remains in flux. The psychological sensitivity of the twentieth century generates claims for novel, as-yet-unrecognized excuses. Some people argue that prolonged social deprivation should excuse criminal behavior. Others maintain that conscientious civil disobedience should excuse acts of political protest. Those with determinist leanings would excuse all criminal acts; indeed, if genes, upbringing, and circumstances determine criminal conduct, there is no rational basis for blaming individuals for violating the criminal law. Carried to this extreme, excuses would engulf the entire criminal law. The practice of blame and punishment would then give way to institutions of social control that focused entirely on the suspect's predicted danger to social interests.

The ongoing controversy about excusing wrong-doers invites attention to the rationale for recognizing and rejecting excuses. The place to begin is with divergent attitudes toward punishment.

Retributive theory. A retributive theory of punishment insists that the actor deserves punishment only if he is personally accountable for violating the law. The assumption is that no one is accountable for unavoidable acts, and excuses argue that the actor could not have avoided committing the criminal act. This standard of "avoidability" should be interpreted normatively. The question always is whether it would be fair under the circumstances to expect the actor to resist the pressures of the situation and abstain from the criminal act. If it would not be fair to expect avoidance of the act, then it cannot be fair to blame and punish the actor for succumbing to the pressures driving him toward the act.

This rationale of excuses rests on the assumption that either internal pressures (insanity, intoxication) or external pressures (duress, natural circumstances) might so intrude upon the actor's freedom of choice that the act committed under pressure no longer appears to be his doing. The act is attributable more to the pressure than to the actor's free choice. If the act is not his, he cannot be blamed for having committed it.

This model of excusing, based as it is on the model of overwhelming pressure, fails to encompass mistake and ignorance of law. In cases such as *Lambert*, the actor does not succumb to pressure; rather, she chooses to commit an act that, given knowledge of the criminal prohibition, she would presumably not choose to commit. In this sense, an act committed through ignorance fails to qualify as voluntary. In cases of mistake and ignorance of law, the actor does not choose to do wrong. Although the case differs from the model of overwhelming pressure, the wrongful act committed through ignorance ought to be excused, precisely as is the act done under pressure.

This retributive rationale of excuses presupposes that the actor is not accountable for the occurrence of the circumstances generating the excuse. If the actor has voluntarily induced his own intoxication, he cannot rely on intoxication to excuse his conduct. If she has been on a hunger strike, she can hardly claim starvation as an excuse for stealing. Similarly, if he could easily have informed himself of his obligations and had some reason to do so, he cannot plausibly claim mistake of law as an excuse. The antecedent culpability precludes a successful claim that the actor is not accountable at the time of committing the wrongful act.

In cases of insanity, intoxication, duress, and personal necessity, two normative questions envelop the analysis of the asserted excuse: whether the actor could fairly have resisted the pressure impelling him toward the act, and whether the actor is accountable for the circumstances generating the pressure. In cases of mistake or ignorance of law, there is only one normative question: whether the actor is accountable for his state of ignorance. So far as legal systems recognize these excuses, the trier of fact (in Anglo-American law, usually the jury) must assess these normative questions in making a judgment of criminal responsibility.

Utilitarian theory. Beginning with Jeremy Bentham (1748–1832), utilitarians have sought to account for recognized excuses by the following argument: As a measure causing pain, punishment should never be imposed when it is pointless. The purpose of punishment is to deter socially undesirable behavior. Punishment is pointless with regard to classes of actors, such as the insane, who are not deterrable. Therefore, nondeterrables should be excused from punishment for their criminal acts.

H. L. A. Hart was among the first to point out that this argument rests on a "spectacular non-sequitur" (p. 19). Bentham's reasoning assumes that the range of potential deterrables is defined by the precise characteristics of the defendant. He did not consider the possibility that punishing an insane or otherwise excused actor might have a deterrent effect on a whole range of potential criminals defined by broader characteristics. Punishing the insane might deter homicide generally; the utilitarian cannot simply assume that punishing excused actors would be pointless.

Utilitarian arguments are often invoked to justify disregarding possible excuses, such as duress, personal necessity, and mistake of law. By disregarding excuses and holding liable those who have unjustifiably violated the law, the criminal sanction arguably serves to induce higher standards of behavior. Disregarding excuses, therefore, may inflict a negative cost on those punished, but the gains to the many might outweigh the costs to the few.

The recognition of excuses expresses tolerance for human weakness, both weakness in succumbing to pressure and a weak resolve to keep abreast of one's legal duties. By rejecting human weakness as a defense, the criminal law takes a stand in favor of ideal human behavior. The law thus becomes our moral teacher. Those otherwise excused might be punished, but only in the name of bringing everyone to a higher standard of behavior.

The refutation of this utilitarian argument requires a shift of attention away from creating a better society toward the imperative of doing justice in the particular case. In *Director of Public Prosecutions v. Lynch*, (1975) A.C. 653, the majority of five judges in the House of Lords expressed this orientation by holding duress available as an excuse in a homicide case, at least in a situation in which the accused merely drove the car to the scene of the murder. Lord Morris rejected the utilitarian view that the law's standard should be higher than the average man can fairly be expected to attain: "The law would be censorious and inhumane which did not recognize the appalling plight of a person who perhaps suddenly finds his life in jeopardy unless he submits and obeys" (671). In *Lovercamp*, the leading case recognizing a defense in cases of escaping prison to avoid a threatened rape, the court reasoned with similar emphasis: "In a humane society some attention must be given to the individual dilemma"

(827; 112). These arguments express compassion for the situation of the accused.

Justification and excuse: similarities and differences

Claims of excuse and of justification have some features in common. In cases of duress or personal necessity, the actor must be aware of the circumstances excusing his conduct; otherwise, it could hardly be said that the circumstances influenced that conduct. Further, these two excuses apply only if the actor responds to an imminent risk of harm. Again, this requirement finds its warrant in the principle that only circumstances overwhelming the actor's freedom of choice should generate excuses. These same requirements appear in justificatory claims, such as those of self-defense and lesser evils, but in that context they express different rationales for limiting the respective defenses.

Three distinctions between claims of justification and of excuse warrant emphasis. First, claims of justification are universal. They extend to anyone aware of the circumstances that justify the nominal violation of the law. If the threatened victim may justifiably defend himself against unlawful aggression, then others in a position to do so may justifiably intervene on his behalf. This feature of universality follows from the justification's rendering the violation right and proper. Excuses, in contrast, are personal and limited to the specific individual caught in the maelstrom of circumstances. This limitation derives from the required element of involuntariness in excused conduct. Sometimes excuses are defined so as to permit intervention on behalf of "relatives or other people close to the actor" who are threatened with imminent harm (German (Federal Republic) Penal Code § 35). The actor's intervening on behalf of this limited circle of endangered people might well be sufficiently involuntary to warrant excuse. Intervention on behalf of strangers is thought to be freely chosen and therefore not subject to excuse.

Second, claims of justification rest, to varying degrees, on a balancing of interests and the judgment that the justified conduct furthers the greater good (or lesser evil). Excuses do not ostensibly call for a balancing of interests. Inflicting harm far greater than that threatened to the actor might well be excused. Yet, indirectly, an assessment of the relation between the harm done and harm avoided might inform our judgment whether the wrongful conduct is sufficient-

ly involuntary to be excused. Committing perjury to avoid great bodily harm would probably be excused, but committing mayhem on several people to avoid minor personal injuries would probably not be. As the gap between the conflicting interests widens, the assessment of the actor's surrendering to external pressures becomes more stringent. This covert attention to the conflicting interests elucidates the normative basis for finding conduct "involuntary."

Third, claims of justification and of excuse derive from different types of norms in the criminal law. Claims of justification rest on norms, directed to the public at large, that create exceptions to the prohibitions of the criminal law. Excuses are different. Excuses derive from norms directed not to the public, but rather to legal officials, judges, and juries, who assess the accountability of those who unjustifiably violate the law. Excusing a particular violation does not alter the legal prohibition. Recognizing mistake of law as an excuse does not change the law; if the excused, mistaken party were to leave the courthouse and commit the violation again, he would clearly be guilty. Neither does recognizing insanity, involuntary intoxication, duress, or personal necessity alter the prohibition against the acts excused on the basis of these circumstances. If someone relies upon the expectation of an excuse in violating the law (say, his ignorance of the law or his being subject to threats), his very reliance creates a good argument against excusing him for the violation. The expectation of an excuse conflicts with the supposed involuntariness of excused conduct.

Identifying excuses

In any given legal system, researchers might encounter difficulty enumerating the recognized excuses. At a certain period of history, certain circumstances might function as an excuse; at a later period the same considerations might be conceptualized as a denial that the act itself is criminal. The fate of the common law excuses *se defendendo* (self-defense) and *per infortunium* (inevitable accident) illustrates this process. In the common law of homicide, both of these defenses generated the exemption from punishment known as "excusable homicide" (Blackstone, pp. 182–187; Cal. Penal Code § 195). Treating these claims as excuses reflected the assumption that any killing of another human being was criminal or wrongful. The excuse did not negate this wrongfulness but rather, in the idiom of civil pleading, merely "confessed" the wrong and sought to "avoid" the consequences.

Today both of these claims are treated as denials that the act is criminal. As noted above, the excuse of *se defendendo* has given way to the statutory justification of self-defense. The excuse of *per infortunium* has undergone a reconceptualization, and functions now in the form of a denial that the killing was either intentional or negligent. Because it is now assumed that a wrongful killing must be either intentional or grossly negligent, the claim of accident challenges the wrongfulness of the killing.

If these excuses have been absorbed into the analysis of wrongfulness, other claims, properly regarded as justificatory, are occasionally treated as excuses. A good example is the claim of *respondeat superior*, or superior orders. This claim arises if a soldier or citizen executes "an order of his superior . . . which he does not know to be unlawful" (Model Penal Code § 2.10). If the order is lawful, then presumably the execution would also be regarded as lawful. A lawful act does not raise a question of excusability. However, if the order is unlawful, the actor's ignorance of the legal quality of the order and of his execution might excuse him by analogy with mistake of law. The Model Penal Code formulation encompasses both of these variations in one provision and locates the section in its chapter devoted primarily to claims of excuse rather than justification. The implicit analogy with duress in Section 2.09 of the Code stresses the coercive, rather than the legitimating, aspect of superior military orders.

Although the distinction between claims of justification and of excuse remains defensible in principle, Anglo-American legal thought has yet to achieve consensus regarding the exact nature not only of superior orders but of duress, personal necessity, and mistake of law.

GEORGE P. FLETCHER

See also ACTUS REUS; JUSTIFICATION: THEORY; MENS REA; MISTAKE; STRICT LIABILITY.

BIBLIOGRAPHY

American Law Institute. *Model Penal Code and Commentaries (Official Draft and Commentaries)*. Philadelphia: ALI, 1985.
ARENELLA, PETER. "Convicting the Morally Blameless: Reassessing the Relationship Between Legal and Moral Accountability." *UCLA Law Review* 39, no. 6 (1992): 1511–1622.
BLACKSTONE, WILLIAM. *Commentaries on the Laws of England* (1765–1769), vol. 4. Reprint. Chicago: University of Chicago Press, 1979.
BRANDT, RICHARD B. "A Utilitarian Theory of Excuses." *Philosophical Review* 78 (1969): 337–361.
CORRADO, MICHAEL LOUIS. *Justification and Excuse in the Criminal Law: A Collection of Essays*. New York: Garland, 1994.
COUGHLIN, ANNE M. "Excusing Women." *California Law Review* 82, no. 1 (1994): 1–93.
DOLINKO, DAVID. "Intolerable Conditions as a Defense to Prison Escapes." *UCLA Law Review* 26, no. 5 (1979): 1126–1182.
DRESSLER, JOSHUA. "Justifications and Excuses: A Brief Review of the Concepts and the Literature." *Wayne Law Review* 33, no. 4 (1987): 1155–1175.
———. *Understanding Criminal Law*, 2d ed. New York: Matthew Bender, 1995.
FLETCHER, GEORGE P. "The Individualization of Excusing Conditions." *Southern California Law Review* 47, no. 4 (1974): 1269–1309.
———. *Rethinking Criminal Law*. Boston: Little, Brown, 1978.
———. "Commentary: Should Intolerable Conditions Generate an Excuse or Justification for Escape?" *UCLA Law Review* 26, no. 6 (1979): 1355–1369.
HART, H. L. A. *Punishment and Responsibility: Essays in the Philosophy of Law*. Oxford, England: Oxford University Press/Clarendon Press, 1968.
HUSAK DOUGLAS N. *Philosophy of Criminal Law*. Totowa, N.J.: Rowman and Littlefield, 1987.
KADISH, SANFORD H. "Excusing Crime." *California Law Review* 75, no. 1 (January 1987): 257–289.
KATZ, LEO. *Bad Acts and Guilty Minds: Conundrums of the Criminal Law*. Chicago: University of Chicago Press, 1987.
LYONS, DAVID. "On Sanctioning Excuses." *Journal of Philosophy* 66 (1969): 646–660.
MOORE, MICHAEL S. "Causation and the Excuses." *California Law Review* 73, no. 4 (1985): 1091–1149.
MORSE, STEPHEN J. "Excusing and the New Excuse Defenses: A Legal and Conceptual Review." *Crime and Justice: An Annual Review of Research*. Edited by Michael H. Tonry. Chicago: University of Chicago Press, 1998, pp. 329–406.
PILLSBURY, SAMUEL H. "The Meaning of Deserved Punishment: An Essay on Choice, Character, and Responsibility." *Indiana Law Journal* 67, no. 3 (1992): 719–752.

ROBINSON, PAUL H. *Criminal Law Defenses.* St. Paul: West Publishing Company, 1984.

SCHOEMAN, FERDINAND. *Responsibility, Character, and the Emotions.* Cambridge: Cambridge University Press, 1987.

SCHOPP, ROBERT. *Automatism, Insanity, and the Psychology of Criminal Responsibility.* Cambridge, England: Cambridge University Press, 1991.

SENDOR, BENJAMIN B. "Mistakes of Fact: A Study in the Structure of Criminal Conduct." *Wake Forest Law Review* 25, no. 4 (1990): 707–782.

EXCUSE: DURESS

The defense of duress is typically invoked when someone has been pressured into committing a crime by another person's threat. According to the Model Penal Code, an actor is excused in committing a crime if "he was coerced to do so by the use, or the threat to use unlawful force against his person or the person of another, that a person of reasonable firmness in his situation would have been unable to resist" (Section 209(1)). The defense has been raised, for instance, by a chiropractor who claimed to have been forced to file false medical claims in behalf of a gangster who threatened to kill him otherwise. It was raised by a wife who claimed that the only reason she helped her husband commit a bank robbery is that he would have killed her if she had not. It was raised by a drug smuggler who was caught with several cocaine-filled balloons in his stomach: he argued that both he and his family would have been killed if he hadn't done as he did. Likewise for the driver of the getaway car in a terrorist hit; and the member of a Trinidad commune who killed the girlfriend of another commune member on the instructions of the commune leader. In each of these cases the perpetrator of a serious crime insisted that the duress of being threatened with death, or of seeing his family threatened with death, should excuse him and should result in his acquittal.

The defense has an ancient lineage. It was already recognized in Roman law. Renowned commentators—Blackstone and Hale, for example—and countless judges over the centuries have treated it as a well-established part of the common law. Yet despite this ancient lineage, there are periodic calls for its abolition and persistent questions about its scope and rationale.

The nature of the threat

What sort of threat will justify the invocation of the defense? First, the threat has to be quite serious. It will not suffice for the defendant to say that unless he had agreed to help another man break into a bank, the man would have taken some of his own property. Second, the threat has to be illegal. It will not suffice for the defendant to say that unless he had committed a bank robbery, he would not have had the money to repay his mortgage and would have lost his house. Third, the threat has to be directed either at the defendant or at a member of the defendant's family. What if it is the daughter of a close friend of the defendant whom the defendant is acting to protect? That's probably not enough for a valid duress claim.

A fourth and quite puzzling aspect of the threat is that it has to have a human source to trigger the duress defense. In other words, it is not enough that the defendant finds himself in a situation in which terrible harm will befall him unless he commits a crime. The terrible harm that might befall him must emanate from a human threat. To see what that means, consider the case of a driver whose car has been commandeered by an escaping prisoner, and who is being forced at gunpoint to drive that prisoner to his hideout. As he is heading down a narrow mountain road at breakneck speed, he comes across a drunk lying in the middle of the street. He would like to stop to push the drunk aside, but the escaping prisoner says he will shoot the driver unless he keeps driving, and so he runs the man over. If the driver is later charged with murder, he might well qualify for the duress defense. But suppose instead that when the driver is heading down that mountain road there is no escaping prisoner by his side trying to prevent him from stopping. Unfortunately, however, his brakes are not working; and if he were to try to avoid hitting the drunk by swerving he would plunge into the adjacent abyss. Not wanting to die, he runs the drunk over instead. If he is later charged with murder, he would almost certainly not qualify for the duress defense, because the threat of death that he averted by killing emanated not from a person but from "nature." Yet in a sense there is not all that much of a difference between the two situations. In both the driver is confronted with the choice between killing the drunk on the pavement or dying himself (in the first situation, by being killed by the escaping prisoner, and in the second situation, by falling into the abyss). Nevertheless in the one case, the terrible choice he faces will excuse him, but in the other case it will not.

Why should the source of the threat make a difference? A typical if not wholly satisfactory answer is provided by the drafters of the Model Penal Code: "There is [this] significant difference between the situation in which an actor [commits a crime] under the threat of unlawful human force and when he does so because of a natural event. In the former situation, the basic interests of the law may be satisfied by prosecution of the agent of unlawful force; in the latter circumstance, if the actor is excused, no one is subject to the law's application" (Section 2.09(3)). In other words, if the threat is human, there will generally be someone for us to punish, the person who issued the threat. But if the threat is "natural," then the only human agent available for punishment is the defendant. Not everyone has been convinced by this reasoning. Why does it matter whether there is or is not someone for us to punish, they ask. Isn't the only relevant question whether the driver who faces a terrible choice really deserves to be punished?

The nature of the crime

Some think that duress, if it is sufficiently severe, will excuse any crime. According to the traditional common law position, however, killings, and maybe even treason, can never be excused by duress. In recent times, this issue was most vividly posed in *Lynch v. Director of Public Prosecutions*, the aforementioned British case involving someone who had been pressured by terrorists to drive their getaway car for them while they executed their hit, and in *Abbot v. The Queen*, another British case, this one involving the member of a commune who had been pressured by the commune's leader to kill the girlfriend of another fellow member. In several lengthy opinions, the House of Lords worried that if we fail to excuse someone who kills because he will otherwise himself be killed we are essentially punishing people for not being heroes, and that seems unduly exacting. On the other hand, if we fail to punish we may be giving a

charter to terrorists, gangleaders and kidnappers. A terrorist of notorious violence might, e.g., threaten death to A and his family unless A obeys his instructions to put a bomb with a time fuse set by A in a certain passenger aircraft and/or in a thronged market, railway station or the like. A, under duress, does obey his instructions and as a result, hundreds of men, women and children are killed or mangled. Should the contentions made in behalf of [the defendant in this case] be correct, A would have a complete defense

and, if charged, would have to be acquitted and set at liberty. Having now gained some real experience and expertise, he might again be approached by the terrorist who would make the same threats and exercise the same duress under which A would then give a repeat performance, killing even more men, women and children. Is there no limit to the number of people you may kill to save your life and that of your family? (*Abbot v. The Queen*; quoted in Katz, p. 68)

For a while the House of Lords split the difference, by granting a duress defense to those who merely assisted in a killing, like Lynch, but denying it to those who actually committed the killing, like Abbott. That difference came to seem too unprincipled and was later abandoned; the duress defense was once more unavailable for all cases involving homicide, whether the defendant had participated in the killing as a principal or as a mere accomplice.

Controversy has also surrounded the availability of the duress defense to prisoners who break out of prison to escape threatened rapes, assaults, or other unbearable aspects of prison life. Technically the duress defense is a little hard to apply to such cases, since the fleeing prisoner is not really being coerced into fleeing, but rather is simply fleeing to avoid being raped, beaten, or killed. But this is not the main thing that has worried courts in granting the defense. Their real worry is a practical one, namely that granting it would unduly encourage prison escapes (*People v. Unger*; *People v. Harmon*; *People v. Lovercamp*).

The Model Penal Code, and the American jurisdictions that follow it, do not exclude any crime from the scope of the duress defense.

The mistaken defendant

What if the defendant is mistaken in thinking he is being threatened? Suppose he misunderstood; suppose he mistakenly read menacing implications into an adversary's genuinely innocent remark that "he hoped he would have a long and healthy life." If his mistake is reasonable, he is probably still entitled to claim the defense. A reasonable misunderstanding is generally deemed deserving of protection. But what if he was unreasonable? What if a reasonable person would not have dreamed of reading a threat into such innocuous language? Some jurisdictions would then automatically deny him the defense. Others take a more refined approach. They allow the defendant to invoke the defense if he is charged with intentional wrongdoing, but not if he is merely charged with an offense involving unreasonable risk-taking. So, for instance, if someone commits a murder under the unreasonable misimpression that he will be killed unless he does so, he would still be entitled to plead duress. But suppose he is merely charged with manslaughter (which is usually understood to refer to reckless killings); he would then not be able to invoke the defense. That makes good sense: when he intentionally killed someone under the unreasonable misimpression that if he did not do so he would himself be killed, he committed the equivalent of an unexcused, reckless killing.

The semiculpable defendant

Courts have also been much troubled by the case of the defendant who has kept bad company and thus gotten himself into the situation where someone thinks to bear pressure on him to commit a crime: the defendant who joins a gang and is then rightfully fearful about leaving it or about not doing what is asked of him, lest he be killed in retribution. Some jurisdictions deny the duress defense altogether in such cases, in which, as the Model Penal Code puts it, "the actor recklessly placed himself in a situation in which it was probable that he would be subjected to duress" (Section 2.09(2)). Other jurisdictions grant the excuse in cases of intentional wrongdoing, but deny it for crimes of recklessness. (In other words, the defendant can plead duress to a charge of murder, but not to one of manslaughter; he can plead it to a charge of mayhem, but not to one of reckless endangerment.)

Of course there will be considerable disagreement over whether the defendant is being subjected to duress because he "recklessly placed himself in a situation which it was probable that he would be subjected to duress." Should Abbott, the man who joined that Trinidad commune whose leader asked him to kill the girlfriend of another commune member, be judged to have done so? Should the prisoner who flees prison in the face of an impending rape or assault be so judged? (After all, he committed crimes that made it not unlikely that he would be caught and put in the company of other dangerous criminals.) The answer is unclear.

The unreasonably fearful defendant

What if the defendant just is not very courageous, in fact is neurotically fearful and easily moved to commit a crime even just to escape a threat that someone else with more fortitude might have withstood? Usually, the law will then deny him the defense. The law insists on a reasonable amount of fortitude. To be sure, there is some elasticity in the way many codes are written. The Model Penal Code refers to threats that "a person of reasonable firmness in the [defendant's] situation would have been unable to resist." The reference to the defendant's situation allows us to consider many of the circumstances that might make someone unusually fearful—"stark, tangible factors that differentiate the actor from another, like his size, strength, age, or health," as the Model Penal Code (Section 2.09(1)) puts it—but it is certainly not meant to include the fact that the defendant just happens to be possessed of an unusually pusillanimous temperament. Still, there are many mysteries about which circumstances should be taken into account in judging the reasonableness of the defendant's submission to a threat. Consider the hypothetical scenario posed by one commentator about "Frieda, an aspiring novelist [with] a day job in a jewelry store. Clarice steals the only manuscript copy of the novel Frieda has been working on for seven years, and threatens to destroy it unless Frieda leaves the store's door unlocked and the burglar alarm off so that Clarice can burglarize it (which Clarice proceeds to do)" (Kaplan et al., p. 681). Ordinarily we would expect a reasonable person to tolerate the destruction of a piece of his property rather than commit a crime. Are we to take into account Frieda's special hopes and ambitions in judging her? The answer is not obvious.

The imminence of the threat

Suppose the defendant is told that unless he helps a would-be bank robber, he is going to be killed some months in the future. Many codes would refuse the duress defense because the threat is not imminent. It is unclear why. Sometimes the imminence requirement is justified on the grounds that there are things that can still be done to avert a nonimminent threat. But of course that need not always be true. An alternative justification for the imminence requirement is that unless a threat is imminent, a reasonable defendant just would not feel pressured enough to commit a crime.

Brainwashing

Master Sergeant William Olsen was captured during the Korean War by the Communist forces in late 1950 and taken to the Kangye prisoner of war camp. There the Chinese who ran the camp set out to "reeducate" him and his fellow prisoners as to the true nature of the war, namely that "they were the victims of the warmongers and were the aggressors in Korea" (*U.S. v. Olsen*, 20 C.M.R. 461 (1955)). This "reeducation" was in no way haphazard. It was systematic and relentless, involving countless hours of lecturing, group discussion, and interrogation. The Chinese called this treatment of the POWs "lenient policy," because it was short on threats and long on "persuasion." Over the course of the war, it proved remarkably successful. It got American POWs to do things the Germans during World War II had never gotten them to do. They informed on each other, frustrated each other's escape attempts, and in one way or another almost all collaborated with the enemy. The capstone of the Chinese strategy was "start small and build," a technique that the psychologist Robert Cialdini describes thus:

Prisoners were frequently asked to make statements so mildly anti-American or pro-Communist as to seem inconsequential. ("The United States is not perfect." "In a Communist country, unemployment is not a problem.") But once these minor requests were complied with, the men found themselves pushed to submit to related yet more substantive requests. A man who had just agreed with his Chinese interrogator that the United States is not perfect might then be asked to make a list of these "problems with America" and to sign his name to it. Later he might be asked to read his list in a discussion group with other prisoners. "After all, it's what you believe, isn't it?" Still later, he might be asked to write an essay expanding on his list and discussing these problems in greater detail.

The Chinese might then use his name and his essay in an anti-American radio broadcast beamed not only to the entire camp but to other POW camps in North Korea as well as to American forces in South Korea. Suddenly he would find himself a "collaborator," having given aid and comfort to the enemy. Aware that he had written the essay without any strong threats or coercion, many times a man would change his image of himself to be consistent with the deed and with the new "collaborator" label, often resulting in even more extensive acts of collaboration. (Cialdini, p. 76)

The issue that arose in the aftermath of the war was whether soldiers who had committed treason might argue that "brainwashing" of the kind Cialdini here describes constitutes a kind of duress. Generally courts have refused to extend the notion of duress this far. After all, the kind of "coercive persuasion" involved usually did not contain actual threats of physical harm—that's what makes it brainwashing. But many commentators have insisted that in at least some such cases the defendant comes to be so far in the thrall to some power as to warrant the invocation of the excuse nonetheless. The most famous recent case in which duress-by-brainwashing was unsuccessfully argued is that of Patty Hearst, the newspaper heiress, who was kidnapped by a group calling itself the Symbionese Liberation Army and who let herself be "persuaded" to participate in a bank heist. Since she was not actually forced to participate, but did so "voluntarily," she was denied the duress excuse.

Superior orders: husbands and wives

A soldier who knowingly obeys an illegal order from a superior will not be able to invoke the duress defense, unless he was threatened with great physical harm for disobedience. Strangely enough, in days of yore, a wife who obeyed her husband's order to commit a crime, automatically was granted the duress defense. That rule has now been entirely repudiated.

Rationale

Why do we have the law of duress? Its justification has been as controversial as its scope. One simple justification is due to Thomas Hobbes, the seventeenth-century political philosopher and author of *Leviathan*. According to Hobbes, we grant the duress defense because it simply would not do any good to threaten someone subject to duress with punishment. He would still not be moved to act any differently. "If a man, by the terror of present death, be compelled to do a fact against the law, he is totally excused, because no law can oblige a man to abandon his own preservation . . . [for] a man would reason thus: If I do it not, I die presently; if I do it, I die afterwards; thereby by doing it, there is time of life gained" (Part 2, Chapter 27). This is not a very satisfactory line of argument. First, it is not true that the defendant who is subject to duress cannot be deterred from committing a crime. If the punishment threatened is more severe than the ill treatment being threatened by the criminal, deterrence is possible. Some situations of duress involve threats against someone's family. If the law countered by threatening the man with a lengthy prison sentence, he might well desist the temptation to save his family by committing a crime. Sir James Stephens, the famous nineteenth-century criminal law commentator, famously put the matter thus: "Surely it is at the moment when the temptation to [commit] the crime is strongest . . . that the law should speak most clearly and emphatically to the contrary" (Kadish and Schulhofer, p. 901). In addition, there is the fact that we do not punish merely to deter, but to mete out just retribution. Thus it really is irrelevant that the defendant acting under duress cannot be deterred. The question is whether he deserves to be punished.

A second justification offered for the duress defense is that the defendant does not deserve to be punished because he did the right thing. If I am threatened with being killed unless I help out in a burglary, is it not perfectly appropriate for me to commit the burglary? Isn't preserving my own life more important than preserving someone else's property? Given the choice between two evils—my death or someone else's being burglarized—isn't the burglary the lesser of those evils? There are three difficulties with this way of justifying the duress defense. First, we do not actually need the duress defense to exonerate the defendant who breaks a law when doing so is the lesser of two evils. The criminal law recognizes a separate defense, sometimes referred to as the choice-of-evils defense, sometimes as the defense of necessity, which provides that "conduct which the actor believes to be necessary to avoid a harm or evil to himself or to another is justifiable [if] the harm or evil sought to be avoided by such conduct is greater than that sought to be prevented by the law defining the offense charged" (MPC, Section 3.02(a)). A second difficulty with this way of justifying the duress defense is that many duress cases do not involve defendants who chose the lesser of two evils. The duress defense might well be claimed by someone who helped kill several persons in order to save his own life. He clearly did not choose the lesser of two evils; but he still might merit being excused. A third difficulty with saying the defendant did the right thing is that we are not really moved to let the defendant off because he did the right thing even if he did the right thing, but because we feel sorry for him and are inclined to forgive him for having yielded to intolerable pressure.

A third rationale sometimes proposed for the duress defense is that somehow what the defendant did was not fully voluntary. He was in the thrall of some other person. As the British case *Regina v. Hudson* put it, "the will of the accused has been overborne by threats of death or serious personal injury so that the commission of the alleged offense [is] no longer the voluntary act of the accused" (Regina v. Hudson 2 All E.R. 244, 246 (C.A. 1971)). But to many commentators this does not make much sense. A person facing a terrible choice is not lacking in volition, he is lacking in good choices. A person choosing to escape execution by executing someone else is not like someone acting out of reflex, or in an epileptic seizure, or during a hypnotic trance. Those are instances of genuinely involuntary behavior. Not so the person acting under duress.

A fourth rationale for the duress defense simply argues that it would be unfair to punish someone for failing to stand up to the extraordinary pressure exerted during a situation of duress. The law cannot ask people to be heroes. As the Model Penal Code commentary puts it, it would be unfair to punish if "judges are not prepared to affirm that they . . . could comply with the law if their turn to face the problem should arise" (Section 2.09(2)).

A final rationale offered for the duress defense is that the defendant in such cases is usually displaying extremely laudable character traits. If he is committing a crime to protect his family, he is showing the kind of filial devotion that we generally admire. If he is committing the crime to protect his own life, he is showing an instinct for self-preservation that we think on the whole desirable. It is true that under the circumstances these laudable character traits are prompting him to act in not so laudable ways. But that just shows that a proclivity to commit bad actions under special circumstances is the price of having a generally good character. That, the argument goes, should lead us to excuse the defendant as a kind of noble miscreant.

LEO KATZ

See also ACTUS REUS; EXCUSE: THEORY; JUSTIFICATION: NECESSITY; JUSTIFICATION: SELF-DEFENSE; MENS REA; PRISONS: PROBLEMS AND PROSPECTS.

BIBLIOGRAPHY

American Law Institute. *Model Penal Code and Commentaries*. Philadelphia: ALI, 1980.

BLACKSTONE, WILLIAM. *Commentaries on the Laws of England (1765–1769)*, vol. 4. Chicago: University of Chicago Press, 1979.

CARR, CRAIG L. "Duress and Criminal Responsibility." *Law and Philosophy*. 10 (1991): 161.

CIALDINI, ROBERT. *Influence: The New Psychology of Persuasion*. New York: Morrow, 1984. Pages 76–77.

DRESSLER, JOSHUA. "Exegisis of the Law of Duress: Justifying the Excuse and Searching for Its Proper Limits." *Southern California Law Review* 62 (1989): 1331.

————. *Understanding Criminal Law*. New York: Matthew Bender/Irwin, 1995. Chapter 23.

FINGARETTE, HERBERT. "Victimization: A Legalist Analysis of Coercion, Deception, Undue Influence, and Excusable Prison Escape." *Washington & Lee Law Review* 42 (1985): 65.

FINKELSTEIN, CLAIRE. "A Philosophical Account of the Defense in Law." *Arizona Law Review* 37 (1995): 251.

FLETCHER, GEORGE. *Rethinking Criminal Law*. Boston: Little, Brown, 1978. Chap. 10.

HALE, MATTHEW. *The History of Pleas of the Crown, vol. 1*. Edited by W. A. Stokes and E. Ingersoll. Philadelphia: Small, 1847.

HITCHLER, WALTER HARRISON. "Duress as a Defense in Criminal Cases." *Virginia Law Review* 4 (1917): 519.

HOBBS, THOMAS. *The Leviathan*. New York: Cambridge University Press.

KADISH, SANFORD H., and SCHULHOFER, STEPHEN J., (eds.). *Criminal Law and its Processes: Cases and Materials,* 6th edition. New York: Aspen Publishers, 1995.

KAPLAN, JOHN; WEISBERG, ROBERT; and BINDER, GUYORA (eds.). *Criminal Law: Cases and Materials,* 4th edition. Gathersburg, N.Y.: Aspen Law and Business, 2000.

KATZ, LEO. *Bad Acts and Guilty Minds*. Chicago: Univ. of Chicago Press, 1987.

NEWMAN, LAWRENCE, and WEITZER, LAWRENCE. "Duress, Free Will, and the Criminal Law." *Southern California Law Review* 30 (1957): 313.

NOZICK, ROBERT. "Coercion." In *Philosophy, Science, and Method: Essays in Honor of Ernest Nagel*. New York: St. Martin's Press, 1969. Page 440.

STEPHENS, JAMES. *History of Criminal Law in England*.

WASLIK, MARTIN. "Duress and Criminal Responsibility." *Criminal Law Review* 1977: 453.

CASES

Abbot v. The Queen, (1976) 3 All ER 140 (Privy Council).

U.S. v. Contento-Pachon, 723 F.2d 691, 693 (9th Cir. 1984).

People v. Harmon (1974), 53 Mich. App. 482, 220 N.W.2d 212.

Regina v. Hudson, 2 All E.R. 244, 246 (C.A. 1971).

People v. Lovercamp (1974), 43 Cal. App. 3d 823, 118 Cal. Rptr. 110.

Lynch v. Director of Public Prosecutions of Northern Ireland (1975) 1 All ER 913.

U.S. v. Olsen, 20 C.M.R. 461, 462 (1955).

People v. Romero, 10 Cal. App. 4th 1150, 13 Cal. Rptr. 2d 332 (1992).

State v. Toscano, 74 N.J. 421, 378 A.2d 755 (1977).

People v. Unger, 66 Ill. 2d 333, 362 N.E.2d 319 (1977).

EXCUSE: INFANCY

The infancy defense, which dates back to the common law and is still recognized in some form or another in the vast majority of jurisdictions, bars the prosecution of children below a specified age (age seven at common law) and presumptively precludes prosecution of older minors (ages seven to fourteen at common law) in the adult criminal justice system (although, under modern statutes, children in the latter group are still eligible for prosecution in juvenile delinquency proceedings).

Origin and rationale

At common law, children below the age of seven were deemed *doli incapax*—irrebuttably presumed to be incapable of forming criminal intent and therefore immune from prosecution for a crime. Children between the ages of seven and fourteen were presumptively *doli incapax* but that presumption could be rebutted by "very strong and pregnant evidence" by the state that the child had the "discretion to judge between good and evil" and "understood what he did" (Hale, pp. 26–27). According to William Blackstone, the infancy defense reflected both a judgment about the impropriety of exacting punishment upon those who were not responsible for their actions and the practical consideration that categorically immunizing all children from prosecution could "propagat[e] a notion that children might commit . . . atrocious crimes with impunity" (pp. 22–24). The infancy defense was carried over into the criminal law of the United States along with other traditional concepts of English law, and it shaped the course of early prosecutions of children. Several states codified the doctrine in their penal codes.

The chronological distinctions drawn by the infancy defense comport (albeit, not neatly) with classic social scientific theories about child development and maturation, particularly the works of Anna Freud and Erik Erikson on children's mental functioning and the works of Jean Piaget and Lawrence Kohlberg on children's moral growth. Current psychological research on children's maturity and mental capacity supports the view that "decision-making capacities increase through childhood into adolescence and that, although there is great variability among individuals, preadolescents and younger teens differ substantially from adults in their abilities" (Scott and Grisso, pp. 137, 157).

Modern status

The infancy defense has been largely superseded by the establishment of a dual adult/ juvenile justice system in which (1) the juvenile court has jurisdiction over prosecutions of children below a certain age (usually set at ages sixteen, seventeen, or eighteen), although typically "waiver" or "transfer" statutes provide for adult criminal prosecution of children at the upper end of the juvenile court's age bracket if they are charged with enumerated serious crimes; and (2) in some states, a juvenile court statute or case law categorically bars the prosecution of very young children (usually following the common law in designating the age at seven, although some states set the minimum age at ten). Adult penal code statutes in some states explicitly refer to the infancy defense in denominating children who fall within the juvenile court's jurisdiction as ineligible for adult court prosecution unless the state shows at a waiver or transfer hearing that the child should be deemed criminally responsible for his or her acts. (See, e.g., N.Y. Penal Code § 30.00. See also *Model Penal Code* § 4.10 (Official Draft 1985), "Immaturity Excluding Criminal Conviction; Transfer of Proceedings to Juvenile Court.")

In essence, the foregoing structure tracks the original contours of the infancy defense by immunizing very young children from prosecution and by treating most older minors as presumptively ineligible for adult criminal prosecution. What this approach leaves uncertain, however, is what, if any, role the infancy defense should play in juvenile delinquency cases. Most of the state courts that have addressed the issue have declared that the infancy defense is inapplicable to juvenile court prosecutions because it was intended to guard children from the harshness of the adult penal system and therefore has no relevance to a rehabilitation-oriented juvenile court system. (See, e.g., *Gammons v. Berlat*, 144 Ariz. 148, 696 P.2d 700 (Ariz. 1985); *In re Tyvonne*, 211 Conn. 151, 558 A.2d 661 (Conn. 1989); *In the Interest of G.T.*, 409 Pa. Super. 15, 597 A.2d 638 (Pa.

1990).) Some courts, however, have relied upon the common law doctrine to construe the applicable statutes as prohibiting prosecution of young children who lack the capacity to appreciate the wrongfulness of their actions or to form the mental element of the charged offense. (See *In re William A.*, 393 Md. 690, 698–699, 548 A.2d 130, 134 (1988), infancy defense is "a firmly established principle of common law" and therefore juvenile code's silence on subject must be construed as signifying legislative intent that defense remain in effect. See also *In the Matter of Robert M.*, 110 Misc.2d 113, 116, 441 N.Y.S.2d 860, 863 (N.Y. Fam. Ct. 1981) (although finding traditional infancy defense to be inapplicable to delinquency cases, court relies on common law and social scientific literature to construe juvenile code as prohibiting conviction of those children whose "immaturity . . . negatives the requisite specific intent" to commit charged crime).)

The infancy defense and concepts akin to it are likely to play an increasingly important role in both adult and juvenile court in the coming years. In the 1980s and 1990s, due at least in part to high-profile cases of youth violence and politicians' calls for aggressive responses, there have been significant increases in the number of children transferred to adult court for prosecution and there appear to be increases in the number of juvenile court prosecutions of very young children. At the same time, emerging psychological data are raising significant questions about the capacity of even older adolescents to make competent waivers of rights and other judgments expected of criminal defendants. As a result, there may be greater attention paid to existing infancy defense statutes that apply to adult criminal prosecutions and further litigation on the applicability of the defense to juvenile court. Moreover, a social scientist has suggested that the data available thus far calls for the adoption of a new standard of "adjudicative competence," which would prohibit adult court prosecutions of adolescents who are less capable than adults to understand the nature of the proceedings and to participate meaningfully in their own defense (see Grisso and Schwartz, forthcoming).

Although the infancy defense is framed in a way that makes it relevant solely at the guilt-innocence stage of a criminal trial, the doctrine's underlying rationale also supports the treatment of the young age of the offender as a factor that should mitigate punishment. Indeed, this reasoning is necessarily implicit in the case law deeming the defense to be inapplicable to a juvenile court system that is designed to rehabilitate, not punish, offenders. The criminal justice system has, in various ways, recognized that youth is relevant to mitigation of punishment (e.g., in death penalty statutes and sentencing guidelines that treat youth as a mitigating factor and in judges' sentencing decisions in individual cases) but the legislatures and courts thus far have not adopted a categorical approach to the subject of youth at sentencing. Indeed, the Supreme Court has held that the Eighth Amendment's cruel and unusual punishment clause does not bar execution of children who were at least sixteen at the time of the crime (*Stanford v. Kentucky*, 492 U.S. 361 (1989)) even though several states' statutes and international conventions prohibit the execution of individuals who were under the age of eighteen at the time of the crime.

RANDY HERTZ

See also AGE AND CRIME; EXCUSE: THEORY; JUVENILE JUSTICE: HISTORY AND PHILOSOPHY; JUVENILE JUSTICE: JUVENILE COURT; JUVENILES IN THE ADULT SYSTEM.

BIBLIOGRAPHY

BAZELON, LARA. "Note. Exploding the Superpredator Myth: Why Infancy is the Pre-Adolescent's Best Defense in Juvenile Court." *New York University Law Review* 75 (April 2000).
BLACKSTONE, WILLIAM. *Commentaries on the Law of England.* Philadelphia: Robert H. Small, 1825.
GRISSO, THOMAS, and SCHWARTZ, ROBERT G., eds. *Youth on Trial: A Developmental Perspective on Juvenile Justice.* Chicago: University of Chicago, 2000.
HALE, MATTHEW. *The History of the Pleas of the Crown.* Dublin: E. Lynch, 1860.
SCOTT, ELIZABETH S., and GRISSO, THOMAS. "The Evolution of Adolescence: A Developmental Perspective on Juvenile Justice Reform." *Journal of Criminal Law and Criminology* 88, no. 1 (1997): 137–189.
WALKOVER, ANDREW. "The Infancy Defense in the New Juvenile Court." *UCLA Law Review* 31, no. 3 (1984): 503–562.

EXCUSE: INSANITY

If a person pleads "not guilty by reason of insanity" (NGRI), that plea means that the person committed the underlying act (that would have been criminal had she had the requisite *mens rea*, or guilty mind), but, because of mental illness, is not to be held responsible for that act. A series of perplexing and difficult questions remains: What should the test be to determine if a defendant is not criminally responsible for her act? If a person is found NGRI, what procedures are to be followed subsequent to the insanity acquittal? And, what do we know about the use of the plea, its success rate, and its implications for those who plead it?

Notwithstanding centuries of jurisprudential evolution, the insanity defense doctrine remains incoherent. Most judges, legislators, scholars, mental health professionals, social policy makers, jurors, journalists, and the public at large would agree with this proposition. This consensus is consistent whether the observer is a retentionist, a modified retentionist, an expansionist, or an abolitionist. Moreover, fixation on questions fundamentally irrelevant to the core jurisprudential inquiry of whom we shall exculpate has resulted in doctrinal stagnation. Immobilized by this irresoluble debate, we continue to ignore even more fundamental questions, such as why we feel the way we do about the "insane" and why, in further structuring the insanity defense, we remain willfully blind to new scientific and empirical realities.

The development of the insanity defense has tracked the tension between psychodynamics and punishment, and reflects our most profound ambivalence about both. On the one hand, we are especially punitive toward persons with mental disabilities who have been charged with crime, characterized by Deborah Scott and her colleagues as "the most despised and feared group in society" (1982); on the other, we recognize that in some narrow and carefully circumscribed circumstances, exculpation is—and historically has been—proper and necessary. This ambivalence infects a host of criminal justice policy issues that involve mentally disabled criminal defendants beyond insanity defense decision-making: on issues of expert testimony, mental disability as a mitigating (or aggravating) factor at sentencing and in death penalty cases, and the creation of a "compromise" guilty but mentally ill (GBMI) verdict. And the dissonances, tensions, and ambivalences reflected in insanity defense policy continue to control the public's psyche.

This entry will proceed in this manner. First, it will review the development of substantive insanity defense doctrine, and procedures followed after an insanity acquittal. Next, it will consider the impact of the John Hinckley case on subsequent doctrinal developments. Then, it will examine the empirical myths that underlie much of the insanity defense debate. Finally, it will look briefly at the abolition movement.

Development of insanity defense doctrine

Pre-*M'Naghten* history. The development of the insanity defense prior to the mid-nineteenth century tracked both the prevailing scientific and popular concepts of mental illness, "craziness," responsibility, and blameworthiness. In existence since at least the twelfth century, the defense has always aroused more discussion than any other topic of substantive criminal law, despite that fact that there were few insanity pleas entered prior to the mid-eighteenth century. Prior to the 1843 *M'Naghten* decision, the substantive insanity defense went through three significant stages: the "good and evil" test, the "wild beast" test, and the "right and wrong" test.

"Good and evil." The "good and evil" test apparently first appeared in a 1313 case involving the capacity of a child under the age of seven. The test reflected the moral dogmata of the medieval theological literature. The insane, like children, were incapable of sinning against their will since, according to the research done by Bernard Diamond and a colleague, man's freedom "is restrained in children, in fools, and in the witless who do not have reason whereby they can choose the good from the evil (1233)."

"Wild beast." The "wild beast" test appeared in *Rex v. Arnold*, an 1812 case in which the defendant had shot and wounded a British Lord in a homicide attempt. Judge Tracy instructed the jury that it should acquit by reason of insanity in the case because "a mad man . . . must be a man that is totally deprived of his understanding and memory, and doth not know what he is doing, no more than *a brute, or a wild beast*, such a one is never the object of punishment."

The emphasis was on lack of *intellectual ability*, rather than the violently wild, ravenous beast image that the phrase calls to mind; the test continued to be used until at least 1840.

"Right and wrong." The "right and wrong" test (the true forerunner of *M'Naghten*) emerged in two 1812 cases; in the second of the two, the jury was charged that it must decide whether the defendant "had sufficient understanding to distinguish good from evil, right from wrong . . ." (*Bellingham's Case*, pp. 477, 671). The test was expanded upon in 1840 in *Regina v. Oxford* where the jury was told that it must determine whether the defendant, "from the effect of a diseased mind," knew that the act was wrong, and that the question that must thus be answered was whether "he was quite unaware of the nature, character, and consequences of the act he was committing" (546–47).

Even with these rigid tests in place, the public's perceptions of abuse of the insanity defense differed little from its reactions in the aftermath of the Hinckley acquittal nearly a century and a half later. The public's representatives demanded an "all or nothing" sort of insanity, a conceptualization that has been "peculiarly foreign" to psychiatry since at least the middle of the nineteenth century.

M'Naghten. In 1843, the "most significant case in the history of the insanity defense in England" (Perlin, Jurisprudence, at 79) arose out of the shooting by Daniel M'Naghten of Edward Drummond, the secretary of the man he mistook for his intended victim: Prime Minister Robert Peel. After nine medical witnesses testified that M'Naghten was insane, and after the jury was informed that an insanity acquittal would lead to the defendant's commitment to a psychiatric hospital, M'Naghten was found not guilty by reason of insanity (NGRI).

In response to Queen Victoria's fury over the verdict, the House of Lords asked the Supreme Court of Judicature to answer five questions regarding the insanity law, and the judges' answers to two of these five became the *M'Naghten* test:

[T]he jurors ought to be told in all cases that every man is presumed to be sane, and to possess a sufficient degree of reason to be responsible for his crimes, until the contrary be proved to their satisfaction; and that to establish a defence on the ground of insanity, it must be clearly proved that, at the time of the committing of the act, the party accused was labouring under such a defect of reason, from disease of the mind, as not to know the nature and quality of the act he was doing; or, if he did know it, that he did not know he was doing what was wrong (722).

The M'Naghten Rules reflected a theory of responsibility that was outmoded far prior to its adoption, and which bore little resemblance to what was known about the human mind, even at the time of their promulgation. Nonetheless, with almost no exceptions, they were held as sacrosanct by American courts that eagerly embraced this formulation, and codified it as the standard test "with little modification" in virtually all jurisdictions until the middle of the twentieth century.

Post-*M'Naghten* developments.

Irresistible impulse. There was some interest in the post-*M'Naghten* years in the so-called irresistible impulse exception that allowed for the acquittal of a defendant if his mental disorder moved him to be unable to resist committing an offense he fully understood to be wrong. However, this formulation was not more than a transitory detour in the development of an insanity jurisprudence. Where it has generally been applied, it has been used in conjunction with *M'Naghten*, rather than by itself.

Durham. The first important theoretical alternative to *M'Naghten* emerged in the District of Columbia in the 1954 case of *Durham v. United States.* Writing for the court, Judge David Bazelon rejected both the *M'Naghten* and the irresistible impulse tests on the theory that the mind of man was a functional unit, and that a far broader test would be appropriate. *Durham* thus held that an accused would not be criminally responsible if his "unlawful act was the product of mental disease or mental defect" (1874–75).

Durham was the first modern, major break from the *M'Naghten* approach; as a result, the District of Columbia became a laboratory for consideration of the details of insanity, in its fullest substantive and procedural ramifications. Within a few years, however, *Durham* was judicially criticized, modified, and ultimately dismantled by the D.C. Circuit. The test's burial was completed by the 1972 decision in *United States v. Brawner* to adopt the Model Penal Code/American Law Institute test.

United States v. Brawner. *Brawner* discarded *Durham*'s "product" test, but added a *volitional* question to *M'Naghten*'s cognitive inquiry. Under this test, a defendant would not be responsible for his criminal conduct if, as a result of mental disease or defect, he "lack[ed] substantial capacity either to appreciate the criminality of his conduct or to conform his conduct to the requirements of law" (979).

Although the test was rooted in *M'Naghten*, there were several significant differences. First, the test's use of the word "substantial" was meant to respond to case law developments that had required "a showing of total impairment for exculpation from criminal responsibility" (p. 87). Second, the substitution of the word "appreciate" for the word "know" showed that "a sane offender must be emotionally as well as intellectually aware of the significance of his con-

duct" (p. 87), and "mere intellectual awareness that conduct is wrongful when divorced from an appreciation or understanding of the moral or legal import of behavior, can have little significance" (p. 87). Third, by using broader language of mental impairment than had *M'Naghten*, the test captured both the cognitive and affective aspects of impaired mental understanding. Fourth, the test's substitution in the final proposed official draft of the word "wrongfulness" for "criminality" reflected the position that the insanity defense dealt with an impaired moral sense rather than an impaired sense of legal wrong.

It was assumed that the spreading adoption of *Brawner* would augur the death of *M'Naghten*, an assumption that—in the light of the attempted assassination of then-President Ronald Reagan and the subsequent passage of the Insanity Defense Reform Act (IDRA)—has proven to be totally inaccurate. *Brawner*, did, however, serve as the final burial for the *Durham* experiment.

Guilty but mentally ill (GBMI). Perhaps the most important post-*Brawner* development in substantive insanity defense formulations has been the adoption in over a dozen jurisdictions of the hybrid "guilty but mentally ill" (GBMI) verdict, adopted, ostensibly, in the words of a Michigan state case (*People v. Seefeld*), to "protect the public from violence inflicted by persons with mental ailments who slipped through the cracks of the criminal justice system" (290 Mich. App. 123, 124 (ct. app. 1980)).

The rationale for the passage of GBMI legislation was that the implementation of such a verdict would decrease the number of persons acquitted by reason of insanity, and would assure treatment of those who were GBMI within a correctional setting. A GBMI defendant would purportedly be evaluated upon entry to the correctional system and be provided appropriate mental health services either on an in-patient basis as part of a definite prison term or, in specific cases, as a parolee or as an element of probation.

Practice under GBMI statutes reveals that the verdict does little or nothing to ensure effective treatment for mentally disabled offenders. As most statutes vest discretion in the director of the state correctional or mental health facility to provide a GBMI prisoner with such treatment as she "determines necessary" (p. 65), the GBMI prisoner is not ensured treatment beyond that available to other offenders. A comprehensive study of the operation of the GBMI verdict in Georgia revealed that only three of the 150 defendants who were found GBMI during the period in question were being treated in hospitals.

Post-insanity acquittal procedures. In 1983, the Supreme Court—in *Jones v. United States*—made it clear that different procedural rules could apply to individuals hospitalized pursuant to an insanity acquittal than to persons who had been involuntarily civilly committed. The *Jones* court—over a strong and impassioned dissent—concluded that, because a successful insanity defense established beyond a reasonable doubt that the defendant committed the underlying criminal act, it was reasonable to conclude that such a person remained dangerous, mentally ill, and in need of treatment. Thus, it was not unconstitutional to force an insanity acquittee to bear the burden of proof at a release hearing, nor was it unconstitutional for such a person to be institutionalized for a longer period of time than would have been permissible had she been given the maximum sentence for the underlying crime.

Some states provide more liberal procedures. For instance, in *State v. Krol* (a case that predates *Jones* by eight years), the New Jersey Supreme Court found that there was little difference between commitments initiated through a civil process and those begun through a criminal process, and provided substantially identical procedures for both universes.

Hinckley and its aftermath

The insanity acquittal of John W. Hinckley for the attempted murder of President Ronald Reagan in 1981 galvanized the American public in a way that led directly to the reversal of 150 years of study and understanding of the complexities of psychological behavior and the relationship between mental illness and certain violent acts. The public's outrage over a jurisprudential system that could allow a defendant who shot an American president on national television to plead "not guilty" (for *any* reason) became a river of fury after the jury's verdict was announced.

Sensational trials such as Hinckley's consume the hearts and minds of the American public. They reflect our basic dissatisfaction with the perceived incompatibility of the due process and crime control models of criminal law, and with the notion that psychiatric "excuses" can allow a "guilty" defendant to "beat a rap" and escape punishment. Such dissatisfaction leads to a predictable response, especially when the defen-

dant—like Hinckley—is perceived as one not sufficiently "like us" so as to warrant empathy or sympathy. As Loren Roth has suggested, when a "wrong verdict" is entered in a sensational trial, the American public may simply be nothing more than a "bad loser" (Perlin, Borderline, at 1380).

Members of Congress responded quickly to the public's outrage by introducing twenty-six separate pieces of legislation designed to limit, modify, severely shrink, or abolish the insanity defense; the debate on these bills illuminates with clarity the character of the legislative decision-making process. Statements by legislators introducing these bills or by Reagan Administration spokespersons supporting them reflected the fears and superstitions that have traditionally animated the insanity debate, as well as the public's core ambivalence about mentally disabled criminal defendants.

The legislation ultimately enacted by Congress—legislation that closely comported with the public's moral feelings—returned the insanity defense to status quo ante 1843, the year of *M'Naghten*. Besides relocating the burden of proof in insanity trials to defendants (18 U.S.C. § 17), establishing strict procedures for the hospitalization and release of defendants found not guilty by reason of insanity (18 U.S.C. § 4243 et seq.), and severely limiting the scope of expert testimony in insanity cases (Federal Rules of Evidence 704 (b)), the IDRA discarded the ALI–Model Penal Code test, and adopted a more restrictive version of *M'Naghten*, by specifying that the level of mental disease or defect that must be shown to qualify be "severe" (18 U.S.C. § 17(a)).

Prior to the Hinckley trial, the burden of proof in all federal courts (and in about half the states) was on the prosecution to prove a defendant's sanity beyond a reasonable doubt. Many observers placed the "blame" for the jury's subsequent acquittal on this allocation, and the question of burden shifting became a major subject of controversy at the subsequent Congressional insanity defense hearings. The IDRA responded to these concerns and placed the burden of proof in insanity defense cases on the defendant, and specified a burden of proof of "clear and convincing evidence."

This change was significant for two main reasons. First, symbolically, it underscored Congress's dissatisfaction with a system that appeared to make it "easier" for jurors to acquit in insanity cases. Second, empirically, by making the quantum greater than a preponderance (previously, the standard allocation in jurisdictions where the burden was on the defendant to prove insanity), it gave researchers the opportunity to investigate the "real life" impact of both the burden shift (as to party) and the especially heavy quantum of proof that the defendant will be responsible to prove.

The states quickly followed the lead of the federal government. Two-thirds of all states reevaluated the defense; as a result, twelve states adopted the guilty but mentally ill (GBMI) test, seven narrowed the substantive test, sixteen shifted the burden of proof, and twenty-five tightened release provisions in the cases of those defendants found to be NGRI. Three states adopted legislation that purported to abolish the defense, but actually retained a mens rea exception.

Empirical data and myths

Researchers agree that, in the small universe of successful insanity defense pleaders, a person with a history of major mental illness, who has sought help for that illness, and whose victim is a member of the immediate family (certainly a non-stranger) will be most likely to be found NGRI by a jury. Both successful and unsuccessful insanity pleaders are more frequently single, caucasian, somewhat older, and better educated than the usual defendant group, unemployed at the time of the insane offense, and with a history characterized by chronic unemployment, prior psychiatric treatment, drug abuse, alcohol abuse, and previous arrests.

In the wake of the Hinckley verdict, commentators began to examine carefully the "myths" that had developed about the insanity defense, in an effort to determine the extent to which this issue has been distorted in the public eye. The research shows that (1) the insanity defense opens only a small window of nonculpability; (2) defendants who successfully use the NGRI plea "do not beat the rap"; and, perhaps more importantly, (3) the tenacity of these false beliefs in the face of contrary data is profound.

Myth #1: The insanity defense is overused. All empirical analyses have been consistent: the public at large and the legal profession (especially legislators) dramatically and grossly overestimate both the frequency and the success rate of the insanity plea, an error that is undoubtedly abetted by the media's bizarre depictions, distortions, and inaccuracies in portraying individuals with mental illness charged with crimes.

The insanity defense is used in only about 1 percent of all felony cases, and is successful just about one-quarter of the time.

Myth #2: Use of the insanity defense is limited to murder cases. In one jurisdiction where the data have been closely studied, contrary to expectations, slightly less than one-third of the successful insanity pleas entered over an eight-year period were reached in cases involving a victim's death. Further, individuals who plead insanity in murder cases are no more successful in being found NGRI than persons charged with other crimes.

Myth #3: There is no risk to the defendant who pleads insanity. Defendants who asserted an insanity defense at trial, and who were ultimately found guilty of their charges, served significantly longer sentences than defendants tried on similar charges who did not assert the insanity defense. Unsuccessful NGRI pleaders are incarcerated for a 22 percent longer time than individuals who never raise the plea (Braff, Arvantes, Steadman, *Detention Patterns of Successful and Unsuccessful Insanity Defendants*, 21 Criminal. 439, 445 (1983)). The same ratio is found when only homicide cases are considered.

Myth #4: NGRI acquittees are quickly released from custody. Of the entire universe of individuals found NGRI over an eight-year period in one jurisdiction, only 15 percent had been released from all restraints; 35 percent remained in full custody, and 47 percent were under partial court restraint following conditional release. A comprehensive study of California practice showed that only 1 percent of insanity acquittees were released following their NGRI verdict and that another 4 percent were placed on conditional release; the remaining 95 percent were being hospitalized. In other recent research, Stephen Golding and his colleagues discovered, in their study of all persons found NGRI in the Canadian province of British Columbia over a nine-year period, that the average time spent in secure hospitalization or supervision was slightly over nine and one-half years.

Myth #5: NGRI non-murderer acquittees spend much less time in custody than do defendants convicted of the same offenses. Contrarily, two-thirds of the NGRI acquittees—those who are not murderers—spend almost double the amount of time that defendants convicted of similar charges spend in prison settings, and often face a lifetime of post-release judicial oversight. In California, while the length of confinement for individuals acquitted by reason of insanity on murder charges was less than for those convicted, defendants found NGRI for other violent crimes were confined twice as long as those found guilty of such charges, and those found NGRI of nonviolent crimes were confined for periods over nine times as long.

Myth #6: Criminal defendants who plead insanity are usually faking. This is perhaps the oldest of the insanity defense myths, and is one that has bedeviled American jurisprudence since the mid-nineteenth century. Of the 141 individuals found NGRI in one jurisdiction over an eight-year period, there was no dispute that 115 were persons with schizophrenia (including 38 of the 46 cases involving a victim's death), and in only three cases was the diagnostician unwilling or unable to specify the nature of the patient's mental illness. Also, most studies show that 80–84 percent (see Perlin, Jurisprudence, at 111 n.178), depending on study, of NGRI defendants have significant histories of prior hospitalizations.

Myth #7: Most insanity defense trials feature "battles of the experts." The public's false perception of the circus-like "battle of the experts" is one of the most telling reasons for the rejection of psychodynamic principles by the legal system. A dramatic case such as the *Hinckley* trial thus "reinforced the public's perception that the insanity defense is characterized by battles of experts [who] overwhelm" the jury, engendering judicial and public skepticism as to the ability of psychiatrists to actually come to reasoned and reasonable judgments in cases involving mentally disabled individuals charged with crime.

The empirical reality is quite different. In a Hawaii survey, there was examiner congruence on insanity in 92 percent of all cases; in Oregon, prosecutors agreed to insanity verdicts in 80 percent of all cases. Most importantly, these are not recent developments: over thirty-five years ago, a study of the impact of the Durham decision in Washington, D.C., found that between two-thirds and three-quarters of all insanity defense acquittals were uncontested. In short, the empirical evidence refuting this myth has been available to judges, legislators, and scholars since almost a decade prior to the adoption of the ALI–Model Penal Code test in *Brawner*.

Myth #8: Criminal defense attorneys—perhaps inappropriately—employ the insanity defense plea solely to "beat the rap." Attorneys representing mentally disabled defendants have—for decades—been routinely criticized for seeking refuge in the insanity defense

as a means of technically avoiding a deserved conviction. In reality, the facts are quite different. First, the level of representation afforded to mentally disabled defendants is frequently substandard. Second, the few studies that have been done paint an entirely different picture; lawyers also enter an insanity plea to obtain immediate mental health treatment for their client, as a plea-bargaining device to insure that their client ultimately receives mandatory mental health care, and to avoid malpractice litigation. Third, the best available research suggests that jury biases exist relatively independent of lawyer functioning, and are generally not induced by attorneys.

Since the mid-1980s, researchers and other scholars have been patiently rebutting these myths. The publication by Henry Steadman and his colleagues of their extended multi-jurisdiction study of virtually every empirical facet of insanity defense pleading proves—beyond any doubt—that the basic tenets are mythic. The extent to which the dissemination of these data alters the terms of the insanity defense debate will reveal whether these myths, in fact, can be reinterpreted by lawmakers and the general public.

The abolitionist movement

While the movement to abolish the insanity defense dates to the turn of the century, its contemporaneous revival can be traced to the Nixon Administration's unsuccessful attempts to limit its use to cases where the defendant, by mental disease or defect, "lacked the state of mind required as an element of the offense charged" (S.1, 94th Cong., 1st sess., 6522 (1975). Perlin, unpacking at 670). This proposed limitation has been characterized as the "lemon squeezer" exception: the defense would apply only where the defendant thought the strangulation-victim's head was a lemon.

Henry Steadman and his colleagues have published important data giving us some inklings as to what actually happens when abolition is attempted. Their research reveals that, basically, "abolition" in Montana was a pretext. First, "abolition" had no meaningful statistical impact on the number of defendants pleading NGRI. Defendants continued to allege that they lacked the requisite mens rea for criminal responsibility.

Second, defendants who previously would have been found NGRI are now found incompetent to stand trial. Two-thirds of these were subsequently committed indefinitely to state hospitals where they were frequently treated on the same units as patients who had been found NGRI prior to abolition "reform." In short, the insanity statutes were reformed, but the detention system was not. It is certainly possible that some of the post-"abolition" pleas were the result of defense counsel wanting to "flag" for the court that the defendants were seriously mentally ill, and in need of psychiatric hospitalization. This is precisely the same strategy often employed by counsel in jurisdictions where the defense has not been abolished.

It is not yet clear what impact Steadman's empirical breakthrough will have on politically motivated abolitionist measures. If the Montana experience is a representative one, then the full measure of the abolition charade is clear. The defense is "abolished" in name, but the plea is entered for pretextual reasons. Severely mentally ill criminal defendants are treated in the same wards of the same forensic hospitals to which they would have been sent had they been found NGRI. This suggests the meretriciousness of much of the politically based abolition movement: voters are being told that their representatives are "doing something" about the crime problem, but only the labels describing the patients' forensic status change.

Conclusion

The insanity defense has always been part of the fabric of criminal law. It is used rarely, successfully more rarely, and its "successful" use generally brings with it significant costs to the pleader (in terms of both stigma and length of institutional stay). The defense remains a prisoner of both behavioral and empirical myth; although these myths bear virtually no resemblance to reality, they have come to symbolize the public's perception of the defense and the plea. It is doubtful that any other area of criminal law is more poorly understood.

MICHAEL L. PERLIN

See also COMPETENCY TO STAND TRIAL; DIMINISHED CAPACITY; EXCUSE: THEORY; MENS REA; MENTALLY DISORDERED OFFENDERS; PSYCHOPATHY.

BIBLIOGRAPHY

BAZELON, DAVID. *Questioning Authority: Justice and Criminal Law.* New York: Knopf, 1988.

BONNIE, RICHARD. "The Moral Basis of the Insanity Defense." *American Bar Association Journal* 69 (1983): 194–197.

CALLAHAN, LISA; MAYER, CONNIE; and STEADMAN, HENRY. "Insanity Defense Reform in the United States—Post-Hinckley." *Mental and Physical Disability Law Reporter* 11 (1987): 54–59.

CALLAHAN, LISA; McGREEVY, MARGARET; ROBBINS, PAMELA; and STEADMAN, HENRY. "The Volume and Characteristics of Insanity Defense Pleas: An Eight-State Study." *Bulletin of the American Academy of Psychiatry and Law* 19 (1991): 331–338.

CAPLAN, LINCOLN. *The Insanity Defense and the Trial of John W. Hinckley, Jr.* Boston: Godine, 1984.

DRESSLER, JOSHUA. "Justifications and Excuses: A Brief Review of the Concepts and the Literature." *Wayne Law Review* 33 (1987): 1155–1175.

———. *Understanding Criminal Law.* 2d ed. New York: Matthew Bender, 1995.

Federal Rule of Evidence 704(b).

FENTIMAN, LINDA. "'Guilty But Mentally Ill': The Real Verdict is Guilty." *Boston College Law Review* 12 (1985): 601–653.

FINGUETTE, HERMAN. *The Meaning of Criminal Insanity.* Berkeley: University of California Press, 1972.

GOLDING, STEPHEN, et al. "The Assessment, Treatment, and Community Outcome of Insanity Acquittees." *International Journal of Law and Psychiatry* 13 (1989): 281–307.

GOLDSTEIN, ABRAHAM. *The Insanity Defense.* New Haven, Conn.: Yale University Press, 1967.

Insanity Defense Reform Act 1988. 18 U.S.C. § 17.

MICKENBERG, IRA. "A Pleasant Surprise: The Guilty But Mentally Ill Verdict Has Succeeded in Its Own Right and Successfully Preserved the Insanity Defense." *University of Cincinnati Law Review* 55 (1987): 943–996.

Model Penal Code. 1955 (tentative draft No. 4) § 4.01.

MOORE, MICHAEL S. *Law and Psychiatry: Rethinking the Relationship.* New York: Cambridge University Press, 1984.

———. *Placing Blame: A General Theory of the Criminal Law.* Oxford, UK: Clarendon Press, 1997.

MORRIS, NORVAL. *Madness and the Criminal Law.* Chicago: University of Chicago Press, 1982.

MORSE, STEPHEN. "Excusing the Crazy: The Insanity Defense Reconsidered." *Southern California Law Review* 58 (1985): 777–836.

Pasewark, Richard, et al. "Successful and Unsuccessful Insanity Plea Defendants in Colorado." *Journal of Psychiatry and Law* 15 (1987): 55–71.

Perlin, Michael L. *Mental Disability Law: Civil and Criminal.* Charlottesville, Va.: The Michie Company, 1989. Supplemented yearly.

———. "Unpacking the Myths: The Symbolism Mythology of the Insanity Defense." *Case Western Reserve Law Review* 40 (1989–1990): 599–731.

———. "Psychodynamics and the Insanity Defense: 'Ordinary Common Sense' and Heuristic Reasoning." *Nebraska Law Review* 69 (1990): 3–70.

———. *The Jurisprudence of the Insanity Defense.* Durham, N.C.: Carolina Academic Press, 1994.

———. "The Insanity Defense: Deconstructing the Myths and Reconstructing the Jurisprudence." In *Law, Mental Health, and Mental Disorder.* Edited by Bruce D. Sales and Daniel W. Shuman. Pacific Grove, Calif.: Brooks/Cole, 1996. Pages 341–359.

———. "'The Borderline Which Separated You From Me': The Insanity Defense, the Authoritarian Spirit, the Fear of Faking, and the Culture of Punishment." *Iowa Law Review* 82 (1997): 1375–1426.

———. "'Big Ideas, Images, and Distorted Facts': The Insanity Defense, Genetics, and the 'Political World.'" In *Genetics and Criminality: The Potential Misuse of Scientific Information in Court.* Edited by Jeffrey R. Botkin, William M. McMahon, and Leslie Pickering Francis. Washington, D.C.: American Psychological Association, 1999.

Platt, Anthony, and Diamond, Bernard. "The Origins of the 'Right and Wrong' Test of Criminal Responsibility and Its Subsequent Development in the United States: An Historical Survey." *California Law Review* 54 (1966): 1227–1260.

Ray, Isaac. *Medical Jurisprudence of Insanity,* 3d ed. Boston, Mass.: Little, Brown, 1853.

Rodriguez, Joseph, et al. "The Insanity Defense Under Siege: Legislative Assaults and Legal Rejoinders." *Rutgers Law Journal* 14 (1983): 397–430.

Roth, Loren. "Preserve but Limit the Insanity Defense." *Psychiatric Quarterly* 58 (1986–1987): 91–105.

Scott, Deborah C., et al. "Monitoring Insanity Acquittees: Connecticut's Psychiatric Security Review Board." *Hospital and Community Psychiatry* 41 (1990): 980–984.

Slobogin, Christopher. "The Guilty But Mentally Ill Verdict: An Idea Whose Time Should Not Have Come." *George Washington Law Review* 53 (1985): 494–527.

Steadman, Henry. *Reforming the Insanity Defense: An Evaluation of Pre- and Post-Hinckley Reforms.* New York: Guilford, 1993.

Steadman, Henry, et al. "Factors Associated with a Successful Insanity Plea." *Archives of General Psychiatry* 35 (1983): 773–782.

Steadman, Henry, et al. "Maintenance of an Insanity Defense Under Montana's 'Abolition' of the Insanity Defense." *American Journal of Psychiatry* 146 (1989): 357–360.

Wexler, David. "An Offense-Victim Approach to Insanity Defense Reform." *Arizona Law Review* 26 (1984): 16–25.

CASES

Bellingham's Case, Old Bailey Session Papers 263 (1812) (no. 433).
Durham v. United States, 214 f. 2d 862 (D.C. Cir. 1954), *overruled* in *United States v. Brawner,* 471 f. 2d (D.C. Cir. 1972).
Jones v. United States, 463 U.S. 354 (1983).
M'Naghten's Case, 8 Eng. Rep. 718 (1843).
Regina v. Oxford, 9 Carr, & P. 525 (1840).
Rex v. Arnold, 16 How. St. Tr. 695 (1724).
State v. Krol, 344 A. 2d 289 (N.J. 1975).
United States v. Brawner, 471 F. 2d 969 (D.C. Cir. 1972).

EXCUSE: INTOXICATION

The importance of intoxication as a criminal defense can be easily exaggerated. In many cases the defense is legally barred, where available it is often rejected on factual grounds by the decision maker, and even when successful it normally serves to reduce the level of conviction rather than excuse entirely. Yet intoxication remains of great interest to the student of criminal law, for intoxication arguments raise the full range of responsibility issues, from criminal intent to problems with rationality and self-control.

Voluntary intoxication

Whether a voluntarily intoxicated person may assert a so-called intoxication defense in a criminal case will depend on: (1) whether the jurisdiction permits intoxication evidence to be used to negate the criminal intent, or mens rea, required for the offense; and (2) if so, whether it appears likely that the accused actually did lack the required mens rea because of intoxication.

Courts have long emphasized that evidence of voluntary intoxication goes only to the narrow issue of mens rea, such as intent to steal or intent to kill. Defendants may not claim excuse based on intoxication-induced personality change or associated loss of self-control, even though these effects may be central to the intoxicant's criminogenic effect. The usual rationale for this position is that the person who chooses to become intoxicated must take the consequences of that choice, especially if those consequences prove dangerous to others. The criminal law's policy also accords with its presumption of unitary personal identity. The law presumes that every individual human is a single responsible entity, regardless of the often dramatic personality chances caused by mood, intoxication, or circumstance.

Beginning in the nineteenth century, English and American courts began to allow defendants to use voluntary intoxication in arguments about mens rea. In a compromise between general principles of culpability, which argue for unrestricted use of intoxication evidence, and public safety worries about the dangers of the intoxicated, which point the law in the opposite direction, courts developed the specific intent doctrine. Defendants may use evidence of voluntary intoxication to negate a form of mens rea known specific intent, but not those—more common—forms of mens rea known as general intent (*People v. Hood*, 463 P.2d 370 (Cal. 1969); *D.P.P. v. Majewski*, (1976) All.E.R. 142). Thus the critical distinction is whether the particular crime is one of specific or general intent.

To illustrate, consider a case in the United States where a defendant is charged with first-degree premeditated murder, a crime of specific intent. The defendant may argue that because of inebriation he lacked the specific intent—the premeditation—necessary for the offense. He may argue that intoxication meant he acted without the cool and calculated resolve to kill that is premeditation. If the decision-maker agrees, but finds that all other elements of the offense are established, the defendant will be convicted of some lesser, general intent form of homicide.

The specific intent approach to intoxication has proven highly durable for a number or reasons. The specific versus general intent distinction suggests a hierarchy of mental states that seems to accord with the effects of intoxication. We know that intoxication commonly interferes with higher levels of mental functioning. The approach also has a built-in public safety limit in its restriction to specific intent crimes. The widespread availability of general intent offenses means that few intoxicated harm-doers will go entirely unpunished. Nevertheless, the doctrine has some major flaws.

Courts and commentators have long noted that the line between general and specific intent is often obscure, dependent more on the form of words and accidents of historical interpretation than on principled distinctions. In different jurisdictions, or at different times, the same offenses can be oppositely characterized. For example, depraved-heart murder is sometimes labeled a crime of general intent and sometimes one of specific intent (*People v. Whitfield*, 868 P.2d 272 (Cal. 1994) (specific intent); *People v. Langworthy*, 331 N.W.2d 171 (Mich. 1982) (general intent)). The doctrine's public safety limitation in reality proves unreliable; especially in areas of more modern criminal legislation, there may be no general intent crime, with the result that voluntary intoxication can support a complete excuse. Nor does the specific versus general distinction necessarily track the seriousness of offense. One of the most serious criminal offenses, rape, is a general intent crime, while less serious offenses such as burglary and larceny are categorized specific intent crimes. Finally, the specific versus general intent distinction does not in fact involve a hierarchy of higher and lower mental functioning. In most instances voluntary intoxication does not negate specific intent, though it might—if allowed—negate general intent.

In an effort to avoid the manifold difficulties of specific intent analysis, the drafters of the influential Model Penal Code eliminated the specific intent distinction in favor of four basic mens rea forms: purposely, knowingly, recklessly, and negligently (section 2.02). With regard to voluntary intoxication the Code states that such evidence may be used to negate purposely or knowingly mens reas. Intoxication is explicitly barred from consideration of recklessness mens rea; it is definitionally barred from negligence analysis because a judgment of negligence depends on the defendant having grossly deviated from the conduct of a the reasonable person in the situation—and the reasonable person is a sober one (sections 2.08, 2.02(d)).

The Model Penal Code's approach to voluntary intoxication has been praised for its clarity, but has drawn its own criticisms, particularly with regard to the recklessness exclusion. How is a fact finder to know what a particular person would have realized if sober? Even more troubling, the exclusion appears inconsistent with the

Code's general presumption that actual awareness of criminally significant facts is critical to culpability.

We now move to the second set of voluntary intoxication issues: assuming the law allows defendants to argue no mens rea based on intoxication, will the argument work? Will the judge or jury agree that proof of mens rea fails due to intoxication? Here we confront a deliberate irony of voluntary intoxication doctrine: as a general rule it is most available where it is least likely to work, and least available where it would be most likely to work.

Although generally allowed as a matter of law under both the specific intent doctrine and the Model Penal Code, most arguments that an accused lacks an intentional mens rea will prove implausible on the facts of the case. For example, two men after an afternoon's drinking fall into an argument and then engage in a fight. One pulls out a deadly weapon and uses it to fatal effect. How likely is it that the man who killed the other lacked the purpose to kill because of intoxication? Here the prosecution might use intoxication to bolster its proof of mens rea by arguing that intoxication inspires more powerful emotions, especially anger, and less self-control, making it more likely that an intoxicated—and enraged—person will retaliate by trying (i.e., intending) to kill or do grave bodily injury. Thus the intoxicated defendant probably did act with the required mens rea.

Now consider crimes that involve careless wrongdoing, those bearing the mens rea of recklessness. In these cases under both the Model Penal Code (with its recklessness exclusion) and the specific intent doctrine (where reckless offenses are usually labeled general intent), attacks on mens rea via intoxication are generally barred. Note that if allowed, the accused in such cases might often have a plausible factual argument that he or she did not realize the risks of her conduct because of intoxication. While the prosecution may counter here that intoxication—especially alcohol intoxication—does not so much make the person unaware of risk as unconcerned about it, most lawmakers have feared that jurors will not recognize this distinction.

Doctrinal reform and the trend toward elimination

In the last three decades of the twentieth century, a number of Anglo-American jurisdictions have considered important reforms in voluntary intoxication doctrine. These reform movements have gone in opposite directions, one urging more liberal use of intoxication evidence and the other urging more restrictions on its employment.

Proponents of liberalization have argued that intoxication evidence should be used without restriction to ensure that only persons proven to have acted in conscious disregard of risk should receive serious punishment. To the extent that dangerous conduct might be excused by this approach, proponents have urged the creation of a new offense of dangerous drinking, where culpability would rest on drinking under circumstances likely to lead to wrongful conduct. A proposal of this kind was recently rejected in England, but the no-restriction approach to intoxication evidence has been judicially adopted in some parts of Australia and New Zealand (*R. v. O'Connor* (1980) 54 A.J.L.R. 349 (Australia); *Kamipeli* (1975) 2 N.Z.L.R. 610 (New Zealand)).

In the United States, reform generally has moved toward further restriction of intoxication evidence, with a significant minority of American states recently deciding to either further restrict or prohibit mens rea arguments based on voluntary intoxication (e.g., Ariz. Rev. Stat. Ann. sec. 13-503; Mont. Code Ann. sec. 45-2-203). These changes have raised issues both of constitutionality and justice.

The constitutionality of barring voluntary intoxication evidence under federal law was largely resolved by the U.S. Supreme Court in *Montana v. Egelhoff* (518 U.S. 37 (1996)). In that decision a majority of the justices agreed that Montana's statute barring consideration of intoxication as to mens rea was consistent with the U.S. Constitution's due process requirement that the prosecution prove every essential element of a criminal offense beyond a reasonable doubt. The court's majority was split on why the statute passed constitutional muster, however.

The majority justices disagreed on both the reach of the U.S. Constitution's due process clause and the proper categorization at Montana's statute. Justice Anthony Scalia, writing for a plurality, held that the statute represents a bar on certain mens rea evidence, but that it was permissible because due process allows states wide latitude in establishing rules of evidence. Thus a state may bar certain evidence relevant to an element of the offense as to which the prosecution has the burden of proof, without effecting an unconstitutional shift in the overall burden of proof. In her concurrence, Justice Ginsburg read the Montana statute as a rule of substantive criminal law and voted to uphold on the ground that states have broad latitude to define crimes as they wish, including creating, modifying, or eliminating defenses to those crimes. Meanwhile the four dissenters argued that the statute impermissibly shifted the burden of proof on an essential element of the offense—mens rea—and so violated due process.

Restrictions on intoxication evidence as to mens rea also raise significant justice issues. If, as the criminal law generally presumes, serious blame and punishment require proof of mens rea, then barring important evidence about mens rea is unjust. Only a few counterarguments are available. First, proponents of restriction might argue that the evidentiary bar simply eliminates confusion about mens rea because, as we have seen, intoxication evidence rarely negates criminal intent. Yet there remain some cases where it does. Proponents most commonly argue that a person's fault in becoming drunk makes the person responsible for all subsequent wrongs. This conflates two quite different forms of misconduct, however. Choosing to drink to excess is hardly the moral equivalent of choosing to violently attack or kill another, for example.

A third approach to reform would concentrate on mens rea rather than on intoxication doctrine. If instead of requiring proof of awareness of harm-doing for serious criminality, the law required proof of a demonstrated attitude of indifference to harm-doing, then intoxication evidence could be freely allowed, consistent with both justice and public safety concerns. Under this approach intoxication evidence might in some cases bolster the prosecution's case by demonstrating lack of concern for harm-doing while in other cases might assist the defense by suggesting less culpable reasons for disregard of risk.

Involuntary intoxication

Intoxication is involuntary if the accused took the intoxicant without awareness of its intoxicating nature or if the consumption was coerced. A person claiming this affirmative defense generally must show both that the intoxication was involuntary and that it either: (1) negated the mens rea required for the offense; or (2) created a state of irrationality or loss of self-control similar to insanity.

Involuntary intoxication is most commonly claimed by individuals who take substances unaware that they may be intoxicating, either because they mistook the identity of the substance or its likely effects (*Carter v. State*, 710 So.2d 110 (Fla. Ct. App. 1998) (mistaking anti-depression drug for over-the-counter pain killer); *People v. Scott*, 194 Cal.Rptr. 633, 146 Cal.App.3d 823 (1983) (unknowing ingestion of hallucinogen in punch at a party causing a psychotic episode two days later); *City of Minneapolis v. Altimus*, 238 N.W.2d 851 (Minn. 1976) (ignorance about effect of prescription drugs). On occasion the accused may claim pathological intoxication, a rare condition of extreme and unforeseen susceptibility to an intoxicant (Model Penal Code § 208(5)(c)). A defendant may also claim involuntary intoxication on the ground that the taking of the intoxicant was coerced by another.

Once involuntary intoxication is shown, the defendant may argue lack of mens rea due to intoxication. This argument may be used regardless of the form of mens rea. Under involuntary intoxication there is no distinction between general or specific intent and no recklessness exclusion under the Model Penal Code. On occasion, courts give the offense a broad interpretation to find a form of mens rea relevant to involuntary intoxication (as in *Carter*; knowing intoxication required for driving under the influence where involuntary intoxication was alleged).

The defendant may also argue that involuntary intoxication created a state of temporary insanity. In most jurisdictions, involuntary intoxication may substitute for the mental disease or disorder element of the insanity test. Then the accused must show a major deficit in rationality or in capacity for control, depending on the jurisdiction's test for insanity (*Torres v. State*, 585 S.W.2d 746 (Tex.Cr.App. 1979)).

Finally, a defendant who was involuntarily intoxicated may be able to argue that intoxication rendered him unconscious, thus negating proof of a voluntary act (*R. v. Quick* (1973) All E.R. 347). Generally this argument is not available for voluntary intoxication, as most courts hold the individual responsible for choosing to risk loss of consciousness (*People v. Velez*, 221 Cal.Rptr. 631 (Ct. App. 1985); but c.f. *R. v. O'Connor*).

Conceptually distinct from involuntary intoxication is what has been called "settled insanity," a severe mental disorder that may result from heavy drinking over a long period and that may produce psychosis. Legally this condition falls under insanity, for the person suffers from a long-standing mental disorder not dependent on actual intoxication. Also to be distinguished are those individuals with significant mental problems who become intoxicated; their criminal responsibility should be analyzed under the rules of either voluntary intoxication or insanity based on underlying mental illness.

SAMUEL H. PILLSBURY
HERBERT FINGARETTE
ANN FINGARETTE HASSE

See also ACTUS REUS; ALCOHOL AND CRIME: BEHAVIORAL ASPECTS; ALCOHOL AND CRIME: THE PROHIBITION EXPERIMENT; ALCOHOL AND CRIME: TREATMENT AND REHABILITATION; DIMINISHED CAPACITY; DRINKING AND DRIVING; DRUGS AND CRIME: LEGAL ASPECTS; MENS REA.

BIBLIOGRAPHY

ASHWORTH, ANDREW. *Principles of Criminal Law.* 2d ed. Oxford, U.K.: Clarendon Press, 1995.
DRESSLER, JOSHUA. *Understanding Criminal Law.* 2d ed. New York: Matthew Bender/Irwin, 1995.
KEITER, MICHAEL. "Just Say No Excuse: The Rise and Fall of the Intoxication Defense." *Journal of Criminal Law and Criminology* 87 (1997): 482.
HORDER, JEREMY. "Sobering Up? The Law Commission on Criminal Intoxication." *Modern Law Review* 58 (July 1995): 534.
MITCHELL, CHESTER N. "The Intoxicated Offender—Refuting the Legal and Medical Myths." *International Journal of Law and Psychiatry* 11 (1988): 11.
ORCHARD, GERALD. "Surviving with Majewski—A View From Down Under." *Criminal Law Review* (1993): 426.
PARKER, ROBERT NASH, with REBHUN, LINDA-ANNE. *Alcohol and Homicide: A Deadly Combination of Two American Traditions.* Albany, N.Y.: State University of Albany Press, 1995.
PILLSBURY, SAMUEL H. "Crimes of Indifference." *Rutgers Law Journal* 49 (1996): 105.
SHINER, ROGER. "Intoxication and Responsibility." *International Journal of Law and Psychiatry* 13 (1990): 9.
SWEITZER, BRETT G. "Implicit Redefinitions, Evidentiary Proscriptions, and Guilty Minds: Intoxicated Wrongdoers after *Montana v. Eglehoff.*" *University of Pennsylvania Law Review* 146 (1997): 269.

EYEWITNESS IDENTIFICATION: CONSTITUTIONAL ASPECTS

The classic eyewitness identification takes place in court, with the witness pointing to the defendant and stating "That's the perpetrator." Such identifications are usually preceded by out-of-court identifications, using one of three procedures: (1) lineups, in which a witness is asked to pick a suspect out of a line of people; (2) showups, in which a witness is shown just one suspect and asked whether that suspect was involved in the incident at issue; or (3) photo arrays, in which a witness is asked to pick a suspect's photo out of an array of photos. Constitutional challenges to those procedures have focused on four provisions: the Fourth Amendment's prohibition on unreasonable searches and seizures; the Fifth Amendment's prohibition of compelled self-incriminating testimony; the injunction in both the Fifth and Fourteenth Amendments that government not deprive persons of life or liberty without due process of law; and the Sixth Amendment's guarantee of assistance of counsel and the right to confront witnesses. Each of these challenges are discussed below. Also discussed are two other issues: the process for determining whether an identification procedure was unconstitutional and the admissibility of identifications that are the "fruit" of a constitutional violation.

Search and seizure

The Supreme Court has held that a person does not have a reasonable expectation of privacy in personal characteristics that are exposed to the public, such as one's visage or the sound of one's voice (*United States v. Dionisio*, 410 U.S. 1, 14 (1973)). Thus, viewing a face in a lineup or showup is not a "search" for purposes of the Fourth Amendment prohibition of unreasonable searches and seizures. However, the Court has also held that the police "seizure" of a person for the purpose of subjecting him or her to an identification procedure does implicate the Fourth Amendment (*Hayes v. Florida*, 470 U.S. 811, 816 (1985); *Davis v. Mississippi*, 394 U.S. 721, 724 (1969)). Under these circumstances, the police need, at a minimum, reasonable suspicion that the person is involved in the crime, unless the person is being used as a distractor and is already in custody, in which case no suspicion is necessary.

Self-incrimination

Because the Fifth Amendment privilege against self-incrimination prohibits only compulsion of "testimony," the Supreme Court has held that the government does not violate that Amendment when it compels a person to stand in a lineup, wear certain clothes, and speak for the purposes of voice identification (*Holt v. United States*, 218 U.S. 245, 252–3 (1910); *Schmerber v. California*, 384 U.S. 757, 764 (1966). These actions, while possibly helpful to the prosecution's case against the person and therefore "self-incriminating," are considered "non-testimonial."

Due process

The first Supreme Court case to apply the due process clause to pretrial eyewitness identification procedures intimated that any procedure that unnecessarily suggested to the eyewitness that the defendant was the perpetrator would be declared unconstitutional (*Stovall v. Denno*, 388 U.S. 293, 301–02 (1967)). Although the Court ultimately upheld the one-on-one confrontation in that case because it was "imperative" (the eyewitness was confined to a hospital bed and near death), its language suggested that this "widely condemned" procedure would not have been permitted had there been time to arrange a lineup or photo array. Subsequent to *Stovall* some lower courts adopted a "per se" rule to the effect that unnecessarily suggestive identification procedures should lead to exclusion of identifications thereby produced.

Within a decade, however, the Court made clear that reliability, not unnecessary suggestiveness, is the "linchpin" of due process analysis (*Neil v. Biggers*, 409 U.S. 188, 198–9 (1972); *Manson v. Braithwaite*, 432 U.S. 98, 114 (1977)). The reliability of an eyewitness identification, according to the Court, is to be gauged by the eyewitness' opportunity to view the perpetrator, the degree of attention the eyewitness is able to direct at the perpetrator, the accuracy of any description the eyewitness gives, the witness's level of certainty about the identification, the time between the crime and the eyewitness identification, and like factors. Thus, in *Biggers*, the Court held constitutional a one-on-one confrontation that occurred several months after the crime, because the witness had been with the perpetrator for well over fifteen minutes, had refused to identify the perpetrator during previous lineups

and showups, and was certain of her identification. In *Braithwaite*, an identification of the defendant from a single photo placed on the eyewitness's desk was upheld because the eyewitness viewed the perpetrator for two to three minutes, was a trained police officer, gave a detailed description of the perpetrator, identified the defendant from the photo within two days, and was certain of his identification.

Rights to counsel and confrontation

In *United States v. Wade*, 388 U.S. 218 (1967), a companion case to *Stovall*, the Supreme Court held that persons subjected to lineups after they have been indicted are entitled to the assistance of counsel under the Sixth Amendment. Subsequently, it held that the right to counsel also attaches at post-charge showups (*Moore v. Illinois*, 434 U.S. 220 (1977)). There is no right to counsel at a photo array, however, whether it occurs prior to or after formal charging (*United States v. Ash*, 413 U.S. 300 (1973)). These cases raise three significant issues: How are photo arrays distinguishable from lineups and showups for purposes of the right to counsel? Why does the right to counsel attach only after formal charge? And what is the role of counsel when the right attaches?

Wade justified its decision by concluding that "there is grave potential for prejudice, intentional or not, in the pretrial lineup" and that counsel can "avert [that] prejudice and assure a meaningful confrontation [of it] at trial." In other words, counsel is needed to make sure the lineup is properly conducted and, if he or she fails in that goal, to record its flaws and expose them at later proceedings through cross-examination and presentation of other evidence. Without counsel, defendants would clearly be unable to accomplish the first goal (recording flaws), because they are not trained to notice irregularities and may not even see them, especially if they take place behind a one-way mirror. Even if they do detect problems, defendants are almost as useless in assisting counsel in the second goal (exposing flaws), because their word will be pitted against that of the police or prosecutor.

This rationale supporting counsel's presence at lineups would seem to apply with even more force to photo arrays, since the defendant is not present at the latter type of identification procedure; here defense counsel hoping to expose procedural irregularities is entirely dependent on the police and the eyewitness, who are unlikely to be disposed to help. Yet it was the defendant's absence at the photo array that led the Court, in *Ash*, to reject a right to counsel claim at the latter type of identification procedure. Because the defendant's absence at the photo array means he is not confronted with the "intricacies of the law and the advocacy of the public prosecutor," the Court reasoned, there is no need for counsel at such procedures. Of course, lineups and showups do not involve such confrontations either. The Ash majority also noted that a photo array is more easily reproduced at trial than a lineup procedure but, as the dissent pointed out, the conduct of the police and witness during the photo identification is as important as the array itself in determining reliability. *Ash* seemed to reject *Wade*'s reasoning, but did not overturn it.

There is no right to counsel even at lineups and showups if they take place prior to the formal charging of the defendant (which is usually the case). This was the holding in *Kirby v. Illinois*, 406 U.S. 682, 690 (1972), which construed the Sixth Amendment's language guaranteeing the assistance of counsel "in all criminal prosecutions" to apply only to actions that occur after the initiation of "adversary judicial criminal proceedings . . . by way of formal charge, preliminary hearing, indictment, information, or arraignment." Of course, if counsel is useful in terms of detecting, preventing, or exposing suggestiveness, that would be as true prior to formal charging as after that event. Setting the Sixth Amendment threshold at arrest might make more sense. But in *Kirby*, presaging *Ash*, the Court insisted that only at formal charging is the defendant "faced with the prosecutorial forces of organized society, and immersed in the intricacies of substantive and procedural criminal law" to the extent necessary to require the assistance of counsel.

When the right to counsel does attach, counsel's role is unclear. *Wade* states that counsel can both "avert prejudice" and "assure a meaningful confrontation [of it] at trial." The first role, with its intimation that counsel can suggest changes in procedures, is more active than the second, which implies that the attorney should function as an observer who will then use the observations to the client's advantage at later proceedings. It is unlikely the *Wade* Court meant to give counsel authority to compel particular police procedures. At most, lower courts have held, counsel should be able to make objections and preserve them for the record if police fail to heed them (e.g., *People v. Borrego*, 668 P.2d 21 (Colo.App.

1983)). Moreover, many lower courts have held that counsel is allowed access only to the identification itself, not to collateral components of it such as witness descriptions of the perpetrator or post-procedure interviews of the witnesses (e.g., *United States v. Bierey*, 588 F.2d 620 (8th Cir. 1978)). If the only role of counsel is observation of the procedure, a videotape or snapshot might be constitutionally sufficient; Wade itself recognized that "substitute counsel" may be permissible under the Sixth Amendment.

Process for determining admissibility

The prosecution bears the burden of proving that a waiver of the right to counsel at the identification procedure was voluntary and intelligent, and it also bears the burden of proving that an in-court identification was not tainted by an earlier unconstitutional identification procedure, while the defendant bears the burden of showing a due process violation. Normally, a pretrial "suppression" hearing is held to determine whether a constitutional violation occurred and the identification should be excluded. But in *Watkins v. Sowders*, 449 U.S. 341, 349 (1981), the Supreme Court held that, at least when the defendant makes a due process claim, the admissibility issue may be determined in the presence of the jury, because the issue raised by such claims—whether the identification is reliable—is "the very task our system must assume juries can perform." However, the Court held that pretrial determinations of admissibility "may often be advisable" and perhaps even "constitutionally necessary" if, for instance, the presence of the jury inhibits the attorney's cross-examination of those who conducted the procedure.

Fruits analysis

Even an identification made during a properly conducted procedure may be excluded if it is considered the "fruit" of a constitutional violation. But such exclusions are rare. For instance, social science suggests that identifications made during suggestive procedures can taint later identifications. But courts routinely hold that these later identifications are based on an "independent" memory of the criminal event, using the same types of factors that inform the reliability analysis (e.g., opportunity to view the act). Sometimes identification procedures are properly conducted, but the presence of the suspect in the lineup or showup is the result of an illegal detention under the Fourth Amendment, as described above. The resulting identification may be deemed inadmissible "fruit" of the detention, but a subsequent in-court identification will usually be admissible if the judge finds it is based on an independent recollection of the criminal event (*United States v. Crews*, 445 U.S. 463 (1980)). Because an illegal arrest is not a bar to subsequent prosecution (*Frisbie v. Collins*, 342 U.S. 519 (1952)), the defendant's presence in court and any untainted identification that occurs there is not unconstitutional.

CHRISTOPHER SLOBOGIN

See also CONFESSIONS; COUNSEL: RIGHT TO COUNSEL; CRIMINAL PROCEDURE: CONSTITUTIONAL ASPECTS; EYEWITNESS IDENTIFICATION: PSYCHOLOGICAL ASPECTS; POLICE: POLICE OFFICER BEHAVIOR.

BIBLIOGRAPHY

GRANO, JOSEPH D. "Kirby, Biggers, and Ash: Do Any Constitutional Safeguards Remain against the Danger of Convicting the Innocent?" *Michigan Law Review* 72, no. 4 (1974): 717–794.

GROSS, SAMUEL. "Loss of Innocence: Eyewitness Identification and Proof of Guilt." *Journal of Legal Studies* 16 (1987): 395–453.

LEVINE, FELICE J., and TAPP, JEAN L. "The Psychology of Criminal Identification: The Gap from *Wade* to *Kirby*." *University of Pennsylvania Law Review* 121, no. 3 (1973): 1079–1131.

POLSKY, LEON B.; UVILLER, H. RICHARD; ZICCARDI, VINCENT J.; and DAVIS, ALAN J. "The Role of the Defense Lawyer at a Lineup in Light of the *Wade*, *Gilbert*, and *Stovall* Decisions." *Criminal Law Bulletin* 4, no. 5 (1968): 273–296.

READ, FRANK T. "Lawyers at Lineups: Constitutional Necessity or Avoidable Extravagance?" *UCLA Law Review* 17, no. 2 (1969): 339–407.

ROSENBERG, BENJAMIN. "Rethinking the Right to Due Process in Connection with Pretrial Identification Procedures: An Analysis and a Proposal." *Kentucky Law Journal* 79 (1991): 259–316.

WHITEBREAD, CHARLES, and SLOBOGIN, CHRISTOPHER. *Criminal Procedure: An Analysis of Cases and Concepts*, 4th ed. New York: Foundation Press, 2000. See chaps. 17–18.

CASES

Davis v. Mississippi, 394 U.S. 721 (1969).
Frisbie v. Collins, 342 U.S. 519 (1952).
Hayes v. Florida, 470 U.S. 811 (1985).
Holt v. United States, 218 U.S. 245 (1910).
Kirby v. Illinois, 406 U.S. 682 (1972).
Manson v. Braithwaite, 432 U.S. 98 (1977).
Neil v. Biggers, 409 U.S. 188 (1972).
People v. Borrego, 668 P.2d 21 (Colo. App. 1983).
Schmerber v. California, 384 U.S. 757 (1966).
Stovall v. Denno, 388 U.S. 293 (1967).
United States v. Ash, 413 U.S. 300 (1973).
United States v. Bierey, 588 F.2d 620 (8th Cir. 1978).
United States v. Crews, 445 U.S. 463 (1980).
United States v. Dionisio, 410 U.S. 1 (1973).
United States v. Wade, 388 U.S. 218 (1967).
Watkins v. Sowders, 449 U.S. 341 (1981).

EYEWITNESS IDENTIFICATION: PSYCHOLOGICAL ASPECTS

Eyewitness identification refers to a type of evidence in which an eyewitness to a crime claims to recognize a suspect as the one who committed the crime. In cases where the eyewitness knew the suspect before the crime, issues of the reliability of memory are usually not contested. In cases where the perpetrator of the crime was a stranger to the eyewitness, however, the reliability of the identification is often at issue. Researchers in various areas of experimental psychology, especially cognitive and social psychology, have been conducting scientific studies of eyewitness identification evidence since the mid-1970s. Today, there exists a large body of published experimental research showing that eyewitness identification evidence can be highly unreliable under certain conditions. In recent years, wrongful convictions of innocent people have been discovered through post-conviction DNA testing; these cases show that more than 80 percent of these innocent people were convicted using mistaken eyewitness identification evidence (Scheck, Neufeld, and Dwyer; Wells et al., 1998). These DNA exoneration cases, along with previous analyses of wrongful convictions, point to mistaken eyewitness identification as the primary cause of the conviction of innocent people.

The three distinct phases of memory

Psychologists commonly partition memory into three distinct phases. The first phase is *acquisition*. The acquisition phase refers to processes involved in the initial encoding of an event and the factors that affect the encoding. Problems in acquisition include the effects of expectations, attention, lighting, distance, arousal, and related factors that control the types, amount, and accuracy of the encoded information. Eyewitnesses to crimes often witness the event under poor conditions because the event happens unexpectedly and rapidly. Attention may be focused on elements that are of little use for later recognition of the perpetrator, such as focusing on a weapon.

The second phase is *retention*. Information that is acquired must be retained for later use. Memory generally declines rapidly in the initial time periods and more slowly later in what psychologists describe as a negatively decelerating curve. Importantly, new information can be acquired during this slower phase and mixed together with what was previously observed to create confusion regarding what was actually seen by the eyewitness and what was perhaps overheard later. Loftus's well-known experiments on misinformation, for example, show that witnesses will use false information contained in misleading questions to create what appear to be new memories that are often dramatically different from what was actually observed.

The final phase is the *retrieval* phase. Two primary types of retrieval are recall and recognition. In a recall task, the witness is provided with some context (e.g., the time frame) and asked to provide a verbal report of what was observed. In a recognition task, the witness is shown some objects (or persons) and asked to indicate whether any of them were involved in the crime event. Retrieval failures can be either errors of omission (e.g., failing to recall some detail or failing to recognize the perpetrator) or errors of commission (e.g., recalling things that were not present or picking an innocent person from a lineup). Problems at any of the three phases of memory lead to unreliability.

The distinction between estimator variables and system variables

The scientific eyewitness identification literature has tended to rely on a distinction between *estimator variables* and *system variables* (Wells, 1978). Estimator variables are those that affect the accuracy of eyewitness identifications, but cannot be controlled by the criminal justice system. System variables also affect the accuracy of eyewitness identifications, but the criminal justice system can control those variables. Estimator

variables tend to revolve around factors involved in the acquisition phase, such as lighting conditions, distance, arousal, the presence of weapons, and so on. System variables tend to revolve around factors involved in the retrieval phase, such as the structure of a lineup, instructions given to witnesses prior to viewing a lineup, and so on.

The methods used in the scientific eyewitness identification evidence typically involve staging live crimes or showing video events to people. Because the events are created by the researchers, it is known with certainty who the actual "perpetrator" was and the performance of eyewitnesses in picking him/her from a lineup can be scored systematically. These eyewitnesses can also be asked to indicate their confidence in the identification decision, thereby permitting analyses of the relation between confidence and accuracy. Systematic manipulations to key variables (e.g., structure of lineup) allows for a causal analysis of variables that affect identification accuracy, eyewitness confidence, and the relation between the two.

Estimator variables. One of the estimator variables that has received considerable attention is the race of the perpetrator relative to the race of the eyewitness (Bothwell, Brigham, and Malpass). A consensus now exists that it is more difficult to identify the face of a stranger from another race than to identify the face of a stranger from one's own race (Meissner and Brigham). There appears to be an element of symmetry to this effect. For instance, white Americans have more difficulty identifying the faces of black Americans than they do of other white Americans, and black Americans have more difficulty identifying the faces of white Americans than they do of black Americans. The precise mechanisms underlying this problem are not fully understood, although most evidence suggests that it is largely a matter of experience rather than prejudice. Another estimator variable that is frequently cited is *weapon focus*. Experiments suggest that the presence of a weapon draws attention toward the weapon and away from the weapon-holder's face, resulting in less reliable identification performance by eyewitnesses (Steblay, 1992). Stress, fear, and arousal have rarely been studied with regard to identification evidence (as opposed to recall) and the problems with studying these variables in an ecologically valid manner are complex. Gender, intelligence, and personality factors appear to be weakly, if at all, related to the tendency to make correct or mistaken identifications (Cutler and Penrod).

System variables.   Scientific understanding of system variables has progressed more rapidly than it has for estimator variables. A primary reason for this is that the "payoff" for understanding system variables may be higher than it is for estimator variables, leading researchers to invest more in system variable research than in estimator variable research. This difference in payoff owes to the fact that an understanding of system variables can inform the criminal justice system about ways to improve the accuracy of eyewitness identification evidence.

System variable research has focused primarily on four factors, namely the instructions to eyewitnesses, the content of a lineup, the presentation procedures used during the lineup, and the behaviors of the lineup administrator. In attempting to understand the importance of these system factors, it is useful to describe briefly the process through which mistaken identifications seem to occur. A dominant account of the process of eyewitness identification that has emerged is the *relative judgment process*. According to this account, eyewitnesses tend to select the person from the lineup who most closely resembles the perpetrator relative to the other members of the lineup. This process works reasonably well for eyewitnesses as long as the actual perpetrator is in the lineup. When the actual perpetrator is not in the lineup, however, there is still someone who looks more like the perpetrator than the remaining members of the lineup, thereby luring eyewitnesses to pick that person with surprising frequency.

The relative judgment process leads to a rapid understanding of why is it critical to instruct eyewitnesses that the actual perpetrator might or might not be present in the lineup before showing the lineup to eyewitnesses. Experiments show that failure to instruct eyewitnesses in this manner leads to a very high rate of choosing, even when the actual perpetrator is not present (Malpass and Devine, 1981a). Proper instructions warning the eyewitness that the perpetrator might not be present do not eliminate the relative judgment tendency altogether, but they do reduce the magnitude of the problem. Importantly, proper instructions lead eyewitnesses to less often mistakenly pick someone when the perpetrator is not in the lineup, but have little effect on their ability to pick the perpetrator when the perpetrator is in the lineup. The result of proper instructions is a net improvement in eyewitness identification performance (Steblay, 1997).

The relative judgment process also has implications for how investigators should select *lineup fillers*. A lineup filler is a known-innocent member of a lineup. Normally, a lineup will have one suspect and several (five or more) fillers whose primary purpose is to prevent the eyewitness from simply guessing. If an eyewitness is merely guessing, then odds against selecting the suspect are N:1 (where N is the number of fillers). However, if investigators use fillers who do not fit the general description of the suspect (as provided previously by the eyewitness) whereas the suspect does fit that description, then the lineup is said to be biased against the suspect. As predicted by the relative-judgment process, lineups in which the fillers do not fit the description of the perpetrator lead eyewitnesses toward picking the suspect, even if the suspect is innocent, because the suspect most closely resembles the perpetrator relative to the other lineup members. Making sure that each lineup member fits the general verbal description of the perpetrator does not lead eyewitnesses to fail to recognize the perpetrator when he is in the lineup, but it does help prevent mistaken identifications of the innocent suspect when the actual perpetrator is not in the lineup (Wells, Rydell, and Seelau, 1993).

Procedures for lineups

Eyewitness researchers have called the usual procedure for lineups the *simultaneous procedure* because all members of the lineup are presented at one time. Simultaneous procedures tend to encourage eyewitnesses to compare one lineup member to another lineup member and hone in on the one who looks most like the perpetrator.

An alternative procedure, based on sequential presentation methods, was developed and tested in 1985 (Lindsay and Wells). The *sequential procedure* presents the eyewitness with one lineup member at a time and requires the eyewitness to make a yes/no decision on each lineup member before viewing the next lineup member. The sequential procedure prevents the eyewitness from merely making a decision as to which lineup member looks most like the perpetrator. Although eyewitnesses can compare the person being viewed at any given time to ones viewed previously, they cannot be sure what the next lineup member will look like. Hence, eyewitnesses must largely abandon the strategy of simply picking the person who looks most like the perpetrator and instead compare each lineup member to their memory of the perpetrator. The sequential procedure has proven itself superior to the simultaneous procedure. When the actual perpetrator is in the lineup, the chances of selecting that person are nearly identical with the simultaneous and sequential procedures. When the actual perpetrator is not in the lineup, on the other hand, the simultaneous procedure produces a considerably higher rate of mistaken identifications than does the sequential procedure. As with proper instructions and proper selection of fillers, the sequential procedure results in a net improvement in eyewitness identification performance. This result is one of the most replicated findings in the eyewitness identification literature and appears to be quite robust.

A major concern of eyewitness researchers has been the behavior of the lineup administrator (Wells et al., 1998). This concern has been especially stressed with regard to photographic lineups, which constitute the majority of initial identifications of criminal suspects. In the United States, courts have held that the suspect has no right to have counsel present for photographic identification procedures. Accordingly, photographic identification procedures are almost always administered by the case detectives with no other observers present. The case detectives are well aware of which lineup member is the suspect because they are the ones who developed the suspect in the first place and put the lineup together. The experimenter expectancy effect, well known in psychology, occurs when the person (e.g., an experimenter) is aware of the desired response and unintentionally (even without awareness) influences the subject to give the desired response. In a lineup situation, verbal and nonverbal interactions between the witness and the investigator should be of great concern because the eyewitness is supposed to use only his or her memory, free from external influences, to make the decision. Recent research indicates that the knowledge of the person administering the lineup can influence the eyewitness to pick the wrong person when the lineup administrator has the wrong person as the suspect (Phillips, McAuliff, Kovera, and Cutler). For this reason, eyewitness researchers have argued strongly that the person who administers the lineup should not be aware of which person in the lineup is the suspect. This solution is known in science as double-blind testing and researchers have been trying to get the criminal justice system to adopt this simple but effective technique for improving the integrity of the identification process.

Eyewitness confidence

Throughout the eyewitness identification literature there has been a great deal of interest in the issue of eyewitness confidence. Research has shown that the confidence of an eyewitness is the principal determinant of whether or not jurors will believe that an eyewitness made an accurate identification (Lindsay, Wells, and, Rumpel). Early research suggested that there was no relation between the confidence with which eyewitnesses made identifications and the accuracy of those identifications. Later research has shown that there is a relation between eyewitness identification confidence and accuracy, although it is not a strong relation (Sporer, Penrod, Read, and Cutler). Under very favorable conditions (e.g., a good view, a fair lineup), the correlation between confidence and accuracy is probably somewhere around .40. For purposes of comparison, consider that the correlation between a person's height and a person's gender is .71. This means that confidence is a poorer predictor of accuracy than height is a predictor of gender. Importantly, research also shows that current procedures by law enforcement are probably harming the already-modest relation between eyewitness identification confidence and accuracy. Specifically, eyewitnesses are commonly given *confirming feedback* after they identify a suspect. This feedback takes many forms, such as "Good, that's the guy we thought it was" or "You got him!" Research shows that feedback of this sort to eyewitnesses who are in fact mistaken leads the eyewitnesses to recall that they were highly confident at the time of the identification (Wells and Bradfield). This confidence inflation effect is stronger for eyewitnesses who were in fact mistaken than for eyewitnesses who identified the actual perpetrator, leading to a diminution of the confidence-accuracy relation. This feedback problem is another factor leading eyewitness researchers to strongly advocate double-blind testing with lineups. Repeated questioning of eyewitnesses tends to have similar confidence-inflating properties such that eyewitnesses tend to become more confident in their incorrect reports with repeated questioning (Shaw and McClure).

Cooperation between eyewitness researchers and the criminal justice system

Some of the battle between eyewitness research findings and the criminal justice system is fought out in the courtroom via issues concerning expert testimony by psychologists on these issues. Beginning in the late 1990s, however, elements of cooperation between eyewitness researchers and the criminal justice system yielded some success (Wells et al., 2000). A project initiated by the U.S. Department of Justice under the auspices of the National Institute of Justice convened a panel and working group of eyewitness researchers, prosecutors, police, and defense lawyers to develop national guidelines for law enforcement. These guidelines, informed by eyewitness research findings, were published in 1999 (Technical Working Group for Eyewitness Evidence). The guidelines include descriptions of how eyewitnesses should be instructed prior to viewing a lineup, how fillers should be selected for lineups, how to conduct a sequential lineup procedure, and warnings against giving feedback to eyewitnesses following their identification decisions. The process of including eyewitness researchers in the development of these guidelines was unique and might hold great promise for the future of the interface between the criminal justice system and social science.

GARY L. WELLS

See also EYEWITNESS IDENTIFICATION: CONSTITUTIONAL ASPECTS; SCIENTIFIC EVIDENCE.

BIBLIOGRAPHY

BOTHWELL, ROBERT K.; BRIGHAM, JOHN C.; and MALPASS, ROY S. "Cross Racial Identification." *Personality and Social Psychology Bulletin* 15 (1989): 19–25.

CUTLER, BRIAN L., and PENROD, STEVEN D. *Mistaken Identification: The Eyewitness, Psychology, and the Law.* New York: Cambridge University Press, 1995.

GOLDSTEIN, ALVIN G.; CHANCE, JANE E.; and SCHNELLER, GREGORY R. "Frequency of Eyewitness Identification in Criminal Cases: A Survey of Prosecutors." *Bulletin of the Psychonomic Society* 27, no. 1 (1989): 71–74.

HUFF, RONALD; RATTNER, ARYE; and SAGARIN, EDWARD. "Guilty until Proven Innocent." *Crime and Delinquency* 32 (1986): 518–544.

LINDSAY, ROD C. L., and WELLS, GARY L. "Improving Eyewitness Identification from Lineups: Simultaneous Versus Sequential Lineup Presentations." *Journal of Applied Psychology* 70 (1985): 556–564.

LINDSAY, ROD C. L.; WELLS, GARY L.; and RUMPEL, CAROLYN. "Can People Detect Eyewitness Identification Accuracy within and between Situations?" *Journal of Applied Psychology* 66 (1981): 79–89.

LOFTUS, ELIZABETH F., *Eyewitness Testimony.* Rev. ed. Cambridge, Mass: Harvard University Press, 1996.

LOFTUS, E. F., and KETCHAM, K. *Witness for the Defense: The Accused, the Eyewitness, and the Expert Who Puts Memory on Trial.* New York: St. Martin's Press, 1991.

LOFTUS, E. F., and DOYLE, J. M. *Eyewitness Testimony: Civil and Criminal,* 3d ed. Charlottesville, Va.: Lexis Law, 1997.

MALPASS, ROY S., and DEVINE, PATRICIA G. "Eyewitness Identification: Lineup Instructions and the Absence of the Offender." *Journal of Applied Psychology* 66 (1981): 482–489.

MEISSNER, CHRISTIAN A., and BRIGHAM, JOHN C. "Thirty Years of Investigating the Own-Race Bias in Memory and Faces: A Meta-Analytic Review." *Psychology, Public Policy, & Law.* Forthcoming.

PHILLIPS, MARK R.; MCAULIFF, BRADLEY D.; KOVERA, MARGARET B.; and CUTLER, BRIAN L. "Double-blind Photoarray Administration as a Safeguard against Investigator Bias." *Journal of Applied Psychology* 84 (1999): 940–951.

SCHECK, BARRY; NEUFELD, PETER; and DWYER, JIM. *Actual Innocence.* New York: Random House, 2000.

SHAW, JOHN S., III, and MCCLURE, KIMBERLY A. "Repeated Postevent Questioning Can Lead to Elevated Levels of Eyewitness Confidence." *Law and Human Behavior* 20 (1996): 629–654.

SPORER, SIEGFRIED; PENROD, STEVEN; READ, DON; and CUTLER, BRIAN L. "Choosing, Confidence, and Accuracy: A Meta-Analysis of the Confidence-Accuracy Relation to Eyewitness Identification Studies." *Psychological Bulletin* 118 (1995): 315–327.

STEBLAY, NANCY M. "A Meta-Analytic Review of the Weapon Focus Effect." *Law and Human Behavior* 16 (1992): 413–424.

———. "Social Influence in Eyewitness Recall: A Meta-Analytic Review of Lineup Instruction Effects." *Law and Human Behavior* 21 (1997): 283–298.

Technical Working Group for Eyewitness Evidence. *Eyewitness Evidence: A Guide for Law Enforcement.* Washington, D.C.: U.S. Department of Justice, Office of Justice Programs, 1999.

WELLS, GARY L. "Applied Eyewitness Testimony Research: System Variables and Estimator Variables." *Journal of Personality and Social Psychology* 36 (1978): 1546–1557.

WELLS, GARY L., and BRADFIELD, AMY L. "Good, You Identified the Suspect:" Feedback to Eyewitnesses Distorts their Reports of the Witnessing Experience. *Journal of Applied Psychology* 83 (1998): 360–376.

WELLS, GARY L.; MALPASS, ROY S.; LINDSAY, ROD C. L.; FISHER, RONALD P.; TURTLE, J. W.; and FULERO, SOLOMON. "From the Lab to the Police Station: A Successful Application of Eyewitness Research." *American Psychologist* 55 (2000): 581–598.

WELLS, GARY L.; RYDELL, SHEILA M.; and SEELAU, ERIC P. "On the Selection of Distractors for Eyewitness Lineups." *Journal of Applied Psychology* 78 (1993): 835–844.

WELLS, GARY L.; SMALL, MARK; PENROD, STEVEN; MALPASS, ROY S.; FULERO, SOLOMON M.; and BRIMACOMBE, C. A. ELIZABETH. "Eyewitness Identification Procedures: Recommendations from Lineups and Photospreads." *Law and Human Behavior* 22 (1998): 603–647.

F

FAMILY ABUSE AND CRIME

Since the early 1970s, violence in the family has been transformed from a private concern to a criminal justice problem. Violence in intimate relationships is extensive and is not limited to one socioeconomic group, one society, or one period in time. Every type and form of family and intimate relationship has the potential of being violent.

In 1998, a National Academy of Sciences panel assessing family violence interventions defined family violence:

Family violence includes child and adult abuse that occurs between family members or adult intimate partners. For children, this includes acts by others that are physically or emotionally harmful or that carry the potential to cause physical harm. Abuse of children may include sexual exploitation or molestation, threats to kill or abandon, or lack of emotional or physical support necessary for normal development. For adults, family or intimate violence may include acts that are physically and emotionally harmful or that carry the potential to cause physical harm. Abuse of adult partners may include sexual coercion or assaults, physical intimidation, threats to kill or harm, restraint of normal activities or freedom, and denial of access to resources. (National Research Council, p. 19)

There are three main sources of data on family violence: (1) clinical data; (2) official report data; and (3) social surveys. Clinical studies carried out by psychiatrists, psychologists, and counselors are a frequent source of data on family violence. This is primarily because clinicians have the most direct access to cases of family violence. Official reports constitute a second source of data on family violence. In the United States, there is abundant official report data on child maltreatment (because of mandatory reporting laws). On the other hand, few other countries have enacted mandatory reporting laws, and thus most nations rely on official data from hospitals or criminal justice agencies for their estimates on the extent of violence and abuse of children. There is no tradition of officially reporting spouse abuse in the United States or other countries, with the exception of a handful of states in the United States that collect data on spouse abuse.

Each of the major data sources has its own validity problems. Clinical data are not representative, and few investigators gathering data from clinical samples employ comparison groups. Official records suffer from variations in definitions, differing reporting and recording practices, and biased samples of violent and abusive behaviors and persons. The biases of social survey data on intimate violence include inaccurate recall, differential interpretation of questions, and intended and unintended response error.

Risk and protective factors

There has been debate regarding the risk and protective factors for family violence. Some advocates argue that violence cuts across all social groups, while others agree that it cuts across social groups, but not evenly. Some researchers and practitioners place more emphasis on psychological factors, while others locate the key risk factors among social factors. Still a third group places the greatest emphasis on cultural factors, for example, the patriarchal social organization of societies.

One note of caution is that, when basing an analysis of risk and protective factors on clinical data or official report data, risk and protective factors are confounded with factors such as labeling bias or agency or clinical setting. Researchers have long noted that certain individuals and families are more likely to be (correctly or incorrectly) labeled as offenders or victims of family violence, and, similarly, some individuals and families are insulated from being (correctly or incorrectly) labeled or identified as offenders or victims. Social survey data are not immune to confounding problems either, as social or demographic factors may be related to a subject's willingness to participate in a self-report survey and the tendency to provide socially desirable responses.

An important caveat is that any listing of risk and protective factors may unintentionally convey or reinforce a notion of single-factor explanations for family violence. No phenomenon as complex as family violence can be explained with a single-factor model.

Social and demographic risk factors

The major social and demographic risk factors for family violence appear to be the following:

Age. One of the most consistent risk factors is the age of the offender. As with violence between nonintimates, violence is most likely to be perpetrated by those between eighteen and thirty years of age. Relative youth is not a risk factor for elder abuse, although the rate of elder abuse is lower than the rate of the other forms of family violence.

Sex. Similarly with nonintimate violence, men are the most likely offenders in acts of intimate violence. However, the differences in the rates of offending by men compared to women are much smaller for violence in the family than with violence outside the home. Men and women experience similar rates of child homicide, although women appear more likely to be offenders when the child victim is young (under three) and males are the more likely offenders when the child victim is older.

Income. Although most poor parents and partners do not use violence toward intimates, self-report surveys and official report data find that the rates of all forms of family violence, except sexual abuse, are higher for those whose family incomes are below the poverty line than for those whose income is above the poverty line.

Situational and environmental factors

Stress. Unemployment, financial problems, being a single parent, being a teenage mother, and sexual difficulties (such as sexual dysfunction or impotence) are all factors that are related to violence, as are a host of other stressor events.

Social isolation and social support. Researchers often find that people who are socially isolated from neighbors and relatives are more likely to be violent in the home. Social support appears to be an important protective factor. One major source of social support is the availability of friends and family for help, aid, and assistance. The more a family is integrated into the community and the more groups and associations they belong to, the less likely they are to be violent.

The intergenerational transmission of violence. The notion that abused children grow up to be abusive parents and violent adults has been widely expressed in the literature on child abuse and family violence. Psychologists Joan Kaufman and Edward Zigler conclude that the best estimate of the rate of intergenerational transmission appears to be 30 percent (plus or minus 5 percent). Although a rate of 30 percent is substantially less than the majority of abused children, the rate is considerably more than the between 2 and 4 percent rate of abuse found in the general population. Byron Egeland and colleagues conducted a longitudinal study of high-risk mothers and their children. They found that mothers who had been abused as children were less likely to abuse their own children if they had emotionally supportive parents, partners, or friends. In addition, the abused mothers who did not abuse their children were described as "middle class" and "upwardly mobile," suggesting that they were able to draw on economic resources that may not have been available to abused mothers who abused their children.

Evidence from studies of parental and marital violence indicate that while experiencing violence in one's family of origin is often correlated with later violent behavior, such experience is not the sole determining factor. When the intergenerational transmission of violence occurs, it is likely the result of a complex set of social and psychological processes. Although experiencing and witnessing violence is believed to be an important risk factor, the actual mechanism by which violence is transmitted from generation to generation is not well understood.

Gender inequality. One of the important risk factors for violence against women is gender inequality. The greater the degree of gender inequality in a relationship, community, and society, the higher are the rates of violence toward women.

Presence of other violence. A final general risk factor is that the presence of violence in one family relationship increases the risk that there will be violence in other relationships. Thus children in homes where there is domestic violence are more likely to experience violence than are children who grow up in homes where there is no violence between their parents. Moreover, children who witness and experience violence are more likely to use violence toward their parents and siblings than are children who do not experience or see violence in their homes.

Research on victims

Compared to research on offenders, there has been somewhat less research on victims of family violence that focuses on factors that increase or reduce the risk of victimization. Most research on victims examines the consequences of victimization (e.g., depression, psychological distress, suicide attempts, symptoms of post traumatic stress syndrome, etc.) or the effectiveness of various intervention efforts.

Children. The very youngest children appear to be at the greatest risk of being abused, especially for the most dangerous and potentially lethal forms of violence. Not only are young children physically more fragile and thus more susceptible to injury, but their vulnerability makes them more likely to be reported and diagnosed as abused when injured. Older children are underreported as victims of abuse. Adolescent victims may be considered delinquent or ungovernable, and thus thought of as contributing to their own victimization.

Early research suggested a number of factors that raise the risk of child abuse. Low birth weight babies, premature children, and handicapped, retarded, or developmentally disabled children were all described as being at heightened risk of being abused by their parents or caretakers. However, a more recent review of studies that examined the child's role in abuse calls into question many of these findings (Starr). One major problem is that few earlier investigators used matched comparison groups. Newer studies fail to find premature or handicapped children being at higher risk for abuse.

Marital partners. Studies that examine the individual and social attributes of victims of marital violence are difficult to interpret. It is often unclear whether the factors found among victims were present before they were battered or are the result of the victimization. Such studies often use small, clinical samples and fail to have comparison groups.

Battered women have been described as dependent, having low esteem, and feeling inadequate and helpless. Descriptive and clinical accounts consistently report a high incidence of depression and anxiety among samples of battered women. Sometimes the personality profiles of battered women reported in the literature seem directly opposite. While some researchers describe battered women as unassertive, shy, and reserved, other reports picture battered women as aggressive, masculine, frigid, and masochistic.

Gerald Hotaling and David Sugarman reviewed the wife abuse literature and examined risk markers for abuse. They found few risk markers that identify women at risk of violence in intimate relations. High levels of marital conflict and low socioeconomic status emerged as the primary predictors of increased likelihood of wife assault.

Elder victims. Research on elder abuse is divided on whether elder victims are more likely to be physically, socially, and emotionally dependent on their caretakers or whether it is the offender's dependence on the victim that increases the risk of elder abuse. Conventional wisdom suggests that it is the oldest, sickest, most debilitated, and dependent elders who are prone to the full range of mistreatment by their caretakers. However, the sociologist Karl Pillemer has found that dependency of the victim is not as powerful a risk factor as perceived by clinicians, the public, and some researchers.

Theoretical models of family violence

The first people to identify a problem often shape how others will perceive it (Nelson, p. 13). Child abuse and neglect, the first form of family violence to receive scholarly and public attention, was identified by the medical profession in the early 1960s. The initial conceptualizations portrayed abuse and violence between intimates as a rare event, typically caused by the psychopathology of the offender. The perception of the abuser, or violent offender, as suffering from some form of psychopathology has persisted, in part because the first conceptualization of family violence was the guiding framework for the work that followed. The psychopathological or psychiatric conceptualization has also persisted because the tragic picture of a defenseless child, woman, or grandparent subjected to abuse and neglect arouses the strongest emotions in clinicians and others who see and/or treat the problem of intimate violence. There frequently seems to be no rational explanation for harming a loved one, especially one who appears to be helpless and defenseless.

Family violence has been approached from three general theoretical levels of analysis: (1) the intra-individual level of analysis, or the *psychiatric model*; (2) the *social-psychological* level of analysis, and (3) the sociological or *socio-cultural* level of analysis.

The psychiatric level focuses on the offender's personality characteristics as the chief determinants of violence and abuse of intimates, although some applications focus on the individual personality characteristics of the victims. The psychiatric level includes theoretical approaches that link personality disorders, character disorders, mental illness, alcohol and substance abuse, and other intra-individual processes to acts of family violence.

The social-psychological model assumes that violence and abuse can best be understood by careful examination of the external environmental factors that impact on the family, on family organization and structure, and on the everyday interactions between intimates that are precursors to acts of violence. Theoretical approaches that examine family structure, learning, stress, the transmission of violence from one generation to the next, and family interaction patterns fit the social psychological level.

The socio-cultural level provides a macro-level of analysis. Violence is examined in light of socially structured variables such as inequality, patriarchy, or cultural norms and attitudes about violence and family relations.

A number of sociological and psychological theories have been developed to explain family violence. They are outlined below.

Social learning theory. Social learning theory proposes that individuals who experienced violence are more likely to use violence in the home than those who have experienced little or no violence. The theory's central proposition is that children who either experience violence themselves or who witness violence between their parents are more likely to use violence when they grow up. The family is the institution and social group where people learn the roles of husband and wife, parent and child. The home is the prime location where people learn how to deal with various stresses, crises, and frustrations. In many instances, the home is also the site where a person first experiences violence. Not only do people learn violent behavior, but also they learn how to justify being violent. For example, hearing a father say "this will hurt me more than it will hurt you," or a mother say, "you have been bad, so you deserve to be spanked," contribute to how children learn to justify violent behavior.

Exchange theory Exchange theory proposes that domestic violence and child abuse are governed by the principle of costs and benefits. Abuse is used when the rewards are greater than the costs. The private nature of the family, the reluctance of social institutions and agencies to intervene—in spite of mandatory child abuse reporting laws or mandatory arrest laws for spouse abuse—and the low risk of other interventions reduce the costs of abuse and violence. The cultural approval of violence as both expressive and instrumental behavior raises the potential rewards for violence. The most significant reward is social control, or power.

Feminist theory. Feminist theorists see violence toward women as a unique phenomenon that has been obscured and overshadowed by what they refer to as a "narrow" focus on domestic or family violence. The central thesis is that economic and social processes operate directly and indirectly to support a patriarchal (male dominated) social order and family structure. Patriarchy is seen as leading to the subordination of women and causes the historical pattern of systematic violence directed against women.

An ecological perspective

The *ecological perspective* is an attempt to integrate the three levels of theoretical analysis (individual, social-psychological, and socio-cultural) into a single theoretical model. The theory rests on three levels of analysis: the relationship between the organism and environment, the interacting and overlapping systems in which human development occurs, and environmental quality. The ecological model proposes that violence and abuse arise out of a mismatch of parent to child and family to neighborhood and community. The risk of abuse and violence is greatest when the functioning of the children and parents is limited and constrained by developmental problems. Children with learning disabilities and social or emotional handicaps are at increased risk for abuse. Parents under considerable stress, or who have personality problems, are at increased risk for abusing their children. These conditions are worsened when social interaction between the spouses or the parents and children heighten the stress or make the personal problems worse. Finally, if there are few institutions and agencies in the community to support troubled families, then the risk of abuse is further raised. The psychologist James Garbarino identifies two necessary conditions for child maltreatment. First, there must be cultural justification for the use of force against children. Second, the maltreating family is isolated from potent family or community support systems. The ecological model has served as a perspective to examine other forms of family violence.

A model of sexual abuse

The sociologist David Finkelhor reviewed research on the factors that have been proposed as contributing to sexual abuse of children and has developed what he calls a "Four Precondition Model of Sexual Abuse." His review suggests that all the factors relating to sexual abuse can be grouped into one of four preconditions that need to be met before sexual abuse can occur. The preconditions are:

1. A potential offender needs to have some motivation to abuse a child sexually.
2. The potential offender has to overcome internal inhibitions against acting on that motivation.
3. The potential offender has to overcome external impediments to committing sexual abuse.
4. The potential offender or some other factor has to undermine or overcome a child's possible resistance to sexual abuse.

Interventions and policy

Protecting children. All fifty states enacted mandatory reporting laws for child abuse and neglect by the late 1960s. These laws require certain professionals (or in some states, all adults) to report cases of suspected maltreatment. When a report is made, protective service workers investigate to determine if the child is in need of protection, and whether the family is in need of assistance. Although a wide array of options are available to child-protection workers, they typically have two basic ways to protect a victim of child abuse: (1) Removing the child and placing him or her in a foster home or institution; or (2) providing the family with social support, such as counseling, food stamps, day care services, and so on.

Neither solution is ideal. There are risks in both. Children who are removed from abusive homes may well be protected from physical damage, but still suffer emotional harm. The emotional harm arises from the fact that abused children still love and have strong feelings for their parents and do not understand why they have been removed from their parents and homes. Often, abused children feel that they are responsible for their own abuse. Abused children frequently require special medical and/or psychological care and it is difficult to find a suitable placement for them. They could well become a burden for foster parents or institutions that have to care for them. Therefore, the risk of abuse might even be greater in a foster home or institution than in the home of the natural parents.

Leaving children in an abusive home and providing social services involves another type of risk. Most protective service workers are overworked, undertrained, and underpaid. Family services such as crisis daycare, financial assistance, suitable housing, and transportation services are often limited. This can lead to cases in which children, reported as abused, and investigated and supervised by state agencies, are killed during the period the family was supposedly being monitored. Half of all children who are killed by caretakers are killed after they have been reported to child welfare agencies (Gelles).

The most effective intervention for preventing child maltreatment is home health visitation. Among children of poor, unmarried teenage mothers who were provided with the full complement of home visits by a nurse during the mother's pregnancy and for the first two years after birth, confirmed cases of child abuse and neglect were reported to the state child protection agency in 4 percent of the cases. Subsequent follow-ups of the home health visiting intervention demonstrated its long-term effectiveness. However, the effectiveness varied depending on the populations receiving the service, the community context, and who made the visits (nurses or others) (Olds et al.).

Other evaluations of interventions for child maltreatment have found that the more services a family received, the worse the family got and the more likely children were to be maltreated. Lay counseling, group counseling, and parent education classes resulted in more positive treatment outcomes. The optimal treatment period appeared to be between seven and eighteen months. The projects that were successful in reducing abuse accomplished this by separating children from abusive parents, either by placing the children in foster homes or requiring the maltreating adult to move out of the house.

Protecting women. There are a number of options available to women who either want to escape or be protected from partner violence. One option is to call the police. Evaluations of mandatory arrest policies find that, overall, arrest alone does not prevent future occurrences of domestic violence. Men who were employed or married when arrested for domestic violence were less likely to reabuse their partners. However, men who were unemployed when they were arrested were actually more likely to be violent after they were arrested compared to unemployed men who were not arrested.

A second possibility is for the woman to go to a shelter or safe house. Researchers find that the effects of shelters seem to depend on the attributes of the victims. When a victim is actively engaged in taking control of her life, a shelter stay can dramatically reduce the likelihood of new violence.

Researchers have also evaluated group programs developed for violent men. They determined that the programs were ineffective in reducing men's violence, regardless of the length or type of program (Levesque).

Conclusion

Characteristics of the child, parent, partners, family, social situation, community, and society are related to which family members are abused and under what conditions. Individual and emotional characteristics, psychological characteristics, and community factors, such as cultural attitudes regarding violence, are moderated and influenced by family structure and family situations. In addition, power and control are common features of nearly all forms of family and intimate violence. Thus, interventions and prevention efforts need to focus on the importance of power and control, and on the functions of the family system, if family and intimate violence are to be effectively treated and prevented.

RICHARD J. GELLES

See also CRIME CAUSATION: PSYCHOLOGICAL THEORIES; CRIME CAUSATION: SOCIOLOGICAL THEORIES; DOMESTIC VIOLENCE; FAMILY RELATIONSHIPS AND CRIME; FEMINISM: CRIMINOLOGICAL ASPECTS; FEMINISM: LEGAL ASPECTS; GENDER AND CRIME; JUSTIFICATION: SELF-DEFENSE; PREVENTION: COMMUNITY PROGRAMS; SCIENTIFIC EVIDENCE.

BIBLIOGRAPHY

EGELAND, BYRAN; JACOBVITZ, DEBORAH; and PAPATOLA, KATHLEEN. "Intergenerational Continuity of Abuse." In *Child Abuse and Neglect: Biosocial Dimensions*. Edited by R. Gelles and J. Lancaster. New York: Aldine de Gruyter, 1987.

FINKELHOR, DAVID. *Child Sexual Abuse: New Theory and Research*. New York: Free Press, 1984.

GARBARINO, JAMES. "The Human Ecology of Child Maltreatment." *Journal of Marriage and the Family* 39 (1977): 721–735.

GELLES, RICHARD J. *The Book of David: How Preserving Families Can Cost Children's Lives*. New York: Basic Books, 1996.

HOTALING, GERALD, and SUGARMAN, DAVID. "A Risk Marker Analysis of Assaulted Wives." *Journal of Family Violence* 5 (1990): 1–13.

KAUFMAN, JOAN, and ZIGLER, EDWARD. "Do Abused Children Become Abusive Parents?" *American Journal of Orthopsychiatry* 57 (1987): 186–192.

LEVESQUE, DEBORAH *Violence Desistance among Battering Men: Existing Intervention and the Application of the Transtheoretical Model of Change*. Ph.D. diss. University of Rhode Island, 1998.

National Research Council. *Violence in Families: Assessing Prevention and Treatment Programs*. Washington, D.C.: National Academy Press, 1998.

NELSON, BARBARA J. *Making an Issue of Child Abuse: Political Agenda Setting for Social Problems*. Chicago: University Chicago Press, 1984.

OLDS, DAVID L.; HENDERSON, JR., CHARLES R.; TATELBAUM, ROBERT; and CHAMBERLIN, ROBERT. "Preventing Child Abuse and Neglect: A Randomized Trial of Nurse Home Visitation." *Pediatrics* 77 (1986): 65–78.

PILLEMER, KARL. "The Abused Offspring are Dependent: Abuse is Caused by the Deviance and Dependence of Abusive Caretakers." In *Current Controversies on Family Violence*. Edited by Richard Gelles and Donileen Loseke. Newbury Park, Calif.: Sage Publications, 1993.

STARR, RAYMOND. H., JR. "Physical Abuse of Children." In *Handbook of Family Violence*. Edited by Vincent B. Van Hasselt, Randall L. Morrison, Alan S. Bellack, and Michael Hersen. New York: Plenum, 1988. Pages 119–155.

FAMILY RELATIONSHIPS AND CRIME

"The most important part of education," said the Athenian in Plato's *Laws*, "is right training in the nursery" (li. 643). Through acceptance of Freudian theory, this ancient belief gained new credibility during the first half of the twentieth century. According to Freudian theory, successful socialization begins with an early attachment to the mother, an attachment that must later be modified by a conscience, or "superego," that develops through identification with a parent of the child's own sex (Freud). In the case of a young boy, the theory continues, attachment to the mother leads to the boy's jealousy of his father, but fear of his father's anger and punishment forces the child to control his incestuous and antisocial desires. Because Freud argued that the development of conscience for males depends on attachment to the mother and identification with the father, psychoanalytic explanations of crime focused on paternal absence and maternal deprivation. These emphases continue to guide psychological theories and research despite the decline in popularity of Freudian theory.

Toward the mid-twentieth century, sociological theories became influential. First Charles Cooley and then George Herbert Mead proposed that people develop self-concepts that reflect how they believe they are perceived by "significant others" (Mead). These self-concepts motivate a person's actions. The parents provide the first group of significant others from whom a child acquires a sense of identity. If parents are neglectful or abusive, the child develops self concepts that tend to lead to associations with others who similarly denigrate the value of individuals. Edwin Sutherland suggested in the 1930s that both delinquent and nondelinquent behavior is learned from "differential associations" with others who have procriminal or anticriminal values. Children reared by families with "criminalistic" values would accept a criminal lifestyle as normal. Children neglected by their families would be more strongly influenced by nonfamilial associates, some of whom might be procriminal (Sutherland and Cressey).

The second half of the twentieth century witnessed development of explanations for crime that took into account both psychological and sociological processes. Most popular among them are the "control theories," which assume that all people have urges to violate society's conduct norms and that people who abide by the norms do so because of internal and external controls. These controls trace to the family through "bonding" (internal control) and discipline (external control).

Control theories rest on an assumption that deviance is natural and that only conformity must be learned. Social learning theories, on the other hand, assume that both prosocial and antisocial activities are learned. They claim that a desire for pleasure and for avoidance of pain motivates behavior, and hence they focus on rewards and punishments. Social learning theories employ the notion of vicarious conditioning to explain how people learn by watching and listening, and direct attention toward the influence of parents as models for behavior and as agents for discipline. Some theorists, however, question the assumption that self-interested pleasure and pain govern all voluntary choices.

Regardless of what theory is used to explain how behavior is learned, Western cultures place a heavy burden on families through assigning responsibility for child rearing to them. Families in such cultures must transmit values so as to lead children to accept rules that they are likely to perceive as arbitrary. It should be no surprise, therefore, to find that family life bears a strong relation to juvenile delinquency (Kazdin). Perhaps the most significant changes in thinking during the last quarter of the twentieth century have been methodological. Increasingly, social scientists have become aware of retrospective and expectational biases, biases that occur when people are asked to recall their experiences—particularly when they have theories about the way people react to events of certain types. These biases affect data collection and interpretation. To overcome these biases, newer studies have used longitudinal approaches, studying people through time. These longitudinal studies provide a basis for reassessing theories about family relations and crime.

Single-parent families and crime

In contemporary Western societies, a nuclear family structure has been idealized. Conversely, deviations from this structure have been blamed for a variety of social problems, including crime. One of the signs of change, however, has been acknowledgment that not all single-parent families are "broken." Another has been renewed examination of family dynamics in a context in which effects of having a single parent in the home can be considered apart from concomitant poverty, or effects of poor supervision and disruptive child rearing.

Classical theories endorsed the popular view that good child development requires the presence of two parents. This view seemed to have been corroborated by studies showing that the incidence of broken homes was higher among delinquents than among the nondelinquents with whom they were compared. In line with the Freudian tradition, many believed that paternal absence resulted in over-identification with the mother. According to this view, delinquency is one symptom of compensatory masculine "acting-out." The theory purports also to explain why delinquency is prevalent among blacks and the poor, groups with high rates of single-parent families.

If delinquency were a response to excessive maternal identification, however, the presence of a stepfather should reduce the criminogenic effects of paternal loss. This does not occur. In fact, studies have consistently shown higher rates of delinquency for boys who had substitute fathers than those having no fathers in the home (Glueck and Glueck; Hirschi; McCord, McCord, and Thurber).

Despite the frequency with which both the popular press and participants in the legal system blame "broken" homes for failures to socialize children as willing participants in an ordered social system, their conclusion goes well beyond the facts. Research that takes into account the role of parental conflict, stress, or socioeconomic conditions in relation to single-parent families fails to show that single-parent families contribute disproportionately to crime.

Because poverty is related to both crime and single-parent families, studies that confound socioeconomic status and family structure have tended to nourish the belief that single-parent families account for crime (Crockett, Eggebeen, and Hawkins). Studies within a particular social class, however, show that neither British nor American children from single-parent homes are more likely to be delinquent than are their similarly situated classmates from two-parent families. Disruptive parenting practices and behavior account for most of the apparent effects of single-parent families on crime (Capaldi and Patterson; Gorman-Smith, Tolan, and Henry; McCord; De-Klyen, Speltz, and Greenberg).

Family conflict is particularly criminogenic (McCord; Rutter; West & Farrington), and the choice to divorce must typically be made by parents who do not get along. David Farrington found that marital disharmony of their parents, when boys were fourteen, predicted subsequent aggressive behavior among boys who had not been previously aggressive. Tracing the lives of a group of men forty years after they had participated in a youth study, Joan McCord contrasted effects of conflict between parents with effects of parental absence. Compared with boys raised in quarrelsome but intact homes, boys reared by affectionate mothers in broken homes were half as likely to be convicted of serious crimes. Criminality was no more common among those reared solely by affectionate mothers than among those reared by two parents in tranquil homes.

Michael Rutter was able to disentangle effects of parental absence and effects of parental discord in his study of children whose parents were patients in a London psychiatric clinic. Among those who had been separated from their parents, conduct disorders occurred only if the separations were the result of parental discord. Among those still living with both parents, disorders occurred when there was parental conflict. Furthermore the children's behavior improved when they were placed in tranquil homes.

No one has taken the position that single-parent families are superior to good two-parent families. But good two-parent families are not the option against which an adequate comparison of single-parent families ought to be measured. For many children, the option to living in a single-parent household is living with an alcoholic or aggressive father or living in the midst of conflict. Recent research has resulted in a considerable amount of evidence to suggest that if the remaining parent provides strong and supportive guidance, offspring in single-parent homes are no more likely to become delinquents than if there are two good parents in the home (Matsueda and Heimer).

Parental attachment and crime

The nuclear family structure places a special burden on parents. Because they are seen to be the primary socializing agents, parents are expected to provide warmth and protection as well as guidance. Conversely, absence of affection and inadequate discipline have been seen as sources of crime.

Psychoanalytic perspectives encouraged the use of case materials to develop facts for a science of human behavior. The view that maternal deprivation has dire effects on personality gained support from case histories documenting maternal rejection in the backgrounds of aggressive youngsters and from studies of children reared in orphanages, many of whom became delinquents. Indeed, John Bowlby suggested that the discovery of a need for maternal affection during early childhood paralleled the discovery of "the role of vitamins in physical health" (p. 59).

Critics of the conclusions reached in these studies noted the selective nature of retrospective histories and pointed out that institutionalized children not only lack maternal affection but also have been deprived of normal social stimulation. They wondered, as well, whether a father's affection was irrelevant. Around mid-century, several studies suggested that paternal affection had effects similar to those of maternal affection. For example, Travis Hirschi compared the impact of paternal affection with that of maternal affection in his study of California students. Hirschi's analysis indicated that the two parents were equally important and, moreover, that attachment to one parent had as much beneficial influence on the child as attachment to both.

Most of the evidence on parental attitudes toward their children has depended on information from adolescents who have simultaneously reported their parents behavior and their own delinquencies. Because these studies are based on data reporting delinquency and socialization variables at the same time and by the same source, they are unable to disentangle causes from effects.

Evidence from adolescents' reports of interactions with their parents when they were fifteen and of their own delinquency when they were seventeen years old suggests that friendly interaction with parents may deter delinquency (Liska and Reed). Relying on adolescents to report about their parents' child-rearing behavior assumes that the adolescents have correctly perceived, accurately recall, and honestly report the behavior of their parents. There are grounds for questioning these assumptions.

Experimental studies show that conscious attention is unnecessary for experiences to be influential, so salient features of their socialization may not have been noticed by the adolescents. Studies have also shown that reports of family interaction tend to reflect socially desirable perspectives. To the extent this bias afflicts adolescents' reports, real differences in family upbringing tend to blur. When parents report on their own behavior, they are likely both to have a limited and biasing perspective and to misrepresent what they are willing to reveal.

A handful of studies have used measures of parent-child interaction not subject to the biases of recall and social approval. Robert Sampson and John Laub reanalyzed data from the files compiled by Sheldon and Eleanor Glueck. Using multiple sources for information about parent-child relations, they found that parental rejection was a strong predictor of criminality. After coding case records based on home observations for a period of approximately five years, Joan McCord retraced 235 members of the Cambridge Somerville Youth Study. She found that those who had mothers who were self-confident, provided leadership, were consistently nonpunitive, and affectionate were unlikely to commit crimes. Thus, studies on emotional climate in the home present consistent results. Like parental conflict, negative parent-child relations enhance the probability of delinquency. Parental affection appears to reduce the probability of crime. Not surprisingly, parental affection and close family ties tend to be linked with other features of family interaction.

Variations in discipline and crime

Psychoanalytic theory postulates that development of the superego depends on the "introjection" of a punitive father. This perspective generated research on successive training for control of oral, anal, and sexual drives and on techniques for curbing dependency and aggression. Although resultant studies failed to produce a coherent picture showing which disciplinary techniques promoted a strong conscience and which decreased antisocial behavior, they focused attention on the relationship between discipline and deviance. Studies less closely tied to psychoanalytic theory have considered various types of punishment and used such concepts as firmness, fairness, and consistency in analyzing relationships between discipline and crime.

The Gluecks found that incarcerated delinquent boys rarely had "firm but kindly" discipline from either parent, yet a majority of the nondelinquents with whom they were compared experienced this type of discipline. Parents of delinquents were more likely to use physical punishment and less likely to supervise their sons. Hirschi characterized discipline by asking if the parents punished by slapping or hitting, by removing privileges, and by nagging or scolding.

He found that use of these types of discipline was related to delinquency, a conclusion which suggests that such punishments promoted the behaviors they were "designed to prevent" (p. 102).

Several longitudinal studies investigating effects of punishment on aggressive behavior have shown that punishments are more likely to result in defiance than compliance. Power and Chapieski studied toddlers one month after they had started walking unassisted and again a month later. The sample, drawn from Lamaze classes, was middle class, with mothers at home. Among them, "Infants of physically punishing mothers showed the lowest levels of compliance and were most likely to manipulate breakable objects during the observations" (p. 273). Additionally, six months later, the same infants showed slower development as measured by the Bayley mental test scores.

Crockenberg and Litman studied two year olds in the laboratory, where they measured the infants' obedience to requests and interviewed their mothers about discipline and family life. The same mother-child pairs were studied a month later in their homes during meal preparation and mealtime. After controlling other types of maternal behavior, the observers' ratings indicated that negative control was related to defiance in both settings.

Similarly, spanking seems counterproductive for children preparing to enter school. Strassberg, Dodge, Pettit, and Bates recruited families in three cities as they registered the children for kindergarten. Parents present in the home reported their disciplinary practices over the prior year. The children were subsequently observed in their classrooms. Children spanked by their mothers or fathers displayed more angry, reactive aggression in the kindergarten classrooms than did those who did not receive physical punishments.

In 1997, McCord analyzed the effects of corporal punishment based on biweekly observation of 224 parents and their sons over an average period of five and one-half years. In addition to measuring the use of corporal punishment in the home, each parent was rated in terms of warmth expressed toward the child. At the time of these ratings, the sons were between the ages of ten and sixteen. Thirty years later, the criminal records of the subjects were traced. Regardless of whether or not a father was affectionate toward his son, his use of corporal punishment predicted an increased likelihood that the son would subsequently be convicted for a serious crime.

Regardless of whether or not a mother was affectionate toward her son, the mother's use of corporal punishment predicted an increased likelihood that the son would subsequently be convicted for a serious violent crime.

Punishment is not necessary to rear an emotionally healthy, behaviorally adaptable, and socially responsible child. Nevertheless, most American adults experienced at least some punishment, typically physical punishment, when they were children. Most use some physical punishment in raising their children. Therefore it is clear that healthy development can occur when physical punishment has been used. Although in the short run, punishments may stop unwanted behavior, they also increase the likelihood that children will learn to use force to get what they want. The use of punishments also endanger the parent-child relationship, a relationship that often provides a foundation for subsequent familial ties.

Punishment is only one of several aspects of effective parenting. Others include holding clear standards of conduct and rules of behavior and communicating these clearly to children. Communication is promoted through attending to what children are doing, monitoring behavior so that parental reactions to unwanted behavior are contingent on that behavior and so that misbehavior can be prevented.

General socialization and crime

In studying the impact of family on delinquency, long-term studies are particularly helpful, providing information for judging whether parental rejection and unfair discipline precede or follow antisocial behavior. For two decades, David Farrington and Donald West traced the development of 411 working-class London boys born between 1951 and 1953. When the boys were between eight and ten years old, their teachers identified some as particularly difficult and aggressive. Social workers visited the homes of the boys in 1961 and gathered information on the parents' attitudes toward their sons, disciplinary techniques used, and compatibility between the parents. In 1974, as the boys reached maturity, each was classified as noncriminal (if there were no convictions) or, according to his criminal record, as a violent or a nonviolent criminal. Farrington and West found that the families most likely to produce criminals had been quarrelsome, provided little supervision, and included a parent with a criminal record.

Furthermore, boys whose parents had been harsh or cruel in 1961 were more likely than their classmates to acquire records for violent crimes. Parental cruelty was actually a more accurate selector of boys who would become violent criminals than was the child's early aggressiveness.

Other longitudinal studies show antecedents to aggression and antisocial behavior similar to those found by Farrington and West. McCord found that maternal rejection and lack of self-confidence, paternal alcoholism and criminality, lack of supervision, parental conflict, and parental aggressiveness permitted predictions of adult criminality that were more accurate than those based on a person's own juvenile offense record. In studying Swedish schoolboys, Dan Olweus found that ratings of maternal rejection, parental punitiveness, and absence of parental control predicted aggressiveness. Descriptions of the family had been obtained from interviews with the parents when the boys were sixth-graders, and aggressiveness was evaluated by the boy's classmates three years later. In her Finnish longitudinal study, Lea Pulkkinen discovered that lack of interest in and control of the fourteen-year-old child's activities, use of physical punishments, and inconsistency of discipline tended to lead to criminality by the age of twenty.

All of these studies suggest that delinquents have parents who act unfairly or who are too willing to inflict pain, whereas the parents of nondelinquents provide consistent and compassionate attention. Community variations may account for the fact that some varieties of family life have different effects in terms of delinquency in different communities. In general, consistent friendly parental guidance seems to protect children from delinquency regardless of neighborhoods. But poor socialization practices seem to be more potent in disrupted neighborhoods.

In sum, family life influences delinquency through providing offspring with predispositions regarding how to cope with life outside the family. Children reared by affectionate, consistent parents are unlikely to commit serious crimes either as juveniles or as adults. On the other hand, children reared by parents who neglect or reject them are likely to be greatly influenced by their community environments. When communities offer opportunities and encouragement for criminal behavior, children reared by neglecting or rejecting parents are likely to become delinquents.

Siblings and crime

Studies of family relationships and crime have commonly centered on parent-child influence. Generally, if included at all, siblings are mentioned only in passing. Daniel Glaser, Bernard Lander, and William Abbott, however, focused on siblings when asking why some people become drug addicts. Three pairs of sisters and thirty-four pairs of brothers living in a slum area of New York City responded to questions asked in interviews by a former addict and a former gang leader. One member of each pair had never used heroin, whereas the other had been an addict. Results of this study suggested that the typical addict was about two years younger than the nonaddicted sibling, spent less time at home, left school at a younger age, and began having relationships with persons of the opposite sex when younger. The interviews did not yield evidence of systematic differences between addicts and their siblings regarding parental affection or expectations for success. Like the Finnish adolescents studied by Pulkkinen, and the British delinquents in the Farrington and West sample, the addicts appear to have had peers for their reference groups. Unfortunately, relatively little is known about why some children adopt peers instead of family as reference groups.

Differences in sex, intelligence, and physique provide partial answers to why one child in a family develops problems and another does not. In addition, several studies show that even after controlling for family size (delinquents tend to come from larger families), middle children are more likely to be delinquents than are their oldest or youngest siblings. Rutter suggests that parental actions could be the determinant, with delinquent children tending to be those who were singled out for abuse by quarreling parents.

Farrington and West analyzed criminal records among the families of the 411 London boys they studied. Having a criminal brother, they discovered, was approximately as criminogenic as having a criminal father. Data from Minnesota confirm the apparent criminogenic impact of sibling criminality. In 1974, Merrill Roff traced criminal records of approximately thirteen hundred sets of siblings born between 1950 and 1953. Males whose siblings had juvenile court records were about one and a half times as likely to have court records themselves as were those whose siblings did not have such records. Furthermore, those whose brothers had been juvenile delinquents were about twice as likely to have adult criminal convictions as those who were the only juvenile delinquents in the family.

Marriage and crime

Although crimes within the family typically go unrecorded, violence between husband and wife accounts for a significant proportion of recorded criminal assaults and homicides. Additionally, as has been noted above, criminal parents tend to rear delinquent children. Apart from these facts, relatively little is known about the relationship of crime to marriage.

Two links between crime and age of marriage have been forged in the literature. First, several studies suggest that delinquents marry at younger ages than do nondelinquents. Second, criminality tends to decline at about the time that marriage takes place. Perhaps because of the popular belief that marriage has a settling effect, researchers have sometimes concluded that marriage reduces crime. Yet at least three accounts of the relationship between marriage and crime can be given. Delinquents may marry when they are ready to settle down, delinquents who are less criminally inclined may be more likely to marry (with marriage marking no change in motivation), or marriage may produce change.

One of the few studies with information sufficient to test whether marriage has a palliative effect is by Farrington and West. They compared men who married between the ages of eighteen and twenty-one with unmarried men at age twenty-one. The two groups had similar histories to the age of eighteen. These comparisons failed to show that marriage reduces delinquency.

Family intervention and crime

Because studies of the causes of crime implicate parents, treatment strategies have been aimed at changing parental behavior. Alan Kazdin summarized research on parent management training by noting that it "has led to marked improvements in child behavior" (p. 1351). One long-term follow-up study of home visiting during the first pregnancies of women suggest that such visits produce reductions in juvenile crime (Olds et al.). Unmarried pregnant women were randomly assigned to have a visiting nurse or to be in a comparison group. Those whose mothers received the home visits had less than half as many arrests fifteen years later. Evidence is mounting that training in parental skills can be successful, although more work is neces-

sary both to develop effective strategies across a variety of cultural environments and to assure that the most dysfunctional families receive the training.

Interpreting the data

After World War II, scientists began to study socialization by producing in microcosm conditions that seemed important for understanding personality development. Early studies generally reflected the psychoanalytic perspective. Aggression was conceived as instinctual, and conscience was thought of as a "superego" that developed from identification with a parent. As Freudian influence declined, researchers began to consider alternative theories.

Laboratory experiments showing that observing aggression can produce aggressive behavior suggest why punitive parents may tend to have aggressive offspring. Imitation of aggression in the laboratory increases when aggression is described as justified. Parents who justify their use of pain as punishment may foster the idea that inflicting pain is appropriate in other contexts.

Much effort has been expended in investigating the role played by rewards and punishments in teaching children how to act. Although it has been demonstrated that prompt feedback increases conformity to norms, some studies also show the paradoxical effects of rewards and punishments. Rewards sometimes decrease performance, and punishments sometimes increase forbidden actions. These studies suggest that use of rewards and punishments can create ambiguous messages. Similar ambiguities may affect parent-child relationships. Lax discipline and the absence of supervision, as well as parental conflict, could increase delinquency because they impede communication of the parents' socializing messages.

JOAN MCCORD

See also CONTRIBUTING TO THE DELINQUENCY OF MINORS; DOMESTIC VIOLENCE; EDUCATION AND CRIME; FAMILY ABUSE AND CRIME; HOMICIDE: BEHAVIORAL ASPECTS; RAPE: BEHAVIORAL ASPECTS; RAPE: LEGAL ASPECTS; SEXUAL OFFENSES: CONSENSUAL.

BIBLIOGRAPHY

BOWLBY, JOHN. *Maternal Care and Mental Health*. New York: Schocken Books, 1966.

CAPALDI, D. M., and PATTERSON, G. R. "Relations of Parental Transition to Boys' Adjustment Problems: I. A Linear Hypothesis. II. Mothers at Risk for Transitions and Unskilled Parenting." *Developmental Psychology* 27 (1991): 489–504.

COOLEY, CHARLES H. *Human Nature and the Social Order.* (1920). Introduction by Philip Rieff. Foreword by George Herbert Mead. New York: Schocken Books, 1964.

CROCKENBERG, S., and LITMAN, C. "Autonomy as Competence in 2-Year-Olds: Maternal Correlates of Child Defiance, Compliance, and Self-assertion." *Developmental Psychology* 26 (1990): 961–971.

CROCKETT, L. J.; EGGEBEEN, D. J.; and HAWKINS, A. J. "Father's Presence and Young Children's Behavioral and Cognitive Adjustment." *Journal of Family Issues* 14, no. 3 (1993): 355–377.

DEKLYEN, M.; SPELTZ, M. L.; and GREENBERG, M. T. "Fathering and Early Onset Conduct Problems: Positive and Negative Parenting, Father Son Attachment, and the Marital Context." *Clinical Child and Family Psychology Review* 1 (1998): 3–21.

FARRINGTON, D. P. "The Family Backgrounds of Aggressive Youths." In *Aggression and Antisocial Behaviour in Childhood and Adolescence.* Edited by L. A. Hersov and M. Berger. Oxford, U.K.: Pergamon, 1978.

FARRINGTON, DAVID P., and WEST, DONALD J. "The Cambridge Study in Delinquent Development (United Kingdom)." In *Prospective Longitudinal Research in Europe: An Empirical Basis for Primary Prevention of Psychosocial Disorders.* Edited by Samoff A. Mednick and Andre E. Baert. New York: Oxford University Press, 1981. Pages 137–145.

FREUD, SIGMUND. *New Introductory Lectures on Psycho-Analysis.* New York: W. W. Norton, 1964.

GLASER, DANIEL; LANDER, BERNARD; and ABBOTT, WILLIAM. "Opiate Addicted and Non-addicted Siblings in a Slum Area." *Social Problems* 18 (1971): 510–521.

GLUECK, SHELDON, and GLUECK, ELEANOR T. "Unraveling Juvenile Delinquency." New York: Commonwealth Fund, 1950.

GORMAN-SMITH, D.; TOLAN, P. H.; and HENRY, D. "The Relation of Community and Family to Risk among Urban-Poor Adolescents." In *Where and When: Historical and Geographical Aspects of Psychopathology.* Edited by P. Cohen, C. Slomkowski, and L. N. Robins. Mahwah, N.J.: Lawrence Erlbaum Associates, 1999.

HIRSCHI, TRAVIS. *Causes of Delinquency.* Berkeley: University of California Press, 1969.

KAZDIN, A. E. "Parent Management Training: Evidence, Outcomes, and Issues." *Journal of the American Academy of Child and Adolescent Psychiatry* 36, no. 10 (1997): 1349–1356.

LISKA, A. E., and REED, M. D. "Ties to Conventional Institutions and Delinquency: Estimating Reciprocal Effects." *American Sociological Review* 50 (August 1985): 547–560.

MATSUEDA, R. L., and HEIMER, K. "Race, Family Structure, and Delinquency: A Test of Differential Association and Social Control Theories." *American Sociological Review* 52 (December 1987): 826–840.

MCCORD, JOAN. "A Longitudinal View of the Relationship between Paternal Absence and Crime." In *Abnormal Offenders, Delinquency, and the Criminal Justice System.* Edited by J. Gunn and D. P. Farrington. Chichester, John Wiley, 1982. Pages 113–128.

———. "Long-term Perspectives on Parental Absence." In *Straight and Devious Pathways from Childhood to Adulthood.* Edited by L. N. Robins and M. Rutter. Cambridge, U.K.: Cambridge University Press, 1990.

———. "Family Relationships, Juvenile Delinquency, and Adult Criminality." *Criminology* 29, no. 3 (1991): 397–417.

———. "Family as Crucible for Violence: Comment on Gorman-Smith et al." *Journal of Family Psychology* 10, no. 2 (1996): 147–152.

MCCORD, J.; MCCORD, W.; and THURBER, E. "Some Effects of Paternal Absence on Male Children." *Journal of Abnormal and Social Psychology* 64, no. 5 (1962): 361–369.

MEAD, GEORGE HERBERT. *Mind, Self and Society from the Standpoint of a Social Behaviorist.* Edited with an introduction by Charles W. Morris. Chicago: University of Chicago Press, 1962.

OLDS, D. L.; HENDERSON, C. R.; COLE, R.; ECKENRODE, J.; KITZMAN, H.; LUCKEY, D.; PETTITT, L.; SIDORA, K.; MORRIS, P.; and POWERS, J. "Long-term Effects of Nurse Home Visitation on Children's Criminal and Antisocial Behavior: 15-year Follow-up of a Randomized Controlled Trial." *Journal of the American Medical Association.* 280 (1998): 1238–1244.

OLWEUS, DAN. "Familial and Temperamental Determinants of Aggressive Behavior in Adolescent Boys: A Causal Analysis." *Developmental Psychology* 16 (1980): 644–660.

PLATO. "Laws." *The Dialogues of Plato,* vol. 2. Translated by B. Jowett. New York: Random House, 1937. Pages 407–703.

POWER, T. G., and CHAPIESKI, M. L. "Childrearing and Impulse Control in Toddlers: A Naturalistic Investigation." *Developmental Psychology* 22, no. 2 (1986): 271–275.

PULKKINEN, LEA. "Search for Alternatives to Aggression in Finland." *Aggression in Global Perspective*. Edited by A. P. Goldstein and M. Segall. Elmsford, N.Y.: Pergamon, 1983. Pages 104–144.

ROFF, MERRILL. "Long-Term Follow-up of Juvenile and Adult Delinquency with Samples Differing in Some Important Respects: Cross-validation within the Same Research Program." *The Origins and Course of Psychopathology*. Edited by John S. Strauss, Haroutun M. Babigian, and Merrill Roff. New York: Plenum, 1977. Pages 323–344.

RUTTER, MICHAEL. "Epidemiological Strategies and Psychiatric Concepts in Research on the Vulnerable Child." *The Child in His Family: Children at Psychiatric Risk. International Yearbook for Child Psychiatry and Allied Disciplines*, vol. 3. Edited by E. James Anthony and Cyrille Koupemik. New York: Wiley, 1974. Pages 167–179.

SAMPSON, R. J., and LAUB, J. H. *Crime in the Making: Pathways and Turning Points Through Life*. Cambridge, Mass.: Harvard University Press, 1993.

STRASSBERG, Z.; DODGE, K. A.; PETTIT, G.; and BATES, J. E. "Spanking in the Home and Children's Subsequent Aggression Behavior toward Kindergarten Peers." *Development and Psychopathology* 6, no. 3 (1994): 445–461.

SUTHERLAND, EDWIN H., and CRESSEY, DONALD R. *Criminology* (1924–). 10th ed. Philadelphia: Lippincott, 1978.

WEST, DONALD J., and FARRINGTON, DAVID P. *The Delinquent Way of Life: Third Report of the Cambridge Study in Delinquent Development*. London: Heinemann, 1977.

FEAR OF CRIME

Criminal events provoke many emotions from the general public—outrage, sadness, anger, disgust, shock. One of those emotions, public fear of crime, has drawn concerted attention from social scientists since the late 1960s. One reason for that attention is a simple but sobering fact: The number of people who experience fear of crime during any particular period is enormously greater than the number of people who will actually become victims of crime. To illustrate, about 40 to 50 percent of respondents in national surveys each year report that they are afraid to walk alone at night in the vicinity of their home, and more than half say that becoming a victim of crime is something that they personally worry about. By contrast, the chances of actually becoming a victim of crime each year are considerably smaller, ranging from fewer than one in ten thousand persons per year for homicide to about one in ten to twenty households per year for residential burglary. Fear of crime, then, is a much larger social problem than crime itself (Warr, 1994, 1995).

The phrase "fear of crime" is sometimes loosely used to describe a variety of attitudes, perceptions, or feelings about crime (e.g., concern about the moral decline of the country, the deterioration of neighborhoods, or mistrust of strangers). Used properly, however, the term *fear* refers to a particular emotion, that is, a feeling of apprehension or dread caused by an awareness or expectation of danger. Psychologists often use the word *fear* to describe reactions to immediate threats (a stranger moves toward you with a weapon in his hand) and the term *anxiety* to describe reactions to possible future events (e.g., what will happen when I walk home tonight or go to the store?). Criminologists rarely honor this distinction, however, and conventionally speak of "fear of crime" even when what they have in mind is anxiety about crime.

Perceptions of risk

Research on fear of crime consistently indicates that the proximate cause of fear is the *perceived risk* of victimization, or an individual's subjective probability that a crime will occur to them. That may seem like an obvious fact, but the relation between fear and perceived risk is more complex than it might appear, and it is critical to understanding fear. Not all people, for example, react to the same risk in the same way. The degree of risk that is sufficient to terrify an elderly woman, for example, might scarcely elicit a reaction from a nineteen-year-old male (Warr, 1987). Individuals also differ as to what constitutes a risk; a wrong phone number or obscene phone call may signify little or nothing to one person, but imply a threat of imminent danger to another.

Perceived risk is also crucial to understanding the degree to which different crimes are feared. There is a natural tendency to assume that fear is directly proportional to the perceived seriousness of crimes, meaning that people fear very serious offenses (homicide or robbery, for example) more so than less serious crimes (residential burglary or auto theft). But that would be true only if people perceived all crimes to be equally likely. In the real world, there is enormous variation across crimes in the perceived risk of victimization as well as the perceived seriousness of crimes, and neither of these factors alone is a sufficient condition for fear. In order to provoke strong fear, an offense must be perceived to be both serious and likely. Although it may seem surprising, homicide is not among the most highly feared crimes in the United States because, despite its seriousness, it is (correctly) viewed as an unlikely event. By contrast, the most feared offense in the United States is residential burglary when no one is home, a crime that is perceived to be fairly serious and rather likely (Warr and Stafford; Warr 1994, 1995).

Just how people form perceptions of risk is not clearly understood, although mass media news coverage of crime seems to have a substantial impact on public perceptions of crime (Warr, 2000). In everyday life outside the home, people often encounter cues or signs that imply heightened risk and thus incite fear. One of those cues is darkness, a particularly potent sign of danger. Another is novelty, or exposure to new places. Rather than arousing fear, a cue that acts to alleviate fear is the presence of other people—even strangers—in the immediate vicinity. Individuals generally feel safer in public places when other people are around—unless, of course, those other people themselves appear to be dangerous. One category of persons that is particularly frightening to many people is young males (especially groups of young males), and young males even seem to frighten one another (Warr, 1990).

These cues aside, a number of investigators have sought to identify the physical and social features of neighborhoods—litter and trash, graffiti, transients, broken windows, abandoned homes, and other so-called signs of incivility—that seem to mark areas as dangerous places (Ferraro, 1995). Research indicates that these signs are in fact correlated with fear, but this finding is difficult to interpret because places that have signs of incivility also tend to have high crime rates, and it is therefore difficult to isolate the cause of fear (is it crime or signs of crime?).

Gender and age

Although fear of crime is quite common in our society, it is substantially more common in some population groups than others. Women, for example, are significantly more prone to fear of crime than are men. The large difference in fear between men and women shows itself not only in self-reports of fear, but also in the behav-

ioral repertoires of the sexes. Women, for example, are far more likely than men to report that they stay at home at night or that they avoid leaving the house alone. One of the factors that seems to underlie the differences between the sexes is the extraordinary fear that many women feel toward one crime—rape. Evidence indicates that rape is feared more than any other crime among younger women (those under about thirty-five years of age), that it is perceived to be approximately as serious a crime as homicide, and that rape is a "master offense" that lurks behind fear of other crimes (e.g., residential burglary, obscene phone calls). So central is rape to the fears of women that one is tempted to speculate that, for many women, fear of crime is fear of rape (Warr, 1984, 1985; Ferraro, 1996).

Fear of crime varies not only by gender, but by age as well. The evidence here is more complex, however. Early studies reported a simple positive relation between age and fear, but more recent, offense-specific, studies reveal that age differences in fear are apparent only for some offenses, and that even in those cases fear is not consistently related to age in a monotonic fashion. Using national data and aggregating over offenses, Ferraro (1995) found fear to be strongest among middle-aged individuals (ages forty-five to fifty-four in his study) and among the very youngest adults (eighteen to twenty-four).

Altruistic fear

Nearly all research to date has concentrated on the fear that individuals feel for their own personal safety. People, however, can and often do feel fear for other persons as well, an emotion that has been referred to as *altruistic fear*. Parents, for example, ordinarily exhibit strong concern for their children—especially young children—and often take vigorous precautions to protect them. Similarly, married couples often fear for one another's safety, although husbands are more likely to worry about their wives than vice versa. Altruistic fear appears to be more common than personal fear and evidently inspires many day-to-day precautions against crime.

Effects of fear

To criminologists and sociologists, the importance of fear ultimately lies in its consequences for individuals, neighborhoods, and for society as a whole. Research suggests that the consequences of fear in the U.S. are widespread and sometimes grave (Warr, 1994, 2000). Nearly all Americans, for example, take some precautions in their everyday lives, if only minor ones like locking doors or leaving lights on. Of the many precautions that citizens employ, the most frequently reported is *spatial avoidance*, or avoiding places that are believed to be dangerous. In many cities, entire regions of the urban landscape—certain parks, neighborhoods, beaches, downtown sectors, commercial areas, or industrial districts—are effectively off limits to a large segment of the population because of their reputations as "dangerous places." Fearful individuals are also less likely to leave their homes at night, travel alone, answer their doors, or travel on foot. The proportion of urban women who engage in these sorts of precautions is nothing short of startling, exceeding 40 percent in some cities (Warr, 1994).

Fear of crime can have devastating long-term effects for neighborhoods, according to research by Skogan. Once fear of crime sets in, established, higher-income residents move away, only to be replaced by new arrivals with weaker commitments to the neighborhood. Residents frequently withdraw from community life, further eroding residents' control of the neighborhood. Some analysts believe that fear of crime has contributed to a general decline in the quality of life in the United States, restricting individual freedom and producing a "fortress society."

However severe consequences, fear is a natural and essential protective mechanism, and fear of crime has undoubtedly prevented many people from becoming victims of crime. It is when fear is *out of proportion to objective risk*, however, that it becomes dysfunctional for an organism or for a group. One frequently overlooked benefit of fear is that it sometimes draws communities together in common purpose and enhances social solidarity. Evidence for this can be seen in such community activities as neighborhood crime watch programs, "take back the night" marches, police/community liaison programs, and similar local initiatives. The challenge today is to insure that the public is fully and accurately informed about the risks of criminal victimization, and that public fear of crime is not needless or excessive.

MARK WARR

See also AGE AND CRIME; MASS MEDIA AND CRIME; PREVENTION: POLICE ROLE; PUBLIC OPINION AND CRIME.

BIBLIOGRAPHY

FERRARO, KENNETH F. *Fear of Crime: Interpreting Victimization Risk.* Albany: State University of New York Press, 1995.

———. "Women's Fear of Victimization: Shadow of Sexual Assault?" *Social Forces* 75 (1996): 667–690.

SKOGAN, WESLEY G. *Disorder and Decline: Crime and the Spiral of Decay in American Neighborhoods.* New York: Free Press, 1990.

SKOGAN, WESLEY G., and MAXFIELD, MICHAEL G. *Coping with Crime: Individual and Neighborhood Reactions.* Beverly Hills, Calif.: Sage, 1981.

WARR, MARK. "The Accuracy of Public Beliefs about Crime." *Social Forces* 59 (1980): 456–470.

———. "Fear of Victimization: Why Are Women and the Elderly More Afraid?" *Social Science Quarterly* 65 (1984): 681–702.

———. "Fear of Rape among Urban Women." *Social Problems* 32 (1985): 238–250.

———. "Fear of Victimization and Sensitivity to Risk." *Journal of Quantitative Criminology* 3 (1987): 29–46.

———. "Dangerous Situations: Social Context and Fear of Victimization." *Social Forces* 68 (1990): 891–907.

———. "Altruistic Fear of Victimization in Households." *Social Science Quarterly* 73 (1992): 723–736.

———. "Public Perceptions and Reactions to Violent Offending and Victimization." In *Understanding and Preventing Violence.* Vol. 4, *Consequences and Control.* Edited by Albert J. Reiss, Jr. and Jeffrey A. Roth. Washington, D.C.: National Academy Press, 1994. Pages 1–66.

———. "Poll Trends: Public Opinion on Crime and Punishment." *Public Opinion Quarterly* 59 (1995): 296–310.

———. "Fear of Crime in the United States: Avenues for Research and Policy." In *Crime and Justice 2000.* Vol. 4, *Measurement and Analysis of Crime and Justice.* Washington, D.C.: National Institute of Justice, 2000.

WARR, MARK, and STAFFORD, MARK C. "Fear of Victimization: A Look at the Proximate Causes." *Social Forces* 61 (1983): 1033–1043.

FEDERAL BUREAU OF INVESTIGATION: HISTORY

The agency now known as the Federal Bureau of Investigation (F.B.I.) has an interesting history. While today the agency enjoys extraordinary prestige and status, and is quite encompassing in its authority and jurisdiction, the agency has a rather humble, and at times scandalous and controversial, past. The purpose of this entry is to trace the evolution of the Federal Bureau of Investigation from its beginnings to its current modern-day form.

Before the beginning of the F.B.I.

At the time of the ratification of the U.S. Constitution, there was not a need or a desire for an elaborate system of policing in the United States. At this time, with few federal laws, the policing function was almost exclusively a responsibility of local government. Policing communities was quite informal, consisting most often of volunteers assigned to the "watch" who would guard the village or town at night, and, later on, during the day. Local control of the police function was a desirable feature of American policing because, ideally, it allowed residents to have input into how policing was conducted in their community. The desire for local control also helped explain why the framers of the Constitution were resistant to the idea of an all-powerful national police force.

The enforcement of the few federal laws that were in existence at this time was the responsibility of a small corps of federal agents and marshals. Again, there was no need or desire for a specialized mechanism to conduct criminal investigations at the federal level.

It was not until the mid 1800s that formal municipal police departments were created and these institutions were primarily located in the large and rapidly growing cities of the eastern United States (e.g., Boston, Philadelphia, New York). Municipal police detectives, those with primary responsibility for criminal identification and apprehension, did not appear until the late 1800s, and this development occurred largely in response to public concern about increasing crime.

In the mid- to late 1800s, the Justice Department, having no investigators of its own, borrowed agents from other federal offices to assist in investigative matters and also used agents from the Pinkerton Detective Agency, a private investigative agency. Pinkerton had investigative and operational advantages over governmental agents; namely, the agency operated without concern for cumbersome political jurisdictional lines, it had a well-developed system of internal communication and record-keeping, and it had

a system in place to share information with the investigative services of foreign nations.

In the early 1900s, an increase in urbanization and crime along with technological changes (namely, the automobile) placed extraordinary demands on the police. With a more mobile population and jurisdictional lines more easily crossed, the need for state and federal law enforcement agencies became apparent.

The beginning of the F.B.I.

President Theodore Roosevelt initially asked the U.S. Congress to create a federal detective force in 1907. Congress opposed President Roosevelt's idea on the official grounds of the long-cited public disdain for an all powerful federal law enforcement agency. However, unofficially, it was significant that in 1906 two members of Congress had been prosecuted for fraud, the investigation of which was conducted by the Justice Department using agents from another federal agency. As a result, many members of Congress were concerned about giving the executive branch of government more investigative power (power perhaps to conduct more investigations of those individuals in the legislative branch). Along with denying President Roosevelt's request, Congress passed legislation that prohibited the Justice Department from using investigators from other federal agencies. Not to be stopped by Congress, in 1908 President Roosevelt created the Bureau of Investigation by executive order and directed Attorney General Charles Bonaparte to develop the agency within the Department of Justice. Twenty permanent and eighteen temporary investigators were hired. The action on the part of President Roosevelt led to considerable political conflict and to many political battles between Congress and the president. The fear of Congress was that the Bureau of Investigation was going to act as a sort of secret police—and, in fact, these fears were quickly substantiated in 1909 when it was learned that agents from the bureau had regularly opened the mail of Senator Benjamin Tillman, one of the bureau's most vocal opponents.

The early days

With the turmoil surrounding its creation, it is not surprising that during the first years of its operation (1910s) the Bureau of Investigation was entrenched in scandal. (Actually, the entire history of the F.B.I. can be viewed as being rather scandalous, as discussed below.) However, at the same time, it was slowly becoming accepted as a law enforcement agency and assigned law enforcement responsibilities. For example, in 1910 Congress pasted the Mann Act, which prohibited the transportation of females across state lines for immoral purposes. Responsibility for the enforcement of the law was given to the Bureau of Investigation. Other statutes followed, prohibiting the transportation of stolen goods, vehicles, and obscene materials.

In 1916, with three hundred agents, and in the face of war in Europe, the bureau was given power to conduct counterintelligence and anti-radical investigations. In 1919, the country experienced a series of bombings with targets ranging from police departments to banks (and included the residence of Attorney General A. Mitchell Palmer). These actions were believed to be the responsibility of communists and others who were "un-American." The bombings and their aftermath became known as the "Red Scare." In response to the bombings, Attorney General Palmer established the General Intelligence Division (GID) within the Justice Department to increase significantly the ability to store information on radicals and those suspected of being sympathetic to radicals. An individual by the name of John Edgar Hoover was named the head of the GID.

In 1920, using information from the GID, Attorney General Palmer authorized a series of raids (to be known as the "Palmer Raids") in thirty-three cities across the country that resulted in more than five thousand arrests of people believed to be un-American or communists. The plan was to then deport the individuals who were arrested. The problem was that most of the people arrested were not radicals at all. The courts ordered many of those arrested to be released. In 1921, during congressional hearings on the conduct of the GID and the Bureau during the Palmer raids, Attorney General Palmer and Hoover fiercely defended their Bureau of Investigation, and the actions of their agents.

Enter J. Edgar Hoover

Calvin Coolidge was elected president in 1923 and, in the aftermath of the Palmer raids, one of his first tasks was to reform the Justice Department, the Bureau of Investigation in particular. Harlan Fiske Stone, former Dean of Columbia University Law School and critic of the Palmer raids was appointed to head the Justice

Department as attorney general. On 10 May 1924 Attorney General Stone offered J. Edgar Hoover the directorship of the Bureau of Investigation on an acting basis. It was after Roger Baldwin, founder of the American Civil Liberties Union, sent a favorable recommendation to the attorney general that Hoover was named the permanent director of the bureau.

J. Edgar Hoover was born 1 January 1895 in Washington, D.C. After graduation from high school he worked at the Library of Congress and attended George Washington University Law School. Upon graduation from law school in 1917 he went to work as a clerk in the Department of Justice.

When Hoover was appointed Director of the Bureau of Investigation in 1924, the bureau had 441 agents. At the direction of Attorney General Stone, Hoover cut the staff to 339 agents by 1929. During his first few days as director, Hoover went through the personnel files and identified agents that should be fired. Agents that were not fired were retrained. Hiring standards were raised and training in law or accounting was required. A training school was established for various skills and for learning the procedures of the bureau. According to Hoover, promotion would be based on performance, not seniority. Control and standardization were the themes that reflected his management style. Even early on, Hoover was well aware of the importance of public support in fighting crime. In remarks prepared for the Attorney General in 1925, he wrote: "The Agents of the Bureau of Investigation have been impressed with the fact that the real problem of law enforcement is in trying to obtain the cooperation and sympathy of the public and they cannot hope to get such cooperation until they themselves merit the respect of the public" (F.B.I., 1997). Hoover served as director of the Bureau of Investigation (later the F.B.I.) for forty-eight years—until his death in 1972. Without question, J. Edgar Hoover was the most influential man in the history of the F.B.I.

The gangster era and the rise of crime

In the late 1920s through the 1930s, numerous high-profile crimes and criminals took center stage with J. Edgar Hoover and his agents, who became known as "G-Men." Gangsters, in particular, became larger than life, capturing the imagination of millions of Americans. Gangsters like "Machine Gun" Kelly, "Pretty Boy" Floyd, "Baby Face" Nelson, John Dillinger, Al Capone,

"Ma" Barker, and others became notorious heroes. Director Hoover rose to the challenge, and with the assistance of Hollywood and detective fiction writers, he was able to portray his agents (and himself) as mythical foes of the gangsters. While gangsters were portrayed as public enemies, the Bureau of Investigation's G-Men were cop-heros, and J. Edgar Hoover was top-cop.

Even beyond this skillful portrayal, Hoover was able to make the good battle against gangsters a personal struggle and to use the public's interest to his and the bureau's advantage. For example, in 1933 four of the bureau's agents and several police officers were escorting bank robber Frank "Jelly" Nash to Levenworth Prison when they were ambushed by three men with machine guns. Three officers and one agent were killed. At least in partial response to this tragic event, Congress passed nine major crime bills giving Hoover much more authority and power. Congress also authorized agents to carry firearms for the first time.

In 1932 the nation was transfixed by the news of the kidnapping and murder of the infant son of Charles and Anne Lindbergh. Kidnapping laws were passed by Congress and the Bureau of Investigation was made responsible for this and other kidnapping investigations. When the kidnapper was apprehended, it was due more to the work of the Treasury agents on the case and an attentive gas station worker (who wrote down the license plate number of the kidnapper's vehicle) than skillful investigatory work on the part of the bureau. Nevertheless, J. Edgar Hoover was able to take credit and reap the political rewards.

The bureau was not immune from bungled investigations. John Dillinger proved a case in point. When bank robber John Dillinger escaped from jail on 3 March 1934, the bureau mounted a full-scale operation to catch him. For two months Dillinger eluded the bureau's traps. Then Agent Purvis received a tip that Dillinger and members of his gang were hiding in Little Bohemia, a resort in Wisconsin. As agents converged on the lodge, several men ran from the area. As they drove away, agents fired on them, killing one and seriously injuring the others. As it turned out, these men were not part of Dillinger's gang. Dillinger and his associates had escaped through a back window. This latest failed attempt to capture Dillinger was a major embarrassment to Hoover and the bureau. Dillinger became public enemy number one. Acting on another tip several weeks later, Purvis shot and killed Dillinger as he left a theater. Purvis got the glory as the man who got Dillinger (and later "Baby Face" Nelson) and Hoover resented it.

Even with its relatively short history, by the mid-1930's Hoover had marshalled the imagery to argue convincingly that the Bureau of Investigation protected American citizens from communists, gangsters, and even kidnappers. By most accounts, it was masterful public relations. But there was more. Starting in 1935 a series of G-men movies were produced. Hollywood's film codes and censorship laws only allowed gangsters in movies if they were being captured or killed by agents of the bureau. Hoover became public hero number one.

Through the 1920s and 1930s, the bureau embarked on several initiatives, each of which helped solidify its reputation as the top law enforcement agency in the country. For example, Hoover received authorization and funding for a national fingerprint identification service, and in 1924 the Bureau's Identification Division was created. The Bureau would serve as the national repository and clearinghouse for fingerprint records, and it began a campaign to collect fingerprints from every American. Representatives of the bureau even went door-to-door in an effort to collect prints.

In 1930 the bureau began administering the Uniform Crime Report (UCR) and began to serve as the central clearinghouse for information on crimes as reported by local, state, and federal police and law enforcement agencies. While there were (and continue to be) serious problems with the UCR as a measure of crime, this mechanism placed crime control, and information about crime, as a central responsibility of the bureau and portrayed the bureau as a supervisory entity to other law enforcement agencies.

In 1932, with a borrowed microscope and a few other pieces of equipment, the bureau's laboratory opened. During its first year of operation, the laboratory conducted 963 examinations—nearly all of which involved examinations of handwriting in extortion cases (F.B.I., 1990).

In 1935 the Bureau began operation of the National Police Academy (later known as the F.B.I. National Academy) to train select local police officers in investigative methods. Also in 1935, the bureau changed its name to the Federal Bureau of Investigation (F.B.I.).

The new challenges of World War II

With the rise of totalitarianism abroad, a new concern with internal enemies developed. At the request of President Franklin D. Roosevelt in 1936, the F.B.I. expanded information collection on the domestic activities of Communists and radicals. By 1939 Hoover had re-established the General Intelligence Division. The war years provided the F.B.I. with a powerful rationale for monitoring political radicals. In addition, the passage of the Smith Act in 1940 provided a legal basis for F.B.I. domestic security investigations. The Smith Act made it a crime to advocate or conspire to advocate the forceful overthrow of the government. During the early 1940s, the F.B.I. underwent dramatic growth, with the number of employees nearly doubling, from 7,420 to 13,317, and the number of agents doubling to 5,702 during the same period.

In the early 1940s the bureau began resorting to more intrusive investigative techniques, wiretaps in particular, but also physical surveillance, elaborate record keeping, mail openings, and warrantless searches. Sometimes the bureau's monitoring activities went beyond the expected targets (like Communists) to less likely ones, like First Ladies. While President Roosevelt was quite supportive of Hoover and the F.B.I., Mrs. Roosevelt was not. In fact, Hoover considered her an enemy of the F.B.I., and she likely considered the F.B.I. an enemy of hers. In response to Eleanor Roosevelt's criticism of the F.B.I., the First Lady and her assistants became the targets of investigations that were designed to intimidate her and, eventually, did silence her criticism. Despite her protests, the investigations continued and the F.B.I. obtained damaging information on Mrs. Roosevelt that included evidence of extramarital relationships (Powers, 1987).

The fruits of this and other unofficial investigations by the Bureau become the basis of what was been referred as Hoover's secret files (Gentry, 1991). The creation of these secret files got a boost with some official action in 1947. In 1947, the executive branch established the Federal Employee-Loyalty Security Program, which in its final form required that each federal agency conduct investigations of its personnel. This information was to be forwarded to the F.B.I. for further investigative work or for filing. In addition, as part of this program, the F.B.I. was given responsibility for conducting investigations of presidential appointees, Supreme Court nominees, and individuals in other high-level positions. With this responsibility, the bureau exercised extraordinary influence in determining who filled high-level governmental positions,

given the bureau's latitude to investigate some people more thoroughly than others.

The rise of organized crime

The 1950s saw a decreasing concern with domestic Communism and an increasing concern with organized crime. As early as 1951, Senator Estes Kefauver had presided over a highly publicized U.S. Senate investigation of organized crime. The event that focused public attention on the problem most directly, however, was the discovery in 1957 of a gathering of major criminal figures at the home of gangster Joseph Barbara in upstate New York. Senate crime hearings were organized and the counsel for the investigating committee was Robert F. Kennedy. With his brother John F. Kennedy's election to the presidency in 1960 and his own confirmation as attorney general in 1961, Robert Kennedy was determined to increase law enforcement pressure on organized crime. Both Kennedys supported new crime laws that strengthened the bureau's jurisdiction in organized crime cases. Aggressive use of wiretaps continued unabated.

After President Kennedy was assassinated in 1963 and Attorney General Kennedy resigned in 1964, the F.B.I.'s organized crime effort slackened briefly, and in 1965, President Lyndon B. Johnson ordered a halt to all electronic eavesdropping not related to national security. But interest in the area was renewed in 1967 with the report of President Johnson's Task Force on Organized Crime. By this time, Hoover had gathered so much information on friends and foes alike, and was so well liked (or feared), that he was virtually untouchable. In fact, President Johnson signed an executive order allowing J. Edgar Hoover to serve as director of the F.B.I. indefinitely.

The administration of President Richard M. Nixon continued to maintain law enforcement pressure on organized crime. In 1970, Congress enacted the most far-reaching law ever directed against organized crime—the Organized Crime Control Act. This statute authorized special grand juries to investigate organized crime and provided for granting witnesses immunity for the use of their testimony.

Civil rights and Vietnam

The F.B.I. had a prominent role in combating race-related violence in the 1960s. Particularly significant was the F.B.I. investigation into the disappearance of three civil rights workers in Mississippi. Bureau agents identified and interviewed Ku Klux Klan members in Mississippi and offered payment for information concerning the missing persons. The case finally broke in August 1964, and six people were convicted of violating the victims' civil rights. From this point on, F.B.I. agents throughout the South became increasingly involved in combating racist violence, but often did using techniques previously reserved for dealing with organized crime and Communists.

The F.B.I. became involved in matters relating to the Vietnam War protests. In June 1970, President Nixon created a working group of representatives from the F.B.I., the Central Intelligence Agency (CIA), the Defense Intelligence Agency, and the National Security Agency to consider the need for more extensive domestic intelligence activities in light of the disorders taking place across the United States. Although the Bureau was reluctant to get involved in this initiative, Hoover did agree to install seventeen telephone taps on newsmen and White House employees suspected of receiving and leaking secret information. When the details of the F.B.I.'s wiretaps were revealed, the damage to the bureau was far-reaching.

On 9 March 1971 a small F.B.I. office in Media, Pennsylvania, was burglarized by a group that called itself the Citizen Commission to Investigate the F.B.I. Hundreds of documents that cast light into the secret operations of the F.B.I. were taken. The documents told the story of widespread surveillance and wiretapping of various groups including the Black Panthers, the Jewish Defense League, and the Ku Klux Klan. Some of the documents made reference to COINTELPROs (Counter-Intelligence Programs), the code name given by the F.B.I. to operations aimed at disrupting or even destroying political and social protest groups identified as subversive; these programs were in operation from 1956 to 1971. The public learned that the F.B.I. was guilty of extensive invasion of privacy. The F.B.I. was under siege. Senator Edward Kennedy called for Hoover's resignation. Even President Nixon was growing cold to Hoover, as Hoover was viewed as unresponsive to many of Nixon's investigative requests (Powers, 1987). The legacy of J. Edgar Hoover came to an end with his death on 2 May 1972.

In the aftermath of Hoover

With additional details of the COINTELPRO files made public in 1973, Congress established committees to investigate the intelligence community. During the course of the hearings, the process of internal F.B.I. reform was continued. In the spring of 1976 the new director, Clarence Kelley, terminated most domestic security investigations. Later, in 1976, the Justice Department issued guidelines aimed at regulating future F.B.I. domestic intelligence activities. These guidelines restricted the circumstances under which domestic security investigations could be initiated, limited the techniques that could be used, and restrained the bureau in its use of informants.

In 1978 Kelly was replaced with William Webster. In 1982, following an increase in terrorist activities abroad, Webster made counterterrorism a top F.B.I. priority. The F.B.I. was involved in numerous espionage cases during the mid-1980s—so many that the press dubbed 1985 "the year of the spy." Throughout the 1980s, the F.B.I. and other federal law enforcement agencies also devoted substantial attention and resources to the illegal drug trade. In 1982 the attorney general gave the F.B.I. concurrent jurisdiction with the Drug Enforcement Administration (DEA) over narcotics violations in the U.S. This increase in attention lead to numerous well-publicized drug seizures and arrests, and led to the dismantling of significant drug rings. Webster also gave increased investigative priority to white collar crimes and public corruption. High-profile investigations on this front included ABSCAM (an investigation of corruption among congressmen) and GREYLORD (an investigation of corruption in the Cook County Illinois court system).

The contemporary F.B.I.

In May 1987, William Webster left the F.B.I. to become director of the CIA and Williams Sessions became the new director of the F.B.I. With the formal dissolution of the Soviet Union, national security matters were less of a concern. In 1992, the F.B.I. reassigned three hundred special agents from foreign counterintelligence duties to violent crime investigations across the country. At the same time, the F.B.I. laboratory began using DNA technology in solving crimes (and prosecuting suspects).

Following controversial and allegedly politically-motivated allegations of ethics misconduct,

692   FEDERAL BUREAU OF INVESTIGATION: HISTORY

Director Sessions was removed from office in July 1993. Shortly after, Louis Freeh was appointed director of the F.B.I. Director Freeh was viewed as an ambitious reformer with high ethical character. With Freeh, the F.B.I. continued its commitment to hire and promote more women and minorities. It is also during this time that the work of the Behavioral Science Unit of the Bureau became an infamous—psychological profiling of suspects based on their crimes (particularly serial homicide) became very well known—but little understood—activity of the bureau. The authority of the F.B.I. into other matters continued to expand as well. For example, in 1996 the Health Insurance Portability and Accountability Act and the Economic Espionage Act were passed by Congress. These new statutes enabled the F.B.I. to significantly strengthen its ability to investigate health care fraud and the theft of trade secrets and intellectual property, respectively. Other emerging areas of responsibility today include the investigation of crimes involving the Internet, including so-called cyber attacks against businesses and governmental agencies.

The structure of the modern F.B.I.

As of 2000, the F.B.I. had approximately 11,400 Special Agents and over 16,400 other employees. About 10,000 employees were assigned to the F.B.I. headquarters in Washington, D.C., while the remainder were assigned to field installations. The total annual budget for the F.B.I. approximates three billion dollars. The F.B.I. is headed by a director and supported by a deputy director. There are eleven assistant directors. F.B.I. field offices are located in fifty-six major cities (fifty-five in the United States, one in Puerto Rico). Each field office is supervised by a Special Agent in Charge (SAC), except in Los Angeles, New York City, and Washington, D.C., where the office is supervised by an Assistant Director in Charge (ADIC). F.B.I. field offices conduct business through the field office headquarters and through satellite offices. To facilitate investigations abroad, the F.B.I. maintains a network of Legal Attache Offices. These offices are located in U.S. embassies in thirty-eight countries around the world (F.B.I., 1999).

The F.B.I. provides numerous types of assistance and support to local police agencies. For example, the F.B.I. crime laboratory is a full-service forensic science laboratory that provides scientific examinations free of charge to any law enforcement agency (given the existence of state operated and funded crime laboratories, local agencies rely primarily on them for their forensic analysis needs). Analysis capabilities include documents, fingerprints, DNA, explosives, firearms, tool marks, toxicology, and tire treads, among others. The laboratory also maintains databases on everything from types of shoe prints and lipstick to types of feathers and rope (F.B.I., 1999).

The F.B.I. also maintains and operates the National Crime Information Center (NCIC). Established in 1967, its purpose is to maintain a computerized filing system of criminal justice information (stolen vehicles, guns, missing persons, etc.) available through a computer network. On average, approximately 1.3 million inquiries are made every day from the over 100,000 terminals located in police agencies across the country (F.B.I., 1999).

The F.B.I. offers training assistance to law enforcement agencies through the F.B.I. National Academy and other training programs. The curriculum of the National Academy includes college courses in law, management, forensic science, and health and fitness, among other disciplines. Since 1935, over thirty thousand students have graduated from the academy.

The F.B.I. also provides other types of operational assistance to federal, state, and local law enforcement agencies (see F.B.I., 1999, for a complete list of services provided). For instance, through the Child Abduction and Serial Killer Unit (CASKU), agents provide psychological profiles of offenders and offer other investigative assistance. The Critical Incident Response Group (CIRG) provides training and operational support in crisis management and hostage negotiations situations. The F.B.I. Hostage Rescue Team and SWAT Programs are part of the CIRG. Evidence Response Teams (ERTs) are located in each field office and specialize in organizing and conducting evidence recovery operations from crime scenes.

F.B.I. investigations in the 1990s

Since the early 1990s, the F.B.I. has been involved in numerous high-profile criminal investigations. It is perhaps, at least in part, because of the F.B.I.'s involvement in these extraordinary investigations that the bureau continues to enjoy high status and prestige. For instance, the F.B.I. had the lead role in the investigation of the bombing of the Alfred P. Murrah Federal Building in Oklahoma City that occurred on 19 April

1995. This bombing remains the worst terrorist attack ever to occur on American soil, killing 168 and wounding approximately 700. Within two days of the bombing, and with some good fortune, agents had a perpetrator, Timothy McVeigh, in custody. Agents identified part of the vehicle that carried the explosives and traced it to a rental shop. This eventually led to the identification and conviction of McVeigh.

In February 1993 a massive explosion at the World Trade Center in New York City killed six people, injured 1,042, and caused over $500 million in damage. Similar to the Oklahoma City bombing, the vehicle that carried the explosives was traced to a rental shop. This information eventually led to the arrests of four of the perpetrators. Six perpetrators in all were identified and each was sentenced to 240 years in prison.

As a result of the investigation into the World Trade Center bombing, in 1993 F.B.I. agents disrupted the plans of a group of Muslim fundamentalists to blow-up simultaneously various places in New York City: the Holland and Lincoln tunnels, the United Nations building, and the Jacab Javits Federal Building. Through the use of surveillance and undercover infiltration, eight suspects were arrested and sentenced to prison.

Other recent skillful, high-profile investigations by the F.B.I. that have resulted in apprehensions include the bombing of Pan Am Flight 103 on 21 December 1988, which killed more than 260 people; the case of CIA officer Harold James Nicholsen, who was arrested by the F.B.I. in 1996 and charged with committing espionage on behalf of Russia; and the U.S. Embassy bombings in Kenya and Tanzania, which occurred on 7 August 1998 and resulted in the death of over 350 people. Three individuals were arrested shortly after the embassy bombings.

Equally high profile but rather unsuccessful investigations of the F.B.I. have cast a shadow on the effectiveness of the F.B.I. and serve as a reminder that what was once true is still true: that the F.B.I is not immune from error. For example, in 1992, agents from the F.B.I. and ATF surrounded the home of Randy Weaver in Idaho, a white supremacist who was wanted on gun violations. During the course of the siege, federal agents fatally shot Weaver's wife and son.

The catastrophic burning of the Branch Davidian compound in Waco Texas in 1993 raised serious questions about the role of the F.B.I. in causing the fire. Subsequent investigations and inquiries into the incident revealed that the F.B.I. agents had in fact used incendiary devices in the attack, contrary to Attorney General Janet Reno's orders. However, it has not been definitively determined what role, if any, these devices played in starting the fire that killed the eighty-six people inside the compound.

With the UNABOMBER case—the name UNABOMB was derived from UNiversity and Airline BOMbing, the perpetrator's early targets—the F.B.I. successfully apprehended the perpetrator, but it took almost eighteen years to do it. Beginning in 1978 and continuing through 1995, sixteen bombs were mailed to, or placed with, various individuals. The bombings resulted in three deaths and twenty-three people injured. In 1996 the bomber requested that his "manifesto" be published in two widely circulated newspapers. With the request granted and the manifesto published, the perpetrator was identified by his own brother, who read the manifesto in the newspaper and alerted the F.B.I. that the writing resembled that of his brother, Ted, who lived in a one-room shack in Montana. Agents converged on the shack and arrested Ted Kaczynski in the midst of bombmaking equipment, supplies, and instructions. He was sentenced to life in federal prison without the possibility of parole.

The F.B.I. investigation of the Olympic Park bombing in Atlanta in 1996, which killed two people and injured 111, serves as another example of the bureau's mixed success. The F.B.I. targeted Richard Jewell, a security guard who was working at the park at the time of the explosion. The F.B.I. has come under considerable criticism for focusing on Jewell (some say smearing him) on the basis of scant evidence. The focus on Jewell may have prevented investigators from pursuing other leads and others suspects. The bombing remains unsolved.

A final comment

The F.B.I. (as well as all other law enforcement agencies in the United States) faces an inescapable paradox: repress criminal behavior but do not violate the civil liberties of citizens in the process. In tracing the evolution of the F.B.I., one finds that the bureau has done both: it has worked to protect freedom but at times it has violated freedom. Ultimately, a knowledgeable citizenry that can distinguish between the protection of freedom and the unjust violation of freedom may be an important prerequisite for ensuring the fair exercise of discretion among those charged with enforcing the law. This entry has provided a step toward such an understanding.

STEVEN G. BRANDL

See also FEDERAL CRIMINAL JURISDICTION; FEDERAL CRIMINAL LAW ENFORCEMENT; ORGANIZED CRIME; POLICE: HISTORY; POLICE: CRIMINAL INVESTIGATIONS; SCIENTIFIC EVIDENCE.

BIBLIOGRAPHY

COUNTRYMAN, VERN. "The History of the F.B.I.: Democracy's Development of a Secret Policy." In *Investigating the F.B.I.* Edited by Pat Watters and Stephen Gillers. New York: Doubleday, 1973.

Federal Bureau of Investigation. *F.B.I.: Facts and History.* Washington, D.C.: U.S. Department of Justice, 1990.

———. *History of the Federal Bureau of Investigation.* Washington, D.C.: Office of Public and Congressional Affairs, 1997.

———. *Your F.B.I.* Washington, D.C.: Office of Public and Congressional Affairs, 1999.

GENTRY, CURT. *J. Edgar Hoover: The Man and His Secrets.* New York: Penguin Books, 1991.

HORAN, JAMES D. *The Pinkertons: The Detective Dynasty that Made History.* New York: Crown, 1968.

POWERS, RICHARD. *Secrecy and Power: The Life of J. Edgar Hoover.* New York: The Free Press, 1987.

PRESTON, WILLIAM. *Aliens and Dissenters: Federal Suppression of Radicals, 1903–1933.* Cambridge, Mass.: Harvard University Press, 1963.

THEOHARIS, ATHAN. *Spying on Americans: Political Surveillance from Hoover to the Huston Plan.* Philadelphia: Temple University Press, 1978.

UNGAR, SANFORD J. *F.B.I.* Boston: Little, Brown and Company, 1976.

WHITEHEAD, DON. *The F.B.I. Story: A Report to the People.* Foreword by J. Edgar Hoover. New York: Random House, 1956.

FEDERAL CRIMINAL JURISDICTION

Since the founding of the United States, the authority to define and punish crimes has been divided between the states and the federal government. Before the Civil War the United States exercised jurisdiction over only a narrow class of cases in which the federal interest was clearly dominant if not exclusive. Since the Civil War, federal criminal jurisdiction has been gradually expanding to subjects previously the exclusive province of the states. Because the bulk of these provisions have been intended to supplement state law and not to supersede, the overlap between federal and state jurisdictions has been increasing.

Origins

The federal government has no general authority to define and prosecute crime. The Constitution created a federal government with only limited delegated powers; federal authority was confined to matters, such as foreign relations, that are not subject to effective governance by individual states. Any power not expressly granted to the central government was reserved to the states and to the people. General police powers and the bulk of criminal jurisdiction were not granted to the federal government, and accordingly were uniformly recognized to be reserved to the states.

The Constitution explicitly authorizes the federal government to prosecute only a handful of crimes: treason, counterfeiting, crimes against the law of nations, and crimes committed on the high seas, such as piracy. Each of these offenses involves a subject, such as foreign relations, over which the federal government has exclusive authority. All other federal criminal jurisdiction rests on a less explicit but more flexible and expansive source of constitutional authority: the grant to Congress of power to pass legislation "necessary and proper" to the implementation of any enumerated federal power (Art. I, § 8). The first Congress clearly assumed that the necessary-and-proper clause authorized Congress to enact criminal sanctions to effectuate various enumerated federal powers. Indeed, the first general criminal legislation included a number of offenses clearly dependent upon the necessary-and-proper clause. For example, the Constitution empowers the federal government to raise and support an army, and the first Congress established criminal penalties for such conduct as larceny of federal military property.

Several early decisions of the U.S. Supreme Court confirmed Congress's discretionary authority to define federal crimes not enumerated in the Constitution. Although the federal government had only the authority delegated to it in the Constitution, the Court's expansive construction of the necessary-and-proper clause in *McCulloch v. Maryland*, 17 U.S. (4 Wheat.) 316, 416–417 (1819) established that Congress has broad discretion to employ criminal sanctions when it deems them helpful or appropriate to the exercise of any federal power.

Before the Civil War there were few federal crimes and little overlap between federal and state criminal jurisdiction. Only the states exercised general police powers. Congress authorized federal criminal sanctions where necessary to prevent interference with, or injury to, the federal government. The principal antebellum federal crimes were (1) acts threatening the existence of the central government, such as treason; (2) misconduct by federal officers, such as acceptance of a bribe; (3) interference with the operation of the federal courts, such as perjury; and (4) interference with other governmental programs, including obstruction of the mails, theft of government property, revenue fraud, and bribery or obstruction of government personnel. These were matters of paramount, if not exclusive, federal concern. Since the federal government's programs and activities were relatively few, the last category of cases was correspondingly narrow. Federal law did not reach crimes against private individuals, which were the exclusive concern of the states. The only major exception to this pattern came in geographic areas under exclusive federal maritime or territorial jurisdiction, where Congress exercised general police powers because no state had jurisdiction. Only in those areas where federal jurisdiction was exclusive, as in the District of Columbia, did Congress adopt criminal penalties for antisocial conduct—such as murder or robbery of private individuals—that posed no direct threat to the central government.

The expansion of federal jurisdiction after the Civil War

After the Civil War, Congress significantly expanded the scope of federal criminal jurisdiction. For the first time Congress sought to extend the federal criminal law to a variety of subjects clearly within the scope of the state's general police powers. Although the Supreme Court's decisions rendered the civil rights legislation largely ineffective, the Court upheld the bulk of this new federal legislation, which was intended to complement existing state criminal law.

Civil rights legislation. The most immediate consequence of the Civil War was the ratification of the Thirteenth, Fourteenth, and Fifteenth Amendments to the Constitution, which, respectively, abolished slavery and forbade the states to deny to any citizen the right to vote, or the privileges and immunities of federal citizenship; provided due process; and provided equal protection of the law. Each amendment gave Congress enforcement authority, and Congress implemented them by passing a series of civil rights statutes between 1866 and 1875. The Reconstruction legislation, however, not only implemented the new prohibitions against unconstitutional state action, but also purported to extend federal jurisdiction to reach private conduct clearly within the realm of the states' traditional police powers. The Court promptly nullified many of the key provisions of the legislation, holding that the civil rights amendments had given Congress no new authority to criminalize the acts of one private citizen against another, and the provisions that were not invalidated or repealed remained "a dead letter on the statute book" for more than sixty years (Schwartz, vol. 1, p. 10). Not until the middle of the next century did decisions such as *United States v. Guest*, 383 U.S. 745 (1966), signal a greater willingness to uphold portions of the Reconstruction legislation proscribing private conspiracies to interfere with rights guaranteed by the Fourteenth Amendment.

Regulation of the mails and commerce. The most important post–Civil War development was the enactment of the first federal criminal penalties for the misuse of facilities under federal control in a manner that caused injury to private individuals, not to the government itself. The first significant step in this direction was the adoption of criminal penalties for the misuse of the mails—facilities provided by the government—to effectuate fraudulent schemes or to distribute lottery circulars and obscene publications.

The next step was the adoption of penalties for misconduct involving the use of interstate facilities, such as railroads, which are subject to federal regulation under the commerce clause. The scope of the earliest provisions was very narrow. For example, the interstate transportation of explosives and of cattle with contagious diseases was made criminal. Some of the later provisions were far broader. The Sherman Act of 1890 outlawed attempts to monopolize and conspiracies to restrain interstate commerce. The Interstate Commerce Commission Act of 1887 was particularly significant because it set the pattern for subsequent legislation that established a federal regulatory framework for an administrative agency, and a comprehensive scheme of civil and criminal sanctions.

No single factor explains the new congressional willingness to expand the scope of federal criminal jurisdiction. The Civil War had forced supporters of the Union to adopt a more flexible and expansive interpretation of the federal government's powers, and the expanded concept of federal power continued to influence the postwar Congress. A strong and politically active antivice movement campaigned for legislation at the state level and then for complementary federal legislation. But clearly the most significant factor influencing Congress was the dramatic postwar economic expansion and growth in interstate commerce, fueled by the development of a national rail system and, to a lesser extent, by the earlier development of the telegraph system and large waterways such as the Erie Canal. The unprecedented growth in interstate transportation and commerce created new national problems that demanded new national solutions.

The constitutionality of many of the new criminal laws was challenged because they allowed federal prosecution of conduct—such as fraud—that was traditionally subject only to state regulation. The first case to reach the Supreme Court, *In re Rapier*, 143 U.S. 110 (1892), involved criminal penalties for misuse of the mails. Although the Court upheld federal authority to punish misuse of the mail facilities furnished by the government, that rationale did not apply to interstate commerce, which is regulated, but not created, by the federal government. The first decision sustaining federal criminal jurisdiction under the commerce clause came in the *Lottery Case (Champion v. Ames)*, 188 U.S. 321 (1903), in which a sharply divided Court upheld the federal prohibition against transportation of lottery tickets across state lines. Since Congress, like the states, might deem wide-scale gambling by lottery to be injurious to public morals, the majority held that Congress should be able to employ its power over interstate commerce to assist the states in suppressing lotteries. The Court emphasized that the federal prohibition in question "supplemented the action" of the states, which might otherwise be "overthrown or disregarded by the agency of interstate Commerce" (pp. 356–357).

In the two decades after the Court's decision in the *Lottery Case*, Congress enacted additional criminal prohibitions involving interstate commerce. The most important were the prohibitions against the distribution in interstate commerce of adulterated or misbranded food or drugs, interstate transportation of women for immoral purposes, and interstate transportation of stolen motor vehicles (Conboy, pp. 319–321). The other significant legislation passed during this period was the Harrison Act of 1914, a comprehensive federal statute dealing with narcotics. The Harrison Act's detailed regulatory scheme, including criminal penalties, was upheld as a proper exercise of the power to tax, despite the fact that it was intended to accomplish a regulatory purpose in addition to raising revenue (*United States v. Doremus*, 249 U.S. 86 (1919)).

Prohibition.   The effort to prohibit the sale and distribution of liquor culminated in 1919 with the ratification of the Eighteenth Amendment, which gave "concurrent" enforcement power to the states and the federal government. The express constitutional grant of concurrent jurisdiction was without precedent. In practice, the enforcement burden was borne largely by the federal government, and it resulted in a phenomenal increase in the number of federal prosecutions. Prohibition cases accounted for more than one-half of all federal prosecutions every year between 1922 and 1933. In 1932, the peak year, approximately sixty-six thousand of the ninety-two thousand federal criminal cases involved Prohibition (Rubin, p. 497). The Eighteenth Amendment was repealed in December 1933.

The continuing expansion of federal jurisdiction after Prohibition

Federal jurisdiction never receded to its relatively narrow pre-Prohibition scope. In 1933, the Senate authorized a special committee to investigate racketeering, kidnapping, and other forms of crime; the committee reported that "the prevalence, atrocity and magnitude of the crimes then being committed and the apparent inability of the then existing agencies to cope with them, constituted the main reason" for congressional action in "a field which had, until then, been regarded as a matter primarily of local or State concern" (U.S. Congress, p. 38). By 1937, seventeen statutes proposed by the committee had been enacted, and the committee's work ultimately led to the adoption of federal criminal penalties for interstate transmission of extortionate communications, interstate flight to avoid prosecution, interstate transportation of stolen property, bank robbery, sale or receipt of stolen property with an interstate origin, and extortion or robbery affecting interstate commerce, as well as the first federal firearms legislation (pp. 40–54). The federal securities laws, including criminal as well as civil sanctions, were also enacted during this period.

Congress's authority to adopt criminal legislation under the commerce power was already well established, but the new legislation demonstrated Congress's growing willingness to assert jurisdiction over an increasingly broad range of conduct clearly within the states' traditional police powers. The proponents of the legislation candidly recognized that much, if not all, of the conduct involved was already prohibited by the criminal codes of most states, but they argued that the states' enforcement had been ineffective. The new federal criminal legislation was adopted during the same sessions in which Congress enacted a sweeping program under the commerce clause in an effort to combat the Depression.

In the decades after the 1930s the scope of the federal government's criminal jurisdiction continued to expand. The Mail Fraud Act and the prohibitions against extortion or robbery affecting interstate commerce were given particularly broad interpretations, and they proved to be adaptable to a wide range of conduct, including bribery and other corrupt conduct of state and local officials.

New legislation was also adopted. Of particular importance were the criminal provisions adopted to secure compliance with the expanding network of federal regulations. For example, beginning in 1935, Congress attempted the comprehensive regulation of national labor relations, and it subsequently established criminal penalties for conduct such as extortion or bribery of union officials and embezzlement or graft in connection with welfare and pension benefit funds. Similarly, criminal penalties were included in the regulatory schemes dealing with such matters as occupational health and safety, water pollution, and coal mine safety. Congress adopted a variety of piecemeal legislation dealing with narcotics and other dangerous drugs, and in 1970 it replaced this patchwork with a comprehensive drug control statute, including both a civil regulatory regime and criminal provisions, enacted under the authority of the commerce clause.

Nationwide concern with organized crime led to the adoption of several significant statutes between 1961 and 1970. The first provision, the Travel Act, authorized criminal penalties for interstate travel intended to facilitate gambling, narcotic traffic, prostitution, extortion, and bribery—illegal activities frequently associated with organized crime. In 1968, Congress authorized criminal penalties for extortionate credit transactions because loansharking was providing funds for organized crime. In 1970 Congress enacted legislation intended to help in the investigation of organized crime, and penalties for syndicated gambling; the most controversial portion of the bill was RICO, the Racketeer Influenced and Corrupt Organizations Act of 1970, as amended, 18 U.S.C. §§ 1961–1968, which supplemented traditional conspiracy law by making it a serious federal offense to participate in a criminal "enterprise" through a "pattern of racketeering activity." In order to prevent organized crime from infiltrating legitimate businesses, RICO also made it a federal offense to invest funds, derived from racketeering activity into any enterprise in interstate commerce (Bradley, pp. 839–845).

In most instances the new federal criminal provisions were intended to supplement, not supplant, related state criminal provisions, and accordingly, in a growing number of cases the same conduct could be prosecuted under either state or federal law, at the prosecutors' discretion. Successive federal and state prosecutions were also permissible because the Court interpreted the double jeopardy clause as a bar only to reprosecution by the same sovereign (*Bartkus v. Illinois*, 359 U.S. 121 (1959)).

Modern challenges to the expansion of federal jurisdiction

Despite the absence of any general police power, Congress has employed various federal powers, particularly the commerce clause, the power to tax, and the postal power, to expand federal criminal jurisdiction dramatically. Both courts and commentators have expressed concern that the balance between federal and state authority has been fundamentally altered, and that federal criminal jurisdiction now greatly exceeds its proper sphere. Critics charge that federal jurisdiction extends to many cases where there is no significant federal interest, and that an overload of criminal cases places an unwarranted strain on the federal courts. The substantial overlap of federal and state law also permits the imposition of different sentences on persons who engage in the same conduct, depending upon whether they are prosecuted under state or federal law, leaving largely unfettered discretion in the hands of federal prosecutors, who decide whether to bring federal charges.

In 1995 the Supreme Court made headlines with the first decision in nearly sixty years to hold that a federal statute exceeded the commerce power. *United States v. Lopez*, 514 U.S. 549 (1995), held that Congress had exceeded its authority in making it a federal crime to possess a handgun in a school zone. This decision was heralded as the first step in the process of restricting federal criminal jurisdiction, but its effect has been relatively minor. Although a number of district courts initially issued rulings invalidating various federal statutes on the authority of *Lopez*, both the Supreme Court and the federal circuit courts responded by giving *Lopez* a relatively restrictive reading. Despite continued uneasiness with the increase in the number of federal criminal statutes and the growth in the federal caseload, no constitutional theory has emerged that would restrict federal criminal jurisdiction while also recognizing the interstate and international character of virtually all commerce and the need for broad federal regulatory authority in many areas. Moreover, despite support for restricting federal criminal jurisdiction from many groups, including the American Bar Association and the Judicial Conference, there is strong countervailing political pressure to continue the expansion to deal with violent offenses and juvenile crime. It therefore seems unlikely that the federal criminal justice system will shrink back to a more restricted sphere.

SARA SUN BEALE

See also BANK ROBBERY; COUNTERFEITING; DRUGS AND CRIME: LEGAL ASPECTS; ECONOMIC CRIME: ANTITRUST OFFENSES; ECONOMIC CRIME: TAX OFFENSES; FEDERAL BUREAU OF INVESTIGATION: HISTORY; GUNS, REGULATION OF; JURDISDICTION; KIDNAPPING; MAIL: FEDERAL MAIL FRAUD ACT; ORGANIZED CRIME; RICO (RACKETEER INFLUENCED AND CORRUPT ORGANIZATIONS ACT); SEDITION AND DOMESTIC TERRORISM; TERRORISM; TREASON.

BIBLIOGRAPHY

ABRAMS, NORMAN, and BEALE, SARAH SUN. *Federal Criminal Law and Its Enforcement*, 3d ed. St. Paul, Minn.: West Group, 2000.
BRADLEY, CRAIG M. "Racketeers, Congress, and the Courts: An Analysis of RICO." *Iowa Law Review* 65 (June, 1980): 837–897.
CONBOY, MARTIN. "Federal Criminal Law." In *Law: A Century of Progress, 1835–1935*, vol. 1. Edited by Alison Reppy. New York: New York University Press, 1937. Pages 295–344.
GAINER, RONALD L. "Federal Criminal Code Reform: Past and Future." *Buffalo Criminal Law Review* 2 (1998): 45–159.
MARION, NANCY E. *A History of Federal Crime Control Initiatives, 1960–1993*. Westport, Conn.: Praeger, 1994.
MOOHR, GERALDINE SZOTT. "The Federal Interest in Criminal Law." *Syracuse Law Review* 47, no. 4 (summer 1997): 1127–1181.
RUBIN, EDWARD. "A Statistical Study of Federal Criminal Prosecution." *Law and Contemporary Problems* 1 (October 1934): 494–508.
SCHWARTZ, BERNARD, ed. *Statutory History of the United States: Civil Rights*. 2 vols. New York: Chelsea House, 1970.
SCHWARTZ, L. B. "Federal Criminal Jurisdiction and Prosecutors' Discretion." *Law and Contemporary Problems* 13, no. 1 (winter 1948): 64–87.
STACY, TOM, and DAYTON, KIM. "The Underfederalization of Crime." *Cornell Journal of Law and Public Policy* 6, no. 2 (winter 1997): 247–324.
STRAZZELLA, JAMES A., ed. "The Federal Role in Criminal Law." *The Annals of the American Academy of Political and Social Science* 543 (1996): 9–166.
Symposium. "Federalization of Crime: The Roles of the Federal and State Governments in the Criminal Justice System." *Hastings Law Journal* 46, no. 4 (April 1995): 965–1338.
Task Force on the Federalization of Criminal Law, American Bar Association. *The Federalization of Criminal Law*. Washington, D.C.: American Bar Association, 1999.
U.S. Congress, Senate Committee on Commerce. "Crime and Criminal Practices." S. Rep. No. 1189. 75th Cong., 1st sess. Washington, D.C.: Government Printing Office, 1937.
WELLING, SARAH N.; BEALE, SARAH SUN; and BUCY, PAMELA H. *Federal Criminal Law and Related Actions: Crimes, Forfeiture, the False Claims Act and RICO*. 2 vols. St. Paul, Minn.: West Group, 1998.

FEDERAL CRIMINAL LAW ENFORCEMENT

Cases investigated and prosecuted by the federal criminal enforcement authorities often capture national attention. Terrorist bombings, official corruption, insider securities trading, organized crime enterprises, international drug conspiracies—all have been targeted by the "Feds," as have bank robberies, environmental crimes, illegal immigration, and foreign espionage, to name just a few. For all the attention it gets, however, what is most surprising about the federal enforcement apparatus is its small size, at least when compared to the network of state and local enforcement agencies, which have primary responsibility for patrolling the streets and pursue most of the crimes that happen on or off them. In 1996, for example, only 74,493 federal officers were authorized to carry guns and make arrests, against 663,535 full-time sworn state and local officers (36,813 in New York City alone).

Structural characteristics

While the fragmentation of state and local law enforcement can easily be explained by the nature of state and local government in the United States, what some might find surprising is the extent of fragmentation within the supposedly unitary federal system. As of 1996, twenty-seven federal agencies each had at least one hundred law enforcement officers, and fourteen of those had five hundred or more. The four biggest agencies are the Immigration and Naturalization Service (INS) (12,403 officers with arrest and firearms authority, including Border Patrol agents, immigration inspectors, criminal agents, and detention officers), responsible for locating and apprehending illegal aliens; the Federal Bureau of Prisons (11,329 officers), which maintains order in federal correctional facilities; the U.S. Customs Service (9,749 officers), which, in addition to its border inspection duties, is charged with investigating smuggling and money laundering cases; and the Federal Bureau of Investigation (F.B.I.) (10,389 officers, mostly special agents), whose broad portfolio includes terrorism, white-collar crime, bank robberies, organized crime, espionage, narcotics trafficking, kidnapping, official corruption, and health-care fraud. Some of the smaller federal agencies are the Drug Enforcement Administration (DEA) (2,946 officers); the U.S. Secret Service (3,185 agents and protective officers), which investigates credit card and computer fraud and counterfeiting cases, in addition to its protective responsibilities; the Bureau of Alcohol, Tobacco, and Firearms (ATF) (1,869 officers), whose authority extends to include arson and explosives; the Internal Revenue Service (IRS) (3,784 officers); the U.S. Postal Inspection Service (3,576 officers); and the U.S. Marshals Service (2,650 officers).

These investigative agencies are not even housed in a single executive department. INS, F.B.I., DEA and the U.S. Marshals Service (which, among other things, tracks fugitives, transports prisoners prior to sentence, and protects witnesses and federal court personnel) are part of the Department of Justice. The Secret Service, ATF, the Customs Service, and IRS report to the Secretary of the Treasury. Postal Inspectors—whose jurisdiction over mail fraud sweeps in a broad array of criminal activity—are part of the U.S. Postal Service. In addition, criminal investigations are conducted by personnel within various regulatory agencies, including the Securities & Exchange Commission, the Environmental Protection Agency, the Food and Drug Administration, and such executive departments as Agriculture (which, among other things, investigates food stamp fraud), Labor (concerned with labor racketeering), and Interior (which includes the U.S. Park Police).

Prosecuting authority is somewhat less fragmented than investigatory authority in the federal system. As a formal matter—except in extraordinary cases involving an independent counsel—all federal prosecutors report to the Attorney General of the United States. Yet there is still a considerable degree of decentralization. The huge majority of federal criminal cases are brought not by the litigating units of the Justice Department like the Criminal, Antitrust, and Civil Rights Divisions, which are under the direct control of assistant attorney generals in Washington, D.C., but by the ninety-four U.S. attorneys' offices, each headed by a presidential appointee responsible only to the Attorney General and the Deputy Attorney General. U.S. attorneys, like assistant attorney generals, generally change with presidential administrations, but they preside over offices that, like the Department's litigating units, are generally staffed by lawyers whose tenure is not based on political allegiances. Although the freedom of the U.S. attorneys' offices is far from absolute, and there are many mechanisms through which "Main Justice" (as the Washington bureaucracy is often called) can assert authority over a recalcitrant office, U.S. attorneys have a long tradition of independence from Washington. This independence is in part rooted in history, since the U.S. attorneys' offices were prosecuting cases before the Justice Department was even created (in 1870), but it also reflects a desire by the Department, and perhaps even more, by Congress, that prosecutorial discretion—even with respect to nationally applicable laws—be exercised by those most attuned to the needs and values of the diverse communities they serve.

This relative decentralization affects the types of criminal cases that are prosecuted in federal court. Even when the Attorney General of the United States announces a national initiative for the prosecution of particular criminal activity, the degree of compliance by U.S. attorneys' offices across the country will vary considerably, and will often be a function of local priorities. Perhaps the most important force in the direction of national priorities comes from the enforcement agencies, which are as a whole quite centralized, and which are primarily responsible for initiating the cases that the U.S. attorneys' offices pursue.

The mix of cases prosecuted in federal court arises out of these diverse influences. And the discretion exercised by enforcement agencies, in the first instance, and by federal prosecutors thereafter, is enormous. Because the scope of federal criminal jurisdiction is so great, and the size of the federal enforcement apparatus so small in comparison, federal enforcers have a great advantage over their state and local counterparts: even as their resource limitations largely free them from being held responsible for policing any particular "beat," they can still be confident that they will have a criminal statute to fit any antisocial conduct they choose to pursue. Some kinds of cases must be brought federally, either because state agencies legally cannot proceed, or because the federal government has primary jurisdiction in the matter. This category includes federal program frauds and intrusions on federal proprietary or security interests. Outside this category, however, are a broad array of potential cases in which federal and state authorities have overlapping interests, and where federal involvement will generally occur only when federal enforcers have made a strategic decision to deploy their resources. In recent years, much of this deployment has occurred in the narcotics area, at least when judged by the number of cases filed. Of the 39,291 cases filed by U.S. attorneys' offices in fiscal 1997, for example, 11,935 involved drug offenses, and 6,248 involved "violent crime" (there is some overlap between these categories); the remainder, for the most part, involved fraud, theft, corruption, immigration, and regulatory offenses.

Sources of structural fragmentation: history and politics

The number and often overlapping responsibilities of the federal enforcement agencies reflect a history of ad hoc responses to particular enforcement problems against a backdrop of expanding federal jurisdiction. Not surprisingly, the first agencies to develop were those meeting the basic needs of a minimalist national government. Indeed, the roots of the Postal Inspection Service date back to before the framing of the Constitution, when Postmaster General Benjamin Franklin found a need to ensure the integrity of the mails. In 1789 Congress created the Revenue Cutter Service of the U.S. Customs office, to deal with smuggling, and the U.S. Marshals Service, to ride circuit with the Supreme Court and perform other duties. The Secret Service was created in 1865 to fight counterfeiting, and later, in 1901, after the assassination of President William McKinley, was given protective duties. In 1908, a small Bureau of Investigation was created within the Department of Justice, to reduce that department's reliance on Secret Service agents. By 1924 this unit had received a new chief, J. Edgar Hoover, and in 1935 became the Federal Bureau of Investigation, with a growing number of responsibilities, from kidnappings to "subversion" and counterespionage.

As the taxation jurisdiction of the Treasury Department grew, so too did that department's readiness to create units to carry out licensing and taxation enforcement functions. In 1919, the Bureau of Internal Revenue (forerunner of the IRS) formed a criminal investigation unit to investigate criminal tax violation. That same year also saw the onset of Prohibition, which led, in 1920, to the creation of a Prohibition Unit within Treasury, charged with enforcing the nationwide ban on the "manufacture, sale, or transportation of intoxicating liquors for beverage purposes." In 1932, a year before Prohibition's repeal, these enforcement functions were transferred to the Justice Department, but Treasury continued to have tax and regulatory responsibilities in this area. Eventually, in 1972, alcohol, tobacco, and firearm enforcement functions were removed from the IRS and given to the newly created ATF, whose mission was later expanded to include arson investigations. In 1973 certain Treasury Department functions in the narcotics enforcement area were transferred to the Drug Enforcement Administration, newly created within the Justice Department. The DEA also inherited the functions of the Justice Department's Bureau of Narcotics and Dangerous Drugs. In 1982, with the intensification of the federal "war on drugs," the F.B.I. was given concurrent jurisdiction (with DEA) over narcotics violations in the United States.

The fragmented structure of the federal enforcement apparatus cannot simply be attributed to historical accident and bureaucratic rivalries, however. It reflects Americans' deep-seated suspicion of concentrated government power, especially in the criminal justice area. There never has been a single "national police force," and there likely never will be. Even J. Edgar Hoover, perhaps the most bureaucratically aggressive director of the F.B.I. (the only agency that conceivably could assume this role), was always careful to disclaim any ambition on this score. The division of responsibilities among agencies also promotes the development of expertise and specialized resources.

Agency fragmentation serves other purposes as well, such as allowing the President and/or Congress, or others, to exercise more control in certain enforcement areas. Efforts in the 1980s and early 1990s to end the overlap in agency responsibilities by merging the DEA into the F.B.I. were defeated in part because legislators wanted to ensure the continued existence of an agency committed solely to narcotics enforcement that was unable to shift resources to other areas. The efforts of gun control opponents to eliminate the ATF came to a sudden (albeit perhaps temporary) halt in 1982 when the lobbyists learned that firearms enforcement functions and personnel were to be transferred from the politically weak ATF to the Secret Service, which, because of its counterfeiting and protective functions, would have been far less vulnerable to political pressure.

Coordination challenges

When two or more units have overlapping spheres of responsibility, competition between them can spur each to greater innovation and superior performance. That at least is the lesson of market theory. And there is some validity to the theory, when applied to the federal enforcement establishment, where competition among agencies can enhance performance and group esprit, and can ensure that no one agency controls policymaking in a particular operational sphere. If necessary, one agency can even be used to investigate alleged misconduct by another.

With these benefits can come severe disadvantages, however. Competition between agencies can be wasteful if each strives simply to look better in the appropriations process. The failure to share information can seriously impede the prosecution of complex criminal activity that is not fully understood by any one agency. And the loss can be even greater if, in the absence of coordination, one agency actually disrupts the operations of another by, say, targeting someone who is an active informant for another agency. One of the critical challenges facing the federal enforcement establishment is thus to keep the benefits of fragmentation while minimizing its costs.

Some efforts to coordinate enforcement activity occur in Washington, through personal and institutionalized relationships between agency leaders and their political superiors. Other efforts occur in the field, through interagency contacts and, increasingly, through the establishment of task forces. Between 1966 and 1990, organized crime "strike forces" were established in fourteen major cities. These units—comprised of representatives of eleven investigative agencies at one point—and prosecutors reporting to the Organized Crime and Racketeering Section in Washington targeted "traditional" organized crime (La Cosa Nostra) as well as some nontraditional criminal enterprises. Although Attorney General Richard Thornburgh merged the strike forces into the local U.S. attorneys' offices in 1990, in order to end occasional turf battles between prosecutors reporting to Washington and those reporting to U.S. attorneys, these units continue to operate within the new framework. In 1982 the task force model was extended to the narcotics area with the establishment of thirteen regional units, the Organized Crime Drug Enforcement Task Forces. These units, formed to target high-level trafficking, include personnel from the DEA, F.B.I., IRS, INS, U.S. Marshals, Customs Service, and Coast Guard.

Another way in which interagency coordination is promoted in the field is through the actions of the U.S. attorneys' offices. Although federal agents sometimes seek legal support—for example, search warrant applications—from state and local prosecuting offices, and those offices will sometimes seek indictments in cases that have been investigated by federal agents, federal agents will generally go the local U.S. attorney's office first for search warrants, grand jury subpoenas, electronic surveillance applications, and other such legal assistance, as well as for indictments. A U.S. attorney's office will therefore find itself at the center of most federal enforcement activity in its district, and can ensure, at the very least, that two different agencies are not on a collision course. It may even be able to promote affirmative cooperation. Within the Justice Department, only the Attorney General and the Deputy Attorney General have hierarchical authority over federal enforcement agencies, and, as noted, many federal enforcement agencies are not even housed with the Justice Department. Nonetheless, a U.S. attorney's office's status as gatekeeper to the federal courts—since agencies cannot prosecute cases without it—gives it considerable influence on agency operations within its jurisdiction.

Determining the federal role

A second challenge facing federal law enforcement agencies is devising a role that addresses national enforcement priorities but still reflects their own special capabilities (and limitations). As political pressure has propelled federal agencies to target violent crime, such a balance has become increasingly difficult to strike. A drive-by shooting may be precisely the sort of crime that the police are best able to address and that they should be held responsible for addressing. But the shooting may be part of a broader pattern of racketeering by a well-structured gang that funds itself with interstate drug trafficking and gets its weapons from out of state. Such an enterprise would be a fitting target for a federal agency that is undeterred by state boundaries and that, lacking broad patrol obligations, can strategically invest its resources in high-impact cases.

As this scenario suggests, a key to the efficient allocation of scarce federal resources will often be coordination with state and local police, particularly in the sharing of information. This in itself will often require striking a difficult balance, because all law enforcement agencies are traditionally protective of their investigative data, and because federal enforcers may also find themselves investigating police corruption or civil rights violations. But no federal agency or agencies can ever hope to duplicate the informational networks available only to a force with broad patrol responsibilities. To promote effective coordination, federal agencies have, here too, turned to the task force model, working with state and local units to target specific criminal organizations or specific types of criminal activity, like narcotics trafficking, terrorism, or bank rob-

beries. Federal agencies have also cultivated the goodwill of state and local authorities by providing access to federal funds and equipment, and by assisting them in the interstate aspects of those authorities' own investigations.

Occasionally, state or local enforcers will complain of intrusions by federal agencies into areas of traditional local concern. Given the degree of statutory overlap between the state and federal systems, however, what is remarkable is not the occurrence of such disputes but their relative infrequency. Spurred by their own needs, and sometimes by political pressure from congressional delegations protecting local interests, federal enforcers have generally developed close working relationships with state and local authorities.

As federal enforcement agencies operate in the twenty-first century, they will increasingly find themselves facing similar coordination issues arising out of their efforts to combat criminal activity that crosses national boundaries. At least for now, state and local authorities are rarely equipped to investigate and prosecute, for example, a fraud on an American bank perpetrated by a foreign national sitting at a computer thousands of miles away. The task will thus fall to federal enforcers, who will not be able to proceed without assistance from foreign authorities, and who therefore must develop cost and information sharing arrangements that will encourage such cooperation.

DANIEL C. RICHMAN

See also DRUGS AND CRIME: LEGAL ASPECTS; ECONOMIC CRIME: ANTITRUST OFFENSES; ECONOMIC CRIME: TAX OFFENSES; FEDERAL BUREAU OF INVESTIGATION: HISTORY; FEDERAL CRIMINAL JURISDICTION; FORFEITURE; KIDNAPPING; MAIL: FEDERAL MAIL FRAUD ACT; ORGANIZED CRIME; PROSECUTION: PROSECUTORIAL DISCRETION; PROSECUTION: UNITED STATES ATTORNEY.

BIBLIOGRAPHY

ABRAMS, NORMAN, and BEALE, SARA SUN. Federal Criminal Law and Its Enforcement, 2d ed. St. Paul, Minn.: West Publishing Co., 1993.
CUMMINGS, HOMER, and MCFARLAND, CARL. Federal Justice: Chapters in the History of Justice and the Federal Executive. New York: Macmillan, 1937.
EISENSTEIN, JAMES. Counsel for the United States: U.S. Attorneys in the Political and Legal Systems. Baltimore, Md.: Johns Hopkins University Press, 1978.

GELLER, WILLIAM A., and MORRIS, NORVAL. "Relations between Federal and Local Police." In *Modern Policing.* Edited by Michael Tonry and Norval Morris. Chicago, Ill.: University of Chicago Press, 1992. Pages 231–348.

GLAZER, ELIZABETH. "Thinking Strategically: How Federal Prosecutors Can Reduce Violent Crime." *Fordham Urban Law Journal* 26, no. 3 (March 1999): 573–606.

MCGEE, JIM, and DUFFY, BRIAN. *Main Justice: The Men and Women Who Enforce the Nation's Criminal Laws and Guard Its Liberties.* New York, N.Y.: Simon & Schuster, 1996.

RICHMAN, DANIEL C. "Federal Criminal Law, Congressional Delegation, and Enforcement Discretion." *UCLA Law Review* 46, no. 3 (February 1999): 757–814.

U.S. Department of Justice, Bureau of Justice Statistics. *Federal Law Enforcement Officers, 1996.* Washington, D.C.: U.S. Government Printing Office, 1998.

U.S. Department of Justice, Bureau of Justice Statistics. *Sourcebook of Criminal Justice Statistics 1997.* Washington, D.C.: U.S. Government Printing Office, 1998.

WILSON, JAMES Q. *The Investigators: Managing F.B.I. and Narcotics Agents.* New York, N.Y.: Basic Books, 1978.

FEMINISM: CRIMINOLOGICAL ASPECTS

Feminist perspectives in criminology developed in reaction to silences and gaps in mainstream criminology. According to the critique that feminists began to mount in the late 1960s and early 1970s, mainstream or traditional criminology was inadequate in five key respects: (1) it focused almost exclusively on male offenders; (2) it was androcentric in its understandings and interpretations of crime; (3) it paid little attention to crime victims; (4) it ignored sex differences in criminal justice processing; and (5) it disregarded the dynamics of gender and power. Although criminology claimed to be an objective social science, the field itself (feminists charged) was deeply biased and implicated in the maintenance of male domination. Feminist criminologists have aimed at including women in analyses of crime, taking power differentials into account, and contributing toward the elimination of inequalities based on gender and other personal characteristics.

The critique

Feminist critics of the late 1960s and early 1970s found criminology lacking in five major respects; many of them would repeat these same criticisms today.

(1) Mainstream criminology has focused almost exclusively on male offenders. It was perhaps natural for mainstream criminologists to focus primarily on male subjects, given that males have comprised the great majority of offenders across time and place. Nonetheless, feminist critics argued, much might be learned about the causes of crime from studying low-rate as well as high-rate offenders. Why should criminologists not also investigate why females are less likely than males to break the law?

Feminists further argued that the use of all-male samples had led to theories of offending that in fact applied only to males, even though most advertised themselves as general explanations of crime. For example, Travis Hirschi, in formulating his well-known control theory of delinquency, deliberately excluded the female subjects on whom data were available in his original sample (p. 35, n. 3). "Since girls have been neglected for too long by students of delinquency, the exclusion of them is difficult to justify," Hirschi admitted, expressing a "hope to return to them soon" (pp. 35–36, n. 3). However, he has not. Titled *Causes of Delinquency,* Hirschi's book is in fact a study of the causes of male delinquency. Most other criminologists, too, assumed a male norm, placing boys and men at the center of their discussions and making women "invisible" (Belknap).

(2) Mainstream criminology is androcentric in its understandings and interpretations of crime. Feminists found little to admire even in the work of those few criminologists who had focused on female crime; this work, the critics maintained, analyzed female lawbreaking from a patriarchal point of view. Relying on cultural stereotypes, Cesare Lombroso, W. I. Thomas, Otto Pollak, and others who in the past had discussed female crime tended to sort women into two opposing categories, good woman or bad woman, madonna or whore (Feinman), leaving little room for ordinary mortals in between. Criminologists defined the law-abiding woman as passive, obedient, chaste, and childlike while describing the criminal woman as aggressive, defiant, sexually impure, and unbecomingly adult, even masculine in nature. These stereotypes had little to do with actual women, feminists objected; they sexualized and condemned women criminals instead of treating them objectively; they reinforced the paternalistic view that good women are those who are submissive and docile; and they bolstered the double standard of sexual morality that accords men but not women sexual autonomy.

Feminists used prostitution to exemplify how criminologists sexualized female crime while remaining silent about the economic pressures that force some women into crime. Some criminologists had attributed prostitution to nymphomania, others to a hatred of men stemming from underlying lesbian tendencies, but few had recognized that disadvantaged women often lack economic alternatives. The Gluecks and other criminologists went so far as to condemn prostitutes as carriers of sexually transmitted diseases. Before the late 1960s, one could search the criminological literature in vain for recognition that prostitution usually involves two parties, a man as well as a woman, and that diseases are more likely to be transmitted by the clients than the service providers, who routinely take measures against infection. In the case of prostitution as in that of other crimes, the effect of criminological commentaries was to make women offenders seem sexually abnormal and even evil while exonerating whatever males were involved.

One of the most egregious failures of traditional criminology in the feminist view was its insistence on interpreting crimes against women from a male perspective. To exemplify this point, critics pointed to Menachem Amir's 1971 study, *Patterns in Forcible Rape*. Nineteen percent of the victims in his sample had arrest records, Amir reported, assuming that negative information on victims was relevant; many had been arrested for sexual misconduct, and 20 percent had a "'bad' reputation." Some rapists had used "temptation" to overcome their victims while others used "verbal coercion"; in only 13 percent of the cases had the offender used "physical aggression"—a finding that implied most victims had actually been "asking for it." Moreover, in 19 percent of the cases, the victim had "precipitated" her own rape, a conclusion Amir based on rapists' own accounts. In studies of incest and domestic violence, too, mainstream criminologists interpreted crimes against women from the vantage point of the male offender, suggesting that men are more credible than women and likely to be falsely accused.

(3) Mainstream criminology has paid little attention to crime victims. One of the chief feminist complaints against traditional criminology was its relative disinterest in victimization and its tendency, when discussing crimes in which women were the primary victims, to blame the victim. Domestic homicide was said to be victim-precipitated in many cases, as was wife battering. Incest was a problem of seductive teenage stepdaughters, not of power imbalances within the family or male views of women as sexual property, while stranger violence might be provoked by women who wore tight sweaters and drank alone in bars. Home was the safest place for women to be, mainstream criminologists concluded, ignoring the huge volume of domestic violence against women.

(4) Mainstream criminology has ignored sex differences in criminal justice processing. Feminists also faulted mainstream criminologists with either ignoring or underestimating the impact of gender on criminal justice processing. Taking a male norm for granted, conventional criminologists assumed that justice officials treated women the same as men or more leniently. They did not investigate whether the system reacts differently to male and female defendants or to different types of female defendants. They did no research on whether women are punished more harshly than men for sex offenses and public order crimes. Even though criminologists had no empirical evidence for assuming that women fared the same as men or better in the criminal justice system, they were not interested in testing the assumption.

(5) Mainstream criminologists have disregarded the dynamics of gender and power. Feminists further charged that traditional criminologists had failed to investigate the interplay of male power, female economic dependency, and abusive male-female dynamics. While mainstream criminology presented itself as an objective social science concerned with all crime, it was in fact masculinist, deeply biased against women, and riddled with hidden agendas for perpetuating male power. Thus criminology itself served to reinforce the status quo and ensure continuance of female subordination.

Development of feminist perspectives

Over the thirty years of their development, feminist perspectives in criminology have evolved through three stages, each lasting roughly a decade: a mobilization stage, 1968–1977; a maturation stage, 1978–1987; and a stage of differentiation that began around 1988 and continues into the present.

Stage 1: mobilization. During the decade 1968–1977, feminists mobilized for criminological reforms on two fronts, in grassroots organizations and within the academy. The grassroots movement began with nonacademic women organizing at the grassroots level to help the victims of rape, spouse abuse, and incest by setting up hotlines, establishing shelters to which battered women could flee with their children, and raising public awareness through marches and rallies. They also worked with lawyers and legislators to achieve rape law reform. These grassroots organizers called for nonhierarchical relationships, consciousness raising, and victim empowerment. A literature began to accrete around their work, some of it produced by professional authors such as Susan Brownmiller (*Against Our Will*, 1975), some published by activists themselves (e.g., Martin, 1976); this literature led to reforms in mainstream criminology, especially in its treatment of female victims. Many of these activists perceived a radical, hostile divide between men and women, a perception that persists in the work of so-called radical feminists such as Andrea Dworkin, Catharine MacKinnon, and members of the group Women Against Pornography.

The second front on which the feminizers of criminology mobilized during this first stage was within the academy. Three academic criminologists, working independently and indeed in ignorance of one another's efforts, issued the first in-house challenges to traditional criminology. Canadian Marie-Andrée Bertrand exposed the myth of sexual equality before the law. Britisher Frances Heidensohn asked why female crime rates are lower than those of males and why conventional criminologists showed so little interest in this issue. And Dorie Klein, an American, revealed the sexist biases of the literature on female crime. The first stage ended with the publication of the first book-length critique of mainstream criminology, Carol Smart's *Women, Crime, and Criminology: A Feminist Critique* (1976).

In a related development, feminists in law schools produced legal theory that helped frame and validate the reform efforts of grassroots activists and academic criminologists. Feminist legal theorists of this period concentrated on exposing ways in which the law operates to perpetuate women's economic, political, and social disadvantages (Smart, 1990/1998). Although there was little direct interaction between the two sets of academic feminists, the legal theorists created an intellectual context for the criminologists and to some extent authenticated their enterprise.

During this first developmental stage, the concepts of *sex*, *sexism*, and *equality* were central to feminist work in criminology. Arguments tended to be framed in terms of a struggle between the sexes, male and female; critiques were posed in terms of sexism, or male bias against women; and demands were based on the idea of equality. What feminists sought was to be treated the same as men. Few noticed that this ideal involved the internalization and promotion of male standards. Moreover, feminists assumed and fostered solidarity among women, paying little attention to divisions created by age, race, sexual orientation, or social class.

Stage 2: maturation. During the decade 1978–1987, the feminist enterprise came to maturity by developing its agendas, establishing footholds within the academic world, and producing a substantial body of literature. Whereas first-stage feminists had usually worked in isolation, the graduation of a significant number of feminists with doctoral degrees in criminology and related areas now created opportunities for alliances and collaborations. When these feminists assumed editorial positions on journals, reviewed manuscripts for publishers, or were invited by book editors or conference organizers to contribute a chapter or deliver a talk, feminist work received a hearing.

In the early 1980s, feminists established the Division on Women and Crime, the first section within the American Society of Criminology, thus creating another forum for feminist work and offering members routes to professional office. Researchers laid the groundwork for studies of women in policing (Martin), in the courts (Kruttschnitt), in prisons (Rafter) and prison reform (Freedman), and as victims (Dobash and Dobash). Textbooks began to appear, opening up the possibility of courses in women and crime and of training a new generation of feminist criminologists. Toward the end of this period, Meda Chesney-Lind published an important review of the literature on women and crime, one sign of its maturity.

Sex, a concept that had figured prominently in the first stage, was replaced in the second stage by the concept of gender. Although variously defined, "gender" was generally used to denote socially constructed differences between males and females. Whereas first-stage theorists had been concerned about sexism, a problem that could be fixed by achieving the ideal of equality, second-stage theorists were concerned about gender inequality, a more intractable problem that included the very nature of law and organizations, which now appeared to be gendered and masculine institutions. Doubts emerged about the wisdom of pursuing equality, the first-stage ideal, because it now became clear that to be equal meant to adopt masculine standards and values.

Stage 3: differentiation. The third stage, kicked off in 1988 with a major review of accomplishments to date (Daly and Chesney-Lind), has been characterized in part by highly specific research projects built on the groundwork established in the second stage. The new work includes sophisticated empirical studies of court processing (e.g., Albonetti); victimization studies assessing violence against women (Bachman, forthcoming; Koss); reconceptualizations of the implications of criminal justice policy (e.g., Miller, ed.); and research on particular prison issues (Human Rights Watch; Morash, Bynum, and Koons). One result of third-stage activity has been documentation of previously unrecognized differences between women and men, among groups of women, and in the practices of various courts and prisons (e.g., Kruttschnitt, Gartner, and Miller, forthcoming). Another result has been the opening up of new territory for theorizing about difference and its criminal-justice effects. Also characteristic of this third stage is an internationalization of feminist work in criminology, starting formally with a 1991 conference in Quebec (Bertrand, Daly, and Klein, eds.) and continuing through smaller conferences and individual initiatives (Rafter and Heidensohn, eds.). This cross-fertilization has sensitized feminists to national differences and to some extent refocused them on global problems such as female circumcision and child prostitution.

During this third stage, the concept of gender evolved even further from its roots in biological sex differences as feminists became concerned with intersectionalities or the ways in which gender is cross-cut by such variables as age, class, race, and sexual preference, creating a multiplicity of ways of being masculine, feminine, something in between, or something entirely different. As the concept of gender fragmented, it gave rise to work on masculinities and crime (e.g., Messerschmidt). Definitions of the key criminological problems also splintered into issues of "multiple inequalities" (Daly and Maher, eds., p. 11). Feminists concentrated more on crime and crime control, less on problems presented by mainstream criminology, which despite some accommodations to the feminist critique has remained remarkably impervious to change. In fact, by the end of the third decade, some feminists had turned away from criminology itself (Daly and Maher, eds.; Rafter and Heidensohn, eds.), refusing to let mainstream criminologists set their political or research agendas.

NICOLE RAFTER

See also DOMESTIC VIOLENCE; FAMILY ABUSE AND CRIME; FEMINISM: LEGAL ASPECTS; GENDER AND CRIME; PRISONS: PRISONS FOR WOMEN; PROSTITUTION; RAPE: BEHAVIORAL ASPECTS; RAPE: LEGAL ASPECTS.

BIBLIOGRAPHY

ALBONETTI, CELESTA A. "Sentencing Under the Federal Sentencing Guidelines: Effects of Defendant Characteristics, Guilty Pleas, and Departures on Sentence Outcomes for Drug Offenses, 1991–1992." *Law & Society Review* 31, no. 4 (1997): 789–822.

AMIR, MENACHEM. *Patterns of Forcible Rape.* Chicago: University of Chicago Press, 1971.

BACHMAN, RONET. "Estimates of Violence Against Women: A Comparison of the National Crime Victimization Survey and the National Violence Against Women Survey." *Violence Against Women.* (May 2000).

BELKNAP, J. *The Invisible Woman: Gender, Crime, and Justice.* Belmont, Calif.: Wadsworth, 1996.

BERTRAND, MARIE-ANDRÉE. "The Myth of Sexual Equality Before the Law." In *Proceedings of the Fifth Research Conference on Delinquency and Criminality.* Montreal: Quebec Society of Criminology, 1967.

BERTRAND, MARIE-ANDRÉE; DALY, KATHLEEN; and KLEIN, DORIE. eds. *Proceedings of the International Feminist Conference on Women, Law and Social Control, 1991.* Vancouver, B.C.: International Centre for the Reform of Criminal Law and Criminal Justice Policy, 1992.

BROWNMILLER, SUSAN. *Against our Will: Men, Women and Rape.* New York: Bantam, 1975.

CHESNEY-LIND, MEDA. "Women and Crime: The Female Offender." *Signs* 12, no. 1 (1986): 78–96.

DALY, KATHLEEN; and CHESNEY-LIND, MEDA. "Feminism and Criminology." *Justice Quarterly* 5, no. 4 (1988): 498–538.

DALY, KATHLEEN; and MAHER, LISA, eds. *Criminology at the Crossroads: Feminist Readings in Crime and Justice.* New York: Oxford University Press, 1998.

DOBASH, R. W.; and DOBASH, R. P. *Violence Against Women: A Case Against Patriarchy.* New York: The Free Press, 1979.

FEINMAN, CLARICE. *Women in the Criminal Justice System.* New York: Praeger, 1980.

FREEDMAN, ESTELLE B. *Their Sisters' Keepers: Women's Prison Reform in America, 1830–1930.* Ann Arbor: University of Michigan Press, 1981.

GLUECK, ELEANOR; and GLUECK, SHELDON. *Five Hundred Delinquent Women.* New York: Knopf, 1934.

HEIDENSOHN, FRANCES M. "The Deviance of Women: A Critique and an Enquiry." *British Journal of Sociology* 19, no. 2 (1968): 160–175.

HIRSCHI, TRAVIS. *Causes of Delinquency.* Berkeley: University of California Press, 1969.

Human Rights Watch Women's Rights Project 1996. *All Too Familiar: Sexual Abuse of Women in U.S. State Prisons.* New York: Human Rights Watch, 1996.

KLEIN, DORIE. "The Etiology of Female Crime: A Review of the Literature." *Issues in Criminology* 8, no. 2 (1973): 3–30.

KOSS, MARY P. "The Measurement of Rape Victimization in Crime Surveys." *Criminal Justice and Behavior* 23, no. 1 (1992): 55–69.

KRUTTSCHNITT, CANDACE. "Social Status and Sentences of Female Offenders." *Law & Society Review* 15 (1980–1981): 247–265.

KRUTTSCHNITT, CANDACE; GARTNER, ROSEMARY; and MILLER, AMY. "Doing Her Own Time? Examining the Impact of Life Experiences in the Context of the Old and the New Penology." In the journal *Criminology* (August 2000).

MARTIN, DEL. *Battered Wives.* New York: Pocket Books, 1976.

MARTIN, SUSAN. *"Breaking and Entering": Policewomen on Patrol.* Berkeley: University of California Press, 1980.

MESSERSCHMIDT, JAMES W. *Masculinities and Crime: Critique and Reconceptualization of Theory.* Lanham, Md.: Rowman & Littlefield, 1993.

MILLER, SUSAN L. ed. *Crime Control and Women.* Thousand Oaks, Calif.: Sage, 1998.

MORASH, MERRY; BYNUM, TIM S.; and KOONS, BARBARA A. *Women Offenders: Programming Needs and Promising Approaches.* National Institute of Justice Publication No. 171668. Washington, D.C.: National Institute of Justice, 1998.

RAFTER, NICOLE H. *Partial Justice: Women in State Prisons, 1800–1935.* Boston: Northeastern University Press, 1985. Published in 2d ed. *Partial Justice: Women, Prisons, and Social Control.* New Brunswick: Transaction Publishers, 1990.

RAFTER, NICOLE H.; and HEIDENSOHN, FRANCES, eds. *International Feminist Perspectives in Criminology: Engendering a Discipline.* Buckingham, U.K.: Open University Press, 1995.

SMART, CAROL. *Women, Crime and Criminology.* London: Routledge Kegan Paul, 1976.

———. "Feminist Approaches to Criminology, or Post-modern Woman Meets Atavistic Man." In *Feminist Perspectives in Criminology.* Edited by Loraine Gelsthorpe and Allison Morris. Buckingham, U.K.: Open University Press, 1990. Reprinted in *Criminology at the Crossroads: Feminist Readings in Crime and Justice.* Edited by Kathleen Daly and Lisa Maher. New York: Oxford University Press, 1998. Pages 21–36.

SPOHN, CASSIA; GRUHL, JOHN; and WELCH, SUSAN. "The Impact of the Ethnicity and Gender of Defendants on the Decision to Reject or Dismiss Felony Charges." *Criminology* 25 (1987): 175–191.

FEMINISM: LEGAL ASPECTS

Even according to its critics, feminism has been one of the most important influences on the substantive criminal law in the past fifty years. Feminism has changed legal understandings of rape and battering as well as the law of homicide and self-defense. Indeed, there is a growing awareness and body of scholarship showing that feminist concerns are not simply limited to "women's" crimes—crimes either committed by female defendants (such as battered women who kill their husbands) or crimes disproportionately affecting women (such as rape and battering). Instead, the feminist critique emerges within the criminal law anywhere gender is found, namely anywhere the law reflects social norms about women, men, and their relationships. What follows considers four different feminist approaches: the call to equality, to subjectivity, to norms, and to civil rights.

Early efforts to reform the law of rape and battering

Early efforts to inject feminist consciousness within the criminal law emphasized formal equality. And, not surprisingly, feminist concern and writing tended to focus on those crimes that appeared to burden women unequally—battering and rape. Early feminist writers urged that stereotypes about women infected legal understandings and prevented adequate law enforcement. They stressed, for example, that prosecutors often failed to "believe" women because of these stereotypes. A short skirt, a messy past, or an intimate relationship were all reasons to assume that the victim had consented, provoked the incident, or fabricated it for manipulative reasons. This credibility gap resonated widely and became a part of the culture's understanding about why rape and assault laws had failed to protect women.

Based on this shift in cultural understanding, major efforts were launched in the 1970s to reform the law of rape and battering. In the case of battering, efforts focused on a new civil system of redress: A grassroots shelter movement advocated new laws authorizing emergency stay-away orders and criminal and civil penalties for violating those orders. In the case of rape, a national task force coordinated efforts to amend state rape statutes, recalibrating and renaming rape statutes, imposing gender neutral language, and limiting marital rape exceptions. While reform in the area of battering focused on prevention, legal doctrine itself was the target of much of the rape reform movement. Requirements of resistance, and corroboration of witnesses, were soon viewed with skepticism by judges and scholars. Legislatures enacted rape shield laws as courts jettisoned jury instructions warning that rape complaints were to be viewed with peculiar suspicion. By the end of the 1980s, the substantive criminal law of rape and the enforcement of domestic violence laws bore little resemblance to that which governed decades earlier.

The second wave critique of rape law

By the 1980s, feminist theory had brought to bear upon rape law two significant and influential critiques—those of Catharine MacKinnon and Susan Estrich. MacKinnon argued that rape was part of a larger problem of female subordination. Rape law was not fundamentally about punishing forceful sexual acquisition, MacKinnon argued, but instead was intended to perpetuate male dominance by achieving female subordination. Since rape law did not prohibit much that was coercive sex, it legitimized male sexual aggression, thus encouraged women to seek male protection, and thereby reinforced the dominant position of men in society generally. Rape law defined rape for men, creating "rapists," and thus leaving men free to achieve sexual acquisition by other coercive means. MacKinnon's critique created substantial controversy by appearing to equate much that society viewed as consensual with coercive sex and, thus, rape. Ultimately, and despite this controversy, MacKinnon's work would breed not only a new generation of feminist criticism of rape law but would also help to push legislators and others to consider rape law as emblematic of the ways in which the state might perpetuate women's inequality even as it purported to reject that same inequality.

The second critique, by Susan Estrich, relied on more traditional ways of talking about the problems of rape law within the context of criminal law doctrine. Estrich's immediate point was that rape law envisioned a particular kind of violence that made the only kind of "real rape" to be rape by strangers. In contrast, Estrich offered an account of the "simple rape," a rape accomplished without "extra" violence and often by intimates, as "real rape." Estrich's account helped to focus substantial public attention on the problem of acquaintance rape, forcing students and scholars to question whether the criminal law had chosen to focus on a stereotyped version of the knife-wielding rapist to the exclusion of the more common and troubling cases of intercourse accomplished against the victim's wishes. Although this debate raised serious questions about the meaning of force in the law of rape, much of the debate centered on questions of consent. Soon, criminal law scholars began to focus on questions of mental state and whether and what the defendant needed to know about the victim's consent to constitute rape. Estrich took the position that the defendant could be held liable for rape based on a negligent mistake about consent, a proposition considered controversial from a traditional criminal law standpoint as inconsistent with a liability regime based on the defendant's consciousness of wrongdoing.

The Estrich and MacKinnon critiques changed the way that rape law was taught in classrooms across America. But their influence was not without sustained criticism. Indeed, the entire feminist focus on rape came under significant attack. Popular skeptics urged that, by equating rape with consensual sex, the feminist critique was prudery in disguise. Other critics charged that feminists were simply exaggerating the problem and engaged in a highly publicized debate about the precise number of rapes in the country. Some legal critics put forth reform proposals that sought to separate "truly" coercive rapes from "sexual misunderstandings." Even feminists' traditional allies began to urge that the feminist account was partial. Critical race theorist Angela Harris and criminal law scholar Dorothy Roberts argued that white feminists had occluded rape as a means of racial domination, obscuring the ways in which black women experienced rape as the oppression of the "master's" free sexual access.

Partly in response to these developments, feminist scholarship turned more explicitly to consider questions of coercion and autonomy. Lynne Henderson reminded students and scholars that rape law's idea of force and consent was built upon social understandings of coercion that amounted to "scripts" of male innocence and female guilt. From here, new questions were asked about whether a policy of laissez-faire reform, popular in 1970s reform efforts, truly served women or, instead, left them to "bargain" for sex from a position of weakness (Hirshman and Larson). Views of statutory rape laws shifted dramatically because of this new emphasis. In the 1970s, many feminists supported the deregulation of sex between minors. By the 1990s, critics charged that statutory rape reforms had failed to recognize the degree to which, in the name of sexual "freedom" for minors, the law actually sanctioned forceful and exploitative encounters (Oberman; Olsen).

The quest for equality in rape law continues. Periodically, questions arise as to whether rape reform has really accomplished as much as it promised. It has been argued, for example, that feminists have been too quick to believe in the success of their critique. Some have maintained that despite ancient reforms the law remains too much the same. Elimination of the resistance requirement in theory, for example, has not eliminated resistance in fact because courts typically require a showing of something more than lack of consent to find rape (Schulhofer). Similarly, it has been argued that, despite apparent elimination of the spousal exception to rape rules, there is still no parity between rape by a stranger and rape by an intimate (West; Nourse, 2000). Finally, controversy remains about the true nature of consent in a world where norms about sexual relations are changing (Schulhofer).

Pornography and violence

Catharine MacKinnon's critique of rape law was a small part of a larger argument about the social subordination of women. That critique has focused attention not only on violence itself but also on representations of violence. MacKinnon

argued that pornographic representations of women as subordinated objects (for example, women who experienced rape as pleasure) was central to the construction of a sexuality of dominance and inequality: "[p]ornography is a means through which sexuality is socially constructed. . . . It constructs women as things for sexual use and constructs its consumers to desperately want women to desperately want possession and cruelty and dehumanization." Thus, MacKinnon goes on to state, "through pornography, among other practices, gender inequality becomes both sexual and socially real." (MacKinnon, 1989, pp. 139–140).

MacKinnon worked with Andrea Dworkin to draft a model anti-pornography ordinance that attacked both the violence of the pornography industry and its portrayals of violently subordinated women. The groundbreaking ordinance, adopted in Indianapolis in 1984, defined pornography as a practice that discriminated against women; it thus explicitly linked the law's notion of discrimination to violence against women. The Indianapolis law provided a civil cause of action to those victimized by pornography, allowing them to sue makers and distributors of pornography for damages caused by harmful representations. The two principal classes of potential plaintiffs envisaged by the statute were women who had been coerced into making pornographic films and battered or raped women who could show that the abusers' use of pornographic material had contributed to the abuse.

The MacKinnon fight against pornography proved to be quite controversial among feminists because it appeared to impinge on free speech and liberal ideals of choice. Critics argued that the MacKinnon/Dworkin ordinance invited censorship and played into Victorian notions of women as asexual beings. Liberal feminists argued that women should be able to decide for themselves the kind of material they found enjoyable, sexually arousing, or dominating. Critics further predicted that the ordinance would have a chilling effect upon representations of unorthodox sexual conduct, including the sexual conduct of lesbians and gays. Supporters of the ordinance replied that the statute was being misconstrued by critics and that it did not attempt to censor all sexually explicit material but only discriminatory representations that harmed and subordinated women. The harm in question, they argued, was not so vague as to prohibit all explicit material but, rather, a form of harm with an evidentiary basis that had to be proved in court. In *American Booksellers Ass'n. v. Hudnut* (771 F.2d 323 (7th Cir. 1985)), aff'd, 475 U.S. 1001 (1986)), the Seventh Circuit court of appeals struck down the Indianapolis ordinance as unconstitutional. Admitting, at least for the sake of argument, the statute's premise that pornography did subordinate women, the court of appeals nevertheless concluded that the law was a content-based regulation impermissible under the First Amendment. According to the court, the statute's definition of pornography was the equivalent of "thought control," establishing an "'approved' view of women."

The pornography battle revealed a significant rift within feminism between liberal and dominance feminists. That debate has certainly tempered enthusiasm for dominance-feminism. Yet, MacKinnon's argument has proved influential in other guises. For example, despite the failure of the Indianapolis ordinance, a statutory definition of pornography similar to MacKinnon's was ultimately sustained by the Supreme Court of Canada in *Regina v. Butler* (89 D.L.R. 4th (S.C.C. 1992)). MacKinnon's notion of "harm"—the harm caused by pornographic imagery—has been invoked in other debates within the criminal law, in particular, debates about hate crime statutes. More importantly, the link between violence and discrimination has proved quite influential, both legally and politically. Indeed, despite the judicial criticism of MacKinnon's ordinance, by 1990, legislators began to propose a federal statute linking civil rights to anti-female violence.

The call of perspective: self-defense

Feminist influence in the criminal law has not been limited to questions of either rape or assault, subordination or formal equality. It has also focused attention on questions of perspective and difference. Self-defense law has been influenced quite dramatically by feminists' insistence that the law failed to accommodate women's "different" perspective. In the case of battered women, for example, feminists urged that the law failed to incorporate the lived experience of battering and lacked the kind of nuanced, contextualized standard necessary for fair adjudication of self-defense claims. As a result, feminists urged the need for legal standards and evidentiary reforms appropriate to women's difference.

The call to perspective led to three important developments in the law of self-defense and

elsewhere. First, courts adjudicating criminal cases involving female defendants were asked to address whether the proper legal standard was consistent with "women's particular viewpoint and experience." And some courts did, indeed, adopt legal standards applying the perspective of the "reasonable woman" or the "reasonable battered woman" (Cahn). Second, defense lawyers sought introduction at trial of battered woman syndrome testimony (Schneider). Relying upon the work of social psychologists and others, appellate courts in some cases and legislatures in others began to acknowledge that juries did not understand the different position of women in battering relationships, their perceptions of harm, and their difficulties in leaving. Third, in some cases, governors were urged to award clemency to battered women whose experience had been excluded at trial. In 1990, for example, Governor Richard Celeste of Ohio granted clemency to more than twenty battered women convicted of killing or assaulting the men who abused them on the theory that these women had been convicted under legal and evidentiary rules that failed to consider the relevancy of prior battering to their claims. Governor Schaefer of Maryland followed the next year with several commutations, which led to similar campaigns in other states.

While some feminists urged the need to contextualize the battered woman's situation, others emphasized the degree to which the law of self-defense was skewed toward the male image of a barroom brawl. Some argued that the rules of self-defense were inherently biased against women and that this applied to a variety of questions about the nature of the threat, the degree of its imminence, the proportionality of the response and the duty to retreat. Was it really a fair fight, they asked, if women are typically far less able to respond with their fists? Was it proper to assume that, if the woman had a weapon, it made her violence disproportionate? Did the retreat rule simply impose a duty to "leave" the relationship? Did exceptions to the retreat rule for cases occurring in the home impose an undue burden on those most likely to be victimized in the home?

Debate about these questions soon came to be standard fare for criminal law courses. Juxtaposing controversial cases, like Bernhard Goetz's subway shooting, with battered women's claims, casebooks presented a portrait of law in flux. Much of this debate still centers on controversial cases like the decision of the North Carolina Supreme Court in *State v. Judy Norman* (378 S.E. 2d

8 (N.C. 1989)). Norman's case was an egregious one. She had been abused for almost two decades; her husband had forced her into prostitution, made her sleep on the floor and other indignities; she had tried to kill herself and, when she sought aid, her husband told the paramedics to let her die. Following upon these events, Norman killed her husband in his sleep. For this act she was convicted of homicide and the North Carolina Supreme Court refused to rescind that ruling based on the defendant's claim of self-defense. For some feminists, *Norman* is representative of the problems of a law that assumes the battered woman who kills to be a vigilante rather than a victim of her circumstances. For critics, to accept Norman's claim of self-defense is to invite lawlessness. Although much legal commentary has been devoted to the *Norman* case, and its meaning for self-defense law, some feminists have questioned whether this is the proper focus of the legal inquiry, urging that most battered women kill in confrontational situations, not as in *Norman* while the man is sleeping (Maguigan).

Over time, there were some changes in the doctrine of self-defense, notably a tendency by courts to be more sympathetic to a "subjectified" standard. The most significant development associated with this contextualized approach, however, was evidentiary: the rapidly spreading approval of battered woman syndrome testimony by appellate courts. Reliance on such evidence moved from murder and assault cases to cover a wide variety of claims and defenses: Posttraumatic stress disorder or battered woman syndrome has been used by defendants under the rubrics of temporary insanity, diminished capacity, and duress in cases as various as fraud, child abuse, and manslaughter. Battered woman syndrome has been borrowed by prosecutors to prove criminal intent in murder prosecutions and to explain why a battered woman might not report the violence or refuse to testify. More controversially, analogues to battered woman syndrome, such as battered child syndrome and other excuses based on prior abuse, have appeared to burgeon in the wake of the success of battered woman syndrome testimony.

Not surprisingly, battered woman syndrome has become quite controversial. High profile cases in which male defendants have sought to borrow the arguments of battered women have caused many traditional scholars to doubt the wisdom of the syndrome, to question its scientific validity, and to emphasize its ability to encourage "abusive excuses" (Wilson; Faigman). This criticism has not gone unnoticed by feminists. Some have openly voiced doubts about whether "reasonable woman" standards perpetuate the very stereotypes that feminists have fought hard to overcome (Cahn). Others have worried that the subjectivity of the standard tends to undermine "women's agency," reimposing ancient images of women as helpless victims (Coughlin; Schneider). Others have suggested that the focus has been on the wrong problem, urging that one needs no special rule, no syndrome, to fit women within conventional self-defense doctrine. Instead, these feminists argue that the real problem is with our image of the battered woman and the law—our image of a woman killing a helpless man rather than a woman trying to leave (Mahoney) or a woman battling a knife (Maguigan).

The power of norms: provocation

In the late 1990s, criminal law scholars interested in feminism focused on new topics and old topics in new ways. From the original focus on "women's crimes," such as rape and battering, attention has turned toward the way in which gender norms affect more conventional distinctions within the criminal law, such as the line between murder and manslaughter. Some of this work has served to highlight the role of emotion in the law and how ideas of emotion may carry with them gender norms that influence doctrines as various as duress, provocation, and even the voluntary act requirement (Kahan and Nussbaum). At the core of the shift in thinking is a move not only from surface equality or special treatment of women but toward a recognition of the ways in which cultural norms about relationships may be played out in all criminal law doctrines (Nourse, 2000).

At the center of this work is the provocation doctrine, which divides murder from manslaughter and, in some states, aggravated from less serious assaults. Provocation has been controversial among feminists for some time on the theory that it was a "male-focused" doctrine (Taylor). In the 1980s, this controversy was often targeted on the "cooling time" requirement in the law. Much feminist criticism focused on a widely taught California case, *People v. Berry* (556 P. 2d 777 (Cal. 1976)), in which a defendant choked his wife to unconsciousness, returned to her home to wait for her for twenty hours, killed her, and claimed, with an appellate court's approval, that he was entitled to argue that he killed in the "heat of passion" (Coker). In the 1990s, however, this kind of argument erupted in the public sphere in response to a widely publicized case in Maryland, in which Kenneth Peacock shot his wife several hours after he found her in bed with another man. In explaining his October 1994 decision to impose a minimal sentence on Peacock, Maryland Judge Robert B. Cahill stated, "I seriously wonder how many married men, married five years or four years would have the strength to walk away, but without inflicting some corporal punishment . . . . I shudder to think what I would do" (Schafran, p. 1064).

The Peacock case ignited public protest and a judicial investigation because the judge articulated the normality of "punishing" women for violating the "rules of relationship." This, in turn, raised new questions about the provocation doctrine. Under conventional criminal law approaches toward provocation, it was thought simply "natural" that a defendant did not have the power to resist the passions inspired by an unfaithful wife. Legal scholarship in the late 1990s, however, challenged the philosophical and normative bases of the idea of emotion as "irrational" or "compelling," suggesting instead that claims of passion were in fact partial claims of reason (Kahan and Nussbaum). Under this view, the provoked killer's claim for our compassion is not simply a claim for sympathy; "it is a claim of authority and a demand for our concurrence" in the reasons for his emotion (Nourse, 1997). This kind of critique made it easy for feminists to emphasize the degree to which the "rationality" of certain emotions may depend less upon psychology than upon social understandings of gender.

The focus on emotion and norms also helped to reinforce earlier shifts in feminist thought away from focusing on women's victimization rather than their agency. In 1991, Martha Mahoney argued persuasively that battered women should not be viewed as victims but as agents, as women who were "trying to leave" relationships rather than women who were inexplicably "staying." New work on provocation tended to confirm Mahoney's efforts to shift the conversation toward women's efforts to leave. Just as self-defense law had failed to see battered women as "agents" seeking to separate from relationships, so too provocation law had failed to see that many of the cases denominated as ones of "passion" were in fact cases in which women had left or were trying to leave (Nourse, 1997). From this

perspective, the provocation doctrine, it was argued, was less about protecting "emotion" than about protecting male prerogatives to enforce relationships; indeed, the provocation doctrine seemed to protect, in emotional guise, those who battered and stalked (Coker).

Questions about gender norms and the criminal law are likely to continue in debates about the law of homicide. Serious questions remain, for example, about the ways in which the law incorporates gender norms within the idea, not only of passion, but of time. This is important because of controversies about "imminence" in self-defense claims brought by women and "cooling time" in provocation claims made by men. Some studies tend to show that men and women kill in different circumstances: Although women tend to kill when physically attacked, men tend to kill when their wives leave or are unfaithful. If this is right, then one set of doctrines, self-defense, is likely to govern female murder defendants and another set of doctrines, provocation, to govern the male defendants. This raises the question whether different emotion and timing rules in fact govern these claims and, if so, whether these claims are in fact different because they absorb social norms of gender. Put another way, they raise questions about why the criminal law has tended to see the cuckold-killer as a victim of his own emotions but the battered wife killer as a vigilante.

Criminal law, sex, and civil rights

If feminism has had a strong influence on criminal law statutes, doctrine, and scholarship, it has also spurred efforts to attack questions of inequalities by means of federal law. In 1994, the Congress passed and the president signed the Violence Against Women Act, a federal statute rendering changes in federal criminal law and creating a new "gender-motivated crime" subject to civil rights protection.

The Violence Against Women Act includes several kinds of provisions relevant to the criminal law. Some of its provisions specifically target existing federal criminal law and seek to encourage states to reform their criminal laws relating to rape and domestic violence. For example, the bill requires that states provide "full faith and credit" to other states' domestic violence orders; offers incentives to states to increase law enforcement; and authorizes programs to advance the treatment of women victimized by violence, ranging from rape education and prevention to training state and federal judges. In two respects, however, the act makes significant, and controversial, changes in federal and state criminal laws.

The act provides, for the first time, federal penalties and prosecution for "domestic violence" crimes. State law enforcement officials had complained to Congress that, in some situations, batterers avoided prosecution or apprehension by moving across state lines. In response to such complaints, the Congress created a federal criminal statute addressing battering. One provision of the act makes it unlawful to travel across a state line with the intent to injure a spouse or intimate partner and then to commit a crime of violence during or as a result of that travel. Another provision asserts federal jurisdiction over conduct involving interstate travel with the intent to violate a domestic violence protective order. Thus, assuming the requisite intent and resulting injury, a defendant who attacks his wife may be charged, under federal law, for battery, rape, homicide, or kidnapping, as long as there is the requisite interstate travel. The constitutionality of this provision has been upheld despite attack on the ground that, like most traditional criminal jurisdiction of the federal government, these provisions require interstate travel.

More importantly, and certainly more controversially, the Violence Against Women Act created the first civil rights remedy for victims of crimes "motivated by gender." This provision aimed at discriminatory violence, permitting women to sue for injuries inflicted by gender-motivated crimes. The congressional hearings leading to enactment of the Violence Against Women Act compiled a lengthy record of the failure of states, in law and in practice, to provide adequate legal remedies to women. These hearings also emphasized the ways in which rape and battering can be acts of sex discrimination.

In May of 2000, the Supreme Court of the United States struck down the civil rights portion of the Violence Against Women Act in *United States v. Morrison* (529 U.S. 598 (2000)). The court ruled on federalism grounds, holding that the federal government had no constitutional power to legislate a remedy aimed at discriminatory violence against women. The court rejected the argument that the federal government could act under the commerce clause, holding that Congress had no power to legislate under that clause unless economic activity was involved. The court also held the Fourteenth Amendment in-

applicable because the remedy attacked private conduct rather than state-sponsored discrimination. Feminists decried this result, urging that the Supreme Court had misconstrued the remedy as a crime measure rather than an antidiscrimination statute. They also questioned whether the case was really about federalism, pointing out that many states had filed briefs supporting the constitutionality of the provision as consistent with states' rights.

VICTORIA NOURSE

See also DOMESTIC VIOLENCE; EXCUSE: DURESS; FEMINISM: CRIMINOLOGICAL ASPECTS; HATE CRIMES; HOMICIDE: LEGAL ASPECTS; JUSTIFICATION: SELF-DEFENSE; SCIENTIFIC EVIDENCE.

BIBLIOGRAPHY

BALOS, BEVERLY, and FELLOWS, MARY LOUISE. *Law and Violence Against Women: Cases and Materials on Systems of Oppression.* Durham, N.C.: Carolina Academic Press, 1994.
CAHN, NAOMI. "The Reasonable Woman Standard in Theory and in Practice." *Cornell Law Review* 77 (September 1992): 1398–1446.
CHAMALLAS, MARTHA. *Introduction to Feminist Legal Theory.* Gaithersburg, Md.: Aspen Law and Business, 1999.
COKER, DONNA K. "Heat of Passion and Wife Killing: Men Who Batter/Men Who Kill." *Southern California Review of Law and Women's Studies* 2 (1992): 71–130.
COUGHLIN, ANNE M. "Excusing Women." *California Law Review* 82 (January 1994): 1–93.
ESTRICH, SUSAN. "Rape." *Yale Law Journal* 95 (May 1986): 1087–1184.
FAIGMAN, DAVID L. "Note: The Battered Woman Syndrome and Self-Defense: A Legal and Empirical Dissent." *Virginia Law Review* 72 (April 1986): 619–647.
HARRIS, ANGELA P. "Race and Essentialism in Feminist Legal Theory." *Stanford Law Review* 42 (February 1992): 581–615.
HENDERSON, LYNNE. "Rape and Responsibility." *Law and Philosophy* 11 (1992): 127–177.
HIRSHMAN, LINDA R., and LARSON, JANE E. *Hard Bargains: The Politics of Sex.* New York: Oxford University Press, 1998.
KAHAN, DAN, and NUSSBAUM, MARTHA. "Two Conceptions of Emotion in the Criminal Law." *Columbia Law Review* 96 (March 1996): 269–374.
MACKINNON, CATHARINE. *Feminism Unmodified.* Cambridge, Mass.: Harvard University Press, 1987.

———. *Toward a Feminist Theory of the State*. Cambridge, Mass.: Harvard University Press, 1989.

MAGUIGAN, HOLLY. "Battered Women and Self-Defense: Myths and Misconceptions in Current Reform Proposals." *University of Pennsylvania Law Review* 140 (December 1991): 379–485.

MAHONEY, MARTHA. "Legal Images of Battered Women: Redefining the Issue of Separation." *Michigan Law Review* 90 (October 1991): 1–94.

NOURSE, VICTORIA. "Where Violence, Relationship, and Equality Meet: The Violence Against Women Act's Civil Rights Remedy." *Wisconsin Women's Law Journal* 11 (1996): 1–36.

———. "Passion's Progress." *Yale Law Journal* 106 (March 1997): 1331–1448.

———. "The 'Normal' Successes and Failures of Feminism and the Criminal Law." *Chicago-Kent Law Review* 75, no. 3 (2000): 951–978.

OBERMAN, MICHELLE. "Turning Girls Into Women: Re-Evaluating Modern Statutory Rape Law." *Journal of Criminal Law and Criminology* 85 (1994): 15–79.

OLSEN, FRANCES. "Statutory Rape: A Feminist Critique of Rights Analysis." *Texas Law Review* 63 (November 1984): 387–432.

ROBERTS, DOROTHY E. "Rape, Violence, and Women's Autonomy." *Chicago-Kent Law Review* 69 (1993): 359–388.

SCHAFRAN, LYNN HECHT. "There's No Accounting for Judges." *Albany Law Review* 58 (1995): 1063–1085.

SCHNEIDER, ELIZABETH M. "Particularity and Generality: Challenges of Feminist Theory and Practice in Work on Woman-Abuse." *NYU Law Review* 67 (June 1992): 520–568.

SCHULHOFER, STEPHEN J. *Unwanted Sex: The Culture of Intimidation and the Failure of the Law.* Cambridge, Mass.: Harvard University Press, 1998.

SIEGEL, REVA. "The Rule of Love: Wife Beating as Prerogative and Privacy." *Yale Law Journal* 105 (June 1996): 2117–2207.

TAYLOR, LAURIE J. "Comment: Provoked Reason in Men and Women: Heat-of-Passion Manslaughter And Imperfect Self-Defense." *UCLA Law Review* 33 (August 1986): 1679–1735.

The Violence Against Women Act, 42 U.S.C. 13981 (Civil Rights provisions); 18 U.S.C 2261–2262 (Criminal provisions).

WALKER, LENORE E. *The Battered Woman.* New York: Harper & Row, 1979.

WEST, ROBIN L. "Equality Theory, Marital Rape, and the Promise of the Fourteenth Amendment." *Florida Law Review* 42 (1990): 45–79.

WILSON, JAMES Q. *Moral Judgment: Does the Abuse Excuse Threaten our Legal System?* New York: HarperCollins, 1997.

FORFEITURE

Forfeiture is the loss or confiscation of one's property in consequence of a crime, offense, or breach of obligation. It is an ancient practice sustained by differing rationales through the centuries. In biblical times, religious ideas supported the view that property causing death was "guilty" and had to be destroyed as a form of expiation. In medieval England, offending property was forfeited to the king for religious purposes in a practice known as deodand. Later, these forfeitures became a source of crown revenue, and confiscation was justified as a penalty for carelessness.

Early English law also permitted forfeiture of one's estate upon conviction of treason or other felony. The theory behind estate forfeitures was that criminal acts were a breach of the king's peace and warranted a loss of property. By statute, English law also provided for the forfeiture of property, such as ships or cargo, used in violation of the customs and revenue laws. Customs and revenue forfeitures were actions *in rem*, that is, actions taken directly against the property. Unlike felony forfeitures, which required a prior conviction of a wrongdoer, custom and revenue forfeitures proceeded directly against a thing and did not depend on the conviction of anyone for anything. In the nineteenth century, England abolished deodand practice and, by 1870, eliminated most felony and treason forfeitures.

The deodand tradition never took root in the United States. Nor did the practice of forfeiture of estate as a consequence of a felony conviction. Indeed the U.S. Constitution (Art. III, sec. 3, cl.2) specifically limits the forfeiture of one's estate as a punishment for treason, and Congress, in 1790, prohibited forfeiture of one's estate as a consequence of a federal criminal conviction. The forfeiture concept that did flourish was the confiscation of property as a means of enforcing customs and revenue laws. Beginning in 1789, Congress enacted laws permitting the confiscation of contraband and the ships used to transport contraband, such as vessels transporting illegal munitions. These laws also authorized seizure of any goods imported or exported in violation of tariff obligations.

As in English practice, U.S. contraband, customs, and revenue forfeitures were accomplished by civil in rem proceedings that named the property itself as the defendant. Since the proceeding was against the thing, the owner had no personal liability beyond the value of his interest in the thing, and forfeiture was permissible even though an owner was not guilty of any crime and did not know of the offending use of his property. By seizing property subject to customs laws, the government could prevent an errant ship and its cargo from simply sailing away, and it could secure its revenues even if the ship owner could not be located. And if the items seized were contraband or dangerous, forfeiture enabled the government to remove the property from circulation and prevent harm to the public.

Modern forfeiture laws

Although Congress expanded its postcolonial use of forfeiture to reach other forms of property, such as misbranded food or illegal distillery equipment, modern forfeiture law dates specifically to 1970. In that year Congress passed two seminal statutes. The first, the Comprehensive Drug Abuse Prevention and Control Act of 1970 (21 U.S.C. § 881) marked the dawn of contemporary drug forfeiture practice. It authorized the government to seize and forfeit contraband drugs, drug manufacturing and storage equipment, and any conveyances used to transport drugs. With subsequent amendments, this law has been applied to embrace an ever-widening list of properties, including assets having a remote connection to illegal drug activity. The law now permits forfeiture of property *intended* to be used in a drug transaction and property used or intended to be used to *facilitate* a drug crime. The government has confiscated, for example, entire residences based on a small-scale drug sale on the premises and cars merely driven to meetings where drugs deals were discussed.

The second statutory foundation of modern forfeiture law was the Racketeer Influenced and Corrupt Organizations Act (RICO) (18 U.S.C. §§ 1961–1968). This law, together with criminal forfeiture provisions of the Comprehensive Drug Abuse Prevention and Control Act, rekindled the long dormant idea of using forfeiture of assets as a significant form of criminal punishment. Under RICO, a person convicted of a racketeering offense faces not only prison and a fine but also the loss of any interest in his criminal enterprise and any property, including legitimate businesses, connected to or derived from the racketeering activity. The potential scope of

RICO is astounding. For example, in *Alexander v. United States*, 509 U.S. 544 (1993), the owner of various businesses dealing in sexually explicit materials was convicted of federal obscenity law violations and racketeering. The racketeering offenses were based on a finding that seven items sold in thirteen Minnesota adult stores were obscene and represented a long-running pattern of illegal activity. In addition to a prison term and a hefty fine, the district court ordered forfeiture of all of the defendant's inventory, stores, vehicles, and $9 million acquired in the illegal enterprise.

Although the most popular and well-known use of forfeiture involves seizure of assets connected to drug violations, property is subject to forfeiture under a broad array of federal and state laws. There are over 150 federal laws permitting some form of forfeiture, and almost every state has one or more statutes authorizing confiscation of property. Federal laws permit, for example, forfeiture of property connected to violations of gun laws, gambling laws, liquor laws, customs laws, securities laws, income tax laws, obscenity laws, telemarketing laws, and even wildlife protection laws. A particularly potent statute is the Money Laundering Control Act of 1986, as amended (18 U.S.C. §§ 981, 982), which provides for criminal and civil forfeiture of property involved in or traceable to money laundering and banking related offenses.

The government justifies modern forfeiture law as a highly successful device for taking the profit out of crime and destroying criminal enterprises that tend to continue operating even if some involved individuals are jailed. But forfeitures have become very profitable for the government, and a significant portion of law enforcement revenue now depends on aggressive pursuit of forfeitable property. The central, although not exclusive, clearinghouse for federal forfeiture proceeds is the Asset Forfeiture Program of the Department of Justice. Officials reported that, in 1995, net deposits to the Asset Forfeiture Fund totaled $487.5 million dollars, and that, between 1985 and 1995, the fund received more than $4.3 billion in forfeited property. Since 1989, fund receipts have averaged one-half billion dollars per year and reached $600 million in 1999. A marked jump in forfeiture receipts coincided with the passage of legislation in 1984 that created the fund and permitted drug forfeiture proceeds to be funneled back to the police agencies that seized them.

Monies from the Asset Forfeiture Fund are used for a variety of purposes but the lion's share, about one half, is paid to state and local law enforcement agencies based upon their participation in forfeiture actions. In a practice known as *equitable sharing*, local agencies ask the federal government to adopt their forfeiture cases. The federal government assumes control, subtracts its expenses, and then returns the bulk of the amount to the local agency to be used solely for law enforcement needs. This payback arrangement allows local law enforcement to evade state legislative or constitutional requirements that may mandate that forfeited property be turned over to the state treasury or used to pay for non-law enforcement needs such as schools.

Even apart from federal equitable sharing arrangements, state and local jurisdictions have developed their own forfeiture programs and have netted millions in property. The total value of forfeited assets from all jurisdictions is unknown, but press accounts report that huge sums have been acquired. For example, between 1989 and 1992, the Sheriff's Office in Volusia County, Florida, seized $8 million in cash in roadside stops of motorists. Although the office returned about half of the money in settlements, it still retained $4 million over the three-year period.

Given the broad scope of modern forfeiture laws and the large sums that law enforcement agencies stand to keep for themselves, critics have charged that forfeiture decisions are driven more by the pursuit of revenue than legitimate law enforcement goals. They cite police tactics such as the *reverse sting* where police sell drugs to buyers, sometimes in drive-by transactions. The focus is on buyers, not suppliers. And the buyer will likely not be prosecuted, because the objective is the cash and the car. A New York City police commissioner explained why drug agents who work the I-95 *drug corridor* target suspects on the southbound lanes, and not those traveling northbound from Florida to New York City. Those traveling south are more likely to have drug proceeds while those traveling north are more likely to have drugs. Law enforcement can spend forfeitable cash; it must destroy contraband drugs.

The distinction between criminal and civil forfeiture

Modern forfeiture law is entirely statutory, and the precise practices permitted depend on each enactment. Nevertheless there are broad patterns that allow a general description of how forfeiture laws operate. The central, defining characteristic is whether a statute permits criminal or civil forfeiture. Although both criminal and civil forfeiture laws are powerful weapons in the hands of law enforcement, these two types of forfeiture function in fundamentally different ways.

Criminal forfeiture is an *in personam* proceeding, that is, an action taken against the individual as part of a criminal case. A prosecutor triggers a criminal forfeiture by including within an indictment a forfeiture count describing the property to be confiscated. To suffer the penalty of forfeiture, the defendant must first be found guilty of the underlying offense, such as drug trafficking or money laundering. In the underlying criminal proceeding, the defendant enjoys all of the rights of the criminally accused such as right to counsel and a presumption of innocence. The criminal forfeiture is, however, an element of the defendant's sentence, not the underlying offense. It is thus an additional punishment imposed on the defendant, over and above a fine or imprisonment. Its closest ancestor is the English forfeiture of estate for felonious behavior or treason.

Upon a finding of forfeiture, the court enters an order authorizing seizure of the identified property. The property may already be in government hands if, after a hearing, the prosecutor convinced the court that there was a substantial likelihood that the defendant would be convicted and that there was an immediate need to protect the property. Under most statutes, property subject to criminal forfeiture includes the defendant's interest in any proceeds from the criminal violation and any property, such as cars, houses, or tools, used or intended to be used to commit or facilitate the violation. Under such expansive terms, criminal forfeiture can reach a wide range of property, and it may be valued far in excess of any fine authorized for the underlying crime. Almost all criminal forfeiture statutes also permit the government to confiscate the defendant's interest in other property as *substitute assets* if the forfeitable property was hidden, transferred, commingled, or diminished in value.

Criminal forfeiture affects only the defendant's interest in the tainted property and not the property itself. Third parties having a claim against the property, such as joint tenants or persons having security interests, do not lose their interests by virtue of a criminal forfeiture order. But the government may pursue forfeitable property in the hands of third parties, and third parties face significant hurdles in protecting their interests. First they face dissipation of their interests as they generally may not press their claims until the criminal proceeding is concluded. Second, after a court has entered an order of forfeiture and notice is given, third parties must act swiftly and convincingly. Typically they have thirty days to file their claims and, at a later hearing, must prove, by a preponderance of evidence, that they have a superior title in the property or are bona fide purchasers.

Although significant forfeitures have occurred in connection with criminal actions, the most explosive forfeiture activity has come in the area of civil forfeiture. This is not surprising since the procedures permitting such forfeitures are congenial to the government, and since civil forfeiture does not depend on the government meeting the arduous task of proving someone guilty of a crime. Under federal law and most state civil forfeiture laws, the government may seize property from anyone once it has probable cause to believe that the property is contraband, proceeds of a crime, or used or intended to be used in the commission of a crime. Probable cause is the weakest of all evidentiary burdens requiring only a *fair probability* that property is forfeitable.

Civil forfeiture is an action in rem, that is, a proceeding directed against "guilty" property and not against any person having an interest in the property. Civil forfeiture is a direct descendant of revenue and customs laws and, as a result, many federal forfeiture rules of practice are based on admiralty and customs procedures. In most cases, civil forfeiture laws permit the government to seize property without giving the owner notice or any prior opportunity to object. Once the property owner or claimant is notified that a seizure has occurred, he or she may contest the action, but they must do so speedily. Typically the property owner must file a claim within twenty days and post a bond. At a hearing on the matter, once the government discharges its small burden of proving probable cause to forfeit, the burden shifts to the property owner to show, by a preponderance of the evidence, that the property is "innocent."

Because the forfeiture proceeding is a civil proceeding, the property owner enjoys none of the procedural protections ordinarily associated with a criminal trial, such as appointed counsel or a presumption of innocence. To escape a civil forfeiture, a property owner must prove that there was no underlying offense, or that, if there was an offense, the property was not connected to it. Owners may not defend by saying that they were not involved in any criminal activity or did not know that the property was used for criminal purposes. Many federal and state statutes soften this harsh limitation by recognizing a so-called *innocent owner* defense. Property owners may avoid a forfeiture order if they prove they had no knowledge of any wrongdoing and did all that was reasonably possible to prevent wrongdoing. However, since it is virtually impossible for property owners to prove that they could not have been more cautious, the innocent owner defense has proved to be difficult to claim. For example, parents who lost their car because their son used it to transport drugs were denied the innocent owner defense because, although knowing absolutely nothing of the illegal activity, they knew the son had a minor criminal record.

Constitutional challenges

As forfeitures have soared, those harmed, particularly innocent third parties, have raised various constitutional challenges. Parties have claimed that civil forfeiture which permits summary, no-notice seizures of property, allows the government to take property on minimal proof that it was tainted with illegality, shifts the burden of proof of innocence to the property owner, and denies minimal procedural due process guaranteed by the Fifth and Fourteenth Amendments. With one exception, the federal courts have been unsympathetic.

In *United States v. James Daniel Good Real Property*, 510 U.S. 43 (1993), the Supreme Court modestly heightened procedural protections by limiting the government's authority to seize certain property with no advance notice or opportunity to be heard. At least with respect to real property, such as houses or farms, the Court held that, absent exigent circumstances, procedural due process requires *pre-seizure* notice and an opportunity to be heard. While the ruling is a welcome development for property owners, including apartment dwellers, it applies only to real property. Cars, boats, planes, currency, and other *movables* remain automatically covered by the *exigent need* to seize-first-and-ask-questions-later.

Substantively, parties have argued that, as applied in particular circumstances, forfeiture laws also violate the excessive fines clause of the Eighth Amendment, constitute double jeopardy

718   FORFEITURE

under the Fifth and Fourteenth Amendments, and are fundamentally unfair to innocent owners under principles of substantive due process. With the exception of the excessive fines attack, the courts have essentially rebuffed these claims as well. And, as with the challenges to forfeiture procedures, they have done so largely based on long historical acceptance of the forfeiture remedy.

The Eighth Amendment provides that excessive fines shall not be imposed. The Supreme Court has held that a fine is a monetary penalty exacted for some offense and, specifically, that a forfeiture is a fine if it is punishment for an offense. In *United States v. Bajakajian*, 524 U.S. 321 (1998), the Court concluded that criminal forfeitures are fines because they are additional penalties imposed on defendants for criminal behavior. In *Bajakajian* the defendant pleaded guilty to failing to report that he was transporting more than $10,000 in currency outside of the United States. In addition to a term of probation and a conventional fine of $5,000, the government sought criminal forfeiture of the entire amount that the defendant sought to remove from the country, namely $357,144. In the only Supreme Court case ever to find a fine excessive, whether a criminal forfeiture or otherwise, the Court held that confiscation of $357,144 for a currency violation was "grossly disproportional" to the gravity of the offense and, therefore, excessive. The defendant's crime was solely a reporting violation, unrelated to any other criminal activity, and the harm caused was minimal.

In *Bajakajian*, the Court left intact its earlier ruling from *Austin v. United States*, 509 U.S. 602 (1993), that civil forfeitures, too, could be fines and could be unconstitutionally excessive. But *Bajakajian* clouded the rationale for applying the excessive fines clause to civil, as opposed to criminal forfeitures. *Austin* said that civil forfeitures were historically understood to be punishment, and the only question was whether they were grossly disproportionate and, hence, excessive. Not all civil forfeitures are disproportionate. It is perfectly proportionate to seize drugs or other contraband, no matter how valuable, because, by definition, that property is illegal to possess. It is also perfectly proportionate to seize the proceeds of a crime offense since criminals should not profit from their wrongdoing. Gross disproportionality potentially arises when the government seizes *instrumentalities* (i.e., property used to commit or to facilitate a crime) especially if it is prop-

erty owned by someone uninvolved in the criminal activity itself. In *Bajakajian* the Court seemed to say, however, that no traditional or historically accepted civil forfeitures, whether of contraband, proceeds, or instrumentalities, could ever be considered punishment. Only those modern in rem forfeitures that "blurred the traditional distinction between civil *in rem* and criminal *in personam* forfeiture" could be punishment and, thus, limited by the excessive fines clause. But the Court's new distinction in *Bajakajian* 524 U.S. at 331 was never explained, and the application of the excessive fines clause to modern civil forfeiture is now in doubt.

Parties have also raised double jeopardy claims to challenge forfeitures. The double jeopardy clause provides protection against being twice tried or punished for the same offense. It is inapplicable to criminal forfeitures because the imposition of criminal punishment such as jail and forfeiture is imposed in a single criminal proceeding. But defendants claimed that a criminal penalty imposed in a criminal case followed by a separate civil forfeiture arising out of the same facts, or vice versa, was double punishment. The idea was derailed in *United States v. Ursery*, 518 U.S. 267 (1996). Civil forfeitures, the Court said, were primarily civil regulatory measures that encouraged people to insure that their property was not used for illicit purposes. The Court noted that although forfeitures may have some punitive aspects, historically they were not regarded as punishment, and viewed in their entirety were not so punitive as to render them a form of double jeopardy punishment.

A final, doomed constitutional challenge to civil forfeiture rested on the claim that applying forfeiture to seize the property of innocent owners was a violation of substantive due process because it was arbitrary and irrational. Seizing the property of innocent owners does make sense if the property is contraband. It is also rational to seize property that constitutes traceable proceeds of crime, even in the hands of innocent third parties. The idea is that in deciding between harm to the innocent third party and closing off avenues for criminals to launder their profits, a legislature may rationally choose to frustrate the criminal. Moreover a third party, like a lawyer, may be in a position to consider whether property was obtained from a known or suspected criminal. But even the Supreme Court seemed to acknowledge that forfeitures applied to innocent persons whose property was simply used by another to commit a crime could be irrational.

In *Calero-Toledo v. Pearson Yacht Co.*, 416 U.S. 663 (1974) the Court upheld the forfeiture of a yacht because a single marijuana cigarette was found on board. The lessor boat company had no knowledge of the drug use but failed to show what degree of care it used in supervising how the boat was used. The Court upheld the forfeiture saying it might induce lessors to exercise greater care. At the same time, the Court also observed that it would be difficult to reject the constitutional claim of an owner who was innocent and proved he had done all that he could do to prevent the illicit use of his property. But that is precisely what a plurality of the Court did in *Bennis v. Michigan*, 516 U.S. 442 (1996) where it permitted the forfeiture of an innocent wife's interest in a car seized from her husband.

In *Bennis*, the husband had been convicted of an indecent act with a prostitute in the vehicle. The wife's interest was sacrificed even though she had absolutely no awareness that her husband had behaved or would behave as he did. Nevertheless, the plurality reasoned that there was long-standing precedent permitting forfeiture against innocent owners and that such forfeitures serve purposes such as preventing further illicit use of the property. Justice Clarence Thomas, writing separately, said that forfeiture of property of innocent owners was valid because it was blessed by history and that the case was a reminder that the Constitution did not prohibit everything that was intensely undesirable. His comments underline the reality that, except for the requirement of pre-seizure notice to seize real property and some boundaries on grossly disproportionate criminal forfeitures, the constitution places very few limits on the use of a practice courts have described as harsh and oppressive. They also make clear that if reforms do come, they must come from the legislatures that originally created and successively broadened modern criminal and civil forfeiture.

MARY M. CHEH

See also BURDEN OF PROOF; CIVIL AND CRIMINAL DIVIDE; COUNSEL: RIGHT TO COUNSEL; CRIMINAL JUSTICE PROCESS; DRINKING AND DRIVING; DRUGS AND CRIME: LEGAL ASPECTS; FEDERAL CRIMINAL JURISDICTION; FEDERAL CRIMINAL LAW ENFORCEMENT; POLICE: CRIMINAL INVESTIGATIONS; PROSECUTION: PROSECUTORIAL DISCRETION; SENTENCING: PROCEDURAL PROTECTION.

BIBLIOGRAPHY

BLUMENSON, ERIC, and NILSEN, EVA. "Policing for Profit: The Drug War's Hidden Economic Agenda." *The University of Chicago Law Review* 65 (1998): 1.
CHEH, MARY M. "Can Something This Easy, Quick, and Profitable Also Be Fair? Runaway Civil Forfeiture Stumbles on the Constitution." *New York Law School Review* 39 (1994): 1–2.
KESSLER, STEVEN L. *Civil and Criminal Forfeiture: Federal and State Practice.* Updated periodically. Deerfield, Ill.: West Group, 1993.
SMITH, DAVID B. *Prosecution and Defense of Forfeiture Cases.* New York: Matthew Bender & Co., Inc., 1981. Updated periodically.
U.S. Department of Justice. *Annual Report of the Department of Justice Asset Forfeiture Program: Fiscal Years 1995 and 1996.* Washington, D.C.: U.S. Department of Justice, 1996

CASES

Alexander v. United States (1993).
Austin v. United States (1993).
Bennis v. Michigan (1996).
Calero-Toledo v. Pearson Yacht Co. (1974).
United States v. Bajakajian (1998).
United States v. James Daniel Good Real Property (1993).
United States v. Ursery (1996).

FORGERY

The law against forgery is designed to protect society from the deceitful creation or alteration of writings on whose authenticity people depend in their important affairs. A person who, with the purpose of deceiving or injuring, makes or alters a writing in such a way as to convey a false impression concerning its authenticity is guilty of forgery in its contemporary sense.

History

The law of forgery may have originated with an early Roman law (c. 80 B.C.) that prohibited falsification of documents describing the passing on of land to heirs. The precise scope of what was considered forgery at common law is not universally agreed upon, but a statute passed in the time of Queen Elizabeth I (An Act against forgers of false deeds and writings, 5 Eliz. 1, c. 14 (1562) (England)) prohibited forgery of publicly recorded, officially sealed documents with the intent to affect the title to land, as well as the knowing use of such documents as evidence in court. In the first major expansion of the law's coverage, a 1726 decision declared that a false endorsement on an unsealed private document was indictable both under the Elizabethan statute and at common law (*Rex v. Ward*, 92 Eng. Rep. 451 (K.B. 1726)). Writing only half a century later, William Blackstone was able to declare, after referring to several contemporary statutes, that "there is now hardly a case possible to be conceived wherein forgery, that tends to defraud, whether in the name of a real or fictitious person, is not made a capital crime" (*250). Blackstone defined common law forgery, which he also called *crimen falsi*, as "the fraudulent making or altering of a writing to the prejudice of another man's right." Pillory, fines, and imprisonment were the penalties in those rare cases that were not subject to capital punishment (*247).

American law of forgery

As with their English antecedents, early American prohibitions of forgery focused more on the types of documents covered than on clarifying the definition of the crime itself. As a result, a rather technical body of case law developed. The most important effort to simplify and rationalize the law was the American Law Institute's Model Penal Code of 1962, variations of which were gradually adopted by the states. However, the principal federal forgery statute, which prohibits false making, forgery, or alteration of any writing for the purpose of obtaining or receiving any sum of money from the United States government, has remained virtually unchanged since its enactment (An Act for the punishment of frauds committed on the government of the United States, ch. 38, 3 Stat. 771 (1823)). This law, codified under 18 U.S.C. § 495 (1999), contains no definition of its central term, *forges*, and has been authoritatively interpreted by the United States Supreme Court to cover only that conduct which was understood as forgery in 1823 (*Gilbert v. United States*, 370 U.S. 650 (1962)). The definition of *forgery* applied in a state prosecution is determined by the statutes of that state and by start-court interpretation of those laws.

Interpretative issues. The problems of interpretation in forgery prosecutions may be grouped around the three key elements of the common law offense: false making, writing, and intent to defraud.

Although a few jurisdictions have held to the contrary, the notion of false making in forgery generally refers only to a document's authenticity and not to the veracity of any factual assertions within it. A written statement may be full of lies and used to cheat, but this does not make it a forgery; on the other hand, an otherwise legitimate deed on which the date of filing has been altered, or the name of one person has been signed by another without permission, is a forgery. Similarly, a document with a genuine signature that has been procured by fraud or trickery is generally not considered a forgery, although a few jurisdictions have held that it is.

In the absence of a contrary statute, a writing is not considered forged unless it might deceive a person of ordinary observation or prudence. Moreover, unless the legislature has prescribed otherwise, the writing must have some apparent legal efficacy in terms of private or public rights; if it is completely innocuous or void on its face, it cannot be a forgery. For example, a check that requires two signatures but has only one cannot be a forgery, even if the one signature which appears is false. In addition, because only writings are covered, the fraudulent simulation of valuable objects, as in art forgery, is nor within the traditional definition.

In forgery, the mens rea (culpable state of mind) is generally an intent to defraud, meaning a purpose to deceive or cheat another person or entity out of his or its legal due. There is no requirement that the intent involve a potential advantage to the forger, or that the fraudulent intention be successfully achieved.

Defenses and evidence. There are three principal defenses to charges of forgery. First, a person may have, or believe he has, the authority to sign another's name; or an alteration may be intended to correct what is genuinely believed to be an error in a document. In either event, there would be no intent to defraud, and probably no false making. Second, even if the document is clearly forged, the prosecution may not be able to prove by legally admissible evidence that the accused is the person who forged it. Finally in a surprising number of cases, it is difficult to prove that the writing is not genuine. For example, the true payee often has a motive to deny receiving and cashing a check, so that a duplicate may be issued.

The testimony of a layperson is admissible evidence to identify handwriting with which he is familiar. However, where the issue is either the identity of the forger or the genuineness of the document, an expert questioned-document examiner will often have to make comparisons between the writing at issue and known exemplars of the handwriting of both the accused and the true payee. The techniques of scientific analysis sometimes do not provide a satisfactory answer, and the prosecution consequently fails.

Related offenses

The knowing use of forged writings has been prohibited as a separate offense at least since "uttering or publishing as true" certain forged writings was made a capital crime in 1729 (An Act for the more effectual preventing and further Punishment of Forgery, Perjury, and Subornation of Perjury, 2 Geo. 2, C. 25 (1729) (Great Britain) (repealed)). Under modern statutes, uttering is usually covered in the section dealing with forgery and carries the same maximum penalty as forgery itself. Mere possession of a forged instrument is generally not a crime until an attempt is made to use ("utter or publish") it. However, under federal law it is an offense knowingly and with fraudulent intent to transport a forged traveler's check or "security" (defined to include a check) in interstate commerce (18 U.S.C. § 2314 (1999)).

One who achieves a dishonest financial advantage by the use of a forged instrument may also be convicted of fraud, false pretenses, or theft by deception. But passing a worthless check, even when accompanied by misrepresentations or intent to defraud, is regarded only as a species of theft or false pretenses, not as uttering or forgery, so long as the checking account and signature are genuine. However, if the account does not exist or if the drawee bank or maker is fictitious, several states' laws treat the passing of the check as a separate offense or even as a form of forgery. Finally, it has often been pointed out that only a restrictive definition of writing permits any distinction to be drawn between forgery and counterfeiting.

The future of forgery laws

The highly influential Model Penal Code recommended that the technical restrictions on forgery laws be abolished and that both uttering and counterfeiting be consolidated with forgery (Model Penal Code, 1962, § 224.1; 1960, commentary on § 224.1). The Code defined *forgery* with specificity and included unauthorized alteration of a writing. It also included the making, completing, executing, authenticating, issuing, or transferring of a writing that misrepresents its time, place, or sequence of execution, or its authority, or that purports to be a copy of which there was no genuine original. *Writing* was defined broadly to include all forms of recording information, money, credit cards, trademarks, and "other symbols of value, right, privilege, or identification." The "purpose to defraud or injure anyone" was retained as an element. The offense would be graded: forgery of money, scamps, and other instruments issued by the government or representing interests in property would be a serious felony; forgery of a will, deed, contract, or other writing having legal efficacy would be a less serious felony; and any other type of forgery would be a misdemeanor. In a separate provision, the Code recommended punishing as a misdemeanor the fraudulent simulation of objects, such as art forgery, which creates a false appearance of "value because of antiquity, rarity, source, or authorship" (1962. § 224.2). The United States National Commission on Reform of Federal Criminal Laws made a similar set of recommendations in 1971 (§ 1751).

By 1980, at least twenty-three states had followed this lead in whole or in substantial part (Model Penal Code, 1980, commentary on § 224.1). Although some jurisdictions will undoubtedly retain a distinction between forgery and counterfeiting, more are likely to adopt the Model Penal Code's approach.

PETER GOLDBERGER
DAN M. KAHAN

See also COUNTERFEITING.

BIBLIOGRAPHY

American Law Institute. *Model Penal Code and Commentaries: Official Draft and Revised Comments*, vol. 2. Philadelphia: ALI, 1980.
———. *Model Penal Code: Proposed Official Draft.* Philadelphia: ALI. 1962.
———. *Model Penal Code: Tentative Draft No. 11.* Philadelphia: ALI. 1960.
BAKER, JAY NEWTON. *Law of Disputed and Forged Documents: Cases, Illustrations.* Charlottesville, Va.: Michie Co., 1995.
BLACKSTONE, WILLIAM. *Commentaries on the Laws of England (1765–1769)*, vol. 4. Reprint. University of Chicago Press, 1979.

U.S. National Commission on Reform of Federal Criminal Laws. *Final Report*. Washington, D.C.: The Commission, 1971.
———. *Working Papers*. vol. 2. Washington, D.C.: The Commission, 1970.

WHARTON, FRANCIS. *A Treatise on the Criminal Law of the UnitedStates*. 2d ed. Philadelphia: James Kay, Jr. & Brother, 1852.

G

GAMBLING

Gambling can be defined broadly as participation in any risk-taking activity. In law gambling is defined as a bet or wager (*consideration*), on a probability game or a sporting event (*chance*), with the hope of winning a payoff or prize (*FCC v. American Broadcasting Co.*, 347 U.S. 284 (1954)). From a public health perspective, activities such as day trading in stocks, commodities, and futures markets have been said to mimic gambling games.

Gambling has never in law or custom been considered inherently evil (*malum in se*). Why then is betting—or accepting bets—sometimes considered a crime? Reasons that can be singled out include the belief that gambling undermines the work ethic, is destructive of personality, invites fraud and deception, and engenders social decay. Such a view of gambling, although present in most English-speaking countries, is a minority viewpoint, especially in the United States, where a variety of gambling forms are permitted under differing legal regimes. These include casinos, lotteries, wagering on horse or dog races, electric gaming devices and slot machines, jai-alai, and Internet gambling.

The historical lottery

Lotteries were popular—and remain so—because they present a rare opportunity to accumulate capital by luck alone. Despite Puritan opposition, the British Parliament authorized numerous lotteries between the sixteenth and nineteenth centuries. "By 1775," asserted the Royal Commission on Lotteries and Betting in 1933, "the lottery had become virtually an annu-

al event." The lottery made its entrance into American history for much the same reasons. Lotteries were said to be the "reall and substantiall food, by which Virginia hath been nourished" (Ezell, p. 8). No American governmental entity—with the exception of post–World War II Nevada or possibly nineteenth-century Louisiana—has ever been dependent upon gambling revenues for so large a proportion of its budget as was the British government. Not until the early nineteenth century, as the lottery became more widespread in England and dependence upon it increased, did its enemies gather enough influence to destroy it. England saw the last of its state lotteries in 1823.

England's Puritan opposition to lotteries reinforced America's opponents of gambling. By the 1840s and 1850s, most of the South began to feel the anti-lottery pressure, and lotteries seem to have been relatively unpopular by the time of the Civil War. National opposition to the lottery strengthened Louisiana's anti-lottery forces, who captured the governor's office and a majority of the legislature. Consequently, Louisiana discontinued its lottery. With the twentieth century approaching, lotteries vanished from the American scene.

The contemporary lottery

No state-sponsored lotteries appeared in the United States until 1964. In that year, conservative New Hampshire adopted a sweepstakes. The state had no sales or income tax, and already derived more than 60 percent of its revenues from "sin taxes" on horse racing, liquor, tobacco, and beer. From the late 1960s onward, most states searched for alternative revenue sources. Gambling became a prime candidate, particularly through the lottery, off-track betting, and casino gambling. Politicians often welcome legal gambling since it does not depend on the coercive power of the state.

Lottery revenues were often referred to as "painless" although legislators recognized that the burden of providing such revenues fell disproportionately upon identifiable income strata. The lottery is usually a regressive source of public revenue since persons who occupy lower-income positions have the most incentive to purchase lottery tickets. Although lottery ticket purchases are voluntary, so is the purchase of most goods and services, which are taxed at a rate considerably lower than the usual percentage that states take before lottery payoffs.

As states compete with one another for the lottery market, novel ways are developed to stimulate demand. States advertise and market lotteries through the following means: frequent drawings; inexpensive tickets; better chances of prize-winning; higher payoff ratios; attractive prizes (including a larger first prize); simpler buying, drawing, and paying procedures; fast notice of results; and the opportunity for players to choose their own ticket numbers. The move from state lottery prohibition to promotion in half a century is remarkable, but not entirely unprecedented given the lottery's fluctuating history of acceptance and rejection in England and the United States.

Extent of gambling

According to the 1976 report of the U.S. National Commission on the Review of the National Policy toward Gambling, 80 percent of Americans favored the legalization of some form of gambling, and two-thirds had actually gambled, signaling widespread public acceptability. Roughly a quarter of a century later, acceptance had escalated into embrace. The 1999 National Gambling Impact Study Commission, which described the intervening period as "transformative," found that by 1999 more than forty states had legalized pari-mutuel racetracks and betting; thirty-seven states had established lotteries, and several others were considering introducing them. Casino gambling expanded from Nevada to Atlantic City, New Jersey, and then nationwide to the gulf coast of Mississippi, to New Orleans, to Midwestern cities on riverboats, to Detroit, and to western mining towns. The immense transformation has been accompanied by an ac-

ceptance of gambling in mainstream culture. The winning lottery numbers in ever bigger jackpot games are routinely announced on the evening news. Racetrack betting takes place over the telephone and in off-track neighborhood betting parlors in New York City. "Legions of employees" testified to the National Gambling Impact Commission about the hope and opportunities that casino jobs have brought to their families. Others, however, told tales of families devastated by problem gambling, of blight and sleaze, of a work ethic undercut by the pursuit of easy money.

When made criminal, gambling is quintessentially a victimless crime. Players rarely, if ever, call police to report that an illegal bookmaker has taken their bet. New York City's Knapp Commission found systemic corruption where police regularly received payoffs from illegal bookmakers and numbers racketeers. In recognition of this, and the consequent difficulties of enforcement, the trend in gambling law and policy has been away from strict prohibition to regulation, with distinctions made according to type and sponsorship of gambling activity. This is not entirely new. Even at common law, gambling was not criminal if the game of chance was played privately. Only when conducted openly or notoriously, and where inexperienced persons were fleeced, was gambling a crime. Most gambling statutes imposed minor misdemeanor penalties for public social gambling, with somewhat harsher penalties for gambling with a minor. Gambling by a professional player might be classified as a felony. The 1976 National Gambling Commission gave considerable attention to state criminal laws prohibiting gambling—and found that they were more widely violated than any other type of prohibition. Criminal violation of state gambling laws was scarcely an issue for the National Gambling Impact Commission. Instead, the Commission focused on social policy and consequences of the widespread growth and acceptance of legal gambling.

Gambling and organized crime

Federal criminal law monitors organized crime and gambling through the Gaming Devices Act of 1951 (Johnson Act, 18 U.S.C. & 1804), which prohibits interstate transportation of gaming devices; the Racketeering Influenced and Corrupt Organization Statutes (RICO, 18 U.S.C. & 1961 et. seq.); and amendments made in 1985 to the Bank Secrecy Act (31 U.S.C. &

103), also known as the Currency and Foreign Transactions Reporting Act). The latter act requires several cash intensive businesses, and explicitly casinos, to report cash transactions in amounts greater then $10,000. In addition, the Money Laundering Control Act of 1986 and the Treasury Department's Financial Crimes Enforcement Network were enacted to "establish, oversee, and implement policies to prevent and detect money laundering" (U.S. Treasury Order No. 105–108).

The federal interest in casino gambling can be traced to Nevada's casino gambling industry, which was established and developed by well-known organized crime figures. Although not all casinos have connections to organized-crime, such roots have at times become visible. During the 1970s, a number of casinos were found by Nevada authorities and the U.S. Department of Justice to be infiltrated by organized crime families who controlled union pension funds that facilitated casino expansion.

The introduction of strong regulatory measures by the states has been a factor in enabling casino gambling to expand throughout the United States. Moreover, gambling enterprises are typically owned and run by major hotel and leisure industry companies, whose stocks are publicly traded, reviewed by financial analysts and the Securities and Exchange Commission as well as by federal and state law enforcement agencies. In the 1980s only two U.S. jurisdictions, Nevada and New Jersey, had legalized casinos, in good part restrained by the industry's history of organized crime connections and financing. By the year 2000, twenty-eight states had legalized some form of casino gambling, usually in resorts, such as in Biloxi, Mississippi, or on riverboats. Detroit, Michigan, was the only major industrial United States city to have legalized casinos. Approximately 260 casinos were located on Indian lands, with many more expected, especially in California, in the twenty-first century.

Native American tribal gambling

The U.S. Supreme Court issued a landmark decision in *California v. Cabazon Band of Mission Indians*, 480 U.S. 202 (1987), holding that California had no authority, on Indian lands, to enforce its criminal statutes forbidding bingo. The Court declared that gambling is a legitimate tourist activity, like hunting and fishing, for Indians to exploit. Congress passed the Indian Gaming Regulatory Act (IGRA) in 1988 to provide a statutory basis for conducting gambling on Indian lands. IGRA divides gambling into three classes: Class I consists of traditional tribal games; Class II consists of games such as bingo, lotto, and punch cards. If these games, such as charity bingo, are permitted by a state and do not violate federal law, they may be conducted on Indian lands without state approval. Class III consists of all other games, especially casino games, parimutuel racing, and jai alai. To introduce casino gaming, IGRA requires states to negotiate compacts with Indians. From 1988, when IGRA was passed, to 1997, revenues from tribal gaming grew more than thirtyfold from $212 million to $6.7 billion (National Gambling Impact Study Commission, p. 6–1,2).

Nevertheless, disputes have arisen between states and Indian tribes over the requirements of IGRA in the areas of regulation, the scope of permitted gambling activities, and the requirement that states negotiate in good faith with tribes. The U.S. Supreme Court, in *Seminole Tribe of Florida v. Florida*, 517 U.S. 44 (1996), held that, under the Eleventh Amendment, Congress was forbidden from authorizing suits by Indian tribes to bring states to the bargaining table to negotiate a gaming compact. This decision, in effect, invalidated the good faith negotiation requirement of IGRA.

By no means, however, did the *Seminole* decision portend an end to the expansion of Class III (casino) gambling sponsored by Indian tribes. States could voluntarily negotiate with Indian tribes, as Connecticut had earlier with the Mashantucket Pequot tribe, who built and ran the highest-grossing casino in the world. In September 1999, California's governor and legislature ratified gaming compacts with fifty-seven tribes. In March 2000, California voters passed a constitutional proposition ratifying these compacts and legalizing a major expansion of Indian casino gambling in California.

Gambling: personality and social costs

Fun, excitement, and the occasional thrill of winning seem to motivate most gamblers. Whatever else may be said against it, gambling is not physically risky. Some psychologists have even argued that gambling can be psychologically beneficial because some gamblers affirm their existence and worth by using skills in a risky setting (Kusyszyn). Other psychiatrists compare the excitement of gambling to the intoxication of drugs. A psychologist who interviewed members of Gamblers Anonymous seems to agree: "The compulsive gambler continues to bet because the action has come to be a refuge from thought of the outside world. His anxieties associated with his wife, family, debts, or job disappear when he concentrates on money and action" (Livingston, p. 55).

Pathological gambling is often cited as a major cost of gambling's expansion. A Harvard University sponsored meta-analysis of research on gambling found that 2.9 percent of gamblers had in the previous year reported "disordered and pathological" gambling. The lifetime rate was 5.4 percent. This was low as compared to alcohol dependence and abuse (9.7%, previous year; 23.5% lifetime). Disordered gamblers often experience "co-morbidity," that is, other life problems, such as alcoholism or drug abuse.

Those citing the social costs of gambling usually include, in addition to pathological or disordered gambling, its attraction to youth, elevated crime rates, suicide rates, family problems, bankruptcy, and the corruption of legislators. However, since gambling also provides economic benefits through employment opportunity, economic renewal of declining resorts and urban areas, and taxation, legal gambling has become an increasingly attractive option for many communities. As expansion has continued, at the turn of the century a backlash has occurred, with several states declining to introduce lotteries or casinos.

Internet gambling

Five federal statutes address Internet gambling, particularly the Wire Act (18 U.S.C. & 1084), which makes illegal the use of "wire communications" to assist with placing bets or wagers. The Wire Act's applicability to the Internet is nevertheless questionable in an era of wireless cellular and satellite technologies.

Several states, including Nevada, Texas, Illinois, and Louisiana, have introduced or passed legislation specifically prohibiting Internet gambling. Nevertheless, the large majority of Internet gambling sites, along with their owners or operators, are beyond the reach of state attorneys general.

On 17 July 2000, the U.S. House of Representatives voted down the Internet Act, legislation that sought to shut down many new online gambling sites—the number of such sites was estimated at between seven hundred and one thousand—most of which operated beyond U.S. borders. Proponents of the legislation included

an unusual coalition of Nevada gaming interests, major sports leagues, and Christian conservatives. Proponents cited the potential dangers of Internet gambling, including the undermining of the integrity of sporting events; the potential for defrauding unsophisticated gamblers; the ease of access by children; an increase in gambling addictions; and the need to preserve state revenues from legal, state-run gambling.

Opponents carried the day arguing that the legislation would drive online gambling underground; tamper with the Internet economy; invade Internet privacy; and be difficult to enforce against sophisticated but inexpensive technologies. Even assuming that law enforcement could develop the technological capacity to detect violations, provisions allowing for prosecution of gamblers would require enormous expansion of federal law enforcement to obtain and administer search warrants and subpoenas. Also cited were issues of jurisdiction, comity, and sovereignty, especially where other countries have chosen, or likely will choose, to regulate, that is, license and tax, Internet gambling.

Most basic to the legal and social issues of Internet gambling is the reality that cyberspace transcends borders. Consequently, Internet gambling markets are inherently global, undermining the traditional territorial basis for legal regulation of borders. Governments have the power to grant licenses and to tax within their sovereign territory. The Internet makes it possible to supply the demand for gambling "services" such as blackjack, poker, sports, or horse race betting outside any state or national borders, and without paying gambling privilege taxes. State-licensed casinos in the United States are taxed on their winnings at 7.75 to 8 percent, as in Nevada and New Jersey, and to two to three times that amount in some riverboat states. Internet purveyors will be able to offer better odds to price-sensitive gambling consumers. Will gamblers demand better odds from land-based gambling sites, such as casinos and racetracks? Will states be forced to lower gambling taxes? Will cyberspace gambling replace sited gambling or increase the demand for it? At the onset of the twenty-first century, predictions are difficult. Nevertheless, most commentators agree that gambling on the Internet will increase, perhaps exponentially, as the new century unfolds—and with uncertain but feared consequences regarding gambling taxation, the social costs of expanded gambling, and the viability of present control systems through licensing, taxation, and enforcement.

JEROME H. SKOLNICK

See also CRIMINALIZATION AND DECRIMINALIZATION; OR-
GANIZED CRIME; POLICE: POLICING COMPLAINANTLESS
CRIMES; VICTIMLESS CRIME.

BIBLIOGRAPHY

BARTHELME, FREDERICK, and BARTHELME, STE-
VEN. *Double Down: Reflections on Gambling and
Loss.* Boston: Houghton Mifflin, 1999.

BLAKEY, G. ROBERT. "State Conducted Lotteries:
History, Problems, and Promises." *Journal of
Social Issues* 35, no. 3 (1979): 62–86.

———, et al. *The Development of the Law of Gambling: 1776–1976.* Washington, D.C.: U.S. Department of Justice, Law Enforcement
Assistance Administration, National Institute
of Law Enforcement and Criminal Justice,
1977.

CHRISTIANSON, E. M.; SINCLAIR, S.; and CABOT, A.
N. "Internet Gambling: Who Regulates?"
11th International Conference on Gambling
and Risk-Taking. Las Vegas, Nevada, 15 June
2000.

CLOTFELTER, CHARLES T., and COOK, PHILIP J.
Selling Hope: State Lotteries in America. Cambridge, Mass.: Harvard University Press,
1989.

CORNISH, D. B. *Gambling: A Review of the Literature
and Its Implications for Policy and Research.*
Home Office Research Study no. 42. London:
Her Majesty's Stationery Office, 1978.

DEVEREUX, EDWARD C., JR. *Gambling and the Social
Structure. A Sociological Study of Lotteries and
Horse Racing in Contemporary America.* 2 vols.
Edited by Harriet Zuckerman and Robert K.
Merton. New York: Arno Press, 1980.

DOMBRINK, JOHN, and THOMPSON, WILLIAM N.
Success and Failure in Campaigns for Casinos.
Reno: University of Nevada Press, 1990.

DOSTOYEVSKY, FYODOR M. "The Gambler." In
The Gambler; Bobok; A Nasty Story. Translated
with an introduction by Jessie Coulson. Baltimore: Penguin Books, 1966.

DOWNES, D. M., et al. *Gambling, Work, and Leisure.
A Study across Three Areas.* London: Routledge
& Kegan Paul, 1976.

EADINGTON, WILIAM R., ed. *Gambling and Society:
Interdisciplinary Studies on the Subject of Gambling.* Springfield, Ill.: Thomas, 1976.

———. "The Evolution of Corporate Gambling
in Nevada." *Nevada Review of Business and Economics* 6 (1982): 13–22.

EADINGTON, WILLIAM R. and CORNELIUS, J. A.,
eds. *Gambling Behavior and Problem Gambling.*
Reno, Nev.: Institute for Gambling and Commercial Gaming, 1993.

EZELL, JOHN SAMUEL. *Fortune's Merry Wheel. The
"Lot" in America.* Cambridge, Mass.: Harvard
University Press, 1960.

GEERTZ, CLIFFORD. "Deep Play: Notes on the Ba-
linese Cock-fight." *The Interpretation of Cultures: Selected Essays.* New York: Basic Books,
1973. Pages 412–453.

GOFFMAN, ERVING. "Where the Action Is." *Interaction Ritual. Essays on Face-to-face Behavior.*
Chicago: Aldine, 1967. Pages 242–270.

HALLIDAY, JON, and FULLER, PETER, eds. *The Psychology of Gambling.* New York: Harper and
Row, 1975.

HAWKINS, WILLIAM. *A Treatise of the Pleas of the
Crown, or a System of the Principal Matters Relat-
ing to That Subject, Digested under Their Proper
Heads.* 5th edition. London: Worrall, 1771.

KAPLAN, H. ROY. *Lottery Winners: How They Won
and How Winning Changed Their Lives.* New
York: Harper and Row, 1978.

The Knapp Commission Report on Police Corruption.
Report of the New York City Commission to
Investigate Allegations of Police Corruption
and the City's Anti-corruption Procedures.
Foreword by Michael Armstrong. New York:
Braziller, 1972.

KORN, DAVID A., and SHAFFER, HOWARD J. "Gambling and the Health of the Public." *Journal of
Gambling Studies* 15, no. 4 (1999): 289–365.

KUSYSZYN, IGOR. "Compulsive Gambling: The
Problem of Definition." *The International Journal of the Addictions* 13 (1978): 1095–1101.

LIVINGSTON, JAY. "Compulsive Gamblers: A Culture of Losers." *Psychology Today,* March
(1974): 51–55.

MANGIONE, THOMAS W., and FOWLER, FLOYD J.,
JR. "Enforcing the Gambling Laws." *Journal of
Social Issues* 35, no. 3 (1979): 115–128.

Pennsylvania Crime Commission. *Report on Police
Corruption and the Quality of Law Enforcement in
Philadelphia.* St. David's, Pa.: The Commission,
1974.

Royal Commission on Gambling. *Final Report.*
Cmnd. 7200. London: Her Majesty's Stationery Office, 1978.

Royal Commission on Lotteries and Betting,
1932–1933. *Final Report.* Cmnd. 434 1. London: His Majesty's Stationery Office, 1933.

National Gambling Impact Study Commission.
Final Report, 1999. World Wide Web document. http://www.ngisc.gov/reports

SHAFFER, H. J.; HALL, M. N.; and VANDER BILT,
J. *Estimating the Prevalence of Disorder Gambling*

Behavior in the United States and Canada: A Meta Analysis. Boston: Presidents and Fellows of Harvard College, 1997.

SKOLNICK, JEROME H. *House of Cards: Legalization and Control of Casino Gambling.* Boston: Little, Brown, 1978.

SKOLNICK, JEROME, and DMBRINK, JOHN. "Legal Aspects of Public Gaming." Symposium. *Connecticut Law Review* 12 (1980): 661–947.

"The Social Risks of Casino Gambling." *Psychology Today*, July (1979), pp.: 52–58, 63–64.

TREVELYAN, GEORGE MACAULEY. *English Social History: A Survey of Six Centuries, Chaucer to Queen Victoria.* 2d edition. London: Longmans, Green, 1946.

U.S. National Commission on the Review of the National Policy Toward Gambling. *Gambling in America: Final Report.* Washington, D.C.: The Commission, 1976.

CASES

California v. Cabazon Band of Mission Indians, 480 U.S. 202 (1987).

FCC v. American Broadcasting Co., 347 U.S. 284 (1954).

Seminole Tribe of Florida v. Florida, 517 U.S. 44 (1996).

GENDER AND CRIME

Gender is the single best predictor of criminal behavior: men commit more crime, and women commit less. This distinction holds throughout history, for all societies, for all groups, and for nearly every crime category. The universality of this fact is really quite remarkable, even though many tend to take it for granted.

Most efforts to understand crime have focused on male crime, since men have greater involvement in criminal behavior. Yet it is equally important to understand female crime. For example, learning why women commit less crime than men can help illuminate the underlying causes of crime and how it might better be controlled.

This discussion of gender and crime first reviews both current and historical information on the rates and patterns of female crime in relation to male crime. The discussion is followed by a consideration of theoretical explanations of female crime and gender differences in crime. Finally, the authors briefly outline a "gendered" approach to understanding female crime that takes into account the influence of gender differences in norms, in socialization, in social control, and in criminal opportunities, as well as psychological and physiological differences between men and women.

Comparisons of criminal behavior between different groups—such as men and women—use data from a variety of sources. One of the most widely used sources is arrest data from the U.S. Federal Bureau of Investigation's Uniform Crime Reports (UCR), collected from the nation's law enforcement agencies and tabulated by the Federal Bureau of Investigation (F.B.I.). Other sources include surveys of victimization experiences, such as the U.S. Bureau of Justice Statistics' National Crime Vicitimization Survey (NCVS); surveys of self-reported offending behavior, such as the National Youth Survey (Elliot and Ageton); and case studies based on autobiographical accounts or interviews with and observation of individual offenders and gangs. The discussion starts with a consideration of what can be learned from arrest data, and then briefly touches on the insights to be gained from other sources. Any comparison of male and female criminality must acknowledge important similarities as well as differences.

Similarities in male and female offending rates and patterns

Both males and females have low rates of arrest for serious crimes like homicide or robbery; and high rates of arrest for petty property crimes like larceny-theft, or public order offenses such as alcohol and drug offenses or disorderly conduct. In general, women tend to have relatively high arrest rates in most of the same crime categories for which men have high arrest rates. For example, rates of homicide are small for both sexes (about 17 offenders for every 100,000 males, about 2 offenders per 100,000 females), as compared to larceny rates, which measure about 800 offenders per 100,000 males and 380 offenders per 100,000 females.

Male and female arrest trends over time or across groups or geographic regions are similar. That is, decades or groups or regions that have high (or low) rates of male crime tend to also have high (or low) rates of female crime. For example, in the second half of the twentieth century, the rates of arrest for larceny-theft increased dramatically for both men and women; and declined even more dramatically for both men and women in the category of public drunkenness. Similarly, states or cities or countries that have higher than average arrest rates for men also have higher arrest rates for women (Steffensmeier, 1993; Steffensmeier, Allan, and Streifel).

Male and female offenders have similar age-crime distributions, although male levels of offending are always higher than female levels at every age and for virtually all offenses. The female-to-male ratio remains fairly constant across the life span (Steffensmeier and Streifel, 1991). The major exception to this age-by-gender pattern is for prostitution, where the age-curve for females displays a much greater concentration of arrests among the young, compared to an older age-curve for males. A variety of factors account for this difference. For example, males arrested under a solicitation of prostitution charge may be men old enough to have acquired the power to be pimps or the money to be customers—men who often put a premium upon obtaining young females. The younger and more peaked female age curve clearly reflects differing opportunity structures for crimes relating to prostitution. Older women become less able to market sexual services, whereas older men can continue to purchase sexual services from young females or from young males. The earlier physical maturity of adolescent females also contributes to their dating and associating with older male delinquent peers.

Female offenders, like male offenders, tend to come from backgrounds marked by poverty, discrimination, poor schooling, and other disadvantages. However, women who commit crime are somewhat more likely than men to have been abused physically, psychologically, or sexually, both in childhood and as adults.

Differences between male and female offending patterns

Females have lower arrest rates than males for virtually all crime categories except prostitution. This is true in all countries for which data are available. It is true for all racial and ethnic groups, and for every historical period. In the United States, women constitute less than 20 percent of arrests for most crime categories.

Females have even lower representation than males do in serious crime categories. Since the 1960s in the United States, the extent of female arrests has generally been less than 15 percent for homicide and aggravated assault, and less than 10 percent for the serious property crimes of burglary and robbery.

Aside from prostitution, female representation has been greatest for minor property crimes

such as larceny-theft, fraud, forgery, and embezzlement. Female arrests for these crime categories has been as high as 30 to 40 percent, especially since the mid-1970s. The thefts and frauds committed by women typically involve shoplifting (larceny-theft), "bad checks" (forgery or fraud), and welfare and credit fraud—all compatible with traditional female consumer/domestic roles.

Trends in female crime relative to male crime are more complex. Some writers claim that female crime has been increasing faster than male crime, as measured by the percentage of female arrests. This has clearly been true in the case of minor property crimes, where the percentage of female arrests had about doubled between 1960 and 1975 (from around 15 to 30 percent or more), with slight additional increases since then. Smaller but fairly consistent increases are also found for substance abuse categories, but they remain less than 20 percent for all categories. The same can be said of major property crimes (which remain less than 10 to 15%). However, the percentage of female arrests has declined for other categories like homicide and prostitution; and it has fluctuated for still other categories such as aggravated assault and drug-law violations (see Steffensmeier, 1993, for a review of trends and explanations).

The patterns just described are corroborated by other sources of data. The National Crime Victimization Survey asks victims about the gender of offenders in crimes where the offender is seen. The percentage of female offenders reported by victims is very similar to (or lower than) the female percentage of arrests for comparable categories. Self-report studies also confirm the UCR patterns of relatively low female involvement in serious offenses and greater involvement in the less serious categories.

From a variety of sources, it is clear that females are less involved in serious offense categories, and they commit less harm. Women's acts of violence, compared to those of men, result in fewer injuries and less serious injuries. Their property crimes usually involve less monetary loss or less property damage.

Females are less likely than males to become repeat offenders. Long-term careers in crime are very rare among women. Some pursue relatively brief careers (in relation to male criminal careers) in prostitution, drug offenses, or minor property crimes like shoplifting or check forging.

Female offenders, more often than males, operate solo. When women do become involved with others in offenses, the group is likely to be small and relatively nonpermanent. Furthermore, women in group operations are generally accomplices to males (see Steffensmeier, 1983, for a review). And males are overwhelmingly dominant in the more organized and highly lucrative crimes, whether based in the underworld or the "upperworld."

Females are far less likely than males to become involved in delinquent gangs. This distinction is consistent with the tendency for females to operate alone and for males to dominate gangs and criminal subcultures. At the onset of the twenty-first century, female gang involvement was described as a sort of "auxiliary" to a male gang. By the 1980s and 1990s, gang studies found somewhat increased involvement on the part of girls (perhaps 15%), including some all-female gangs. Regardless, female gang violence has remained far less common than male gang violence.

The criminal justice system's greater "leniency" and "chivalry" toward females may explain a portion of the lower official offending rates of women in comparison to men. Likewise, the justice system's tendency to be relatively less lenient and chivalrous toward females today may help explain recent increases in levels of female arrests. Although there appear to be relatively small differences between adult women and men in likelihood of arrest or conviction, women defendants do appear to have a lower probability of being jailed or imprisoned. This difference appears to be related to a variety of factors: pregnancy, responsibilities for small children, the greater likelihood to demonstrate remorse, as well as perceptions that women are less dangerous and more amenable to rehabilitation (Daly; Steffensmeier, Ulmer, and Kramer).

Explaining female offending

Social, biological, economic, and psychological explanations have been used to develop theories to explain why women commit crime, as well as why they commit less crime than men. The number and complexity of these theories has expanded greatly in recent years as part of the growing body of work on gender both in criminology and in the social sciences more generally.

Early social science views. Early explanations of female crime reflected prevailing views regarding crime and human behavior more generally. During the late 1800s and early 1900s, theories of human behavior tended to be deter-

ministic. In criminology this perspective was apparent in theories attributing crime to either biological or social factors beyond the control of individuals. Psychological explanations of crime emerged as psychological theories gained prominence. At the same time, major sociological explanations of crime (differential association, anomie, social disorganization) were emphasizing social and cultural factors that could account for female as well as male criminality.

During the first half of the twentieth century, most explanations of female crime were ancillary to explanations of male criminality. Lombroso, for example, linked both male and female crime to biological predisposition. Early sociological explanations generally rejected biological determinism and offered sociocultural interpretations of both male and female crime as well as of gender differences in crime. Sociocultural views were manifest in criminology textbooks published between 1920 and 1960 (see the review in Steffensmeier and Clark). Whatever the orientation, biological or sociocultural, most criminologists focused primarily on male criminality. Female offending was largely ignored.

Theorists emphasizing the causal role of biological and psychological factors in female crime typically postulated that criminal women exhibited masculine biological or psychological orientations. Lombroso viewed female criminals as having an excess of male characteristics. He argued that, biologically, criminal females more closely resembled males (both criminal and normal) than females.

Similarly, Freud argued that female crime results from a "masculinity complex," stemming from penis envy. According to Freud, all females suffer from penis envy, but most are able to make a healthy adjustment to the realization that they do not have a penis. Those who cannot successfully resolve their penis envy overidentify with maleness and are likely to act out in criminal ways. Both Lombroso and Freud, then, viewed the female criminal as biologically or psychologically male in orientation.

While some theorists linked female crime to "masculinity," others saw it as distinctly feminine. Eleanor and Sheldon Glueck's studies of adult and juvenile delinquents suggested that female crime reflected the inability of certain women—especially those from disadvantaged neighborhood and family contexts—to control their sexual impulses. The Gluecks also subscribed to the theme of the woman offender as a pathetic creature, a view that characterized much of criminological writings in the 1930s.

Otto Pollak's *The Criminality of Women* is the most important work on female crime prior to the modern period. The book summarized previous work on women and crime, and it challenged basic assumptions concerning the extent and quality of women's involvement in criminal behavior. Pollak himself explained female crime and the gender gap with reference to a mix of biological, psychological, and sociological factors.

Pollak is the first writer to insist that women's participation in crime approaches that of men and is commensurate with their representation in the population. He argues that the types of crimes women commit—shoplifting, domestic thefts, thefts by prostitutes, abortions, perjury—are underrepresented in crime statistics for a variety of reasons: easy concealment, underreporting, embarrassment on the part of male victims, and male chivalry in the justice system.

Pollak consistently emphasizes the importance of social and environmental factors, including poverty, crowded living conditions, broken homes, delinquent companions, and the adverse effects of serving time in reform schools or penitentiaries. Pollak also noted that there is considerable overlap in causative factors for delinquency among girls and boys, and women and men.

Yet another fundamental theme of Pollak's work is the attribution of a biological and physiological basis to female criminality. Pollak stresses the inherently deceitful nature of females, rooted particularly in the passive role assumed by women during sexual intercourse. Also significant are the influences of hormonal and generative phases (e.g., menstruation, pregnancy, and menopause) on female criminality.

In sum, in comparison to explanations for male offending, some early explanations of female crime placed greater emphasis on biological and psychological factors. Nevertheless, early sociological explanations of female crime, stressing sociocultural factors, were also commonplace. Criminology textbooks, in particular, offered an interpretation of female offending and the gender gap that took into account gender differences in role expectations, socialization patterns and application of social control, opportunities to commit particular offenses, and access to criminally oriented subcultures—all themes that have been further developed in more recent accounts (see reviews in Steffensmeier and Clark 1980; Chesney-Lind 1986).

Recent developments

A rich and complex literature on female criminality has emerged over the past few decades. One view received an extraordinary amount of media attention during the late 1960s and the 1970s. This was the argument that "women's liberation" could help explain the apparent narrowing of the disparity between female and male arrest rates. This was a revival of a view long current in criminology, that gender differences in crime could be explained by differences in male and female social positions. This plausible notion gave rise to the "gender equality hypothesis": as social differences between men and women disappear under the influence of the women's movement, so should the differences in crime disappear.

This interpretation of the "dark side" of female liberation was welcomed enthusiastically by the media. However, other criminologists have pointed to the peculiarity of the view that improving girls' and women's economic conditions would lead to disproportionate increases in female crime when almost all the existing criminological literature stresses the role played by poverty, joblessness, and discrimination in the creation of crime (Chesney-Lind, 1997; Miller; Steffensmeier, 1980, 1993). This and other weaknesses in the gender equality hypothesis have been discussed at length elsewhere, as have more plausible explanations for the narrowing of differences for specific categories of crime. (Recall that gender differences in arrest rates have by no means narrowed for all categories, actually increasing for some and remaining the same for others.)

Another issue receiving much attention is whether traditional theories of crime, developed by male criminologists to explain male crime, are equally useful in explaining female crime, or whether female crime can only be explained by gender-specific theories. Causal factors identified by traditional theories of crime such as anomie, social control, and differential association-social learning appear equally applicable to female and male offending (Steffensmeier and Allan, 1996).

For both males and females, the likelihood of criminal behavior is increased by weak social bonds and parental controls, low perceptions of risk, delinquent associations, chances to learn criminal motives and techniques, and other access to criminal opportunities. In this sense, traditional criminological theories are as useful in understanding overall female crime as they are in understanding overall male crime. They can also help explain why female crime rates are so much lower than male rates: for example, females develop stronger bonds and are subject to stricter parental control, but have less access to criminal opportunity.

On the other hand, many of the subtle and profound differences between female and male offending patterns may be better understood by a gendered approach. Recent theoretical efforts, often drawing from the expanding literature on gender roles and feminism, typically involve "middle-range" approaches aimed at explaining this or that dimension of female criminality by linking it to specific aspects of the "organization of gender" (a term used here to denote identities, arrangements, and other areas of social life that differ markedly by gender). These approaches are reviewed briefly next, after which we discuss a broader gendered paradigm that offers a general theoretical framework for understanding female criminality and sex differences in offending.

Cloward and Piven, for example, argue that the persistence of gender segregation in the society at large differentially shapes the form and frequency of male and female deviance. Limits on women's opportunities in the paid workforce, in conjunction with their more extensive domestic responsibilities, constrain the deviant adaptations available to women. As a result, "the only models of female deviance which our society encourages or permits women to imagine, emulate and act out are essentially privatized modes of self destruction" (p. 660).

Harris makes a comparable point when he argues that societies are structured such that all behaviors are "type-scripted." These "type-scripts" specify acceptable and unacceptable forms of deviance for various categories of social actors including men and women. As a result of these type scripts, "it is unlikely or impossible for women to attempt assassination, robbery, or rape" (p. 12). Instead, consistent with gendered type scripts and roles (e.g., consumer, domestic), women are much more heavily involved in minor thefts and hustles such as shoplifting, theft of services, falsification of identification, passing bad checks, credit card forgery, welfare fraud, and employee pilferage.

Steffensmeier argues that underworld sex segregation adds further structural constraints on female levels of offending, particularly in the more lucrative venues. "Compared to their male counterparts, potential female offenders are at a disadvantage in selection and recruitment into criminal groups, in the range of career paths, and access to them, opened by way of participation in these groups, and in opportunities for tutelage, increased skills, and rewards" (1983, p. 1025). It is hardly surprising, therefore, that female involvement in professional and organized crime continues to lag far behind male involvement. Women are hugely underrepresented in traditionally male-dominated networks that engage in large-scale burglary, fencing operations, gambling enterprises, and racketeering (Commonwealth of Pennsylvania; Steffensmeier, 1986).

Broidy and Agnew have speculated that the dynamics of gender shape both the types of strains males and females are exposed to and the emotional and behavioral responses available to them, thus leading to distinctly different outcomes. Aggressive, externalizing behavioral responses are acceptable for males in various environments, whereas such responses are less commonly available to females. Thus, female responses to strain are more likely to be nonaggressive and/or self-destructive.

Chesney-Lind (1997) further clarifies the different strains faced by females in her depiction of the differential impact of gender dynamics on the lives and experiences of boys and girls growing up in similar neighborhood and school environments. Specifically, gender-based socialization patterns set the stage for the sexual victimization and harassment of girls. It is this victimization that often triggers girls' entry into delinquency as they try to escape abusive environments. Girls attempting to run away from abuse often end up in the streets with few legitimate survival options, so they gravitate toward crime, drug-use and -dealing, and sexual exchange transactions. Thus, the role of interpersonal victimization in female paths to crime often involves a circular dynamic in which victimization places some females at high risk for offending, which in turn puts them at risk for further victimization (Daly; Gilfus). This dynamic is especially problematic for minority and low income women whose risks for both crime and victimization are already heightened by limited access to resources (Arnold; Richie).

Figure 1

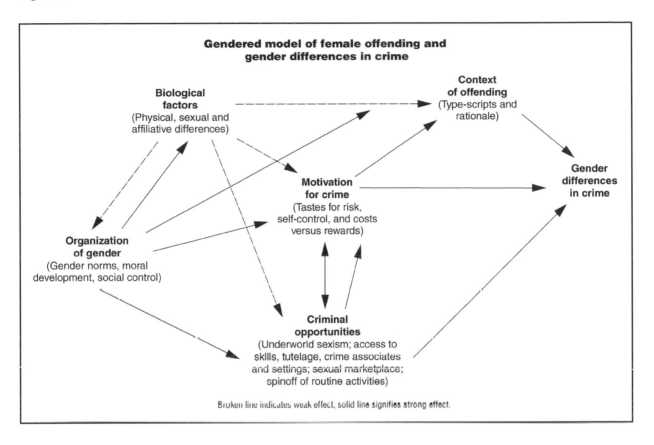

A gendered paradigm of female offending and the gender gap

Steffensmeier and Allan (1996, 2000) provide another attempt to build a unified theoretical framework for explaining female criminality and gender differences in crime. This perspective incorporates factors suggested by other theorists. Depicted in Figure 1, their framework recognizes that (1) causal patterns for female crime often overlap those for male crime, but also (2) that continued profound differences between the lives of women and men produce varying patterns of female and male offending.

At least five areas of life tend not only to inhibit female crime and encourage male crime, but also to shape the patterns of female offending that do occur: gender norms, moral development and affiliative concerns, social control, physical strength and aggression, and sexuality. These five areas overlap and mutually reinforce one another and, in turn, condition gender differences in criminal opportunities, motives, and contexts of offending. Key points are summarized here.

Gender norms. Female criminality is both inhibited and molded by two powerful focal concerns ascribed to women: (1) role obligations (daughter, wife, mother) and the presumption of female nurturance; (2) expectations of female beauty and sexual virtue. Such focal concerns pose constraints on female opportunities for illicit endeavors. The constraints posed by child-rearing responsibilities and other nurturant obligations are obvious. Moreover, the frequency of derivative identities restrains deviance on the part of women affiliated with conventional males; however, wives or girlfriends of criminals may be pushed into the roles of accomplices.

Femininity stereotypes are the antitheses of those qualities valued in the criminal subculture (Steffensmeier, 1986); therefore, crime is almost always more destructive of life chances for females than for males. In contrast, the dividing line between what is considered masculine and what is criminal is often thin.

Finally, expectations of female sexuality may restrict the deviant roles available to women to those of sexual media or service roles. Female fear of sexual victimization reduces female exposure to criminal opportunity through the avoidance of bars, nighttime streets, and other crime-likely locations.

Moral development and affiliative concerns. Compared to men, women are more likely to refrain from crime due to concern for others. This may result from gender differences in moral development and from socialization toward greater empathy, sensitivity to the needs of others, and fear of separation from loved ones (Gilligan). This predisposition toward an "ethic of care" restrains women from violence and other behavior that may injure others or cause emotional hurt to those they love. Men, on the other hand, are more socialized toward status-seeking behavior and may therefore develop an amoral ethic when they feel those efforts are blocked.

Social control. The ability and willingness of women to commit crime is powerfully constrained by social control. Particularly during their formative years, females are more closely supervised and discouraged from misbehavior. Risk-taking behavior is rewarded among boys but censured among girls. Careful monitoring of girls' associates reduces the potential for influence by delinquent peers (Giordano et al.). Even as adults, women find their freedom to explore worldly temptations constricted.

Physical strength and aggression. The weakness of women relative to men—whether real or perceived—puts them at a disadvantage in a criminal underworld that puts a premium on physical power and violence. Muscle and physical prowess are functional not only for committing crimes, but also for protection, contract enforcement, and recruitment and management of reliable associates.

Sexuality. Reproductive-sexual differences, coupled with the traditional "double standard," contribute to higher male rates of sexual deviance and infidelity. On the other hand, the demand for illicit sex creates opportunities for women for criminal gain through prostitution. This in turn may reduce the need for women to seek financial returns through serious property crimes. Nevertheless, although prostitution is a money-making opportunity that women may exploit, it is a criminal enterprise still largely controlled by men: pimps, clients, police, businessmen.

Collectively, the above aspects of the organization of gender serve to condition and shape additional features of female offending, including criminal opportunity, criminal motives, and contexts of crime.

Access to criminal opportunity. Limits on female access to legitimate opportunities put further constraints on their criminal opportunities, since women are less likely to hold jobs such as truck driver, dockworker, or carpenter, that would provide opportunities for theft, drug dealing, fencing, and other illegal activities. In contrast, abundant opportunities exist for women to commit and/or to be caught and arrested for petty forms of theft and fraud, for low-level drug dealing, and for sex-for-sale offenses.

Like the upperworld, the underworld has its glass ceiling. The scarcity of women in the top ranks of business and politics limits their chance for involvement in price-fixing conspiracies, financial fraud, and corruption. If anything, women face even greater occupational segregation in underworld crime groups, at every stage from selection and recruitment to opportunities for mentoring, skill development, and, especially, rewards (Steffensmeier, 1983; Commonwealth of Pennsylvania).

Motivation. The subjective willingness of women to engage in crime is limited by factors of the organization of gender, but amplified by criminal opportunity. Being able tends to make one more willing. Female as well as male offenders tend to be drawn to criminal activities that are easy and within their skill repertoire, and that have a good payoff and low risk. Women's risk-taking preferences differ from those of men (Hagan; Steffensmeier, 1983; Steffensmeier and Allan, 1996). Men will take risks in order to build status or gain competitive advantage, while women may take greater risks to protect loved ones or to sustain relationships. Criminal motivation is suppressed in women by their greater ability to foresee threats to life chances and by the relative unavailability of female criminal type scripts that could channel their behavior.

Context of offending. The organization of gender also impacts on the often profound differences in the contexts of female and male offenses. Even when the same offense is charged, there may be dramatic differences in contexts, such as the setting, presence of other offenders, the relationship between offender and victim, the offender's role in initiating and committing the offense, weapon (if any), the level of injury or property loss/destruction, and purpose of the offense (Daly; Steffensmeier, 1983, 1993). Moreover, female/male contextual differences increase with the seriousness of the offense.

J. Miller's qualitative study of male and female robbery clarifies how gender shapes the context of robbery, even when motives are the same. Males typically target other males, and their robberies often involve direct confrontation, physical violence, and guns. Females most often target other females and seldom use guns. When women do rob men, they may carry a gun, but they are more likely to soften the target with sex than with actual violence. Miller concludes that male and female robbery may be triggered by similar social and cultural factors, but that gender shapes the actual manner in which those robberies are enacted.

Spousal murders also illustrate striking male-female differences in context (Dobash et al.). The proposition that wives have as great a potential for violence as husbands has had some currency among criminologists (Straus and Gelles). Although in recent years wives are the perpetrators in only about one-fourth of spousal murders, in earlier decades they were the perpetrators in nearly one-half of the spousal murders. But suggestions of similar aptitude conceal major differences. Wives are far more likely to have been victims, and they turn to murder only when in mortal fear, after exhausting alternatives. Husbands who murder wives, however, are more likely to be motivated by rage at suspected infidelity, and the murder often culminates a period of prolonged abuse of their wives. Some patterns of wife-killing are almost never found when wives kill husbands: murder-suicides, family massacres, and stalking.

The various aspects of the organization of gender discussed here—gender norms, moral and relational concerns, social control, lack of strength, and sexual identity—all contribute to gender differences in criminal opportunity, motivation, and context. These factors also help explain why women are far less likely than men to be involved in serious crime, regardless of data source, level of involvement, or measure of participation.

Summary

The majority of girls and women involved in the criminal justice system have committed ordinary crimes—mostly minor thefts and frauds, low-level drug dealing, prostitution, and misdemeanor assaults against their mates or children. Some of them commit crime over several years and serve multiple jail or prison terms in the process. But they are not career criminals, and women are far less likely than men to be involved in serious crime. These generalizations hold true regardless of data source, level of involvement, or measure of participation.

The gender gap for criminal offending is remarkably persistent across countries, population subgroups within a given country, and historical periods. This persistence can be explained in part by historical durability of the organization of gender and by underlying physical/sexual differences (whether actual or perceived). Human groups, for all their cultural variation, follow basic human forms.

Recent theory and research on female offending have added greatly to our understanding of how the lives of delinquent girls and women continue to be powerfully influenced by gender-related conditions of life. Profound sensitivity to these conditions is essential for understanding gender differences in type and frequency of crime, for explaining differences in the context or gestalt of offending, and for developing preventive and remedial programs aimed at female offenders.

DARRELL STEFFENSMEIER
EMILIE ALLAN

See also DOMESTIC VIOLENCE; FAMILY ABUSE AND CRIME; FEMINISM: CRIMINOLOGICAL ASPECTS; FEMINISM: LEGAL ASPECTS; PRISONS: PRISONS FOR WOMEN; PROSTITUTION.

BIBLIOGRAPHY

ADLER, FREDA. *Sisters in Crime: The Rise of the New Female Criminal.* New York: McGraw-Hill, 1975.

ARNOLD, REGINA. "The Processes of Criminalization of Black Women." In *The Criminal Justice System and Women.* Edited by B. Price and N. Sokoloff. New York: McGraw-Hill, 1995. Pages 136–146.

AUSTIN, ROY L. "Recent Trends in Official Male and Female Crime Rates: The Convergence Controversy." *Journal of Criminal Justice* 21 (1993): 447–466.

BOWKER, LEE H. *Women, Crime and the Criminal Justice System.* Lexington, Mass.: Heath, 1978.

BROIDY, LISA, and AGNEW, ROBERT. "Gender and Crime: A General Strain Theory Perspective." *Journal of Research in Crime and Delinquency* 34 (1997): 275–306.

Bureau of Justice Statistics. *National Crime Victimization Survey.* Washington, D.C.: U.S. Department of Justice, 1980–1998.

CAMPBELL, ANN. *The Girls in the Gang.* Oxford, U.K.: Basil Blackwell, 1984.

CHESNEY-LIND, M. "Women and Crime: The Female Offender." *Signs* 12 (1986): 78–96.

———. *The Female Offender.* Thousand Oaks, Calif.: Sage, 1997.

CLOWARD, RICHARD, and PIVEN FRANCIS. "Hidden Protest: The Channeling of Female Protest and Resistance." *Signs* 4 (1979): 651–669.

Commonwealth of Pennsylvania. *Organized Crime in Pennsylvania: The 1990 Report.* Conshohocken, Pa.: Pennsylvania Crime Commission, 1991.

DALY, KATHLEEN. *Gender, Crime, and Punishment.* New Haven, Conn.: Yale University Press, 1994.

DENNO, DEBORAH. "Gender, Crime and the Criminal Law Defenses." *Journal of Criminal Law and Criminology* 85, no. 1 (1994): 80–180.

DOBASH, RUSSELL; DOBASH, R. EMERSON; WILSON, MARTIN; and DALY, MARY. "The Myth of Sexual Symmetry in Marital Violence." *Social Problems* 39 (1992): 71–91.

ELLIOT, DELBERT, and AGETON, SUZANNE. "Reconciling Race and Class Differences in Self-Reported and Official Estimates of Delinquency." *American Sociological Review* 45 (1980): 95–110.

Federal Bureau of Investigation. *Uniform Crime Reports: Crime in the United States.* Washington, D.C.: Department of Justice, 1980–1998.

FREUD, SIGMUND. *New Introductory Lectures.* New York: Norton, 1933.

GILFUS, MARY. "From Victims to Survivors to Offenders: Women's Routes to Entry and Immersion into Street Crime." *Women and Criminal Justice* 4 (1992): 63–89.

GILLIGAN, CAROL. *In a Different Voice: Psychological Theory and Women's Development.* Cambridge, Mass.: Harvard University Press, 1982.

GIORDANO, PEGGY; CERNKOVICH, STEPHEN; and PUGH, MARTIN. "Friendships and Delinquency." *American Journal of Sociology* 91 (1986): 1170–1203.

GLUECK, SHELDON, and GLUECK, ELEANOR. *Five Hundred Delinquent Women.* New York: Knopf, 1934.

HAGAN, JOHN. *Structural Criminology.* New Brunswick, N.J.: Rutgers University Press, 1989.

HAGAN, JOHN; SIMPSON, JOHN; and GILLIS, A. R. "Class in the Household: A Power Control Theory of Gender and Delinquency." *American Journal of Sociology* 92 (1987): 788–816.

HARRIS, ANTHONY. "Sex and Theories of Deviance: Toward a Functional Theory of Deviant Type-scripts." *American Sociological Review* 42 (1977): 3–16.

JAMES, JENNIFER. "Prostitutes and Prostitution." In *Deviants: Voluntary Action in a Hostile World.* Edited by E. Sagarin and F. Montanino. New York: Scott, Foresman, 1977.

LOMBROSO, CEASAR, and FERRARO, WILLIAM. *The Female Offender.* London: Fisher Unwin, 1895.

MILLER, ELEANOR. *Street Women.* Philadelphia: Temple University Press, 1986.

MILLER, JO. "Up it Up: Gender and the Accomplishment of Street Robbery." *Criminology* 36 (1998): 37–65.

MORASH, MERRY, and CHESNEY-LIND, MEDA. "A Reformulation and Partial Test of the Power Control Theory of Delinquency." *Justice Quarterly* 8 (1991): 347–377.

POLLAK, OTTO. *The Criminality of Women.* Philadelphia: University of Pennsylvania Press, 1950.

RICHIE, BETH. *The Gendered Entrapment of Battered, Black Women.* London: Routledge, 1996.

SIMON, RITA. *The Contemporary Woman and Crime.* Rockville, Md.: National Institute of Mental Health, 1975.

SIMPSON, SALLY, and ELLIS, LISA. "Doing Gender: Sorting Out the Caste and Crime Conundrum." *Criminology* 33 (1975): 47–81.

STEFFENSMEIER, DARRELL. "Sex Differences in Patterns of Adult Crime. 1965–1977: A Review and Assessment." *Social Forces* 58 (1980): 1080–1108.

———. "Sex-segregation in the Underworld: Building a Sociological Explanation of Sex Differences in Crime." *Social Forces* 61 (1983): 1080–1108.

———. *The Fence: In the Shadow of Two Worlds.* Totowa, N.J.: Rowman and Littlefield, 1986.

———. "National Trends in Female Arrests, 1960–1990: Assessment and Recommendations for Research." *Journal of Quantitative Criminology* 9 (1993): 413–441.

STEFFENSMEIER, DARRELL, and ALLAN, EMILIE. "Gender and Crime: Toward a Gendered Theory of Female Offending." *Annual Review of Sociology* 22 (1996): 459–487.

———. "Gender, Age, and Crime." In *Handbook of Contemporary Criminology,* 3rd ed. Edited by J. Sheley. New York: Wadsworth, 2000.

STEFFENSMEIER, DARRELL; ALLAN, EMILIE; and STREIFEL, CATHY. "Development and Female Crime: A Cross-national Test of Alternative Explanations." *Social Forces* 68 (1989): 262–283.

STEFFENSMEIER, DARRELL, and CLARK, ROBERT. "Sociocultural vs. Biological/sexist Explanations of Sex Differences in Crime: A Survey of American Criminology Textbooks, 1919–1965." *American Sociologist* 15 (1980): 246–255.

STEFFENSMEIER, DARRELL, and TERRY, ROBERT. "Institutional Sexism in the Underworld: A

View from the Inside." *Sociological Inquiry* 56 (1986): 304–323.

STEFFENSMEIER, DARRELL, and STREIFEL, CATHY. "The Distribution of Crime by Age and Gender Across Three Historical Periods—1935, 1960, 1985." *Social Forces* 69 (1991): 869–894.

STEFFENSMEIER, DARRELL; ULMER, JEFFREY; and KRAMER, JOHN. "The Interaction of Race, Gender, and Age in Criminal Sentencing: The Punishment Cost of Being Young, Black, and Male." *Criminology* 36 (1998): 763–798.

STRAUS, MURRAY, and GELLES, RICHARD. *Physical Violence in American Families*. New Brunswick, N.J.: Transaction, 1990.

GRAND JURY

History of the grand jury

The English origin of the grand jury commonly is traced to the Assize of Clarendon, issued by Henry II in 1166. The Assize required that criminal accusations thereafter be "presented" by juries composed of twelve "good and lawful men" selected from the township. The Assize was designed to strengthen royal judicial authority. The jurors were familiar with the local scene and could present charges that otherwise might not be known to the crown's representatives. They were required to accuse all whom they suspected and faced substantial fines if they failed to make appropriate accusations. Following the jury's accusation, the defendant was subjected to trial, typically by ordeal.

By the end of the fourteenth century, the English criminal justice process had turned to trial by jury rather than by ordeal, and the original jury had been divided into two separate juries. The trial of guilt was before a twelve-person petit jury, and the accusatory jury was expanded to twenty-three persons, chosen from the entire county. This jury became known as *le grand inquest*, which probably explains its eventual title of grand jury. At this point, the grand jury remained essentially an accusatory body that assisted the Crown in ferreting out criminals. Accusations were either initiated by the jurors themselves, acting on the basis of their own knowledge or information received from complainants, or were initiated by a representative of the Crown, often a justice of the peace, who supported his accusation with the testimony of witnesses who appeared before the grand jury. Where the accusation was initiated by the jury it-

self, the jury's written charge was titled a "presentment." Where the accusation was based on a case placed before the jury by the Crown's representative, the jury's charging document was titled an "indictment." The Crown's representative ordinarily would place a proposed indictment before the grand jury, and if the jury found the Crown's evidence sufficient to proceed, it issued the indictment as a "true bill." If it found the evidence insufficient, it returned a finding of *ignoramus* ("we ignore it") or, in later years, "no bill."

It was not until the late seventeenth century that the grand jury, refusing to indict two prominent critics of the king, achieved its reputation as a safeguard against the oppression and despotism of the Crown. In the case of Stephen Colledge, charged with making treasonous remarks, the grand jury refused to indict, notwithstanding considerable pressure from the Lord Chief Justice. In the case brought against the earl of Shaftesbury, the Crown's representative sought to place more pressure on the grand jury by presenting witnesses publicly rather than privately before the jurors alone, as had been past practice. The jurors nevertheless refused to indict. Colledge was subsequently indicted by a different grand jury, convicted, and executed, and the earl of Shaftesbury fled the country to avoid a probable indictment by a new grand jury. The grand jury nevertheless had established its reputation as an independent screening agency capable of resisting the pressure of the Crown.

This view of the grand jury as the "people's panel" was reinforced in the American colonies, where grand juries refused to indict numerous opponents of the Crown. Thus, the infamous prosecution of John Peter Zenger for seditious libel was brought by a prosecutor's information—a charging instrument issued by the prosecutor alone—because grand juries twice refused to issue indictments. It was with such cases in mind that those who drafted the Bill of Rights required grand jury review of prosecutions. The first clause of the Fifth Amendment prohibits prosecutions for all serious crimes "unless on a presentment or indictment of a Grand Jury." The reference to presentments recognized the grand jury's continued authority to bring accusations on its own initiative. Indeed, the colonial grand juries had exercised that authority even against the wishes of the Crown.

At the start of eighteenth century, the grand jury was a key participant in the criminal justice processes of both the states and the federal government. As commentators later noted, the grand jury provided both the "shield" and the "sword" of the criminal justice system. In screening proposed indictments put before it by the prosecution (or private complainants), it shielded potential defendants from mistaken or vindictive prosecutions. In pursuing through its own investigative powers possible crimes that had come to its attention through the jurors' knowledge of the community, it provided a sword against criminals whose activities might otherwise have escaped prosecution. Moreover, particularly in western states, the grand jury took on a broader "public watchguard" role as it investigated and issued public reports on governmental misfeasance that did not involve criminal behavior (a practice that continues today in many states).

Over the eighteenth century, two major developments substantially altered the use of the grand jury to screen potential charges and to investigate possible criminal activity. First, sharp criticism of the grand jury as a costly and inefficient screening body produced a strong movement to eliminate the requirement of prosecution by indictments, and to give prosecutors the option of instituting prosecution by a prosecutor's information supported by a magistrate's finding of probable cause at a preliminary hearing. In 1859, Michigan became the first state to adopt such a reform, and in 1884, the Supreme Court in *Hurtado v. California*, 110 U.S. 516 (1884), upheld the authority of the states to authorize felony prosecutions by information following a preliminary hearing bindover. *Hurtado* reasoned that the Fourteenth Amendment's due process clause (prohibiting the deprivation of life, liberty, or property without due process of law) required adherence only to "fundamental principles of liberty and justice which lie at the base of all our civil and political institutions," and prosecution by indictment was not such a fundamental principle. Admittedly, the indictment process, by requiring grand jury screening provided a valuable safeguard against the arbitrary exercise of prosecutorial authority; but other modes of proceeding could also provide such protection, as illustrated by the preliminary hearing and as recognized in the English common law, which had authorized prosecution of all misdemeanors and certain felonies without indictments. Following *Hurtado*, there was a gradual movement of the states away from mandatory prosecution of felonies by indictment, although

that did not become a majority position until the twentieth century.

Second, a combination of the establishment of professional police forces and the granting to public prosecutors of a virtual monopoly over the decision to prosecute (largely eliminating private prosecutions) significantly altered the grand jury's investigative role. The growth of police investigative capacity lessened the need for grand jury's use of its investigative authority. Where private complainants sought an investigation and prosecution, they went to the police rather than to the grand jury. Indeed, in many jurisdictions, the authority of the grand jury to charge by presentment was eliminated. Cases came to the grand jury through the prosecutor, and when the special investigative powers of the grand jury were needed, they were exercised at the direction of the prosecutor, who served as the jury's legal advisor.

The grand jury retained the authority to initiate an investigation that the prosecutor opposed or to carry an investigation beyond what the prosecutor requested, and such "runaway" grand jury investigations did occur on rare occasions (usually by a grand jury that obtained judicial appointment of a special prosecutor). In large part, however, the grand jury investigations that came to bolster the modern grand jury's reputation as an engine for uncovering corruption in government, combating white collar crime, and undercutting organized crime were initiated and led by prosecutors. The same was true of those investigations that sullied the grand jury's reputation by suggesting that its investigative authority had been used for partisan political purposes. During the Vietnam War era, a flurry of such investigations at the federal level, directed at the alleged criminal activity of radicals (but seemingly operating more to harass than to produce supportable indictments), led to the adoption of reform legislation in various states. That legislation enhanced the rights of grand jury witnesses, providing, for example, that they could be accompanied by their attorneys in testifying before the grand jury. In the federal system, such reform legislation failed to gain legislative support, although the Justice Department did adopt as internal policy guidelines several requirements protective of witnesses and the targets of investigation (e.g., advising witnesses of their rights).

Structure

Certain elements of the legal structure of the grand jury relate primarily to either one or the other of its functions, but there are three basic structural features that influence both its screening and investigative roles—jury composition, jury independence, and the secrecy of jury proceedings.

Grand jury composition. In most jurisdictions grand jurors are drawn from the same constituency, and selected in the same manner, as the jury panel for petit jurors. The federal system and a majority of the states use a random selection system, where jurors are selected at random from a voter registration list or similar list. A smaller group of states use a "discretionary" selection system, under which jurors are selected by local judges or jury commissioners, usually on the basis of recommendations by various community leaders. Both selection systems seek representation reflecting a cross section of the community. The U.S. Supreme Court has long held that an indictment is constitutionally invalid if issued by a grand jury chosen through a racially discriminatory selection procedure. Many authorities conclude that the Court also would invalidate an indictment if the grand jury selection procedure failed to meet the other basic nondiscrimination requirement, that the jurors be drawn from a "fair cross section" of the community.

Grand jury independence

Relationship to the prosecutor. Independence from the prosecutor is, of course, basic to the grand jury's shielding function. In its investigative function, although the grand jury is expected to work in cooperation with the prosecutor, some degree of independence also is assumed. Thus, the legal structure of the grand jury seeks to ensure the jury's independence of the prosecutor, while allowing the jurors, as a group of laypersons, to take advantage of the professional expertise of the prosecutor. The prosecutor's position as the "legal advisor" to the grand jury illustrates these dual objectives. The prosecutor serves as the primary source of advice on issues of law arising in grand jury proceedings, but the grand jury always retains the authority to seek further legal advice from the court. Similarly, although the prosecutor must be available to examine witnesses who testify before the grand jury, many jurisdictions also recognize a right of the grand jurors to exclude the prosecutor if they so desire.

The grand jury, at least theoretically, also has the final say on the evidence presented before it. Some jurisdictions require the grand jury to listen to any witnesses presented by the prosecutor, but others still recognize the common law authority of the grand jury to refuse to hear such evidence. In all jurisdictions, the grand jury is free to seek additional evidence beyond that offered by the prosecutor. Jurors have authority to ask witnesses questions that go beyond the prosecutor's examination, and they also have authority to require the prosecutor to subpoena additional witnesses. Available data indicate, however, that grand juries only infrequently exercise their authority to override the prosecutor in determining the scope of their proceedings.

Relationship to the court. Although often characterized as an "independent body," the grand jury is also recognized to be an "arm of the court." The court cannot order the grand jury to indict or refuse to indict, but in most jurisdictions it can substantially influence what matters are considered by the grand jury. Thus, many states recognize the authority of the judge impaneling the grand jury to require the grand jury to undertake a particular investigation or to consider particular evidence where necessary to prevent a miscarriage of justice. More significantly, the prosecutor's authority to compel witnesses to testify before the grand jury rests on the use of judicially enforced subpoenas, and the court may refuse to enforce subpoenas if it determines that they are being misused. Since the impaneling judge is not present during the grand jury proceedings and is unaware of the particulars of grand jury activity, the exercise of judicial supervision to preclude grand juror or prosecutorial misconduct depends upon that conduct being brought to the judge's attention by the prosecutor, the grand jurors, a subpoenaed party, or other persons familiar with the proceedings.

In *United States v. Williams*, 504 U.S. 36 (1992), the Supreme Court suggested that federal courts have very limited supervisory control over the grand jury. The federal courts may use that limited authority to ensure that the grand jury abides by limits imposed under the Constitution, federal statutes, or the Federal Rules of Criminal Procedure. However, the federal courts may not create their own "common law" limits upon grand jury proceedings, as they do for their own trial court proceedings, as that would be inconsistent, the Court noted, with the "grand jury's functional independence from the judicial branch" (504 U.S. 48).

Grand jury secrecy. The requirement that the grand jury hear evidence in a closed proceeding grew out of the Crown's attempt to pressure the grand jury in the earl of Shaftesbury's case by presenting its witnesses at a public hearing. By the time of the adoption of the Fifth Amendment, it was firmly established that all grand jury proceedings were to be secret, with only the final result, if an indictment, made known to the public. The secrecy of the proceedings no longer was designed simply to protect the jurors from improper pressures. As noted by the Supreme Court in *United States v. Procter and Gamble Co.*, 356 U.S. 677 (1958), grand jury secrecy came to be justified on several grounds:

(1) to prevent the escape of those whose indictment may be contemplated; (2) to insure the utmost freedom to the grand jury in its deliberations, and to prevent persons subject to indictment or their friends from importuning the grand jurors; (3) to prevent subornation of perjury or tampering with the witnesses who may testify before grand jury and later appear at the trial of those indicted by it; (4) to encourage free and untrammeled disclosures by persons who have information with respect to the commission of crimes; (5) to protect the innocent accused who is exonerated from disclosure of the fact that he has been under investigation, and from the expense of standing trial where there was no probability of guilt. (356 U.S. 682)

Although the justifications for secrecy continue to be accepted, there has been a gradual movement over the years toward narrowing its scope. This movement has been supported by two lines of reasoning: (1) that the former, broader requirements often went beyond what was needed to serve the justifications for secrecy; and (2) that it is necessary to balance against those justifications other, equally important interests.

Perhaps the most significant loosening of secrecy requirements has occurred in the exemption of the grand jury witness from the obligation of secrecy. In all jurisdictions, the prosecutor, grand jurors, and grand jury stenographer are prohibited from disclosing what happened before the grand jury, unless ordered to do so in a judicial proceeding. In the vast majority of jurisdictions, witnesses are no longer under such an obligation. They may disclose what they wish to whomever they wish. A major objective of grand jury secrecy is to keep a target from learning of the investigation, and thus to preclude his probable flight or attempt to tamper with witnesses.

However, a witness questioned about another is now free to inform that person of the grand jury's interest in his activities. The witness exemption was adopted partly because it was thought that requiring secrecy of the witness was unrealistic and unenforceable, particularly where the target is a relative or friend of the witness.

Another significant change in secrecy requirements has been the gradual expansion of the disclosure made to the indicted defendant. At one time, the defendant had no access to the testimony before the grand jury that led to his indictment. Today, however, in almost every jurisdiction, if a witness who testified before the grand jury later testifies at trial, the defendant will be given a transcript of the grand jury testimony of that witness for possible impeachment use. Roughly a dozen states take the further step of providing the defendant with a complete transcript of all relevant testimony before the grand jury. Insofar as secrecy requirements encourage otherwise reluctant witnesses to assist the grand jury, that encouragement is likely to be lost through extensive postindictment disclosures.

Grand jury screening

Federal prosecutions. The Fifth Amendment provides that except in certain military cases, "no person shall be held to answer for a capital, or otherwise infamous crime, unless on a presentment or indictment of a Grand Jury." The reference to "otherwise infamous crimes," has been interpreted, in light of historical practice, as encompassing all felonies (offenses punishable by imprisonment for a term exceeding one year). Thus, the net effect of the Fifth Amendment provision is to establish grand jury screening as the constitutional right of any person charged in a federal court with a felony offense. Since the provision is designed to protect the interests of the defendant, it does not require grand jury review when the defendant knowingly and voluntarily waives the use of an indictment. In such cases, and in prosecutions for misdemeanors, the federal prosecutor ordinarily will proceed by information.

State prosecutions. Only eighteen states continue to make a grand jury indictment mandatory for all felony prosecutions (absent a voluntary waiver). Most do not allow waiver for capital offenses, so such prosecutions always are brought by indictment. Four additional states require prosecution by indictment for capital offenses or both capital and life-imprisonment offenses, but not for other felonies.

The remaining twenty-eight states permit prosecution by information for all felonies. These states grant the prosecutor the option of proceeding by indictment, but in several states that option is entirely theoretical, as grand juries do not exist. In most of the states permitting the information option, convening a grand jury is a realistic option, but one that is rarely used. Prosecutors proceed by indictment rather than information only where they have a special reason for doing so (e.g., the case was originally brought to the grand jury because the prosecutor had need for its investigative authority, the prosecutor desires to avoid the preliminary hearing that would be required if the prosecutor proceeded by information, or the case is politically sensitive and the prosecutor seeks to share responsibility for the charging decision with the grand jury). However, an occasional prosecutor in a state permitting prosecution by information may have a general preference for proceeding through the grand jury and bring most felony charges by indictment.

Screening procedures

Presenting the prosecutor's case. The prosecutor's grand jury presentation ordinarily begins with an explanation of a proposed indictment and a summary of the evidence that will be offered to support it. The evidence is then presented through the testimony of witnesses or the introduction of documents. In many jurisdictions (but not the federal), the prosecution has an obligation to produce, in addition to supporting evidence, any further evidence that it knows to be exculpatory. Thus, if a lineup produced conflicting eyewitness identifications, the prosecutor must make the jury aware of that conflict and not simply present the one eyewitness who identified the accused. The prosecutor's disclosure obligation is limited, however, to evidence obviously exculpatory and material. The prosecutor need not assume the role of a defense counsel and introduce all the evidence that a defense counsel might have wished to offer.

Although grand jury proceedings are secret, persons often are informed—for example, after being arrested—that charges against them will be presented to the grand jury. The grand jury proceeding is not an adversary proceeding, however, and those persons have no right to present their own evidence to that body. The potential defendant may request the opportunity to testify before the grand jury, but conventional wisdom deems that a risky tactic, as it subjects the potential defendant to cross-examination by the prosecution in a setting in which neither counsel (in most jurisdictions) nor the judge (in all jurisdictions) is present. Should such a request be presented, most jurisdictions hold that the grand jury can reject or grant the request at its discretion. Several states, however, give the potential defendant a right to testify if he so chooses, and they may permit him to be accompanied by counsel.

Evidentiary restrictions. All jurisdictions require that the testimonial privileges of a witness be recognized in grand jury proceedings. Beyond that, there is considerable variation in the applicability of rules of evidence that would govern at trial. A small group make these evidentiary rules fully applicable. Among indictment jurisdictions, those that generally favor application of the rules of evidence will recognize one or more broad exceptions to the rules of evidence. Those exceptions typically are designed to remove the burden of testifying from persons whose testimony ordinarily would not present a significant credibility issue (e.g., forensic experts).

Most indictment jurisdictions, and many information jurisdictions, simply refuse to apply the rules of evidence (other than testimonial privileges) to grand jury proceedings. In these jurisdictions, prosecutors may use any type of evidence without regard to whether it could be used at trial. Thus, prosecutors need not have key witnesses themselves testify, but may simply introduce statements the witnesses gave to the police, even though those statements would be inadmissible hearsay at trial. In *Costello v. United States*, 350 U.S. 359 (1956), the Supreme Court held that the prosecutorial practice of relying entirely on hearsay did not violate the Fifth Amendment. The Court stressed that historically, the grand jury was a "body of laymen" whose "work was not hampered by rigid procedural rules" (350 U.S. 362).

Standard for indictment. In many states the grand jury is directed to indict only if the evidence before it establishes probable cause to believe that the accused committed the felony charged; in others, it is directed to indict "when all the evidence taken together, if unexplained or uncontradicted, would warrant a conviction of the defendant." The first standard is very much like that applied by a preliminary-hearing magistrate. The second is a somewhat more rigorous standard, being similar to the standard applied by a trial judge in ruling on a motion for directed acquittal. No matter which standard applies in the particular jurisdiction, the jurors need not be unanimous in their conclusion that it is met. At common law, a vote of a majority (twelve out of twenty-three jurors) was sufficient to indict. Many jurisdictions now permit smaller grand juries, but require a somewhat higher percentage of votes for indictment (for example, twelve out of sixteen).

In some jurisdictions, generally those applying the rules of evidence, a defendant may challenge an indictment as not supported by sufficient evidence. To sustain such a challenge, the court must find that the evidence before the grand jury, even if read in a light most favorable to the state, did not meet the applicable standard for indictment. Other jurisdictions refuse all challenges to the sufficiency of the evidence before the grand jury. They stand by the standard suggested in *Costello*, that "an indictment returned by a legally constituted and unbiased grand jury, . . . if valid on its face, is enough to call for a trial on the merits" (350 U.S. 363).

The debate.   Few criminal justice issues have been the subject of such prolonged and heated debate as the comparative merits of prosecution by indictment and prosecution by information. Critics of prosecution by indictment tend to fall into two categories. First, there are those who see the screening grand jury as no more than a rubber stamp for the prosecutor. They point to various indictment jurisdictions in which grand juries have refused to indict in less than three percent of their cases. The legal structure of the grand jury, these critics argue, gives it only theoretical independence; in light of the prosecution's ready access to investigative resources, its legal expertise, and its close working relationships with the grand jurors, it is inevitable that the grand jurors will follow the prosecution's lead on whether the evidence is sufficient to proceed.

Supporters of grand jury screening offer a quite different reading of grand jury independence and the statistics on refusals to indict. They argue that a low rate of refusals to indict simply indicates that prosecutors, respecting independent grand jury review, have themselves eliminated the weaker cases. The success of grand jury screening, supporters note, is evidenced by the high percentage of indictments that produce convictions and the very small percentage that result in dismissals for want of substantial evidence (opponents respond that dismissals on the prosecutor's own motion and negotiated pleas to lesser offenses are more common, and they may cover flaws in grand jury screening). Reference is also made to the experience in jurisdictions in which prosecutors do not screen so carefully and in which grand juries have refused to indict in as many as 15 percent of their cases.

A second group of critics acknowledge that the grand jury has some value as a screening agency, but believe that preliminary hearing is a better screening procedure. They contend that an independent magistrate, an adversary proceeding, and an open hearing clearly make the preliminary hearing the more effective procedure for eliminating unwarranted prosecutions. Grand jury supporters respond that the grand jury is the better screening agency because its strength lies where screening is most needed—in those cases where special factors, such as the involvement of politics or racial animosity, will probably result in unjust accusations. Lay participation permits the grand jury to evaluate the prosecution's case in light of community notions of justice and fairness. Indeed, the grand jury has the recognized authority to "nullify" the law by refusing to indict, notwithstanding legally sufficient evidence.

Grand jury investigations

In contrast to their division on the use of the grand jury as a screening agency, both indictment and information jurisdictions use the grand jury as an investigative body. Although the extent of that use varies, the grand jury tends to be treated as a specialized investigative agency needed for a limited class of offenses. Compared to police investigations, grand jury investigations are expensive, time-consuming, and logistically cumbersome. However, the grand jury offers distinct investigative advantages where investigators must unravel a complex criminal structure, deal with victims reluctant to cooperate, or obtain information contained in extensive business records. Criminal activities presenting such investigative problems ordinarily relate to public corruption (e.g., bribery), misuse of economic power (e.g., price fixing), widespread distribution of illegal services and goods by organized groups (e.g., gambling syndicates), and threats of violence used by organized groups (e.g., extortion schemes).

The subpoena to testify

Significance. A major investigative advantage of the grand jury is its use of the *subpoena ad testificandum*, a court order directing a person to appear and testify before the grand jury. If the police wish to take a person into custody for questioning, they must have the probable cause required by the Fourth Amendment to justify the seizure of a person. Even then, the person has no duty to answer police questions. Moreover, if the person does answer and lies, his lying will not constitute a crime in most jurisdictions. If the prosecution, on the other hand, wishes to question a person before the grand jury, it may simply utilize the subpoena to testify, which avoids all of these obstacles. A subpoena to testify can be obtained without a showing of probable cause and, in general, without even a lesser showing that the person subpoenaed is likely to have relevant information. The compulsion of a subpoena to testify has long been held not to fall within the Fourth Amendment, since it does not involve taking a person into custody. Moreover, as various courts have noted, the grand jury (or the prosecutor acting on its behalf) may utilize subpoena authority on no more substantial grounds than "tips" or rumors. This enables the grand jury to serve as "a grand inquest, a body with powers of investigation and inquisition, the scope of whose inquiries is not limited narrowly by questions of propriety or forecasts of the probable result of the investigation" (*Blair v. United States*, 250 U.S. 273, 282 (1919)).

Unlike the person questioned by a police officer, the subpoenaed witness is compelled to answer questions before the grand jury unless the witness can claim an evidentiary privilege, such as the marital privilege or the privilege against self-incrimination. If the witness refuses to testify without such legal justification, the witness will be held in contempt and subjected to incarceration. Ordinarily, the recalcitrant witness will be held in "civil contempt," which means the witness will be released when willing to testify, or if unwilling, when the grand jury term ends. Criminal contempt is available if the grand jury no longer has need for the witness' testimony, and it commonly carries a jail term of several months to a few years. If the witness testifies and fails to tell the truth, the witness may be prosecuted for perjury since the testimony is given under oath. Here the potential prison term is substantially longer.

Safeguards. The granting of subpoena authority to grand juries rests, in part, on the premise that extensive safeguards are available to prevent misuse of that authority. Judicial discussions of subpoena authority frequently note, for example, that the grand jury witness retains the same evidentiary privileges that would be available to a witness at trial. In particular, a witness who may be involved in a criminal enterprise can always exercise the privilege against self-incrimination, refusing to respond whenever his answer might provide "a link in the chain of evidence needed to prosecute" (*Hoffman v. United States*, 341 U.S. 479, 486 (1951)). Indeed, if the witness is a potential target for indictment, the prosecutor may be required to inform the witness specifically, before he gives testimony, of his right to claim the privilege.

Courts also have stressed that the grand jury itself provides protection against misuse of the subpoena power. The grand jurors, it is noted "have no axes to grind and are not charged personally with the administration of the law" (Justice Black's dissent, U.S. 330, 346–347 (1957)). If questioning or other prosecutorial tactics offend their sense of justice, they may direct the prosecutor to discontinue (seeking the assistance of the court, if necessary). A final safeguard is the supervisory authority of the court issuing the subpoena. As the Supreme Court has noted, that court has the continuing obligation, if other safeguards fail, to prevent "the transformation of the grand jury into an instrument of oppression" (*United States v. Dionisio*, 410 U.S. 1, 12 (1973)).

Right to counsel. A primary legal reform urged by critics of grand jury investigations is the increased availability of counsel for witnesses. Because the witness is not an "accused" person (even if the target of the investigation), the Sixth Amendment right to counsel does not apply. Only a few jurisdictions have provisions requiring appointment of counsel to assist witnesses who are indigent. Even if a witness has counsel, the witness in most jurisdictions cannot have counsel accompany him before the grand jury. These jurisdictions view the presence of the witness' counsel before the grand jury as disruptive and inconsistent with grand jury secrecy. They will, however, permit the witness to interrupt his testimony and leave the grand jury room for the purpose of consulting with counsel just outside the grand jury room. Counsel for witnesses claim that this practice is not adequate, because witnesses do not always realize that they need legal advice in responding to a particular question. Moreover, witnesses often are fearful that they will appear to have "something to hide" if they too frequently leave the room to consult with counsel. Roughly twenty states do permit witnesses to be assisted by counsel within the grand jury room. These jurisdictions strictly limit the lawyer to giving advice to the witness, thereby seeking to prevent counsel from turning the grand jury examination into an adversary proceeding by making arguments to the grand jury.

Subpoena duces tecum.   The *subpoena duces tecum* (a court order directing a person to bring with him specified items in his possession) gives the grand jury the capacity to obtain physical evidence in a manner very similar to its capacity to obtain testimony. This subpoena is used primarily to obtain business records and other documents in investigations of white-collar crimes. However, it has also been used to require a suspect to provide such identification evidence as fingerprints or handwriting samples. A subpoena duces tecum, in contrast to a search warrant, does not require a showing of probable cause. Although the subpoena does direct the subpoenaed person to search his files and bring forth specified documents, it does not authorize the police or prosecutor themselves to search the premises for those files. The only Fourth Amendment limitation imposed upon the subpoena duces tecum relates to its breadth. A subpoena may not encompass such a wide range of material as to impose an unreasonable burden on the subpoenaed party.

The safeguards applicable to the subpoena ad testificandum also apply to the subpoena duces tecum. However, the privilege against self-incrimination is far less likely to apply to a subpoena duces tecum. The privilege extends only to individuals, and therefore cannot be raised, to subpoenas requiring production of documents belonging to corporations or similar entities, notwithstanding potential incrimination to the persons who authored or possessed the documents. Moreover, even with respect to personal records, the privilege tends to be limited to private documents personally prepared by the subpoenaed individual. Since the writing of the previously prepared document was not itself compelled, the only compelled testimonial element occurs in the acknowledgments that may be inherent in the act of productions—that is, acknowledging that the document exists, that it is possessed by the person presenting it, and that it is the document described in the subpoena. Where the document is not private and personally prepared, compelling those acknowledgments often will not be viewed as seeking testimony because existence, posses-

sion, and the document's authenticity already will be known as "foregone conclusions." As the privilege extends only to testimonial disclosures, it also has no applicability to subpoenas requiring production of fingerprints or similar identification evidence.

Immunity grants.   Perhaps the most significant advantage of the grand jury investigation is the availability of the immunity grant. An immunity grant is a court order that, in effect, supplants the witness' self incrimination privilege. Since the privilege prohibits compelling a witness to give testimony that may be used against him in a criminal case, the privilege can be rendered inapplicable by precluding such use of the witness' compelled testimony. An immunity grant does exactly that. It directs the witness to testify and protects him against use of his testimony in any subsequent criminal prosecution.

The Supreme Court has held that to be effective, the immunity grant must guarantee against further use of both the witness's testimony and any evidence derived from that testimony (*Kastigar v. United States*, 406 U.S. 441 (1972)). Moreover, if a subsequent prosecution is brought, the prosecution bears the burden of establishing that all of its evidence was derived from a source independent of the immunized testimony. As a practical matter, unless the prosecution had a fully prepared case before the witness was granted immunity, it will be most difficult to prosecute successfully for a criminal activity discussed in immunized testimony. Many states simply grant the witness what is commonly called "transactional immunity." They bar any prosecution for a transaction discussed in the immunized testimony, without regard to the possible independent source of the prosecutor's evidence.

JEROLD H. ISRAEL

See also ARRAIGNMENT; CONFESSIONS; CRIMINAL JUSTICE PROCESS; PRELIMINARY HEARING; PROSECUTION: PROSECUTORIAL DISCRETION; SEARCH AND SEIZURE.

BIBLIOGRAPHY

BEALE, SARA SUN; BRYSON, WILLIAM; FELMAN, JAMES; and ELSTON, MICHAEL. *Grand Jury Law and Practice*, 2d. St. Paul, Minn.: Westgroup, 1998.

BLANK, BLANCHE. *The Not So Grand Jury*. Lanham, Md: University Press of America, 1993.

BRENNER, SUSAN, and LOCKHART, GREGORY. *Federal Grand Jury Practice*. St. Paul, Minn.: West Publishing, 1996.

CLARK, LEROY D. *The Grand Jury: The Use and Abuse of Political Power.*. New York: Quadrangle, 1975.

FRANKEL, MARVIN E., and NAFTALIS, GARY P. *The Grand Jury: An Institution on Trial.* New York: Hill & Wang, 1977.

LAFAVE, WAYNE; ISRAEL, JEROLD; and KING, NANCY. *Criminal Procedure.* 2d ed. St. Paul, Minn.: Westgroup, 1999, chapters 8 and 15.

LIEPOLD, ANDREW. "Why Grand Juries Do Not (And Cannot) Protect the Accused." *Cornell Law Review* 80 (1995): 260.

SCHWARTZ, HELENE E. "Demythologizing the Historic Role of the Grand Jury." *American Criminal Law Review* 10 (1972): 701–770.

YOUNGER, RICHARD D. *The People's Panel: The Grand Jury in the United States, 1634–1941.* Providence, R.I.: Brown University Press, 1963.

CASES

Blair v. United States, 250 U.S. 273 (1919).
Costello v. United States, 350 U.S. 359 (1956).
Hoffman v. United States, 341 U.S. 479 (1951).
Hurtado v. California, 110 U.S. 516 (1884).
Kastigar v. United States, 406 U.S. 441 (1972).
United States v. Dionisio, 410 U.S. 1, 12 (1973).
United States v. Procter and Gamble Co., 356 U.S. 677 (1958).
United States v. Williams, 504 U.S. 306 (1992).

GUILT

Introduction

The drama of guilt is enacted upon a wider stage than that set by law. Betraying a friend, lying subtly to oneself, or perhaps even telling an injurious truth to another are among the many types of conduct that may give rise to some guilt—but not necessarily to legal guilt. The subject of this article is legal guilt. But because this legal concept is arguably weighted with moral significance, the relationship between it and moral guilt is also addressed.

The concept of legal guilt has a circumscribed role, not only within life but within the law itself. Judgments of guilt are neither to be identified with, nor implied by, judgments of invalidity or judgments of civil liability. A marriage or a will may be found invalid; this implies nothing about one's guilt in failing to satisfy the conditions required for a valid marriage or will. A judgment in a civil action in favor of a plaintiff

and against a defendant does not by itself, even if the defendant has been found to be at fault, imply anything about the defendant's guilt. The legal concept of guilt is restricted to the criminal law, and it is within this area of law that verdicts of guilt are rendered. Consideration of this practice of rendering verdicts is essential if one is to grasp the nature of legal guilt.

The verdict of guilt

The verdicts of guilty and not guilty are legally significant acts that are embedded in a complex rule-defined practice in which charges are leveled, hearings held, and judgments rendered. What is a verdict? As distinguished from the factual assumptions underlying it, a verdict is not a statement of fact that one is or is not guilty as charged. Verdicts themselves are neither true nor false, but valid or invalid. If challenged, they may be "set aside," but not because they are false. It is an essential characteristic of verdicts that they make things happen rather than state what is so. If a verdict is valid a person becomes, by virtue of that fact, either guilty or not guilty before the law. This concept of legal guilt is referred to here as "legally operative guilt."

A number of issues related to the practice of rendering verdicts of guilt will be considered. First, what conditions must be satisfied if a verdict is to be valid? Second, what does it mean to be guilty in the legally operative sense? Third, what presuppositions underlie the legal practice of rendering verdicts of guilt? Fourth, what functions are served by this legal practice? Finally, is there a concept of legal guilt different from that of legally operative guilt, and if so, how are the different concepts related?

Validity conditions for verdicts. There is a common understanding as to what communicative behavior in what settings constitutes a verdict. Thus, for example, persons without legal authority may state their opinions about a defendant's guilt or reach moral judgments upon the matter, but without legal authority they cannot render legal verdicts. Only when a verdict has been rendered can its validity or invalidity be considered. Verdicts must be in compliance with rules that define the conditions to be satisfied if they are to be legally operative. These rules regulate such matters as the form and substance of the verdict, the conditions in which it is arrived at, and the setting in which it is delivered. Thus, a verdict may be set aside because of uncertainty in its formulation, as when it is unclear which of two defendants charged with an offense has been found guilty; because it has been announced in the absence of the defendant; because of misconduct by those charged with rendering it; or because of a lack of evidence to support it.

The meaning of legally operative guilt. What does it mean to be guilty before the law in the legally operative sense? The verdict itself is a formal pronouncement of condemnation by an authoritative social organ. In being declared guilty, one is branded. One's status is thereby transformed into that of the legally condemned. Being thus branded, one is set apart from others and placed in a condition that requires correction. Guilt, by its very nature, calls for something to be done. Further, being legally guilty in the operative sense implies that the guilty person is properly subject to punishment. Any legal practice restricted to establishing one's liability to make reparations or restitution, or restricted to providing compensation, would differ fundamentally from the legal practice of determining guilt. None of these alternative practices necessarily implies either condemnation or the idea of conduct causing injury to society, and thus of owing society something.

Presuppositions of the practice. A number of background conditions are presupposed by a legal practice embodying the concept of guilt. These are conditions whose presence makes intelligible the practice and whose absence would reasonably cause doubt about the existence of this particular practice.

First, a verdict of guilt presupposes the belief that there is a condition of guilt logically independent of the verdict. There are facts to be determined, and they relate, of course, to a person's being in fact guilty—what shall be referred to as "factual legal guilt." As a corollary, it is also presupposed that those charged with rendering verdicts will reflect on the evidence presented to them relating to the criminal charge and will not resort to such arbitrary devices for determining guilt as flipping coins.

Second, a verdict of guilt presupposes that the person adjudged guilty is the same person charged with having committed the offense. There would be an oddity, for example, in rendering a verdict against a person who at the time of conviction, because of severe amnesia, was believed to lack any sense of continuity with the person claimed to have committed the offense. Again, society could conceivably penalize close relatives of escaped felons in order to deter escapes, but in such a practice, verdicts of guilt would not be rendered against the unfortunate relatives. Liability to suffer penalties is not equivalent to being judged guilty.

Third, the practice presupposes that individuals adjudged guilty have the capacity to comprehend the significance of the verdict and of the punishment prescribed. Verdicts have a communicative function, and among the persons addressed are those convicted of crime. Verdicts would lose their point if they were addressed to individuals who did not comprehend their significance as condemnatory and who were at a loss to understand why suffering was to be imposed upon them.

A fourth consideration, connected with this last point, is more speculative: perhaps a general commitment throughout society to the norms established by law, to the values they support, and to the legitimacy of the practice that has been established is necessary in order to determine violations and guilt. Without these elements the legal practice of finding guilt would be transformed into one in which individuals with power merely enforced their will upon others. In such circumstances the normative basis of the practice would crumble, condemnation would inevitably fall upon deaf ears, and punishment would become merely a matter of making another suffer.

Finally, the social practice embodying guilt presupposes beliefs in an established order of things, in an imbalance to that order caused by wrongdoing, in the undesirability of alienation, and in the possibility of restoration. Unlike the concepts of pollution or shame, for example, the concept of guilt arises in a world in which people conceive of guilty wrongdoing as disrupting a valued order of things. This produces instability and sets the guilty person apart from others, but nevertheless also creates a situation that may be righted by sacrificial or punitive responses. Punishment, although it has other explanations as well, in this conception is a mode of righting imbalances through exaction of a debt owed by the guilty to society. The debt, once exacted, brings about rejoinder. Given this conception, the person branded as guilty is so branded because he has set himself apart by wrongdoing. "Guilt" then adheres to the guilty like a stain and weighs like a burden, and punishment serves both to purify and relieve. Punishment as a response to guilt is thus freighted with symbolic significance, and major shifts in how it is conceived would imply transformation in the legal practice of which it and guilt are now a part.

Functions served by the practice of rendering verdicts of guilt.   Practices come into existence and persist for a variety of reasons. They may also, once in existence, serve interests that were not factors leading to their genesis. The universal fascination with crime and punishment strongly suggests that deep emotional needs may be gratified by the legal practice of rendering verdicts of guilt. It seems clear that these needs are better served by the drama of a public trial and conviction than by the growing phenomenon of the plea bargain.

Determinations of guilt and the infliction of punishment upon the guilty convey as nothing else can that there are indeed norms in effect in society and that they are to be taken seriously. Guilt determinations allay anxiety through reassurance that one's social world is orderly and not chaotic: it is a structured space in which not everything is permitted, where there are limits to conduct, and where retribution may be expected if these limits are breached. The practice also provides reinforcement for one's hope that in this world one is not merely a helpless victim, for guilt is founded upon the idea that individuals are responsible for what they do. Moreover, judging persons to be legally guilty permits a societally approved deflection of aggressive impulses. Punishment, like war, may allow for aggression without our suffering guilt as a consequence.

Finally, life outside the law, when issues of guilt and innocence arise, is filled with complexity, ambiguity, and irresolution. It is a virtue of law to make matters neater than they are outside the law, and to make smooth the rough edges of human interaction. The law presents a drama in which one is either guilty or not guilty and in which the guilty meet with their just deserts. Real life is, of course, quite different, but the law with its relative definiteness and its institutionalized means of retribution at least partially satisfies our longing for an ideal world.

Legally operative guilt and factual legal guilt.   Some might argue that legally operative guilt is the entire substance of the concept of legal guilt, for, after all, what is more closely connected with legal guilt than liability to punishment? On the other hand, jurors are asked to consider whether a person is in fact guilty before they reach a verdict of guilt. What sometimes justifies setting aside a verdict is a judgment that the evidence of guilt—factual legal guilt—is insufficient to justify the verdict. This seems to establish that we possess a concept of legal guilt that is logically independent of a verdict of guilt, for it is a concept that guides those charged with reaching a verdict. Thus, it would seem wise to acknowledge the presence of two legal concepts of guilt and to address oneself to their relationship.

Factual legal guilt

We have seen that the norms governing the practice of rendering verdicts require that those charged with the responsibility consider the evidence relevant to factual legal guilt. In our own system of criminal law a verdict of guilt is to be returned only if it is believed beyond a reasonable doubt that the defendant is indeed guilty. Although the verdict is not a statement of fact, it presupposes beliefs about the facts. This brings us to a consideration of the nature of factual legal guilt. When is a person guilty in this sense?

First, conduct is normally a prerequisite for legal guilt. This means that a person must actually commit a certain act. It is not enough for him to merely think of doing it, nor is it enough for him simply to have a status of a certain kind, such as being a member of a certain race. Second, the conduct must normally be conscious. Individuals are not guilty for what they do while asleep. Third, there must be legal wrongdoing. Even the most egregious moral wrong does not occasion legal guilt unless the wrong is also a legal one. Fourth, one must have the capacity to appreciate the significance of the norms applicable to one. Animals and infants, for example, do not have the ability to experience guilt. Finally, it is normally a prerequisite for legal guilt that there be conscious fault or culpability with respect to wrongdoing, that is, there must be a "guilty mind" (mens rea). Whatever defeats one's fair opportunity to behave otherwise than he did— typically some reasonable ignorance of fact or limitation on his freedom of action—may excuse him.

These conditions are common to most legal systems. But how do they relate to the concept of legal guilt? Are there limitations on what legal systems can do with regard to specifying conditions for guilt? Here there are logical and, arguably, moral constraints on legal practice. The law could, imaginably, impose penalties upon individuals merely because of their race. In such a case, however, it would be odd to describe the defendant as having been found guilty. Some of the above criteria, then, may be essentially connected with the concept of legal guilt, in that failure to satisfy them would imply that the concept had no application.

The connection that factual legal guilt has with our moral conceptions of guilt is less clear: moral fault is not essential for legal guilt. Nevertheless, there may be a connection between legal guilt and moral fault that is more than merely accidental. As discussed above, the legal practice of rendering verdicts of guilt has special significance. Individuals who are guilty are viewed as justifiably condemned and as having set themselves apart from the community by disregarding its basic values. To this extent, a number of the conditions for being morally guilty—among them conditions related to a fair opportunity to behave otherwise than one did—are presuppositions of legal guilt as well. On this view, a system that allowed generally for a finding of guilt in conflict with certain moral constraints would be one that used existing institutions of the criminal law in a way fundamentally at odds with certain of its basic presuppositions. Prevention and social control would replace crime and punishment as these are now understood. Even today, when legal doctrine permits conviction of those without fault, it seems that something on the order of a lie is being perpetrated. This is because such convictions create the false impression that the guilty are insufficiently committed to the community's norms, whereas in the case of those not proved to be at fault this has not been established.

Moral and legal guilt

How are these concepts related beyond what has been suggested above? There can, of course, be moral guilt without legal guilt, legal guilt without moral guilt, and a range of instances in which the two overlap. Earlier, there were listed a number of examples of what might occasion moral guilt without legal guilt. To this list might be added those cases where compliance with evil laws creates moral guilt. Since it is sometimes morally right to violate an iniquitous law, it follows that there may be legal guilt without moral guilt. From a consideration of crimes such as murder, where generally those factually guilty are morally guilty as well, it is evident that the two overlap.

Moral and legal guilt may differ significantly. There is no concept in morality comparable to legally operative guilt; one is never morally guilty merely by virtue of being judged as such. Moral guilt is always factual guilt. Further, the law may specify in a relatively arbitrary way the norms that regulate conduct and the circumstances under which violation of these norms incurs guilt. But for moral guilt the norms and the conditions to be satisfied for incurring guilt are entirely immune from deliberate human modification.

Moreover, legal guilt is restricted to those situations in which a wrong is done to society. It is not enough that someone's personal rights have been violated. For the most part, however, moral wrongs that establish guilt arise in situations where another's rights have been violated; the guilt is not necessarily done to the society that conceives itself as threatened by the conduct. Thus, those in a position to condemn or forgive are those whose rights have been violated, and not some party that stands in an institutionally defined relationship to the wronged party.

Further, in being morally guilty there is no implication of being justifiably liable to punishment. There may be entitlement to criticize and to be resentful or indignant, but in a variety of situations where moral guilt arises, either the wrong done is not appropriately viewed as punishable, or the relationship (for example, between friends) is in no way seen as righted by punishment. What is essential for restoration in the moral sphere is such emotions and attitudes as guilt, contrition, and repentance. In addition, the objects of moral guilt differ from those generally of concern to the law. Maxims such as "the law aims at a minimum; morality at a maximum" and "the law is concerned with external conduct; morality with internal conduct" draw attention to the different emphases of law and morality. Finally, moral guilt may remain forever in doubt once all the facts are in. Moral reflection allows for the judgment that a person is and yet is not guilty; this depends on one's perspective, which is not precisely defined by any authoritative pronouncement. Thus, there is no need for moral reflection ever to come to rest.

The sense of guilt

What is the sense of guilt, and how is it related, if at all, to law? Guilt is a human sentiment that manifests itself in our inhibition from doing what we believe to be wrong and in our feeling guilty when we do what we believe to be wrong. Thus, it operates both in a forward- and a backward-looking manner. In this respect it resembles conscience, which "doth make cowards of us all" and which, when we disobey its dictates, makes us conscience-stricken. Guilt is the feeling most closely connected with wrongdoing, taking as its object belief in wrongdoing. What, more precisely, is it to feel guilt?

A person who feels guilt holds certain beliefs and is disposed to feel and act in certain specific ways. First, one is attached to avoiding wrong, and the mere fact that one has done wrong causes a feeling of pain. Second, just as there is a special satisfaction connected with thinking of oneself as the creator of what is valuable, so there is a special dissatisfaction that derives from the realization that one has been responsible for wrongdoing. This is partly because one sees oneself as a destroyer of value. Third, in feeling guilt one turns on oneself the criticism and hostility that, if another had acted in the same way, would have been directed at that person. Fourth, there is a sense of unease caused by one's feeling alienated from those to whom one is attached. Finally, the sense of unpleasantness associated with guilt is connected with carrying a burden from which one longs to be relieved. One feels obliged to confess, to make amends, to repair, and to restore. A further sense of unpleasantness is caused by one's resistance to do these things, owing to fear and perhaps pride, and the unease experienced until they are done.

How, if at all, is the human disposition to feel guilt related to the legal practice, described above? Individuals are often adjudged guilty and do not feel guilt. They may believe themselves innocent of the charge; they may believe that, although legally wrong, what they did was morally obligatory; or they may not have the requisite degree of internalization with regard to the law generally or to a particular law. Although all this is possible and no doubt even common, vulnerability to the feeling of guilt may be connected with the legal practice embodying the concept of guilt. For, as has been claimed, among the practice's presuppositions is a general acceptance of the authority of society's norms and of the institutions applying them. This seems to imply that individuals generally are liable, when violating the norms, to having their sense of guilt activated. If it were otherwise, condemnation and punishment would no longer have the significance that they do.

The future of guilt

From Ezekiel we learn:

The soul that sins shall die. The son shall not suffer for the iniquity of the father, nor the father suffer for the iniquity of the son; the righteousness of the righteous shall be upon himself, and the wickedness of the wicked shall be upon himself [18:20].

These words mark a dramatic change in prior practices related to guilt; it was individualized. With Christianity another dramatic change slowly came about: the inner life of the moral agent assumed an importance it earlier did not have. Our own age may now be witness to a drama of equal significance. Through a confluence of factors—philosophical determinism, the development of the behavioral sciences, the ideology of sickness and therapy, and utilitarianism—the very foundations of the concept of legal guilt have been placed in question.

The assault on guilt has moved along a number of parallel fronts. There are those who claim that the presuppositions upon which guilt depends are not in fact valid. Here one encounters either metaphysical lines of argument, or more empirically grounded theories asserting the existence of causative factors in every case that should exempt the wrongdoer from blame. This line of argumentation is evident in the modern tendency to see antisocial conduct as a matter for therapy, not punishment. Moreover, even if one were to acknowledge the reality of the conditions required for the appropriate application of the concept of guilt, it is sometimes claimed that we cannot have reasonable grounds for believing that these conditions are ever present. Skepticism of this kind may incline its adherents to urge foregoing concern with culpability at the time of the offense charged. Attention should focus rather upon what was in fact done—something observable—and, once this is determined, one should then concentrate on what would be the best disposition of the responsible party, given that party's condition at the time of trial. The orientation is almost entirely toward the future and away from the past.

Finally, some are prepared to say that the conditions for guilt are valid, that we can know them, and yet that it is a mistake to continue the practice. Guilt and punishment are viewed by some as fundamentally irrational modes of viewing human conduct—relics from a superstitious past in which suffering is seen as magically erasing evil. From this perspective it is never a former evil that justifies infliction of present pain, only a future good to be realized.

These, then, are some of the strains of discontent with guilt. It is not always evident from a particular critique precisely what the implications are for customary ways of proceeding. For example, philosophical determinists do not customarily urge abandoning the criminal law. It remains unclear, too, whether the law, an institution intertwined so closely with our moral way of looking at things, could be fundamentally changed without a corresponding transformation in moral conceptions and in such moral feelings as guilt and indignation. Nonetheless, the above critiques may gradually modify morality as we have known it, and guilt may conceivably appear as strange to future generations as the world against which Ezekiel was rebelling appears to us.

Powerful assaults have been mounted upon guilt and punishment. They have not gone unanswered, and have in fact mobilized tenacious defenses of customary ways of thinking about human beings. Few ages in history have spoken to the issue of human responsibility with the power and force of our own. Some have insisted that humans are basically free, that they often choose their own enslavement, and that by taking their past wrongs seriously they can redeem themselves. For those of this persuasion the law, with all its imperfections, embodies recognition of the truth of human responsibility and daily reenacts the drama of human waywardness, of wrongdoing, and of its being righted.

HERBERT MORRIS

See also CRIME: DEFINITION; EXCUSE: THEORY; JUSTIFICATION: THEORY; MENS REA; PUNISHMENT; STRICT LIABILITY; VICARIOUS LIABILITY.

BIBLIOGRAPHY

BRETT, PETER. An Inquiry into Criminal Guilt. London: Sweet & Maxwell, 1963.
DRESSLER, JOSHUA. "Reflections on Excusing Wrongdoers: Moral Theory, New Excuses, and the Model Penal Code." Rutgers Law Journal 19, no. 3 (1988): 671–716.
DURKHEIM, ÉMILE. The Division of Labor in Society. Translated by George Simpson. New York: Free Press, 1947.
FEINBERG, JOEL. Doing and Deserving Essays in the Theory of Responsibility. Princeton NJ: Princeton University Press, 1970.
FREUD, SIGMUND. Civilization and Its Discontent (1930). Translated by James Strachey. London: Hogarth Press, 1961.
HART, H. L. A. Punishment and Responsibility: Essays in the Philosophy of Law. Oxford, England: Clarendon Press, 1968.
LEWIS, H. D.; HARVEY, J. W.; and PAUL, G. A. "The Problem of Guilt" (Symposium). Proceedings of the Arisiotelian Society, supp. vol. 21 (1947): 175–218.
MILLER, WILLIAM IAN. The Anatomy of Disgust. Cambridge, Mass.: Harvard University Press, 1997.
MOBERLY, WALTER HAMILTON. The Ethics of Punishment. London: Faber & Faber, 1968.
MOORE MICHAEL. Placing Blame. Oxford, England: Oxford University Press, 1997.
MORRIS, HERBERT. On Guilt and Innocence: Essays in Legal Philosophy and Moral Psychology. Berkeley: University of California Press, 1976.
———. "The Decline of Guilt." Ethics 99, no. 1 (1988): 62–76.
MURPHY, JEFFRIE G., and HAMPTON, JEAN. Forgiveness and Mercy. Cambridge, England: Cambridge University Press, 1988.
NIETZSCHE, FRIEDRICH. "On the Genealogy of Morals." Basic Writings of Nietzsche. Translated by Walter Kaufmann. New York: Random House, 1968.
PIERS, GERHARDT, and SINGER, MILTON B. Shame and Guilt: A Psychoanalytic and a Cultural Study. New York: Norton, 1971.
PILLSBURY, SAMUEL H. Judging Evil: Rethinking the Law of Murder and Manslaughter. New York: New York University Press, 1998.
RAWLS, JOHN. A Theory of Justice. Cambridge, Mass.: Harvard University Press/Belknap Press, 1971.
RICOEUR, PAUL. The Symbolism of Evil. New York: Harper & Row, 1967.
ROSS, ALF. On Guilt, Responsibility, and Punishment. London: Stevens, 1975.
SAKS, ELYN R. Jekyll on Trial: Multiple Personality Disorder and Criminal Law. New York: New York University Press, 1997.

GUILTY PLEA: ACCEPTING THE PLEA

A guilty plea consists of a defendant admitting having committed one or more of the crimes charged and a court agreeing to accept that admission and to sentence the defendant. Ordinarily, a guilty plea occurs after defense counsel has bargained with the prosecution and obtained some concession—for example, a reduction of the charges, an agreement not to file other charges, or a stipulation with respect to the position the prosecution will take at sentencing. Nevertheless, defendants have a right to plead guilty without a prosecutor's agreement, provided that they plead to all the crimes charged. Defendants sometimes pursue this course in unwinnable or minor cases an which they believe a plea will encourage the presiding judge to impose a lenient sentence.

The nature of guilty pleas

The main purpose of a guilty plea is to produce a final conclusion to a criminal case. Once a defendant enters a guilty plea, the prosecutor has no further obligation to introduce evidence of the defendant's guilt. A pleading defendant waives the right to raise most objections to police, prosecutorial, or judicial behavior that could have been raised on appeal after a trial and conviction. However, the defendant may still appeal issues relating to the guilty plea process, to events that occur after the guilty plea (e.g., improprieties in sentencing), to the essential invalidity of the court's "jurisdiction," and to a limited number of constitutional violations. The Supreme Court has had difficulty identifying dividing lines for which constitutional issues may be raised post-plea. Appellate courts also have upheld the ability of prosecutors to demand, as part of a plea bargain, a waiver of the right to appeal some issues relating to sentencing. In general, the courts have shown a strong preference for maintaining the finality of guilty pleas.

In other respects, guilty pleas have the same consequences as guilty verdicts. The judgments of conviction carry the identical evidentiary value and ramifications for future proceedings—including the same potential for sentence enhancement and for forfeiture of assets. In many jurisdictions, a guilty plea or guilty verdict forecloses defendants from suing their lawyers for malpractice.

Some jurisdictions recognize pleas that are not guilty pleas in the traditional sense. The most common alternative is the nolo contendere, "Alford," or "non vult" plea. It enables defendants to accept the consequences of a guilty verdict without admitting that they committed the offense. A nolo plea has most of the consequences of a guilty plea; the potential sentence is identical and the judgment is considered a conviction. The plea is useful when both sides want to dispose of a case in order to reduce their risks, but the defendant simply cannot admit guilt.

The nolo plea differs from a guilty plea in two significant respects. It may not be used against a defendant in a *civil* case as an admission or as proof that defendant committed the underlying crime. And the defendant can publicly continue to deny guilt. Because of these differences, a defendant has no right to enter a nolo plea unless the prosecutor and court agree to accept it.

In some jurisdictions, guilty pleas may be entered conditionally, by agreement with the prosecutor or under some institutionalized program. Typically, these pleas are suspended while the defendant is given an opportunity to satisfy conditions of the plea agreement. If the defendant fulfills the requirements, the plea is vacated and the charges dropped; if the defendant fails, the guilty verdict becomes final. The most common conditional pleas involve pretrial diversion programs and traffic programs requiring participation in traffic school.

A different form of conditional plea, which few jurisdictions recognize, entitles defendants to admit committing a crime but to preserve appellate issues that might preclude a conviction. The logic of these pleas is that, when only legal issues have potential merit, it is wasteful to proceed with trial just to preserve the defendant's right to appeal. Moreover, if legal issues raise matters of public importance—such as police misconduct in Fourth Amendment cases—the appellate courts should be able to hear them. In most states, a defendant wishing to concede guilt but to retain the right to appeal would need to obtain the prosecutor's agreement to a jointly "stipulated trial," in which both sides agree upon all the facts in a bench trial. Prosecutors, who engage in plea bargaining to reduce the risk of acquittals and to avoid expending resources on appeals, rarely agree to stipulated trials.

A defendant's excuse for criminal conduct ordinarily is irrelevant to the defendant's plea. Excuses are raised as affirmative defenses at trial or left for sentencing. A few states, however, require defendants to identify particular affirmative defenses as part of the plea—requiring, for example, a plea of not guilty by reason of insanity.

The plea process

Early in any prosecution, a defendant is brought before a judicial officer for arraignment. There, the judge advises the defendant of the charges, appoints counsel if necessary, and requires the defendant to enter a guilty or not guilty plea. In serious matters, the judge ordinarily will not accept a guilty plea at the arraignment unless satisfied that the defendant has been advised by counsel to enter the plea.

A defendant may change a not guilty plea to guilty at any time. Guilty pleas usually occur before trial, because prosecutors will offer concessions to avoid the risky and resource-intensive trial process. Occasionally, however, pleas occur after both parties have reassessed their chances of success in light of trial developments.

There is some question about the disclosure obligation of prosecutors before a plea is entered. Defendants need not accept a bargain until discovery is complete. But prosecutors may not be willing to offer as good a bargain late in the process. There is a strong argument that disclosure of at least constitutionally mandated discovery—including exculpatory material—should be required if defendants are to make rational judgments about the risks they face.

Once a guilty plea has been entered, the defendant is sentenced just like someone convicted after trial. However, the plea agreement may include sentencing concessions by the prosecutor, such as a promise to propose a particular sentence or not to take any position at sentencing. Some plea agreements specify a sentence to be imposed. Because sentencing is the court's prerogative, the presiding judge has the option of agreeing to impose this sentence or rejecting the plea agreement.

After sentencing, pleading defendants have the same time to appeal as convicted defendants. The issues that they may raise on appeal are limited. Additional procedures exist for attacking pleas collaterally. But because of the system's interest in finality and the reality that many defendants regret their decisions to plead guilty once incarcerated, courts restrict the grounds for undoing pleas.

The elements of guilty pleas

Valid guilty pleas have three basic elements. The court accepting the plea must have jurisdiction. The defendant must be competent to make the decision to plead guilty. Due process requires that the decision be voluntary and reasonably well-informed.

Competence and voluntariness are linked. Because plea agreements are conceptualized as rational bargains, it is important for courts to satisfy themselves that defendants have exercised free will. A mentally incompetent defendant or one under the influence of drugs or alcohol is legally unable to enter a voluntary plea. The standards for mental incompetence are similar to the standards for competence to stand trial; namely, whether the defendant can understand the proceedings and has "sufficient present ability to consult with his lawyer with a reasonable degree of rational understanding."

The concept of voluntariness extends further. It is easier to list factors that may make pleas involuntary than to identify a general standard for voluntary pleas. When a defendant enters a plea because of terror, threats, or *improper* inducements, the plea is not voluntary. On the other hand, a defendant's fear of the real consequences of not pleading guilty or the defendant's desire to receive concessions will not vitiate a plea. Otherwise, most pleas would be invalid. The dividing line is elusive.

Equally complicated is the question of how well defendants must understand the consequences of pleading. At a minimum, defendants must be made aware of the main constitutional rights being relinquished. These include the privilege against self-incrimination, right to trial by jury, and right to confront one's accusers. Defendants also must understand the nature of the charges against them and the maximum possible sentence. But when a defendant turns out to have been confused or to have received bad advice regarding such matters as the likelihood of winning at trial or of receiving leniency, courts have not been generous in deeming pleas involuntary. The opinions weigh the need to provide due process against the system's need for finality in guilty plea judgments.

Extraneous factors may require rejection of superficially valid pleas. One example is prosecutorial misconduct. The courts have rejected guilty pleas induced by threats, misrepresentations, overcharging, and broken promises by prosecutors. However, plea negotiations often involve posturing and puffing by the lawyers on both sides. The degree of compulsion created by such prosecutorial conduct is key to the decision of whether the conduct rendered a plea involuntary or violated due process.

The presence of competent defense counsel is relevant to an assessment of both voluntariness and defendant's separate constitutional right to effective assistance of counsel. When a defendant proceeds *pro se* or when the defendant's lawyer represents the defendant poorly (or is constrained by a conflict of interest), prosecutorial misconduct is more likely to force a plea and render a defendant's decision uninformed. As a result, courts hesitate to accept a guilty plea unless competent counsel is present. At a minimum, a court must assure itself that a defendant understands the right to counsel before accepting a waiver of counsel in connection with a plea. Conversely, the presence of active counsel may mitigate a court's sense that threats or fear prevented a defendant from making a voluntary, rational choice.

Judicial misconduct also can undermine plea agreements. Judges have statutory obligations in accepting pleas. Failure to fulfill these obligations does not automatically justify withdrawal of a plea. On the other hand, a judge's overinvolvement in plea negotiations may coerce defendants into accepting bargains, fearing retaliation for failure to do so. Some jurisdictions forbid any judicial involvement in negotiations. Even where no clear rule exists, judicial interference increases the possibility that a plea will later be deemed involuntary.

Statutory and procedural requirements

Numerous protections against faulty pleas exist. Most important are the right to counsel and the requirement of judicial supervision of plea agreements. To avoid guilty pleas becoming subject to collateral attack, most jurisdictions have adopted prophylactic procedures governing the plea process. These typically require judges to provide defendants key information and to satisfy themselves that each plea is voluntary and intelligent. Failure to implement the statutes may open a plea to subsequent attack. However, because the statutory requirements often exceed constitutional requirements, reviewing courts may overlook technical flaws in the proceedings as harmless error.

Guilty plea proceedings consist of an inquiry into the voluntariness of the bargain and the factual basis for the conviction. The presiding judge must inquire into the nature of the bargain, including all inducements, and into the facts that the prosecution could prove to support the charges. The best procedures require courts to engage in a dialogue with defendants through which defendants themselves show their understanding of the charges, the elements of the crime, the nature of the bargain, and the range of possible consequences of pleading guilty. In the course of this inquiry, the court also must satisfy itself that defendant is competent and understands the extent and nature of the rights being waived.

Following these procedures insulates most guilty pleas from subsequent challenge. They help ensure that a court will not accept a plea when there are indications that defendant is incompetent, the plea is involuntary, or a factual basis for conviction is lacking. When defense counsel appears to suffer from a conflict of interest or appears ineffective, the court must inquire into those deficiencies as well. Thus, by the time a subsequent court is asked to review the plea, the record usually is clear that the plea was voluntary, intelligent, and—though regretted by the defendant—a product of fair bargaining.

Subsequent challenges

Courts and legislatures hesitate to allow defendants who later find themselves dissatisfied to undo plea agreements. Nevertheless, occasions exist in which fairness demands reconsideration. Three mechanisms for challenging pleas exist. Defendants may seek to withdraw pleas, before sentencing or thereafter. Defendants may challenge pleas or sentences on appeal. Defendants may raise legal objections after the time for appeal has elapsed, through habeas corpus or other statutory procedures.

It is easier to withdraw a guilty plea before sentencing than thereafter. Federal and some state statutes authorize only pre-sentencing withdrawal. Their logic is that plea withdrawals before sentencing put the parties in the same position as before an agreement was reached. Thus, defendants are likely to request withdrawal only for a good reason. After sentencing, on the other hand, all defendants dissatisfied with their sentences will seek to undo their pleas. The longer the period that has passed, the more difficult it becomes for the prosecution to prove its case.

Accordingly, defendants may seek pre-sentencing withdrawal for any "fair and just reason." A few courts have interpreted this standard as permitting automatic withdrawal unless the prosecutor shows prejudice. Most, however, require defendants to present some substantial justification for withdrawal. Jurisdictions that allow post-sentencing withdrawal impose a higher standard: defendants must show that "manifest injustice" will occur if withdrawal is refused.

After sentencing, a defendant may challenge the plea or sentence on direct appeal, provided that the appeal is filed within statutory time limits. Direct appeal offers advantages over other forms of collateral attack, because defendants may raise all legal and constitutional objections to the plea process without having to overcome jurisdictional hurdles. The grounds for successful appeal are, however, limited. Most claims of pre-plea police misconduct and evidentiary deficiencies are not cognizable.

In practice, most challenges to guilty pleas occur after the time for appeal has expired. They typically take the form of habeas corpus petitions, motions for new trials, or other state-specific post-conviction relief mechanisms. In deference to the government's interest in finality of judgments, these remedies all impose procedural obstacles to successful prosecution. Even if a petition survives these, courts ordinarily will not reverse guilty pleas unless a defendant can establish that a significant constitutional error has occurred and that maintaining the plea would produce manifest injustice.

FRED C. ZACHARIAS

See also APPEAL; ARRAIGNMENT; COUNSEL: RIGHT TO COUNSEL; COUNSEL: ROLE OF COUNSEL; CRIMINAL JUSTICE PROCESS; GUILTY PLEA: PLEA BARGAINING; PROSECUTION: PROSECUTORIAL DISCRETION.

BIBLIOGRAPHY

ADELSTEIN, RICHARD P. *The Negotiated Guilty Plea: An Economic and Empirical Analysis.* New York: Garland, 1985.

American Bar Association. *Standards for Criminal Justice Prosecution Function and Defense Function,* 3d ed. Washington, D.C.: American Bar Association, 1993, 3–4.1 to 3–4.3; 4–6.1 to 4–6.2.

ALSCHULER, ALBERT W. "Plea Bargaining and its History." *Columbia Law Review* 79 (January 1979): 1.

BOND, JAMES E. *Plea Bargaining and Guilty Pleas,* 2d ed. New York: Clark Boardman & Co., 1982.

KAMISAR, YALE; LAFAVE, WAYNE R.; and ISRAEL, JEROLD. *Modern Criminal Procedure,* 8th ed. St. Paul, Minn.: West Publishing Co., 1994.

LAFAVE, WAYNE R., and ISRAEL, JEROLD. *Criminal Procedure §§ 21.1–21.6,* 2d ed., St. Paul, Minn.: West Publishing Co., 1992.

LANGBEIN, JOHN H. "Understanding the Short History of Plea Bargaining." *Law and Society Review* 13 (1979): 261.

SCHULHOFER, STEPHEN J. "Plea Bargaining as Disaster." *Yale Law Journal* 101 (1992): 1979.

SCOTT, ROBERT E., and STUNTZ, WILLIAM J. "Plea Bargaining as Contract." *Yale Law Journal* 101 (June 1992): 1909.

ZACHARIAS, FRED C. "Justice in Plea Bargaining." *William & Mary Law Review* 39 (March 1998): 1121.

CASES

Blackledge v. Perry, 417 U.S. 21 (1974).
Bordenkircher v. Hayes, 434 U.S. 357 (1978).
Boykin v. Alabama, 395 U.S. 238 (1969).
Brady v. United States, 397 U.S. 742 (1970).
Godinez v. Moran, 509 U.S. 389 (1993).
Henderson v. Morgan, 426 U.S. 637 (1976).
Hill v. Lockhart, 474 U.S. 52 (1985).
Hollaway v. Arkansas, 435 U.S. 475 (1978).
Kercheval v. United States, 274 U.S. 220 (1927).
Lefkowitz v. Newsome, 420 U.S. 283 (1975).
McCarthy v. United States, 394 U.S. 459 (1969).
Menna v. New York, 423 U.S. 61 (1975).
McMann v. Richardson, 397 U.S. 759 (1970).
North Carolina v. Alford, 400 U.S. 25 (1970).
Parker v. North Carolina, 397 U.S. 790 (1970).
Ricketts v. Adamson, 483 U.S. 1 (1987).
Santobello v. New York, 404 U.S. 257 (1971).
United States v. Hyde, 520 U.S. 670 (1997).
United States v. Timmreck, 441 U.S. 780 (1979).
Tollett v. Henderson, 411 U.S. 258 (1973).
United States v. Broce, 488 U.S. 563 (1989).
White v. Maryland, 373 U.S. 59 (1963).

STATUTES

Fed. R. Crim. P. 11.
Fed. R. Crim. P. 32(e).

GUILTY PLEA: PLEA BARGAINING

"There is no glory in plea bargaining," writes Professor George Fisher. "In place of a noble clash for truth, plea bargaining gives us a skulking truce . . . . Plea bargaining may be . . . the invading barbarian. But it has won all the same" (p. 859). In the late 1990s, 94 percent of the convictions of state-court felony defendants in the seventy-five largest U.S. counties were by guilty plea rather than trial (Bureau of Justice Statistics, 1999, p. iv). Similarly, 94 percent of all federal-court felony convictions were by guilty plea (Bureau of Justice Statistics, 2000, p. 51). Professor John Langbein, a prominent plea bargaining critic, suggests that Americans replace the word *all* in the Constitutional declaration, "The Trial of all Crimes . . . shall be by jury," with the words *virtually none* (Langbein, 1992). Plea bargaining has made our criminal justice system far more administrative than adjudicative in character.

Definition and types of bargaining

Plea bargaining consists of the exchange of any actual or apparent concession for a plea of guilty. Nevertheless, the term sometimes is used informally to include discussions about other things. For example, when a prosecutor offers favorable treatment to a defendant in exchange for the defendant's testimony against other suspected offenders, the prosecutor may refer to this offer as plea bargaining. Similarly, a defense attorney who approaches a prosecutor to seek a dismissal of pending criminal charges may refer to their discussion as plea bargaining. These uses of the term, however, seem imprecise. An unqualified dismissal of charges involves neither a plea nor an exchange, and a prosecutor's exchange of concessions for a suspect's or a defendant's testimony may occur without the entry of a plea of guilty.

Under the definition offered above, plea bargaining does not include pretrial diversion. Although diversion is often the result of a bargain and may be granted in exchange for concessions (for example, a defendant's agreement to participate in a specified treatment program), it does not lead to a conviction on a plea of guilty. Instead, if the defendant complies with the required conditions, the pending charges are dismissed, and the case is thus "diverted" from the criminal justice system.

It is common to distinguish between *express* and *implicit* plea bargaining. Express bargaining occurs when a defendant or his representative negotiates directly with a prosecutor, a trial judge, or (very rarely) another official concerning the benefits that may follow the entry of a plea of guilty. Implicit bargaining, by contrast, occurs without face-to-face negotiations. Officials—sentencing judges especially—establish a pattern of treating defendants who plead guilty more leniently that those who exercise the right to trial, and defendants therefore come to expect that the entry of guilty pleas will be rewarded.

The concessions officials may offer for a plea of guilty are almost unlimited. Typically, a prosecutor agrees to reduce a single charge against a defendant to a less serious offense (for example, by substituting a charge of manslaughter for one of first-degree murder), to reduce the number of charges against a defendant (for example, by dismissing four bad-check charges when the defendant pleads guilty to one), or to recommend a particular sentence to the court (one the defendant is likely to regard as more lenient than the anticipated sentence after a conviction at trial). Bargaining for a reduction in either the number or severity of criminal charges is referred to as *charge bargaining*. Bargaining for a favorable sentence recommendation by the prosecutor (or bargaining directly with a trial judge for a favorable sentence) is referred to as *sentence bargaining*.

In cases of sentence bargaining, trial judges in a substantial number of jurisdictions must either impose sentences no more severe than those recommended by prosecutors or else afford defendants an opportunity to withdraw their guilty pleas. Even when trial judges are legally free to depart from bargained prosecutorial sentence recommendations, they tend to do so infrequently.

Although charge bargaining and sentence bargaining are the most common forms of plea bargaining, they are not the only ones. In *fact bargaining*, a prosecutor agrees not to contest a defendant's version of the facts or agrees not to reveal aggravating factual circumstances to the court. This form of bargaining is likely to occur when proof of an aggravating circumstance would lead to a mandatory minimum sentence or to a more severe sentence under sentencing guidelines. A prosecutor also may agree to provide leniency to a defendant's accomplices, withhold damaging information from the court, influence the date of the defendant's sentencing, arrange for the defendant to be sent to a particular correctional institution, request that a defendant receive credit on the sentence for time served in jail awaiting trial, agree to support the defendant's application for parole, attempt to have charges in other jurisdictions dismissed, arrange for sentencing in a particular court by a particular judge, provide immunity for crimes not yet charged, or simply remain silent when a recommendation otherwise might be unfavorable.

The development of plea bargaining

Guilty pleas have been regarded as a sufficient basis for conviction from the earliest days of the common law. In treating a guilty plea as conclusive, common law nations depart from the law of most nations on the European Continent. In serious cases, these nations do not treat any form of confession as an adequate basis for dispensing with trial (although trials are likely to be simpler and to focus mostly on sentencing issues when defendants do not contest their guilt).

Compared to the long Anglo-American history of guilty pleas, the history of plea bargaining seems relatively short. The criminal justice system long has rewarded some forms of cooperation by defendants—notably, cooperation in procuring the conviction of other alleged offenders. Nevertheless, only occasional instances of plea bargaining have been discovered prior to the nineteenth century. For example, scholars who have studied eighteenth-century felony prosecutions in the Old Bailey in London report no sign of plea bargaining. To the contrary, the judges of the Old Bailey urged defendants who offered to plead guilty to reconsider and stand trial.

Although plea bargaining in felony cases before the nineteenth century was rare, nontrial dispositions in minor misdemeanor cases may have been the subject of express or implicit bargains. A misdemeanor court could permit a plea of *nolo contendere*, which allowed a defendant to submit to conviction and pay a fine without admitting guilt. Judges, however, did not allow *nolo* pleas in serious cases, and in early nineteenth-century America, guilty pleas typically accounted for a minority of felony convictions. When occasional cases of plea bargaining began to appear in reported decisions in the second half of the century, appellate judges voiced strong disapproval of the practice. Despite this disapproval, plea bargaining became routine in many places before the end of the century. Plea bargaining remained a low-visibility activity, however, until crime commission studies in the 1920s revealed how extensive it had become.

Among the historical developments that may have contributed to the growth of plea bargaining were (1) the increasing complexity of the trial process (which may have led to the greater use of nontrial procedures both for economic reasons and because officials sought to avoid the "technicalities" of trial); (2) expansion of the substantive criminal law (particularly the enactment of liquor-prohibition statutes); (3) increasing crime rates; (4) larger case loads; (5) the frequent political corruption of urban criminal courts at and after the turn of the twentieth century; (6) the greater use of professionals in the administration of criminal justice (police, prosecutors, and defense attorneys); and (7) the increasing statutory power of prosecutors.

A comparative perspective

Plea bargaining is common in England, Canada, and most other nations of the British Commonwealth. As recently as 1979, however, a noted law review article proclaimed that Germany was a "land without plea bargaining" (Langbein, 1979). Not only was the formal plea of guilty unknown in serious cases in Germany, but prosecutors and judges did not promise or negotiate for in-court confessions. Even implicit concessions were unlawful, and because German trial procedure was simpler and more straightforward than English and American procedure, concessions for confession were unnecessary.

This law review article's claim was plausible when it was made, but it did not remain accurate. European and American criminal justice systems have become more alike, and most of the movement has come on the European side. As trials in Germany and elsewhere became longer and more adversarial, as complex prosecutions for white-collar crime came before the courts in greater numbers, and as case loads increased, German prosecutors offered concessions to defendants not to contest their guilt. Italy, in fact, formally instituted a system of plea bargaining by statute. Plea bargaining remains less frequent in Continental Europe than in England and America. One German observer declares that "some kind of bargaining takes place in roughly twenty to thirty percent of all cases" (Herrmann, p. 756). Moreover, debate about the propriety of plea bargaining, which has faded in America, remains lively in Germany. The recent history of Continental jurisdictions seems to teach the same lesson as our own history. The more elaborate and adversarial the trial process becomes, the less likely it is to be used.

Operation of the plea bargaining system

As the following remarks may suggest, the day-to-day operation of the plea bargaining system cannot be neatly captured in a simple description:

In attending . . . conferences on plea bargaining, I have been struck by the extent to which people who should understand this subject . . . sound like the blind man describing the elephant. One scholar may begin by declaring that plea bargaining usually produces the same result as trial. When two experienced lawyers can use their expertise to predict the probable outcome of a trial, they are very likely to agree; and once this happens, there is no longer any need for the trial to be held. Another scholar then suggests that trial is often a capricious process whose results cannot be predicted. When a case goes to trial one either "wins big" or "loses big." The goal of plea bargaining is not to produce the *same* result as trial but to "vector" the risks of litigation and to reach a more sensible middle ground. Still another academic then contends that the object of plea bargaining is neither to produce the same results as trial nor to vector the risks of litigation. The goal is to escape altogether the irrationalities of an overly legalized trial system and . . . to achieve "substantive justice" without regard to technicalities. Then [another] lawyer . . . proclaims that all of this misses the point. A lawyer's object in plea bargaining is to take as much as possible from the other side by threat, bluster, charm, bluff, campaign contributions, personal appeals, friendship, or whatever else works. Finally some cynic . . . says that sometimes the dominant motivation is for lazy lawyers and judges to take the money and go home early. Of course, to some extent, all of these things are happening at the same time. The disagreement, if not wholly illusory, merely concerns the relative size of the trunk, tail, legs, ears, and side. (Alschuler, 1981, p. 691 n. 103)

In view of the different forms that plea bargaining may take and the many considerations that may influence it, mathematical models of plea negotiation of the sort developed by economists generally seem artificial to practicing lawyers. A few of the major operational issues are discussed below.

The "sentence differential." Defendants in America plead guilty in overwhelming numbers partly because they believe this action is likely to lead to more favorable treatment than conviction at trial. The U.S. Sentencing Commission reported that, prior to the implementation of the Federal Sentencing Guidelines, the sentences of federal defendants who pleaded guilty were 30 to 40 percent less severe than those of comparable defendants convicted at trial. The Commission's 1987 Guidelines authorized a substantial sentence reduction for a defendant's "acceptance of responsibility," and in 1992, the Commission authorized a further reduction for "assist[ance] in the prosecution of [the defendant's] own misconduct by . . . timely notifying authorities of his intention to enter a plea of guilty." The benefits of both of these "adjustments" are typically added to whatever sentencing benefits a defendant can obtain through charge bargaining and fact bargaining with prosecutors.

Most prosecutors and defense attorneys can describe cases in which defendants rejected plea bargaining offers and then were sentenced far more severely after convictions at trial. In *Bordenkircher v. Hayes*, 434 U.S. 357 (1978), for example, a defendant charged with forging an $88 check rejected the prosecutor's offer to recommend a five-year sentence in exchange for a plea of guilty. The prosecutor then re-indicted the defendant as a habitual offender, and following his conviction at trial, the defendant was sentenced

to a mandatory life term. The U.S. Supreme Court upheld the defendant's reindictment, conviction, and sentence.

At the same time, defendants may be influenced to plead guilty not only by accurate perceptions that more severe treatment will follow convictions at trial but also by inaccurate perceptions, by a desire to avoid the "process costs" of a trial (such costs as the loss of wages resulting from court appearances), by the lack of plausible defenses, and sometimes by remorse.

The significance of case load pressures. It is commonly suggested that the practical inability to provide trials to more than a small minority of defendants accounts for the predominance of plea negotiation. Some scholars, however, have sought to refute the "myth" that case load pressures "cause" plea bargaining (e.g., Heumann).

Financial pressure certainly is not the only reason for plea bargaining, and the reduction or elimination of this pressure would not automatically bring plea bargaining to an end. Prosecutors still would have incentives to bargain in cases in which they doubted their ability to secure convictions at trial and in other situations as well. At the same time, prosecutors and other officials regularly mention case load pressure as one important reason for their plea bargaining practices. The best conclusion probably is that case load pressures are indeed a cause of plea bargaining but not a necessary cause.

The principal actors in the bargaining process

Prosecutors. In making plea agreements, prosecutors are influenced by a variety of concerns. As mentioned above, one important motivation is the apparent need to induce large numbers of guilty pleas in order to keep criminal case loads within manageable proportions. This administrative concern sometimes leads prosecutors to offer greater concessions in complex cases whose trials are likely to consume substantial amounts of time than in more routine prosecutions.

In addition, prosecutors almost universally report that they consider the strength or weakness of the state's evidence an important bargaining consideration. On the theory that "half a loaf is better than none," they offer greater concessions to defendants who appear to have a substantial chance of acquittal than to defendants without plausible defenses. Indeed, in some situations, prosecutors may bluff defendants into pleas of guilty by concealing case weaknesses that would make conviction at trial impossible. The practice of "bargaining hardest when the case is weakest" may suggest that "the greatest pressures to plead guilty are brought to bear on defendants who may be innocent" (Alschuler, 1968, p. 60).

Frequently, the issue compromised through plea bargaining is not whether the prosecutor has charged "the right person." Rather, the parties compromise a legal issue (such as the admissibility of evidence) or a mixed issue of fact and law (such as intention, causation, insanity, or self-defense).

Prosecutors plainly are influenced by the equities of individual cases (the seriousness of the defendant's alleged crime, the defendant's prior criminal record, and so on). At times, prosecutors are influenced as well by their personal views of the law the defendant is accused of violating. Moreover, although the victim of the crime has been called the forgotten person in plea bargaining, many prosecutors give substantial weight to the desires of victims.

In most of the roles described above, prosecutors enter plea agreements primarily because these bargains seem to offer greater benefit to the state than the alternative of trial. On occasion, however, prosecutors bargain for more personal reasons. Through plea bargaining, a prosecutor can avoid much of the hard work of preparing cases for trial and of trying them. In addition, prosecutors can use plea bargaining to create seemingly impressive conviction rates. The desire to be liked and to enjoy comfortable relationships with coworkers also may influence plea bargaining practices. So may the desire for professional advancement either within a prosecutor's office or after leaving it. Although most prosecutors probably do not deliberately sacrifice the public interest to their personal goals, the bargaining process is beset by conflicts of interest, and prosecutors may rationalize decisions that serve primarily their own interests.

One persistent issue is the extent to which prosecutors "overcharge" in the effort to induce pleas of guilty. Do they charge more serious crimes than the circumstances of their cases seem to warrant, or a greater number of offenses than seems warranted, in an effort to induce defendants to plead guilty to the "proper" crimes? Deliberately filing unfounded charges to gain plea bargaining leverage is undoubtedly rare, but both the likelihood of plea bargaining and other strategic concerns may lead prosecutors to con-strue the available evidence and to file charges at the highest level that the evidence will permit. Prosecutors often file charges that they intend to press to conviction only when defendants insist on standing trial.

Defense attorneys. Although bargaining with unrepresented defendants once was common, it is now unusual except in traffic cases and other minor cases. In the main, defense attorneys seek to advance their clients' interests through plea bargaining in much the same way that prosecutors seek to advance the public interest. They recommend plea agreements to a client primarily when the concessions that the client has been offered seem to overbalance the client's chances of acquittal.

Again, however, there are substantial conflicts of interest. Private defense attorneys commonly are paid in advance, and their fees do not vary with the pleas their clients enter. Once an attorney has pocketed the fee, the attorney's personal interest may lie in disposing of a client's case as rapidly as possible—that is, by entering a plea of guilty. Even conscientious attorneys may find their judgments colored to some extent by this economic consideration. Moreover, not all defense attorneys are conscientious. "Cop-out lawyers" who plead virtually all of their clients guilty sometimes represent large numbers of defendants for relatively low fees. Some of these lawyers have been known to deceive their clients in the effort to induce them to plead guilty.

Appointed attorneys may suffer a similar conflict of interest. The relatively small amount that an appointed attorney is likely to receive for representing an indigent defendant may seem inadequate compensation for a trial, but this amount may seem substantially less inadequate as a fee for negotiating a plea of guilty.

Unlike private lawyers and other appointed attorneys, public defenders are salaried lawyers whose compensation does not vary with the time their individual cases require. Nevertheless, public defenders are usually overworked, and some defenders seem to view plea bargaining in all but the most exceptional cases as necessary to the effective management of their case loads.

In theory, the decision to enter a plea of guilty is the defendant's rather than the attorney's. Nevertheless, many defense attorneys speak of "client control" as an important part of the plea negotiation process. When clients are reluctant to follow their advice, these attorneys may use various forms of persuasion, including threats to discontinue their representation, in an effort to lead the clients to what the attorneys regard as the appropriate course of conduct.

The serious problem of providing effective representation in the plea bargaining process often has been neglected. Observers simply assume that defense attorneys will perform the protective role the criminal justice system assigns to them and will advise guilty pleas only when these pleas are likely to advance their clients' interests. This view of the defense attorney's role is often more romanticized than real.

Trial judges. Although prosecutors and defense attorneys are the principal actors in the plea bargaining process, judicial participation in this process is far from rare. This participation may take various forms. In some courts, trial judges conduct in-chambers conferences and offer to impose specified sentences when defendants plead guilty. In others, judges offer suggestions to prosecutors and defense attorneys, describe how they have treated certain cases in the past, or indicate a probable range of sentences.

Judges who do not participate in any form of explicit bargaining may engage in implicit bargaining by treating a defendant's guilty plea as a reason for substantially reducing the penalty imposed. Judges may also further the goals of plea bargaining by deferring routinely to prosecutorial plea bargaining decisions. Primarily on the theory that judicial plea bargaining is more coercive that prosecutorial bargaining, some authorities have argued that judges should be prohibited from engaging in this practice. This position has been adopted in rules and appellate decisions in a number of jurisdictions, including the federal courts.

Plea bargaining and sentencing guidelines

The statute that created the U.S. Sentencing Commission in 1984 directed it to promulgate policy statements concerning the acceptance or rejection of plea agreements by judges. The legislative history of this statute revealed Congress's concern that plea bargaining could undermine the equality in sentencing it sought to achieve. When the Commission submitted its Sentencing Guidelines to Congress in 1987, however, it declared: "The Commission has decided that these initial guidelines will not in general make significant changes in current plea negotiation practices . . . . The Commission will collect data on the courts' plea practices and will analyze this infor-

mation . . . . In light of this information and analysis, the Commission will seek to further regulate the plea agreement process as appropriate" (U.S. Sentencing Commission, p. 1.8). Thirteen years after this statement, the Commission apparently was still studying the issue. With one unimportant exception, state sentencing guidelines have imposed no limits on plea bargaining at all.

Sentencing guidelines have tended to transfer sentencing discretion from judges to prosecutors. Indeed, guidelines that appear to mandate tough sentences but leave plea bargaining unconstrained sometimes mimic the "good-cop, bad-cop" stratagem for obtaining confessions at the stationhouse. The sentencing commission, the "bad-cop," threatens the accused with harsh treatment. The prosecutor, the "good-cop," then offers to save the accused from the threatened guidelines sentence in exchange for a plea of guilty. Substantial sentencing discretion remains—except for defendants who exercise the right to trial.

Of course much depends on the extent to which prosecutors do approve less severe treatment than sentencing guidelines prescribe when defendants plead guilty. Federal prosecutors seem to have undercut guidelines less than state prosecutors, and although researchers have discovered at least occasional guidelines evasion through plea bargaining in every federal district studied, the extent of this evasion varies substantially from one district to the next (see Schulhofer and Nagel).

Evaluations of plea bargaining

Prior to the mid-1960s, most courts and scholars tended to ignore plea bargaining, and when discussions of the practice occurred, it usually was critical. The crime commissions of the 1920s, for example, described plea bargaining as a lazy form of prosecution that resulted in undue leniency for offenders. In 1967, however, both the American Bar Association and the President's Commission on Law Enforcement and Administration of Justice approved the concept of plea bargaining. Like these national study groups and like virtually all American courts, most scholars have tended to approve of plea negotiation, at least in broad outline. One departure from the pattern was the 1973 report of the National Advisory Commission on Criminal Justice Standards and Goals, which recommended the abolition of all forms of plea bargaining within five years.

Plea negotiation raises substantial legal and constitutional issues. For one thing, common law courts traditionally treated a confession as involuntary when it had been induced by a promise of leniency from a person in authority. The application of this rule to plea bargaining would have rendered all bargained guilty pleas invalid. Moreover, a guilty plea waives the constitutional right to trial and subordinates trial rights such as the right to confront one's accusers. Under the "doctrine of unconstitutional conditions," waivers of constitutional rights often are held invalid when they have been required as a condition for receiving favorable governmental treatment.

Despite these substantial issues, the Supreme Court under Chief Justice Earl Warren all but ignored plea bargaining during the period of its "due process revolution." One decision at the very end of the Warren Court era seemed to call certain plea bargaining practices into question (*United States v. Jackson,* 390 U.S. 570 (1968)). The Supreme Court did not pass directly upon the constitutionality of plea bargaining, however, until 1970 and 1971 when, in a series of cases, it approved the practice. The Court saw the presence of counsel as a significant safeguard of fairness in plea negotiation, and it emphasized that plea bargaining may result in a mutuality of advantage partly because the defendant limits the probable penalty while the state conserves scarce resources (*Brady v. United States,* 397 U.S. 742 (1970); *McMann v. Richardson,* 397 U.S. 759 (1970); *Santobello v. New York,* 404 U.S. 257 (1971)).

The Supreme Court has required that plea agreements be honored, and it has held that certain procedures must be followed in accepting pleas of guilty. The Court also has held that in some circumstances a trial judge constitutionally may accept a guilty plea submitted by a defendant who claims to be innocent (*North Carolina v. Alford,* 400 U.S. 25 (1970)).

Apart from the legal contentions noted above, critics of plea bargaining have advanced a number of objections to it. They have argued that plea bargaining undercuts the requirement of proof beyond a reasonable doubt and that plea negotiation is substantially more likely than trial to result in the conviction of innocent defendants. They also maintain that plea bargaining results in unjust sentencing. In their view, this practice turns the defendant's fate on a single tactical decision, which, they say, is irrelevant to desert, deterrence, or any other proper objective of criminal proceedings. Some critics maintain that plea bargaining results in unwarranted leniency for offenders and that it promotes a cynical view of the legal process.

Critics of plea bargaining also object to the shift of power to prosecutors that plea bargaining has effected, noting that sentencing judges often do little more than ratify prosecutorial plea bargaining decisions. They maintain that, even more clearly, plea bargaining makes figureheads of the probation officers who prepare presentence reports after the effective determination of sentence through prosecutorial negotiations. Plea negotiation, they say, very frequently results in the imposition of sentences on the basis of incomplete information. In light of the conflicts of interest that beset prosecutors, defense attorneys, and trial judges, the critics sometimes contend that plea negotiation subordinates both the public's interest and the defendant's to the interests of criminal justice administrators. In their view, the practice also warps both the initial formulation of criminal charges and, as defendants plead guilty to crimes less serious than those that they apparently committed, the final judicial labeling of offenses. Finally, critics suggest that plea bargaining deprecates human liberty and the purposes of the criminal sanction by "commodifying" these things—that is, treating them as instrumental economic goods.

Defenses of plea bargaining fall into three main categories. First, some defenders maintain that it is appropriate as a matter of sentencing policy to reward defendants who acknowledge their guilt. They advance several arguments in support of this position—notably, that a bargained guilty plea may manifest remorse, an acceptance of responsibility, or a willingness to enter the correctional system in a frame of mind that may afford hope for rehabilitation over a shorter period of time than otherwise would be necessary.

A second defense treats plea bargaining, not primarily as a sentencing device, but as a form of dispute resolution. Some plea bargaining advocates maintain that it is desirable to afford the defendant and the state the option of compromising factual and legal disputes. They observe that if a plea agreement did not improve the positions of both the defendant and the state, one party or the other would insist upon a trial. These defenders view plea bargaining as essentially indistinguishable from settling a civil lawsuit.

Finally, some observers defend plea bargaining on grounds of economy or necessity. Viewing plea negotiation less as a sentencing device or a form of dispute resolution than as an administrative practice, they argue that society cannot afford to provide trials to all the defendants who would demand them if guilty pleas were unrewarded—or, at least, that there are more appropriate uses for the additional resources that an effective plea bargaining prohibition would require. Sometimes these defenders add that any attempt to prohibit plea bargaining would prove ineffective and would merely drive the practice underground.

Abolition and reform efforts

The claim that plea bargaining is a "practical necessity" derives support from the high percentage of criminal cases resolved by guilty pleas. Nevertheless, plea bargaining opponents sometimes suggest that existing resources could be allocated more effectively by providing less elaborate trials to greater numbers of defendants. They point, for example, to the practices of cities in which the frequent use of informal nonjury trials has resulted in guilty-plea rates far lower than those of other jurisdictions (see Schulhofer). Moreover, they observe that it is difficult to know the extent to which trial rates would increase if plea bargaining were prohibited; a substantial number of defendants lacking plausible defenses might plead guilty without the inducements now provided by plea bargaining.

The most notable American effort to abolish plea bargaining began in Alaska in 1975. Evaluations of this reform by the Alaska Judicial Council five and fifteen years later revealed that "[p]lea bargaining effectively was prohibited in most Alaska cases for about 10 years. The prohibition did not, as far as could be measured, cause major disruption to the justice system. The screening portion of the policy resulted in better police investigations and stronger cases" (Carns and Kruse, p. 317). Although Alaska's plea bargaining prohibition led to a 30 percent increase in the number of trials, the absolute number of trials remained small. A substantial majority of convictions continued to be by guilty plea. Despite the increased trials, court delay was reduced, possibly because of a reduction in the dilatory tactics that plea bargaining had encouraged. The Judicial Council reported that the plea bargaining ban led to substantial increases in sentence severity in some crime categories but to no increases in others. Largely because supervising prosecutors in the mid-1980s did not share the critical view of plea bargaining that had impelled the

ban, plea bargaining reemerged in Alaska. The state's plea bargaining prohibition formally ended in 1993.

One plea bargaining reform—that of placing plea agreements "on the record"—has been adopted in nearly all American jurisdictions. In earlier decades, guilty-plea defendants usually were expected to (and did) declare that no promises had been made to induce their pleas. Today the practice of plea negotiation is generally avowed, and the terms of individual plea agreements are often recorded when guilty pleas are accepted.

One common focus of reform efforts is the role of the trial judge. Some reformers advocate substantially less judicial involvement in plea negotiations; others, substantially more. Some reformers also hope to limit the extent of the sentence differential between defendants who plead guilty and those who exercise the right to trial.

Some prosecutors' offices have formulated internal guidelines to regulate plea negotiation and other forms of discretionary decision-making. These guidelines have been designed both to reduce discretion and to afford office administrators greater control over their subordinates. Nevertheless, the variables that influence plea negotiation are so numerous and so complex that it is difficult to reduce them to a formula. Many guidelines—for example, those promulgated by the U.S. Department of Justice—have been so general as to provide only minimal constraints on prosecutorial discretion. Moreover, even reasonably specific guidelines sometimes have proven ineffective in practice.

Conclusion

Plea negotiation will remain central to the American criminal justice system for the foreseeable future. Nevertheless, as the President's Commission on Law Enforcement and Administration of Justice observed in 1967, "Few practices in the system of criminal justice create a greater sense of unease and suspicion than the negotiated plea of guilty" (p. 9). Plea bargaining raises fundamental issues of sentencing policy, of the propriety of compromising questions of criminal guilt, and of the use of governmental inducements to secure waivers of constitutional rights.

ALBERT W. ALSCHULER

See also COUNSEL: RIGHT TO COUNSEL; COUNSEL: ROLE OF COUNSEL; CRIMINAL JUSTICE PROCESS; CRIMINAL PROCEDURE: COMPARATIVE ASPECTS; GUILTY PLEA: ACCEPTING THE PLEA; INFORMAL DISPOSITION; PROSECUTION: COMPARATIVE ASPECTS; PROSECUTION: PROSECUTORIAL DISCRETION.

BIBLIOGRAPHY

ALSCHULER, ALBERT W. "The Prosecutor's Role in Plea Bargaining." *University of Chicago Law Review* 36 (1968): 50–112.

———. "The Defense Attorney's Role in Plea Bargaining." *Yale Law Journal* 84 (1975): 1179–1314.

———. "Plea Bargaining and Its History." *Columbia Law Review* 79 (1979): 1–43.

———. "The Changing Plea Bargaining Debate." *California Law Review* 69 (1981): 652–730.

———. "Implementing the Criminal Defendant's Right to Trial: Alternatives to the Plea Bargaining System." *University of Chicago Law Review* 50 (1983): 931–1050.

Bureau of Justice Statistics. *Felony Defendants in Large Urban Counties, 1966: State Court Processing Statistics.* U.S. Department of Justice, NCJ 176981. Washington, D.C.: U.S. Department of Justice, 1999.

———. *Compendium of Federal Justice Statistics, 1998.* U.S. Department of Justice, NCJ 180258. Washington, D.C.: U.S. Department of Justice, 2000.

CARNS, TERESA WHITE, and KRUSE, JOHN A. "Alaska's Ban on Plea Bargaining Reevaluated." *Judicature* 75 (1992): 310–317.

EISENSTEIN, JAMES, and JACOB, HERBERT. *Felony Justice: An Organizational Analysis of Criminal Courts.* Boston: Little, Brown, 1977.

FISHER, GEORGE. "Plea Bargaining's Triumph." *Yale Law Journal* 109 (2000): 857–1086.

HERRMANN, JOACHIM. "Bargaining Justice: A Bargain for German Criminal Justice?" *University of Pittsburg Law Review* 53 (1992): 755–776.

HEUMANN, MILTON. *Plea Bargaining: The Experiences of Prosecutors, Judges, and Defense Attorneys.* Chicago: University of Chicago Press, 1977.

LANGBEIN, JOHN H. "Land without Plea Bargaining: How the Germans Do It." *Michigan Law Review* 78 (1979): 204–255.

———. "On the Myth of Written Constitutions: The Disappearance of Criminal Jury Trial." *Harvard Journal of Law and Public Policy* 15 (1992): 119–127.

President's Commission on Law Enforcement and Administration of Justice, Task Force on the Administration of Justice. *Task Force Report: The Courts.* Washington, D.C.: The Commission, 1967.

RUBINSTEIN, MICHAEL L.; CLARKE, STEVENS H.; and WHITE, TERESA J. *Alaska Bans Plea Bargaining.* Washington, D.C.: U.S. Department of Justice, National Institute of Justice, 1980.

SCHULHOFER, STEPHEN J. "Is Plea Bargaining Inevitable?" *Harvard Law Review* 97 (1984): 1037–1107.

SCHULHOFER, STEPHEN J., and NAGEL, ILENE H. "Plea Negotiations under the Federal Sentencing Guidelines: Guideline Circumvention and Its Dynamics in the Post-Mistretta Period." *Northwestern University Law Review* 91 (1997): 1284–1316.

U.S. Department of Justice, Law Enforcement Assistance Administration, National Advisory Commission on Criminal Justice Standards and Goals. *Courts.* Washington, D.C.: The Commission, 1973.

U.S. Sentencing Commission. *Sentencing Guidelines and Policy Statements.* Washington, D.C.: U.S. Gov. Printing Office, 1987.

CASES

Bordenkircher v. Hayes, 434 U.S. 357 (1978).
Brady v. United States, 397 U.S. 742 (1970).
McMann v. Richardson, 397 U.S. 759 (1970).
North Carolina v. Alford, 400 U.S. 25 (1970).
Santobello v. New York, 404 U.S. 257 (1971).
United States v. Jackson, 390 U.S. 570 (1968).

GUNS, REGULATION OF

There are approximately as many guns in civilian hands in the United States as there are people, more than 250 million (Kleck, pp. 96–97). Most are rifles and shotguns used primarily for recreation, but a growing proportion, perhaps one-third, are handguns, which are usually purchased for personal or home defense. Between the late 1960s and late 1970s, violent crime rates in the United States increased very rapidly. The robbery rate increased nearly six-fold, and the murder rate nearly doubled, peaking at about 10 in 100,000 in 1979 (Polsby). During this same period, the American public rapidly acquired an inventory of tens of millions of new handguns, as well as even more rifles and shotguns. Many opinion leaders blamed the escalating rates of violent crime on the increased private ownership of firearms, and proposed various kinds of gun control laws to deal with the problem.

Four main policies constitute *gun control* as the term is used in common conversation:

- Laws and regulations meant to prohibit, or to impose regulatory burdens on, civilian importation, manufacture, sale, or possession of certain weapons or classes of weapons;
- Laws requiring people who want to buy firearms to wait out a "cooling off" period between purchasing a weapon and taking delivery of it;
- Laws requiring people who want to buy firearms to undergo background checks to ensure that they are not legally ineligible for some reason, such as having a criminal record, to purchase or own such weapons;
- Efforts by municipalities and occasionally by private philanthropies to buy guns from members of the public at a stated price with no questions asked (often called gun buyback programs).

Many other sorts of efforts by the criminal justice system to deter or minimize the abuse of firearms, such as aggravating punishments for the use of a firearm in the commission of a crime, or directly confronting and discouraging potential abusers of firearms, are practically never called "gun control." "Gun control," in other words, usually refers to the set of public policies whose main purpose is suppress or slow down the *supply* of firearms to the general public. It usually does not include the (much less politically controversial) policies meant to reduce potential abusers' *demand* for firearms.

Gun control laws usually are based on the assumption that there is a regular relationship between the availability of weapons to members of the general public and the rate at which crimes, especially homicides and suicides, occur in a given population. Numerous scholars have made some version of this claim (e.g., Zimring; Cook; Kellermann and Reay; Duggan). Note that this claim is not that better-armed populations are automatically more criminous than less well armed populations, as there may be many other differences, such as age, income, wealth, education, and so on, that much more powerfully predict extreme deviant behavior than any "access to a gun" variable could ever do. Rather, the contention is that if one could hold constant the characteristics of a population and vary only the accessibility of firearms, one should expect to see higher rates of murder and suicide among the better-armed, and lower rates among the less well armed populations.

More guns, more crime

The most important and influential evidence for the claim that guns are a vector of violent crime is found in the work of Zimring and Hawkins, whose comparison of the crime, violence, and lethal outcomes rates of various countries leads them to the conclusion that forms the title of their study: *Crime Is Not the Problem*. What is the problem, then? Guns—at least as a first approximation. For example, if one compares the rates of assault or robbery in the United States with other Anglophone countries (e.g., Australia, New Zealand, Canada, England, and Wales), America's statistics appear normal; most of those countries' rates of crime are quite similar to that of the United States. Similarly, if one compares burglary rates in London and New York City, one finds rather similar numbers. But in terms of lethal outcomes of crimes—crimes that end with somebody getting killed—the U.S. experience is far more deadly than that of other English-speaking countries. Polsby and Kates (1998) argue that differences in the populations and cultures of these countries offer an explanation for this phenomenon.

Prohibition

For purposes of the present discussion prohibition means either legally forbidding civilian ownership of weapons of a certain class or heavily burdening ownership with the practical effect of prohibition. In the second sense, machine guns and artillery pieces have been prohibited by federal law even though a few civilians—collectors and hobbyists—comply with the onerous legal requirements that are imposed on the possession of such weapons. In the first sense, sawed-off shotguns are prohibited by federal law; handguns by the laws of a number of cities such as Washington, D.C., or Chicago and a few of its northern suburbs (Morton Grove, Winnetka, Evanston, Highland Park); Saturday night specials (cheap, easily concealed handguns), variously defined, by the laws of a few jurisdictions; and so-called assault weapons, variously defined, by federal law and the laws of a number of states.

The two principal questions posed by any prohibition law is whether it will have its intended effect and, if so, whether it will have unintended effects. Both these questions have theoretical and empirical aspects.

Intended effect. It is reasonable to ask why one should, a priori, expect weapons prohibitions to work at all. Prohibitions are enforced by means of criminal penalties, but the penalty assessed for violating a weapon law as such will always be minor in comparison to the penalty that is specified for using a weapon to commit a murder or armed robbery. Persons who are not deterred by the greater penalty are not likely, as a rule, to be deterred by the lesser. The entire freight of behavior modification that such laws can be expected to effect should be on people who are highly unlikely to utilize weapons in crime. Supposing that prohibitory laws have any effect at all, one should expect them first of all and most significantly to affect the behavior of persons who are disposed voluntarily to obey the law—who obey as a habit of social life and not as a calculation about the probability of being apprehended and punished in any given instance. Equally, one should expect to see the tardiest and most trivial obedience to such laws among persons who are not disposed to obedience to law. Accordingly, in the real world of weapons prohibition one should expect to see, if any effect at all, a perverse change in the distribution of weapons in society, with those least disposed to crime disarming themselves and those most disposed to crime disarming themselves, if at all, at a slower rate. Moreover, if it is true that weapons, as a tool of criminals, become more valuable as they can be introduced into transactions where defenders (shopkeepers, homeowners, and so on) are increasingly less likely themselves to be armed, one should actually expect prohibitory laws to "cause" a certain amount of crime. A more circumspect conclusion is reached by Kleck and Patterson (1993), whose study of the effect of nineteen different gun control laws on gun ownership levels and rates of violent crimes, controlling for numerous potential confounding factors, found no consistent evidence for the effectiveness of these laws.

Unintended consequences. The most ambitious econometric study ever attempted of the effects of gun control on crime reached the conclusion that liberalizing the terms on which civilians might carry concealed weapons had a significant and constructive effect on the rate of murders, robberies, burglaries, and rapes (Lott and Mustard). The explanation for this effect seems, in fact, to be the oldest theory of modern criminology, namely that of general deterrence (Beccaria). As predatory behavior becomes more expensive, there will be, other things equal, less predatory behavior. The implication is that restricting civilian access to firearms can reasonably

be called a "cause" of crime, at least certain kinds of crime—the kinds that involve interpersonal confrontations in which direct intimidation is a factor.

Suicide. Suicide differs from other homicide in that perpetrators more seldom have a background of deviant behavior. Suicide is overwhelmingly a phenomenon of the old and the sick; in fact, suicide rates are the highest in segments of the population in which homicide rates are the lowest—and vice versa. National rates of suicide are among the most stable of public health statistics. The suicide rate in the United States is approximately 11 or 12 in 100,000 of population, and handguns have been rapidly increasing as the method of choice for suicide. A number of studies have attempted to relate an individual's access to handguns to his probability of committing suicide (see Kleck). The methodological problem for such studies is that of causation: does possession of a gun increase a person's likelihood of suicide, or do people who mean to commit suicide go out and get guns? It may be the case that access to a firearm modestly increases the risk of suicide. Other means of self-destruction, though numerous, are imperfect substitutes for firearms, which are cheap, effective, and easy to use. This fact might also serve to explain why handguns are increasingly becoming the instrument of choice for suicides. There appears to be negligible evidence, however, that gun control laws can realistically be used to keep weapons out of the hands of those contemplating suicide.

Waiting periods

Laws that require purchasers of firearms to wait for one or more days between purchasing weapons and taking possession of them are based on the idea that a certain number of homicidal attacks are impulsive, rage-driven affairs, and that a cooling-off period might lower the danger of this sort of homicide. Lott found no evidence that waiting periods did in fact affect rates of homicide or other crimes, nor did Kopel in an earlier study. If there is any evidence in favor of this form of gun control, it is anecdotal in nature.

Gun buy-back programs

The premise of programs in which people turn in unwanted weapons to authorities, with no questions asked—sometimes in exchange for cash or something of value—is that firearms are, in effect, mischief waiting to happen, and that the fewer firearms in civilian hands, the better. Buy-back programs have been favorites of newspaper editorialists and anti-gun advocates (e.g., Editorial, *Chicago Tribune*; Seibel), but even some scholars generally friendly to gun control (e.g., Callahan, Rivara, and Koepsal; Romero, Wintemute, and Vernick), have found no credible evidence that such programs affect rates of crime or have a favorable impact on public safety.

Background checks

The federal Brady law requires purchasers of handguns to submit to background checks prior to taking delivery of a handgun, and the laws of some states, like Illinois, make background checks mandatory for all firearms purchases. The purpose of these laws is to establish that the purchaser is not a criminal, fugitive, known substance abuser, or in other ways legally disqualified from possessing a firearm. So long as the background check is carried out within a few minutes, such laws impose little burden on gun buyers. For this reason, they have not been especially controversial. There appears, however, to be no persuasive evidence that such laws affect crime or indeed that they have any impact on criminals' acquisition of weapons. As a leading researcher on the subject has said, there are apparently "serious limits on the results one can reasonably expect from controls applied only to voluntary (nontheft) transfers such as gun sales. One cannot substantially reduce the flow of water through a sieve by blocking just a few of the holes, especially if one cannot block the largest ones" (Kleck, p. 93).

Conclusion

Gun control laws invite two questions. First, how do firearms laws affect the distribution of guns in a given population; second, how does the pattern of firearms dispersion in that population affect its likelihood of engaging in crime. It must be said that there is relatively little evidence in the United States for the proposition that laws can effectively get people to give up guns they already own or to refrain from acquiring new weapons. The relationship between firearms dispersion, crime, and violence is difficult to sort out. While criminals often use guns to commit crimes, seek firearms for this purpose, and probably commit a different number and kind of crime when they have guns than when they do

not, it is undeniably also true that guns are effective in the same applications for which police officers use them—deterring aggression. One should expect to see guns where one sees criminals, but also where honest people are fearful of criminals. There is little persuasive evidence in favor of gun control as a crime reduction technique and some probability that, in some circumstances, additional regulation might have a perverse effect.

DANIEL D. POLSBY

See also FEAR OF CRIME; PREVENTION: ENVIRONMENTAL AND TECHNOLOGICAL STRATEGIES; PUBLIC OPINION AND CRIME; VIOLENCE.

BIBLIOGRAPHY

BECCARIA, CESARE. *An Essay on Crimes and Punishments* (1764). Boston: International Pocket Library, 1983.
CALLAHAN, CHARLES M.; RIVARA, FREDERICK P.; and KOEPSAL, THOMAS D. "Money for Guns: Evaluation of the Seattle Gun Buy-Back Program." *Public Health Reports* (July 1994): 472.
COOK, PHILIP J. "The Technology of Personal Violence." *Crime and Justice, Annual Review of Research.* Edited by Michael Tonry. Chicago: University of Chicago Press, 1991.
DUGGAN, MARK. *More Crime, More Guns* (National Bureau of Economic Research working paper no. W7967, October, 2000).
Editorial. "317 Down, Millions More to Go." *Chicago Tribune*, 29 December 1993, sec. 1, p. 14.
KELLERMANN, ARTHUR L., and REAY, DONALD T. "Protection or Peril? An Analysis of Firearms-Related Deaths in the Home." *New England Journal of Medicine* 314 (1986): 1557–1560.
KLECK, GARY. *Targeting Guns.* Hawthorne, N.Y.: Aldine de Gruyter, 1997.
KOPEL, DAVID B. *Why Gun Waiting Periods Threaten Public Safety.* Golden, Colo: Independence Institute, 1993.
LOTT, JOHN R., JR. *More Guns, Less Crime.* Chicago: University of Chicago Press, 1998.
LOTT, JOHN R., JR., and MUSTARD, DAVID. "Crime, Deterrence and Right-to-Carry Concealed Handguns." *Journal of Legal Studies* 26 (1997): 1–68.
LUDWIG, JENS. "Gun Self-Defense and Deterrence." *Journal of Crime and Justice* 27 (2000): 363–417.
POLSBY, DANIEL. "The False Promise of Gun Control." *Atlantic Monthly* (March, 1994), pp. 57–70.

POLSBY, DANIEL, and KATES, DON. B., JR. "American Homicide Exceptionalism." *University of Colorado Law Review* 69 (1998): 969–1007.

ROMERO, MICHAEL P.; WINTEMUTE, GAREN J.; and VERNICK, JON S. "Characteristics of a Gun Exchange Program, and an Assessment of Potential Benefits." *Injury Prevention* 4 (1998): 206–210.

SEIBEL, TOM. "Rodriguez Touts Gun Turn-In." *Chicago Sun-Times,* 25 January 1994, p. 6.

ZIMRING, FRANKLIN. "Is Gun Control Likely to Control Violent Killings?" *University of Chicago Law Review* 35 (1968): 721–737.

ZIMRING, FRANKLIN, and HAWKINS, GORDON. *Crime is Not the Problem.* New York: Oxford University Press, 1998.

H

HABEAS CORPUS

Habeas corpus is shorthand for a variety of *writs* or legal pleadings seeking to bring a person within a court's power. Of the many habeas corpus writs, the most celebrated and significant is the writ of habeas corpus *ad subjiciendum*, the "Great Writ," which requires an official or person who holds another in custody to produce the person so that a court can inquire into the legality of the detention. In contemporary practice, this writ is most commonly used to challenge the legality of criminal convictions and sentences, though it is also used to challenge the legality of pretrial detentions and the legality of custody in other settings, including immigration, mental health, and military contexts. Other habeas writs are available for distinct purposes, such as to make a prisoner available to testify in court (*ad testificandum*) or to ensure that a prisoner is brought before the proper court for prosecution (*ad prosequendum*).

Origins and history

Habeas corpus in its most familiar form (*ad subjiciendum*) has played an important role in Anglo-American history as a safeguard of individual liberty. Indeed, the availability of habeas relief was at the center of the struggle between Crown and Parliament in the seventeenth century, when Parliament objected to lawless detentions for which no judicial remedies were forthcoming. Infamous deprivations of liberty led to extensive criticism and protest, as English citizens were often held for significant periods without trial and without recourse. Ultimately, Parliament prevailed with the enactment of the Habeas Corpus Act of 1679, which specifically authorized (indeed, required) habeas relief under certain circumstances with substantial penalties for noncompliance.

The English protection of the writ of habeas corpus was quite influential during the framing period of the United States, with both states and the federal government adopting statutory and constitutional guarantees of the writ. Indeed, the federal constitutional guarantee prohibiting the suspension of habeas corpus is one of only two federal constitutional provisions that explicitly refers to and protects a particular remedy ("the Privilege of the Writ of Habeas Corpus shall not be suspended, unless when in Cases of Rebellion or Invasion the public Safety may require it" (Art. I, §9)).

Constitutional protection of the writ of habeas corpus

One central question surrounding the suspension clause concerns the nature and scope of its protection. As an initial matter, the clause does not declare that the writ of habeas corpus must be made available (as was proposed but not adopted during the constitutional convention), but rather suggests that once established it cannot be withdrawn (barring rebellion or invasion). In *Ex Parte Bollman*, 8 U.S. (4 Cranch) 75 (1807), Chief Justice Marshall nonetheless suggested that Congress's creation of habeas jurisdiction in the Judiciary Act of 1789 was likely the result of its perceived "obligation" to give "life" to the constitutional provision. Under Chief Justice Marshall's reasoning, the clause protects federal judicial power to grant writs of habeas corpus, though many scholars have argued that the clause was intended to protect state judicial power from federal intervention. When a state court sought to secure the release of an abolitionist who had been convicted in a federal proceeding of aiding and abetting a fugitive slave, the Court decisively rejected the notion that state habeas enjoys any federal constitutional protection, insisting instead that state courts lack power to interfere with persons imprisoned under the authority of the federal government (*Ableman v. Booth*, 62 U.S. (21 How.) 506 (1858)). That Congress appears to have initially extended the writ to federal prisoners alone suggests that the suspension clause, at least as an initial matter, was not understood to afford protections to persons held in state custody; recent scholarship, though, challenges the notion that the Judiciary Act of 1789 should be understood to have deprived federal courts of habeas power with respect to state prisoners.

During the early nineteenth century, Congress gradually extended the scope of federal habeas jurisdiction to certain classes of state prisoners in response to specific threats to federal power. When South Carolinians declared federal tariffs unconstitutional at the climax of the nullification controversy, President Andrew Jackson feared that federal officers seeking to enforce the tariffs would be subject to state interference. On President Jackson's initiative, Congress authorized federal judges to exercise habeas jurisdiction in cases involving federal or state prisoners confined for acts committed in pursuance of federal law. Less than a decade later, following a diplomatic crisis that ensued when New York tried a British citizen who had attempted to prevent American assistance to Canadian rebels during the winter revolt of 1837–1838, Congress again expanded federal habeas jurisdiction to permit federal review of cases involving federal or state prisoners who are subjects or citizens of a foreign state.

The most significant statutory expansion of the writ occurred in the wake of the Civil War. The Judiciary Act of 1867 extended the writ to all persons, federal or state, restrained of liberty in violation of federal law. Today, the term "federal habeas" is invariably used to describe challenges by state prisoners, as federal habeas jurisdiction for federal prisoners has essentially been replaced by a separate comprehensive federal postconviction scheme whose substantive scope is basically congruent with the habeas remedy that it displaced (28 U.S.C. § 2255).

An additional question surrounding the suspension clause concerns which branch of government can withhold the writ in response to rebellion or invasion. This question took on great significance at the beginning of the Civil War. Just over two weeks after shots were fired on Fort Sumpter, President Abraham Lincoln issued an order to Commanding General Winfield Scott permitting him to suspend the writ. When John Merryman was subsequently arrested for his participation in the destruction of bridges in Baltimore, military officials refused to respond to a writ before Chief Justice Taney. The Chief Justice wrote a scathing opinion denying the legality of President Lincoln's purported suspension (*Ex parte Merryman*, 17 F. Cas. 144 (C.C.D. Md. 1861) (No. 9487)), arguing that it is Congress and not the president in whom the Constitution vests such power. President Lincoln publicly disagreed with the opinion (and did not honor it), and Congress subsequently declared its retroactive approval of President Lincoln's military actions. In 1863, Congress also specifically authorized President Lincoln to suspend the writ whenever in the course of the "present rebellion" he judged it to be necessary.

The scope of federal habeas corpus

The most controversial question surrounding federal habeas corpus concerns its appropriate role. This question has two components: how has federal habeas corpus functioned historically and how should it function today? The English version of the writ secured by the Habeas Corpus Act of 1679 primarily afforded a mechanism for challenging unauthorized pretrial detentions. The earliest habeas practice in the United States, both state and federal, likewise focused on defendants' rights against warrantless detentions and denials of bail. But throughout the nineteenth and early twentieth centuries, prisoners sought, and in some cases received, habeas review of claims challenging criminal convictions.

Scholars disagree about the scope of federal habeas review during this period. One prominent scholar, Professor Paul Bator, famously insisted that federal habeas was simply not available to persons convicted by courts of competent jurisdiction; though federal habeas courts sometimes entertained an expansive conception of "jurisdiction," on Bator's view federal habeas was not generally a forum for revisiting legal or factual determinations after trial.

More recent scholarship asserts that federal habeas has always permitted some post-conviction review of federal constitutional claims. One of the leading treatise authors on federal habeas, Professor James Liebman, maintains that the scope of federal habeas review during the nineteenth and early twentieth centuries was intimately connected to the availability of other forms of federal review of federal claims. On this view, the U.S. Supreme Court continually adjusted the scope of habeas review in both the state and federal prisoner cases based on whether some other federal jurisdictional vehicle was available to address substantial federal claims. In the federal prisoner context, for example, this thesis explains why the scope of federal habeas for federal prisoners diminished after Congress established federal appellate review of criminal convictions in 1891. In the state prisoner context, this account explains why the scope of habeas corpus increased when federal review as of right through writ of error became largely discretionary.

Yet another influential view argues that federal habeas review has always been quite broad, but that state prisoners rarely prevailed because of the narrowness of federal constitutional protections. According to this position, denials of habeas relief in landmark cases such as *Frank v. Magnum,* 237 U.S. 309 (1915), in which the Court rejected a claim of mob domination and jury intimidation at trial, were predicated on the Court's narrow readings of the due process clause. Frank lost, on this view, not because the Court refused to consider the merits of his constitutional claim via federal habeas, but because, as a matter of due process, state-court review of a mob-domination claim was constitutionally sufficient. Hence, when federal constitutional protections for state prisoners increased dramatically during the 1960s, the significance of federal habeas increased as well, and not necessarily because the nature of federal habeas itself had been altered.

The dispute surrounding the historic role of federal habeas is not merely academic. Although habeas corpus has both statutory and constitutional roots, the Court has repeatedly focused on historical practice in deciding the appropriate reach of the writ. Indeed, in a much-publicized decision concerning the scope of federal habeas review, two factions of the Court offered conflicting historical accounts to support their respective views as to whether federal habeas courts should defer to state court determinations of mixed law-fact determinations (*Wright v. West,* 505 U.S. 277 (1992)).

The emergence of modern federal habeas corpus

By the mid-twentieth century, the Court cemented federal habeas's role as a vehicle for challenging the lawfulness of state criminal convictions (*Brown v. Allen,* 344 U.S. 443 (1953)). Most importantly, the Court indicated that state court legal determinations were not binding on federal habeas courts, and that such courts should address federal constitutional claims *de novo.*

At the time *Brown* was decided, federal habeas review remained quite limited, because few federal constitutional protections had been extended to state prisoners. But during the 1960s, the Court "constitutionalized" criminal procedure and read the due process clause of the Fourteenth Amendment to encompass virtually all of the protections of the Fourth, Fifth, Sixth, and Eighth Amendments. In addition, the Court adopted relatively lenient rules concerning state procedural defaults. The Court characterized federal habeas review as an independent civil action rather than as a formal appeal of a state court judgment and refused to apply the independent and adequate state ground doctrine to bar procedurally defaulted claims on federal habeas. Instead, the Court held that if a state inmate failed to properly raise a federal constitutional claim in state court, the issue would nonetheless be cognizable on federal habeas unless the inmate had deliberately bypassed state procedural rules (*Fay v. Noia,* 372 U.S. 391 (1963)). As a result, federal habeas increasingly became a robust forum for vindicating the federal constitutional claims of state prisoners. Not surprisingly in light of these developments, the sheer volume of federal habeas petitions grew dramatically in the four decades following *Brown.* Although Justice Jackson had complained of a "haystack" of federal habeas petitions in *Brown,* the 541 petitions filed in 1951 had become 12,000 by 1990.

Relationship of federal habeas to state postconviction

The availability, scope, and significance of state postconviction review has changed dramatically over the past half century. Prior to the 1950s, state postconviction remedies consisted almost entirely of common law writs, most prominently habeas corpus and coram nobis. These writs did not generally afford state inmates a meaningful opportunity to adjudicate federal constitutional issues.

State habeas corpus, like its federal counterpart, had originally served primarily as a vehicle for challenging pretrial or extrajudicial detentions. When state inmates invoked habeas to challenge their continued detention after conviction, state courts did not view the writ as a basis for revisiting every legal issue bearing on the conviction. Rather, state courts often described their inquiry as confined to "jurisdictional" questions and they repeated the black letter rule that habeas relief was available only if the challenged conviction was not merely "voidable" but absolutely "void." The jurisdictional limitation rendered state habeas an unpromising means of addressing federal constitutional claims because such claims were not ordinarily thought to undermine the basic authority of the trial court to conduct the proceedings leading to the challenged conviction.

Coram nobis, on the other hand, was the traditional postconviction mechanism for revisiting convictions based on non-record facts. Coram nobis was available in the court of conviction—not in a reviewing or appellate court—and it did not generally extend to pure legal error. Moreover, coram nobis did not afford relief unless the newly found facts would have resulted in a different judgment. Accordingly state coram nobis remedies also seemed an unlikely means of vindicating federal constitutional rights.

The problem of state enforcement of federal constitutional rights, though, was not simply a matter of putting ancient writs to modern uses. In the first half of the century, states seemed less than zealous in protecting defendants' rights. Perceived state hostility to federal rights and irregularities in state criminal procedures—including the absence of effective postconviction review—no doubt encouraged federal courts to review state convictions for constitutional error through federal habeas corpus.

As federal habeas review of federal constitutional claims became more common and intrusive with the Warren Court's extraordinary expansion of due process rights for state prisoners, states had strong incentives to develop more extensive postconviction procedures. These procedures protected state convictions from federal review in two important respects: first, state fact-finding in postconviction would ordinarily earn deference in federal court, allowing state courts to shape the future federal habeas litigation; second, additional postconviction opportunities for state prisoners meant additional opportunities to enforce state procedural rules, leading to increased forfeitures in federal court.

The expansion of state postconviction review, though welcome in some respects, has unfortunately also delayed federal habeas review of federal claims. Of course, some delay is unavoidable if state courts are to assume initial responsibility for adjudicating federal rights; if states fail to provide a forum for non-record claims, inmates must litigate these claims in the first instance on federal habeas. But state postconviction review also delays federal review of record claims that could be fully adjudicated in the state courts on direct appeal (without any additional recourse to state postconviction). Delays between state court resolution and federal habeas resolution of record claims contributes to the perception—and reality—that federal habeas undermines the finality of state convictions.

Overall, the dynamic interplay between federal habeas and state postconviction has produced a tremendously burdensome system for reviewing federal claims. Concerns about the adequacy of state criminal justice systems led to the recognition of federal constitutional rights and the expansion of the federal remedy of habeas corpus. Robust federal habeas in turn led to widespread adoption of extensive state postconviction proceedings, primarily to limit intrusive federal court review. The introduction of extensive state postconviction proceedings substantially delays federal review of federal claims and increases the costs of ultimately granting relief in federal court. Recognizing these costs, Congress and the Court have in recent years erected labyrinthine obstacles to merits review on federal habeas.

The proceduralization of federal habeas corpus

Just as the Warren Court's "revolution" of criminal procedure became a target of extensive criticism, federal habeas's role in implementing the revolution also came under attack. Some critics argued that federal habeas had become excessively intrusive on legitimate state interests, notably the finality of state criminal convictions and comity for state courts. Other critics noted that the habeas remedy had strayed far from its historic common law roots as primarily a pretrial remedy. Despite regular efforts to limit federal habeas legislatively in the three decades after *Brown*, though, Congress refused to enact any meaningful habeas reform.

Nonetheless, the Supreme Court took the lead in reshaping and restricting the scope of the habeas forum. First, the Court imposed stricter rules governing procedural defaults, shifting the burden to petitioners to justify failing to comply with state procedural rules. These strict rules applied even in capital cases, with the result that a death-row inmate could lose all federal review of his constitutional claims based on his attorney's filing a state habeas appeal three days late (*Coleman v. Thompson*, 501 U.S. 722 (1991)). In addition, the Court adopted more onerous requirements for filing both same-claim and new-claim successive habeas petitions, essentially limiting state prisoners to one opportunity to litigate federal claims—not one opportunity to litigate each federal claim—in federal court even if new facts or new law subsequently confirmed or revealed additional constitutional violations.

Perhaps the most significant Court-initiated reform concerned its limitation on the retroactive availability of "new" constitutional law on federal habeas. Prior to the mid-1960s, the Court drew no important distinctions between inmates' claims seeking the benefit of new law and those seeking vindication of clearly established or long-standing constitutional doctrines. All decisions enforcing the constitutional rights of criminal defendants were simply presumed to have full retroactive effect. But the unprecedented expansion of criminal defendants' rights after the incorporation decisions prompted the Court to limit the impact of the growing constitutional criminal protections. At first, the Court adopted a balancing test that led to the retroactive application of some but not all of the new constitutional decisions. More recently, the Court adopted a presumptive rule prohibiting petitioners from seeking the benefit of new law on habeas; under the Court's approach, a federal habeas petitioner can avoid the nonretroactivity bar against new-law claims only if the rule sought (or established in a recent decision) renders the underlying conduct of the petitioner unpunishable or represents a "watershed" contribution to the criminal justice system that substantially increases the reliability of the guilt-innocence determination (*Teague v. Lane*, 489 U.S. 288 (1989)).

The nonretroactivity doctrine has been of extraordinary practical significance. The Court's expansive conception of "new" law, which focuses on whether a petitioner's claim was "clearly dictated" by prior precedent, has blocked retroactive application of many decisions far less dramatic or path-breaking than the Warren Court rulings that had given rise to the doctrine. At the same time, courts have construed the exceptions quite narrowly. Few new rules prohibit states from punishing certain conduct at all, and, in the numerous retroactivity cases litigated at the Supreme Court level, the Court has declined to identify any new rule as sufficiently fundamental to command retroactive application.

By the early 1990s, the Court's procedural default, successive petition, and nonretroactivity decisions had significantly eroded state inmates' efforts to receive federal review of the federal lawfulness of their convictions via federal habeas corpus. In addition, the infamous 1995 bombing of the Alfred P. Murrah Federal Building in Oklahoma City led Congress to substantially revisit the scope of federal habeas review for the first time in over 125 years. The resulting legislation, the Anti-Terrorism and Effective Death Penalty Act (AEDPA), was signed within days of the first anniversary of the Oklahoma City bombing. Whereas the previous habeas statute had extended the writ to all persons held in violation of the Constitution or laws or treaties of the United States, the AEDPA additionally requires that the challenged state adjudication "resulted in a decision that was contrary to, or involved an unreasonable application of, clearly established Federal law, as determined by the Supreme Court of the United States" (28 U.S.C. §2254(d)). The Court has recently construed this language as replacing the de novo standard articulated in *Brown* (*Williams v. Taylor*, 526 U.S. 1050 (1999)). According to the Court, this language requires federal habeas courts to sustain "reasonable" but "wrong" state court adjudications of federal rights. In addition, the AEDPA imposes a new limitations period on filing federal habeas petitions and further cuts habeas review of successive petitions.

The Court-initiated procedural obstacles to habeas review, together with the new "reasonableness" standard of review of the AEDPA, have transformed federal habeas into an enormously complex forum. Instead of debating whether a state prisoner's conviction or sentence violates federal constitutional norms, the parties and federal courts devote extraordinary resources attempting to resolve questions of procedural default, retroactivity, and the "reasonableness" of state court decision-making. In some respects, the current scope of federal habeas for state prisoners could be viewed as a compromise between advocates of federal supervision over state criminal processes and defenders of state autonomy. The compromise protects the fundamental jurisdictional power of the federal courts to review unconstitutional convictions of state prisoners. Yet the compromise increasingly saddles such jurisdiction with arcane and often insurmountable procedural barriers. For many critics, this state of affairs should be lamented because it sustains the appearance of extensive federal supervision of federal rights despite the reality of truncated and increasingly limited review.

Habeas corpus and capital punishment

The enormous growth of procedural obstacles on federal habeas, as well as the new limitations period established in the AEDPA, have made it extremely difficult for unrepresented petitioners, acting *pro se*, to receive federal review of their constitutional claims. As a result, the bulk of meaningful federal habeas litigation now involves death-sentenced inmates, for whom Congress recently established a statutory right to counsel on federal habeas. Death-row petitioners often focus their habeas litigation on the federal lawfulness of state death penalty procedures. When the Court first subjected state death penalty schemes to federal constitutional scrutiny in the early 1970s, the popular perception was that the Court was deciding the constitutional rightness or wrongness of the death penalty as a punishment. In 1976, the Court made clear that the death penalty was a permissible punishment so long as states developed adequate systems for ensuring its reliable and equitable administration.

The notorious subsequent history reveals the development of extremely intricate, difficult-to-apply doctrines that have plunged states and petitioners into a morass of confusing litigation concerning states' obligations in their administration of the death penalty. This litigation eventually arrives in federal court with the result that federal habeas has become less a broad forum for enforcing the federal rights of state prisoners generally than the inevitable battleground for enforcing or overturning state death sentences and elaborating the meaning of the Eighth Amendment in capital cases. The drafters of the AEDPA undoubtedly understood this when they equated "effective death penalty" with diminished federal habeas corpus.

The role of federal habeas in supervising state death penalty schemes has also prompted a reexamination of the scope of habeas review. Throughout American legal history, as a matter of black letter law, federal habeas could not serve as a forum for relitigating the accuracy of criminal convictions. But death-row inmates insisted that the difference in kind between capital punishment and imprisonment should require federal habeas relief where extremely strong evidence of actual innocence surfaces after trial and the state courts refuse to provide any posttrial mechanism for evaluating new evidence of innocence. In making this argument, capital defense lawyers borrowed from Judge Henry Friendly's influential article insisting that innocence should not be irrelevant to the availability of federal habeas review. But whereas Judge Friendly focused on innocence as a limiting principle, to restore habeas to its purported roots as an exceptional remedy, advocates for capital defendants sought to establish actual innocence as a separate and independent basis for habeas relief. In a much-observed case, the Court ultimately denied habeas relief to a death-sentenced inmate whose only claim was his actual innocence of the crime (*Herrera v. Collins*, 506 U.S. 390 (1993)). But the Court's decision ultimately turned on the petitioner's lack of sufficient new evidence of innocence, and the Court did not dispositively rule on the cognizability of such "bare-innocence" claims.

The future of federal habeas for state prisoners

Federal habeas corpus for state prisoners is presently in a precarious position. For its critics, federal postconviction review of state criminal convictions is an unjustifiable intrusion into state criminal justice systems. Such review subjects state court decisions to review in the lower federal courts (as opposed to the U.S. Supreme Court) often years after trial. To this extent, current federal habeas corpus departs from the traditional norm of hierarchical appeals to a final court in a timely manner. Moreover, federal habeas review as a practical matter has become a vehicle for extensive federal intervention in state death penalty practices.

For its defenders, federal habeas provides the lone meaningful opportunity for federal courts to have the last say regarding the content of federal law. Recognizing that discretionary Supreme Court review is not a practical means of supervising state court compliance with federal constitutional norms, federal habeas serves as an essential surrogate to review by the Court.

As the Court and Congress impose new and substantial procedural obstacles to federal habeas review, there is less reason to believe that federal habeas will provide much incentive for state courts, in the famous words of Justice Harlan, "to toe the constitutional mark" (*Mackey v. United States,* 401 U.S. 667 (1971)). The increased proceduralization will also take federal habeas far from its origins as a broad means of inquiring into the lawfulness of custody. In his ringing dissent decrying the Court's refusal to grant the writ in the face of a mob-dominated trial, Justice Holmes insisted that "*habeas corpus* cuts through all forms and goes to the very tissue of the structure" and "comes in from the outside, not in subordination to the proceedings, and although every form may have been preserved opens the inquiry whether they have been more than an empty shell" (*Frank v. Mangum,* 237 U.S. 309 (1915)). The future of federal habeas corpus will ultimately turn on whether federal enforcement of federal law is regarded as a desirable norm or an unnecessary and unjustified departure from state control over the federal rights of state prisoners.

JORDAN M. STEIKER

See also AMNESTY AND PARDON; APPEAL; CAPITAL PUNISHMENT: LEGAL ASPECTS; COUNSEL: RIGHT TO COUNSEL; CRIMINAL PROCEDURE: CONSTITUTIONAL ASPECTS; CRIMINAL JUSTICE PROCESS; EXCLUSIONARY RULE; GUILT; PRISONERS, LEGAL RIGHTS OF.

BIBLIOGRAPHY

BATOR, PAUL M. "Finality in Criminal Law and Federal Habeas Corpus for State Prisoners." *Harvard Law Review* 78 (1963): 441–528.

CHEN, ALAN K. "Shadow Law: Reasonable Unreasonableness, Habeas Theory, and the Nature of Legal Rules." *Buffalo Criminal Law Review* 2 (1999): 535–634.

"Developments in the Law: Federal Habeas Corpus." *Harvard Law Review* 83 (1970): 1038–1280.

DUKER, WILLIAM F. *A Constitutional History of Habeas Corpus.* Westport, Conn.: Greenwood, 1980.

FREEDMAN, ERIC M. "Milestones in Habeas Corpus: Part I. Just Because John Marshall Said It, Doesn't Make It So: *Ex Parte Bollman* and the Illusory Prohibition on the Federal Writ of Habeas Corpus for State Prisoners in the Judiciary Act of 1789." *University of Alabama Law Review* 51 (2000): 531–602.

FRIENDLY, HENRY J. "Is Innocence Irrelevant? Collateral Attack on Criminal Judgments." *University of Chicago Law Review* 38 (1970): 142–172.

HOFFMAN, JOSEPH L. "Substance and Procedure in Capital Cases: Why Federal Habeas Courts Should Review the Merits of Every Death Sentence." *University of Texas Law Review* (2000): 1771–1803.

HURD, ROLLIN C. *A Treatise on the Right of Personal Liberty, and on the Writ of Habeas Corpus,* 2d ed. Albany, N.Y.: W.C. Little & Co, 1876.

LIEBMAN, JAMES S. "Apocalypse Next Time?: The Anachronistic Attack on Habeas Corpus/Direct Review Parity." *University of Columbia Law Review* 92 (1992): 1997–2097.

———. "More Than 'Slightly Retro': The Rehnquist Court's Rout of Habeas Corpus Jurisdiction in *Teague v. Lane.*" *New York University Review of Law and Social Change* 18 (1990–1991): 537–635.

LIEBMAN, JAMES S., and HERTZ, RANDY. *Federal Habeas Corpus Practice and Procedure,* 2d ed. Charlottesville, Va.: The Michie Co., 1994.

OAKS, DALLIN H. "Habeas Corpus in the States: 1776–1865." *University of Chicago Law Review* 32 (1965): 243–288.

PELLER, GARY. "In Defense of Federal Habeas Corpus Relitigation." *Harvard Civil Rights and Civil Liberties Law Review* 16 (1982): 579–691.

STEIKER, JORDAN. "Innocence and Federal Habeas." *University of California at Los Angeles Law Review* 41 (1993): 303–389.

———. "Incorporating the Suspension Clause: Is there a Constitutional Right to Federal Habeas Corpus for State Prisoners?" *University of Michigan Law Review* 92 (1994): 862–924.

———. "Restructuring Post-Conviction Review of Federal Constitutional Claims Raised by State Prisoners: Confronting the New Face of Excessive Proceduralism." *University of Chicago Legal Forum* (1998): 315–347.

———. "Habeas Exceptionalism." *University of Texas Law Review* (2000): 1703–1730.

TUSHNET, MARK, and YACKLE, LARRY. "Symbolic Statutes and Real Laws: The Pathologies of the Antiterrorism and Effective Death Penalty Act and the Prison Litigation Reform Act." *Duke Law Journal* 47 (1997): 1–86.

YACKLE, LARRY W. *Postconviction Remedies.* Rochester, N.Y.: Lawyers Co-Operative Publishing Co., 1981.

———. "The Misadventure of State Post-Conviction Remedies." *New York University Review of Law and Social Change* 16 (1987–1988): 359–394.

———. "A Primer on the New Habeas Corpus Statute." *University of Buffalo Law Review* 44 (1996): 381–449.

———. "The Figure in the Carpet." *University of Texas Law Review* (2000): 1731–1770.

CASES

Ableman v. Booth, 62 U.S. (21 How.) 506 (1858).
Brown v. Allen, 344 U.S. 443 (1953).
Coleman v. Thompson, 501 U.S. 722 (1991).
Ex Parte Bollman, 8 U.S. (4 Cranch) 75 (1807).
Ex Parte Merryman, 17 F. Cas. 144 (C.C.D. Md. 1891) (No. 9487).
Fay v. Noia, 372 U.S. 391 (1963).
Frank v. Magnum, 237 U.S. 309 (1915).
Herrera v. Collins, 506 U.S. 390 (1993).
Mackey v. United States, 401 U.S. 667 (1971).
Williams v. Taylor, 526 U.S. 1050 (1999).
Wright v. West, 505 U.S. 277 (1992).

HATE CRIMES

A hate crime is a crime committed as an act of prejudice against the person or property of a victim as a result of that victim's real or perceived membership in a particular group. Many of the most notorious hate crimes have been murders, such as the racially motivated murder of James Byrd, Jr., in Texas in 1998 or the homophobic-motivated murder of Matthew Shepard in North Dakota later that same year. The vast majority of hate crimes, however, are cases of assault or vandalism.

The critical identifying element of hate crimes is the bias motivation of the perpetrator. The distinguishing factor can be obscured by the very term *hate crime*, which is the popular term used in connection with bias-motivated violence. In fact, *bias crime* is a more accurate label. Many if not most crimes are motivated by hatred of one kind or another. Not every crime that is motivated by hatred for the victim is a bias crime. Hate-based violence causes a bias crime only when this hatred is connected with antipathy for a group, such as a racial or ethnic group, or for an individual because of membership in that group. In some form, virtually every state in the United States expressly criminalizes bias crimes.

Elements of bias crimes

Bias crime statutes in the United States encompass crimes that are motivated by the race, color, ethnicity, national origin, or religion of the victim. Many reach sexual orientation or gender as well, and some include other categories such as age or disability. Bias crime laws may either create a specific crime of bias-motivated violence or raise the penalty of a crime when committed with bias motivation.

The key factor in identifying an actor as a bias criminal is the motivation for the conduct. Bias crimes are unusual but not unique in their focus on motivation rather than the traditional focus on intent. Some scholars have criticized bias crime laws on this basis, a critique that is addressed below.

There are two analytically distinct, albeit somewhat overlapping models of bias crimes. These models may be referred to as the *discriminatory selection model* and the *group animus model*. (In this terminology, *group* is used to represent all group characteristics that constitute bias crimes, such as ethnicity, race, or religion.)

The discriminatory selection model of bias crimes defines these crimes in terms of the perpetrator's selection of his victim. It is irrelevant why an offender selected his victim on the basis of race or other group; it is sufficient that the offender did so. The discriminatory selection model received much attention because it was a statute of this model that was upheld by the Supreme Court in *Wisconsin v. Mitchell*, 508 U.S. 476 (1993). The group animus model of bias crimes defines crimes on the basis of a perpetrator's animus for the group of the victim and the centrality of this animus in the perpetrator's motivation for committing the crime. Florida and Massachusetts, among other states, have adopted group animus bias crimes laws. Many and perhaps most cases of discriminatory selection are in fact also cases of group animus bias crimes, but not all. A purse snatcher, for example, who preys solely on women, finding it more efficient to grab purses than to pick wallets out of men's pockets, would have discriminatorily selected a victim on the basis of gender, but not with group animus.

Most states with bias crime laws have adopted statutes that draw on both models. These laws provide enhanced sentences for crimes committed "because of" or "by reason of" the victim's real or perceived membership in a particular group. Although these statutes lack explicit reference either to discriminatory selection or animus, they share attributes of both. "Because of" statutes look to the perpetrator's selection of the victim. In addition, particularly in those states that require a finding of maliciousness, "because of" statutes are akin to animus as well.

Under any of these models, bias crimes can arise out of mixed motivation where the perpetrator of a violent crime is motivated by a number of different factors in the commission of the crime, bias among them. To constitute a bias crime, the bias motivation must be a substantial motivation for the perpetrator's criminal conduct. Under the Supreme Court decision in *Apprendi v. New Jersey*, 120 S.Ct. 2348 (2000), all elements of a bias crime must be submitted to a jury (or judge as a trier of fact) and proven beyond a reasonable doubt; a sentence enhancement for a bias crime may not be imposed on a finding by preponderance of evidence by the sentencing judge.

How bias crimes differ from other crimes

The justification for bias crime laws turns primarily on the manner in which bias crimes differ from other crimes. Bias crimes cause greater harm than *parallel crimes*, that is, those crimes that lack a prejudicial motivation but are otherwise identical to the bias crime. This is true on three levels: harm to the individual victim, the victim's group or community, and the society at large.

Bias crimes generally have a more harmful emotional and psychological impact on the individual victim. The victim of a bias crime is not attacked for a random reason (e.g., the person injured during a drive-by shooting) nor for an impersonal reason (e.g., the victim of a violent robbery). Rather the victim of a bias crime is attacked for a specific, personal reason: for example, race, religion, ethnicity, or sexual orientation. Moreover, the bias crime victim cannot reasonably minimize the risks of future attacks because the victim is unable to change the characteristic that made him a victim in the first place. The heightened sense of vulnerability caused by bias crimes is beyond that normally found in crime victims. Studies have suggested that the victims of bias crimes tend to experience psychological symptoms such as depression or withdrawal, as well as anxiety, feelings of helplessness, and a profound sense of isolation.

The impact of bias crimes reaches beyond the harm done to the immediate victim or victims of the criminal behavior. There is a more widespread impact on the "target community"—that is, the community that shares the race, religion, ethnicity, or other group characteristic of the victim. The target community experiences bias crime in a manner that has no equivalent in the public response to parallel crimes. The reaction of the target community goes beyond mere sympathy with the immediate victim. Members of the target community of a bias crime perceive that crime as if it were an attack on themselves directly and individually.

Finally, the impact of bias crimes may spread beyond the immediate victims and the target community to the general society. This effect may be seen on a number of levels, and includes a spectrum of harms from the very concrete to the most abstract. On the most prosaic level—but by no means least damaging—the isolation effects discussed above have a cumulative effect throughout a community. Members of the community, even those who are sympathetic to the plight of the victim family, may be reluctant to place themselves or their children in harm's way, and will shy away from socializing with the victims, thus exacerbating the problems associated with social isolation.

Bias crimes cause an even broader injury to the general community. Such crimes violate not only society's general concern for the security of its members and their property but also the shared value of equality among its citizens and racial and religious harmony in a heterogeneous society. A bias crime is therefore a profound violation of the egalitarian ideal and the antidiscrimination principle that have become fundamental not only to the American legal system but to American culture as well. Indeed, when a legislature defines the groups that are to be included in a bias crime law, it unavoidably makes a normative statement as to the role of certain groups or characteristics. Bias crime laws are concerned with those characteristics that implicate social fissure lines, divisions that run deep into the social history of a culture. Thus every bias crime law in the United States includes race as a category; racial discrimination, with its earliest roots in slavery, is the clearest example of a social fissure line in American society. Strong cases can similarly be made for the other classic bias crime categories—color, ethnicity, religion, and national origin. When a state legislature debates the inclusion of other categories to its bias crime law, the debate is partly over the place of those groups in society. Drafting the scope of a bias crime law is necessarily a process that includes the locating of social fissure lines.

Scope of the problem

Although there is some reason to believe that the level of bias crimes increased over the last two decades of the twentieth century, it remains difficult to gauge whether the bias crime problem has actually worsened. During the 1980s, public concern over the level of bias-motivated violence in the United States rose dramatically. Such concern and the consequent enactment of bias crime statutes across the United States probably stemmed, at least in part, from an apparent worsening of the bias crime problem. Statistics from both independent and governmental data-gathering organizations support the conclusion that bias crime increased over the course of the 1980s and, to a large extent, leveled off during the 1990s. These statistics, however, remain inconsistent and incomplete. Moreover, the statistics gathered toward the end of the 1980s and throughout the early to mid-1990s reflected not only a growth in the bias crime problem, but also a growth in legislative and administrative awareness of the problem.

In general, experts and commentators on bias crime agree that these crimes had, throughout the mid and late 1980s and early 1990s, increased annually. The main organizations that collect data on the subject of bias-motivated violence—the Anti-Defamation League, the Southern Poverty Law Center, and the National Gay and Lesbian Task Force—all reported such persistent growth.

In 1990 Congress passed the Hate Crime Statistics Act (HCSA) in an effort to provide official statistics concerning the level of bias crimes. Under this act, the Department of Justice must collect statistics on the incidence of bias crimes in the United States as a part of its regular information-gathering system. The Attorney General delegated the development and implementation of the HCSA to the Federal Bureau of Investigation's Uniform Crime Reporting Program for incorporation among its sixteen thousand voluntary law enforcement agency participants. Beginning with the HCSA's implementation in 1991 and through the early 1990s, the F.B.I. documented a general rise in bias crimes. However, these figures, like those reported by other data-gathering organizations, remain vulnerable to charges of inaccuracy. Because the F.B.I.'s numbers simply mirror the numbers reported by

state and local law enforcement agencies, and because agency participation under the HCSA is voluntary, the completed data more aptly reflect popular perception of the bias crime problem rather than the problem itself.

There is a mutual-feedback relationship between the bias crime problem and both the popular perception and official response to the problem. A perceived increase in bias crime as fostered by independent data-gathering and reporting leads to increased public concern regarding such crimes. Such concern leads, in succession, to legislative and administrative response, to increased official reporting, and, in effect, to an even greater perceived increase in bias crime. Thus, problem and perception conflate, and the apparent growth in bias crime becomes not simply a reflection of increased hatred and apathy (as the statistics alone would suggest) but also an indication of increased understanding and action (as the increased response to the problem suggests).

On the other hand, there is reason to believe that, despite increased bias crime reporting by police agencies, a majority of bias crime victims do not report incidents at all. Victims' distrust of the police, language barriers, and fear of either retaliation by the offender or public exposure generally may well lead to systemic underreporting of bias crimes.

In addition to all of the problems with measuring the current level of bias crimes, there is a significant problem with establishing a baseline for a meaningful comparison. Data collection on the levels of bias crimes prior to the mid-1980s was virtually nonexistent. For example, it was not until 1978 that the Boston City Police Department became the first law enforcement agency to track bias-motivated crimes; it was not until 1981 that Maryland became the first state to pass a reporting statute.

It is thus not possible to say with confidence the extent to which bias crimes are increasing and the extent to which the increase is one of perception. However, the obvious relationship between perception and problem in no way undercuts the severity of the problem. Whatever the difficulties of measuring bias crime levels with precision, the existence of a serious level of bias-motivated crime is confirmed. Moreover, the mutual-feedback relationship between the level of bias crime and the popular perception of this level does not necessarily undermine a determination of the severity of the problem. As the understanding of what constitutes a bias crime is broadened, that which may have been dismissed as a "prank" in an earlier time is now properly revealed as bias-motivated criminal conduct. This does not mean that bias crimes are being overcounted; rather it means that previously these crimes were undercounted.

Critique of bias crimes

The enhanced punishment of bias-motivated violence has been criticized on a number of grounds. One critique argues that bias crime laws punish thoughts and not criminal acts. This critique itself takes two forms: a constitutional argument that bias crime laws violate the First Amendment right to free expression of ideas, and a criminal law theory argument that bias crime laws improperly focus on motivation rather than mens rea. An additional critique, which applies only to federal bias crime laws, involves questions of federalism and the constitutional authority for such legislation.

The free expression challenges to bias crime laws were the subject of a great deal of scholarly attention as well as a number of judicial opinions. Judicial consideration of the issue culminated in two Supreme Court decisions, *R.A.V. v. City of St. Paul*, 505 U.S. 377 (1992), which struck down a municipal cross-burning ordinance, and *Wisconsin v. Mitchell*, which upheld a state law that provided for increased penalties for bias crimes. Three general positions have emerged among observers concerning the challenge to bias crime laws based in principles of free expression. One position argues that bias crime laws unconstitutionally punish thought because the increased punishment is due solely to the defendant's expression of a conviction of which the community disapproves. A second position permits the enhanced punishment of bias crimes, arguing that bias motivations and hate speech are not protected by the First Amendment. Ironically, these two opposing positions share a common premise: that bias crime laws do involve the regulation of expression.

The third position distinguishes between hate speech and bias crimes, protecting the former but permitting the enhanced punishment of the latter. This has been understood in two related ways. One approach is based on the distinction between speech and conduct, protecting hate speech as the former and punishing bias crimes as the latter. This is the approach adopted by the Court in *Wisconsin v. Mitchell*. An alternative approach focuses on the perpetrator's state of mind, and distinguishes behavior that is intended to communicate from behavior that is intended to cause focused and individualized harm to a targeted victim.

The critique that bias crime laws punish bad thoughts rather than criminal acts also has been based on criminal law doctrine. This argument criticizes bias crime laws for impermissibly straying beyond the punishment of act and purposeful intent to reach the punishment of motivation. The argument rests on the assertion that motive can be distinguished from mens rea, based on the formal distinction between motive and intent: intent concerns the mental state provided in the definition of an offense in order to assess the actor's culpability with respect to the elements of the offense, whereas motive concerns the cause that drives the actor to commit the offense.

Several responses have been made to this critique. First, as a matter of positive law, concern with the punishment of motivation may be misplaced. Motive often determines punishment. In those states with capital punishment, the defendant's motivation for the homicide stands prominent among the recognized aggravating factors that may contribute to the imposition of the death sentence. For instance, the motivation of profit in murder cases is a significant aggravating factor adopted in most capital sentencing schemes. Bias motivation itself may serve as an aggravating circumstance. In *Barclay v. Florida*, 463 U.S. 939 (1983), the Supreme Court explicitly upheld the use of racial bias as an aggravating factor in the sentencing phase of a capital case. The Court reaffirmed *Barclay* in *Dawson v. Delaware*, 503 U.S. 159 (1992).

A second response to this critique of bias crime laws more broadly questions the usefulness of the formal distinction between intent and motive, arguing that the decision as to what constitutes motive and what constitutes intent largely turns on what is being criminalized. Criminal statutes define the elements of the crime and a mental state applies to each element. The mental state that applies to an element of the crime is "intent" whereas any mental states that are extrinsic to the elements are "motivation." The formal distinction, therefore, turns on the elements of the crime. What is a matter of intent in one context may be a matter of motive in another. There are two equally accurate descriptions of a bias-motivated assault: the perpetrator possessed a (i) mens rea of purpose with respect to the assault along with a *motivation* of bias; or (ii) a mens rea of purpose with respect to the parallel crime of assault and a mens rea of purpose with respect to assaulting this victim because of group identification. The defendant in description (i) "intends" to assault the victim and does so because the defendant is a bigot. The defendant in description (ii) "intends" to commit an assault and does so with both an intent to assault and a discriminatory or animus-driven intent as to the selection of the victim. Both descriptions are accurate. The formal distinction between intent and motive may thus bear less weight than some critics have placed upon it. Whether bias crime laws punish motivation or intent is not inherent in those prohibitions. Rather the distinction mirrors the way in which the law describes these crimes.

The federalism challenges to the constitutionality of a federal bias crime law arise from the fact that the vast majority of bias crimes are state law crimes that are motivated by bias. The question of constitutional authority for a federal bias crime law is especially pressing after the Supreme Court's decisions in *United States v. Morrison*, 120 S.Ct. 1740 (2000), striking down the civil remedy provisions of the Violence Against Women Act, and *United States v. Lopez*, 514 U.S. 549 (1995), striking down the Federal Gun-Free Zones Act. Each decision held that the legislation in question exceeded Congress' authority under the commerce clause. It is partially for this reason that, at the time of writing, there is no pure federal bias crimes statute. Bias motivation is an element of certain federal civil rights crimes such as 18 U.S.C. § 245. Moreover, in 1994, Congress directed the U.S. Sentencing Commission to promulgate guidelines enhancing the penalties for any federal crimes that are motivated by bias. These statutes, however, cover only a small range of cases involving bias motivation.

After *Morrison* and *Lopez*, the commerce clause, the constitutional authority for civil rights legislation during the 1960s barring discrimination in public accommodations, housing, and employment, is a more doubtful source for constitutional authority for a federal bias crime law. A more promising source for such authority may lie in the post–Civil War constitutional amendments, at least for bias crimes involving racial, ethnic, and possibly religious motivation. In enacting section 245, Congress expressly relied, in part, upon the Fourteenth and Fifteenth Amendments as authority for the federalization of bias-motivated deprivation of certain specified rights individuals hold under state law. Not all bias crimes deprive the victim of the ability to exercise

some right under state law. It has been argued, however, that the Thirteenth Amendment as well provides constitutional authority for a federal bias crime law. The modern view of the Thirteenth Amendment, articulated in *Jones v. Alfred H. Mayer*, 392 U.S. 409 (1968), and *Runyon v. McCrary*, 427 U.S. 160 (1976), understands the amendment as a constitutional proscription of all the "badges and incidents" of slavery, authorizing Congress to make any rational determination as to what constitutes a badge or incident of slavery and to ban such conduct, whether from public or private sources. The abolition of slavery in the Thirteenth Amendment, although immediately addressed to the enslavement of African-Americans, has been held to apply beyond the context of race to include ethnic groups and perhaps religions as well. The Thirteen Amendment would not, however, provide constitutional authority for elements of a federal bias crime law reaching sexual orientation, gender, or other categories.

FREDERICK M. LAWRENCE

See also CRIME: DEFINITION; GENDER AND CRIME; MENS REA; RACE AND CRIME; SENTENCING: DISPARITY.

BIBLIOGRAPHY

ALTSCHILLER, DONALD. *Hate Crimes: A Reference Handbook.* Santa Barbara, Calif.: ABC-CLIO, Inc., 1999.
Anti-Defamation League of B'nai B'rith. *Hate Crimes Laws: A Comprehensive Guide.* New York: Anti-Defamation League, 1994.
BOWLING, BENJAMIN. *Violent Racism: Victimisation, Policing, and Social Context.* Oxford, U.K.: Clarendon Press, 1998.
Bureau of Justice Assistance, U.S. Department of Justice. *A Policymaker's Guide to Hate Crimes.* Washington, D.C.: Department of Justice, 1997.
DILLOF, ANTHONY. "Punishing Bias: An Examination of the Theoretical Foundations of Bias Crime Statues." *Northwestern University Law Review* 91 (1997): 1015.
KELLY, ROBERT J., ed. *Bias Crime: American Law Enforcement and Legal Responses.* Chicago: University of Illinois, 1991.
JACOBS, JAMES B., and POTTER, KIMBERLY. *Hate Crimes: Criminal Law and Identity Politics.* New York: Oxford University Press, 1998.
LAWRENCE, FREDERICK M. "The Punishment of Hate: Toward a Normative Theory of Bias-

Motivated Violence." *Michigan Law Review* 93 (1994): 320.

———. *Punishing Hate: Bias Crimes Under American Law*. Cambridge, Mass.: Harvard University press, 1999.

LEVIN, JACK, and MCDEVITT, JACK. *Hate Crimes: The Rising Tide of Bigotry and Bloodshed*. New York: Plenum Press, 1993.

WANG, LU-IN. *Hate Crimes Law*. St. Paul, Minn.: Clark, Boardman & Callaghan, 1997.

SYMPOSIA

"Penalty Enhancement for Hate Crimes." *Criminal Justice Ethics* 11 (1992): 3–63.

"Papers of a Symposium on Hate Crime Legislation: Hate Crimes—Propriety, Practicality and Constitutionality." *Annual Survey of American Law* 93 (1992): 483–636.

CASES

Apprendi v. New Jersey, 120 S. Ct. 2348 (2000).
Barclay v. Florida, 463 U.S. 939 (1983).
Dawson v. Delaware, 503 U.S. 159 (1992).
Jones v. Alfred H. Mayer, 392 U.S. 409 (1968).
R.A.V. v. City of St. Paul, 505 U.S. 377 (1992).
Runyon v. McCrary, 427 U.S. 160 (1976).
Wisconsin v. Mitchell, 508 U.S. 476 (1993).

HOMICIDE: BEHAVIORAL ASPECTS

Homicide is the killing of one human being by another. As a legal category, it can be criminal or noncriminal. Criminal homicides are generally considered first-degree murder, when one person causes the death of another with premeditation and intent, or second-degree murder, when the death is with malice and intent but is not premeditated. Voluntary manslaughter usually involves intent to inflict bodily injury without deliberate intent to kill; involuntary manslaughter is negligent or reckless killing without intent to harm. Noncriminal forms include excusable homicide, usually in self-defense, and what is called justifiable homicide, as when a convicted offender is executed by the state. The classification of any homicide as either criminal or noncriminal, or of a death as either a homicide, an accident, or a natural death, is not the same in all time periods or across all legal jurisdictions. What is considered a homicide death varies over time by the legal code of given jurisdictions and by the interpretations and practices of agencies responsible for reporting deaths. When cars were first introduced into the United States, for example, deaths resulting from them were classified by some coroners as homicides, although now they are generally labeled accidental unless caused by negligence. An abortion may be considered a criminal homicide or the exercise of a woman's reproductive choice. Homicide statistics, like those of many other crimes, reflect definitions and legal interpretations that vary over time and space. Agencies responsible for reporting deaths influence how a death is reported. Roger Lane describes, for example, that coroners in early twentieth-century America were paid to determine the cause of deaths on a fee-for-service basis. The same fee was paid no matter how difficult the case, and in some cases, the fee was collected from the convicted offender. In difficult cases or those for which the coroner might not expect payment, as when a newborn was killed by an indigent woman, the cause of death might be reported as suffocation of the infant rather than as a homicide. Criminal homicide reflects the political processes that affect all definitions of crime.

Sources of data on homicide

Homicide data generally derive from either health or police agencies. There are two major sources of international data; one complied by the United Nations in *World Health Statistics Annual* and the other by the International Criminal Police Organization (Interpol), which was established in 1950. The national police agency of each country reports the number of that country's homicides for every two-year period. *World Health Statistics Annual* publishes the cause of death, including homicide, for each reporting country. These statistics, which have been collected since 1939, are the joint product of the health and statistical administration of many countries and the office of the United Nations and the World Health Organization. Problems in the use of these sources include lack of consistent definitions and interpretations across jurisdictions and lack of consistent reporting by all countries. Some countries, including most in Africa and many in Asia, do not routinely report (LaFree). Furthermore, there are few validation procedures to assess the accuracy of the data. For a summary of difficulties with these data sources, see LaFree.

Within the United States there are two major national sources of data on homicide: the National Center for Health Statistics (NCHS) and the

Federal Bureau of Investigation *Crime in the United States* (known as the Uniform Crime Reports, which is published annually). The NCHS data derive from coroners and medical examiners, who forward death certificates to the center's Division of Vital Statistics. These data focus solely on the homicide victim and generally include information on the cause of death and the age, race, and sex of the victim. Data about offenders, victim offender relationships, and motives are not included. The various states entered this national reporting system at different times. Prior to the 1930s, when the system became fully national, the data available depended on which states and cities were included. Boston was the first entrant, and in general there were data from the East Coast cities very early. Boston had death data in 1880, Pennsylvania in 1906, and Washington, D.C., in 1880. Other states, such as Georgia and Texas, entered the registry much later—in 1922 and 1933, respectively. In establishing trends, then, there is difficulty in obtaining national data before 1930.

The Uniform Crime Reports, a voluntary national data-collection effort, began in 1930 and gradually accumulated reporting police districts. Homicide reports are detailed and include information on both victims and offenders and, since the 1970s, on victim-offender relationships. This system is the only national one with information on homicide offenders and includes information on crimes classified by size of population, state, county, and Standard Metropolitan Statistical Area. Although there are some problems with the use of the Uniform Crime Reports data, they are commonly used in studies of homicide.

In general, information on the number of homicides in the nation reported by NCHS and the UCR show relatively high agreement. However, there is variation, sometimes substantial, when comparing the two sources on such questions as age or ethnic background of the victim. A discussion of these differences are found in Riedel.

Although the UCR and NCHS are the most commonly used national data sources for studies of homicide, the National Incident Based Reporting System (NIBRS), which is under development, may become an important source in homicide research. This system originated as a result of the 1982 F.B.I. Bureau of Justice Statistics task force comprehensive evaluation and redesign of the UCR program. When fully implemented there will be more detailed data at the national level than are currently available (Reidel).

In addition to these national sources, researchers have records of specific homicide cases, available either from medical examiners' offices or from police departments. Such records are richer in detail than those at the national and international levels and provide more specific evidence on time and location of homicides, alcohol and drug involvement, sequence of events leading to victim-offender confrontations, and the like. Locally based data can be used to augment those compiled nationally and are useful for describing homicide events in detail. There is extensive long-term city level information available from police records in Chicago (Block), St. Louis (Decker, 1993; Rosenfeld), Philadelphia (Wolfgang; Zahn, 1997) as well as other cities. These data are available in analyzed form from the publications of the authors, and are also available from the Inter-University Consortium for Political and Social Research (ICPSR) at the University of Michigan and at their web site (http://www.umich.edu). Most of these studies rely on the model established by Marvin Wolfgang in his classic study *Patterns in Criminal Homicide* (1949).

Cross-national patterns of criminal homicide

Although there are problems in using international crime statistics because of differing definitions and methods in classifying the phenomenon, both Interpol and the United Nations data nonetheless offer useful information on homicide rates in different countries. Cross-national studies of homicide are generally based on either WHO or Interpol data. There are a number of problems with these sources including lack of representation of many countries (e.g., Africa, Asia, former Communist countries). Lack of consistency in reporting is also a problem. Gary LaFree, in summarizing these problems, supports an earlier assessment by Kalish, who said, "It is risky to quote a crime rate for a particular country for a particular year without examining rates for other years, and, whenever possible, rates from other sources" (quoted in LaFree, p. 138).

Despite these difficulties, studies confirm that, in general, Central and South American nations have high rates of homicide. In fact, Colombia is frequently the nation with the highest homicide rate. Also, several former Soviet block nations tend to have high homicide rates, notably the countries of the Russian Federation. Countries with the lowest homicide rates tend to be Western European nations. Japan often has the lowest rate of homicide. Again, it is important to note differential reporting from some areas of the world. There is only one African nation that has somewhat consistent reporting to the WHO from year to year (Mauritius). Few Asian countries, including the Middle Eastern countries, are represented. Table 1 shows worldwide homicide rates drawn primarily from the World Health Organization.

Researchers have tried to explain why there are differences in rates between countries. In his summary of these studies, LaFree notes several explanations. The most consistent finding is that the greater the difference between the rich and the poor in a country, the higher the country's homicide rate. Some research shows that the difference between the rich and poor has a stronger effect on homicide rates in areas that are densely populated. However, it does not appear that the number of people unemployed in a country or the degree of population density alone is related to its homicide rate. It is important to emphasize that the difference between the rich and poor groups in a country, in terms of income and education, has the most effect on a country's homicide rate.

Another explanation for differences in homicide rates is the varying levels of economic development across nations. Economic development refers to, for example, the per capita gross national product, the number of telephones, radios, or newspapers in a country, the amount of energy used, and the amount of industry and technology in a country. Most research shows that the less economic development in a country, the higher its homicide rate. For example, Japan is an economically developed country, as are many Western European nations, and they have low homicide rates. The obvious exception to this generalization is the United States, which is highly developed economically but also has a high homicide rate. Reasons for this exception are not clear, although patterns of gun ownership by individuals may have a bearing on it.

Other explanations for differences in national homicide rates relate to the makeup of a country's population. Some researchers suggest that the number of teenagers and young adults in a country is related to higher homicide rates, but findings are inconsistent. Other studies contend that the number of different linguistic, racial,

Table 1

Worldwide homicide rates

Country	Year reported	Rate per 100,000 pop.	Source
Colombia	1994	78.5	a
Russian Federation	1995	30.8	a
El Salvador	1991	27.4	b
Puerto Rico	1992	23.8	b
Kazakhstan	1995	19.4	a
Brazil	1992	19.0	b
Mexico	1995	17.1	a
Venezuela	1994	15.7	a
Bahamas	1995	15.1	a
Ukraine	1996	15.0	b
Kyrgyzstan	1995	12.2	a
Trinidad/Tobago	1994	11.4	a
United States	1994	9.4	a
Romania	1995	7.7	a
Northern Ireland	1995	7.0	a
Albania	1993	6.0	c
Argentina	1993	4.4	a
Hungary	1995	3.5	a
Croatia	1995	3.3	a
Chile	1994	2.9	a
Finland	1995	2.9	a
Poland	1995	2.8	a
China (urban)	1994	2.5	c
China (rural)	1994	2.2	c
Slovakia	1995	1.9	a
Australia	1994	1.8	a
Czech Republic	1995	1.8	a
Korea	1995	1.8	a
Singapore	1995	1.8	a
Belgium	1992	1.7	a
Canada	1995	1.7	a
Italy	1993	1.7	a
Kuwait	1994	1.7	b
Portugal	1995	1.7	a
New Zealand	1993	1.5	c
Israel	1995	1.4	a
Mauritius	1995	1.4	a
Greece	1995	1.3	a
Switzerland	1994	1.3	c
Denmark	1996	1.2	a
Netherlands	1995	1.2	a
France	1994	1.1	a
Germany	1995	1.1	a
Austria	1995	1.0	a
Spain	1994	0.9	a
Sweden	1995	0.9	a
England/Wales/Scotland	1995	0.8	a
Malta	1996	0.8	a
Norway	1994	0.8	a
Ireland	1993	0.6	a
Japan	1994	0.6	c

aWorld Health Organization. *World Health Statistics Annual, 1996*. Geneva: World Health Organization, 1998.
bUnited Nations. *Demographic Yearbook, 49th Issue*. New York: United Nations, 1997.
cWorld Health Organization. *World Health Statistics Annual, 1995*. Geneva: World Health Organization, 1996.

ethnic, or religious groups in a country influence the homicide rate. However, there has been little evidence showing that a greater number of such groups are related to higher homicide rates. One relationship that has been consistently associated with homicide rates is increasing population growth. The faster a country's population is growing, the higher its homicide rate tends to be.

Patterns of criminal homicide in the United States

While comparative studies have focused on the broad question of rates of homicide, studies in the United States examine how the rates change through time, which groups are affected, and the relationships between victims and offenders. Zahn and McCall summarize national homicide trends in the twentieth century. While national data from the early twentieth century are not readily available, they conclude that the homicide rate increased moderately between 1900 and 1933. After the mid-1930s, when data are more reliable, rates dipped sharply then rose between 1933 and 1974. The rates declined through 1964, although this decline was briefly interrupted by a short increase in the three years after World War II. After 1964, the rates began to rise from 6.1 per 100,000 in 1967 (UCR), to 9.7 in 1974, to an all-time high of 10.2 in 1980. Overall, the United States homicide rate doubled from the mid 1950s to 1980. After 1980, the homicide trend fluctuated, dropping to 7.9 in 1985, going up to 9.8 in 1991, and then decreasing through the late 1990s. In 1998, the UCR reported a homicide rate for the United States of 6.3, which represents the lowest U.S. homicide rate since 1967. In general, the highest homicide rates of the twentieth century in the United States occurred during the 1970s, 1980s, and early to mid-1990s, whereas the lowest rates occurred during the late 1950s.

There are consistent differences in rates of homicide victimization between males and females, blacks and whites, and young and old. In terms of age difference, homicide victimization rates are generally higher for young adults, especially young adult males. In the past, the highest rates have occurred for the age group twenty-five to thirty-four, followed by fifteen to twenty-four year olds. In the 1990s, the rates for most age groups declined, but the rates for these two groups continued to increase. By 1989, the fifteen to twenty-four-year-old group converged with and then surpassed the twenty-five to thirty-four-year-old group. In 1993, the homicide rate for fifteen to twenty-four year olds was 23.5 per 100,000 (*Vital Statistics*) and 19.5 for the twenty-

five to thirty-four year olds. Zahn and McCall, who summarized these trends, point out that shift in the age structure of homicide is one of the most important changes in the patterns of homicide during the twentieth century.

Reynolds Farley has reported that age-adjusted homicide rates during the period 1940–1977 were about six times greater for men than for women. Race and gender-specific victimization rates from vital statistics from 1968 to 1997 confirm this, with a black male rate of 47 per 100,000 in 1997, compared to 6.7 per 100,000 for white males. (The rate for black females in that year was 9.3 and for white females 2.3.) Explanations for why racial minorities are overrepresented as both victims and offenders of homicide have focused on income inequality between racial groups as well as racial segregation in housing. Segregation into areas with few economic resources may lead to frustration and hostility that increase violence. Such isolation may also undermine the ability of the community to mobilize community residents for crime prevention activities (Peterson and Krivo).

The low rates of victimization and offending for women as compared to men are not adequately explained. Differences in social inequality do not seem to be as important, and various studies have confirmed that there has not been a great escalation of female homicide rates accompanying women's increased participation in the labor force in the United States. While males dominate as victims and offenders when considering the homicide rate overall, gender patterns differ greatly in reference to a specific type of homicide, intimate partner homicide. Only in the area of partner homicides do women's offending rates approach that of men; even here, however, women are twice as likely to be killed by their partners as men are by their female partners. Women are more likely to be killed by their male partners than by any other assailant. A substantial majority of homicides committed by women occur in response to male aggression and threat. Other studies show a history of physical abuse and threat by men who eventually kill their victims. It is clear that the link between partner separation and murder is more than incidental, such that when a woman leaves a man he experiences rage that leads to her murder. A summary of research on homicide between intimate partners is found in Browne, Williams, and Dutton.

Victim-offender relationships

Although many relationships occur in human affairs, only some seem to be persistently associated with homicide in the United States. For example, an employee-employer relationship is less frequently associated with homicide than a husband-wife relationship. Unfortunately, information concerning the relation between the victim-offender and reasons for the murder are often difficult to obtain. Each homicide event can be characterized by motive. The descriptions of the motive or of the events by the participants may differ from those of official agencies or of researchers. Definitions used by some researchers for friends, acquaintances, or strangers are sometimes not specified, thus making it difficult to compare various studies of victim-offender relationships. Despite such difficulties, comparisons show that in early U.S. history the major type of homicide in both the North and the South was that of a male killing another male with whom he was acquainted, while they were in a nonwork setting (Lane). In the 1920s and 1930s, homicides that resulted from criminal transactions or justifiable homicides by police, often related to bootlegging and prohibition laws, became more prominent (Boudouris; Lashly).

In the 1940s and 1950s, homicide rates were relatively low and stable. Two types of homicide were most prevalent: homicide between family members, usually husbands and wives, and homicide between two males known to each involved in an argument. From the 1960s into the 1990s, UCR data indicate that homicide between acquaintances and friends was the most predominant form, ranging from a high of 51 percent of the total in 1963 to a low of 34 percent in 1995. The percentage of homicides involving acquaintances dropped during this time, and since 1990 has been superseded by those where the relationship between the victim and offender is unknown. There has also been a decline in family-related homicide, varying from 31 percent of the total in 1963 to a low of 11 percent in 1995.

Based on Uniform Crime Reports, arguments are the predominant precipitating event in homicides, through time. However, in the 1970s and early 1980s there were many homicides in large cities associated with robberies, and in some large U.S. cities in the late 1980s and early 1990s, there was an upsurge of homicides related to narcotics trafficking. The number of homicides for which police do not know the precipitating circumstance showed the greatest increases in the last quarter of the twentieth century in the United States; despite this increase, the majority of homicides still involve victims and offenders who are acquainted.

The Technology of Homicide

Homicide is also characterized by technology, which includes implements used to kill (guns, knives, and clubs) and substances (drugs and alcohol) that may cause or contribute to the crime. The majority of homicides in the United States are committed with a gun, usually a handgun. Uniform Crime Reports in 1998 revealed 65 percent of homicides were committed with a firearm. This percentage has remained relatively constant since 1970. Knives are the second most frequent method used, claiming 13 percent of deaths in 1998. Rates of murder involving guns are higher in the southern regions of the United States and are increasingly prevalent in homicides involving teens and young adults (Fox and Zawitz, 2000). The extent to which gun control would affect the rate of homicide remains an issue of continuing debate. Some researchers suggest that the ready availability of guns in the United States is related to the nation's high rates of criminal homicide, while others suggest that factors associated with the willingness to use guns are also of importance.

There have been attempts to explore the relationship between homicide and the use of alcohol and drugs. Studies that examine alcohol use and homicide commonly examine the percentage of victims, offenders, or both who were drinking at the time of the fatal attack. Wolfgang's study, for example, found that in 64 percent of the homicides in Philadelphia, either the victim or the offender had consumed alcohol. Although much of the literature shows some association between alcohol and homicide, the means by which this association occurs remains problematic. Parker and Auerhahn (1999) suggest that selective disinhibition explains the association. Alcohol impacts judgement, and in potentially violent situations, alcohol will disinhibit norms that constrain individuals from engaging in violent behavior—especially in situations in which violence is seen as likely to result in successful resolution of a dispute. While exact ways in which this occurs remains obscure, some researchers studying the connection suggest that alcohol may be one causal agent in the genesis of homicide. Most researchers agree that alcohol interacts with social contexts and social relationships; it alone, apart from social contexts, does not explain the occurrence of homicide.

The relationship between drugs other than alcohol and homicide poses many of the same problems. Paul Goldstein and colleagues suggested that drugs may be associated with homicide in one of three ways. First, drug use by offenders or victims may alter behavior and increase the likelihood of violence or victimization. Second, some drug users may engage in violent crime accidentally while committing relatively nonviolent crimes aimed at securing money to buy drugs. Third, homicide may be systematically related to the use of illegal substances in that it may involve conflicts between rival drug dealers over territory, settlement for "bad debts" or for "bad drugs," and the like. Studies dealing with the impact of each of these situations have been done, although which, if any, of the three contributes most to the drug-homicide relationship is unknown, since existing studies have produced contradictory results.

Sociological explanations of homicide

There are a number of sociological explanations for homicide. Most explanations have focused on explaining why rates of homicide are different in different groups, for example, minority versus majority groups, or in different regions of the United States, such as South versus North. Two major lines of thought, cultural and social structural, have been most prevalent. While these explanations are not mutually exclusive, debates between advocates of these perspectives have been common. Cultural theorists explain homicides as resulting from learned, shared values and behavior specific to a given group. The basic causes are in the norms and values, transmitted across generations, that are learned by members of a group. Certain subgroups exhibit higher rates of homicide because they are participants in a subculture that has violence as a norm. First developed by Wolfgang in 1958 and later expanded by Wolfgang and Ferracutti in 1967, this position asserts that there is a subculture of violence—that is, a subculture with a cluster of values that support and encourage the overt use of force in interpersonal relations and group interactions. The subculture is reflected in the psychological and behavioral traits of its participants. Ready access to weapons and the carrying of weapons are symbols indicating a willingness to participate in violence and to expect and be ready for retaliation. The development of favorable attitudes toward the use of violence in a subculture involves learned behavior and a process of differential association or identification. In general, violence is a learned shared mode of adaptation for specific groups of people (Wolfgang and Ferracutti).

Social structural explanations have been more pronounced in the 1980s and 1990s. The factors most commonly studied are two features of economic stratification: poverty and income inequality. Poverty refers to absolute economic deprivation wherein persons have difficulty securing the basic necessities for a healthy life, whereas relative deprivation refers to relative lack of material goods, on the premise that the subjective experience of deprivation motivates individuals to violence (Messner and Rosenfeld). Studies show that poverty alone is not consistently linked to homicide, although it is a related component. The inequality hypothesis has also been tested using different units of analysis, that is, neighborhoods, cities, and nations. For subnational units the evidence is somewhat mixed, and at the national level results are very consistent. Nations with high levels of income inequality tend to exhibit high homicide rates. Further refinement of research on the relationship between economics and racial and other forms of inequality needs to continue, as do attempts to integrate cultural and social structural approaches. Studies of factors related to specific types of homicide, such as intimate partner homicide and gang homicide, are also important and are proving more useful in suggesting ways to prevent such deaths than are the more general approaches.

MARGARET A. ZAHN

See also ASSASSINATION; GUNS, REGULATION OF; DOMESTIC VIOLENCE; HOMICIDE: LEGAL ASPECTS; SUICIDE: LEGAL ASPECTS; TERRORISM; VIOLENCE; WAR AND VIOLENT CRIME.

BIBLIOGRAPHY

BLOCK, RICHARD. *Violent Crime: Environment, Interaction, and Death.* Lexington, Mass.: Heath, Lexington Books, 1977.
BOUDOURIS, JAMES. "Trends in Homicide, Detroit 1926–1968." Ph.D. diss. Wayne State University, 1970.
BREWER, VICTORIA E.; and SMITH, M. DWAYNE. "Gender Inequality and Rates of Female Homicide Victimization across U.S. Cities." *Journal of Research in Crime and Delinquency* 32, no. 2 (1995): 175–190.

BROWNE, ANGELA; WILLIAMS, KIRK R.; and DUTTON, DONALD G. "Homicide between Intimate Partners: A 20-Year Review." In *Homicide: A Sourcebook of Social Research*. Edited by M. Dwayne Smith and Margaret A. Zahn. Thousand Oaks, Calif.: Sage, 1999. Pages 149–164.

COOK, PHILIP J.; and MOORE, MARK H. "Guns, Gun Control, and Homicide: A Review of Research and Public Policy." In *Homicide: A Sourcebook of Social Research*. Edited by M. Dwayne Smith and Margaret A. Zahn. Thousand Oaks, Calif.: Sage, 1999. Pages 277–296.

CORZINE, JAY; HUFF-CORZINE, LIN; and WHITT, HUGH P. "Cultural and Subcultural Theories of Homicide." In *Homicide: A Sourcebook of Social Research*. Edited by M. Dwayne Smith and Margaret A. Zahn. Thousand Oaks, Calif.: Sage, 1999. Pages 42–57.

DECKER, SCOTT H. "Exploring Victim-Offender Relationship in Homicide: The Role of Individual and Event Characteristics." *Justice Quarterly* 10, no. 4 (1999): 585–612.

———. "Deviant Homicide: A New Look at the Role of Motives and Victim-Offender Relationships." *Journal of Research in Crime and Delinquency* 33, no. 4 (1996): 427–449.

FARLEY, REYNOLDS. "Homicide Trends in the United States." *Demography* 17, no. 2 (1980): 177–188.

FELSON, R. B.; and TEDESCHI, J. T. "A Social Interactionist Approach to Violence: Cross-Cultural Applications." In *Interpersonal Violent Behaviors: Social and Cultural Aspects*. Edited by R. Barry Ruback and Neil Alan Weiner. New York: Springer, 1995. Pages 153–170.

FOX, JAMES A., and ZAWITZ, MARIANNNE. "Homicide Trends in the United States: 1998 Update." March 2000. www.ojp.usdoj.gov/bjs/homicide/homtrnd.htm.

GAUTHIER, DEANN K., and BANKSTON, WILLIAM B. "Gender Equality and the Sex Ratio of Intimate Killing." *Criminology* 35, no. 4 (1997): 577–600.

GOLDSTEIN, PAUL J.; BROWNSTEIN, HENRY H.; and RYAN, PATRICK J. "Drug-Related Homicide in New York: 1984 and 1988." *Crime and Delinquency* 38, no. 4 (1992): 459–476.

HAWKINS, DARNELL F. "What Can We Learn from Data Disaggregation? The Case of Homicide and African Americans." In *Homicide: A Sourcebook of Social Research*. Edited by M. Dwayne Smith and Margaret A. Zahn. Thousand Oaks, Calif.: Sage, 1999. Pages 195–210.

KAPLAN, MARK S., and GELING, OLGA. "Firearm Suicides and Homicides in the United States: Regional Variations and Patterns of Gun Ownership." *Social Science Medicine* 46, no. 9 (1998): 1227–1233.

KLECK, GARY, and PATTERSON, E. BRITT. "The Impact of Gun Control and Gun Ownership Levels on Violence Rates." *Journal of Quantitative Criminology* 9, no. 3 (1993): 249–257.

LANE, ROGER. *Violent Death in the City: Suicide, Accident, and Murder in Nineteenth-century Philadelphia*. Cambridge, Mass.: Harvard University Press, 1979.

LaFREE, GARY. "A Summary and Review of Cross-National Comparative Studies of Homicide." In *Homicide: A Sourcebook of Social Research*. Edited by M. Dwayne Smith and Margaret A. Zahn. Thousand Oaks, Calif.: Sage, 1999. Pages 125–148.

LASHLY, ARTHUR V. "Homicide in Cook County." *The Illinois Crime Survey*. Chicago: Illinois Association for Criminal Justice, 1929. Chap. 13.

MARTINEZ, RAMIRO, JR., and LEE, MATTHEW T. "Extending Ethnicity in Homicide Research: The Case of Latinos." In *Homicide: A Sourcebook of Social Research*. Edited by M. Dwayne Smith and Margaret A. Zahn. Thousand Oaks, Calif.: Sage, 1999. Pages 211–220.

MESSNER, STEVEN F., and ROSENFELD, RICHARD. "Social Structure and Homicide: Theory and Research." In *Homicide: A Sourcebook of Social Research*. Edited by M. Dwayne Smith and Margaret A. Zahn. Thousand Oaks, Calif.: Sage, 1999. Pages 27–41.

National Center for Health Statistics. *Vital Statistics of the United States* (Vol. 2: Mortality, Pt.A). Washington, D.C.: Government Printing Office, annually.

PARKER, KAREN F.; McCALL, PATRICIA L.; and LAND, KENNETH C. "Determining Social-Structural Predictors of Homicide: Units of Analysis and Related Methodological Concern." In *Homicide: A Sourcebook of Social Research*. Edited by M. Dwayne Smith and Margaret A. Zahn. Thousand Oaks, Calif.: Sage, 1999. Pages 107–124.

PARKER, ROBERT NASH. "Bringing 'Booze' Back In: The Relationship between Alcohol and Homicide." *Journal of Research in Crime and Delinquency* 32, no. 1 (1995): 3–38.

PARKER, ROBERT NASH, and AUERHAHN, KATHLEEN. "Drugs, Alcohol, and Homicide: Issues in Theory and Research." In *Homicide: A Sourcebook of Social Research*. Edited by M. Dwayne Smith and Margaret A. Zahn. Thousand Oaks, Calif.: Sage, 1999. Pages 176–194.

PETERSON, RUTH D., and KRIVO, L. J. "Racial Segregation and Black Urban Homicide." *Social Forces* 71, no. 4 (1993): 1001–1026.

PHILLIPS, JULIE A. "Variation in African-American Homicide Rates: An Assessment of Potential Explanations." *Criminology* 35, no. 4 (1997): 527–556.

RIEDEL, MARC. "Sources of Homicide Data: A Review and Comparison." In *Homicide: A Sourcebook of Social Research*. Edited by M. Dwayne Smith and Margaret A. Zahn. Thousand Oaks, Calif.: Sage, 1999. Pages 78–93.

ROSENFELD, RICHARD. "Changing Relationships between Men and Women: A Note on the Decline in Intimate Partner Homicide." *Homicide Studies* 1, no. 1 (1997): 72–83.

SMITH, M. DWAYNE, and KUCHTA, ELLEN S. "Female Homicide Victimization in the United States: Trends in Relative Risk, 1946–1990." *Social Science Quarterly* 76, no. 3 (1995): 665–672.

WOLFGANG, MARVIN E. *Patterns in Criminal Homicide*. New York: Wiley, 1966. Earlier editions printed in 1949 and 1958.

WOLFGANG, MARVIN E., and FERRACUTTI, FRANCO. *The Subculture of Violence: Towards an Integrated Theory in Criminology*. London: Tavistock, 1967.

ZAHN, MARGARET A. "Changing Patterns of Homicide and Social Policy." Paper presented at the annual meeting of the American Society of Criminology, San Diego, 1997.

ZAHN, MARGARET A., and McCALL, PATRICIA L. "Trends and Patterns of Homicide in the 20th Century United States." In *Homicide: A Sourcebook of Social Research*. Edited by M. Dwayne Smith and Margaret A. Zahn. Thousand Oaks, Calif.: Sage, 1999. Pages 9–23.

HOMICIDE: LEGAL ASPECTS

Introduction

The central theme of the law of homicide is the unique value of human life. While danger to life is an element of many other crimes as well, the law of homicide focuses on it directly, by declaring criminal a wide range of conduct that actually causes a death. Because life is valued so highly, such conduct is prohibited much more generally than conduct causing other kinds of harm. Whereas the criminal law for the most part is concerned with intentional harms, criminal homicide includes not only intentional killing but also a broad range of conduct from which death results unintentionally.

Homicide is the killing of a human being by another human being. (Suicide, insofar as the criminal law deals with it, is treated separately.) A question occasionally arises whether a death satisfies this definition, either because it is not clear whether the victim was a "human being" for this purpose or because it is not clear whether another person's conduct caused the death. Most often, the fact of homicide is not an issue. The difficult questions are whether the homicide is criminal or noncriminal and, if the first, in which category of criminal homicide it belongs.

The victim a human being. When homicide is the issue, the law makes no distinctions among human beings as victims. It is human life as such that is protected, and none of the criteria of worth by which we may classify persons for other purposes is material. Death is the more or less remote end for us all, but it is no less homicide that the life cut short would soon have ended anyway, because of age, ill health, or any other reason.

No question has arisen in any adjudicated case as to whether a living creature who is the victim of a homicide was a human being or belonged to some other species. A problem of definition sometimes arises because it is necessary to determine when, in the process of prenatal or postnatal development, life as a separate human being begins or when, in the process of dying, life as a human being ends. The usual rule is that the victim of a homicide must have been "born alive." The older law required that the fetus have been fully separated from the mother and have a separate existence, including an independent circulatory system; it was sometimes also required that the umbilical cord have been cut. There has been some modification of the requirement of full separation, probably in recognition of the easier and safer conditions of ordinary childbirth. It is still generally the law that the victim must have been born alive, which means that there were signs of separate existence and that the birth was far enough advanced so that it would ordinarily have been completed successfully. The destruction of a fetus before it has reached this stage of development is covered by statutes dealing specifically with abortion or the killing of a fetus.

At the other end of a life, the availability of heroic medical techniques to sustain some of the body's vital functions, including circulation and respiration, after other functions have stopped has raised the question of when life ends. The question may be critical if an organ transplant is contemplated, because it is homicide if a human being, however near death, is killed; a successful transplant requires that the organ be removed before necrosis of tissue sets in. There is scant law to answer the question. In ordinary cases, death is deemed to have occurred when there is absence of a heartbeat and respiration. It has also been urged that irreversible coma or cortical brain death, which involves destruction of the cognitive faculties, is enough to constitute legal death, even if circulatory and respiratory action continue.

Action causing death. If someone acts with the intention to kill another person and the death occurs as he intended, there is no difficulty in establishing that his conduct is the cause of death. If he acts without intending to kill or if he has such intent but the death occurs in an unanticipated way, it may not be obvious whether his conduct or some other contributing factor for which someone else or no one else is criminally responsible should be regarded as the cause of death. Efforts to define more precisely the element of causation in homicide have not taken the law beyond what the concept of causation itself conveys. The matter is left to the trier of fact, who must decide on the basis of common sense and ordinary experience whether to attribute causal responsibility.

Since homicide is constituted by a result rather than a particular kind of action, one can commit homicide by an omission or failure to act, if the omission is the cause of death. In many situations, more than one person has an opportunity to take action that would avert death; it would be an extravagant extension of the notion of causation to say that the failure of each caused the death. Furthermore, the criminal law does not generally impose a duty to aid another, even if aid would avoid serious injury to the other and could easily and safely be given. Accordingly, criminal liability for homicide based on an omission is limited to failure to perform an act that one is otherwise legally required to perform. Liability is not based only on a moral obligation, however plain, arising from the danger to life or any other circumstance.

The most common example of such liability is the death of a dependent child resulting from a parent's failure to provide the ordinary care required by law. The relationship of marriage also imposes on each spouse a duty to care for the other that will sustain liability for homicide. Other relationships, like the employer-employee relationship or the ship's captain-seaman relationship, may also provide a basis for liability; the increasing impersonality of such relationships makes liability doubtful if there is not also some

other basis of liability. A legal duty to act may be prescribed by a statute or regulation or may arise from a specific contractual undertaking or a voluntary undertaking that places the other person in one's care. Even if there was a legal duty to act, a death resulting from an omission is not a criminal homicide unless all the elements of the offense, discussed below, are also present. If a person's omission to perform a legal duty was not intentional or negligent, we should probably not describe it as having caused the death; but in any case, in the absence of the required culpability, the omission would not constitute a crime. Convictions of manslaughter by omission are not as rare as convictions of murder by omission; the latter are not, however, unknown, the most common example being a parent's failure to care for an infant who is intentionally left to die.

When the failure to perform a legal duty manifests the same culpability that establishes liability for an act that causes death, liability for the omission, if death results, is unproblematic. One whose grossly negligent failure to act causes a death is not less guilty than one whose grossly negligent act causes a death. Similarly, if a person's legal duty to act has the effect that no one else will probably act in his place, his deliberate nonperformance with the intent to cause death is not very different from a deliberate act. It may not, however, always be possible to establish a close equivalence between acts and omissions. Doubts of this kind, if they arise, are resolved as part of the requirement that the omission in question be the cause of death.

The notion of causation is usually used disjunctively. Ordinarily, a conclusion that one person has killed another precludes a conclusion that another person's separate conduct has brought about the same death. Provided that the element of causing the death of another is satisfied in each case, there is no rule prohibiting more than one person from being criminally liable for the same death. If both parents of a child, each acting independently, failed to give him adequate care and the child died as a result, they might both be guilty of homicide. Similarly, in theory two persons whose independent acts were each the cause of another's death might both be liable.

Most American jurisdictions have preserved a common law rule that a person cannot be convicted of homicide unless the death occurs within a year and a day after the conduct alleged to have caused the death. The purpose of the rule is to avoid a conviction if the passage of time has rendered the element of causation uncertain. Taking account of advances in medical science, the Model Penal Code and the law of some states have abandoned the rule.

Noncriminal and criminal homicide. Despite the value of life, the law recognizes that in some circumstances other values prevail. The official carrying out of a sentence of death, for example, is a deliberate, carefully planned homicide pursuant to the authority of the state. Killing an enemy in battle during war is another example of justifiable homicide, which the state not only permits but approves. There are in addition a number of situations in which the use of deadly force is permitted even though there is no official purpose to take life. In certain circumstances, deadly force can be used to defend oneself or others against the threat of death or serious injury or to prevent commission of a felony or the escape of a felon. The combination of another strongly supported value and the unavoidable necessity of risking life to protect that value excuses the homicide. If life is not taken intentionally, there is no criminal liability unless the actor's conduct is culpable to the extent specified by the categories of unintentional criminal homicide, the least of which requires substantial negligence. Many unforeseen deaths that can be traced causally to the conduct of a particular person occur simply as accidents for which no one is criminally responsible.

Criminal homicide is everywhere divided into categories that reflect the historical distinction in English law between murder and manslaughter. American statutory formulations have varied the terminology and the precise classifications; many statutes create more than two forms of criminal homicide, for purposes of definition and/or punishment. These variations notwithstanding, it is usually possible to discern a category that corresponds to the common law crime of murder, the paradigm of which is a deliberate killing without legal justification or excuse, and a category that corresponds to the common law crime of manslaughter and comprises killings that either are committed in circumstances which substantially mitigate their intentional aspect or are not intentional. In common speech as well as in the law, *murder* refers to the most serious criminal homicides, and *manslaughter* to those that may be serious crimes for which a substantial penalty is imposed but lack the special gravity of murder.

Murder

The traditional definition of *murder* is that it is a homicide committed with "malice aforethought." That phrase, as it developed in English law, was a technical term referring to the mental state of the actor or to the other equivalent circumstances that qualified a homicide as murder. It did not invariably require malice or forethought. While it is still common to use the phrase in connection with murder, it has no independent descriptive significance. In the common law, there was malice aforethought if the homicide was accompanied by (1) intention to kill; (2) intention to cause serious injury; (3) extreme recklessness or disregard of a very substantial risk of causing death; (4) commission or attempted commission of a felony; or (5) according to some authorities, resistance to a lawful arrest. Modern definitions of murder have clarified and in some respects limited these as elements of the crime of murder. In general, the distinguishing feature of the crime is an intent to kill or a disregard of so plain a risk of death to another that it is treated as the equivalent of an intent to kill.

Intention to kill. All jurisdictions place the intentional killing of another without jurisdiction, excuse, or mitigating circumstances within the category of murder, as the most serious form of criminal homicide. While intentional killings may be classified further into subcategories of greater or lesser gravity, there is no controversy about their general classification as murder. Intent to kill has nothing to do with motive as such. While the circumstances that give rise to the intent may mitigate culpability, the law makes no differentiation between a killing with a benevolent motive, like euthanasia, and any other intentional killing.

Ambiguities in the general use of the concept of "intention" to describe conduct have caused trouble in its use to define murder. If the actor's very purpose is to kill, there is no difficulty. It may be, however, that the death of another is an apparently necessary means to the accomplishment of his purpose but that he would be just as satisfied if it wee achieved otherwise. Or, he may be aware that a death is a substantially certain consequence of his conduct, without wanting or trying to bring it about. Courts have wrestled with the distinctions among such states of mind and sometimes offer elaborate analyses of them in the context of particular facts. While such efforts may help to explain the result based on those facts, they do not yield generalizations beyond the ordinary open use of the concept of intention. In general, if the actor is aware that the likelihood of a death resulting from his conduct goes beyond the level of risk to the level of certainty or near-certainty, the element of intent is satisfied. The availability of another category of murder based on extreme recklessness instead of intent helps to ease the burden of decision in borderline cases.

Since persons who intend to kill unlawfully are not likely to proclaim their intention, murder must often be established without explicit proof of intent to kill. The use of a deadly weapon is ordinarily sufficient to establish that element of the crime. While this result may be based on a "presumption" arising from use of a deadly weapon, the presumption amounts only to the usual inference that a person intends the ordinary and probable consequences of his actions. A killing may be murder even though the actor intended to kill someone other than the person who was the actual victim. Although the killing of that person was not intentional, it is enough that the actor acted with the intent to kill. His intent is sometimes said to be "transferred" to the actual killing.

As one of the most serious crimes, murder has historically been a capital offense. All cases of murder were capital offenses under the common law, which remained unchanged in England until 1957, when the class of capital murders was sharply limited; before then, capital punishment could be avoided only by the exercise of executive discretion to commute the sentence of death. In the United States, the Pennsylvania legislature in 1794 limited capital punishment by distinguishing between intentional killings that are "willful, deliberate or premeditated" and those that are not (Pa. Act of April 22, 1794, ch. 257, § 2, 3 Dallas 599). (The formula was later changed to "willful, deliberate and premeditated.") The former, along with a restricted category of felony murder, discussed below, and killing by poison or lying in wait, were labeled murder in the first degree and remained punishable by death. All other kinds of murder were designated murder in the second degree and were not capital offenses. This distinction and the "degree" labels were adopted elsewhere and continue to be widely used. While the term *willful* by itself does not add to the requirement of intent, the deliberation-premeditation formula calls attention to the difference between someone who kills "in cold blood," fully aware of what he is

doing and determined to bring about the result, and someone who acts intentionally but impulsively, without having turned the plan over in his mind. Courts have repeatedly observed that deliberation and premeditation require no particular period of reflection; a very short time before the plan is formed and, once formed, executed, is enough. For this reason and because it is so unclear what kind or quality of deliberation and premeditation is required, the formula has been criticized for giving juries power to dispense verdicts of different severity without any workable standard to guide them. As much criticized as it has been, and difficult as it has been to apply in close cases, the formula reflects a perceived difference of culpability in the paradigms.

Intention to injure seriously.   The intention to injure that constituted one of the common law's categories of malice aforethought was an intention to cause serious physical injury, stopping short of death itself. Provided that the intended injury is truly serious, so that an accidental death from an ordinary assault is not included, few homicides that fall within this category would not also fall within one of the other categories of murder. Death having in fact been the result, in most cases in which a jury is able to find the necessary intent to injure it will be able to find either an intent to kill or extreme disregard of a risk to life. One of the functions of this category of malice aforethought may indeed have been to relieve somewhat the burden of finding an intent specifically to kill rather than to inflict a serious injury.

The Model Penal Code eliminates intent to injure as a separate basis of liability for murder. The drafters concluded that proper cases for liability of this type will be included without it. The only clear case of murder under the common law that is excluded under the Code is one in which the actor inflicts serious injury while taking express precautions not to kill his victim, and the victim dies anyway. Such a case would in any event fall within some category of criminal homicide—manslaughter, if not murder. On the other hand, retention of the common law classification leaves the possibility that unless the degree of seriousness of the intended injury is emphasized, an unintentional killing not accompanied by the same culpability as an intentional killing will be treated in the same way. Some jurisdictions follow the lead of the Model Penal Code; many others retain this category of murder.

Extreme recklessness.   The common law recognized as the equivalent of an intent to kill an attitude of extreme recklessness toward the life of others. One whose conduct displayed plain disregard for a substantial, unjustified risk to human life was guilty of murder if his conduct caused a death. Various formulas have been used to describe this category of malice aforethought, including phases such as "a depraved mind regardless of human life," "an abandoned and malignant heart," and "a heart regardless of social duty and fatally bent on mischief." Whatever formula is used, the key elements are that the actor's conduct perceptibly creates a very large risk that someone will be killed, which he ignores without adequate justification. The risk must be large, and it must be evident; there must also not be circumstances that make it reasonable to impose such risk on others. It is not necessary that the actor be aware of the identity of the person or persons whose life he endangers or that he have any desire that they be killed. The Model Penal Code sums this up in a requirement of recklessness "under circumstances manifesting extreme indifference to the value of human life" (§ 210.2 (1)(b)).

The scope of this category of murder evidently depends considerably on how "extreme" the actor's conduct has to be. Properly limited, the category includes only conduct about which it might be fairly said that the actor "as good as" intended to kill his victim and displayed the same unwillingness to prefer the life of another person to his own objectives. Examples of such conduct, which have been the basis of convictions for murder, are firing a gun into a moving vehicle or an occupied house, firing in the direction of a group of persons, and failing to feed an infant while knowing that it was starving to death. Expanded much beyond cases of this kind, the category might include conduct involving a high degree of carelessness or recklessness that is nevertheless distinct from an intent to kill and more properly included within some lesser category of homicide.

The question is occasionally raised whether the actor must be aware of the risk he creates, if it would be plain to an ordinary reasonable person. Unless the actor is subject to some personal disability that accounts for his lack of awareness, it is most unlikely that he will be unaware of, rather than simply indifferent to, a plain risk so extreme that murder is in issue. In such a case, the resolution will probably depend on the jurisdiction's treatment of that kind of disability generally. If the disability is accepted as a defense or mitigation generally, then it will avoid the charge of murder; otherwise, the actor's lack of aware-

ness will not help him. Thus, for example, while the Model Penal Code's formulation requires conscious disregard of the risk of death, one who was unaware of the risk because he was drunk could nevertheless be found guilty of murder, because the Code elsewhere provides that self-induced intoxication does not avoid a charge of recklessness as an element of an offense. Aside from special cases of this kind, it is probably safe to conclude that the extreme recklessness that characterizes this category of murder includes a realization of the risk. A lesser degree of risk, of which the actor might be unaware, would suffice for manslaughter but not murder.

Felony murder. The common law crime of murder included a homicide committed by a person in the course of committing (or attempting to commit) a felony. The felon—and, according to the rules of accomplice liability, his accomplices—was guilty of murder even if he had no intent to kill or injure anyone and committed no act manifesting extreme recklessness toward human life. The origin of this doctrine may reflect the difficulty of proving specifically an intent to kill, in circumstances in which the intent to commit a felony may suggest a willingness to kill if necessary and other proof either way is lacking. Felonies under early English law were mostly violent crimes and were in any case punishable by death. An attempt to commit a felony was only a misdemeanor, however; the felony-murder doctrine, which also applied to uncompleted felonies, did change the outcome if a homicide was committed during an unsuccessful attempt.

The number of felonies has increased dramatically under modern law. Statutory felonies include a large number of offenses that, however serious on other grounds, do not ordinarily pose great danger to life. Application of the felony-murder doctrine to them distorts the concept of murder as a crime involving a serious direct attack on the value of human life. The explanation that the intent to commit the felony "supplies" the malice aforethought merely states the conclusion. So also, stretched to its logical limits, the felony-murder doctrine would make a felon guilty of murder even if the victim were killed by someone else trying to prevent the felony, provided it were found that the commission of the felony caused the death. In this way, it was occasionally held that when a policeman fired at felons and the bullet struck and killed a bystander, the felons were guilty of murder.

Far as such a death is from the intentional killing that is the paradigm of murder, one can perhaps understand the attitude that leads to the conclusion that the felon should be liable. If not for the felon's conduct—the commission of the felony—the victim would not be dead, accidentally or not. Since in that sense the commission of the felony is the cause of death and the felon has in any case engaged in criminal conduct, it is easy to hold him responsible for the death as well. Even so, it is not appropriate to describe his conduct as murder if he has not engaged in conduct that seriously endangers life. Murder is not simply homicide, but homicide of a particularly culpable nature because it is accompanied by defined mental states; although willingness to commit a felony is itself culpable, it is not the same as, or equivalent to, the culpability that qualifies a homicide as murder.

While the doctrine of felony murder has sometimes been extended to cases very remote from an intentional killing, the courts and legislatures have quite generally adopted rules to restrict its scope. One restriction that responds to a large number of nonviolent statutory felonies is that the doctrine is applicable only if the underlying felony involves violence or danger to life. Sometimes it is required that the *type* of the underlying felony meet this requirement; or it may be enough if the commission of the felony in the particular circumstances is violent or dangerous. The first approach retains the felony-murder doctrine on its own terms but confines it to a more limited group of felonies; to the same general effect are requirements that the felony have been a felony at common law or that it be *malum in se*. The second approach may create liability in a case not covered by the first; it looks in the direction of a displacement of felony murder by a different rationale based directly on the dangerousness of the actor's conduct.

In many states that have more than one category of murder, the more serious category includes homicides committed in the course of one of a short list of particularly dangerous felonies: usually arson, rape, robbery, and burglary; commonly kidnapping; and sometimes one or two others. All other felony murders are in the less serious category. The Pennsylvania degree statute of 1794, referred to above, made this distinction; only homicides committed in the course of the first four mentioned crimes were murder in the first degree.

The nature of the underlying felony is restricted also by the requirement that it be "independent" of the homicide. Otherwise, every felonious assault from which death results might be prosecuted as murder, by operation of the felony-murder doctrine. Such an outcome would obliterate the common law difference between murder and manslaughter and would treat alike homicides of very different character and culpability. Even so, the requirement of independence has been rejected in a few jurisdictions, which presumably leave it to the good sense of the prosecutor not to reach an inappropriate result. The requirement does not apply if the person who is killed is someone other than the victim of the assault.

Another way of restricting felony murder places strong weight on the element of causation. Mere temporal conjunction of the felony and death has never been sufficient for felony murder; it is necessary at least that the death would not have occurred but for the felony. Some courts have explicitly required more than "but for" causation; the death must be a reasonably foreseeable, or natural and probable, consequence of the felony and must not be attributable primarily to a separate, intervening cause. Various ad hoc rules rejecting felony murder when someone other than the felon or an accomplice actually commits the homicide or when an accomplice is killed take a similar approach, although they refer to the party who kills or is killed rather than to causation as such.

The duration of the period during which the felony-murder doctrine applies is not uniformly defined. Once the felony is in progress, the doctrine certainly applies, but it is possible to end its application sooner or later after the felony is complete or has been abandoned, to include or exclude, in particular, flight from the scene of the felony. Some statutes explicitly include the period of flight. There is no clear general rule, the doctrine usually is applicable if the flight is continuous with the commission of the felony and if it cannot yet be said that the felony has succeeded or failed.

A more general attack on felony murder rejects it entirely and subsumes appropriate cases of homicide in the course of a felony under another category of murder. If a felon acting either with intent to kill or with extreme recklessness commits a homicide, then he is guilty of murder on that basis; the fact that the acts were committed in furtherance of a felony obviously does not count against liability. Reflecting the conclusion that if no element of that kind is present, then the felon's liability for murder is gratuitous, the

Model Penal Code and the statutes of a few states have eliminated the felony-murder doctrine. Elsewhere, there has been a partial displacement of the strict doctrine by allowance of an affirmative defense if the felon's own conduct was not intended to and did not in any way endanger life. Of course, if the commission of a felony is itself deemed sufficient to satisfy the requirement of extreme recklessness (on the ground that a felony of that nature is always extremely dangerous to life), the concept of felony murder is reintroduced with the pretense of a different rationale. The Model Penal Code, for example, notwithstanding its strong criticism of the felony-murder doctrine, provides that recklessness and extreme indifference to the value of human life, which support liability for murder, are presumed if the actor is committing or is in flight after committing, one of half a dozen named violent felonies (§ 210.2(1)(b)). Some courts occasionally criticize the doctrine but preserve its force in particular cases by tenuous application of an alternative basis of liability to the specific facts. England, where the doctrine originated, abolished it by statute in 1957 (Homicide Act of 1957, 5 & 6 Eliz. 2, c. 11, § 1).

The uneven record of legislative and judicial efforts to limit or eliminate the felony-murder doctrine suggests strongly the central themes of the law of criminal homicide. When a death occurs and its occurrence can be attributed to the conduct of an identifiable person who is not blameless, there is a strong impulse to hold that person liable for the death, even if, from his point of view, the death should be viewed as accidental. The law not only reflects considered judgments about culpability; it also reflects an unconsidered effort to find an explanation and assign responsibility for an occurrence as disturbing to our sense of order as an unnatural death.

Resistance to a lawful arrest.   Some of the older accounts of murder under the common law include resistance to a lawful arrest as a category of malice aforethought. Such a rule would impose strict liability for murder on a person whose resistance to a lawful arrest caused a death, even if it were accidental. It is now generally agreed that there is no such independent category of murder, although a statutory provision reflecting the traditional rule survives in a few states. A lawful arrest does not mitigate or excuse conduct in opposition to it, as might an unlawful application of similar physical force. Otherwise, homicide resulting from resistance to a lawful arrest

if not treated differently from other homicide. Even in those states that have a special statutory provision, it is doubtful whether a wholly accidental death would be treated as murder if it did not also satisfy some other category of the crime. (England explicitly abolished this category of murder along with felony murder by means of the Homicide Act of 1957.)

Degrees of murder.   The distinction between first-degree and second-degree murder that the Pennsylvania legislature adopted in 1794 applied to intentional killings and felony murder. The statute referred explicitly to killings "by means of poison, or by lying in wait"; but these were evidently intended simply as examples of "willful, deliberate, or premeditated killing." Statutory provisions differentiating types of murder were subsequently enacted in other states. They typically followed the Pennsylvania formula (including references to poison and lying in wait, which sometimes took on a significance of their own) and occasionally made additional distinctions. As in Pennsylvania, the dominant purpose has been to restrict the imposition of the most severe penalty, whether capital punishment or the longest period of imprisonment. Among other circumstances that may qualify a homicide as first-degree, or capital, murder are the use of torture, destruction of or interference with the operation of a public conveyance, use of an explosive, murder for hire, and killing a public official or someone engaged in law enforcement.

Another approach is taken by the Model Penal Code, which rejects further classification of murder but specifies "aggravating circumstances" and "mitigating circumstances" to be taken into account in the determination of whether to impose capital punishment (§ 210.6). The aggravating circumstances include ones that have been used in statutory degree provisions, such as commission of specified violent felonies. They also include others which reflect a judgment that the special deterrent or preventive effect of the death penalty or an extreme measure of retribution is appropriate, as in the case of a defendant under sentence of imprisonment or previously convicted of murder or a violent felony, or where there has been more than one victim. Mitigating circumstances include aspects of the crime that lessen the defendant's culpability as well as factors about the defendant himself, including his youth and lack of a criminal history. Capital punishment can be imposed only if at lest one aggravating circumstance, and no mitigating circumstance, is present. Decisions of the Supreme Court have imposed constitutional limitations on capital punishment, which appear to require an exercise of discretion in each case pursuant to legislatively prescribed standards. The approach of the Model Penal Code, which meets this test, has been widely adopted. The degree formula is still used to distinguish noncapital murders of unequal culpability; most often, as in the original Pennsylvania statute, the circumstances of first-degree murder are prescribed and other cases are grouped generally as second-degree murder.

Manslaughter

As the common law developed, manslaughter became a residual category that included homicides lacking the very high degree of culpability that characterized the capital offense of murder but not so lacking in culpability as to be noncriminal altogether. The need for an intermediate category of this kind reflects the special significance given to the taking of human life; whereas the criminal law might disregard other kinds of harm that was not fully intentional, it could not disregard a homicide accompanied by any substantial degree of fault.

Two general groupings of manslaughter are distinguished in the common law, although they were treated as a single crime and were punishable similarly. They can be described generally as voluntary manslaughter and involuntary manslaughter, labels that are sometimes used in statutes to refer to separate crimes carrying different penalties, with voluntary manslaughter as the more serious offense. There is considerable variation among current statutory formulas, some of which continue to rely on the understandings of the common law and refer simply to manslaughter without defining it. It is still convenient to consider the crime according to the groupings of voluntary and involuntary manslaughter, those terms being used descriptively, whether or not there is explicit statutory differentiation.

Voluntary manslaughter. The principal category of murder refers simply to a homicide committed with intent to kill, without taking account of circumstances that might mitigate culpability because they explain, and in some measure excuse, the actor's state of mind. Voluntary manslaughter is an intentional homicide that would be murder but for the existence of such mitigating circumstances. It is commonly described as an intentional killing accompanied by additional factors that negate malice afore-

thought. Occasionally, voluntary manslaughter is described as a homicide committed in circumstances that overcome and eliminate an intention to kill. Such statements rely on a concept of intention that includes a measure of reflection; they should not be understood to require the killing be unintentional in the ordinary sense.

Most often, the factor that reduces homicide from murder to involuntary manslaughter is some act of the victim that prompts the intent to kill. The usual rule is that an intentional homicide is manslaughter if the actor was provoked to kill by an adequate provocation and acted while provoked, before sufficient time had passed for a reasonable person to have "cooled off." It is not the provocative acts of the victim as such that reduce murder to manslaughter, but their effect on the actor. The most extreme provocation does not affect the result if it does not deprive the actor of self-control; one who responds to a provocation by cooling killing the person who provoked him is guilty of murder, not manslaughter.

Insisiting that conduct be judged by the standard of a reasonable person, the law tended to develop rather rigid rules about the kinds of provocative act that were adequate; a violent battery by the victim and discovery of the victim committing adultery with one's spouse were the paradigms of adequate provocation. Abuse by means of "mere words" was the paradigm of inadequate provocation. Other, less certain, categories were assault or a threat of assault on oneself or a battery or assault on a near relative. Whatever the nature of the provocation, it was not adequate if the actor responded by intentionally killing someone other than the source of the provocation. If, on the other hand, he directed his response against one whom he mistakenly believed to be the source of the provocation, or if accidentally or negligently he killed someone other than his intended victim, the provocation might be allowed. Rules of this kind are sometimes expressed as a general requirement that the homicidal response related to the nature and source of the provocation.

The cooling-off doctrine, as it is sometimes called, is yet another aspect of the requirement that provocation be adequate. A person is expected to regain control of himself within a reasonable period. Courts have sometimes applied this rule strictly and held that rage prolonged or renewed after enough time to cool off has elapsed does not reduce murder to manslaughter, whatever the actual provocation. Despite the argument that the passage of time and brooding over an injury might reduce rather than increase self-control, which may then be swept away by a slight reminder of the original injury, the evident judgment of the law was that only a sudden provocation adequate in itself should be taken into account.

The current direction of the law is to eliminate categorical restrictions of the provocation that may be adequate. The Model Penal Code eliminates all such restrictions and substitutes a general provision classifying as manslaughter "a homicide which would otherwise be murder [that] is committed under the influence of extreme mental or emotional disturbance for which there is reasonable explanation or excuse" (§ 210.3(1)(b)). This provision leaves it to the trier of fact to determine whether the actor's loss of self-control is reasonably comprehensive, without prescribing in advance what sorts of provocation in what circumstances may meet that standard. A number of jurisdictions have adopted such an approach in whole or part, either by statute or judicial decision.

A distinct but related issue is whether the adequacy of provocation should be measured from the point of provocation should be measured from the point of view of an "ordinary reasonable person" or from the point of view of the actor, taking into account any idiosyncratic features he possesses. A defendant has sometimes claimed that provocation which would have been inadequate for an ordinary person was adequate in his case because of some factor peculiar to himself that made the provocative act unusually disturbing. Once again, the law has tended to relax its earlier insistence on an objective standard—without, however eliminating entirely the requirement that the actor's behavior be objectively comprehensible. The Model Penal Code, for example, provides that the reasonableness of the actor's explanation or excuse for his disturbance "shall be determined from the viewpoint of a person in the actor's situation" (§ 210.3(1)(b)). The commentary to this provision explains that the actor's physical handicaps are surely part of his "situation" but that idiosyncratic moral values are not; for the rest, the commentary observes, the reference to the actor's situation is deliberately ambiguous and leaves the issue to the common sense of the finder of fact.

A provoked intentional killing is the most common example of voluntary manslaughter. There are a number of other situations in which an intentional killing is not altogether excused but the circumstances diminish culpability enough to remove it from the category of murder. In general, such situations are those in which a recognized basis for excusing the killing fails to apply fully because one of its elements is absent; nevertheless, the partial applicability of the excuse mitigates the killing. Thus, for example, a person who kills another in what he believes is necessary self-defense against a threat of death or serious injury is excused entirely if his belief is reasonable. If his belief is unreasonable, the defense of self-defense is not available. Even so, the fact that he acted in response to what he believed was a deadly threat distinguishes the crime from an intentional killing not prompted by such fear. His fear seems as appropriate a basis for mitigation as passion or rage caused by provocation.

Similarly, one who uses deadly force in defense against an actual threat of death or serious injury may not be excused entirely if he provoked the attack or if he did not retreat as required before using deadly force. One may use deadly force to protect another person or to prevent commission of a felony, in circumstances that make these defenses not fully available. In these and similar cases of an imperfect excuse, the intention to kill is in a significant sense responsive rather than original with the actor. That element contradicts the extreme denial of the value of human life that characterizes murder. England and a few jurisdictions in the United States have recognized the possibility that a person's capacity to reflect and weigh the consequences of his conduct may be significantly less than normal, without being so abnormal that the defense of insanity is available. His "diminished capacity" may then provide a basis for reducing an intentional killing from murder to manslaughter. Even where this defense is recognized, it is allowed infrequently and in special circumstances only, lest all objective elements of the distinction between murder and voluntary manslaughter be swept away and replaced by an assessment of the actor's subjective culpability.

Involuntary manslaughter. As the name suggests, involuntary manslaughter comprises homicides that are not intentional and lack the special elements of culpability that qualify certain unintentional killings as murder but are nevertheless deemed too culpable to be excused entirely. The crime is recognized in all states in a variety of statutory formulations, which generally follow the common law pattern and may rely wholly on the common law definition. Whether or not it is explicitly differentiated from voluntary manslaughter by statute, involuntary manslaughter is regarded as a less serious offense and usually punished less severely.

A person whose criminal negligence causes the death of another is guilty of involuntary manslaughter. It is generally agreed that negligence sufficient for liability is considerably greater than what would suffice for civil or tort liability. Such negligence may be characterized simply as "criminal," "gross," or "culpable" negligence; as "recklessness"; or as "reckless" or "wanton" carelessness. The central element is unjustified creation of a substantial risk of serious injury or death. Sometimes it is also required that the actor be aware of and disregard the risk, in which case the standard of culpability is more aptly described as recklessness than as negligence. The standard is measurably lower than the extreme recklessness that suffices for murder.

An alternative basis of liability for involuntary manslaughter under the common law and most statutory provisions is commission of an unlawful act or an unlawful omission from which death results. Although the unlawfulness of the conduct may be indicative of negligence, under this theory it is the unlawfulness, rather than the nature of the risk created by the conduct, that establishes liability. In principle, liability might extend to conduct that is unlawful but not criminal, but in practice, liability us usually restricted to conduct that is criminal (but not a felony that will support felony murder). Where vehicular homicide has not been made a separate offense, violation of a traffic regulation is a common example.

Frequently described as misdemeanor manslaughter, this form of criminal homicide has been criticized on the same grounds as felony murder and limited along the same lines. Paralleling the restriction of felony murder to violent felonies, misdemeanor manslaughter is sometimes limited to offenses that are *malum in se,* lest liability be extended to all the conduct that has been made a misdemeanor by statute. Moreover, the requirement of causation has been applied strictly, courts distinguishing between the illegal aspect of the conduct as a causal factor in the homicide, and merely an attendant circumstance of an accidental death. The tendency of the law, not always stated explicitly in the cases, is to confine misdemeanor manslaughter to situations in which the actor's negligence provides a basis for liability, the illegal act having only evidentiary significance on that issue. Such a development

reflects the same analysis that has led to the restriction or elimination of felony murder as a distinct category of that crime.

A homicide resulting from an unlawful battery or assault on the victim without intent to kill or injure seriously may be treated as manslaughter without express reliance on the misdemeanor manslaughter rule. The intention to injure the victim and the commission of an act to that end are evidently perceived, like criminal negligence, as a sufficient basis for liability if death results, without special emphasis on the illegality of the conduct. Since an unjustified attack is always at least a misdemeanor (*malum in se*), such cases might also be regarded as straightforward examples of misdemeanor manslaughter. (Even if, because of aggravating circumstances, the battery were felonious, the "independence" requirement would preclude application of the felony-murder doctrine.) The Model Penal Code, which rejects the misdemeanor manslaughter rule entirely, eliminates liability for manslaughter when death results accidentally from a battery.

Negligent or vehicular homicide. In much the way that the Pennsylvania degree formula differentiated types of murder in order to limit application of the death penalty, statutes in many jurisdictions provide for a lesser category of involuntary criminal homicide. Commonly called negligent homicide or something similar and treated as a separate offense, the category may also be distinguished simply as a lesser degree of manslaughter. A lower standard of culpability applies than that for manslaughter. In particular, recklessness or conscious disregard of the danger to others is not required. While negligence suffices, it is still more than is needed for civil liability. The precise standard of culpability both as set forth in a statute and elaborated by the courts is likely to depend significantly on the formula used to define involuntary manslaughter, with which it must be contrasted.

In some states, the lesser offense is made specifically applicable to motor-vehicle accidents and labeled "vehicular homicide." Even when a high degree of negligence can be established, juries have frequently been unwilling to convict a driver of manslaughter. The large number of traffic fatalities, often occurring in accidents for which liability is uncertain, has evidently made it easier to perceive such deaths as an ordinary, random incident of driving and has diminished the need to resort to the criminal law for explanation. Reduction of the criminality and the penalty attached to the offense acknowledges these changed attitudes and has made application of some criminal sanction more likely.

Penalties

The decision of the Supreme Court in *Coker v. Georgia*, 433 U.S. 584 (1977) raised considerable doubt as to whether capital punishment is constitutionally permitted for any crime other than homicide. Those jurisdictions that retain capital punishment always include among capital crimes a category of murder, which may be narrowly restricted. The Supreme Court has indicated that, except perhaps in very special circumstances, the Constitution prohibits mandatory imposition of the death sentence. The decision whether to impose sentence of death is made by the judge and/or jury, pursuant to various statutory procedures that generally provide for full consideration of aggravating and mitigating factors.

Whether or not capital punishment is retained, murder is always regarded as one of the most serious offenses, for which (or for the most serious category of which) the law's maximum penalty can be imposed. Most jurisdictions authorize a sentence for murder ranging up to life imprisonment, and a minimum sentence of imprisonment for a substantial number of years, commonly as many as ten or twenty. For the most serious category of murder, some jurisdictions provide a mandatory sentence of life imprisonment. Penalties for manslaughter vary widely. The maximum penalty may be as high as ten or twenty years' imprisonment, and the minimum as little as one or two. If involuntary manslaughter is treated separately, the maximum penalty is less—usually not more than five years' imprisonment. The penalty for negligent homicide or vehicular homicide usually does not exceed three years' imprisonment.

The sentencing provisions of the Model Penal Code are representative of this general pattern. Murder, a felony of the first degree (§ 210.2(2)), is punishable (capital punishment aside) by imprisonment for a minimum of not less than one nor more than ten years and for a maximum of life. Manslaughter, a felony of the second degree (§ 210.3(2)), is punishable by imprisonment for a minimum of not less than one nor more than three years and for a maximum of ten years. Negligent homicide, a felony of the third degree (§ 210.4(2)), is punishable by imprisonment for a minimum of not less than one nor more than two years and for a maximum of five years.

Conclusion

The extent to which criminal homicide can be characterized as a single crime or family of crimes is indicated by the fact that the less serious categories are treated as lesser included offenses within the more serious. In a prosecution for first-degree murder, for example, the jury is likely to be instructed on second-degree murder, as well as voluntary manslaughter and even involuntary manslaughter, if any view of the evidence would support those verdicts. The taking of human life, as the harm to be avoided, rather than a common type or measure of culpability, is what binds the whole together.

That element has been critical in efforts to reform or rationalize homicide offenses according to general principles of the criminal law. Although criminal responsibility is thought not to be properly based on fortuities, whether of not death results from an act is often fortuitous from the point of view of the actor and may have large consequences because the severity of the penalty increases so dramatically if death does result. When the circumstances of a death do not allow one to regard it as an ordinary event in human experience, the need for explanation is strong and includes the assignment of blame if that is plausible.

The replacement of strict rules and categories, such as those that characterized voluntary manslaughter, with more general and open principles that refer directly to our primary concerns, may not further the purpose of rationalizing the law of homicide as much as we should like. The exercise of judgment or discretion is, in the end, guided by the same basic impulses as those that led to the more rigid structure. Thus, for example, despite insistence that the doctrine of felony murder is not consistent with basic premises about criminal responsibility, it persists in one form or another. Perhaps the most significant and constant thread in the long development of the law of homicide has been the progressive narrowing of the application of capital punishment. That has not been the product of greater understanding of the bases of liability for homicide so much as a drawing away from capital punishment as such.

LLOYD L. WEINREB
DAN M. KAHAN

See also ABORTION; ASSASSINATION; CAPITAL PUNISHMENT: LEGAL ASPECTS; CAPITAL PUNISHMENT: MORALITY, POLITICS, AND POLICY; EUTHANASIA AND ASSISTED SUICIDE; SUICIDE: LEGAL ASPECTS.

BIBLIOGRAPHY

American Law Institute. *Model Penal Code and Commentaries: Official Draft and Revised Comments.* Philadelphia: ALI, 1980.

DEVINE, PHILIP E. *The Ethics of Homicide.* Ithaca, N.Y.: Cornell University Press, 1978.

DUFF, R. A. "Implied and Constructive Malice in Murder." *Law Quarterly Review* 95 (1979): 418–444.

GEGAN, BERNARD E. "A Case of Depraved Mind Murder." *St. John's Law Review* 49 (1974): 417–459.

HART, H. L. A., and HONORÉ, ANTONY M. *Causation in the Law.* New York: Oxford University Press, 1959.

HOLLIS, CHRISTOPHER. *The Homicide Act.* Foreword by Gerald Gardiner. London: Victor Gollancz, 1964.

HORDER, JEREMY *Provocation and Responsibility.* New York: Oxford University Press, 1992.

HUGHES, GRAHAM. "Criminal Omissions." *Yale Law Journal* 67 (1958): 590–637.

KADISH, SANFORD H. "Respect for Life and Regard for Rights in the Criminal Law." *California Law Review* 64 (1976): 871–901.

LANE, ROGER. *Murder in America: A History.* Columbus: Ohio State University Press, 1997.

Law Commission. *Imputed Criminal Intent (Director of Public Prosecutions v. Smith).* London: Her Majesty's Stationery Office, 1967.

MORELAND, ROY. *The Law of Homicide.* Indianapolis: Bobbs-Merrill, 1952.

MORRIS, NORVAL. "The Felon's Responsibility for the Lethal Acts of Others." *University of Pennsylvania Law Review* 105 (1956): 50–81.

———, and HOWARD, COLIN. *Studies in Criminal Law.* Oxford: Oxford University Press, Clarendon Press, 1964.

MORRIS, TERENCE, and BLOM-COOPER, LOUIS. *A Calendar of Murder: Criminal Homicide in England since 1957.* London: Michael Joseph, 1964.

NOURSE, VICTORIA. "Passion's Progress: Modern Law Reform and the Provocation Defense." *Yale Law Journal* 106 (1997): 1331–1448.

PILLSBURY, SAMUEL H. *Judging Evil: Rethinking the Law of Murder and Manslaughter.* New York: New York University Press, 1998.

Royal Commission on Capital Punishment (1949–1953). *Report.* Cmd. 8932. London: Her Majesty's Stationery Office, 1953.

SELLIN, THORSTEN, ed. "Murder and the Penalty of Death." *Annals of the American Academy of Political and Social Science* 284 (1952): 1–166.

WECHSLER, HERBERT, and MICHAEL, JEROME. "A Rationale of the Law of Homicide." *Columbia Law Review* 37 (1937): 701–761, 161–1325.

WILLIAMS, GLANVILLE. *The Sanctity of Life and the Criminal Law.* Foreword by William C. Warren. New York: Knopf, 1957.

WOLFGANG, MARVIN E. *Patterns in Criminal Homicide.* Reprint. Criminology, Law Enforcement, and Social Problems Series 211. Montclair, N.J.: Patterson Smith, 1975.

HOMOSEXUALITY AND CRIME

A glance through anthropological and historical records reveals immense cross-cultural variation in the acceptance and repression of homosexual relations between men and between women. So great is this variation that some societies in some eras have imposed capital punishment on men engaging in homosexual acts, while others have held sexual friendships between men to be a social ideal of the most honorable, and even heroic, men. The treatment of homoerotic relations between women has often not been symmetric to those of men, being valued or constrained as much by gender conformity as by sexuality per se. Given this immense variation, the question, especially for western societies, is: How did homosexuality become criminalized, then medicalized, and then, to varying degrees, emancipated from the control of church, government, and other social institutions and reform movements? Today the relevant issue in democratic societies is less about crime and more about how best to assure that law works to guarantee the freedom and equal participation of all, including homosexually interested members of society, in the rights and responsibilities of citizenship. Homosexuality and people identified as homosexuals—lesbians, gay men, bisexuals, and transgendered people—today confront a patchwork of legal injunctions, depending on jurisdiction, that range from unreformed criminal labels to inclusion in antidiscrimination codes.

Cross-cultural conceptions

Anthropological records tend to be uneven in documenting sexual customs and practices around the world, typically reveal more about male attitudes than female, and show a wide range of social attitudes regarding homosexuality. What emerges from the anthropological record is that at least some indigenous societies on every inhabited continent have socially valued relationships that include a homosexual aspect. These relationships fall into a few major patterns typically defined by life stage, gender, status, kinship, or some combination (Adam, 1985; Greenberg; Trumbach). One major pattern, well documented in the Americas and Polynesia, is the "berdache," "two-spirited," or transgendered form where gender fluidity, gender mixing, or gender migration appears to be possible for some men and a few women. In these societies, homosexual relations are part of a larger pattern where men and women take up some or most of the social roles and symbols typical of the other gender and enter into marital relations with other people with conventional gender attributes (Jacobs, Thomas, and Lang; Lang and Vantine). A second major pattern takes the form of hierarchical, military, age-graded, and mentor/acolyte relationships, where adult men who presume control over women's bodies also assume sexual rights over younger, subordinate males (Dover; Herdt; Adam; Halperin). Examples of this pattern have been documented in ancient Greece, medieval Japan, precolonial Africa, and Melanesia.

A third pattern, sometimes overlapping with the first two, orders homosexual relationships along the same kinship lines as heterosexuality. Thus, where particular clan members are considered appropriate marital partners—while unions with members of other clans may be prohibited as incestuous—both males and females of the same clan may be considered appropriate and acceptable partners. There are Australian and Melanesian cultures where, for example, one's mother's brother was considered both an appropriate marital partner for girls and an appropriate mentor (including a sexual aspect) for boys (Adam, 1985). Similarly, in some societies where the accumulation of bride-price is the prerequisite to obtaining a wife, occasionally women with wealth are able to avail themselves of this system to acquire wives and men can provide a corresponding gift to the families of youths whom they take into apprenticeship (Amadiume). These kin-governed bonds have been documented in some societies of Australia, Africa, and Amazonia. These major patterns do not exhaust the full range of cross-cultural homoerotic bonding, nor do they explain the gay and lesbian worlds of today. They do point to the fact that there is no unitary idea of homosexuality in different societies, no single role or attitude toward same-sex sexuality, and thus no predominant conception of social approval or disapproval. It is also clear that there is no intrinsic connection between conceptions of homosexuality and crime. Indeed, in kin-based models of homosexual attachment, socially disapproved or "criminal" relationships would refer to relationships formed between persons of inappropriate clans, regardless of gender. Similarly, in age-graded, mentor-acolyte systems, the relationships considered to be odd, ridiculous, or even criminal are those where older men take a sexually receptive role in relation to younger men, in contravention of social expectations that younger men should assume a receptive role. Homosexuality per se would not be at issue. It is against this backdrop that the western preoccupation with homosexuality as criminal sexual conduct must be explained.

Western traditions

The roots of the political and philosophical traditions of the West are in a society deeply affirmative of homosexual relations of the mentor-acolyte model. Indeed, most of the heroes of ancient Greek mythology had male lovers; the founding of political democracy is attributed to the male couple Harmodias and Aristogeiton, who slew the tyrant Hyppias in 514 B.C.E. (Halperin; Foucault). And Socrates, in unexpurgated translations of the *Symposium*, rhapsodizes about how the love of youths leads to the love of beauty and thus to the love of wisdom. Yet the modern Western tradition has suppressed, denied, and appropriated this homoerotic heritage consigning it to sin, sickness, or crime. The gradual shaping and consolidation of Christian doctrines into the canon law of the Western church articulated by medieval theologians, and the propagation and enforcement of these views by the Roman Catholic Church from the twelfth to fourteenth centuries and onward replaced the heroic friendships valued by the ancients with the idea of the *sodomite* (Jordan, 1997). Like the traditions it suppressed, the *sodomite* cannot simply be equated with modern ideas of the *homosexual*. In ecclesiastical law *sodomy* typically referred to a vague, sometimes comprehensive category of sexual practices that lack pro-natal objectives, including, for example, nonreproductive heterosexual acts and bestiality, as well as homosexual practices. The consolidation of church power through the first millennium of the Christian era included the gradual eradication of indigenous, European forms of sexual friendship (Boswell). By the fifteenth and sixteenth centuries, sodomy became a charge pursued in the West by the Inquisition, with varying degrees of rigor in different countries, along with the church's campaign to suppress Jews, witches, and other forms of religious nonconformity. In the sixteenth through twentieth centuries, Christian orthodoxies, imposed by military conquest on indigenous populations of the Americas, Africa, and Asia, actively extinguished local forms of homosexuality as part of larger campaigns of cultural colonialism, or forced these local forms underground (Trexler; Bleys). The conceptualization of homosexuality as a sinful, nonreproductive sexual act became widely established where governments and empires acted in concert with institutional churches to enforce cultural and juridical dominion over much of the world's population in the Christian realm.

As nation-states emerged from empires in the eighteenth through the twentieth centuries, many of them formalized their criminal codes from the legacy of canon law, depending on the social ingredients that went into state formation and their relation to church control. Nation-states might be thought of as places where particular social groups defined by capital, race, language, religion, gender, and sexuality forge hegemony over a territory (Corrigan and Sayer). These groups institutionalize their own cultures as national cultures, thereby generating a range of subordinated and minority groups who must fend for themselves in an alien world. With the rise of nation-states in the context of a Eurocentric, Christian, modern world-system, the modern conception of homosexuality has emerged, a sexual act attributed to a class of people subject to social sanction and criminal penalty (Adam, 1995; Stychin). As the world economy mobilized masses of people in cities, and as states devised more efficient systems of supervising, regulating, and policing their populations, homosexual men (and later women) began to be affected by the criminal justice systems of Europe. From the early example of the fifteenth century Venetian Republic, to eighteenth-century campaigns to catch and suppress organized sodomy—that is, the nascent gay world—in Britain, Holland, and Switzerland, state agencies (and at least in Britain, Societies for the Reformation of Morals, as well) swept up hundreds of men and some women in their punitive nets. The Dutch cam-

paign alone resulted in seventy executions. The legacy of this nexus of church and state building has been the disciplining of same-sex eroticism, the categorization of its adherents as a people apart, and the invention of homosexuality as a juridical and medical category.

Modernity

The seeds of an alternative to the old order germinated in the Enlightenment, when scientific and humanist thinking, and a rediscovery of the ancient Greek legacy of democratic politics and aesthetics, grew into a countermovement to theocracy. Socio-economic changes occurring in the world system were, at the same time, undermining the aristocratic, landholding classes of Europe and the church that legitimized their rule. The French Revolution is perhaps the most central symbol of the modern social and cultural paradigm that swept aside church and aristocracy in the name of the right of the people to govern themselves rather than submit to the will of monarchs and bishops. The modern French state advanced the idea of the citizen with rights to self-determination regardless of origin or trait. Religion was dethroned from its hegemonic position, deprived of the tools to enforce its will on everyone, and privatized to the realm of personal belief. Everyone could have religion; they just did not have the right to force those around them to believe or to carry out the same moral agenda.

It is perhaps not surprising, then, that this liberal democratic revolution also initiated the disestablishment of sexual orthodoxy, permitting greater individual freedom, and extracting the state from the regulation of homosexuality. With the advent of the Napoleonic legal code, sodomy disappeared from criminal law, and as Napoleon swept through Europe evicting the mainstays of the old order, he left new nation-builders in his wake who founded legal systems without the category of *sodomy*. The modern world of most of western and southern Europe, as well as its territories (principally in Latin America), broke the medieval link between homosexuality and criminality in the early nineteenth century.

Germany, Britain, the United States, and their territories, who held out against Napoleon, remained unreformed for the next century or more. British elites reacted to the French Revolution with widespread crackdowns on dissidents and a wave of imprisonments of men for sodomy. When the German states united under the auspices of Prussia in the late nineteenth century, they retained the Prussian sodomy law, Paragraph 175, and in some instances overturned the decriminalization that had occurred in such component states of the new German empire as Bavaria and Hannover. One Hannover jurist, Karl Ulrichs, became a lifetime advocate against Paragraph 175 and was a precursor to the first organized gay and lesbian movement organization, the Scientific-Humanitarian Committee. Founded in Berlin in 1897, the committee worked for many years to overturn Paragraph 175 in Germany. During the late 1890s in Britain, the primary public event surrounding the criminal labeling of homosexuality was the show trial that condemned Oscar Wilde to two years of hard labor in Reading Gaol.

By the early twentieth century, European nations contained conflicting social forces advancing modern reforms and defending premodern traditions. Gay and lesbian public spaces, now evident in cities throughout the industrialized world, became vulnerable to predation by an array of police, clerics, physicians, moral entrepreneurs, and blackmailers, each with their own agenda. Gay and lesbian voices could only infrequently break through official censorship to participate in the public agenda, and often had to resort to oblique references in science, theater, and literature in order to communicate with each other and to the public. Only in Germany and the Netherlands was there a sufficiently open civil society for above-ground gay and lesbian organizations advocating for change.

With reactionary forces coming to power in Germany in 1933, the law became a tool used to strike out against Jews, national minorities, the disabled, religious dissidents, and homosexuals, with each group falling under criminal sanction and suffering genocide in the Holocaust. Russian Communism under Stalin moved in a similarly authoritarian direction, re-criminalizing homosexuality at a time when the Soviet state was inventing and destroying a wide range of supposed internal enemies. The end of World War II brought little solace to homosexual peoples, as the criminalizing states—most notably the Soviet Union, the United States, the United Kingdom, and the Federal Republic of Germany—showed little sign of reform or even initiated new campaigns of persecution against their gay and lesbian citizens. When ruling elites become fearful during times of national or international upheaval, criminal law is often a tool of repression directed against those imagined to be enemies of national identity and community. Just as Britain included homosexuals in its repression of dissidents during the French Revolution, the Cold War fed state searches for "traitors" and dissidents. In the United States, McCarthyism criminalized a wide range of people imagined to be the "un-American *other*" as "communists" driving many out of their careers and into exile. Again, among its fantasy enemies were homosexuals pursued as "security risks" and forced into jails and mental hospitals (D'Emilio). With the suppression of the early gay and lesbian movement in the Holocaust, the only alternative in the 1950s to the criminal paradigm was the medical view of homosexuality as sickness. While police and courts raided and jailed gay and lesbian meeting places, psychiatrists were busy promoting the redefinition of homosexuality as a psychopathology.

Anglo-American law reform

A thaw in the repressive climate of the post–World War II period occurred on several fronts in the late 1950s. In Britain, as in most western European countries and the United States, gay and lesbian people began to organize in small, cautious groups in major cities. These homophile groups attempted to provide mutual support in an environment characterized by fear and harassment. Criminal laws gave police and citizens alike a warrant to persecute: blackmailers were given free rein to exploit many, gay bashers could act with impunity, gay bars were subject to raids, gays and lesbians were vulnerable to losing their jobs when a newspaper or a gossip informed on them to employers, and some were pressed into mental hospitals and prisons. No one could count on sympathy from courts or professionals when seeking redress against discrimination. Indicative of the times was the 1954 death of Alan Turing, a master cryptographer during World War II responsible for breaking Nazi codes and today recognized as an originator of the modern computer. When his homosexuality was found out by police in 1952, he was forced to undergo destructive hormone treatments and hounded to suicide in 1954 (Hodges). But also in 1954, an unrepentant Peter Wildeblood spoke out against his persecutors in a well-publicized trail by demanding "the right to choose the person whom I love" (Adam, 1995). The courts responded by sending him to prison. Nevertheless, by 1957 a royal commission recommended that private homosexual relations between consenting adults be decriminalized (Weeks). It look another ten years before a Labour government enacted the commission's recommendation during a period when laws were being liberalized on a series of "moral" and family issues, such as divorce and abortion.

In the United States, the Civil Rights movement challenged Americans to practice the legal and democratic ideals professed in the Constitution, and to recognize the racial subordination that violated these ideals. The Civil Rights movement, in turn, opened the way for wide-ranging public debates about other forms of social injustice, and gave courage to other subordinated groups to mobilize for citizenship rights. Students, women, other racial minorities, and gay and lesbian people joined in the New Left demand for democratic participation of disenfranchised groups. The defensive homophile groups of the 1950s gave way to a new militancy of the 1970s as lesbians and gay men shifted from apologetics to a rights discourse. In 1961, Illinois became the first state to decriminalize by adopting the Model Legal Code of the American Law Institute. Twenty years later a bare majority of the states had followed suit either through legislative reform or court rulings, and in 1986 the United States Supreme Court upheld the sodomy laws in the unreformed states (*Bowers v. Hardwick*).

Similar changes were occurring worldwide during the 1960s and 1970s. Canada and Germany decriminalized in 1969, and Australia decriminalized the federal capital and northern territories in 1973, beginning a process that worked its way through state legislatures.

Decriminalization came about as part of a larger set of socio-economic changes that have led to a public rethinking of the meanings and functions of family and sexuality, especially in the advanced, industrial nations. The growth of women in the workforce helped create the foundation for feminist movements and challenged traditional presumptions about gender and family. Women's movements struggled for a right of personal and sexual self-determination, successfully pressing for reform of divorce and abortion laws. Families shifted from being units of production in traditional, agrarian societies, to units of consumption in wage-labor systems, resulting in a fall in the birthrate and a corresponding questioning of pro-natal ideologies. All of these changes are associated with a gradual reconceptualization of marriage as voluntary, egalitarian, and romantic—all criteria that have equal applicability to same-sex unions. Same-sex relationships have been part of this reorganization of the elements of gender, sexuality, and family, and have come to seem less "different" as heterosexual relationships have themselves changed over time. And lesbian and gay people have organized to throw off the disabilities imposed on them by law and psychiatry.

The global view

At the turn of the twenty-first century, criminal penalties for homosexual acts remained part of legal codes primarily in three sets of countries: (1) post-colonial governments of south Asia, Africa, and the Caribbean (many still preserving British laws now abandoned by the United Kingdom itself); (2) mainly southern and Rocky Mountain states of the United States; and (3) Islamic governments of the Arab world and Asia (International Lesbian and Gay Association). Executions of homosexual men were reported in the 1990s in the radical, theocratic states of Iran and Afghanistan, as well as in Saudi Arabia. With the fall of the Soviet Union, most of the newly independent states, including Russia, moved rapidly to decriminalize, but some Caucasus and Islamic republics still retain the Stalinist legal code. There are exceptional instances of the *recriminalization* of homosexuality in recent times as in Puerto Rico and Nicaragua. Recriminalization came about in Nicaragua when church and landowning elites reasserted themselves in government, with U.S. backing, against the former Sandinista revolutionary government.

Criminal law is, of course, not a reliable guide to actual practice. Applied to consenting, sexual behavior, it is necessarily arbitrary and uneven. Enforcement typically relies on vindictive neighbors, police intrusion, or periodic campaigns of persecution dependent on the motivations of political elites and moral entrepreneurs. Because it is a charge that is virtually impossible to disprove, sodomy law has long proven to be a convenient political weapon in the absence of legitimate wrongdoing. Sodomy was a convenient tool for seizing control of the commercial empire of the former Crusaders, the Knights Templar, in the fourteenth century when French and Spanish monarchs grew covetous of their influence. The Nazi regime also used it to discredit and arrest political enemies. In 1998, it proved useful to the Malaysian Prime Minister Mahathir Mohamad, who successfully imprisoned his political rival, finance minister Anwar Ibrahim, on charges of sodomy.

Vibrant gay and lesbian communities flourish in some jurisdictions where sodomy law continues, but is largely a "dead letter," even in places where homosexual people struggle against active discrimination practiced by state and social institutions, including the police and the courts. In other countries, where homosexual "offenses" are off the law books, a range of other discriminatory legislation nevertheless imposes disabilities on the freedom of citizens to love and live with the persons of their choice. Various kinds of sweeping laws regulating "public scandal" and "indecent acts" provide police with broad powers that lead to harassment and intimidation, often directed against gay men, most notably in Latin America and Romania. In the United States and Canada, police and gay communities contest the boundaries between "public" and "private" as men suffer arrest from time to time for sexual speech or conduct typically under the cover of darkness in parks or in bathhouses. Lack of criminal penalty may be no guarantee of freedom of association or freedom of expression. Attempts to form gay and lesbian associations, or simply to gather together on a social basis, may be subject to repression. In many places, the organization of gay and lesbian film festivals or the founding of a gay press have resulted in police action, or in official acquiescence to attacks incited by church officials, criminal gangs, and death squads. Violence against lesbians and gay men continues to flourish in places where police turn a blind eye toward perpetrators, and where courts excuse them when they claim to be reacting against a sexual advance. A number of jurisdictions impose a higher age of consent for homosexual than for heterosexual activity, a remnant of the theory that homosexuality is in need of special, surplus regulation in comparison to heterosexuality.

From criminal to human rights law

In the last decades of the twentieth century, many governments took steps to rectify discriminatory regulations imposed on citizens' freedom to form the sexual and affective relationships of their choosing. As justice, rather than crime, has come to define public discourse around homosexual relations, governments have increasingly recognized their gay, lesbian, bisexual, and transgendered populations as subordinated and vulnerable peoples whose fundamental rights to life, livelihood, and democratic participation have been unjustifiably compromised by social prejudice and misuse of state power. Redress for discrimination experienced in employment or housing was a demand first pressed by many labor unions in the 1970s, and adopted by voluntary associations and municipal governments. Norway became the first country to adopt a national antidiscrimination law in 1981. By the end of the 1990s, human rights legislation including *sexual orientation* as a protected category had become widespread in the European Union, including Sweden, Denmark, Iceland, France, Spain, Finland, the Netherlands, Luxembourg, and Switzerland (International Lesbian and Gay Association). In Canada, human rights law reform came province by province, first with Québec in 1977 and culminating in a Supreme Court decision in 1998 that ordered the last hold-out among the ten provinces to adopt anti-discriminatory law. Australia undertook a similar state-by-state process; New Zealand adopted its law in 1993. The United States shows a much slower movement toward legal reform with only ten of fifty states having human rights laws. One state, Maine, repealed its human rights law in a state-wide referendum. *Sexual orientation* legislation is appearing in other countries that undertook constitutional reform in the 1990s, namely, South Africa, Slovenia, Ecuador, and Fiji. Somewhat more restrictive human rights legislation, applied only to employment, is now in place in Ireland and Israel. Included in some human rights legislation are anti-vilification provisions that prohibit hate propaganda and incitement to violence.

The advent of AIDS in the 1980s introduced a new round in conflicts over sexual regulation. AIDS was seized upon by the traditional opponents of homosexuality as a tool for re-criminalization. While some of the more egregious initiatives have been turned back, a myriad of punitive and exceptional laws are now on the books that limit safe-sex education, pretend to control sexual transmission of HIV, or prohibit travel. The United States has distinguished itself with a law that discriminates against the entry of HIV-positive individuals into the country; as a result, the United States has been boycotted by the leading world AIDS research organization, the International AIDS Society.

The frontier of full citizenship rights at the end of the twentieth century is the legal recognition of same-sex partnerships. Denmark initiated a registered partnership program for same-sex couples in 1989. Norway, Sweden, the Netherlands, and Iceland have followed the Danish precedent, and a supreme court decision in Hungary has included same-sex couples in common law spousal status. Broad legal recognition is now in place in the Canadian provinces of Québec, Ontario, and British Columbia (a federal bill, C-23, is currently before the Canadian Parliament but not yet passed), the Spanish regions of Catalonia and Aragon, and the U.S. states of Hawaii and Vermont. All of these laws, however, fall short of full equality, often barring gay and lesbian couples from full-fledged marriage, adoption, or access to alternative insemination. Beginning with Utah in 1995, a wave of preemptive legislation and referenda swept through the United States to ban "gay marriage," extending in five years to thirty-one states and the federal Congress.

Conclusion

Today gay and lesbian movements and scholars continue to grapple with the legacy of modern and premodern paradigms of sexuality that continue to contend for supremacy in many places. A *queer theory* school of thought, manifested briefly in the early 1990s as a *queer nation* movement, critiques the historical peculiarity of the modern homosexual, calling for its deconstruction. Concepts of sin, crime, and sickness all depend on the peculiar process by which heterosexuals produce and reinforce a category of the sexual other through police, medicine, and the mass media. But on the other hand, the queer critique has become possible only because a great many people have been willing to embrace gay and lesbian identities, which means standing up for a right to love and live with persons of one's choice, and standing against the malevolent designations propagated by states, churches, and culture producers. Today, gay, lesbian, bisexual, and transgendered identities and cultures continue to hold enormous appeal for those struggling in the "pursuit of happiness" against the forces of repression. Pride celebrations have boomed in three decades from a small gathering in New York's Central Park to a worldwide festival, counting among the largest of celebrations in such cities as Toronto, Sydney, and San Francisco, and serving as symbols around which people mobilize for the first time in small towns and new countries. Despite (or perhaps in opposition to) official silence, or active suppression, people are mobilizing as homosexual people in such places as China, Cuba, and Zimbabwe to claim social and cultural space for themselves.

Criminal law remains a tool held in abeyance in some jurisdictions, but nevertheless ready-at-hand when clerics, police, politicians, or other homophobes choose to wrap themselves in the flag of "virtue" by attacking "vice." Vague laws governing censorship, public conduct, and indecency continue to provide warrant for suspending the freedom of speech and association of homosexual people, even where homosexual "acts" are legal. The status of gay and lesbian people today functions as something of an index of the willingness of democratic societies to follow through on their self-proclaimed principles of guaranteeing equality and freedom of their citizens, acting as individuals, in households, and in communities.

BARRY D. ADAM

See also CRIMINALIZATION AND DECRIMINALIZATION; HATE CRIMES; SEX OFFENSES: CONSENSUAL; VICTIMLESS CRIMES.

BIBLIOGRAPHY

ADAM, BARRY D. "Age, Structure, and Sexuality." *Journal of Homosexuality* 11, no. 3–4 (1985): 19–33.
———. *The Rise of a Gay and Lesbian Movement.* New York: Twayne, 1995.
AMADIUME, IFI. *Male Daughters, Female Husbands.* Toronto: DEC, 1980.
BLEYS, RUDI. *Geography of Perversion/Desire.* London: Cassell, 1995.
BOSWELL, JOHN. *Same-Sex Unions in Pre-Modern Europe.* New York: Villard, 1994.
CORRIGAN, PHILIP, and SAYER, DEREK. *The Great Arch.* Oxford: Basil Blackwell, 1985.
D'EMILIO, JOHN. *Sexual Politics, Sexual Communities.* Chicago: University of Chicago Press, 1983.
DOVER, K. J. *Greek Homosexuality.* New York: Vintage, 1978.
FOUCAULT, MICHEL. *The Care of the Self.* History of Sexuality, vol. 2. New York: Pantheon, 1978.
GREENBERG, DAVID. *The Construction of Homosexuality.* Chicago: University of Chicago Press, 1988.
HALPERIN, DAVID. *One Hundred Years of Homosexuality.* New York: Routledge, 1990.
HERDT, GILBERT. *Ritualized Homosexuality in Melanesia.* Berkeley: University of California Press, 1984.
HODGES, ANDREW. *Alan Turing.* New York: Simon & Schuster, 1984.

International Lesbian and Gay Association. http://www.ilga.org.

JACOBS, SUE ELLEN; WESLEY, THOMAS; and LANG, SABINE. *Two Spirit People.* Urbana: University of Illinois Press, 1997.

JORDAN, MARK. *The Invention of Sodomy in Christian Theology.* Chicago: University of Chicago Press, 1997.

LANG, SABINE, and VANTINE, JOHN. *Men as Women, Women as Men.* Austin: University of Texas Press, 1998.

STYCHIN, CARL. *A Nation by Rights.* Philadelphia: Temple University Press, 1998.

TREXLER, RICHARD. *Sex and Conquest.* Ithaca: Cornell University Press, 1995.

TRUMBACH, RANDOLPH. "Gender and the Homosexual Role in Modern Western Culture." In *Homosexuality, Which Homosexuality?* Edited by Dennis Altman et al. London: GMP, 1989.

WEEKS, JEFFREY. *Coming Out.* London: Quartet, 1977.

HUMAN IMMUNODEFICIENCY VIRUS

Human Immunodeficiency Virus (HIV) is usually spread unintentionally, but in the course of sexual or drug-using conduct that is intentional. Since the beginning of the HIV epidemic, criminal law has been proposed, and sporadically deployed, as a means of addressing conduct that exposes others to, or actually infects them with, HIV. This entry surveys the practical, legal, and social issues that arise in the "criminalization" of a public health threat.

The case for criminalizing conduct that spreads HIV is straightforward. People who deliberately or recklessly expose others to or actually infect others with HIV are said to deserve punishment. Such punishment might have the added benefit of deterring others from creating the same risks. Criminal laws certainly express society's disapproval of the conduct, which may provide additional deterrence through social influence. In practice, however, the issue is much more complicated.

Criminalization as a health measure

The public health case for criminalization is weak. Criminal law can be an effective tool of HIV prevention only if it incapacitates or deters the people whose behavior is responsible for a significant proportion of new cases, but criminalization stumbles almost immediately on a paradox. The behavior most widely accepted as wrong—deliberately using HIV as a tool to harm or terrorize another—is too rare to influence the epidemic, whereas the behavior most responsible for spreading the virus—voluntary sex and needle sharing—is difficult and controversial to prohibit. Both the impetus for and opposition to criminalization reflect profound social differences over the acceptability of homosexuality and drug use, and the clash of values those differences entail.

Sex and needle sharing as crime

In principle, a zone of wrongful exposure to HIV can be delineated in terms of autonomy. The risk of HIV transmission through sex is low enough that a person may reasonably choose to run it, but high enough that no one should endanger another without consent. The consent principle embraces the worst cases of deliberate exposure, rape, and fraud, but also the common sexual encounters (or needle sharing) that drive the epidemic. Research indicates that many people who know they are infected with HIV sometimes engage in unsafe sexual or drug-using behavior without informing their partners of their infection. Women, with less power than their male partners, are particularly vulnerable to unwanted sexual risk.

Although most people would probably agree that concealment of one's HIV status from a sex or needle partner is wrong, there are both principled and practical objections to enforcing the norm through criminal law. Sex and drug use are voluntary activities with known (and rather moderate) risks. They are normally conducted under implicit social conventions concerning disclosure, risk-taking, and consent that may not require explicit discussion of infection. Some contend, on libertarian or privacy grounds, that the government simply ought not to be regulating such behavior. Other commentators suggest that sexual interaction is simply too psychologically complicated and socially unsettling to be sensibly analyzed in the terms of culpability offered by criminal law.

Public health professionals have worried that designating such common behavior as criminal could add to the stigma and social risk of getting tested, educated, or treated. They fear that prosecutions, particularly if they involve use of public health records to document prior knowledge of infection, can rend the fabric of privacy and cooperation necessary to effective prevention. Although empirical support for this concern is weak, even a minor negative effect would outweigh the negligible benefits of criminalization for public health.

Research has largely discredited the belief that needle sharing is a social preference in favor of the view that it is a response to the scarcity of new, sterile injection equipment. This scarcity, in turn, is attributable to drug paraphernalia and needle prescription laws designed to prevent drug users from obtaining injection equipment. It is objectionable on principle, as well as counterproductive from a public health perspective, to deliberately prevent individuals from getting sterile syringes while prosecuting those same people for sharing unsterile ones.

Mistrust is the greatest obstacle to criminal law's protection of sexual autonomy and public health. Many people are dubious of the motivation behind criminalization. Many gay men, for example, fear that HIV is used as an excuse to suppress gay sexuality. Moreover, the fact that criminalization initiatives tend to come from more conservative legislators, and are never systematically enforced, fuels suspicion that criminalization is really part of a larger struggle between social factions for normative dominance in matters of sexuality. Sexually-transmitted disease control policies have historically reflected and been a vehicle for the expression of competing social norms about sexual behavior and the status of women and minorities. On this view, criminalization of HIV is of a piece with laws prohibiting sodomy, or denying civil rights protection to gay men and lesbians.

The behavioral impact of criminalization

The population of people spreading HIV is so large, and the resources devoted to detecting and prosecuting exposure crimes so small, that incapacitation can be ruled out as a plausible outcome of current criminalization initiatives. Deterrence is notoriously difficult to assess, but on each of the leading theories of the mechanism of deterrence the suggestion that criminalization will deter people from having sex or sharing needles without disclosure is implausible.

Rational actor theories posit that deterrence rests on some combination of likelihood of detection and severity of punishment. Long imprisonment is a severe punishment for a person with HIV, whose life expectancy is shorter than usual and whose need for the best medical care is greater. The chances of being prosecuted, however, are so low as to undermine the impact of a severe sanction.

Legitimacy-based theories suggest that people may obey the law because they believe it is right to do so, and in particular because they believe that the legal system operates fairly in setting and enforcing norms. The small number of prosecutions tends by itself to make any one appear freakish or arbitrary. More importantly, the criminalization of HIV entails the imposition of disputed norms of sobriety and chastity upon communities that have substantially defined themselves in their rejection or subversion of the values of the dominant groups in society. It seems unlikely that gay men or drug users will change their behavior out of respect for authority.

Criminalization in practice

Prosecutors began charging people with HIV-related crimes early in the epidemic. Nearly all cases involved exposure to the virus, rather than its actual transmission. As many as one hundred prosecutions had been initiated by 1988, when the first reported decisions appeared. In that same year, the final report of the Presidential Commission on HIV recommended that "HIV infected individuals who knowingly conduct themselves in ways that pose significant risk of transmission to others must be held accountable for their actions." By 1999, there were approximately fifty reported cases and at least 200 prosecutions. Thirty states had passed HIV-specific criminal provisions, laws that varied enormously in the conduct they embraced and the penalties they imposed.

The cases fall into three main groups. The most numerous is comprised of instances of the allegedly deliberate use of HIV as a weapon to cause emotional distress or bodily harm. These cases, which have commonly involved biting or spitting, are notable for the high charges (including attempted murder) and long sentences meted out. A smaller group is made up of cases using HIV as a basis for more severe sentencing in cases of prostitution, rape, and child abuse. The third group is comprised of prosecutions, under the Uniform Code of Military Justice, of military personnel who disobeyed "safe-sex" orders to refrain from sexual contact without informing partners of their infection. No more than a handful of civilians have been prosecuted for isolated instances of unsafe sex without disclosure, and no reported cases involve needle sharing.

General criminal law

Depending on the actor's state of mind, actual transmission of HIV by any means could be prosecuted as murder or manslaughter if it resulted in death of the exposed party. In practice, the long latency period of the disease, and old doctrines such as the rule that the fatal act must have occurred within a year and a day of the death to be prosecuted as a murder, may help explain why there is no reported case in the United States.

More commonly prosecuted is the act of exposing someone else to HIV. Available charges include reckless endangerment, assault, assault with a deadly weapon (or aggravated assault), and attempted murder. Reckless endangerment requires proof that the actor placed another at risk of serious bodily harm with conscious disregard of the risk. An assault is established if the actor is proven to have knowingly or purposefully engaged in conduct likely to transmit HIV. Some courts have allowed prosecution for aggravated assault or assault with a deadly weapon on the theory that HIV, or some body part containing HIV, is a weapon. Attempted murder requires a showing that the defendant purposely or knowingly deployed HIV as a weapon of homicide.

Both proponents and opponents of criminalization have been critical of the current approach of the criminal law to HIV cases. Proponents worry that bad actors get off too easily. The long course of the disease makes prosecuting actual transmission as murder impractical. Cases of exposure are also said to be hard to prosecute. A minority of courts have refused to analogize HIV to a deadly weapon, or have ruled that one or two sexual contacts are simply not risky enough to place another at the kind of risk prohibited by assault. Numerous commentators have pointed to a supposed difficulty of proving an intent to harm, particularly where, as the Supreme Court of Maryland ruled, proof of infection alone is not sufficient to establish the defendant's intent to do harm.

Critics worry that both intent and risk are poor tools for assessing HIV cases. They note convictions in numerous assault and attempted murder cases involving very low risk acts like spitting, biting, and throwing infected body fluids. In such cases, and potentially in cases involving voluntary sexual activity, the unacceptability of the risk to jurors can skew their assessment of the likelihood of harm. Critics also worry about the effect of race, class, and the stigma of HIV on the decision-maker's assessment of the defendant's intent. Convictions of biters and spitters for attempted murder are seen as proof that judges and juries can ascribe a homicidal intent to a person with HIV even where the chosen weapon was practically incapable of causing death.

HIV-specific offenses

Concerns about the inappositeness of general criminal law has long led commentators from across the spectrum of opinion to prefer laws specifically defining culpable conduct among people with HIV, but positive legislation has brought neither clarity nor consistency. Many statutes deal only with specific modes of risk creation, such as blood donation or prostitution. Those that address sexual behavior more generally vary in the state of mind and acts addressed, as well as on important issues such as whether condom use or other safe sex practices can be considered in defense.

Two examples illustrate the range of provisions. California's law, one of the narrowest, covers only unprotected sexual activity carried out with the specific intent to infect the other, and states that knowledge of infection alone is not sufficient to satisfy the intent requirement. Idaho's law covers any transfer or attempted transfer of any body fluid, body tissue, or organ to another by a person who knows of his or her infection or any symptom of infection. "Transfer" includes "engaging in sexual activity by genital-genital contact, oral-genital contact, anal-genital contact," without regard to the riskiness of the act or even the use of a condom. Thus in Idaho, a person who has oral sex using a condom but without informing the other is liable to up to fifteen years in prison, whereas the same conduct is not covered by California's law at all. Even without the condom and with a specific intent to infect, such conduct in California would be subject to a maximum of eight years. Absent systematic enforcement, the few prosecutions under these laws have depended upon a happenstance of detection under circumstances that led a prosecutor to charge the crime.

The "extreme case"

Criminalization debate tends to be framed in terms of "willful" or "incorrigible" people who expose large numbers of partners to their infection. An example is NuShawn Williams, who had sex with dozens of women, many of them minors, after being told he was infected. Thirteen of the women were later found to have HIV. Mr. Williams, who is black, claimed to believe that white health officials had falsely told him he was HIV infected in order to discourage him from having sex with white women in the rural area where he was diagnosed. He denied any wish to hurt any of this partners. After public health authorities released his name, he was discovered in a New York City jail. He eventually pled guilty to charges of statutory rape and reckless endangerment and was sentenced to between four and eighteen years in prison.

Proponents of criminalization tend to point to his as the "easy" case: a man, tested and counseled, continues to have sex and infect underage partners with a conscious disregard of the risk. The biggest problem with his case was that he could not be charged with more serious crimes: none of his victims had died, or were likely to predecease Williams himself, while prosecutors in New York reportedly doubted they could prove he had the specific intent to kill required to make out the offense of attempted murder.

If one accepts that he believed he was infected and understood the risks, then perhaps Williams's was an easy case. But this, opponents suggest, is just the problem: Williams's demonic intent was assumed, not proven. For example, his ability to recall the names of most of his partners when questioned by health authorities, which could reasonably be read as proof of fondness and concern, was interpreted by more than one commentator as malignant sexual scorekeeping. For criminalization critics, it is Williams's race, class, and incongruity with his rural setting that made him the "easy" case, and not a basic difference between him and other infected people.

Conclusion

Public health programs prevent HIV through the systematic deployment of interventions designed to change the behaviors that pose the highest risk to the population. Although criminal law is sometimes a useful public health tool, as against HIV it has been applied to a small number of randomly identified cases to punish and deter wrongdoing through action taken against individuals deemed morally culpable. Neither theory nor experience supports the belief that criminal penalties can reduce the rate of HIV's spread.

SCOTT BURRIS

See also ASSAULT AND BATTERY; ATTEMPT; FEAR OF CRIME; HOMOSEXUALITY AND CRIME; POLITICAL PROCESS AND CRIME; RAPE: LEGAL ASPECTS.

BIBLIOGRAPHY

BRANDT, ALLEN M. No Magic Bullet: A Social History of Venereal Disease in the United States Since 1980. New York: Oxford University Press, 1987.
BURRIS, SCOTT; DALTON, HARLON; and MILLER, JUDITH, eds. AIDS Law Today: A New Guide for the Public. New Haven, Conn.: Yale University Press, 1993.
Dangerous Bedfellows, eds. Policing Public Sex: Queer Politics and the Future of AIDS Activism. Boston, Mass.: South End Press, 1996.
GOSTIN, LAWRENCE O., and LAZZARINI, ZITA. "Prevention of HIV/AIDS among Injection Drug Users: The Theory and Science of Public Health and Criminal Justice Approaches to Disease Prevention." Emory Law Journal 46 (1997): 587–696.
GUSFIELD, JOSEPH R. Symbolic Crusade: Status Politics and the American Temperance Movement. Urbana, Ill.: University of Illinois Press, 1963.
MARK, GARY; BURRIS, SCOTT; and PETERMAN, THOMAS. "Reducing Sexual Transmission of HIV from Those Who Know They Are Infected: The Need for Personal and Collective Responsibility." AIDS 13 (1999): 297–306.
STEPHENS, ALAN. "Annotation: Transmission or Risk of Transmission of Human Immunodeficiency Virus (HIV) or Acquired Immunodeficiency Syndrome as Basis for Prosecution or Sentencing in Criminal or Military Discipline Case." American Law Reports 5, vol. 13 (1993): 628–683.
SULLIVAN, KATHLEEN M., and FIELD, MARTHA A. "AIDS and the Coercive Power of the State." Harvard Civil Rights – Civil Liberties Law Review 23 (1988): 139–197.

HUMAN RIGHTS

See CORPORAL PUNISHMENT; CRUEL AND UNUSUAL PUNISHMENT; INTERNATIONAL CRIMINAL JUSTICE STANDARDS.

I

INCAPACITATION

Incapacitation is one of the mechanisms through which prisons contribute to crime prevention. While incarcerated an offender is restrained from committing crimes, at least outside the prison walls, and thus it is said that prisons incapacitate offenders from "additional mischief," as William Blackstone once put it. For at least two hundred years incapacitation has been recognized as one of the legitimate objectives of the criminal law alongside deterrence and retribution, but arguably since the mid-1970s incapacitation may have become the main rationale for imprisonment, certainly in the case of the United States.

Until 1975 the incarceration rate nationwide remained strikingly steady averaging 107 prison inmates per 100,000 residents. Thereafter, and particularly since the early 1980s, the prison population grew at an astonishing rate of 7.2 percent each year, leading to a fourfold increase in the nation's incarceration rate by the end of the century.

The so-called war on drugs was certainly an important factor fueling this colossal expansion of imprisonment. Under this approach, introduced during the first Reagan Administration, stiff criminal sanctions replaced treatment-on-demand as the main weapon of choice to fight the use of illegal substances. The effects of this policy change were dramatic in the extreme. The number of drug inmates increased from just under 24,000 in 1980 to almost 240,000 in 1996. Yet, it would be a mistake to conclude that the shift in imprisonment levels was entirely or even mainly attributable to the change in drug policy. During the period 1980–1996 the number of in-

mates in prison for a violent offense increased by 248,000 whereas inmates serving time for a property offense grew by almost 150,000 prisoners (Blumstein and Beck). The wave of punitiveness did not materialize equally across states and among crime types, but there is no documented instance of a single jurisdiction or crime domain completely sidestepping the trend toward higher levels of punishment (Cohen and Canela-Cacho).

To an important extent, the increase in incarceration levels was the result of the public's cry for swifter and tougher criminal sanctions simply on grounds of retribution, particularly after the proliferation of victims' rights groups. The late 1970s saw not only the demise of the "rehabilitation ideal"—the use of prisons as a tool for the reformation of offenders—but also the rebirth of the notion of prisons as a place of penance. But to a much larger extent, the unprecedented expansion of incarceration reflected almost a blind faith among a large portion of the population and a dominant segment of elected officials that prisons are an effective means, and sometimes the only means, to prevent serious crimes. True, chronic offenders may be beyond rehabilitation and may be essentially immune to deterrence, but, in the words of the celebrated conservative columnist Ben Wattenberg, "a thug in prison can't shoot your sister."

The enactment since 1993 of so-called three-strikes-and-you're-out statutes in twenty-six states (Zimring et al.) is perhaps the best indicator of the public's confidence that crime can be best prevented through incapacitation. These statutes typically provide for mandatory sentences or life imprisonment for offenders convicted of a serious offense and who also have two or more prior convictions for violent or serious crimes. In some states, such as California, the "third-strike" need not be a conviction for a violent offense. These draconian measures have been largely accepted by the public not only as fair policies but as wise ones, premised on the notion that "three times an offender, always an offender," and that society has a right to permanently incapacitate those who cannot control their criminal urges.

This entry reviews the extant scientific literature on incapacitation, in particular studies that have attempted to measure the crime suppression effects of incapacitation. In a subsequent section, the entry reviews current knowledge on patterns of offending behavior that has a direct bearing on incapacitation policy. In this regard it is of special importance to assess what we know and do not know about offenders that are the prime targets of incapacitation, namely those who engage in frequent criminal doings over a long portion of their lives, and that historically have been called habitual offenders, chronic offenders, career criminals, and, more recently, life-course persistent offenders. The entry closes with a brief discussion of new policy developments, some of which continue the trend toward more incapacitation, while other teens seem to offer a reprieve from the era of punitiveness.

The scholarly literature on incapacitation and the measurement of incapacitative effects

The empirical literature on incapacitation is of recent vintage, going back to the early 1970s. Although arguably the most important rationale for imprisonment these days, incapacitation continues to be the least studied of the prison's functions. For the period 1990–1999, the Criminal Justice Abstracts lists only 85 incapacitation publications, compared to 509 for deterrence and 639 for rehabilitation. This gap in publications was substantially more pronounced in the 1980s, for example one incapacitation article for every fourteen articles on deterrence (Zimring and Hawkins).

The works by Cohen (1977, 1983), Zimring and Hawkins, Nagin, and Spelman (2000b) provide an excellent basis to track the evolution of the incapacitation literature over the past twenty-five years. Together they also give us a good portrait of what we know in the domain of incapacitation and, particularly, how well we know it. One important observation is that from the very beginning, scholars of high standing in the crimi-

nal justice academic community have disagreed on the basic point of whether the crime suppression effects of prison-incapacitation are large or small.

The two most important 1970s articles on incapacitation, published in the same issue of the *Law and Society Review* in 1975, illustrate the point. As reviewed by Cohen (1977), the first of these articles, written by David Greenberg, concluded that the crimes prevented by incapacitation amounted to no more than 8 percent of the total crimes actually committed, and perhaps as little as 1.2 percent. The second article was authored by a father-son team of noncriminologists, the Shinnars, and was one in a series of three articles essentially presenting the same model, which ultimately would have a lasting influence on the incapacitation literature. The Shinnars concluded that in the 1970s crimes prevented through incapacitation amounted to 25 percent of crimes committed, three times higher than the upper-bound effect suggested by Greenberg. Moreover, they argued that just as recently as the 1960s, when the risk of incarceration per crime committed was substantially higher, the number of crimes prevented through incapacitation amounted to 120 percent of crimes committed.

Despite substantial progress in methods and theory, disparities in the estimates of incapacitation put together by the best in the discipline continue to be huge, leading Nagin to conclude that "The evidence [about incapacitation] is of limited value in formulating policy. . . . [Predicting] the timing, duration, and magnitude of the impact of incremental adjustments in enforcement penalties remains largely beyond our reach" (Nagin, p. 367).

To understand why measuring incapacitation is such a difficult enterprise one needs to remember that the essence of this exercise is to count crimes that did not occur. Unavoidably, one needs to engage virtual reality and ask questions of the following two basic types: How many crimes would the 162,000 inmates incarcerated in California during the year 2000 have committed had they been free? Or, between 1996 and 1997 California increased its prison population by 9,200 inmates: What difference did that make, if any, in the actual crimes committed during 1997?

In answering these questions empirical evidence readily available to scholars consists of the crime rate, as reported to the police, and the actual imprisonment rate. At first sight, these two variables should provide all we need to assess incapacitation, for intuitively, the more people imprisoned, the larger the number of crimes prevented, and, all other things being equal, the smaller the crime rate.

Unfortunately, this logic can be seriously flawed for various reasons. To begin with, incapacitation and deterrent effects are commingled, a fact recognized since the first works on incapacitation (Cohen, 1977) and, to this day we lack a proven methodology to separate the two. The two effects are commingled because they both respond in the same direction to increases in imprisonment levels. As the prison population increases more offenders are incapacitated but also other would-be offenders may be deterred from committing additional crimes, in light of the higher incarceration risk. Both effects would lead to a reduction in the crime rate.

Second, all other things are hardly constant when imprisonment policies change. In all likelihood the opposite is the case: criminal sanction policies often change following observable changes in crime rates or in a number of other contextual factors that may have an effect on crime. Consider, for example, a situation in which the robbery rate increases by a factor of two, for reasons having nothing to do with the current level of criminal sanctions. In this case one could see an increase in the observed robbery rate and also very likely an increase in the number of people going to prison for robbery. Arguably, the number of prevented robberies via incapacitation would have increased because more robbers would now be in prison; it would be entirely likely that because of the increase in the robbery rate, the criminal sanctions would be further toughened, but still, one would not see a decline in actual robberies. Incapacitation would be expanding but not fast enough to catch up with the expansion in robbery offending. One can play the opposite scenario and easily identify a situation in which the prison population is going down, the number of crimes prevented by incapacitation is going down, and the observed crime rate is also declining.

The important point to keep in mind is that measures of simple correlation between incarceration rates and crime rates are not sufficient to assess incapacitation effects and may very well be misleading. Figure 1 provides a telling illustration of the ambiguous relationship over time between the incarceration and crime rates using California data for the period 1963–1998.

For robbery and burglary Figure 1 displays the crime and incarceration rates as percents of their respective 1963 values. Thus, Figure 1a shows that between 1963 and 1980 the incarceration rate for robbery remained roughly stable whereas during the same period the robbery rate increased by a factor of four. The correlation of the crime and incarceration rates for robbery over this period would be close to zero, as the first was rising sharply and the second was roughly stable. After 1980 and through 1988 the correlation is negative as the imprisonment rate steadily increased and the crime rate steadily decreased. After 1988 and through 1993 the correlation switches to a positive value with the robbery imprisonment rate continuing its assent at a constant rate relative to the prior period while the robbery rate showed a steep increase. The most striking segment of Figure 1a is the story it reveals after 1992. One observes what can be described as a meltdown of the robbery rate at a time when the imprisonment rate for robbery began to flatten. One can find segments of time in Figure 1a to advance claims that the incapacitation effect is either large or irrelevant or actually counterproductive.

The story for burglary displayed in Figure 1b is very different from that of robbery and almost uniformly supportive of the hypothesis that the incarceration and crime rates move in the opposite direction, as expected under the most simple scenario of how incapacitation works. Together Figures 1a and 1b show that the ambiguity of the relationship between incarceration and crime rates occurs not only over time within crime types but also across crime types. This introduces yet another possibility: that incapacitation works for some crimes but not for others.

Estimates of incapacitation

This section presents incapacitation estimates derived from modeling exercises in which various statistical controls were used to overcome the inherent ambiguity between incarceration and crime rates described before. It has been noted that incapacitation estimates vary enormously by source. However, sometimes the differences in estimates are exaggerated because estimates calculated under different metrics are directly compared.

Historically there have been four conceptually different incapacitation measurement systems. The earlier measures were of the type provided by Greenberg and the Shinnars, previ-

Figure 1

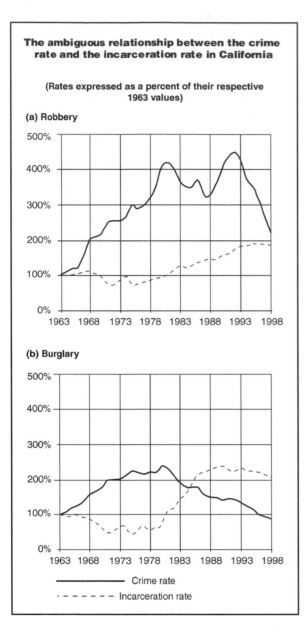

The ambiguous relationship between the crime rate and the incarceration rate in California

(Rates expressed as a percent of their respective 1963 values)

(a) Robbery

(b) Burglary

——— Crime rate

- - - - - Incarceration rate

Table 1

Marginal incapacitation estimates

Source	All crimes	All property crimes	All violent crimes	Robbery	Burglary
Marvel and Moody (1994)	16.6	16.1	0.5	0.46	4.7
Levitt (1996)	14.9	12.5	2.3	1.1	2.6
Zimring and Hawkins (1995)	3.5	3.3	0.2	0.13	2.2
Canela-Cacho et al. (1997)	N/A	N/A	N/A	0.86	2.2

SOURCE: Marvell and Moody 1994, p. 132, Table V; Levitt 1996, p. 345, Table VIII; Zimming and Hawkins 1995, pp. 116–118, Tables 6.5 and 6.6; and Canela-Cacho et al. 1997, pp. 150–151, calculated by the author based on results of Tables 4 and 5, and model described in pages 137–142.

change in the incarceration rate. Finally, a fourth useful measure attempts to measure what could be described as marginal incapacitation, and that is the number of crimes prevented by the incarceration of additional inmates in the event of an expansion in the prison population.

While these four measures are obviously interrelated, numerically they are not equivalent. For example, Levitt provides both elasticity and marginal incapacitation estimates based on the same data and model. The elasticity estimate is fairly small, -.31, suggesting that for a 10 percent increase in incarceration rates the crime rate would be about 3 percent below where it otherwise would have been. To some this would be evidence that incapacitation effects are negligible; yet, the marginal incapacitation estimate that accompanies this elasticity value is 14.9 crimes prevented for each additional inmate joining the prison population, evidence to many of large incapacitation effects.

When comparing incapacitation estimates one needs to make sure that the incapacitation measures in question belong to the same type, otherwise the comparison would be misleading. In this entry the incapacitation estimates discussed below belong to the type previously defined as marginal incapacitation measures (Table 1) or to measures of the elasticity of incapacitation.

The first two sets of estimates presented in Table 1 (Marvell and Moody; Levitt) were obtained using similar methods and data sets. They both rely on a statistical technique called regression analysis to assess changes in the crime rate as a result of changes in the incarceration rate, controlling for other factors that could influence

ously mentioned. In this approach incapacitation is measured by the percent that crimes prevented represent relative to crimes committed, or some variant of this basic calculation, often referred to as the incapacitation effect. More recent measures of incapacitation focus on the number of crimes prevented per offender in prison, using the average or median offending rate of offenders in prison as the basis for that calculation. A third measure favored by economists measures incapacitation as an elasticity, that is, the percent change in the crime rate following a 1 percent that relationship, such as the demographic composition of the population and levels of economic well being. The data informing these two models spans the period 1971 to the early 1990s and includes all states. The Zimring and Hawkins incapacitation estimates (1995) also rely on the relationship between crime and incarceration rates but in a nonregression estimation context, and are based only on California data covering the period 1981 through 1990. These three sets of estimates are comparable in that they provide marginal incapacitation estimates by crime type and for the aggregation of all crimes, and they are all based on aggregate crime and imprisonment rates.

The last set of estimates in Table 1 are an extrapolation specifically prepared for this entry based on results reported by Canela-Cacho and colleagues. The latter estimates are based on a completely different methodology relying on individual offending rates to calculate incapacitation effects rather than aggregates of crime and incarceration rates. The estimates are based on California data and apply to the same time period considered by Zimring and Hawkins. In addition, the individual offending rates used in this approach derive from surveys of prison inmates where offenders have reported their crimes.

Some commonalities in the four sets of estimates are readily apparent. The marginal incapacitation estimates are all substantially higher for burglary than for robbery, and this applies generally to property crimes vis-à-vis violent crimes. In addition, the size of the estimates for marginal burglary incapacitation is virtually the same in the estimates by Levitt, Zimring and Hawkins, and Canela-Cacho and colleagues.

However, the differences across estimates are striking concerning marginal incapacitation for violent crimes. The Marvell and Moody estimate is 2.5 times that of Zimring and Hawkins, whereas Levitt's estimate is 4.6 times that of Marvell and Moody. For robbery, similar differences exist among the four sets of estimates. These differences raise concerns since the Levitt and Marvell and Moody estimates rely essentially on the same data and apply the same genre of statistical models. The estimates of Zimring and Hawkins and Canela-Cacho and colleagues are based on completely different methodologies but they both apply to California during the same time period, and again, with regard to robbery, the estimates are dramatically different. Perhaps the one conclusion we can reach is that substantial uncertainties remain in the size of incapacitation

effects, despite some impressive methodological advances in the measurement of incapacitation.

The crime drop throughout the United States that began in 1992 has given new impetus to the study of incapacitation effects, as scholars are busily trying to explain what contribution imprisonment played, if any, to this large and for the most part unexpected decline. Not surprisingly, in a context where homicide and robbery rates have experienced declines of over 50 percent in seven years, the new rounds of incapacitation estimates tend to be larger than estimates based on data prior to 1992, even when the same methodology is applied. For example, Spelman (2000a) redid Levitt's analysis expanding the data through 1997 and reports an increase in the incapacitation elasticity of 41 percent between 1973 and 1997.

Similarly, some recent work examining the incapacitation effect for homicide reports elasticities of -1.5 to -1.9 (Marvell and Moody, cited in Rosenfeld). Rosenfeld analyzed the decline in homicides in the period 1990–1995 and concluded that the high elasticity estimates just cited are in agreement with his finding, obtained independently, that the homicide rate would have been 28 percent higher absent the incapacitation effect generated by an average annual increase of about 67,000 prison inmates between 1990 and 1995.

It should be noted that the crime types for which incapacitation estimates have been attempted are limited to violent offenses and to some property offenses. No one seriously has entertained the notion that putting one drug dealer behind bars would prevent a number of drug transactions; the incarcerated offender would be easily replaced by someone else in the streets as long as the demand for drugs continues unabated. Such replacement effect is unlikely to apply to offenses like robbery or burglary, except in the context of co-offending where two or more individuals team up to engage in criminal acts. Reiss pointed out that the incarceration of one of the members of a group of two or three offenders acting together need not have an incapacitative effect as the remaining free members of the group could recruit a new member to replace the incarcerated peer.

There are two additional situations that could further negate or at least diminish incapacitation. The first one relates to crime desistence, a phenomenon exhaustively documented in crime research. Simply put, as a result of aging, many offenders stop committing crimes, and thus past a certain point their incarceration yields no incapacitation benefits.

In the second case, incapacitation would initially be effective but would eventually become counterproductive, if as a result of an episode of incarceration, an offender upon release evolves into more serious crimes or engages in the same criminal behaviors but at substantially higher rates. In this instance prisons would have a criminogenic effect, preventing some crimes at first but at the expense of contributing to more serious or to a higher number of crimes in the future.

The incapacitative estimates presented before only indirectly attempt to control for replacement or desistence of offenders following incarceration, and none allow for the possibility that prisons are indeed criminogenic. These omissions further compound the uncertainties surrounding the available incapacitation estimates and show the need to develop yet better measuring techniques and substantially richer data sets.

Offending trajectories and incapacitation policy

One of the most robust findings in criminal justice research is the heterogeneity in offending rates and in deviant behavior generally, across the population. Longitudinal research studies in various countries such as the United States, Canada, England, Denmark, and New Zealand have found that when a group of individuals born the same year (a "birth cohort") are monitored from birth to adulthood a small percentage, typically under 10 percent, account for the majority of crimes generated by the entire cohort. For example, in the now famous study of a birth cohort of Philadelphia boys by Wolfgang and colleagues, 6 percent of boys were responsible for 52 percent of all police contacts generated by the cohort.

In longitudinal cohort studies the vast majority of cohort members do not report any criminal activity when interviewed and do not have an official criminal record. Among those with at least one reported criminal justice contact, 15 to 20 percent often account for about half of the total crimes. Comparable findings have been obtained when analyzing reported offending rates of prison inmates (Chaiken and Chaiken).

The subset of offenders with substantially higher offending rates than the average offender has been the subject of much criminological research, for not only do they represent the natural population in which to study the effect of various factors influencing onset and termination of criminal behavior, but they also constitute a natural target for incapacitation (as well as special deterrence and rehabilitation).

Capitalizing on the existence of high rate offenders, and seeking to achieve large incapacitation levels with low incarceration rates, the controversial policy of selective incapacitation was advanced in the early 1980s by Greenwood and Abrahamse. In the area of incapacitation and even in criminal justice policy generally, few scholarly proposals have generated as much controversy and heated exchanges as the idea of selectively incarcerating offenders based in part on their expected future crimes. Ethical and legal concerns, coupled with the inability to prospectively distinguish with accuracy high and low rate offenders, have precluded the implementation of selective incapacitation policies, even on a trial basis. Instead, what happened was a toughening of criminal sanctions across the board but especially for repeat offenders with multiple prior convictions. For example, the three-strikes-and-you're-out statutes previously discussed impose very long sentences on offenders with two or more prior convictions, presumably because those prior convictions indicate a high criminal propensity. However, the application of this scheme does not call for any predictions of future criminality and treats exactly alike two offenders with the same prior record and the same current offense. Still the foundation of this policy is the existence of chronic offenders whose incapacitation allegedly yields high social returns. It is ironic that to overcome the ethical and legal concerns associated with assigning incarceration terms partly based on unreliable predictions of what an offender may do in the future, we essentially adopted the policy that two prior strikes automatically qualify a convictee as a chronic offender and thus a good target for long incapacitation. Clearly, many false positive predictions result from this policy and apparently its only redeeming grace is that the prediction it implicitly relies on is based on past rather than future behavior.

Since around 1990, much has been learned about high rate offenders as a result of the development of new statistical techniques applied to data sets collected from longitudinal studies. The joining of developmental theories in psychology with the criminal career approach of the 1980s has been particularly fruitful and is a promising source of new policy insights. The criminal career paradigm brought attention to the dimensions of individual offending, namely age of onset of offending, frequency and seriousness of offending, and termination of offending. The approach was particularly helpful in recognizing that crime control policies could differentially affect each of the dimensions of individual offending, and that in turn particular attributes of criminal careers could affect the effectiveness of crime control policies. For example, early on the limits of incapacitation due to of career termination were recognized. Developmental psychology and longitudinal research methods have infused the criminal career paradigm with a theoretical foundation and a much more powerful dynamic outlook. The resulting new approach, often referred to as "criminal trajectory analysis," looks closely at the interaction of personal attributes and external events in the unfolding of an offender's course of criminal acts. The approach is also dynamic in that it seeks to determine how aging affects an individual's trajectory. Important pioneering works in this new tradition are those of Terri Moffitt from the developmental psychology perspective, and of Nagin and Land from the field of quantitative criminology.

The criminal trajectory approach has confirmed that not all offenders have the same propensity to engage in criminal behavior and in deviance generally. Offenders vary in their frequency of deviance involvement as well as in the number of years during which they engage in those behaviors. Typically, these studies find three distinct groups among the members of a cohort with delinquent acts, each with a typical "offending trajectory": adolescent-limited offenders, low-level chronic offenders, and high-level chronic offenders (Nagin et al.; Fergusson et al.). These groups are different in a number of ways, for example the adolescent-limited typically start offending in early adolescence and generally stop offending altogether in early adulthood. In contrast, high-level chronic offenders have their criminal onset during childhood and continue their involvement in crime and deviant behavior for long periods of time. Oftentimes this group consists mostly of children with neuropsychological deficits who have faced disadvantageous social and family environments from day one in their lives.

A very important insight from this new generation of longitudinal studies pertains to the relationship between age and criminal involvement. Even high-level chronic offenders show a declining criminal trajectory after a cer-

tain age, contradicting past notions that high-rate offenders maintain a constant rate of offending while criminally active. This insight is important as it makes clear that some incarceration time will have either declining returns or even, possibly, no returns. Beyond a certain point in an offender's incarceration term, he would not commit additional offenses if free, and thus the rationale for incapacitating him is lost.

The new longitudinal studies may eventually provide us with better ways to prospectively identify high-level chronic offenders among all offenders. The development of that ability need not entail the return of proposals of selective incapacitation, and in fact there is presently no literature in print exploring that possibility. Rather, as we learn to precisely identify the set of conditions, from conception to adulthood, that turn an individual into a high-rate chronic offender, society may be moved to intervene early, and not necessarily in a criminal justice context, to undermine the host of conditions pushing individuals into a trajectory of sustained offending.

The future of incapacitation policies

Various policy developments in the 1990s suggest that the era of punitiveness with emphasis on incapacitation will not be over anytime soon. Two instances of policies along these lines are the passage of "sexual predator laws" and the increasing use of the adult criminal system to prosecute and sanction juveniles as young as fourteen years of age.

Washington state passed the first sexual predators statute in 1990 and thereafter nine other states have enacted basically equivalent laws (Lieb et al.). These statutes target incarcerated sex offenders who are soon to be released having completed their sentences. If the offender can be shown to suffer from a "mental abnormality or personality disorder that makes [him] likely to engage in future predatory acts of sexual violence" (Wash. Rev. Code 71.09.020, emphasis added) the statute authorizes the state to confine the just released inmate for treatment until a jury finds him safe for release. Clearly, the objective of the statute is to extend the incapacitation of these inmates past the end of their incarceration sentence, a sort of "incapacitation beyond punishment."

These statutes have been particularly controversial. Disavowing well-established principles of civil commitment law and practice, the sexual predator statutes do not require a showing that the person is "mentally ill" but instead rely on the malleable concept of "mental abnormality or personality disorder." The former term is limited to diagnosable medical conditions such as schizophrenia; the latter does not have a uniform clinical definition. Some also argue that with the sex predator laws the state is able to apply in series, and essentially based on the same facts, two control mechanisms (criminal sanctions first and then civil commitment) that until now were incompatible with each other. The Supreme Court, however, has found these statutes constitutionally acceptable in two recent rulings (*Seling v. Young*, 121 S.Ct. 727 (2001); *Kansas v. Hendricks*, 521 U.S. 346 (1997), essentially on the ground that the statutes are not punitive and therefore do not constitute double jeopardy, and under the guise that incapacitation of dangerous sexual violent predators is a legitimate exercise of the states' regulatory power to secure public safety.

Thus far the sexual predator statutes have been applied in a very limited number of cases, by one count under 1 percent of all eligible released inmates (Lieb, 1998), and there is no evidence that the same approach will be extended to other violent predators. Still the precedent has been set for a policy of incapacitation beyond the completion of a criminal sentence.

Another telling indicator of the remaining support for tough criminal justice policy for the sake of crime prevention is the shift of underage perpetrators from the juvenile to the adult system. Of all new admissions into prison nationwide, 2.3 percent were children (as young as fifteen, in New York and North Carolina). Despite the sizable declines in violent crime levels since 1992, the public apparently agrees with the proposition that more gains can be achieved by further toughening criminal sanctions. California approved a referendum, by a two-to-one margin, that requires juveniles fourteen years of age or older charged with murder or a serious sex offense to be tried in adult court.

But there are also some promising policy developments for crime control that are not imprisonment-based. There is an impressive body of scientific evidence showing that drug treatment is a very efficient means for crime control, vastly superior to imprisonment in many contexts. Caulkins and colleagues have shown that the resources consumed by mandatory minimum sentences for drug offenders would have greater social returns—in terms of crime control and in other ways—if they were spent in drug treatment facilities. Along the same lines, a large quasi-experimental study of drug and alcohol treatment in California (Caldata) showed that on average every dollar invested in drug treatment yields the equivalent of $7 in social returns, most of it on account of the reductions in criminal behavior of the persons receiving treatment.

It has often been argued that the incarceration of drug users results in little or no incapacitation of serious crimes. That conventional wisdom may or may not hold true. Some rigorous studies have shown that the criminal records of offenders in prison for a drug offense are comparable, in terms of prior violent or property crimes, to the records of offenders in prison for property of violent offenses (Cohen et al.). But the point that drug users may be good targets for incapacitation does not contradict the notion that these same offenders, or at least a fraction of them, are even better targets for drug treatment.

California again is showing the way, in this case with a bold policy that finally heeds the findings of rigorous research that drug treatment pays off. Beginning on 1 July 2001, offenders convicted of a "nonviolent drug possession offense" are sentenced to probation and are required to complete a drug treatment program. This new system will require that the state create a treatment trust fund of almost $700 million for the first six years of the program. In return, the state expects to save up to $250 million a year in state prison operating costs and a one-time savings of $500 million on capital outlay costs. Of course, the attention will not focus on the financial savings from diverting offenders from prisons to drug treatment facilities. We have always known that the latter are substantially less expensive than the former. The focus will be on what happens to the criminal propensities of the diverted offenders: Will a drug offender in treatment not shoot your sister? Will the incapacitation returns on account of drug treatment surpass the incapacitation returns from imprisonment?

The drug treatment initiative is part of a more general trend in what can be called the cost-benefit analysis of imprisonment. Throughout the 1980s and most of the 1990s, scholars probing into the cost-efficiency of prisons posed the question simply in terms of incarcerate or not incarcerate (DiIulio and Piehl; Piehl and DiIulio). Whether prisons pay, in the sense that the benefits of incarceration exceed its costs, is by no means a settled matter (see Spelman, 2000b), but the interesting point is that presently the cost-benefit analysis of incarceration has been expanded beyond its traditional formulation. Greenwood and colleagues (1998) pulled together the best literature on the effectiveness of early interventions in the lives of children at risk of deviant behavior. While we are still awaiting large demonstration programs, the cumulative knowledge acquired to date is suggestive of the notion that, from the standpoint of incapacitating future crimes, an ounce of early intervention is worth a couple pounds of later incarceration. Perhaps the times are ripe to give that policy a real chance.

JOSÉ A. CANELO-CACHO

See also DETERRENCE; PREDICTION OF CRIME AND RECIDIVISM; PROBATION AND PAROLE: HISTORY, GOALS, AND DECISION-MAKING; PUNISHMENT; REHABILITATION; RETRIBUTIVISM; SENTENCING: ALTERNATIVES; SENTENCING: DISPARITY; SENTENCING: GUIDELINES; SENTENCING: MANDATORY AND MANDATORY MINIMUM SENTENCES.

BIBLIOGRAPHY

BLUMSTEIN, ALFRED, and BECK, ALLEN J. "Population Growth in U.S. Prisons, 1980–1996." In Crime and Justice: A Review of Research. Vol. 26. Edited by Michael Tonry and Joan Petersilia. Chicago: University of Chicago Press, 1999. Pages 17–61.
California Department of Alcohol and Drug Programs. Evaluating Recovery Services: The California Drug and Alcohol Treatment Assessment (CALDATA), General Report. Publication No. ADP 94-629. Sacramento, Calif.: California Department of Alcohol and Drug Programs, 1994.
CANELA-CACHO, JOSÉ A.; BLUMSTEIN, ALFRED; and COHEN, JACQUELINE. "Relationship between the Offending Frequency (λ) of Imprisoned and Free Offenders." Criminology 35 (1997): 133–175.
CAULKINS, JONATHAN P.; RYDELL, C. PETER; SCHWABE, WILLIAM L.; and CHIESA, JAMES. "Are Mandatory Minimum Drug Sentences Cost-Effective?" Corrections Management Quarterly 2 (1998): 62–73.
CHAIKEN, MARCIA R., and CHAIKEN, JAN. Varieties of Criminal Behavior. Santa Monica, Calif.: Rand, 1982.
COHEN, JACQUELINE. "The Incapacitative Effect of Imprisonment: A Critical Review of the Literature." In Deterrence and Incapacitation: Estimating the Effects of Criminal Sanctions on Crime Rates. Edited by Alfred Blumstein, Jacqueline

Cohen, and Daniel S. Nagin. Washington, D.C.: National Academy Press, 1977. Pages 187–241.
COHEN, JACQUELINE, and CANELA-CACHO, JOSÉ A. "Incarceration and Violent Crime." In Understanding and Preventing Violence. Consequences and Control. Vol. 4. Edited by A. Reiss and J. F. Roth. Washington, D.C.: National Academy Press, 1994. Pages 296–388.
COHEN, JACQUELINE; NAGIN, DANIEL S.; and WASSERMAN, LAWRENCE. Drug Offenders: How Bad Are They? Pittsburgh, Pa.: Carnegie Mellon University, 1994.
———. "Incapacitation as a Strategy for Crime Control: Possibilities and Pitfalls." In Crime and Justice: A Review of Research. Vol. 5. Edited by Michael Tonry and Norval Morris. Chicago: University of Chicago Press, 1983. Pages 1–84.
DIIULIO, JOHN J., and PIEHL, ANNE MORRISON. "Does Prison Pay? The Stormy National Debate over the Cost-Effectiveness of Imprisonment." Brookings Review 9, no. 4 (1991): 28–35.
FERGUSON, DAVID M.; HORWOOD, L. JOHN; and NAGIN, DANIEL S. "Offending Trajectories in a New Zealand Birth Cohort." Criminology 38 (2000): 525–551.
GOTTFREDSON, STEPHEN D., and GOTTFREDSON, DON M. "Behavioral Prediction and the Problem of Incapacitation." Criminology 32 (1994): 441–474.
GREENWOOD, PETER W., and ABRAHAMSE, ALLAN. Selective Incapacitation. Santa Monica, Calif.: Rand, 1982.
GREENWOOD, PETER W.; MODEL, KARYN E.; RYDELL, C. PETER; and CHIESA, JAMES. Diverting Children from a Life of Crime. Measuring Costs and Benefits. Santa Monica, Calif.: Rand, 1990.
LEVITT, STEVEN D. "The Effect of Prison Population Size on Crime Rates: Evidence from Prison Overcrowding Litigation." The Quarterly Journal of Economics 61 (1996): 319–351.
LIEB, ROXANNE; QUINSEY, VERNON; and BERLINER, LUCEY. "Sexual Predators and Social Policy." In Crime and Justice: A Review of Research. Vol. 23. Edited by Michael Tonry. Chicago: University of Chicago Press, 1998. Pages 43–114.
MARVELL, THOMAS B., and MOODY, CARLISLE E., JR. "Prison Population Growth and Crime Reduction." Journal of Quantitative Criminology 10 (1994): 109–140.
MOFFITT, TERRIE E. "Adolescence-Limited and Life-Course-Persistent Antisocial Behavior: A Developmental Taxonomy." Psychological Review 100 (1993): 674–701.

NAGIN, DANIEL S. "Deterrence and Incapacitation." In *The Handbook of Crime and Punishment.* Edited by Michael Tonry. New York: Oxford University Press, 1998. Pages 345–368.

NAGIN, DANIEL S.; FARRINGTON, DAVID P.; and MOFFIT, TERRIE E. "Life-Course Trajectories of Different Types of Offenders." *Criminology* 33 (1995): 111–138.

NAGIN, DANIEL S., and LAND, KENNETH C. "Age, Criminal Careers, and Population Heterogeneity: Specification and Estimation of a Nonparametric, Mixed Poisson Model." *Criminology* 31 (1993): 327–362.

PIEHL, ANN M., and DiIULIO, JOHN J., JR. "Does Prison Pay? Revisited." *Brookings Review* 13, no. 1 (1995): 20–25.

REISS, ALBERT J. "Co-Offending and Criminal Careers." In *Crime and Justice: A Review of Research.* Vol. 10. Edited by Michael Tonry and N. Morris. Chicago: University of Chicago Press, 1988. Pages 117–170.

ROSENFELD, RICHARD. "Patterns in Adult Homicide: 1980–1995." In *The Crime Drop in America.* Edited by Alfred Blumstein and Joel Wallman. New York: Cambridge University Press, 2000. Pages 130–163.

SPELMAN, WILLIAM. "The Limited Importance of Prison Expansion." In *The Crime Drop in America.* Edited by Alfred Blumstein and Joel Wallman. New York: Cambridge University Press, 2000. Pages 97–129.

———. "What Recent Studies Do (and Don't) Tell Us about Imprisonment and Crime." In *Crime and Justice: A Review of Research.* Vol. 27. Edited by Michael Tonry. Chicago: University of Chicago Press, 2000. Pages 419–494.

WOLFGANG, MARVIN E.; FIGLIO, ROBERT M.; and SELLIN, THORSTEN. *Delinquency in a Birth Cohort.* Chicago: University of Chicago Press, 1972.

ZIMRING, FRANKLIN E., and HAWKINS, GORDON. *Incapacitation. Penal Confinement and the Restraint of Crime.* New York: Oxford University Press, 1995.

ZIMRING, FRANKLIN E.; HAWKINS, GORDON; and KAMIN, SAM. *Punishment and Democracy. Three Strikes and You're Out in California.* New York: Oxford University Press, 2001.

CASES

Kansas v. Hendricks, 521 U.S. 346 (1997).
Selig v. Young, 121 S.Ct. 727 (2001).

INCHOATE OFFENSES

See ATTEMPT; CONSPIRACY; RICO (RACKETEER INFLUENCED AND CORRUPT ORGANIZATIONS ACT).

INFORMAL DISPOSITION

Prosecuting authorities in the American criminal justice system have broad discretion in deciding how to handle a criminal matter. A prosecutor may file formal charges against an individual suspect and pursue a guilty verdict by means of a plea bargain or trial. The vast majority of cases that are processed to a verdict within the criminal justice system result in the conviction and punishment of the offender, with only a tiny percentage resulting in acquittal. Alternatively, a prosecutor (or, in some instances, the police) can dispose of a case by dismissing the charges outright, if the circumstances warrant such a disposition. Principled reasons that a prosecutor might dismiss charges include a determination that there is insufficient evidence to establish guilt beyond a reasonable doubt, the failure of a material witness to cooperate with the prosecution, a determination that the evidence was unlawfully obtained by the police, or for policy reasons. Lying in between these two options is a third reason—to seek a satisfactory disposition through informal means.

The term *informal disposition* refers broadly to the manner of obtaining a final disposition of a criminal matter without reliance on the normal processes of the criminal justice system that would result in conviction of the offender. Informal dispositions are obtained without any judicial determination of guilt or innocence. It should be noted, however, that many of the programs available for informal dispositions may also be utilized as sentencing alternatives for those convicted through the traditional criminal process. Thus, the demarcation between the informal and formal processes may not be clear, but rather may resemble a fine continuum of options available to prosecuting authorities or the police.

A principal form of informal disposition is a process known as "pretrial diversion" by which an alleged offender's case may be transferred into structured programs for rehabilitative purposes, such as mental health treatment or drug or alcohol abuse treatment, or for the payment of restitution and fines or community service. Alternatively, the criminal prosecution may be "deferred" for a period of time with the understanding that unless the person commits a subsequent offense in that period, the charges will be dismissed. Yet another option is to transfer an individual's case to another forum that would provide warnings against future wrongdoing as well as periodic supervision. Examples include the transfer of a minor to juvenile court and the dismissal of domestic violence cases in exchange for the individual's consent to permit community supervision.

Thus, the informal disposition process serves a screening function to determine which cases merit prosecution and which merit an alternative mode of treatment, usually for purposes of rehabilitation. Informal dispositions also serve the purpose of reducing the overburdened criminal caseloads of prosecutors and judges, as well as, in some jurisdictions, public defenders. The drive to reduce caseloads, cut costs, and promote the rehabilitation of offenders who have the potential to become law-abiding citizens has fueled a trend to create innovative new programs and even new forms of "courts" for producing the desired results without resort to the traditional criminal adjudication process. A renewed interest in better serving the needs of victims of crime has also spurred the development of programs for mediating cases between the offender and the victim, in lieu of the formal criminal process.

This entry surveys the primary types of informal dispositions available to the criminal justice system and explores both the availability of such modes of disposition as well as the process by which the decision to proceed informally is made.

The principal types of informal dispositions

In one sense, there is so little uniformity in the types of informal dispositions available that it is nearly impossible to speak generally on the subject. Most states have adopted their own unique statutes on informal dispositions, and courts within the states have begun to establish their own procedural rules to govern certain types of informal dispositions. Furthermore, prosecuting offices may establish their own set of guidelines (Landis). Community groups have proved to be very creative in designing a variety of innovative rehabilitative programs.

In another sense, however, most jurisdictions offer the same basic menu of programs. Generally speaking, informal dispositions take three basic shapes: (1) referrals to structured programs of various types; (2) conditional dispositions; and (3) dismissal or a noncriminal disposition with warnings and supervision.

Referrals to programs. Pretrial diversion, also known as deferred prosecution, is the most common example of an informal disposition. Pretrial diversion involves the referral of individuals, often before arraignment, to rehabilitative or restitution programs in lieu of criminal prosecution. Individuals with plans to enter the military may also qualify for pretrial diversion on the condition that they actually do enter into military service. The individual's criminal charges are dropped upon completion of the treatment program or upon meeting the agreed-upon conditions. Such programs are designed to promote rehabilitation and minimize the stigma that attaches upon conviction.

Offenders who are directed into treatment as a condition of pretrial diversion or deferred adjudication tend to remain in treatment longer than individuals who voluntarily commit themselves for treatment. The length of treatment has been shown to be crucial to the long-term rehabilitation of the individual. Thus, the coercive nature of the imposition of treatment may be more effective in bringing about the desired change in the individual than voluntarily applied treatment. Both the public at large and court personnel are willing to accept community-based diversion programs, a fact bolstered by the increasing number of programs initiated by community groups (Sigler and Lamb).

A wide variety of offenses may qualify for pretrial diversion, and statutes may enumerate the offenses eligible for such treatment. Generally, the categories of offenses eligible for pretrial diversion will include relatively minor offenses for which a person could be sentenced to a jail term. Traffic offenses, for example, would not likely be eligible, since their violation does not ordinarily carry a jail term. On the other hand, a person charged with driving while under the influence of alcohol traditionally has been eligible for pretrial diversion. More recently, however, some legislatures have taken the position that those charged with driving while under the influence of alcohol should be specifically disqualified for participation in pretrial diversion programs. Other categories of offenses generally eligible for pretrial diversion include minor drug charges, bad check writing (false pretenses), petty theft, and domestic violence offenses.

Most cases of domestic violence or maltreatment of children by parents are handled by means of pretrial diversion. Many states require treatment as a condition of pretrial diversion. These cases are rarely prosecuted due to a variety of reasons, such as the concern over the damage to the family unit by removing the culpable parent or spouse. Mandatory treatment has been found to reduce recidivism in these cases, but not in cases involving child sexual abuse (Lederman and Malik). However, drop-out rates are high for battering spouses who are sent to treatment as a condition of pretrial diversion and subsequent prosecution does not often occur (Hanna).

Prosecutors frequently issue criminal "no-contact" orders or criminal protection orders as a condition of pretrial diversion. These orders typically prohibit the defendant from returning to the home or directly or indirectly contacting the victim. Statutes in several states require the issuance of no-contact orders in domestic violence cases. Unlike civil protective orders obtained at the request of the victim, criminal no-contact orders are obtained upon the request of the prosecutor, even over the objection of the victim (O'Connor).

A fierce debate persists in the area of domestic violence with regard to the advantages and disadvantages of mandatory intervention by both police and prosecutors. Most states have implemented statutes requiring a more aggressive approach to family intervention by the police, through the adoption of policies calling for either preferential or mandatory arrest. Similarly, prosecutors have adopted "no drop" policies or preferential prosecution policies. These trends represent the acknowledgment that domestic violence is a serious criminal matter and that the decision whether to treat such assaults as crimes should not be left to the victim (O'Connor). Not surprisingly, some jurisdictions are moving away from pretrial diversion and are beginning to require a conviction before treatment can be ordered.

For other types of offenses, developed programs since the early 1990s give the courts new options for the informal disposition of cases. For example, the large volume of drug cases entering the court system has prompted a search for alternatives to criminal prosecution for alleged offenders who have serious drug abuse problems. A new type of court, known as a "drug treatment court" (DTC), has emerged as a means for implementing court-supervised drug treatment without resort to the formal adjudicative process. Individuals will be brought before a DTC almost immediately after arrest so that they may begin their treatment. Individuals will be required to complete a course of treatment that takes from one to two years to complete. The treatment process involves detoxification, counseling, education, vocational courses, group meetings, urine testing, and weekly court appearances. Failure to complete the program leads to prosecution on the original charges. The charges are dropped, however, upon successful completion. There are approximately two hundred DTCs in the United States today (Reisig). Pretrial diversion into a treatment program may be the only way for some drug offenders to avoid long prison sentences under mandatory sentencing laws that exist in many jurisdictions.

DTCs operate in a fundamentally different way than regular criminal courts in that the roles of the court participants are transformed. The judge, prosecutor, defense counsel, probation officer, law enforcement and correctional officers, and treatment specialists all become part of the "DTC team" and work together in a collaborative effort to motivate the individual to stay in treatment (Hora et al.). As with other diversionary programs, the prosecutor in a DTC screens files for acceptable candidates, but this screening process may be done in cooperation with the defense counsel. The role of defense counsel is not to advance the legal defense of the individual, but to assist the team in motivating the individual to turn away from drug abusing behavior. Treatment providers also attend court sessions and may advise the court of the individual's progress and make recommendations.

Yet another development of fairly recent vintage is the establishment of victim-offender reconciliation programs (VORP), also known as victim-offender mediation programs. VORP programs, which first arrived in the United States in the mid-1970s, had proliferated by the year 2000 (Mika). VORP programs embody a radically different vision of justice often referred to as "restorative justice." Rather than simply serving as a vehicle for streamlining the caseloads of criminal courts or providing some alternative therapeutic treatment for the rehabilitation of offenders, VORP programs are motivated by a concern to serve the needs of the individual victims of crime, as opposed to the interests of the state. The conflict, thus, is viewed as one between individuals. VORP programs bring victims of crime face-to-face with offenders for purposes of informally resolving their conflict. With the assistance of trained mediators, victims and offenders have a meeting to discuss the facts of the case, the impact it has had on their lives, and their feelings about the offense. Each party also has an opportunity to ask questions of one another. The parties then mutually discuss and reach a resolution. The resolution is a written, enforceable agreement signed by the parties that specifies the amount and schedule for delivery of restitution and/or community service (Mika).

Typically, community-based private groups operate VORP programs, and prosecutors, judges, or probation officers refer cases directly to them. Both the program administrators as well as the criminal justice official (typically the prosecutor) screen cases for eligibility. VORP has been used primarily for minor property offenses and cases involving juvenile offenders, although it has also been used by judges as a form of sentencing after conviction in more serious cases, such as rape and even vehicular homicide. Many states have placed statutory limitations on the use of VORP for domestic abuse cases, consistent with the trend to view domestic abuse cases as serious assault offenses and not as trivial family disputes. Ironically, the emphasis on victims' rights may actually increase the use of mediation for more serious felony offenses. Texas, for example, has recently enacted a statute providing for mediation in felony criminal proceedings before the trial court accepts a guilty plea or plea of no contest, but only upon the request of the victim (Rendon).

Victim restitution and community service programs are another alternative community-based program for pretrial diversion that focus on serving the victims of crime. Individuals sent to these programs are put to work doing paid community service, and a part of their pay is turned over to the victim.

For juvenile offenders, a separate set of programs have been established. The juvenile courts themselves may be considered a program that diverts minors from the adult criminal system into a system designed to rehabilitate them without attaching stigma. Most practitioners, however, recognize that juvenile courts involve the same type of formal proceedings as adult criminal courts and a finding of juvenile delinquency can also create stigma. Thus, diversionary programs have been created specifically to remove juvenile offenders from the juvenile courts (Panzer). Some of these are counterparts to the adult versions also available in communities, such as Victim-Offender Mediation Programs and Victim Restitution and Community Service Programs.

Other pretrial diversionary programs have been designed especially for juveniles. For example, "teen courts" have emerged as a community response for handling nonviolent, first-time juvenile offenders. Many such programs originated in the schools as a way to deal with offenses committed at school. The concept has taken root in communities as well, which now accept referrals from the juvenile courts. In teen courts, community teen volunteers typically staff the programs, supervised by adult professionals. Teens may play the roles of prosecutor, defense counsel, judge, and jurors. Teen courts informally adjudicate the offense and, upon finding guilt, may impose sentences of restitution and/or community service. In contrast to the juvenile court process, teen court dispositions do not result in a court record, nor any formal or informal probation record.

"Youth accountability boards" have been developed in other communities to process nonserious juvenile offenses. Panels of three to five volunteer adults serve on such boards. Cases are referred by juvenile probation officers, and the board may accept or reject them. Juveniles who are sent to youth accountability boards appear at a hearing, accompanied by their parents. The board gives the juvenile the opportunity to plead his or her case. If the juvenile is found culpable, the board typically requires the juvenile and the parents to sign a contract that may provide for rehabilitative treatment, curfew, nonassociation with known gang members, restitution, and/or community service. The contract holds the parents financially liable for any restitution that must be paid, and parents may also be required to undergo rehabilitative treatment (Panzer).

Finally, "family conferences" are an innovation imported from New Zealand and Australia. Family conferences bring together a larger group of people to take collective responsibility for a youthful offender and to assist the offender in carrying out his or her agreement. Participants in the conference may include family, friends, teachers, and coworkers. Family conferences are organized by trained police officers, probation officers, or social services. This is not yet a concept that has taken root in the United States. Such programs exist in only a few communities (Kurki).

Conditional dispositions. Deferred adjudication, another extremely common form of informal disposition, permits an individual to avoid obtaining a criminal record, but only after successfully completing a period of time without re-arrest (generally six months) and completing whatever course of treatment the court may impose. The deferred adjudication process requires the individual to plead guilty before the court will order treatment. If after the allotted period the defendant has successfully fulfilled the conditions imposed, then the criminal record for the offense will be expunged. Thus, deferred adjudication operates in a similar manner as pretrial diversion except that deferred adjudication requires a guilty plea before treatment will be ordered.

Warning and supervision. Informal dispositions may take the form of outright dismissals of charges with warnings to the individual to avoid reoffending the law and on the condition that individual will agree to be supervised for a period of time. In juvenile cases, a program called "informal probation" allows a juvenile and his or her parents to avoid even the filing of criminal charges against the juvenile by entering into contract with a juvenile probation officer, who may maintain an office in a police station. Informal probation contracts, usually to be completed in six months, will usually contain several requirements, including a curfew, making adequate grades in school, and avoidance of certain associations (with known gang members, for example). Informal probation also calls for adequate supervision by the probation officer. The contract may also call for the completion of counseling, educational programs, or community service, or the payment of restitution (Panzer). Parental involvement is a key component of informal probation programs. The sufficiency of a parent's supervision of a juvenile may also be monitored (Panzer).

The decision-making process

Traditionally, the decision whether to proceed by means of an informal disposition has usually begun with the defense attorney, and this remains true to date. It is incumbent on defense attorneys to identify those cases that would generally merit informal disposition and request such disposition from the prosecutor, court, and/or program administrator. In some instances, statutes delineate factors that prosecutors and/or courts should consider in making the determination. Factors typically considered relevant to the decision include: the individual's amenability to rehabilitation, motivation in committing the crime, employment record, family ties, age, past

criminal record, and mental and physical condition. For VORP programs, the willingness of both the victim and offender to participate in mediation are central to the referral decision.

Once a defense attorney determines that an individual should be considered favorably for an informal disposition, the next step will depend on the nature of the disposition sought. For pretrial diversion and referral to a rehabilitative program, the program administrator may be the first person to review the individual's request for admission into the program. If the program administrator determines that the individual does qualify for admission, then the next person who considers the request may be the prosecutor or it may be the judge.

Statutes and court rules governing pretrial diversion programs vary, but at least in some places it is no longer within the absolute discretion of the prosecutor whether to refer an individual to pretrial diversion. Some statutes and court rules permit courts to dismiss charges and refer individuals to pretrial diversion, even over the objection of the prosecutor. In other places, the prosecution maintains a veto power over the decision. Efforts were made in the 1970s by highly regarded groups like the American Law Institute (ALI) to convince prosecutors to publish guidelines such as the American Law Institute's (ALI) Model Code of Pre-Arraignment Procedure (1975) to make public the criteria upon which prosecutorial charging decisions are made. For the most part, these efforts have failed, and prosecutors continue to make these decisions without providing the public any means for evaluating the decision-making process.

SANDRA GUERRA

See also ALCOHOL AND CRIME: TREATMENT AND REHABILITATION; DISPUTE RESOLUTION PROGRAMS; JUVENILE JUSTICE: JUVENILE COURT; MENTALLY DISORDERED OFFENDERS; POLICE: COMMUNITY POLICING; POLICE: HANDLING OF JUVENILES; PRETRIAL DIVERSION; PREVENTION: COMMUNITY PROGRAMS; PROSECUTION: PROSECUTORIAL DISCRETION; RESTORATIVE JUSTICE; SENTENCING: ALTERNATIVES; URBAN POLICE.

BIBLIOGRAPHY

"Alternatives to Incarceration for Drug-abusing Offenders." *Harvard Law Review* 111 (1998): 1898–1921.

HANNA, CHERYL. "The Paradox of Hope: The Crime and Punishment of Domestic Violence." *William and Mary Law Review* 39 (1998): 1505–1584.

HORA, HON. PEGGY F.; SCHMA, HON. WILLIAM G.; and ROSENTHAL, JOHN T. A. "Therapeutic Jurisprudence and the Drug Treatment Movement: Revolutionizing the Criminal Justice System's Response to Drug Abuse and Crime in America." *Notre Dame Law Review* 74 (1999): 439–537.

KURKI, LEENA. "Incorporating Restorative and Community Justice Into American Sentencing and Corrections." National Institute of Justice. *Papers From the Executive Sessions on Sentencing and Corrections* 3 (1999): 1–10.

LANDIS, DEBRA T. "Pretrial Diversion: Statute or Court Rule Authorizing Suspension or Dismissal of Criminal Prosecution on Defendant's Consent to Noncriminal Alternative." *American Law Reports* 4th ser., 4 (2000): 147–182.

LEDERMAN, HON. CINDY S., and MALIK, NEENA M. "Family Violence: A Report on the State of the Research." *Florida Bar Journal* 73 (1999): 58–62.

MCDONALD, DOUGLAS C. "Restitution and Community Service." *Crime File Study Guide.* Washington, D.C.: National Institute of Justice, 1988.

MIKA, HARRY. "The Practice and Prospect of Victim-Offender Programs." *SMU Law Review* 46 (1993): 2191–2205.

MISNER, ROBERT L. "Recasting Prosecutorial Discretion." *Journal of Criminal Law and Criminology* 89 (1996): 717–777.

NARDULLI, PETER F. "'Insider' Justice: Defense Attorneys and the Handling of Felony Cases." *Journal of Criminal Law and Criminology* 77 (1986): 379–417.

NIEMEYER, MIKE, and SHICHOR, DAVID. "A Preliminary Study of a Large Victim/Offender Reconciliation Program." *Federal Probation* 60 (1996): 30–34.

O'CONNOR, CHRISTINE. "Domestic Violence No-Contact Orders and the Autonomy Rights of Victims." *Boston College Law Review* 40 (1999): 937–967.

PANZER, CHERI. "Reducing Juvenile Recidivism through Pre-trial Diversion Programs: A Community's Involvement." *Journal of Juvenile Law* 18 (1997): 186–207.

REISIG, MARTIN I. "Rediscovering Rehabilitation: Drug Courts, Community Corrections and Restorative Justice." *Michigan Bar Journal* 77 (1998): 172–176.

RENDON, JOSEFINA MUNIZ. "Mediation in the Criminal Courts." *Houston Lawyer* 35 (1998): 42.

ROBBINS, KALYANI. "No-Drop Prosecution of Domestic Violence: Just Good Policy, or Equal Protection Mandate?" *Stanford Law Review* 52 (1999): 205–233.

SIGLER, ROBERT T., and LAMB, DAVID. "Community-Based Alternatives to Prison: How the Public and Court Personnel View Them." *Federal Probation* 59 (1995): 3–9.

SUBIN, HARRY I.; MIRSKY, CHESTER L.; and WEINSTEIN, IAN S. *Federal Criminal Practice: Prosecution and Defense.* St. Paul, Minn.: West Publishing Co., 1992.

INTELLIGENCE AND CRIME

The study of intelligence in criminological research has ebbed and flowed considerably during the past century. In the first quarter of the 1900s, hundreds of studies categorized criminal offenders as "feebleminded" and "mentally deficient." Fifty studies conducted from 1910 to 1914 identified an average of 51 percent of institutionalized delinquents as feebleminded (Sutherland). In 1931, however, E. H. Sutherland challenged this prevailing view. He compared the IQ scores of adult offenders to those of army draftees—representative of the general population—and the two groups had nearly identical IQ levels. He concluded that intelligence was not a "generally important cause of delinquency" (p. 362). This rejection of IQ was widely accepted in the criminological literature through the mid-1970s. In 1977, Hirschi and Hindelang reviewed a half-dozen well-known empirical studies and concluded that IQ predicted delinquency as strong, if not more strongly, than race and social class—two variables prominently featured in criminological theory. This revisionist perspective stimulated greater interest in IQ and crime over the next two decades. In 1994, Herrnstein and Murray published their highly controversial book *The Bell Curve* in which they argued, among other things, that racial differences in crime rates resulted from racial differences in intelligence. This book has received widespread negative reaction and has possibly created a general backlash against studies of intelligence and crime.

Measuring the size of the IQ-crime correlation

The central question of IQ-crime studies is whether individuals with less intelligence, on average, commit more crime than those with more intelligence. That is, are IQ and crime negatively correlated? The best answer, drawn from previous research, is a qualified "yes." Delinquents and criminals average IQ scores 8 to 10 points lower than noncriminals, which is about one-half a standard deviation. IQ and criminal behavior are negatively correlated at about r = −.20 (Hirschi and Hindelang; Wilson and Herrnstein). Here are five well-known studies that illustrate the correlation between IQ and crime.

Terrie Moffitt and colleagues studied 4,552 Danish men born at the end of World War II. They examined intelligence test scores collected by the Danish army (for screening potential draftees) and criminal records drawn from the Danish National Police Register. The men who committed two or more criminal offenses by age twenty had IQ scores on average a full standard deviation below nonoffenders, and IQ and criminal offenses were significantly and negatively correlated at r = −.19.

Donald Lynam and colleagues studied 430 seventh-grade boys in Pittsburgh, Pennsylvania. They measured both IQ and self-reported participation in delinquent acts. Those boys who committed serious delinquent acts, such as stealing cars, breaking and entering, or selling drugs, scored 8–10 IQ points lower than boys who had not. IQ scores and delinquency were correlated at r = −.22, with the correlation between verbal IQ and delinquency being much stronger than the correlation with performance IQ (r = −.33 versus −.06).

Hakan Stattin and Ingrid Klackenberg-Larsson followed 122 Swedish males from ages three though thirty. They measured IQ at ages three, five, eight, eleven, fourteen, and seventeen and counted the number of registered criminal offenses through age thirty. Frequent offenders, those men with four or more criminal offenses, averaged IQ scores of only 91 points; sporadic offenders averaged 97 IQ points; and nonoffenders averaged a full 102 points. Remarkably, IQ at age three significantly correlated with registered crime at (Spearman's) rho = −.25. IQ at the later ages also correlated with crime at around rho = −.20.

Scott Menard and Barbara Morse studied 257 high school students in San Diego, California, measuring both IQ and self-reported delinquency. IQ was correlated with nonserious crime—such as petty theft, liquor violations, vandalism, truancy, and running away—at r = −.08. IQ was correlated with serious crime—such as gang fights, auto theft, grand theft, and robbery—at r = −.16.

Deborah Denno analyzed data from 987 African American school children in Philadelphia. Her data contained multiple measures of intelligence collected at ages four, seven, and thirteen as well as officially recorded criminal offenses. Chronic, violent offenders consistently had low IQ scores. For example, female chronic offenders were almost four times less likely to be in the top third of verbal-IQ test scores than female nonoffenders. Similarly, male violent offenders scored 10 to 17 percentile points lower on measures of vocabulary, reading, and language than nonoffenders.

In addition to finding a robust IQ-crime correlation, studies have turned up two other empirical regularities worth noting. The first regards two different types of IQ measures: performance IQ (PIQ) versus verbal IQ (VIQ). Performance IQ is measured with nonverbal tests of attention to detail, manual design construction, and visual puzzle solving. Verbal IQ is measured with tests of general factual knowledge, abstract reasoning, mental arithmetic, and vocabulary. Studies have consistently found that criminals have PIQ scores close to the general population but VIQ scores substantially lower. This PIQ > VIQ finding holds even when controlling for race, class, and reading ability (Moffitt), suggesting that verbal intelligence is a more important correlate of criminal behavior than other types of intelligence.

The second regularity regards official versus self-reported measures of crime. While IQ consistently correlates with both of these measures, the correlation between IQ and official measures tends to be somewhat stronger than the correlation with self-reported crime (Hirschi and Hindelang).

Is R = −.20 a meaningful correlation size?

While studies have frequently found that IQ and crime correlate at around r = −.20, they disagree about how to interpret the size of this correlation coefficient. At one extreme, some studies have dismissed the IQ-crime correlation as being simply too small to matter. Menard and Morse concluded that "the association between IQ and delinquent behavior is so weak as to be negligible," and so it "contributes nothing to existing delinquency theory" (pp. 1374, 1347). Likewise, a task force of the American Psychological Association figured that since a correlation of r = −.20 produces an explained variance of only 4 percent

(r^2 =.04), the IQ-crime correlation is "very low" (Siegel, p. 174). At the other extreme, some studies have identified IQ as a critical, if not the fundamental, correlate of crime. Herrnstein and Murray argued that the effect of IQ on crime, as well as other social problems, is so strong that "much of the attention now given to problems of poverty and unemployment should be shifted to . . . coping with cognitive disadvantage" (p. 251).

In between these two extremes is a more sensible interpretation of the IQ-crime correlation as moderately strong. One way to gauge the strength of the IQ-crime correlation is to compare it to other correlates of crime. A study by Wright and others (1999a) looked at social bonds and crime in late adolescence and early adulthood. They found that some social bonds correlated with crime much more strongly (in absolute value) than r = −.20; for example, delinquent friends correlated with crime at r =.40, and living with one's parents correlated at r = −.32. Other social bonds correlated less strongly, for example, full-time employment (r = −.13) and romantic partnerships (r = −.13). Still other social bonds correlated right at r = −.20, including educational achievement, occupational aspirations, and months unemployment. These comparisons show IQ to be a moderately strong, though neither the strongest nor weakest, correlate of crime.

Another way to gauge the IQ-crime correlation is to restate it in more intuitive terms. Rosenthal and Rubin allow for this with their binomial effect size display (BESD), a procedure that translates simple correlations into equivalent experimental results. In this approach a correlation of r = −.20 is equivalent to an experimental intervention that reduces subjects' success rates from 60 percent to 40 percent. Hypothetically, then, randomly assigning high IQs to low-IQ individuals would decrease their criminal behavior by about 30 percent (i.e., from 60 percent to 40 percent)—certainly a meaningful change.

Explaining the IQ-crime correlation

Once the IQ-crime correlation is measured, the next task is to explain it. Why are IQ and crime negatively correlated? Explanations of the IQ-crime correlation typically take one of three approaches, that: (1) IQ and crime are spuriously, not causally, correlated; (2) low IQ increases criminal behavior; or (3) criminal behavior decreases IQ.

A popular argument against IQ as a cause of crime criticizes IQ tests as only measuring middle-class knowledge and values rather than innate intelligence. As a result, the observation that some minority groups and the poor score low on IQ tests simply reflects their diverse cultural backgrounds. These same groups also commit proportionately more crime because they suffer structural disadvantages such as poverty and discrimination. Consequently, the same people who score low on IQ tests also tend to commit more crime, and so IQ and crime are empirically correlated, thus this correlation is not causal but reflects only culturally biased testing of intelligence.

A variation of this argument holds that the structural disadvantages that increase crime rates also reduce educational opportunities thus lessening individuals' ability and motivation to score well on IQ tests. The IQ-crime correlation occurs only because they are both rooted in structural disadvantage, which, in statistical terms, represents a "spurious" correlation.

Although these discrimination hypotheses have wide appeal, they have received fairly little support in empirical studies, for IQ and crime are significantly correlated within race and class groups as well as when statistically controlling for race, class, test-taking ability, and test-taking motivation (e.g., Hirschi and Hindelang; Lynam et al.).

Another argument against IQ as a cause of crime holds that school teachers and administrators treat students differently by perceptions of the students' intelligence—giving negative labels and fewer educational opportunities to less intelligent students. These labels and constrained opportunities, in turn, produce feelings of alienation and resentment that lead students to delinquent peers and criminal behavior (Menard and Morse). As such, society's reaction to intelligence, and not any property of intelligence itself, increases criminal behavior. Unfortunately, few studies have adequately tested this labeling hypothesis.

A final argument against IQ holds that even if all people commit crime with equal frequency, less intelligent people would be less able to evade detection and would be arrested more often. This detection hypothesis has received some empirical support in that IQ scores tend to correlate more strongly with officially recorded crime than self-reported crime. However, most studies still find a significant correlation between IQ and self-reported crime, which is not easily explained by differential police detection (e.g., Moffitt and Silva).

In contrast to the above spurious arguments, some explanations emphasize IQ as a cause of crime. The earliest causal explanation, popular during the early 1900s, portrayed criminals as so "feebleminded" and "mentally deficient" that they could neither distinguish right from wrong nor resist criminal impulses. This feeblemindedness hypothesis, however, lost favor long ago as it became clear that few criminals are actually mentally deficient and most recognize, though may not follow, behavioral norms (Moffitt et al.).

A more recent, and more compelling, causal explanation emphasizes the importance of intelligence—especially verbal intelligence—during childhood socialization. The socialization of children involves constant verbal communication and comprehension of abstract symbols; therefore, children with poor verbal and cognitive skills have greater difficulty completing the socialization process, which puts them at risk of undercontrolled, antisocial behavior. Empirical studies overall have supported this developmental hypothesis (Moffitt, p. 116), and it fits with the especially strong correlation between verbal IQ and crime.

A final causal explanation links IQ to crime through school performance. Less intelligent students do less well in school, which results in academic frustration. This frustration, in turn, weakens their attachment and commitment to schooling, and a weakened bond to school, as per social control theory, allows for more criminal behavior (Hirschi and Hindelang). This school-performance hypothesis has received strong support from empirical studies, and it is probably the most widely accepted explanation of the IQ-crime correlation (Moffitt).

One last approach to IQ and crime deserves mention even though few criminological studies have examined it. Rather than low IQ increasing criminal behavior, criminal behavior might decrease IQ. Many facets of a criminal lifestyle can impair cognitive abilities, including physical injuries, especially head traumas, drug use, and withdrawing from school (Moffitt).

The future of IQ-crime studies

Turning to the future of IQ-crime studies, two questions stand out. Will criminologists continue to study intelligence and crime, and if so, which research questions should be pursued?

Starting with the second question, one issue for future studies involves society's response to intelligence. Menard and Morse hypothesized that school teachers and administrators negatively label low-IQ students thus increasing their risk of criminal behavior. In addition to testing this hypothesis, studies should examine other societal reactions to IQ as well. Stories abound of classmates stigmatizing bright students as "brains" and "geeks," especially in schools with overall low scholastic achievement. Bright students might avoid these negative labels by cutting back on schoolwork and acting out antisocially. Indeed, peers' labels of high-IQ students may cause more harm than officials' labels of low-IQ students.

Another issue for study involves the nature of IQ's effect on criminal behavior. Up until now, causal arguments have assumed that low IQ increases criminal behavior; however, it is possible that in various ways high IQ actually increases criminal behavior. For example, more-intelligent individuals may feel greater confidence of committing crimes without getting caught, which, as per deterrence theory, should lead to more criminal behavior. More-intelligent individuals might also have more opportunities for some crimes, such as white-collar crime. (See Wright et al., 1999b, for a discussion of simultaneous positive and negative causal linkages, between social class and crime.)

An additional issue for study involves the effect of low IQ after a crime is committed. As discussed above, low IQ correlates more strongly with arrests and imprisonment than with self-reported crime (Hirschi and Hindelang), which has been taken as evidence for the detection hypothesis—that low-IQ criminals get caught more easily. Another possibility, though, is that low-IQ criminals experience more negative outcomes once in the criminal justice system. If criminal justice officials, from police officers to judges to parole officers, believe that low intelligence increases criminal behavior, they might prejudge low-IQ criminals as greater risks and correspondingly give them fewer opportunities and harsher punishments.

The question of how to study intelligence and crime, however, is meaningless if few criminologists study it, and this might happen because of its highly politicized nature. Critics have derided IQ-crime causation theories as social Darwinism and as supportive of regressive social policies. Advocates have countered that critics' political preferences have blinded them to empirical realities (Hirschi and Hindelang). This type of conflict dampens research interest in intelligence and crime.

Ultimately, the best answer about whether to study IQ and crime takes a middle path between critics and advocates. Cullen and others exemplify this approach in their critique of *The Bell Curve*. They catalog potentially serious misuses of IQ-crime research in both criminological theory and public policy and strongly encourage researchers to avoid these misuses. At the same time, they also argue not to "throw the baby out the with bathwater" by ignoring the well-documented empirical link between intelligence and crime. Instead, criminologists should accept that "IQ is a criminogenic factor, and, thus, is an individual difference that must be included in theories of crime causation" (p. 403).

BRADLEY R. E. WRIGHT

See also CRIME CAUSATION: BIOLOGICAL THEORIES; CRIME CAUSATION: PSYCHOLOGICAL THEORIES; CRIME CAUSATION: SOCIOLOGICAL THEORIES; CRIMINOLOGY: MODERN CONTROVERSIES; EDUCATION AND CRIME; PREDICTION OF CRIME AND RECIDIVISM.

BIBLIOGRAPHY

CULLEN, FRANCIS T.; GENDREAU, PAUL; JARJOURA, G. ROGER; and WRIGHT, JOHN PAUL. "Crime and the Bell Curve: Lessons from Intelligent Criminology." *Crime & Delinquency* 43 (1997): 387–411.

DENNO, DEBORAH. *Biology and Violence: From Birth to Adulthood.* Cambridge, U.K.: Cambridge University Press, U.K. 1990.

HERRNSTEIN, RICHARD J., and MURRAY, CHARLES. *The Bell Curve: Intelligence and Class Structure in American Life.* New York: The Free Press, 1994.

HIRSCHI, TRAVIS, and HINDELANG, MICHAEL J. "Intelligence and Delinquency: A Revisionist Review." *American Sociological Review* 42: (1997) 571–587.

LYNAM, DONALD R.; MOFFITT, TERRIE E.; and STOUTHAMER-LOEBER, MAGDA. "Explaining the Relationship between IQ and Delinquency: Class, Race, Test Motivation, School Failure, or Self-Control?" *Journal of Abnormal Psychology* 102 (1993): 187–196.

MENARD, SCOTT, and MORSE, BARBARA J. "A Structuralist Critique of the IQ-Delinquency Hypothesis: Theory and Evidence." *American Journal of Sociology* 89 (1984): 1347–1378.

MOFFITT, TERRIE E. "The Neuropsychology of Juvenile Delinquency: A Critical Review." In *Crime and Justice: An Annual Review of Research.* Edited by Noral Morris and Michael Tonry. Chicago: University of Chicago Press, 1990. Pages 99–169.

MOFFITT, TERRIE E.; GABRIELLI, WILLIAM F.; MEDNICK, SARNOFF A.; and SCHULSINGER, FINI. "Socioeconomic Status, IQ, and Delinquency." *Journal of Abnormal Psychology* 90 (1981): 152–156.

MOFFITT, TERRIE E., and SILVA, PHIL A. "IQ and Delinquency: A Direct Test of the Differential Detection Hypothesis." *Journal of Abnormal Psychology* 97 (1988): 330–333.

ROSENTHAL, ROBERT, and RUBIN, DONALD B. "A Simple, General Purpose Display of Magnitude of Experimental Effect." *Journal of Educational Psychology* 74 (1982): 166–169.

SIEGEL, LARRY. *Criminology,* 7th ed. Belmont, Calif.: Wadsworth/Thomas Learning, 2000.

STATTIN, HAKAN, and KLACKENBERG-LARSSON, INGRID. "Early Language and Intelligence Development and Their Relationship to Future Criminal Behavior." *Journal of Abnormal Psychology* 102 (1993): 369–378.

SUTHERLAND, E. H. "Mental Deficiency and Crime." In *Social Attitudes.* Edited by Kimball Young. New York: Holt, Rinehart, and Wilson, 1931. Pages 357–375.

WILSON, JAMES Q., and HERRNSTEIN, RICHARD J. *Crime and Human Nature.* New York: Simon and Schuster, 1985.

WRIGHT, BRADLEY R. E.; CASPI, AVSHALOM; MOFFITT, TERRIE E.; and SILVA, PHIL A. "Low Self-Control, Social Bonds, and Crime: Social Causation, Social Selection, or Both?" *Criminology* 37 (1999a): 479–514.

WRIGHT, BRADLEY R. E.; CASPI, AVSHALOM; MOFFITT, TERRIE E.; MIECH, RICHARD A.; and SILVA, PHIL A. "Reconsidering the Relationship between SES and Delinquency: Causation but Not Correlation." *Criminology* 37 (1999b): 175–194.

INTERNATIONAL CRIMINAL COURTS

A major step to close one of the important gaps in the enforcement system of international criminal law was taken on 17 July 1998 with the adoption of the Rome Statute of the International Criminal Court (Statute) at a diplomatic conference in Rome. The vote was 120 in favor to 7 against (including the United States, China, Iraq, and Israel), with twenty-one abstentions. The Statute provides for the establishment of a permanent international criminal court with jurisdiction over genocide, crimes against humanity, war crimes, and the crime of aggression. As of

January 2001, 139 states, including the United States and Israel, had signed the Statute and 27 of them had ratified it. It is expected to receive the sixty ratifications required under Article 126 for it to enter into force in 2001 or 2002.

Historical background

Until the adoption of the Statute, there was no single instrument containing a comprehensive and widely accepted definition of crimes under international law, and enforcement was left to national courts exercising territorial or universal jurisdiction over these crimes or to ad hoc national or international criminal courts. Although there were occasional ad hoc international criminal courts during the Middle Ages, the first formal proposal to establish a permanent international criminal court was not made until 1872, when Gustave Moynier, one of the founders of the International Committee of the Red Cross, proposed such a court to enforce the 1864 Geneva Convention on the treatment of wounded soldiers. Leading international lawyers of the day dismissed it as impractical. The failure to set up the ad hoc international criminal tribunal envisaged in the Treaty of Versailles (1919) to try the former German emperor for "a supreme offence against international morality and the sanctity of treaties" for his role during the First World War led to numerous proposals between 1920 and 1945 for a permanent international criminal court. Two treaties, adopted by the League of Nations in 1937 at the initiative of France to establish a permanent international criminal court with jurisdiction over terrorist crimes, never entered into force.

At the end of the Second World War, the international community rejected the idea of establishing a permanent court, partly because it would take too long to set one up by treaty, and instead favored establishing two ad hoc international criminal courts to try major suspects of the Axis powers (Germany and Japan) on charges of crimes against peace, war crimes, and crimes against humanity: the International Military Tribunal at Nuremberg (Nuremberg Tribunal) and the International Military Tribunal of the Far East (Tokyo Tribunal). Their judgments were landmarks in international law in holding that the atrocities committed during the Second World War, including those perpetrated against a state's own citizens, were crimes under international law. Such atrocities were of concern to the entire international community, and any individual, regardless of status or rank, could be held criminally responsible. In 1946, the United Nations General Assembly affirmed the principles of international law recognized in the Nuremberg Charter and Judgment. However, both tribunals were criticized by some as applying retroactive justice, selective prosecution, or unfair procedures.

As a result of such criticism, Henri Donnedieu de Vabres, who served as a judge on the Nuremberg Tribunal and had made proposals on the subject, introduced a French proposal in the United Nations (UN) in 1947 to establish a permanent international criminal court. The following year, the UN General Assembly asked the International Law Commission (ILC), a UN body composed of international legal experts, to study the question. However, as a result of hostility to the idea of such a court and concerns about the crime of aggression, particularly by the United Kingdom, the United States, and the USSR, there was little progress on this proposal for more than four decades. In 1954, the ILC adopted a draft Code of Offences against the Peace and Security of Mankind, but it was never incorporated in a treaty, and the 1974 definition of aggression by the General Assembly in Resolution 3314 (XXIX) was widely seen as insufficient for determining individual criminal responsibility. The ILC resumed work on the draft code in the 1980s, but did not complete its work on a Draft Code of Crimes against the Peace and Security of Mankind (1996 Draft Code of Crimes) until 1996.

Work would not have resumed on the proposal for a permanent international criminal court until 1996 but for pressure from two different directions. First, in the 1980s, the German foreign minister, President Mikail Gorbachev of the USSR, and A. N. R. Robinson, the prime minister of Trinidad and Tobago, each called for a permanent court. Second, in May 1993, as a result of international revulsion at the massacres, rapes, and expulsions in the former Yugoslavia, the Security Council, acting under Chapter VII of the UN Charter to restore and maintain international peace and security, established the ad hoc International Criminal Tribunal for the former Yugoslavia (Yugoslavia Tribunal) with jurisdiction over genocide, crimes against humanity, and war crimes committed since 1991 in that region. In November 1994, the Security Council established a second ad hoc tribunal, the International Criminal Tribunal for Rwanda (Rwanda Tribunal), to bring to justice those responsible for genocide, crimes against humanity, and war crimes committed during internal armed conflict in Rwanda in 1994. Between 500,000 and one million members of the minority Tutsi group, as well as moderate members of the Hutu majority, were killed in Rwanda between April and July 1994.

In December 1993, the General Assembly asked the ILC to complete its work on a draft statute for a permanent international criminal court "as a mater of priority" by July 1994. The July 1994 ILC draft statute was considered in an Ad Hoc Committee in 1995 and a Preparatory Committee from 1996 to 1998 before it was adopted by the Diplomatic Conference in 1998. Since then, a Preparatory Commission has been meeting in New York. On 30 June 2000, it adopted draft Elements of Crimes, which under Article 9 must be consistent with the Statute and are to aid the court in interpreting definitions of crimes, and draft Rules of Procedure and Evidence, which also must be consistent with the Statute (Article 51). They are to be considered and adopted by the Assembly of States Parties, along with other supplementary instruments being prepared by the commission.

Jurisdiction, crimes, principles of criminal responsibility, and defenses

The court will have subject matter jurisdiction under Article 5 over four categories of crimes under international law that are committed after entry into force of the Statute: genocide, crimes against humanity, war crimes, and, once it has been defined and a procedure for addressing it agreed, the crime of aggression. Genocide, a term coined in 1944 by Rafael Lempkin, is defined in Article 6 exactly as in Article II of the 1948 Convention for the Prevention and Punishment of the Crime of Genocide.

The concept of crimes against humanity dates to the middle of the nineteenth century. The 1919 Paris Peace Conference investigated such crimes, but U.S. and Japanese objections prevented any prosecutions. However, perpetrators of such crimes were prosecuted in the Nuremberg, Tokyo, Yugoslavia, and Rwanda Tribunals. Crimes against humanity listed in Article 7(1) of the Statute (and further defined in Article 7(2)), include murder, extermination, enslavement, deportation or forcible transfer of population, imprisonment, torture, rape and other crimes of sexual violence, persecution in connection with any other prohibited act, en-

forced disappearance of persons, apartheid, and other inhumane acts. However, such conduct amounts to a crime against humanity only when it is "committed as part of a widespread or systematic attack directed against any civilian population, with knowledge of the attack." Such an *attack*, as defined in Article 7(2), "means a course of conduct involving the multiple commission of acts referred to in paragraph 1 against any civilian population, pursuant to or in furtherance of a State or organizational policy to commit such attack." Despite the misleading term *attack*, and in contrast to the Nuremberg Charter and the Statute of the Yugoslavia Tribunal, which limited the scope of jurisdiction over crimes against humanity to those linked to armed conflict, the Statute requires no link between crimes against humanity and armed conflict or, indeed, any military action, and the *attack* could include legislation.

The court will have jurisdiction under Article 8 (2) (a) and (b) over grave breaches of the 1949 Geneva Conventions and other serious violations of international humanitarian law in international armed conflict, including violations of the Hague Convention IV of 1907 and its Regulations and some violations of Protocol I of the Geneva Conventions. The court also will have jurisdiction under Article 8 (2) (c) to (f) and (3) over violations of international humanitarian law in non-international armed conflict, the most common form of armed conflict today. These include violations of common Article 3 of the 1949 Geneva Conventions and Protocol II to those treaties, as well as certain conduct that would be a violation if it occurred during international armed conflict. These provisions confirm the rapid evolution of international law in the 1990s, as evidenced by the decision of the Appeals Chamber of the Yugoslavia Tribunal in the *Tadić* case, concluding that serious violations of international law in internal armed conflicts entailed individual criminal responsibility; and the Rwanda Statute, which expressly gave the tribunal jurisdiction over serious violations of common Article 3 and Protocol II.

Although Articles 6, 7, and 8 simply define the court's jurisdiction, the United States has expressly recognized that they, as well as the draft Elements of Crimes, largely reflect the state of customary international law today.

Among the most important aspects of the definitions in the Statute are Article 7 (1) (g) and (2) (f), defining the court's jurisdiction over rape, sexual slavery, enforced prostitution, forced pregnancy, enforced sterilization, or any other form of sexual violence of comparable gravity as crimes against humanity, and Article 8 (2) (b) (xxii) and (e) (vi), defining the Court's jurisdiction over analogous war crimes in international and noninternational armed conflict. Inclusion of these crimes was foreshadowed in the 1996 Draft Code of Crimes and is a recognition that such crimes are committed on a large scale throughout the world. It is also a significant advance over the 1945 Allied Control Council Law No. 10 governing trials of Nazis in Germany and the Yugoslavia and Rwanda Statutes, which expressly list rape, but not other crimes of sexual violence, and the Nuremberg and Tokyo Charters, which did not list any crimes of sexual violence.

The court will not have jurisdiction over states for international crimes, a controversial concept rejected by the ILC in 2000, or over crimes committed by legal entities, such as corporations, political parties, or trade unions. Instead, its jurisdiction will limited to crimes committed by individuals over the age of eighteen (Article 26). Individuals may be held criminally responsible under Article 25, not only if they commit or attempt to commit the crime, but also if they order, solicit, or induce others to do so; aid, abet, or otherwise assist others; or assist a group of persons acting with a common purpose. They may also beheld individually criminally responsible pursuant to Article 25 if they directly and publicly incite genocide. Except as otherwise provided in the Statute, Elements of Crimes, or international law, a person may be held criminally responsible only if the material elements of the crime were committed with intent and knowledge (Article 30), thus ruling out a negligence standard for most crimes. The Court will have jurisdiction over persons regardless of government position, including heads of state (Article 27). Military commanders can be found criminally responsible under Article 28 for crimes of subordinates under their effective control when they knew or should have known that the subordinates were committing or about to commit crimes and failed to take all necessary and reasonable measures within their power to prevent or repress the crimes or to submit the mailer to a prosecutor; civilian superiors are criminally responsible under a similar, but somewhat less strict, standard. None of the crimes are subject to a statute of limitations (Article 29).

Superior orders are largely ruled out as a defense under Article 33, and the situations in which such orders would be a defense before the court are extremely narrow. Under certain limited circumstances, criminal responsibility may be excluded under Article 31 because of a mental disease or defect, involuntary intoxication, self-defense, defense of others or certain property, or duress. Mistake of fact is a ground for excluding criminal responsibility under Article 32 only if it negates the mental element; mistake of law about whether a particular type of conduct is a crime is not a ground for excluding criminal responsibility, but mistake of law may be such a ground if it negates the mental element required.

The court will have jurisdiction under Article 12 over crimes committed on the territory of any state party to the Statute or by a national of any state party, regardless where the crime occurred. It will also have jurisdiction over crimes in a situation referred by a non-state party that has made a special declaration. In addition, the court can exercise jurisdiction over crimes committed anywhere in a situation that breaches or threatens international peace and security that has been referred by the Security Council (see below).

The cornerstone of the Statute is the principle of complementarity, as identified in the Preamble, Article 1, and Article 17. This principle has two parts. First, as the Preamble makes clear, states have the primary duty to bring those responsible for these crimes to justice. In the Preamble, the states parties affirm that "the most serious crimes of concern to the international community must not go unpunished and that their effective prosecution must be ensured by taking measures at the national level and by enhancing international cooperation," determine "to put an end to impunity," and recall that "it is the duty of every State to exercise its criminal jurisdiction over those responsible for international crimes." Second, as Article 17 provides, the court will act only when states are unwilling and unable genuinely to investigate and prosecute suspects themselves. In such cases, and when trial is precluded under the principle of *ne bis in idem* (double jeopardy) as defined in Article 20 or the case is not of sufficient gravity, the court is required to determine that the case is inadmissible. In determining whether a state is unwilling, the court shall consider whether the national proceedings were or are being undertaken or the national decision (which would include amnesties, pardons, or similar measures of impunity) was made to shield the person concerned, there was unjustified delay, the proceedings were not independent or impartial, or they were conducted in a manner inconsistent with bringing the person to justice. In determining inability in a particular case, the court shall consider whether, "due to a total or substantial collapse or unavailability of its national judicial system, the State is unable to obtain the accused or the necessary evidence and testimony or otherwise unable to carry out its proceeding." Article 17 does not, however, preclude the court from examining other factors.

There are three ways an investigation can be opened. Article 13 (b) will make ad hoc international criminal tribunals for crimes committed after entry into force of the Statute largely unnecessary. It provides that the Court may exercise jurisdiction over a genocide, crimes against humanity, war crimes, and the crime of aggression if the Security Council, acting pursuant to Chapter VII of the UN Charter, has referred a situation to the prosecutor where such crimes appear to have been committed. Article 13 (a) provides that the court may exercise its jurisdiction over such a crime when a state party has referred a situation to the prosecutor pursuant to Article 14 in which such crimes may have occurred. Article 13 (e) gives the court jurisdiction over a crime when the prosecutor has initiated an investigation pursuant to Article 15. That article authorizes the prosecutor to initiate an investigation based on information from any source, including victims and their families, intergovernmental organizations, and nongovernmental organizations, if authorized to do so by the Pre-Trial Chamber. Regardless which method is used, the prosecutor can be subjected to a lengthy series of admissibility challenges by states (whether the states are parties to the Statute or not) under Article 18, based on the complementarity criteria in Article 17, and admissibility and jurisdictional challenges under Article 19 and judicial scrutiny by the Pre-Trial Chamber before the prosecutor can open or continue an investigation.

Organization of the court

The court will be composed of six organs: the Presidency (consisting of three judges: the president and two vice presidents), three judicial divisions (Pre-Trial, Trial, and Appeals), the Office of the Prosecutor, and the Registry (Article 34). It will have eighteen full-time judges in the three judicial divisions, although that number can be raised by the Assembly of States Parties to meet an increase in the workload (Article 36). Judges must have relevant experience and either estab-

lished competence in criminal law and procedure or in relevant areas of international law, such as international humanitarian law or human rights law. The judges are to be elected by the Assembly of States Parties in a secret ballot for nine-year nonrenewable terms. Article 40 requires that judges be "independent in the performance of their functions," serve full time, and not engage in outside activities that would endanger that independence. Article 42 states that the Office of the Prosecutor "shall act independently as a separate organ of the Court" and members "shall not seek or act on instructions from any external source." The prosecutor and deputy prosecutors must be "persons of high moral character, be highly competent in and have extensive practical experience in the prosecution or trial of criminal cases." They will be elected by the Assembly of States Parties in a secret ballot for a single, nonrenewable term. Article 42 provides for a registrar, elected by the judges, who will be responsible for the administration of the Court. The Registry will include a Victims and Witnesses Unit with responsibility to provide, in consultation with the Office of the Prosecutor, "protective measures and security arrangements, counselling and other appropriate assistance for witnesses, victims who appear before the Court, and others who are at risk on account of testimony given by such witnesses." Its staff must include persons "with expertise in trauma, including trauma related to crimes of sexual violence." To help guarantee their independence, Article 46 provides that judges may only be removed by a two-thirds vote of the Assembly of States Parties and the prosecutor by a majority vote; the registrar may only be removed by a majority of the judges.

Pretrial investigation, trial, appeal, and revision

The procedure to be applied by the court draws upon both common and civil law models, but most aspects of the procedure are so modified that they should be seen as a new international criminal procedure. For example, although the procedure is largely adversarial, judges are expected to assert a greater control of litigation during all phases. Moreover, in carrying out investigations, the prosecutor has a duty to establish the truth, to investigate evidence that is favorable as well as unfavorable to the person under investigation, to respect the interests and circumstances of victims, and to fully respect the rights of persons (Article 54). The prosecutor will be largely dependent on state cooperation to conduct investigations. He or she may conduct investigations on the territory of a state, but apart from the limited exception of a major breakdown in the judicial system when authorized to do so by the Pre-Trial Chamber under Article 57, this may occur only with the consent of the state. In an important innovation, the Pre-Trial Chamber will be able to gather evidence pursuant to Article 56, which may not be available at trial, such as the testimony of a victim or witness.

One of the most important provisions in the Statute, which is likely to have an enormous impact over the long term on national criminal justice systems, is Article 55. It contains a mini-charter guaranteeing the rights of persons during an investigation, and expressly guarantees that suspects questioned by the prosecutor or state authorities acting at the court's request have the right to silence, and the exercise of that right may not be considered in the determination of guilt or innocence. Suspects also have the right to the presence of a lawyer during any questioning. Evidence obtained in violation of these rights can be excluded pursuant to Article 69 (7).

Unless otherwise decided, trials will be at the seat of the court (Article 62). Article 65 requires the Trial Chamber, before accepting an admission of guilt, to determine if the accused understands the nature and consequences of this decision and has made it voluntarily after consulting counsel, and that it is supported by the facts. Discussions between the prosecutor and defense counsel concerning modification of the charges, the admission of guilt, or the penalty are not binding upon the court. The Trial Chamber under Article 64 must "ensure that the trial is fair and expeditious and is conducted with full respect for the rights of the accused and due regard for the protection of victims and witnesses." A broad range of fair trial guarantees are set forth in the Statute, including the prohibitions of retrospective criminality (*nulla crimen sine lege*) (Articles 22 and 24) and punishment (*nulla poena sine lege*), the right to be present (except when disrupting the trial) (Article 63), the presumption of innocence (Article 66), and most of the other rights to fair trial recognized in international instruments, such as Article 14 of the International Covenant on Civil and Political Rights and the Yugoslavia and Rwanda Statutes and Rules of Procedure and Evidence (Article 67). However, proposals to permit the use of anonymous witnesses, as authorized by the Trial Chamber of the Yugoslavia Tribunal in the *Tadić* case, were rejected. Article 70 spells out offenses against the administration of justice, such as perjury and bribery, which can be punished by the court or states parties. Article 72 establishes a complex procedure for safeguarding information where states consider that disclosure would prejudice their national security, and for referral to the Assembly of States Parties when the court concludes that the refusal by a state party to provide such information is not in accordance with the Statute.

Article 77 authorizes the imposition of prison sentences up to life and, in addition to a prison sentence, the court may order a fine and forfeiture of proceeds, property, or assets derived directly or indirectly from a crime. Like the Yugoslavia and Rwanda Statutes, the Statute excludes the death penalty. The prosecutor, as well as the convicted person, may appeal a judgment on the grounds of procedural, factual, or legal error, and may also appeal the sentence; the convicted person may also appeal on other grounds (Article 81). After a final decision on appeal, Article 84 permits a request for revision of a conviction or sentence on the basis of newly discovered evidence that was not available at the time of trial, where this was not the fault of the accused and the evidence could have led to a different verdict. Article 85 permits compensation for unlawful arrest and miscarriages of justice.

The role of victims

The Statute is a major advance in international law with respect to the protection of victims, their participation in the proceedings, and their right to reparations. As stated above, the Statute provides for a Victims and Witnesses Unit, with appropriate expertise, to provide protection and support for victims. Article 68 (1) requires the Court to take "appropriate measures to protect the safety, physical and psychological well-being, dignity and privacy of witnesses," taking into account a number of factors, including whether the crime was one of sexual violence or violence against children, but such measures "shall not be prejudicial to or inconsistent with the rights of the accused and a fair and impartial trial." Such measures may include conducting certain hearings *in camera* or withholding certain evidence prior to the commencement of the trial. Article 15 would permit victims or their families, as other reliable sources, to provide information to the prosecutor that he or she would use to determine whether to open an investigation. Although the Statute does not provide that the victims may be *parties civiles*, as in certain civil law systems such as France, or institute private prosecutions, as in certain common law systems such as the United Kingdom, Article 68 (3) provides that where their personal interests are affected, the court "shall permit their views and concerns to be presented and considered at stages of the proceedings determined to be appropriate by the Court and in a manner which is not prejudicial to or inconsistent with the rights of the accused and a fair and impartial trial." Article 75 requires the court to establish principles relating to reparations, including restitution, compensation, and rehabilitation. The court may award reparations against the person convicted and states parties must give effect to the court's decision.

State cooperation

Article 86 provides that states are under a general obligation to cooperate fully with the court in its investigation and prosecution of crimes. These obligations include the duty to ensure that there are procedures available under national law to cooperate (Article 88), to surrender accused or escaped convicted persons promptly (Article 89), and to provide a wide range of cooperation, such as locating witnesses and evidence, conducting searches and seizures, tracing and freezing assets of the accused with a view toward forfeiture, as well as other assistance not prohibited under national law (Article 93).

Article 98 is a weak point in the Statute. Article 98 (1) provides that the court may not proceed with a request for surrender where it would require the requested state to act inconsistently with respect to its obligations under international law or the diplomatic immunity of a third state, although it is a widely shared view of the drafters that states parties would not be able to assert diplomatic immunity of their nationals to defeat a request to surrender. Article 98 (2) was added at the insistence of the United States to address existing bilateral and multilateral extradition agreements and status of forces agreements (SOFAs) providing for trial of American nationals in the United States or the other states parties. It requires that the court not proceed with a request for surrender that would require a requested state to act inconsistently with its obligations under an international agreement pursuant to

which the consent of a sending state is required, unless consent is obtained.

The Court will not have any prisons, but instead will rely, like the Yugoslavia and Rwanda tribunals, on states to enforce sentences. Articles 103 to 111 provide for the voluntary enforcement of sentences by states under supervision of the court, consistent with widely accepted international treaty standards. States may not modify the sentences without Court approval. Article 109 requires states parties to give effect to fines and forfeitures.

Other matters

Article 112 provides for the establishment of an Assembly of States Parties. Its responsibilities will include adopting recommendations of the Preparatory Commission, providing management oversight of the Court, selecting the judges and the Prosecutor, deciding the budget and determining what action to take when states fail to cooperate with the court. The court is to be funded, as provided in the budget, from assessed contributions of states parties, funds provided by the UN (Article 114), and voluntary contributions (Article 115). Article 119 provides that the Court will settle any dispute concerning its judicial functions, and any other dispute between states parties concerning the interpretation or application of the Statute not settled within three months will be settled by the Assembly of States Parties or, if it so decides, by the International Court of Justice. No reservations may be made to the Statute (Article 120).

Under Article 121, no amendments are possible for seven years after entry into force. Amendments must first be adopted by the Assembly of States Parties or a Review Conference (the first of which must be held under Article 123 within seven years) by consensus or by a two-thirds majority. Except as provided in Article 121 (5), amendments enter into force for all states parties one year after acceptance by seven-eighths of the states parties; states parties that have not accepted the amendment may withdraw from the Statute immediately by giving notice within one year after the amendment enters into force. In contrast, under Article 121 (5), amendments to Articles 5 to 8 (concerning definitions of crime) enter into force for those parties which have accepted them one year after their acceptance. However, if a state party has not accepted an amendment to Articles 5 to 8, then the court may not exercise its jurisdiction regarding a crime covered by that amendment when committed by that state's nationals or on its territory. Certain amendments of an institutional nature can be adopted by the Assembly of States Parties by a two-thirds majority, which will bind all states parties (Article 122). A transitional provision, Article 124, provides that a state party may, when becoming a party to the Statute, declare that, for a period of seven years after entry into force for that state, it does not accept the jurisdiction of the Court with respect to war crimes that are alleged to have been committed by its nationals or on its territory. Only one state, France, which proposed this article, has done so. Article 127 permits states parties to withdraw, effective one year after the notice, but they remain bound by obligations prior to the date of withdrawal.

CHRISTOPHER KEITH HALL

See also ADVERSARY SYSTEM; CRIMINAL PROCEDURE: COMPARATIVE ASPECTS; INTERNATIONAL CRIMINAL JUSTICE STANDARDS; INTERNATIONAL CRIMINAL LAW; WAR CRIMES.

BIBLIOGRAPHY

Amnesty International. *The International Criminal Court: Making the Right Choices—Parts I–V, 1997–1998.* London: Amnesty International. Also available on the World Wide Web at http://www.amnesty.org.

BASSIOUNI, M. CHERIF. *Crimes against Humanity in International Law,* 2d ed. The Hague, London, and Boston: Kluwer Law International, 1999.

BASSIOUNI, M. CHERIF. *The Statute of the International Crime Court.* Ardsley, N.Y.: Transnational Publishers, Inc., 1998.

BASSIOUNI, M. CHERIF, ed. *International Criminal Law,* 2d ed. 3 vols. Irvington-on-Hudson, N.Y.: Transnational Publishers, Inc., 1999.

BRACKMAN, ARNOLD C. *The Other Nuremberg.* New York: Morrow, 1987.

CASSESE, ANTONIO; ESER, ALBIN; GAJA, GIORGIO; and CONOR, ROBERT E. *Justice at Nuremberg.* New York: Harper & Row, 1980.

Coalition for an International Criminal Court. World Wide Web document, 2001. http://www.iccnow.org. Contains text of the court's Statute, draft Elements of International Crime, draft Rules of Procedure and Evidence, and many other documents concerning the court.

DAVID, ERIC. *Principes de droit des conflits armés,* 2d ed. Brussels: Bruylant, 1999.

DAVIDSON, EUGENE. *The Trial of the Germans: An Account of the Twenty-Two Defendants before the International Military Tribunal at Nuremberg.* Columbia, Missouri, and London: University of Missouri Press, 1966.

FERENCZ, BENJAMIN B. *An International Criminal Court, A Step Toward Peace: A Documentary History.* London: Oceana Publications, 1980.

GREEN, LESLIE C. *The Contemporary Law of Armed Conflict,* 2d ed. Manchester, U.K.: Manchester University Press, 2000.

International Committee of the Red Cross. *Commentary on the Additional Protocols of 8 June 1977 to the Geneva Conventions of 12 August 1949.* Geneva: International Committee of the Red Cross, 1987.

International Criminal Tribunal for the Former Yugoslavia. World Wide Web document, 2001. http://www.un.org/icty. Judgments and other documents.

International Criminal Tribunal for Ruwanda. World Wide Web document, 2001. http://www.ictr.org. Judgments and other documents.

KIRSCH, PHILLIPE; PELLET, ALAIN; and SWART, BERT, eds. *International Criminal Law for an International Criminal Court.* Oxford, U.K.: Oxford University Press, 2001.

LEE, ROY S., ed. *The International Criminal Court: The Making of the Rome Statute—Issues, Negotiations, Results.* The Hague, London, and Boston: Kluwer Law International, 1999.

Memorandum by the Secretary-General. "Historical Survey of the Question of International Criminal Jurisdiction." UN Doc. A/CN.4/7/Rev.1 (1949).

MINEAR, ROBERT H. *Victor's Justice: The Tokyo War Crimes Trial.* Princeton: Princeton University Press, 1971.

MORRIS, VIRGINIA, and SCHARF, MICHAEL P. *An Insider's Guide to the International Criminal Tribunal for the Former Yugoslavia.* 2 vols. Irvington-on-Hudson, N.Y.: Transnational Publishers, Inc., 1995.

———. *The International Criminal Tribunal for Rwanda.* 2 vols. Irvington-on-Hudson, N.Y.: Transnational Publishers, Inc., 1998.

PICTET, JEAN. *Commentary on the Four Geneva Conventions of 1949.* Geneva: International Committee of the Red Cross, 1952–1960.

ROLING, B. V. A., and CASSESE, ANTONIO. *The Tokyo Trial and Beyond.* Cambridge, Mass.: Polity Press, 1993.

SCHABAS, WILLIAM. *Genocide in International Law.* Cambridge, U.K.: Cambridge University Press, 2000.

TAYLOR, TELFORD. *The Anatomy of the Nuremberg Trials: A Personal Memoir.* New York: Alfred A. Knopf, 1992.

TRIFFTERER, OTTO, ed. *Commentary on the Rome Statute of the International Criminal Court: Observers' Notes, Article by Article.* Baden-Baden, Germany: Nomos Verlagsgesellschaft, 1999.

TUSA, ANN, and TUSA, JOHN. *The Nuremberg Trial.* New York: Atheneum, 1983.

VARAUT, JEAN-MARC. *Le proces de Nuremberg.* Paris: Perrin, 1992.

VON HEBEL, HERMAN; LAMMERS, JOHAN G.; and SCHUKKING, JOLIEN. *Reflections on the International Criminal Court: Essays in Honour of Adriaan Bos.* The Hague: T. M. C. Asser Press, 1999.

INTERNATIONAL CRIMINAL JUSTICE STANDARDS

International criminal justice standards, including principally the right to a fair trial, have been defined and guaranteed by no less than twenty global and regional human rights treaties and other instruments. The most important are (1) the Universal Declaration of Human Rights; (2) the International Covenant on Civil and Political Rights; (3) the International Convention on the Elimination of All Forms of Racial Discrimination; and (4) the Convention on the Rights of the Child. International humanitarian law, codified in the four Geneva Conventions and two Additional Protocols, ensures the right to a fair trial and related criminal justice standards during periods of internal and international armed conflicts. There are several other treaty and nontreaty standards relating to the role of judges, prosecutors, and lawyers; the protection of detainees/prisoners, juvenile offenders, persons facing the death penalty; and providing safeguards against disappearances and torture. Regional treaties such as the African Charter on Human and Peoples' Rights, the Inter-American Convention on Human Rights, and the [European] Convention for the Protection of Human Rights and Fundamental Freedoms contain fair trial guarantees and other provisions relevant to criminal justice. The most visible and recent elaboration of the right to a fair trial has been in the context of the ad hoc tribunals for the former Yugoslavia and Rwanda as well as the statute for the new permanent International Criminal Court.

Universal declaration of human rights

In 1948 the U.N. General Assembly adopted the Universal Declaration of Human Rights (Universal Declaration), which provides a worldwide definition of the human rights obligations undertaken by all U.N. member states pursuant to Articles 55 and 56 of the U.N. Charter, including several provisions relating to the administration of justice. For example, Article 10 of the Universal Declaration states, "Everyone is entitled in full equality to a fair and public hearing by an independent tribunal, in the determination of his rights and obligations and of any criminal charge against him." Article 11 provides for the presumption of innocence, public trial, "all guarantees necessary for [one's] defence," and the right to be free from retroactive punishment or penalties. Other provisions of the Universal Declaration—for example, as to arbitrary arrest, the right to an effective remedy, the right to be free from torture, the right to security of person, and privacy—are relevant to the criminal justice system and the fairness of the trial process.

International covenant on civil and political rights

Following the adoption of the Universal Declaration, the U.N. Commission on Human Rights drafted the International Bill of Human Rights, which includes the International Covenant on Civil and Political Rights (Civil and Political Covenant). The Civil and Political Covenant entered into force 23 March 1976 as a multilateral treaty (ratified by 144 countries as of 1 November 2000) and establishes an international minimum standard of conduct for all participating governments. The Civil and Political Covenant further elaborates—particularly in its Articles 14 and 15, but also in Articles 2, 6, 7, 9, and 10—upon the criminal justice standards identified in the Universal Declaration. Article 14 of the Civil and Political Covenant recognizes the right in all proceedings to "a fair trial and public hearing by a competent, independent and impartial tribunal established by law." Every person is "equal before the courts and tribunals" under Article 14(1).

Article 14 also distinguishes between the sort of fair hearing required for civil cases, on the one hand, and criminal cases, on the other. Article 14(3) deals with the "minimum guarantees" required in the determination of any criminal charge, the observance of which is not always sufficient to ensure the fairness of a hearing. Among the minimum guarantees in criminal proceedings prescribed by Article 14(3) is the right of the accused to be informed of the charge against him/her in a language that the accused understands; to have adequate time and facilities for the preparation of a defense and to communicate with counsel of one's own choosing; to be tried without undue delay; to examine or have examined the witnesses against the accused and to obtain the attendance and examination of witnesses on one's behalf under the same conditions as witnesses against the accused; to the assistance of an interpreter free of any charge, if the accused cannot understand or speak the language used in court; and the right not to be compelled to testify against oneself or to confess guilt. Article 14 also gives the accused the right to have one's conviction and sentence reviewed by a higher tribunal according to law; to compensation if there was a miscarriage of justice; and not to be subjected to trial or punishment for a second time (*non bis in idem*). Under Article 14(4) juvenile persons have the same right to a fair trial as adults, but are also entitled to certain additional safeguards. Article 15 codifies the principle of *nullum crimen sine lege* (no crime without law) and also gives the accused the benefit of any decrease in penalty that is promulgated after the person has committed an offense. Other relevant provisions of the Civil and Political Covenant forbid torture or cruel, inhuman or degrading treatment or punishment; forbid arbitrary arrest; and require equality before the law.

The Human Rights Committee was established by the Civil and Political Covenant to interpret and apply the Covenant's provisions. The Committee has evolved a considerable jurisprudence on issues relating to the administration of justice—particularly as to the right to a fair trial. For example, many prisoners have complained to the Human Rights Committee that they have not received a prompt trial and the committee has sought to interpret that requirement. In 1984 the Human Rights Committee issued General Comment 13 authoritatively interpreting Article 14 of the Covenant and stating that the right to trial without undue delay relates not only to the time by which a trial should commence, but also to the time by which it should end and judgment be rendered; all stages must take place "without undue delay." It must be ensured, by means of an established procedure, that the trial will proceed "without undue delay," both in the first instance and on appeal.

The Civil and Political Covenant identifies in Article 4 certain rights as nonderogable, that is, those rights which cannot be the subject of suspension during periods of emergency that threatens the life of the nation. While Article 4 does not specify Article 14 (right to a fair trial) as expressly nonderogable, it does mention Articles 7 (prohibition of torture), 15 (*nullum crimen sine lege* (no crime without law)), and 16 (recognition of every person before the law) as nonderogable. Furthermore, the Human Rights Committee has interpreted other nonderogable rights (e.g., the right not to be subjected to arbitrary deprivation of life) as implying that the basic fair trial provisions of Article 14 cannot be suspended during periods of national emergency. The Human Rights Committee will likely strengthen the nonderogable nature of the right to a fair trial by issuing a further General Comment as well as decisions and views on individual cases interpreting the Covenant.

International Convention on the Elimination of All Forms of Racial Discrimination

The Convention of the Elimination of All Forms of Racial Discrimination (Race Convention) entered into force on 12 March 1969, and had been ratified by 156 countries as of 15 November 2000. The preamble proclaims that "all human beings are equal before the law and are entitled without any discrimination to equal protection of the law." This principle of equality before the law is repeated in the opening paragraph of Article 5, which imposes upon state parties the obligation to guarantee this right to everyone, without distinction as to race, color, or national or ethnic origin. Article 2(1) (a) of the Convention affirms that each state party undertakes to ensure that public authorities and public institutions, national and local, shall not engage in acts or practices of racial discrimination against persons, groups of persons, or institutions.

The Committee on the Elimination of Racial Discrimination (CERD) has also interpreted the Race Convention on some aspects of the administration of justice. For example, *L.K. v. the Netherlands* (comm. No. 4/1991) involved de facto housing discrimination by members of the neighborhood where a foreign-born man wished to reside. In its opinion of 16 March 1993, CERD found that the mere existence of a law making discrimination a criminal act was insufficient and decided that the state's obligation to treat instances of racial discrimination with particular attention was missing. The police and judicial proceedings in the case did not afford the applicant effective protection and remedies within the meaning of Article 6 of the Race Convention. The CERD declared that the Netherlands should compensate the author and report back to the Committee on measures taken to remedy the situation.

Convention on the Rights of the Child

The Convention on the Right of the Child entered into force on 2 September 1990, and had been ratified by 191 countries as of 1 November 2000, that is, nearly every county of the world, except Somalia and the United States. The Child Convention elaborates on the rights of juvenile offenders in the Civil and Political Covenant and other treaties.

Articles 12, 37, and 40 are the primary provisions in the Child Convention relevant to the administration of justice. Article 12 safeguards each child's right to be heard in legal proceedings. Article 37(b) provides that "[n]o child shall be deprived of his or her liberty unlawfully or arbitrarily." Furthermore, Article 37 (d) provides that "[e]very child deprived of his or her liberty shall have the right to prompt access to legal and other appropriate assistance, as well as the right to challenge the legality of the deprivation of his or her liberty before a court or other competent, independent and impartial authority, and to a prompt decision on any such action."

Article 40 of the Child Convention addresses the same fair trial issues as Article 14 of the Covenant on Civil and Political Rights. Article 40 of the Child Convention significantly expands fair trial protection to children under the age of eighteen, by using the term "child" instead of "juvenile" used by the Covenant. This expansive approach is also evident when compared to the United Nations Standard Minimum Rules for the Administration of Juvenile Justice (The Beijing Rules, 1985), which defines a juvenile as "a child or young person who, under the respective legal systems, may be dealt with for an offence in a manner which is different from an adult."

Humanitarian law

Common Article 3 of the four Geneva Conventions for the protection of victims of armed conflict (entered into force 21 October 1950, ratified by 188 countries as of 1 November 2000) and Article 6 of Additional Protocol II (entered into force 7 December 1978, ratified by 150 countries as of 1 November 2000) contain fair trial guarantees and other provisions relevant to the administration of justice for times of noninternational armed conflict. For example, Common Article 3(d) prohibits the "passing of sentences and the carrying out of executions without previous judgment pronounced by a regularly constituted court. . . ." Articles 96 and 99–108 of the Third Geneva Convention prescribe the rights of prisoners of war in judicial proceedings, essentially creating a fair trial standard. Articles 54, 64–74 and 117–126 of the Fourth Geneva Convention contain provisions relating to the right to fair trial in occupied territories. Article 75 of Additional Protocol I (entered into force 7 December 1978, ratified by 165 countries as of 1 November 2000) extends fair trial guarantees in an international armed conflict to all persons, including those arrested for actions relating to the conflict.

Other global standards

There are several other global non-treaty standards that relate to criminal justice, including Basic Principles on the Independence of the Judiciary; Basic Principles on the Role of Lawyers; Basic Principles for the Treatment of Prisoners; Basic Principles on the Use of Force and Firearms by Law Enforcement Officials; Body of Principles for the Protection of All Persons under Any Form of Detention or Imprisonment; Code of Conduct for Law Enforcement Officials; Declaration of Basic Principles of Justice for Victims of Crime and Abuse of Power; Declaration on the Protection of All Persons from Being Subjected to Torture and Other Cruel, Inhuman or Degrading Treatment or Punishment; Declaration on the Protection of All Persons from Enforced Disappearances; Draft International Convention on the Protection of All Persons from Enforced Disappearance; Guidelines on the Role of Prosecutors; Standard Minimum Rules for the Treatment of Prisoners; Convention against Torture and Other Cruel, Inhuman or Degrading Treatment or Punishment; Principles on the Effective Prevention and Investigation of Extra-legal, Arbitrary and Summary Executions; Safeguards Guaranteeing Protection of the Rights of Those Facing the Death Penalty; United Nations Guidelines for the Prevention of Juvenile Delinquency (The Riyadh Guidelines); United Nations Rules for the Protection of Juveniles Deprived of Their Liberty; United Nations Standard Minimum Rules for the Administration of Juvenile Justice (The Beijing Rules); and United Nations

Standard Minimum Rules for Non-custodial Measures (The Tokyo Rules). Most of these standards have been drafted by the U.N. Committee on Crime Prevention and Control (which has been replaced by the Commission on Crime Prevention and Criminal Justice); one of the U.N. Congresses on the Prevention of Crime and Treatment of Offenders (which have been held every five years since 1955); the U.N. Commission on Human Rights; and the U.N. Sub-Commission on the Promotion and Protection of Human Rights (formerly the Sub-Commission on the Prevention of Discrimination and Protection of Minorities).

In addition, the Second Optional Protocol to the International Covenant on Civil and Political Rights, aiming at the abolition of the death penalty, entered into force on 11 July 1991, and has been ratified by 44 nations as of 1 November 2000. Furthermore, the Convention (entered into force 22 April 1954) and Protocol (entered into force 4 October 1967, 135 states parties as of 1 November 2000) relating to the Status of Refugees contain a few provisions relating to the rights of refugees in the context of the administration of justice, such as access to the courts, including legal assistance.

Regional standards

European Convention on Human Rights. The Convention for the Protection of Human Rights and Fundamental Freedoms (European Convention on Human Rights or European Convention) entered into force on 3 September 1953, and has been ratified by all forty-one member counties of the Council of Europe. Provisions of the European Convention on Human Rights have enjoyed a very high degree of compliance—both because many countries have incorporated the Convention's provisions into domestic law and because the European Court and Commission's judgments have almost always been obeyed.

Fundamental fair trial guarantees are established in Article 6 of the European Convention. Article 6(1) provides that a person is entitled to a fair and public hearing within a reasonable time by an independent and impartial tribunal established by law. Article 6(1) of the European Convention applies to both "civil rights and obligations" as well as "any criminal charge." Some of the more difficult problems in the interpretation of the European Convention concern the application of Article 6 to noncriminal cases.

Article 6(2) stipulates that a person charged with a criminal offense shall be presumed innocent until proved guilty. Article 6(3)(a–e) addresses many of the same fair trial rights guaranteed in Article 14 of the Civil and Political Covenant. In particular, the accused must be promptly informed of the charges against her in a language she understands; to have adequate time and facilities to prepare her defense; to be allowed to defend herself or receive legal assistance, including free legal assistance if the accused lacks sufficient means and if the interests of justice requires; to examine or have examined witnesses against her; and to have free assistance of an interpreter if she cannot speak the language of the court.

The right to a fair trial holds a position of preeminence in the European Convention, due not only to the importance of the right involved but also to the great volume of applications and jurisprudence that it has generated. More applications to the European Court and Commission involve Article 6 than any other provision of the Convention. The minimum rights enumerated in Article 6(3) are not exhaustive, according to the Commission and the Court. (With the coming into force of Protocol 11 to the European Convention on 1 November 1998, the European Court and Commission have been consolidated into a unified European Court of Human Rights.) The concept has, rather, an open-ended, residual quality, providing ample opportunity, therefore, to infer other rights not specifically enumerated in Article 6(3) within Article 6(1)'s broad protection for a "fair and public hearing."

The European Court and Commission of Human Rights have interpreted the European Convention in light of the cases brought before them and have thus developed the largest single body of international human rights jurisprudence on fair trial and other administration of justice issues. For example, individuals have very frequently raised questions about the right to a speedy trial. The European Court has declared in *Moreira de Azevedo v. Portugal*, 189 Eur. Ct. H.R. (ser. A)(1990), that the European Convention "stresses the importance of administering justice without delays which might jeopardize its effectiveness and credibility," thus highlighting the importance of the maxim "Justice delayed is justice denied." Article 6(1) guarantees the right to trial within a reasonable time in both civil and criminal proceedings. Article 5(3) provides that "everyone arrested or detained . . . shall be brought promptly before a judge . . . and shall be entitled to trial within a reasonable time or to release pending trial."

In regard to criminal proceedings, scrutiny of the reasonable time under Article 6(1) begins at the moment when "the situation of the person concerned has been substantially affected as a result of a suspicion against him" (*Neumeister v. Austria*, 1 E.H.R.R. 91 (1968)) and lasts at least until acquittal, dismissal, or conviction, or until the sentence becomes definite (*Eckle Case*, 51 Eur. Ct. H.R. (ser. A) at 33 (1982)). The European Court and the Commission have said that the reasonableness of the length of proceedings must be assessed in the light of the circumstances of the case and having regard to its complexity, the conduct of the parties, and the authorities dealing with the case (*Bucholz Case*, 42 Eur. Ct. H.R. (ser. A) (1981)).

The European Court considers that the applicant is only required to show diligence in carrying out the procedural steps relating to him or her and to refrain from using delaying tactics (*Union Alimentaria Sanders SA Case*, 157 Eur. Ct. H.R. (ser. A) (1989)). An accused is not held responsible for the delay even if he or she does not request that the proceedings be expedited (*Schouten and Meldrum v. The Netherlands*, 19 E.H.R.R. 390 (1994)). The European Court has held that the accused is under no duty to be more active and is not required to cooperate actively with judicial authorities in connection with criminal proceedings (*Eckle Case*, 51 Eur. Ct. H.R. (ser. A) at 33 (1982)).

Moreover, the European Convention imposes an obligation upon states to "organise their legal systems so as to comply with the requirements of [A]rticle 6(1)" (*Milasi v. Italy*, 119 Eur. Ct. H.R. (ser. A) (1987)). Hence, the European Court found that delays attributable either to a backlog at the Court of Appeals or to the Court of Cassation's desire to hear cases dealing with a similar issue were unjustifiable under Article 6(1) and constituted a violation (*Hentrich v. France*, 18 E.H.R.R. 440 (1994)). Generally, a long period of inactivity in a case is entirely attributable to the state unless it provides a satisfactory explanation for the delay (*Philis v. Greece*, 40 Eur. Ct. H.R. (1997).

Another major element of European "fair trial" jurisprudence is the principle of equality of arms between the accused and the public prosecutor. Under that principle the European Court has examined a number of cases dealing with the position of experts in a proceeding. For example, in the *Bönisch Case*, 92 Eur. Ct. H.R. (ser. A) (1985), the European Court found a lack of equal treatment of the parties because an expert appearing as a witness for the prosecution had a stronger procedural position than another expert appearing for the defense. The witnesses should have been given equal treatment. The European Court further held that Article 6(3), which provides that an accused has the right to examine witness against him or her, is a constituent element of the concept of "fair trial" set forth in Article 6(1). The Court declined to consider a complaint under Article 6(3), but that determination did not preclude it from finding a violation under the more general fair trial grounds of Article 6(1). Each case should thus be examined with regard to the "development of the proceedings as a whole and not on the basis of one particular incident" (*Le Compte v. Belgium*, 58 Eur. Ct. H.R. (ser. A) (1983)).

In addition to the European Convention on Human Rights, the Council of Europe has also promulgated the Convention on Laundering, Search, Seizure and Confiscation of the Proceeds from Crime; the Convention on the Transfer of Sentenced Persons; the European Convention for the Prevention of Torture and Inhuman or Degrading Treatment or Punishment; European Convention on Extradition; the European Convention on Mutual Assistance in Criminal Matters; the European Convention on the Supervision of Conditionally Sentenced or Conditionally Released Offenders; the European Convention on the Transfer of Proceedings in Criminal Matters; the European Convention on the Non-Applicability of Statutory Limitation to Crimes against Humanity and War Crimes; the European Convention on the Suppression of Terrorism; and several other treaties.

African Charter on Human and Peoples' Rights

The African Charter on Human and Peoples' Rights entered into force 21 October 1986, and as of 15 December 1999 had been ratified by all forty-nine African countries except the Sahrawi Arab Democratic Republic. Article 7 of the African Charter guarantees several fair trial rights, including notification of charges, appearance before a judicial officer, right to release pending trial, presumption of innocence, adequate preparation of the defense, speedy trial, examination of witnesses, and the right to an interpreter.

Under Article 26, African states are bound to guarantee the independence of the judiciary, which is a basic requirement for a fair trial. In addition to the above-mentioned guarantees, Articles 3, 4, 5, and 6 of the African Charter also provide for the rights to equality before the law, the equal protection of the law, the inviolability of human beings, as well as guarantees against all forms of degradation of man or any arbitrary arrest or detention.

The African Commission on Human and Peoples' Rights adopted a resolution in March 1992 on the "Right to Recourse Procedure and Fair Trial," which elaborated upon the provisions of the African Charter, including the right to an appeal to a higher court.

American Convention on Human Rights

The American Convention on Human Rights (American Convention) entered in force on 18 July 1978, and as of 15 December 1999 had been ratified by all twenty-four states in the Western Hemisphere. Article 7 of the American Convention provides several criminal justice guarantees, including, for example, the right to notice and to *habeas corpus*. Article 8 deals with the right to a fair trial in a detailed manner, including the right to a hearing, the presumption of innocence, the rights to a free translator and to counsel, the right of the accused not to be compelled to be a witness against himself, the principles of *ne bis in idem* (not twice in the same), and that criminal proceedings be public. Article 9 guarantees freedom from ex post facto laws. The Inter-American Commission on Human Rights also considers the right to compensation for miscarriage of justice as forming part of the right to fair trial under Article 10. Article 25 of the Convention further guarantees the right to "simple and prompt recourse, or any other effective recourse, to a competent court or tribunal for protection against acts that violate his fundamental rights recognized by the constitution or laws of the state concerned or by this Convention, even though such violation may have been committed by persons acting in the course of their official duties."

The Inter-American Commission on Human Rights has interpreted the American Convention on Human Rights and the American Declaration on the Rights and Duties of Man (1948) elaborating the rights necessary for a fair trial. The Inter-American Court of Human Rights, through its adjudicatory and advisory jurisdiction, has also examined violations of human rights related to a fair trial, albeit in only a few cases.

In addition to the American Convention on Human Rights, the Inter-American Convention to Prevent and Punish Torture, Inter-American Convention on Extradition, the Inter-American Convention on Mutual Assistance in Criminal Matters, and the Inter-American Convention on Serving Criminal Sentences Abroad have also been issued under the aegis of the Organization of American States.

International Criminal Tribunal for Former Yugoslavia and Rwanda

On 25 May 1993, the United Nations Security Council adopted resolution 827 (1993) in which it approved the establishment of "an international tribunal for the sole purpose of prosecuting persons responsible for serious violations of international humanitarian law committed in the territory of the former Yugoslavia" after 1 January 1991. Article 15 of the Statute of the International Tribunal authorizes the judges to "adopt rules of procedure and evidence for the conduct of the pre-trial phase of the proceedings, trials and appeals, the admission of evidence, the protection of victims, and witnesses and other matters." Article 20 of the statute provides that the Trial Chambers of the International Tribunal "shall ensure that a trial is fair and expeditious and that proceedings are conducted in accordance with the rules of procedure and evidence, with full respect for the rights of the accused and due regard for the protection of victims and witnesses." Articles 20 through 26 contain more specific provisions relating to the right to a fair trial, judgment, and appeal. In particular, most of the fair trial provisions in Article 14 of the Civil and Political Covenant are reflected in Article 21 of the statute, although the Covenant is not mentioned as such.

Additional articles contain safeguards designed to ensure the impartiality of the tribunal (rules 14–36), ensure the suspect's right to free counsel and the assistance of an interpreter (42), provide for the video- or audio-taping of all suspect questioning (43), contain procedural safeguards for all indictments and arrest warrants (47–61), require that all accused be brought promptly before the tribunal (62), do not allow the suspect to be questioned without counsel present (63), require the prosecution to disclose all exculpatory evidence to the accused (68), allow the judges to close the proceedings to the public in certain circumstances (79), and provide for appeal (107–22) and pardon (123–125) procedures. The Rules of Procedure and Evidence for the Yugoslav Tribunal devote more attention to the rights of victims and witnesses than previous international criminal standards.

On 8 November 1994, the U.N. Security Council adopted resolution 955 (1994) in which it approved the establishment of an "International Criminal Tribunal for the Prosecution of Persons Responsible for Genocide and other Serious Violations of International Humanitarian Law Committed in the Territory of Rwanda and Rwandan Citizens Responsible for Genocide and Other Such Violations Committed in the Territory of Neighboring States," between 1 January 1994 and 31 December 1994. The Rwanda Tribunal has been established in Arusha, Tanzania, but shares the same prosecutor, appellate court, and basic rules of procedure as the Yugoslav Tribunal.

International Criminal Court

Based upon the precedents of the Nuremberg Tribunal established by the London Agreement of 1945, the International Military Tribunal for the Far East (Tokyo Tribunal) established in 1946, trials in Germany under Control Council Law No. 10 (1946), the Yugoslav Tribunal established in 1993, and the Rwanda Tribunal of 1994, a diplomatic conference in Rome adopted a statute of 17 July 1998 for a permanent International Criminal Court (ICC). When the statute has been ratified by at least sixty states, the ICC will begin to bring to justice persons who have been accused of genocide, crimes against humanity, war crimes, and the crime of aggression. On an ad hoc basis, the ICC may also be authorized by the Security Council to handle any situations similar to the former Yugoslavia and Rwanda. As of 15 December 1999, there are ninety-one states that have signed and five that have ratified the ICC Statute.

Many of the international criminal justice standards in the ICC Statute were derived from the Civil and Political Covenant and the rules of the Yugoslav Tribunal. The ICC Statute establishes a structure and rules of procedure for the court and protects the rights of suspects, defendants, victims, and witnesses. Further procedural protections will be developed in coming years.

Conclusion

The United Nations and regional organizations have codified a substantial framework of international criminal justice standards, which have been accepted, albeit not always followed, by most nations and that have begun to be used in the context of international criminal tribunals. In addition to the codified standards, several human rights institutions, including particularly the Human Rights Committee and the European Court of Human Rights, have interpreted and applied criminal justice norms to particular cases and have thus generated an impressive corpus of jurisprudence that lawyers and judges worldwide should consult.

DAVID WEISSBRODT

See also COMPARATIVE CRIMINAL LAW AND ENFORCEMENT: CHINA; COMPARATIVE CRIMINAL LAW AND ENFORCEMENT: ENGLAND; COMPARATIVE CRIMINAL LAW AND ENFORCEMENT: ISLAM; COMPARATIVE CRIMINAL LAW AND ENFORCEMENT: PRELITERATE SOCIETIES; COMPARATIVE CRIMINAL LAW AND ENFORCEMENT: RUSSIA; CRIMINAL PROCEDURE: COMPARATIVE ASPECTS; INTERNATIONAL CRIMINAL COURTS; INTERNATIONAL CRIMINAL LAW; WAR CRIMES.

BIBLIOGRAPHY

ALDERSON, J. C. *Human Rights and the Police.* Strasbourg, Germany: Directorate of Human Rights, 1984.

Amnesty International. *Fair Trials Manual.* London: Amnesty International Publications, 1998.

BASSIOUNI, M. CHERIF. "Human Rights in the Context of Criminal Justice: Identifying International Procedural Protections and Equivalent Protections in National Constitutions." *Duke Journal of Comparative and International Law* 3 (1993): 235–297.

BUERGENTHAL, THOMAS, and KEWENIG, W. "Zum Begriff der Civil Rights in Artikel 6 Absatz 1 der Europaischen Menschenrechtskonvention." *Archiv des Volkerrechts* (1966–1967): 393–411.

CHERNICHENKO, STANISLAV, and TREAT, WILLIAM. *The Right to a Fair Trial, Brief Report Prepared by Mr. Stanislav Chernichenko and Mr. William Treat in Accordance with Resolution 1989/27 of the Sub-Commission on Prevention of Discrimination and Protection of Minorities.* Geneva: United Nations, U.N. Doc.E/CN.4/Sub.2/1990/34, 1990.

———. *The Right to a Fair Trial: Current Recognition and Measures Necessary for its Strengthening, Second Report Prepared by Mr. Stanislav Chernichencko and Mr. William Treat in Accordance with*

Resolution 1990/18 of the Sub-Commission and Resolution 1991/43 of the Commission on Human Rights. Geneva: United Nations, U.N. Doc. E/CN.4/Sub.2/1991/29.

————. *The Right to a Fair Trial: Current Recognition and Measures Necessary for its Strengthening, Fourth Report Prepared by Mr. Stanislav Chernichencko and Mr. William Treat.* Geneva: United Nations, U.N. Doc. E/CN.4/Sub.2/1992/24, 1992.

————. *The Right to a Fair Trial: Current Recognition and Measures Necessary for its Strengthening, Fourth Report Prepared by Mr. Stanislav Chernichencko and Mr. William Treat.* Geneva: United Nations, U.N. Doc. E/CN.4/Sub.2/1993/24, 1993.

————. *The Right to a Fair Trial: Current Recognition and Measures Necessary for its Strengthening, Final Report.* Geneva: United Nations, U.N. Doc. E/CN.4/Sub.2/1994/24, 1994.

GOMIEN, DONNA. "The Future of Fair Trial in Europe: The Contribution of International Human Rights Legal and Political Instruments." *Netherlands Quarterly of Human Rights* 9 (1991): 263–290.

GROTRIAN, ANDREW. *Article 6 of the European Convention on Human Rights: The Right to a Fair Trial.* Strasbourg, Germany: Council of Europe Press, 1994.

RANNAT, MOHAMMED AHMED ABU. *Study in the Administration of Justice.* New York: United Nations, U.N. Doc. E/CN.4/Sub.2/296/Rev.1, 1972.

REYNAUD, A. *Human Rights in Prisons.* New York: Oxford University Press, 1986.

RODLEY, NIGEL S. *The Treatment of Prisoners under International Law,* 2d ed. New York: Oxford University Press, 1999.

SINGHVI, L. M. *The Administration of Justice and the Human Rights of Detainees: Study on the Independence and Impartiality of the Judiciary, Jurors and Assessors and the Independence of Lawyers, Final Report.* Geneva: United Nations, U.N. Doc. E/CN.4/Sub.2/1985/18 and Add. 1–6, 1985.

SLOAN, JAMES. "The International Criminal Tribunal for the Former Yugoslavia and Fair Trial Rights: A Closer Look." *Leiden Journal of International Law* 9 (1996): 478–501.

STAVROS, STEPHANOS. *The Guarantees for Accused Persons under Article 6 of the European Convention on Human Rights: An Analysis of the Application of the Convention and a Comparison with Other Instruments.* Boston: M. Nijhoff, 1993.

SUNGA, LYAL S. *The Emerging System of International Criminal Law, Developments in Codification and Implementation.* Boston: Kluwer, 1997.

United Nations. *Consolidated List of Secretary-General of Provisions in the Various United Nations Standards Relating to Human Rights in the Administration of Justice.* New York: United Nations, U.N. Doc. E/CN.4/Sub.2/1991/26, 1991.

United Nations Centre for Social Development and Humanitarian Affairs. *Study of the Right of Everyone to be Free from Arbitrary Arrest, Detention and Exile.* New York: United Nations, U.N. Doc. E/CN.4/826, Rev.1, 1964.

————. *Compendium of United Nations Standards and Norms in Crime Prevention and Criminal Justice.* New York: United Nations, U.N. Doc. ST/CSD][A/16, 1991.

VAN DIJK, PIETER. *The Right of the Accused to a Fair Trial Under International Law.* Utrecht, Netherlands: Studie-en Informatiecentrum Mensenrechten, 1983.

WEISSBRODT, DAVID S. *Human Rights and Pre-Trial Detention: A Handbook of International Standards Relating to Pre-Trial Detention.* New York: United Nations, U.N. Doc. ST/HR/P/PT/3, 1994.

WEISSBRODT, DAVID S., and WOLFRUM, RÜDIGER, eds. *The Right to a Fair Trial.* Berlin and New York: Springer, 1997.

INTERNATIONAL CRIMINAL LAW

The bulk of criminal law is established and enforced under the national law of individual states, but an increasingly important body of international criminal law has also emerged. It began with a few international procedures developed by states to coordinate the enforcement of their national criminal law and has grown as international law itself has come to proscribe certain acts as crimes.

Since the end of the Thirty Year's War in 1648, the international system has been based on state sovereignty, including each state's jurisdiction over its own territory and citizens. A basic system of international law, defining the rights and obligations of states, was needed to recognize and validate this sovereignty, but this decentralized system has no legislature. Instead, international law must arise from one of three primary sources: treaties, customary international law, or general principles of law. Treaties make binding law for those states that agree to accept them. Rules of customary international law develop when the actions of states, their general and consistent practices, demonstrate their implied consent to those rules. General principles of law, especially when common to the laws of many nations, can also be applied at the international level. Judicial decisions and scholarly writings are recognized as secondary sources of international law, and are especially useful as indicators of changes in customary international law. International crimes, and the other substantive aspects of international criminal law, emerge from these same sources.

The traditional focus of international law has been upon the rights and obligations of states, but international criminal law regulates and punishes the conduct of individuals. Many of the crimes now defined by international law involve violations of the human rights of individuals. These too are now recognized under international law.

International criminal law, as the term is used today, includes those aspects of substantive international law that deal with defining and punishing international crimes, as well as the various mechanisms and procedures used by states to facilitate international cooperation in the investigation and enforcement of national criminal law.

Defining international crimes

Traditionally, international law has defined very few crimes, proscribing only acts generally viewed as a serious threat to the interests of the international community as a whole or to its most fundamental values. For centuries piracy has been recognized as an international crime under customary international law. Slave trading joined the list at the end of the nineteenth century when that practice was outlawed by treaty. As technological advances, along with increasing trade and globalization, have made the world seem smaller, more such crimes have gained recognition.

The basic jurisdiction of any sovereign state includes the right to define and punish crimes. The U.S. Constitution provides (Art. I, sec. 8, col. 10) that Congress shall have power "to define and punish Piracies and Felonies committed on the high Seas, and Offences against the Laws of Nations." Under this provision, Congress may identify and declare criminal under U.S. law, acts that are criminal under international law. Normally this is done by legislation. The domestic law of the United States is part of the fabric of international criminal law insofar as that national law provides for the recognition and punishment of international offenses. It has generally been the practice of the United States to recognize and punish international crimes only when they are embodied in U.S.treaties and implemented by federal legislation.

Some of the key categories of international crimes are briefly discussed below, but this list is far from exhaustive.

Aggression. Throughout history, the world community has sought to prevent war and eliminate aggression. In the Middle Ages, theories on "just" and "unjust" war were formulated. After World War I, efforts to curb war resulted in the establishment of the League of Nations. The Treaty of Versailles of 1919 called for the prosecutions of Kaiser Wilhelm II for waging unjust war, but efforts to carry out this provision were fruitless. The Kellogg-Briand Pact of 1928 provided for the formal renunciation of war as an instrument of national policy. This renunciation became the basis of the London Charter of 8 August 1945, which established in Nuremberg the International Military Tribunal for the prosecution of the major Nazi war criminals, and of the 1946 charter for the International Military Tribunal for the Far East, establishing a similar tribunal in Tokyo. These charters, the indictments and judgments of the tribunals, and the 1947 United Nations resolutions embodying the "Nuremberg Principles," are among the legal sources for considering aggression a "crime against peace." In 1946, the United Nations charter prohibited "aggression," but did not define it.

No real consensus on the meaning of "aggression" was reached until the United Nations' "Definition of Aggression" was agreed upon on 14 December 1974. The definition states that "[a]ggression is the use of armed force against the sovereignty, territorial integrity, or political independence of another state, or in any manner inconsistent with the charter of the United Nations." The definition also enumerates (not exhaustively, however) seven specific examples of aggression and sets forth their legal and political consequences. Thus far, no definition of aggression has been embodied in an international convention, although the issue has been much discussed in the multilateral negotiations. The Statute of the International Criminal Court (ICC), as adopted in Rome in 1998, lists aggression as a crime within the jurisdiction of the ICC, but delays any prosecution for aggression until such time as the parties to the statute can agree upon and adopt a definition of the crime.

Genocide. In 1948, only a few years after the Nazi Holocaust ended, the United Nations General Assembly adopted the text of the Genocide Convention. That text enshrined what was then a new international consensus defining and condemning the crime of genocide. The convention has since achieved very broad international acceptance. According to this definition, genocide occurs when any of five enumerated acts are "committed with intent to destroy, in whole or in part, a national, ethnical, racial or religious group, as such." The enumerated acts include killing members of the group, imposing birth control measures upon them, forcibly transferring children from the group, causing them serious bodily or mental harm, or inflicting on the group conditions deliberately calculated to bring about its physical destruction.

In ratifying the Genocide Convention, the parties "confirm that genocide, whether committed in time of peace or in time of war, is a crime under international law which they undertake to prevent and punish" (Article I). The parties also agree to enact the domestic legislation necessary to provide effective penalties for those committing genocide. This provision anticipates and establishes a decentralized control scheme under which the crimes defined by treaty are subject to enforcement under the national criminal law of states. At the same time, the Genocide Convention also refers to the possibility that those charged with genocide might be tried by "such international penal tribunal as may have jurisdiction" (Article VI). This set the stage for efforts to create a permanent International Criminal Court.

War crimes. The humanitarian law of armed conflict is an outgrowth of centuries of warfare, in the course of which the rules and customs governing the conduct of hostilities have evolved. Its development has been stimulated by military experts who recognize that violence and destruction, in excess of that required by actual military necessity, is not only immoral but also counterproductive to the attainment of the political objectives for which military force is used. The term "war crimes" refers to a broad category of acts prohibited during armed conflict that have come to be recognized as crimes under international law. Most war crimes are defined by treaty, although some are outlawed principally by unwritten customary international law. In some cases, even where there is a treaty prohibiting a specific war crime, the treaty's effectiveness is limited by the fact that many states have failed to sign and ratify it.

The most universally accepted source of rules on the regulation of war is the four Geneva Conventions of 12 August 1949, and their two additional protocols of 1977. Almost every country in the world, including the United States, is a party to the Geneva Conventions. These agreements codify many of the principal rules of international law relating to war crimes. In the national law of the United States, these rules have been incorporated into the Uniform Code of Military Justice. The Geneva conventions obligate each party to prevent and suppress acts contrary to their provisions. They directly incorporate an element of criminal law when they identify and define "grave breaches" of their terms. The parties agree (1) to enact legislation under their domestic law to criminalize these grave breaches; (2) to search for those believed to have committed them; and (3) either to prosecute them or to extradite them to another party that will do so. The enforcement regime applicable to these grave breaches became the model for other treaties establishing international crimes such as the Convention Against Torture.

Persons protected under the Geneva Conventions include wounded, sick, and shipwrecked persons, medical and religious personnel, prisoners of war, and civilians. For the most part, its protections apply to these persons only when they are in the hands of a foreign power. Specific prohibited conduct constituting war crimes includes torture, inhuman treatment, the taking of hostages, the destruction of protected property, physical mutilation, the performing of medical experiments, and refusal to release protected yet detained civilians or military personnel after cessation of active hostilities.

Crimes against humanity. The concept of crimes against humanity was only recently developed, emerging in the early part of the twentieth century, well after the notion of war crimes was developed in the nineteenth century. The Charter of the Nuremberg Tribunal was the first multilateral legal instrument that expressly provided for the prosecution of crimes against humanity as an offense separate from war crimes. The legal concept of crimes against humanity was developed in large part to remedy the argument that international law did not apply to criminal acts directed by a government against its own civilian population, a matter that was traditionally seen as falling exclusively within the sovereignty of a state. The fundamental element in the definition of crimes against humanity is widespread or systematic atrocities committed against civilians, for example, enslavement.

States have often objected to extending international law so far into the domestic sphere of activity, and they have proposed, at various times, a number of additional conditions limiting the application of this concept. The 1945 Nuremberg Charter, for example, authorized prosecution for crimes against humanity only if the alleged crimes were committed in execution of or in connection with a crime against peace or a war crime. It is now generally recognized that crimes against humanity can be committed in time of war or in time of peace, and even if there is no armed conflict as such. Nonetheless, states are still reluctant to endow international institutions with the authority to investigate and or prosecute crimes other than those committed in connection with international armed conflict.

The United Nations has adopted (or at least considered) a number of variations on the definition of crimes against humanity. Among these are a General Assembly resolution endorsing the standards of the Nuremberg Charter, the International Law Commission's Draft Code of Crimes Against the Peace and Security of Mankind, and the Statutes of the two ad hoc international criminal tribunals established by the United Nations in the 1990s. Negotiations leading to the 1998 adoption of the Statute of the International Criminal Court (ICC) produced consensus on a very narrowly defined core concept of crimes against humanity to be applied by that institution.

Torture. The 1984 Convention against Torture and Other Cruel, Inhuman or Degrading Treatment or Punishment (Torture Convention) defines torture as any act by which severe pain or suffering, whether physical or mental, is intentionally inflicted on a person by, or with the consent or acquiescence of, a public official in order to achieve certain purposes. The most common purposes are to obtain information or a confession, punishment, intimidation, coercion, or discrimination/persecution. This definition of torture does not include pain or suffering arising only from, inherent in, or incidental to lawful penal sanctions.

The Torture Convention has achieved very broad acceptance by states. It establishes an enforcement regime similar to that of the 1949 Geneva Conventions, in which the parties agree to make torture punishable under their domestic law and also agree to take the steps necessary to prosecute those offenders within their jurisdiction.

The convention's definition of torture is extremely narrow. It excludes acts of torture committed by individuals in a personal capacity, except in cases where there is some government, or official, complicity. The concept of torture as an international crime is correspondingly constrained.

Drug offenses. The international community has adopted a number of treaties designed to control the illicit production, manufacture, trade, and use of drugs. The 1961 Single Convention on Narcotic Drugs, as amended by its 1972 Protocol, established the International Narcotics Control Board to regulate the production and sale of narcotics, cannabis, and coca leaves. The 1971 Convention on Psychotropic Substances extended this regime to chemical drugs. The 1988 United Nations Convention against Illicit Traffic in Narcotic Drugs and Psychotropic Substances defines internationally recognized drug trafficking offenses and requires the parties to criminalize them under their domestic law. The United States has signed all three of these conventions and incorporated their provisions into law.

Terrorism and threats to civil aviation. Terrorism is an extremely dangerous form of criminal activity that needs suppression at both national and international levels. Unfortunately states have found it impossible, thus far, to agree on a general definition of terrorism as an international crime. The 1999 International Convention for the Suppression of the Financing of Terrorism came closer than ever before to this goal when it defined the offense of providing or collecting funds to be used to carry out terrorist acts. The European Convention on the Suppression of Terrorism, a regional initiative, incorporates a functional definition of terrorism among its parties and creates a relatively strong regional enforcement regime.

There has been broad international acceptance of effective international criminal standards relating to at least two forms of terrorism. The principal treaties on threats to civilian aviation define aircraft hijacking and a number of related crimes and require the parties to suppress them under their national law. This system has become a cornerstone of international civil aviation. Similarly, the International Convention against the Taking of Hostages outlaws this form of terrorism.

Bribery of foreign public officials. The bribery of foreign public officials, first outlawed by the United States in the Foreign Corrupt

Practices Act of 1977, is gaining recognition as a crime under international law. The 1997 Convention on Combating Bribery of Foreign Public Officials in International Business Transactions has been signed by thirty-four countries and entered into effect in February 1999. This treaty sets a general standard to be met by its parties in outlawing such bribes, but does not explicitly require states to impose sanctions on corporations as opposed to individuals. It has also been criticized for its failure to establish any uniform penalties for bribery, and for its failure to ban the tax deductibility of bribes paid to foreign officials. Another concern is that only a small number of states have ratified the treaty so far.

Other international crimes.   Other crimes defined by international conventions include counterfeiting, the theft of cultural property or archeological treasures, the crime of apartheid, and the threat or use of force against internationally protected persons such as diplomats.

Procedural Aspects

International criminal law also consists of procedures for cooperation between states in the execution of their national criminal law.

Under international law, one state cannot exercise its jurisdiction on the territory of another without the agreement of that state. This means that when suspects or evidence relating to a criminal trial in one country are found on the territory of another, cooperation between them is often indispensable. The most common, and most important, of these cooperative procedures are extradition and mutual legal assistance in cases of criminal law. Other important procedures include the transfer of prisoners, the seizure and forfeiture of the illicit proceedings of crime, the recognition of foreign penal judgments, and the transfer of penal proceedings.

Extradition.   Extradition is by far the most important of these cooperative procedures. When a person charged with a criminal violation of the law in one state is physically present on the territory of another, it is via the extradition procedure that the former may request the surrender of the accused from the latter. There is no general obligation of states to extradite under international law, and treaties, bilateral or multilateral, provide the basis for extradition in almost all cases. Extradition treaties establish the reciprocal agreement of the states-parties to extradite, set out the procedures for requesting extradition, and outline the conditions under which it may be granted or refused.

These treaties define a range of extraditable offenses. To form the basis of a request for extradition, an offense must generally be punishable under the laws of both countries. This is known as the principle of *double-criminality*. Among the more controversial provisions commonly found in these treaties is the traditional rule that no person should be extradited for a political offense. This rule severely complicated efforts by the United Kingdom to extradite accused terrorists from the United States until a 1985 US-UK Supplementary Extradition Treaty clarified that such offenses were not to be regarded as offenses of a political nature.

States choose their extradition partners carefully, and need not enter into such treaties with a country if they lack faith in its judicial system. In Europe, a multilateral extradition treaty has been successful in creating a regional regime of extradition. Supplementing bilateral and multilateral extradition treaties are provisions appearing in various multilateral treaties on subjects such as hijacking and the drug traffic, which may also serve as the legal basis for the extradition process. These generally incorporate the obligation to extradite or prosecute, as discussed elsewhere in this entry.

In one prominent 1992 case, the U.S. Drug Enforcement Administration (DEA) attempted to circumvent extradition procedures by kidnapping a suspect in Mexico and bringing him directly to trial in the United States. Mexico strongly objected, arguing that this act violated Mexican sovereignty as well as the U.S.-Mexico extradition treaty. Lawyers for the accused, a Mexican national named Hector Alvarez-Machain, argued that his abduction violated the extradition treaty and that, as a result, he could not be legally tried in the United States. The U.S. Supreme Court, in a very controversial opinion (*United States v. Alvarez-Machain*, 504 U.S. 655 (1992)), ruled 6–3 that the fact of his forcible abduction did not prohibit his trial in a United States court for violations of this country's criminal laws. The decision was based in part on their finding that "the Treaty says nothing about either country refraining from forcibly abducting people from the other's territory or the consequences if an abduction occurs." Mexico, and a number of other countries, reacted by expressing their desire to include an explicit ban on forcible abduction in their extradition treaties. In response, the U.S. government announced that, in the future, it would not be the policy of the

U.S. to carry out such forcible abductions in lieu of extradition.

Mutual legal assistance.   Technically extradition is a form of mutual legal assistance, but the term generally refers to mechanisms for the securing of evidence from a foreign state. This was traditionally done by means of *letters rogatory* (requests by the court of one country for evidence to be taken by the court of another country), which left cooperation within the discretion of the requested state. To remedy this problem, the United States has entered into several bilateral conventions that make the execution of such requests by the treaty partners a matter of course.

Enforcement models

Defining international crimes is only a first step in using criminal law to protect the values and interests of the international community. To be effective, international criminal law must be enforced. There are essentially two ways that this can be done: indirectly, under the jurisdiction and national criminal law of states, or directly, by international courts created for this purpose.

Enforcement presupposes jurisdiction to enforce. International law recognizes that states may prosecute for crimes committed on their territory (*territoriality principle*), by their nationals (*nationality principle*), or against their nationals (*passive personality principle*). Normally a state must have some such link as the basis for its exercise of jurisdiction over a crime. Universal jurisdiction is a special exception to this rule, applicable only to those, such as pirates, whose criminal acts render them *hostes humani generis*, the enemies of all humankind. Under the principle of universal jurisdiction, such a person may be tried not only by states linked to the crime but also by any other state. This extraordinary jurisdiction helps to remedy the inability of the decentralized international system to enforce even its most fundamental laws. It applies today to international crimes such as genocide and torture and may eventually apply to all serious international crimes.

The traditional approach calls for international crimes to be enforced and sanctioned under the national law of a state, even when the international crimes themselves are defined by a multilateral treaty. The parties to the 1949 Geneva Conventions, the Torture Convention, and a number of other international criminal law treaties are thus obliged either to prosecute offenders under national criminal law or to extradite them to a state that is willing to prosecute. The advantage of this approach is that it does not require the creation of new international institutions. Another advantage, at least from the point of view of some governments, is that it does not compromise the sovereignty or other interests of states.

The approach also has several weaknesses. It relies entirely upon states, acting pursuant to their treaty obligations, for the enforcement of international criminal law, yet it provides no mechanism for ensuring their compliance. It also fails to provide a mechanism for the resolution of conflicts between states relating to enforcement, and fails to provide fair trial or other safeguards for alleged offenders.

A unique and innovative model of enforcement was developed to try two Libyan nationals charged with planting the bomb that killed 270 people, mostly Americans and Britons, aboard Pan Am Flight 103 over Lockerbie, Scotland, in 1988. Libya refused to extradite the suspects to the United States, or to Scotland, for trial as demanded by the United Nations Security Council. After enduring years of economic sanctions, Libya finally handed them over for trial by a Scottish court sitting in the Netherlands. One suspect was convicted, the other was acquitted.

The possibility of creating an international criminal court has been discussed for centuries but, until recently, the only major precedents were the international military tribunals of Nuremberg and Tokyo of the 1940s. These tribunals pioneered the use of international criminal courts to hold individuals responsible for serious international crimes. From 1951 to 1953, the United Nations made futile efforts to foster an international criminal court. There was little or no progress on this front for the next forty years. Many governments were concerned that creating an international court with jurisdiction to try national officials for international crimes could compromise state sovereignty. The government of the United States was among those states that shared this view until reports of shocking international crimes brought the issue of international criminal courts back onto center stage.

In 1994 the International Criminal Tribunal for the Former Yugoslavia (ICTY) was created ad hoc by the U.N. Security Council, in response to the atrocities being committed in that region and, in 1995, a second such institution, the International Criminal Tribunal for Rwanda (ICTR), was created on the same model. They represented a major step forward from the Nuremberg and Tokyo precedents. The Nuremberg and Tokyo tribunals were international military tribunals created by the victorious powers of World War II. The ICTY and ICTR were created by the United Nations, and were thus international tribunals in the fullest sense. The intervening development of the international law of human rights also meant that the ICTY and ICTR would need to respect the international fair trial standards that had developed since the post–World War II era.

Each of these institutions could only prosecute for international crimes committed within a specific territory, and neither threatened the interests of states outside the regions concerned. Despite their limitations, the ad hoc tribunals functioned well enough to lay the groundwork for the creation of a permanent International Criminal Court (ICC). Their indictments and decisions did much to clarify the law governing crimes against humanity, genocide, and war crimes. They also demonstrated that international tribunals could act fairly in investigating and prosecuting international crimes.

On 17 July 1998, after three years of periodic preparatory negotiations and a five-week diplomatic conference in Rome, 120 states voted to approve the text of a treaty creating a permanent ICC with jurisdiction to prosecute for genocide, crimes against humanity, and the most serious war crimes. The ICC will officially come into existence when sixty countries have ratified this treaty. Even as the United States signed the ICC treaty in December 2000, there was substantial opposition to the treaty in the U.S. Senate, which must grant its advice and consent before the United States can ratify. The track record of the new ICC may eventually assuage these concerns.

Conclusion

International criminal law has long been limited by the fact that criminal lawyers and criminal law judges rarely work with international law or international cases, while international lawyers and international judges tend to have little experience with criminal law. This changed as the work of the ICTY and ICTR, and the negotiations leading to the birth of a permanent ICC, brought the world's top specialists in international law into contact with specialists in criminal law from the various nations. The result was an unprecedented period of progress for international criminal law.

The jurisdiction of the soon-to-be-established ICC will initially be very limited, but supporters hope that it will grow into a strong, independent, and effective institution of international justice. Critics oppose creating a stronger and more comprehensive system of international criminal law, fearing the loss of state sovereignty and national freedom of action. In light of this persistent attitude, it remains to be seen how far and how effectively the institutionalization of international criminal law will progress in the future.

The practices of state prosecutors in matters of international criminal law have developed in parallel to the development of international criminal courts. In 1999, a Spanish prosecutor's bold attempt to extradite Chilean General Augusto Pinochet from the United Kingdom marked the beginning of a radical new willingness of national authorities to prosecute for international crimes committed on the territory of another state. It also led to a historic decision by the House of Lords affirming that even a former head of state could be prosecuted for the international crime of torture. That case is likely to inspire more such prosecutions in the future, a trend that may prove as significant for the development of international criminal law as the establishment of the permanent International Criminal Court.

BARTRAM S. BROWN

See also INTERNATIONAL CRIMINAL COURTS; INTERNATIONAL CRIMINAL JUSTICE STANDARDS; TERRORISM; WAR CRIMES.

BIBLIOGRAPHY

BASSIOUNI, M. CHERIF. *International Extradition: United States Law and Practice*, 3rd ed. Dobbs Ferry, N.Y.: Oceana Publications. 1996.

———. *International Criminal Law*, 2d ed. 3 vols. Ardsley, N.Y.: Transnational Publishers, 1999.

BROWN, BARTRAM S. "Primacy or Complementarity: Reconciling the Jurisdiction of National Courts and International Criminal Tribunals." *Yale Journal of International Law* 23 (1998): 383–436.

DUGARD, JOHN, and VAN DEN WYNGAERT, CHRISTINE, eds. *International Criminal Law and Procedure*. Aldershot; Brookfield, Vt.: Dartmouth Publishing Co., 1996.

ELAGAB, OMER Y., ed. *International Law Documents Relating to Terrorism*, 2d ed. London: Cavendish, 1997.

GROSS, LEO. "The Peace of Westphalia, 1648–1948." *American Journal of International Law* 42 (1948): 20–41.

RUBIN, ALFRED P. *The Law of Piracy.* Irvington-on-Hudson, N.Y.: Transnational, 1998.

WISE, EEDWARD M., and PODGOR, ELLEN S. *International Criminal Law, Cases and Materials.* New York, N.Y.: Lexis, 2000.

CASES

Regina v. Bartle and the Commissioner of Police for the Metropolis and others Ex Parte Pinochet, 38 I.L.M. 581 (House of Lords, 24 March 1999).

United States v. Alvarez-Machain, 504 U.S. 655 (1992).

United States v. Fawaz Yunis, 924 F.2d 1086 (D.C. Cir. 1991).

TREATIES AND OTHER DOCUMENTS

Charter of the International Military Tribunal, in Agreement for the Prosecution and Punishment of the Major War Criminals of the European Axis (London Agreement), August 8, 1945, 58 Stat. 1544, E.A.S. No. 472, 82 U.N.T.S. 280.

Convention on the Prevention and Punishment of the Crime of Genocide, 9 December 1948, 78 U.N.T.S. 277.

Geneva Convention Relative to the Treatment of Civilian Persons in Time of War, 12 August 1949, 6 U.S.T. 3316, T.I.A.S. No. 3365, 75 U.N.T.S. 287.

Convention for the Suppression of the Unlawful Seizure of Aircraft, signed at the Hague on 16 December 1970, 22 U.S.T. 1641, T.I.A.S. No. 7192.

Convention for the Suppression of Unlawful Acts against the Safety of Civil Aviation, signed at Montreal on 23 September 1971, U.N.T.S. No. 14118, vol. 974, pp. 178–184, 24 U.S.T. 565, T.I.A.S. No. 7570.

Extradition treaty Between the Government of the United States of America and the Government of the United Kingdom of Great Britain and Northern Ireland, 8 June 1972, 28 U.S.T. 227, T.I.A.S. No. 8468.

International Convention on the Suppression and Punishment of the Crime of Apartheid, Nov. 30, 1973, G.A. Res. 3068, 28 U.N. GAOR (No. 50), U.N. Doc.A/9233/Add.1 (1973).

Convention on the Prevention and Punishment of Crimes against Internationally Protected Persons, Including Diplomatic Agents, 14 December 1973, 28 U.S.T. 1975, T.I.A.S. No. 8532.

Definition of Aggression, General Assembly Res. 3314 (XXIX) of 14 December 1974, U.N. G.A.O.R. 29th Sess., Supp. No. 31 (A/9631), p. 142.

International Convention against the Taking of Hostages, 17 December 1979, G.A. Res. 146, UN, GAOR (XXXIV), U.N. Doc. A/34/819.

Convention against Torture and other Cruel, Inhuman or Degrading Treatment or Punishment, G.A. Res. 39/46, annex, 39 U.N. GAOR Supp. (No. 51) at 197, U.N. Doc. A/39/51 (1984).

Supplementary Treaty Concerning the Extradition Treaty between the Government of the United States of America and the Government of the United Kingdom of Great Britain and Northern Ireland, 25 June 1985, 24 I.L.M. 1105 (1985).

United Nations Convention Against Illicit Traffic in Narcotic Drugs and Psychotropic Substances, U.N. Doc. E/CONF.82/15 (1988), reprinted in 28 I.L.M. 493 (1989).

Statute of the International Criminal Tribunal for the Former Yugoslavia, annexed to *Report of the Secretary-general Pursuant to Paragraph 2 of U.N. Security Council Resolution 808,* U.N. GAOR, 19 May 1993, U.N. Doc. S/2-5704 (1993).

Convention on Combating Bribery of Foreign Public Officials in International Business Transactions, opened for signature 18 December 1997, reprinted in 37 I.L.M. 1 (1998).

Rome Statute of the International Criminal Court, U.N. Doc. A/CONF.183/9 (17 July 1998, as corrected by the procés-verbaux of 10 November 1998 and 12 July 1999).

Agreement between the Government of the Kingdom of the Netherlands and the Government of the United Kingdom of Great Britain and Northern Ireland Concerning a Scottish Trial in the Netherlands, 18 September 1998, 38 I.L.M. 926 (1999).

International Convention for the Suppression of the Financing of Terrorism, Adopted by the General Assembly of the United Nations in resolution 54/109 of 9 December 1999, 39 I.L.M. 270 (2000).

INTERPOL

See INTERNATIONAL CRIMINAL LAW.

J

JAILS

Jails are locally administered, short-term confinement facilities, usually run by the county sheriff or city police, which typically hold persons awaiting trial or other proceedings, as well as convicted offenders serving sentences of one year or less. The transiency and diversity of jail inmate populations cause significant problems for jail administrators, and many believe that local control compounds these (Mattick, pp. 830–835). Yet local control and diverse jail functions have deep historical roots, and are not easily changed.

Historical perspective

Among penal institutions, the jail has the longest history. Paradoxically, it is also the one institution about which the least is known. Remote from public view and concern, it has evolved largely by default (Mattick, pp. 782–785). As a place of detention of the accused prior to trial, the jail is traceable to the earliest forms of civilization and government. Although there are no reliable descriptions of ancient places of detention, references are found to murky caves, ramshackle cages of timber (standing or suspended), unscalable pits, and strong poles or trees to which prisoners were tied. By the late medieval period, prisoners were detained in a variety of settings, ranging from fortress dungeons and precipices outside high castle walls, town gates, and bridge abutments to the dank cellars of municipal and privately owned buildings. About the only characteristic shared by these structures was their massive and insurmountably secure nature.

The history of the American jail is firmly embedded in Anglo-Saxon society, which has provided the United States with most of its social institutions. As such, the American jail is a curious hybrid of the tenth-century gaol, whose principal function was to detain persons awaiting trial and those convicted but still awaiting punishment, and the fifteenth- and sixteenth-century houses of correction, with their special function of punishing such minor offenders as debtors, vagrants, prostitutes, and beggars. From its very beginning, the jail's functions were broadly conceived and included punishment and coercion, as well as custody. A punitive intent is evident in the earliest source of information on incarceration, the written laws of Alfred the Great (A.D. 871–899), the most prominent figure in Anglo-Saxon history. Historians have traced the creation of the prototype of the modern jail as a local governmental institution in the English-speaking countries to the year 1166, when England's King Henry II ordered the construction of jails in his realm (Barnes and Teeters, p. 460).

The establishment of the office of county sheriff coincided broadly with the development of the gaol. The sheriff represented the king in the shire or county, the largest division of the kingdom in matters of local government. His duties were to maintain the peace within the shire and to look after the king's revenues. Since rents from his vast estates constituted the king's principal source of revenue, it was the sheriff's duty to collect these rents together with any fines assessed by the courts. As chief executive officer of the county, the sheriff became the ex officio jailer and had custody over suspected and arrested offenders—and thereby the right to control the county gaol. The construction and maintenance

851

of the gaols were the responsibility of the sheriff and the justice of the peace. The sheriff typically contracted, at no salary, with a keeper, since all the prisoner's necessities (including privileges and amenities) were offered on a fee-for-service basis, paid by the prisoner from personal funds, friends' donations, or begging. The schedule of payments varied with the seriousness of the alleged offense and the prisoner's social status. There were also charges for admission to the jail and for discharge, even when prisoners were acquitted after trial.

The American colonists brought with them the customs and institutions of their mother countries. Thus, they established the system of county government, built the first jails, and invested local sheriffs or marshals with the authority to keep the peace and to control the jails. The earliest reference to jails in the United States comes from prerevolutionary Boston, which ordered the construction of a "people pen" in 1632 (Jordan, pp. 140–141). The historical tenacity of these early institutions is seen in the fact that they continue to this very day as the prevailing form of local law enforcement and correction in most of the states. Jails continued their highly limited function in the colonies until the end of the eighteenth century. They detained those awaiting trial when it was feared they might otherwise run away. They also held convicted offenders awaiting sentencing and those unable to discharge contracted debts. However, jails only rarely confined convicted offenders as a means of correction or punishment. In essence, jails facilitated the process of criminal punishment, although they were not themselves instruments of discipline (Rothman, p. 53). At that time, the predominant form of punishment was corporal, with death, physical mutilation, branding, and whipping decreed for the more serious offenses. For lesser offenses the punishment involved public ridicule and humiliation, effectively administered at the stocks, the pillory, the public cage, or the ducking stool. A remarkably wide range of punishment also included fines, banishments, public whippings, or any combination of these options.

Eighteenth-century practices of criminal justice did not survive for long in the nineteenth century. The Quakers of the Pennsylvania and New Jersey colonies were the first to react against the brutality of the harsh British penal codes and practices that had persisted in the New World. Having been at the receiving end of British justice, they sought to eliminate the stocks, the pillory, the branding iron, and the gallows by substituting imprisonment for corporal punishment and the death penalty. The Quakers thus became the earliest American experimenters in penology. Once the colonist had won independence from England, they followed the leadership of the Quakers by rejecting the old punitive laws and rapidly changing their criminal codes. The new codes reflected the classical legal philosophy of the Enlightenment and followed the recommendations of such great social philosophers of that era as Cesare Beccaria, Jeremy Bentham, François-Marie Voltaire, and Samuel Romilly. Thus, the number of crimes punishable by death was greatly reduced, and the predominant form of punishment for most crimes became imprisonment or a fine.

To implement their new laws, Americans had to invent new institutions. In time, individual states began to design and build penal facilities for the incarceration of serious offenders, and the modern prison was born. However, minor offenders continued to be sent to the existing jails, which increasingly became repositories for the petty offender, the vagrant, the debtor, the beggar, the promiscuous, and the mentally ill, as well as the untried. Thus, American jails preceded the prison system, but they acquired their unique and largely contemporary character as a residual function of a larger movement of legal and penal reform (Mattick, p. 784). Historians have yet to pinpoint the period when county jails changed in function from places solely for general detention to places for both detention and incarceration of sentenced minor offenders.

England's local governments had developed penal institutions variously named workhouses, houses of corrections, and reformatories as early as the sixteenth century. Their purpose was to punish by imprisonment persons guilty of religious or political crimes, as well as debtors, and to serve as alternatives to corporal punishment for vagrancy, public drunkenness, prostitution, and juvenile delinquency. By the mid-eighteenth century, these institutions had merged with the local jails (Barnes and Teeters, pp. 460–461). American colonials, in turn, ordered the construction of workhouses as early as 1748, when the New Jersey assembly authorized Middlesex County officials to build a workhouse (as distinct from a poorhouse) for the punishment of rogues, vagabonds, and petty criminals (Rothman, p. 29). However, the concept of the workhouses failed to take root, since few of the colonies provided the funds for their construction, and those that were built tended to merge with the existing poorhouses. As a result, these institutions are more accurately categorized as the forerunners of the American prison, rather than as the direct ancestors of the county jail (Mattick, p. 783).

After the American jail had assumed its combined function of detention and correction in the early nineteenth century, it changed very little save for some minor variations in its clientele (Mattick, pp. 784–785). The combined effects of the juvenile reformatory movement, the establishment of hospitals for the criminally insane, the development of state farms and adult reformatories, and the evolving practice of probation served to divert an increasing number of misdemeanants from the jail. The growth of cities and the development of urban law enforcement agencies brought yet another hybrid: the city jail. It evolved from the temporary police lockup and the need for a place of detention for interrogation and trial purposes. More by default than by intent, city jails came under the jurisdiction of law enforcement agencies and grew into full-fledged jails serving both detainee and sentenced populations. Both types of jails continue today as the crucible into which the vast majority of accused and convicted felons are shunted, along with confined material witnesses and diverse misdemeanants.

Contemporary jails

Fulfilling a multiplicity of functions, modern jails hold accused offenders, either not eligible for bail, or unable to raise bail due to poverty. Jails also hold persons waiting arraignment, trial, conviction, or sentencing. Jails furthermore detain probation, parole, and bail-bond violators and absconders. Jails house inmates for federal and state authorities when prisons are overcrowded. At times, jails may hold the mentally ill pending transfer to mental health facilities. In many jurisdictions, jails temporarily detain juveniles pending transfer to appropriate county or state facilities. Jails, moreover, hold persons wanted by the military or federal authorities and those held in protective custody, for contempt of court, and as material witnesses. Finally, jails hold convicted misdemeanants, usually sentenced to one year or less. Exceptions to this rule include Massachusetts and Pennsylvania, where inmates may serve much longer terms, ranging from one to five years. Also, some states make heavy use of jails for felony as well as misdemeanor sentencing. For example, two-thirds of con-victed felons in Minnesota receive jail sentences of one year or less (Frase, p. 479).

National jail surveys define a jail as a locally administered facility authorized to hold convicted persons and those who have been arraigned in court (which usually occurs within seventy-two hours of arrest). This definition thus excludes so-called drunk tanks, police and court lockups, and all state-run penal institutions for short-term offenders (such as state farms, road and forestry camps, and reformatories). Applying this definition, the 1999 Census of Jails reported that there were 3,365 local jails in about three thousand cities and counties (Bureau of Justice Statistics, 2000). The vast majority of these jails are county facilities under the control of elected sheriffs or a county corrections agency. Over six hundred municipal jails operate under the control of local corrections departments. At midyear 1999, forty-seven of the nation's jails were privately owned or operated under contracts with local governments in seventeen states (Bureau of Justice Statistics, 2000). Six states—Alaska, Connecticut, Delaware, Hawaii, Rhode Island, and Vermont—had integrated state-level prisons and jails. This type of arrangement is usually referred to as a "state unified system" and is controlled by the respective state department of correction and/or department of public safety. The Federal Bureau of Prisons operates a system of metropolitan correctional centers (MCCs). These centers house both pretrial detainees and sentenced inmates and are located in Los Angeles, San Diego, Miami, Chicago, Brooklyn, New York, Manhattan, and in San Juan, Puerto Rico.

The American Correctional Association (2000) categorizes jails by the number of inmates they hold. As such, jails fall into four categories: small, medium, large, and mega-jails. There are over one hundred mega-jails in the United States. Defined as local correctional institutions with more than one thousand beds, mega-jails are located in the nation's largest metropolitan areas. Florida leads the nation with seventeen mega-jails, followed by Texas with thirteen, California with fifteen, and New York with twelve. There are over 500 large jails, defined as local correctional institutions with 250 to 999 beds. There are over 1,200 medium-sized jails defined as local correctional institutions with 50 to 249 beds. Finally, there are over 1,500 small jails, with 1 to 49 beds, making this institution the most frequent modality of all jails.

Jail structure and design characteristics

There is no typical jail. Many jails are part of multipurpose buildings that also serve as the county courthouse, the sheriff's office, or the police station. Others are larger and self-contained. Although it is often charged that most jails are antiquated, the majority of jails were opened between the 1950s and 1980s. Although most jails are small, rural or suburban facilities, almost half of all jailed prisoners are in large urban institutions, which tend to be chronically overcrowded. Many jails utilize double occupancy, perching two or more inmates into cells designed for one. Large numbers of inmates are also housed in dormitories. Many of these arrangements are a far cry from meeting the standards promulgated by the Commission on Accreditation in Corrections. These standards require single celling for maximum security inmates. They also provide that all cells or sleeping areas in which inmates are confined contain thirty-five-square feet of unencumbered space. "Unencumbered" space is defined as usable space not occupied by furnishings or fixtures. When confinement exceeds ten hours per day, a situation found in most jails, the standards call for at least eighty square feet of total unencumbered floor space per occupant (American Correctional Association, 1991).

Architecturally, three generations of jails are discernible since their inception. The first-generation jail design dates back to the eighteenth century. It divided the jail space into inflexible cells and/or cage-like dayrooms. Rows of cells were composed of self-contained cell blocks facing large cages, or "bullpens." Inmates spent their days and nights like caged animals and had little contact with their keepers. Boredom and idleness prevailed, occasionally punctuated by outbursts of violence. Food was passed into the bullpens or cells through slotted doors. While most such jails have been replaced by newer facilities, a few remain along the eastern seaboard and in the northeastern quadrant of the United States. They are characterized by limited access to any sanitary facilities (including toilets) for long periods of time. Access to showers and washrooms is equally limited. Inadequacies such as these, when combined with short supplies of clean bedding, toilet paper, soap and towels, pose serious health and morale problems and clearly contribute to the high rates of infectious diseases found in many jail populations.

The second generation of jails has a linear construction, with multiple-occupancy cells and dormitories aligned along corridors. The latter may be arranged at acute angles creating a spoke-like effect. As was the case with its historic predecessor, the newer version was designed to operate with a minimum of staff. Many such jails utilize closed-circuit television (CCTV) and/or audio surveillance to augment staff supervision and control of the inmates. Again, their design provides little contact between inmates and staff. Supervision is effected by intermittent staff patrols of the jail corridors and technology. About one thousand county and major city jails were built during the 1970s and 1980s, amounting to roughly 30 percent of the nation's jails at that time (National Institute of Corrections, 1985). Despite claims to the contrary, these facilities suffered from the same deficiencies that had plagued their predecessors, including space and program shortages, crowding, inadequate physical separation between different types of inmates, and a myriad of maintenance problems.

While most counties and municipalities doggedly continued to pursue archaic jail designs when building new jails, a third-generation jail began to emerge during the early 1970s. Under the leadership of the U.S. Bureau of Prisons and the Law Enforcement Assistance Administration (LEAA) of the U.S. Department of Justice, several leading architectural firms were commissioned to develop designs for a new generation of prisons and jails. Simultaneously, LEAA funded the development of National Guidelines for the Planning and Design of Regional and Community Correctional Centers for Adults (1971) at the University of Illinois. The guidelines were a direct response to the Omnibus Crime Control and Safe Streets Act of 1968, which focused national attention on corrections under the Part E Amendment of 1971. The guidelines led to the creation of the National Clearinghouse for Criminal Justice Planning and Architecture at the University of Illinois. LEAA through the clearinghouse provided federal support for programs and facilities that were consistent with advanced practices. Interdisciplinary in nature, the guidelines took an open-system approach. This paradigm focuses on the interrelationship between corrections, police, and courts, and envisions interdependent and interrelated agencies and programs that provide a coordinated and consistent response to the nation's crime problems. The guidelines, coupled with federal subsidies and thousands of technical assistance and demonstration projects, became a major turning point in the nation's quest to improve its corrections systems.

What differentiates third-generation jails (and prisons) from its predecessors is that the new designs were driven by the philosophical mandate that humane treatment of the accused and convicted offender must be at the very heart of the correctional enterprise. Concomitant was the idea that programming considerations should determine the physical design of jails and prisons, and that both should be applied to improve the institutional quality of life, enhance facility safety, and effect humane inmate control. The federal Metropolitan Correctional Centers in Los Angeles, San Diego, Miami, Chicago, Brooklyn, Manhattan, and San Juan are third-generation jails, having been constructed between 1974 and 1993. Today, a growing number of such facilities exist in many county and municipal jurisdictions. The differences between the old and new jail designs could not be more pronounced. Many jails are part of multifunction public buildings, sharing space with the courts and related public and social services. Jail intake is often based on an "open booking" concept, with staff seated behind a counter. Inmate housing is based on a pod or module concept. This means that housing is broken into groups ranging from eight to forty-six inmates. Each module is staffed around the clock by specially trained corrections officers. Modules are self-contained, combining the housing of inmates with visiting, programming, recreation, and related activities. The podular design reduces the need for inmate movement, enhances security, and increases contact between inmates and correctional staff. Interior and exterior finishes and furnishings provide a "normalized" environment in most housing areas except those used for discipline and segregation. Most direct supervision jails have carpeting, wood, upholstered furnishings, splashes of color, and considerable natural light. Housing units are also equipped with counters, sinks, drink dispensers, and telephones accessible to inmates in the dayrooms. Many pods have their own exercise machines. Cells have one or two bunks, a desk and seat, running water, intercoms, and sizable windows. Ongoing assessments of the effectiveness of third-generation jails indicate that they have, for the most part, succeeded in providing a safer and more humane environment for staff and inmates alike (Farbstein et al.). Not surprisingly, research has tied the success of the new facility designs to dedicated managerial leadership, improved human relations skills of correctional staff, and extensive training of all involved (Zupan and Menke).

Jail populations

Until 1970, no national data existed on jails and their populations. That year, the U.S. Bureau of the Census conducted the first national census of jails for the Bureau of Justice Statistics. Additional censuses have been conducted in 1972, 1978, 1983, 1988, 1993, and 1999; sample surveys of jails and jail inmates have been carried out in every noncensus year since 1983.

According to the 1999 Census of Jails, local authorities held and/or supervised 687,973 offenders at midyear of 1999, reflecting an increase of 3.5 percent from the previous year. About 12 percent of these offenders were supervised in alternative programs outside the jail facilities, such as day reporting, weekend reporting, electronic monitoring, community service, or work release programs. The remaining 605,943 inmates were confined within the jails. While jail populations remained relatively stable during the 1970s, the picture changes dramatically during the 1980s and 1990s. The past two decades have witnessed a dramatic expansion of incarceration in American jails and prisons. Since 1990, the country's jail population increased on average 4.6 percent per annum (Bureau of Justice Statistics, 2000). However, the most recent count of jail inmates shows that the growth rate from 1998 to 1999 is only half the growth rate recorded between 1990 and 1999 (2.3% compared with 4.6%). As a result, there is some reason for hope that the appalling jail expansion of the past two decades may be finally abating.

As important as jail population counts are for understanding the magnitude of the local corrections problem, they do not begin to explain the full impact jails have on the lives of inmates or on America's system of justice. This is because jail inmates are highly transient populations, with some detainees staying for as little as a few hours and about half of the sentenced population serving six months or less (Bureau of Justice Statistics, 1998). The full importance of jails only emerges when population movement is considered. Jails in the United States admit and release over twenty million people per annum. Jails, therefore, handle more inmates than prisons. With the exception of traffic enforcement encounters, jails touch more lives than does any other agent of the criminal justice system.

During the 1980s and 1990s, jails became dangerously overcrowded due to the rapid increases of jail populations. While many jails systems furiously added bed capacity, inmate populations outpaced most of these efforts. As a result, the occupancy capacity in many jails exceeded 100 percent. For example, in 1990, the rated capacity of local jails, which is the number of beds or inmates assigned by a rating official to facilities in each jurisdiction, was 389,171 beds. Even though 21,402 beds had been added that year in various jurisdictions, the percent of capacity occupied was 104. During much of the 1990s, jail capacity hovered around 97 percent. The first turnaround in these dismal statistics did not come until 1999. That year, the rated capacity of the counties local jails reached 652,321, reflecting an increase of almost forty thousand beds added during a twelve-month period ending at midyear of 1999. This singular spurt in construction of jail bed space brought the occupancy rate down to 93 percent. But little comfort can be taken from this statistic. This is because jail populations vary much at the regional, state, and local levels. For example, in 1999, seven states incarcerated more than half of all local jail inmates: California, Texas, Florida, New York, Georgia, Pennsylvania, and Louisiana. By contrast, ten states with the smallest jail populations each held fewer than three thousand inmates. Collectively, the latter states held only 3.1 percent of the country's total jail population (Bureau of Justice Statistics, 2000). Seven states and the District of Columbia exceeded jail capacity, with occupancy rates falling between 102 and 120 percent. By contrast, the total jail population of six states was below 80 percent.

It is important to note that jail populations bear no close relationship to the size of the population the jail serves or to a particular jurisdiction's crime rates. This fact emerges most clearly when incarceration rates are examined. According to the Bureau of Justice Statistics (2000), the number of jail inmates per 100,000 in the population reached 220 by midyear 1999. Of the seventeen states with rates greater than that for the country, eleven were in the South, four were in the West, one was in the Northeast, and one in the Midwest. States with the largest number of jail inmates per 100,000 population were Louisiana (585), Georgia (421), Tennessee (358), and Florida (337). By contrast, the incarceration rates of four states—Maine (89), North Dakota (92), Iowa (104), and Minnesota (105), were less than half of the national rate. Population size and the crime rate do have a modest effect on the size of jail populations, but other issues have greater

relevance (Klofas). For example, there are substantial variations in statutes, law enforcement, and court practices, the use of alternatives to incarceration, the assumption of state control over local facilities, the closing or opening of correctional facilities, court orders to reduce prison and jail populations, and public opinion. Together, these factors explain much of the variance in the nation's jail incarceration rate.

Characteristics of jail inmates

In contrast with the growth of jail populations, the characteristics of jail inmates have remained predictably stable. Jails are predominantly repositories for young males, minorities, drug addicts, the mentally ill, the poor, and the down and out. According to the Bureau of Justice Statistics (2000) male inmates made up 89 percent of the local jail inmate population in 1999. Females made up 11 percent of jail inmates. However, since 1990, the female jail population has grown at a faster pace (6.8%) compared with males (4.2%). By midyear of 1999, local jails held approximately 1 in every 181 adult men and 1 in 1,538 women in the country. Minorities are a majority in jails. Census data show that African American (non-Hispanics) made up 41.5 percent of the local jail population in 1999. White (non-Hispanics) made up 41.3 percent, Hispanics 15.5 percent, and other races (Asians, Pacific Islanders, American Indians, and Alaska Natives) constituted 1.7 percent. This translates into the fact that African Americans are six times more likely than whites, two and one-half times as likely than Hispanics, and sixteen times more likely than Asians to be incarcerated in local jails (Bureau of Justice Statistics, 2000). Census data for 1999 indicate that over half of all jail inmates (54%) were awaiting court action on their current charges. The remainder (278,400) were serving a jail sentence, awaiting sentencing, or were serving jail time for a probation or parole violation. Examining private jails, the 1999 Census notes that almost fourteen thousand inmates were jailed in privately owned or operated facilities. While the percentage of inmates housed in private jails is still small when compared with public institutions (2.3%), private jails are growing at a remarkably brisk rate. Census data reflect that between 1993 and 1999, privately owned or operated jails increased from seventeen to forty-seven. States with the largest number of jailed inmates in private facilities are Texas (3,469), Tennessee (2,278), Florida (1,931), and

Pennsylvania (1,592). Finally, in 1999 jails held almost ten thousand persons under the age of eighteen. Over 90 percent of these young persons had been convicted or were being held for trial as adults in criminal court.

Criminal record and demographic characteristics

Because of the jail's function as the intake center for the entire criminal justice system, its population is the most heterogeneous and transient of any correctional institution. Recent data on jail inmate stocks reveal a distressed population, frequently in trouble with the law. (National data on the characteristics of jail "flows"—persons admitted to and released from jails—is not available; such data would probably reveal a less criminally experienced group—but a much more heterogeneous, more transient, and more vulnerable one (Frase, pp. 482–483; 501).) Over half of jail inmates were already under the supervision of the courts or corrections at their most recent arrest (Bureau of Justice Statistics, 1998). More than two-thirds of jail inmates had prior sentences to probation or incarceration. Almost half of the inmates had already served three or more sentences. Compared with a 1989 population profile by the Bureau of Justice, offender drug use (marijuana, stimulants, hallucinogens, depressants, and opiates) had increased appreciably. Half of the inmates had used cocaine. Over one-third reported some physical or mental disability. Twenty-five percent of inmates had been treated at some time for mental or emotional problems. Almost half of the jailed women had been physically or sexually abused prior to their admission. Almost 30 percent had been raped. The distribution of offenses for which inmates were being held ranged from violent crimes (26%), to property offenses (27%), to drug offenses (22%), and public-order violations (24%). Pretrial detainees were more likely than convicted inmates to be in jail for serious offenses. Male inmates were nearly twice as likely as female inmates to be in jail for violent crimes. Women were more likely than men to be in jail for drug offenses. Proportionately more African American and Hispanic inmates than whites were in jail for drug offenses. And African American inmates were more likely than whites or Hispanics to be in jail for violence crimes. Among whites, the most common offense was driving while intoxicated (DWI).

Social and demographic characteristics of jail inmates reported by the Bureau of Justice Statistics reinforce the image of a distressed and troubled population (1998). About 2.3 percent of the nation's jail population were under the age of eighteen. Almost one-quarter of jail inmates was between the ages of thirty-five and forty-four, reflecting a growth in the middle-aged population compared with previous years. This finding is consonant with the aging of America's population. More than one-third (36%) of inmates were unemployed before their most recent arrest. By contrast, 64 percent of inmates were employed at the time of their arrest. Of these, almost half worked full time, about 10 percent worked part time, and about 5 percent worked occasionally. In general, inmates had low incomes compared with the general population. Almost half had incomes of less than $7,200 per annum. Almost one-fourth of the inmates received some kind of government assistance: Welfare, Aid to Families with Dependent Children (AFDC), food stamps, Social Security, and Supplemental Security Income (SSI). Only 15.7 percent of the inmates were married. The vast majority (58.6%) were never married. The remainder were widowed, divorced, or separated. The educational attainment of jail inmates is quite limited. Only about 14 percent had some college education (or more); 40 percent were high school graduates; 33 percent had some high school and a full 13 percent had an eighth grade education or less. Jail inmates were over twice as likely to have grown up in a single-parent household. Almost 12 percent had lived in childhood households without any parent. Another 14 percent had lived in a foster home or state agency at some time of their lives. Almost half of the inmates had at least one family member who had been incarcerated. Many had alcohol and drug abuse in their homes. Almost 12 percent of jail inmates were veterans.

Personnel and costs

Given the unprecedented expansion of local, state, and federal imprisonment since around 1975, corrections has turned into a huge enterprise. In 1994, local jails employed an estimated 205,426 persons in various capacities (Bureau of Justice Statistics, 1995). That same year, local governments spent over $11.1 billion to operate the nation's jails (Bureau of Justice Statistics, 1998). Excluding capital expenditures, the average cost to keep one jail inmate incarcerated for one year was $19,903 in 1997. Gender, race, and ethnicity of jail officers and staff reflected the following patterns in 1997: 71.6 percent were male, 28.4 percent were female. Less than 22 percent of local corrections staff was African American. Hispanics, Asian, and other racial minorities were seriously underrepresented when compared to their numbers in the general population (Criminal Justice Institute).

Legal rights of jail inmates

Until the late 1960s, state and federal courts refused litigation by jail and prison inmates against their keepers, preferring a "hands off" doctrine grounded in the constitutional separation of powers between the judicial and executive branches of government. This situation changed during the early 1970s owing to the expansion of defendants' pretrial rights and of judicial review of administrative agency activities. Federal writs of habeas corpus, litigation under the Civil Rights Act of April 20, 1871, 42 U.S.C. section 1983 (1976 & Supp. III 1979), and class action suits have brought relief in the form of release, injunctions, damages, and declaratory judgments for violations of inmates' constitutional rights.

Pretrial detainees are entitled to the presumption of innocence; hence, any imposition of punishment on them constitutes a denial of due process. In *Brenneman v. Madigan*, 343 F. Supp. 128 (N.D. Cal. 1972), the court stated that convicted offenders are denied their liberty in the interest of satisfying such objectives of the criminal law as punishment, restraint, or rehabilitation. Consequently, they have fewer rights than detainees and can be subjected to a range of restrictions and correctional programs. By contrast, pretrial detainees have not been convicted of any crime and therefore should not be treated in the same manner. Since *Brenneman*, a number of courts of appeals adopted the "least restrictive alternative test" for detention, holding that jailers must use the least restrictive means when depriving detainees of their liberty pending trial (*Jones v. Wittenberg*, 323 F. Supp. 93 (N.D. Ohio 1971); *Moore v. Janing*, No. C-72-0-223 (D. Neb. 1976)).

In 1979, the U.S. Supreme Court overruled this test in *Bell v. Wolfish*, 441 U.S. 520 (1979), holding that restrictions on pretrial detainees violate the Constitution only if they affect an independent constitutional right or if they amount to the imposition of punishment. Although confirming that the due process clause prohibits officials from punishing persons awaiting trial, the Court noted that not every condition of confinement amounts to punishment. Thus, it upheld as reasonably related to the effective management of a detention facility such practices as housing two persons in cells designed for one. The Court also held that neither blanket prohibitions on contact visits for pretrial detainees, nor routine body cavity searches of inmates after contact visits, nor random "shakedown" searches violated the constitutional right to due process. However, since most correctional standards recommend single-cell occupancy (with the exception of housing for work release or similar minimum-security programs), contact visits (when appropriate), and protections against unreasonable searches, the *Bell* decision is clearly a backward step for corrections.

Since *Bell*, the determination of whether a particular restriction imposed on pretrial detainees violates due process requires courts to decide whether that restriction is for the purpose of punishment or whether it is reasonably related to a legitimate and nonpunitive governmental purpose (Robbins, 2000). In spite of this legal setback, *Bell* does not affect the rights of convicted prisoners, nor does it affect cases in which any or all aspects of incarceration are challenged in particular facilities. In general, Eighth Amendment prohibitions continue to set a minimum below which jail conditions may not fall. Recent data on jail litigation provide strong evidence of continuing court involvement with jail conditions. Of 112 reporting jail systems, sixteen percent indicated that one or more of jail facilities they were operating were under a court order in 1998. An additional 20 percent noted they were under court-mandated population caps, and 6 percent had facilities under the supervision of a court monitor or master (Criminal Justice Institute, 1998). Finally, definitions of what is considered cruel and unusual punishment will continue to change because of what a previous Supreme Court has called "the evolving standards of decency that mark the progress of a maturing society" (*Trop v. Dulles*, 356 U.S. 86 (1958)).

Organizational characteristics, inspections, and standards

The American jail owes its unique organizational characteristics to the fact that no single unit or branch of government has the power, interest, or resources to alter fundamentally a jail's purpose, organization, management, and operation. Local courts and county grand juries are traditionally charged with inspecting jails. In some jurisdictions their visitations and reports are mandatory. In others, they are merely authorized. Since few grand juries or judges consider jail reform their primary function, jail visits are infrequent and perfunctory at best. In some states, visiting citizens' committees, local officials, fire, health and building inspectors share responsibility for inspecting jails.

In a notable effort to move things forward, some states have assumed statutory responsibility for developing standards for local detention and corrections facilities and for inspecting these jails to oversee compliance. Today, over two-thirds of the states have set standards for their local corrections institutions. In over half of those states those standards are mandatory. Since 1977, the American Correctional Association (ACA) has promulgated Standards for Adult Detention Facilities. As such, the Standards serve as the foundation for accreditation activities involving an increasing number of jails all over the country. The ACA Committee on Standards continually reviews and updates its accreditation standards to ensure that they depict the current professional requirements in the field of corrections. As a result, executive, legislative, and judicial branches of local, state, and federal jurisdictions increasingly refer to the standards as the professional benchmark for judging the quality of a detention operation. ACA standards are reinforced by the publication of national standards promulgated by several professional associations, such as the American Bar Association and the National Sheriff's Association, all of which are actively pursuing jail reform.

Proposals and prospects for jail reform

The history of jail reform is replete with resistance to improvement. When John Howard first published his devastating but valid *The State of the Prisons in England and Wales* in 1777, the modern jail reform movement was born. Howard's purpose was to relieve the wretchedness of the people incarcerated in English jails. Since his time, ideas and knowledge have seldom, if ever, been combined with the resources of the legislative, judicial, and executive branches of government in a sustained, adequately funded effort to bring about lasting solutions. Given that piecemeal reforms and political patchwork have only ameliorated but not solved the American jail problem, more systematic solutions are needed

that transcend the individual jail and that see it for the central and integral part of the criminal justice system that it is.

Until recently, jails have been the forgotten element in corrections. Unlike prisons, they have managed to escape the glare of public scrutiny. But this is no longer the case. Jail reform is currently taking place along the paths previously identified in the literature (Flynn, pp. 73–85; Frase, pp. 494–502; Mattick, pp. 821–843). Each path varies in comprehensiveness and ranges from procedural changes to dramatic realignments of policies, resources, and practices.

The first mode of systematic jail reform involves relatively simple shifts in administrative procedures and policies. It entails expanding the current use of decriminalization, diversion, reduced penetration into the system, and alternatives to incarceration. This approach, coupled with screening out of low-risk, less serious offenders at the pretrial stage and the sentencing of minor offenders to such noninstitutional alternatives as fines, misdemeanant probation and parole, electronic monitoring, day reporting, and community service, is one of the more significant and positive developments in local corrections.

A second mode of jail reform builds upon the first path and looks upon the jail as the focal point of a community rather than as a remote and isolated institution. This view is based on the recognition that jails, for better or for worse, receive, process, treat, impact, and release hundreds of thousands of citizens including drug abusers, alcoholics, the mentally ill, the homeless, and the physically ill (Wallenstein). Jails must deal with a wide range of public health problems, ranging from persons infected with the human immunodeficiency virus (HIV), those with AIDS (acquired immune deficiency syndrome), sexually transmitted diseases, and various forms of hepatitis and tuberculosis. One of the unintended consequences of deinstitutionalizing the mentally ill has been their "diversion" from mental health facilities straight into jails. Jails are receiving a growing number of persons with multiple physical and mental disorders. Recognizing that jails were never meant to function as public hospitals or mental health treatment centers, jail reformers take the position that interactive linkages must be built between the jails and existing service agencies in the community. But linkages are more than just referrals or recommendations. They are true collaborations with sister service agencies and include information sharing from the time detainees or offenders arrive at the jail until they depart. To function properly, the services delivery should be seamless (Wallenstein).

The third mode of jail reform is by far the most dramatic in that it advocates the elimination of local control of detention and correctional functions and seeks to abolish the jail in its present form. This view encourages the development of regional or community based correctional centers as part of an integrated correctional system under regional or state control. At this point, there are many multi-jurisdictional corrections facilities in existence across the country (National Institute of Corrections, 1991). Six states and Washington, D.C., have assumed responsibility for pretrial detention. In addition, some state, regional, and local jurisdictions have replaced their jails with intake (or court) service centers to provide short-term intake screening, diversion of lesser offenders, pretrial and presentence investigations, and coordination of in-house and community-based services and referrals.

The last decade of the twentieth century finally brought forth multiple and varied efforts at jail reform. At this point, it is too early to predict success, given the fierce resistance to reform experienced since the inception of the jail. Nonetheless, there is agreement among scholars and practitioners alike that change must come and that alternative ways must be found to bring relief to the mass of humanity passing through jail doors.

EDITH E. FLYNN

See also BAIL; CRIMINALIZATION AND DECRIMINALIZATION; CRIMINAL JUSTICE PROCESS; CRIMINAL JUSTICE SYSTEM; PRETRIAL DIVERSION; PRISONERS, LEGAL RIGHTS OF; PRISONS: HISTORY; PRISONS: PRISONERS; PRISONS: PRISONS FOR WOMEN; PRISONS: PROBLEMS AND PROSPECTS; SPEEDY TRIAL.

BIBLIOGRAPHY

American Correctional Association. *Standards for Adult Local Detention Facilities,* 3d ed. Lanham, Md.: American Correctional Association in cooperation with the Commission on Accreditation for Corrections, 1991.
———. *Jails and Adult Detention 2000–2001.* Lanham, Md.: American Correctional Association, 2000.
BARNES, HARRY ELMER, and TEETERS, NEGLEY K. *New Horizons in Criminology,* 3d ed. Englewood Cliffs, N.J.: Prentice-Hall, 1959.

Bureau of Justice Statistics. *Profile of Jail Inmates, 1989.* NCJ 129097 (April 1991).
———. *Jails and Jail Inmates 1993–1994.* NCJ-151651 (April 1995).
———. *Profile of Jail Inmates, 1996.* NCJ 164620 (April 1998).
———. *Sourcebook of Criminal Justice Statistics, 1998.* Washington, D.C.: U.S. Government Printing Office. 1998.
———. *Prison and Jail Inmates at Midyear 1999.* NCJ 181643 (April 2000).
Criminal Justice Institute, Inc. *Corrections Yearbook, 1998.* Middletown, Conn.: National Criminal Justice, Inc. 1998.
FARBSTEIN, JAY; LIEBERT, DENNIS; and SIGURDSON, HERBERT. *Audits of Podular Direct-Supervision Jails.* Washington, D.C.: National Institute of Corrections, 1996.
FLYNN, EDITH E. "Jails and Criminal Justice." In *Prisoners in America.* Edited by Lloyd E. Ohlin. Englewood Cliffs, N.J.: Prentice-Hall, 1973.
FRASE, RICHARD S. "Jails." In *Handbook of Crime and Punishment.* Edited by Michael Tonry. New York: Oxford University Press, 1988. Pages 474–506.
JORDAN, PHILIP P. "The Close and Striking Jail." In *Frontier Law and Order: Ten Essays.* Lincoln: University of Nebraska Press, 1970. Pages 140–154.
KLOFAS, JOHN M. "Disaggregating Jail Use: Variety and Change in Local Corrections over a Ten-Year Period." In *American Jails.* Edited by Joel A. Thompson and G. Larry Mays. Chicago: Nelson-Hall Publishers, 1991.
MATTICK, HANS W. "The Contemporary Jails of the United States: An Unknown and Neglected Area of Justice." In *Handbook of Criminology.* Edited by Daniel Glaser. Chicago: Rand McNally, 1974. Pages 777–848.
National Clearinghouse for Criminal Justice Planning and Architecture. *Guidelines for the Planning and Design of Regional and Community Correctional Centers for Adults.* Washington, D.C.: U.S. Government Printing Office, 1971.
National Institute of Corrections. *The Nature of New Small Jails: Report and Analysis.* Champaign, Ill.: KIMME Planning & Architecture, 1985.
———. *Briefing Paper: Regional Jails.* Boulder, Colo.: National Institute of Corrections Information Center, 1992.
ROBBINS, IRA P. *Prisoners and the Law.* St. Paul, Minn.: West Group, 2000.
ROTHMAN, DAVID J. *The Discovery of the Asylum: Social Order and Disorder in the New Republic.* Boston: Little, Brown, 1971.

WALLENSTEIN, ARTHUR. "Intake and Release in Evolving Jail Practice." In *Prison and Jail Administration*. Edited by Peter M. Carlson and Judith Simon Garrett. Gaithersburg, Md.: Aspen Publishers, 1999.

ZUPAN, LINDA L., and MENKE, BEN A. "The New Generation Jail: An Overview." In *American Jails*. Edited by Joel A. Thompson and G. Larry Mays. Chicago: Nelson-Hall Publishers. 1991.

CASES

Bell v. Wolfish, 441 U.S. 520 (1979).
Brenneman v. Madigan, 343 F. Supp. 128 (N.D. Cal. 1972).
Jones v. Wittenberg, 323 F. Supp. 93 (N.D. Ohio 1971).
Moore v. Janing, No. C-72-0-223 (D. Neb. 1976).
Trop v. Dulles, 356 U.S. 86 (1958).

JURISDICTION

The U.S. federal, state, and even local governments have adapted the territorial reach of their criminal laws to permit punishment of "new and complex crimes" when elements of extraterritoriality exist. The proactive extension of its extraterritorial jurisdiction has resulted in transformation of the law of jurisdiction and has led to occasional tension with other governments. While this discussion concerns primarily federal law, similar developments have occurred on a subnational level, where states and even municipalities continually expand their jurisdiction to meet criminal threats from an increasingly borderless world, where technology, transportation, and free-trade developments enable criminals to move money, capital, goods, people, and ideas instantaneously.

This discussion outlines the conceptual bases of jurisdiction and then applies it to recent developments in U.S. law, especially with respect to terrorism, narcotics, and alien smuggling. The article also describes the jurisdiction of military courts-martial, the use of proactive investigative and policing techniques abroad, the limits on the enforcement of foreign penal judgments, and basic principles governing jurisdiction between state and federal courts, and conflict-of-laws in the criminal context.

Constitutional limitations

Generally there is no constitutional bar to the extraterritorial application of domestic penal laws. Prosecutors, if challenged, must be able to show that congressional intent of extraterritorial scope is clear and that the application of the statute to the acts in question does not violate the due process clause of the Fifth Amendment.

Jurisdiction is the power of the state to prescribe and punish crimes, the power of the executive to apply and enforce laws, and the power of courts to adjudicate cases. Since a state's criminal law has no force and effect beyond its territorial limits, except for universal crimes, a criminal offense committed in one state cannot be prosecuted in another. The threshold issue of whether a court has jurisdiction to resolve a pending controversy is fundamental. A court cannot act outside its authority or jurisdiction. Each court has jurisdiction to determine whether it has jurisdiction. If a court determines it has no jurisdiction to decide the merits of a case, the appropriate action is to dismiss.

The five traditional bases of jurisdiction over extraterritorial crimes are: territorial, nationality, protective, passive personality, and universal. Under the "territorial theory," jurisdiction applies to conduct or the effect of which occurs within the territorial boundaries of the state. When an element of an offense occurs within a state, that state has jurisdiction based on subjective territoriality. When an effect or result of criminal conduct impacts the state, but the other elements of the offense occur wholly beyond its territorial boundaries, that state has jurisdiction based on objective territoriality. The "nationality theory" bases jurisdiction on the allegiance or nationality of the perpetrator of offenses proscribed by the state of his allegiance, no matter where the offense occurs. The "protective principle" applies whenever the criminal conduct has an impact on or threatens the asserting state's sovereignty, security, or some important governmental function. The "passive personality theory" applies merely on the basis of the victims nationality. The United States and many other nations have rejected this basis of jurisdiction, although they increasingly have started to invoke it, especially with respect to terrorist crimes. The "universality theory" permits any forum to assert jurisdiction over particularly heinous or universally condemned acts (e.g., genocide and crimes against humanity), when no other state has a prior interest in asserting jurisdiction.

Extraterritorial jurisdiction

The expansion of the theoretical bases of jurisdiction to prescribe, which is based on the thwarted extraterritorial narcotics conspiracy aimed at importation of narcotics into the United States, has been criticized. Various U.S. judicial decisions have expanded the objective territoriality theory to include offenses intended to have an effect on the United States, such as thwarted extraterritorial conspiracies. The decisions are the subject of criticism because, being thwarted, the offenses never actually cause such an effect. Because the extraterritorial conspiracy is thwarted, it arguably causes no significant effect on the asserting state's territory and does not give it jurisdiction.

To combat international narcotics trafficking, the U.S. Congress and the courts have expanded extraterritorial jurisdiction In addition to asserting jurisdiction over thwarted extraterritorial conspiracies, they have enacted laws with extraterritorial jurisdiction over new crimes, such as money laundering, even when such crimes have limited connection with the United States.

In the arrest of General Manuel Noriega, the president of Panama, for narcotics offenses, the United States sent troops into Panama, killing innocent civilians to arrest Noriega. The Noriega case is one of the most celebrated modern examples of the expansion of U.S. extraterritorial jurisdiction because of the use of so much force to arrest a head of state for acts that occurred in Panama (Andreas, p. 37).

In August 1986, the United States enacted the Omnibus Diplomatic Security Act of 1986, providing jurisdiction to extradite or prosecute perpetrators of international terrorism. The act provides for the U.S. prosecution of persons who kill U.S. nationals abroad when the offense was "intended to coerce, intimidate, or retaliate against a government or a civilian population." Hence, U.S. jurisdiction is provided even though the actions occur abroad.

The continued expansion of U.S. territorial jurisdiction to combat organized crime was reflected in U.S. Attorney Zachary W. Carter's announcement on 7 October 1997 of stricter interpretation of U.S. jurisdiction over its territorial waters with regard to regulating casino boats. The new interpretation required casino boats that sail from New York City to travel at least twelve miles from shore before passengers could start gambling. New York City Mayor Rudolph

W. Giuliani had urged federal officials to invoke the twelve-mile start in order to curb organized crime influences (Fried).

The U.S. has broadly extended its extraterritorial jurisdiction to try to ensure that other governments meet their international law obligations to combat transnational organized crime. Under the Foreign Assistance Act of 1961, as amended (the "FAA"), the U.S. Department of State is required to prepare an annual International Narcotics Control Strategy Report (INCSR). The INCSR provides the factual basis for the presidential narcotics certification determinations for major drug-producing or drug-transit countries. The law requires that if the United States does not certify a country for its actions occurring totally outside the U.S., then it must suspend most foreign assistance and vote against multilateral development bank lending to that country.

The statute requires that for each country that received international narcotics assistance in the past two fiscal years, a report must be issued on the extent to which the country has "met the goals and objectives of the United Nations Convention Against Illicit Traffic in Narcotic Drugs and Psychotropic Substances."

The convention requires that parties take legal measures to prohibit, criminalize, and punish all forms of illicit drug production, trafficking, and drug money laundering, to control chemicals that can be used to process illicit drugs, and to cooperate in international efforts to meet these goals. The convention also requires signatory countries, such as the United States to take extraterritorial criminal action over narcotics offenses committed on the high seas, and to cooperate in allowing an investigating state to search vessels flying its flag, and otherwise cooperate in investigations on the high seas.

In October 1995, President Bill Clinton in President Decision Directive (PDD) 42 imposed sanctions under the International Emergency Economic Powers Act (IEEPA), blocking the assets of the leaders, cohorts, and front companies of identified Colombian narcotics traffickers in the United State and in U.S. banks overseas. IEEPA authorities required the U.S. Secretary of the Treasury to impose sanctions, including freezing assets held in U.S. financial institutions, against nations and entities deemed a threat to the national security, foreign policy, or economy of the United States. The directive provides a series of new initiatives: (a) identifying nations that are most egregious in facilitating money laundering, and considering sanctions if after negotiation they do not take adequate steps; (b) using the authority of the IEEPA to block the U.S. assets of cartel leaders and front companies and to bar trade between them and the United States as outlined in Executive Order 12978; (c) negotiating an international Declaration on Citizens' Security and Combating International Organized Crime; (d) developing a legislative package of new authorities to better enable U.S. agencies to investigate and prosecute all aspects of international organized crime; and (e) seeking additional resources to provide increased U.S. anticrime training and assistance to friendly governments.

On 21 October 1995, President Clinton issued Executive Order 12978, under the authority of IEEPA. It finds that the activities of significant foreign narcotics traffickers centered in Colombia and the unparalleled violence, corruption, and harm constitute a usual and extraordinary threat to the U.S. national security and economy. Additionally, U.S. individuals and companies are forbidden from engaging in financial transactions or trade with the identified individuals or enterprises connected to the Colombian Cali Cartel. The Treasury Department identified 359 businesses and individuals whose assets had been blocked since 1995 under authority of the President's Executive Order. As part of the PDD 42 process, an interagency group is reviewing whether measures can be taken against other international criminal cartels (U.S. Department of State, p. 532).

U.S. extraterritorial jurisdiction has expanded to combat alien smuggling. On 9 November 1995 the report of the Interagency Working Group (IWG), "Deterring Alien Smuggling," determined that alien smuggling must be dealt with at its source as well as in those transit countries through which migrants are moved to the United States. The IWG recommended programs to disrupt global smuggling by increasing the awareness of foreign governments. The IWG has helped prepare a model antismuggling law for adoption in the Western Hemisphere and recommended that additional human resources be devoted to combating alien smuggling by expanding U.S. overseas enforcement capability. In June 1997 the Immigration and Naturalization Service (INS) announced a major expansion of its offices overseas to "go to the source" of the immigrant smuggling problem (Andreas, pp. 40–41).

Congress vested in U.S. district courts jurisdiction over offenses punishable by federal law that have been committed within the special U.S. maritime and territorial jurisdiction. Such jurisdiction extends to the high seas, to any other waters within the U.S. admiralty and maritime jurisdiction that remains outside the jurisdiction of any particular state, and to any U.S. aircraft while in flight over the high seas, or over any other waters within the U.S. admiralty and maritime jurisdiction outside the jurisdiction of any particular state.

Courts-martial jurisdiction

Another means by the which the United States exerts extraterritorial jurisdiction is through courts-martial. The three types of courts-martial are general, special, and summary. General courts-martial adhere to the Uniform Code of Military Justice. They have jurisdiction to try any person who is subject to a trial by a military tribunal for violations of the laws of war. Special courts-martial have jurisdiction to try persons subject to the code for noncapital offenses, and capital offenses under regulations prescribed by the President of the United States, who is also authorized to determine punishment. Summary courts-martial have jurisdiction to try persons subject to the code, except officers, cadets, aviation cadets, and midshipmen, for any noncapital offense. No person may be brought to trial, however, if he objects.

Status-of-forces (SOFAs) agreements were created to aid in the determination of which courts have jurisdiction over visiting forces. These agreements established "concurrent jurisdiction," which allowed courts-martial to adhere to both the jurisdictions of the "sending" and "receiving" states. The "sending" state (e.g., the United States over its troops in Germany) retains its ability to perform its military mission by reserving the right to try persons for offenses against the nation or its property (e.g., theft by a U.S. serviceman against U.S. government property), and for offenses borne out of official duty. The "receiving state" retains its territorial sovereignty and jurisdiction over all other offenses (e.g., violent crimes against German nationals) (Bassiouni, p. 119).

The United States and other states engage in proactive policing extraterritorially, such as the use of surveillance, undercover sting operations, controlled deliveries of contraband (whereby the delivery of the contraband is allowed in order to trace and detect the involvement of upper-echelon criminals), and the use of liaison officers whereby federal agencies station officials permanently in foreign countries. States try, as much as possible, to abide by the internal law of the foreign state when conducting investigations.

Traditionally, the United States has not recognized and executed the penal laws of another country. To the extent that authority to recognize foreign penal judgments has existed in the U.S. (e.g., through treaty or statute), such recognition has been restricted. The limited authority to recognize and enforce foreign penal judgments combined with the traditional suspicion with foreign criminal procedure has resulted in decisions that substantially limit the effect accorded criminal judgments abroad. Few statutes specifically refer to convictions in courts of a foreign sovereign. Some statutes expressly exclude such convictions, while most are silent or ambiguous.

As between state and federal courts, a federal court has original jurisdiction over all violations of federal law. In cases where one act constitutes an offense against both a state and the United States, both the federal and state courts have jurisdiction of the offense, unless the U.S. Constitution or an act of Congress gives exclusive jurisdiction to the federal courts. A federal court can obtain jurisdiction over a defendant's non-federal offense where there exists a joinder of a codefendant who is charged with federal violations. If a constitutionally authorized federal nexus exists, the federal government can prosecute crimes anywhere in the United States.

The same act may constitute a crime under a state statute and violate a municipal ordinance. As a result, the courts of the state as well as of the municipality may have jurisdiction over the offense, assuming that the municipality has authority to enact the ordinance. Where two courts have concurrent jurisdiction over the same subject matter, the court that first obtains jurisdiction retains it until the end of the controversy, to the exclusion of the other courts.

The United States and other states employ a type of conflict-of-laws, which is a formula to determine which country's laws to apply in a specific case, or limit the exercise on jurisdiction to prescribe in criminal matters. Even when they have jurisdictional bases, a nation may not exercise jurisdiction to prescribe law with respect to a person or activity having connections with another state when the exercise of such jurisdiction is unreasonable. A state or court will consider various factors in this determination, such as the link of the activity to the territory of the regulating state, that is, the extent to which the activity occurs within the territory, or has substantial, direct, and foreseeable effect upon or in the territory; the connections, such as nationality, residence, or economic activity, between the regulating state and the person principally responsible for the activity to be regulated, or between that state and those whom the regulation is designed to protect; and the likelihood of conflict with regulation by another state.

Proof of jurisdiction beyond a reasonable doubt is an integral element of the state's burden in a criminal prosecution. The state can fulfill its burden of showing that jurisdiction properly lies in a state court by presenting evidence that any or all of essential elements of the alleged offense took place in the state.

In the future a shrinking world guarantees that criminal jurisdiction between national governments and state and local governments will inevitably overlap. Additional means will be required to resolve conflicting jurisdictional claims and negotiate agreements and mechanisms to cooperate in the investigation, adjudication, and supervision of international crimes and criminals.

BRUCE ZAGARIS

See also FEDERAL CRIMINAL JURISDICTION; INTERNATIONAL CRIMINAL COURTS; INTERNATIONAL CRIMINAL LAW; VENUE.

BIBLIOGRAPHY

American Law Institute. "Restatement of the Foreign Relations Law of the United States," § 403. In *Restatement of the Law,* 3d ed. Washington, D.C.: American Law Institute, 1980.

ANDREAS, PETER. "The Rise of the American Crimefare State." *World Policy Journal* 14 (1997): 37, 40.

BASSIOUNI, M. CHERIF, ed. *International Criminal Law,* 2d ed. Ardsley, N.Y.: Transnational Publishers, Inc., 1999.

BLAKESLEY, CHRISTOPHER. *Terrorism, Drugs, International Law, and the Protection of Human Liberty.* Ardsley-on-Hudson, N.Y.: Transnational Publishers, Inc., 1992.

Executive Order No. 12978, 60 Fed. Reg. 54, 579 (1995).

PAUST, JORDAN J.; BASSIOUNI, M. CHERIF; WILLIAMS, SHARON A.; SCHARF, MICHAEL; GURULÉ, JIMMY; and ZAGARIS, BRUCE. *International Criminal Law Cases and Materials.* Durham, N.C.: Carolina Academic Press, 1996.

TORNARITIS, CRITON G. "Individual and Collective Responsibility in International Criminal Law." In *International Criminal Law*. Edited by Cherif Bassiouni. Springfield, Ill.: Charles C. Thomas, 1973. Pages 119–155.

U.S. Department of State. *International Narcotics Control Strategy Report*. Washington, D.C.: Government Printing Office, 1997.

ZAGARIS, BRUCE. "U.S. International Cooperation Against Transnational Organized Crime." *Wayne Law Review* 44 (1998): 1402–1464.

CASE

United States v. Yunis, 681 F. Supp. 896 (D.D.C. 1988), rev'd 859 F.2d 953 (D.C. Cir. 1988).

JURY: BEHAVIORAL ASPECTS

Public praise and criticism for the jury have a long history, and high profile jury trials are a staple of modern press coverage. However, it is only in the past forty years that researchers have published systematic empirical studies of jury behavior. Study of the jury is a particularly thorny project because the jury speaks publicly only through its verdict. At the end of the trial the jury retires to deliberate in the privacy of the jury room. It emerges occasionally to ask a question, but more commonly, only to report its verdict.

The jury in the United States gives no explanation for its verdict and the jurors can return to their pretrial lives without revealing any information about how they arrived at their decisions. Research on the jury, as a result, has relied on a variety of indirect methods, each with strengths and limitations: (1) archival studies of jury case characteristics and verdict patterns (records provide information on large samples of cases, but courts record a limited number of variables); (2) post-trial interviews with jurors (the jurors are reporting on the actual process of reaching a verdict, but what they report is limited to what jurors noticed, accurately recorded, remember, and are willing and able to report); (3) surveys of other trial participants, such as judges and attorneys (these respondents are informed court observers, but they have only indirect information on jury behavior and their reports may be influenced by the verdict); (4) field experiments (these can offer strong evidence on the impact of a legal reform like juror note-taking, but they provide little information on process and are hard to implement successfully); and the most

common approach; (5) simulation experiments (simulations are strong on process information and provide unambiguous causal inference, but generalizability of findings depends on correspondence with dynamics of real jury behavior). By combining these various approaches, researchers have compiled a nuanced, although incomplete, picture of jury behavior.

The role of the jury in the criminal justice system

Most criminal cases, even in the United States, end in dismissals or guilty pleas. In addition, if the case does go to trial and the defendant does not exercise the right to a jury trial, it will be decided by a judge. An estimated 150,000 jury trials occur in state courts and an additional 10,000 (half of them criminal trials) in federal courts. Yet the influence of the jury extends far beyond the trials it actually decides. The terms of a plea agreement and the decision to let a judge decide the case are based on what attorneys and defendants anticipate would happen if the case were decided by a jury.

The jury also plays a political role in the criminal justice system. In addition to deciding cases, the jury is a potential source of legitimacy for the legal system. To the extent that the jury is viewed as representing a fair cross-section of the community, its verdict is likely to be seen as the product of fair consideration and can carry a legitimacy that the decision of the judge, as an employee of the state, may lack. Even when the jury's verdict is unpopular, and even if observers believe that the jury does not fairly represent the community, the jury acts as a lightning rod, insulating the judge and other parts of the state legal system from criticism.

The jury also can act as a conduit for community standards. For example, in evaluating a claim of self-defense, the jury must determine what a reasonable person would be expected to believe, as well as what the particular defendant did believe. Although the jury is charged with applying the law it receives from the judge to the facts, this example illustrates the fuzziness of the division between law and facts. The jury must often inject its understanding of appropriate standards into its fact-finding even while scrupulously following the instructions that the judge provides.

A final political role for the jury is its educative function, identified by Alexis de Toqueville as the jury's great strength. Surveys suggest that more than one-half of American adults have had some personal involvement with the courts; of this sub-group, half have served on a jury. Citizens also receive information and misinformation on the courts from other sources, including the media. The extent to which jury service provides additional or corrective information is unclear, but jury experience tends to make jurors feel more positive about the jury system.

Judge versus jury

One way to evaluate jury behavior is to compare the decisions reached by juries with those reached by judges. Studies of judge-jury agreement reveal substantial, but not uniform agreement. In Kalven and Zeisel's classic study of jury trials, judges reported the jury verdicts for each of the jury trials over which they presided. They also indicated how they would have decided the cases if they had been bench trials. In 78 percent of the cases, the judge and jury agreed on the verdict. In disagreement cases, the judge would have convicted when the jury acquitted in 19 percent of the cases and the jury convicted when the judge would have acquitted in 3 percent of the cases, a net leniency of 16 percent.

When disagreement arose, it was not attributable to case complexity. Cases that the judge rated as high in complexity were no more likely to stimulate disagreement between the judge and jury than were cases that were low in complexity. The disagreements emerged most often (in 45 percent of the disagreement cases) from the combination of a difference in interpretation of the evidence (the jury's traditional fact-finding role) and an issue of values (e.g., the jury's preference for an expanded version of the law of self-defense). Different conclusions about the facts alone accounted for 34 percent of the disagreements, and values alone accounted for only 21 percent of the disagreements.

Kalven and Zeisel collected their data in the late 1950s, but despite many changes in the makeup of the jury pool and the bench, a very similar pattern was found more recently by Heuer and Penrod. In a sample of criminal trials, they obtained a rate of 74 percent agreement, with the judge convicting when the jury would have acquitted in 23 percent of the cases and the jury convicting when the judge would have acquitted in 3 percent of the cases, a net leniency of 20 percent.

A few researchers have examined the impact extra-legal factors, such as inadmissible evidence, or judicial decisions. The results suggest that judges as well as jurors are susceptible to cognitive biases that can influence their verdicts.

How jurors evaluate evidence

The traditional legal model of the jury trial portrays jurors as passive recipients of the evidence and legal instructions. However, empirical studies of jury behavior find jurors to be active processors of incoming information. Early models of jury decision-making included (1) "averaging models," in which jurors assess and weigh each piece of evidence, combining the results to reach a verdict and (2) "Bayesian models," in which jurors consider and evaluate each new piece of information, revising their position on the appropriate verdict in light of their prior position and the additional evidence. These formal models have enjoyed limited success as descriptions of how jurors actually decide cases.

Explanation-based models of jury decision-making, such as Pennington and Hastie's story model, provide an account of jury behavior that comports better with empirical evidence about jury behavior. Consistent with the story model, jurors do not simply record and store the evidence for later use as they receive it. Rather, they actively select and organize the trial evidence to construct a story about what happened. The story they construct is based on the evidence, but jurors also use it to fill in gaps in the evidence by drawing inferences based on their understandings of how the world works. Jurors arrange evidence in the form of a sequence of motivated human actions that include important events, the circumstances of the case, inferences about character, and the parties' motivations and states of mind. By influencing jurors' understanding of what took place, the order in which facts are presented (i.e., in story order rather than witness order) can affect verdicts. No studies have investigated whether the story model provides a reasonable account of decision-making by judges as well as jurors.

Jury composition

The modern American jury is far more heterogeneous and representative of the citizenry at large than was the early English jury or even the American jury in the early twentieth century. Nonetheless, the jury is not a random sample of citizens. It is the product of a multi-stage selection process that typically begins with a list of potentially eligible jurors drawn from voter registration lists and often supplemented by lists of individuals holding drivers' licenses in the general geographic area where the court sits. Prospective jurors may be excused from jury service on the basis of hardship, but losses also arise as a result of geographic mobility, a failure to update the lists, and nonresponse by prospective jurors to a court summons. The loss of prospective jurors in the qualification and summons process results in a systematic underrepresentation of minorities, younger individuals, and those at lower income levels.

The final stage in jury selection occurs when prospective jurors are brought into the courtroom and questioned to determine whether they will serve in the particular case. Those who clearly express preconceived notions about what the verdict in the case should be, and those with clear conflicts of interest, are excused by the judge (the challenge for cause). In addition, the parties can excuse a limited number of prospective jurors without giving a reason (the peremptory challenge). The U.S. Supreme Court has ruled—*Batson v. Kentucky*, 476 U.S. 79 (1986); *J.E.B. v. Alabama ex rel. T.B.*, 511 U.S. 127 (1994)—that peremptory challenges based on race or gender are constitutionally prohibited, but that prohibition fails to eliminate racially and gender motivated challenges because courts generally require the party making the challenge to provide only minimal justification when the opposing party charges that a challenge was improperly motivated. Also, given the small number of jurors challenged in the typical trial, an attorney can generally identify a unique and nondiscriminatory reason for each challenge.

The result of this variety of shaping and sometimes cross-cutting forces is that juries tend to be somewhat more educated, wealthier and older, and less likely to include a representative number of minorities, as compared to the distribution of these groups in the adult population. Although these differences are likely to persist, the American jury today is more representative than ever before, and is more heterogeneous than the juries of other countries with a jury system. Moreover, jury participation is extensive. Surveys indicate that 25 percent of American citizens are likely to serve on a jury trial at some point in their lives.

Individual differences

Attempts to predict juror verdict preferences based upon juror's background characteristics have had limited success. For example, demographic characteristics like gender, race, and age generally account for very little of the variation in jurors' responses. Attitudinal characteristics can be more powerful, albeit also modest, predictors.

Expectations, beliefs, and values affect the way jurors react to evidence. In that respect, jurors are no different from any other decisionmakers, because people ordinarily scrutinize more carefully, and are more likely to reject, information that is inconsistent with their beliefs and expectations. It is generally easier for people to remember theory-consistent information than theory inconsistent information; moreover, ambiguous information tends to be interpreted as theory-consistent.

Some types of legal cases and issues are more likely than others to implicate strongly held beliefs or values. A primary example concerns the death penalty: even among jurors willing to impose the death penalty in some cases, the strength of their support for the death penalty can strongly influence the likelihood that they will vote for a death sentence.

Pretrial publicity

The American constitutional right to a free press occasionally provides the public with information or misinformation about the case that a jury will be asked to decide. Under such circumstances, the constitutional rights to a free press and to a fair trial are potentially at odds. This conflict is not faced in countries like Canada and Great Britain where the press is prohibited from writing about impending trials. For example, pretrial publicity about a defendant's alleged confession can affect the expectations and beliefs of prospective jurors in the United States. Although some limited research indicates that the effects of some types of pretrial publicity are generally small, it also suggests that jury selection and the passage of time may not eliminate them. In some high-profile cases, the legal system faces not only the cost of moving a trial, but also the increasing difficulty of identifying a location that has not been saturated with pretrial media coverage.

The jury's response to experts

Trials increasingly involve the testimony of experts who present technical and scientific evidence. The addition of DNA evidence to the usual range of forensic testimony is a prime example. Surveys of jurors indicate that they find expert testimony to be useful, but they are wary of experts and their potential biases, a factor that can affect an expert's persuasiveness. Jurors typically work hard at trying to understand the content of expert testimony. Motivation, however, is not enough to ensure success and jurors often express concern about their ability to handle complex evidence.

Jurors are instructed to base their verdicts on the evidence presented at trial and legal instructions. However, their ability to fully process the evidence may be reduced if the expert fails to teach as well as attempt to persuade. When faced with technical testimony, jurors look for cues about the trustworthiness of the source, sometimes using the language itself as a cue. When a decision-maker accepts a persuasive message in response merely to cues (e.g., the prestigious credentials or complicated language of the source of the message), and has not processed and evaluated the message itself, the decision-maker is engaging in peripheral (or heuristic) processing. This approach contrasts with the central (or systematic) processing of the expert testimony that occurs if there is a thorough evaluation of the evidence.

There is little evidence to suggest that jurors adopt the position of an expert based solely on peripheral cues. What is more likely to happen is that the juror will reject unintelligible expert testimony. Moreover, unintelligible jargon may lead jurors to give less credence to an expert who displays other evidence of potential bias, such as an unusually high rate of pay.

Jury size and decision rule

Traditional English and American juries consisted of twelve members who were required to reach a unanimous verdict. Some American jurisdictions now permit juries with as few as six members and nonunanimous verdicts of 9–3 or 10–2; England permits a 10–2 verdict if the jury has been unable to reach unanimity within a specified period of time. Reducing jury size increases the likelihood of an aberrant jury verdict. A majority-decision rule tends to reduce the rate of hung juries and to shorten deliberations because jurors in the majority do not need to gain the support of all jury members. It may also result in less thorough deliberations if the deliberators can arrive at a verdict without considering the reasons why there is disagreement among the members of the jury.

Reactions to the law, including nullification

In theory, jurors are expected to apply the law to the facts of the case. However, a verdict rarely reveals whether the jury has applied the judge's legal instructions, or whether the jury has applied the judge's instructions accurately. Thus, trial and appellate courts are left to assume that the jury has followed the judge's instructions when the verdict is consistent with the law under at least one possible interpretation of the facts. Questions about the jury's use of the legal instructions typically arise at the appellate level only in the context of concerns about whether the trial court has stated the legal standard accurately. If the statement of the law comports with the legal standard, questions are rarely raised regarding whether the judge conveyed the standard clearly enough to be correctly applied.

Jurors might fail to follow the judge's instructions on the law if they were either unmotivated or unable to apply the instructions. Empirical studies of the jury show that jurors see themselves as obligated to apply the law, and that they spend a significant portion of their time during deliberations discussing the law. Yet, there is also evidence that legal instructions as they are typically given often fail to provide jurors with helpful legal guidance. Nearly twenty years ago, Elwork, Sales, and Alfini examined juror comprehension of several frequently used jury instructions. They showed not only that comprehension was low, but also that it could be significantly improved if the instructions were rewritten using a combination of psycholinguistic tools and common sense.

More recent work has demonstrated additional ways to facilitate comprehension. The traditional approach to jury instructions is to tell the jury only what it is supposed to do, and to avoid directing attention to any matter that the jury should ignore. But failing to address the erroneous beliefs that jurors do have does not make those beliefs go away, and it does not neutralize them. For example, if jurors are worried about whether a defendant not sentenced to death will be eligible for parole, avoiding any mention of the parole issue during jury instructions can leave jurors believing that a swift release is likely. Jurors come to court with expectations, beliefs, and schemas that can powerfully affect perceptions, attention, and recall. When instructions fail to correct inaccurate legal impressions, they miss the opportunity to provide jurors with a meaningful legal framework.

Although the most common source of deviations from legal standards is a failure of the legal instructions to convey clearly what the appropriate legal standard is, jurors also may deviate from the path outlined in the instructions due to cognitive biases or motivational obstacles. Jurors admonished to disregard particular information may find it difficult to do so. Other legal instructions may ask the jurors to engage in mental gymnastics that are not easy to perform, for example, to use a defendant's criminal record only to assist in evaluating his credibility, but not as evidence of bad character; to forget that they learned about damaging evidence that the judge ruled inadmissible. Yet, jurors may be unwilling or unable to perform the required cognitive adjustments. A series of simulation experiments have illustrated that such inadmissible evidence can affect juror decisions. The remaining question is whether these failures are significantly less likely when the trier of fact is a judge, or whether they represent heuristic patterns of using information that neither a judge nor jury can overcome.

Finally, jurors may depart from the judge's legal instructions when the application of the legal standard to the particular case so substantially violates the jurors' sense of justice that they are persuaded to temper the letter of the law. This conduct has come to be known as "jury nullification." Kalven and Zeisel attributed most of the disagreements they found between judge and jury to evidentiary disputes, reporting that the jury is engaged in only a modest rewriting of the law in cases that are close on the evidence. Yet, even if it is rare, explicit jury nullification of the law plays a central role in conceptions of the jury and has been a source of extensive debate. Although courts have long recognized the power (as opposed to the right) of the jury to nullify, courts and commentators have disagreed about whether juries should be told about that power (*United States v. Dougherty*, 472 F.2d (D.C. Cir. 1972); *United States v. Thomas*, 116 F.3d 606 (2d Cir. 1997)). Empirical research indicates that the distinction between the power and the right matters: when jurors are explicitly instructed that they have the right not to apply the law as the judge describes it, they are more willing to reach verdicts that temper the literal application of the law.

Deliberations

Deliberations resulting in a group verdict distinguish the jury from its chief alternative, the trial court judge, in two ways. First, the jury verdict in principle reduces the likelihood that the decision will represent an idiosyncratic view of a single deviant decision-maker. Second, in theory, deliberations give the jury an opportunity to profit from the resources of its multiple members and to pool its knowledge and sensibilities to resolve differences. Presumably, a jury verdict reflects more than what could be achieved either by a single decision-maker or by mechanically combining or averaging the preferences of the individual members.

The extent to which deliberations actually do affect jury verdicts in criminal cases is in dispute. Some scholars have suggested that jury verdicts simply reflect the position of the majority before deliberations begin. This suggestion is consistent with the verdict-driven jury that takes an immediate vote to see where each juror stands and then focuses its attention on persuading the minority to join the position initially held by a majority of the jurors. When a vote is immediate, it is likely to reflect predeliberation preferences. When a discussion of the evidence precedes a vote (the so-called evidence-driven jury), that vote will be affected by any changes that have occurred as a result of the discussion. Although jurors often call for an immediate vote, discussions can interrupt before a vote is completed, so that first votes often are not immediate and they imperfectly reflect the individual predeliberation preferences of the jurors. Nonetheless, most juries probably do end up reaching a verdict that reflects the majority position that was apparent at the time most of the jurors expressed a verdict preference in deliberations. The majority, using both normative and informational pressure, persuades the minority to accept its position. When the jury in a criminal case is evenly divided on its first vote, some evidence suggests that the "beyond a reasonable doubt" standard will make a not guilty verdict more likely than a guilty verdict.

Reforming jury trials

The jury is regularly the subject of calls for reform. Some proposed reforms, such as those advocating that jurors be permitted to take notes and to submit questions for witnesses during the trial, are modest designed changes to assist jurors in reaching well-considered judgments, to improve the comfort of the conscripted citizens who serve as jurors, and generally to optimize jury performance and juror satisfaction. Other proposed reforms, such as the reduction or elimination of peremptory challenges and the call for greater use of nonunanimous verdicts, have serious potential costs. The remaining question is whether the increasing scholarly literature on jury behavior will inform popular and political discussion.

SHARI SEIDMAN DIAMOND

See also JURY: LEGAL ASPECTS; SENTENCING: ALLOCATION OF AUTHORITY.

BIBLIOGRAPHY

ABRAMSON, JEFFREY. *We, The Jury: The Jury System and the Ideal of Democracy.* New York: Harper Collins, 1994.

DIAMOND, SHARI S., and LEVI, JUDITH. "Improving Decisions on Death by Revising and Testing Jury Instructions." *Judicature* 79, no. 5 (1996): 224–232.

DIAMOND, SHARI S.; CASPER, JONATHAN D.; HEIERT, CAM; and MARSHALL, ANNA-MARIA. "Juror Reactions to Attorneys at Trial." *Journal of Criminal Law and Criminology* 87 (1996): 17–47.

ELWORK, AMIRAM; SALES, BRUCE D.; and ALFINI, JAMES J. *Making Jury Instructions Understandable.* Charlottesville, Va.: Michie, 1982.

ELLSWORTH, PHOEBE C. "Are Twelve Heads Better than One?" *Law and Contemporary Problems* 52 (1989): 205–224.

FUKURAI, HIROSHI; BUTLER, EDGAR W.; and KROOTH, RICHARD. *Race and the Jury: Racial Disenfranchisement and the Search for Justice.* New York: Plenum, 1993.

HASTIE, REID; PENROD, STEVEN D.; and PENNINGTON, NANCY. *Inside the Jury.* Cambridge, Mass.: Harvard University Press, 1983.

HEUER, LARRY, and PENROD, STEVEN D. "Trial Complexity: A Field Investigation of Its Meaning and Effects." *Law and Human Behavior* 18 (1994): 29–51.

HOROWITZ, IRWIN. "The Effect of Jury Nullification on Verdicts and Jury Functioning in Criminal Trials." *Law and Human Behavior* 9, no. 1 (1985): 25–36.

KALVEN, HARRY, JR., and ZEISEL, HANS. *The American Jury.* Chicago, Ill: University of Chicago Press, 1966.

LIEBERMAN, JOE, and SALES, BRUCE D. "What Social Science Teaches Us about the Jury Instruction Process." *Psychology, Public Policy, and Law* 3 (1997): 589–644.

MACCOUN, ROB J. "Experimental Research on Jury Decision Making." *Science* 244, no. 4908 (1989): 1046–1450.

MUNSTERMAN, G. THOMAS, and MUNSTERMAN, JANICE T. "The Search for Jury Representativeness." *Justice System Journal* 11, no. 1 (1986): 59–78.

PENNINGTON, NANCY; and HASTIE, REID. "Evidence Evaluation in Complex Decision Making." *Journal of Personality & Social Psychology* 51, no. 2 (1986): 242–258.

SAKS, MICHAEL J., and MARTI, MOLLIE W. "A Meta-Analysis of the Effect of Jury Size." *Law and Human Behavior* 21, no. 5 (1997): 451–467.

SANDYS, MARLA, and DILLEHAY, RONALD C. "First-ballot Votes, Predeliberation Dispositions, and Final Verdicts in Jury Trials." *Law and Human Behavior* 19, no. 2 (1995): 175–195.

SMITH, VICKI L., and STUDEBAKER, CHRISTINA A. "What Do You Expect?: The Influence of People's Prior Knowledge on Crime Categories on Fact-finding." *Law and Human Behavior* 20, no. 5 (1996): 517–532.

THAMAN, STEPHEN. "Europe's New Jury Systems: The Cases of Spain and Russia." *Law and Contemporary Problems* 62 (1999): 233–259.

CASES

Batson v. Kentucky, 476 U.S. 79 (1986).

J.E.B. v. Alabama ex rel. T.B., 511 U.S. 127 (1994).

United States v. Dougherty, 472 F.2d 1113 (D.C. Cir. 1972).

United States v. Thomas, 116 F.3d 606 (2d Cir. 1997).

JURY: LEGAL ASPECTS

In 1791, the Sixth Amendment of the U.S. Constitution guaranteed every criminal defendant the right to trial "by an impartial jury of the State and district wherein the crime shall have been committed." This provision was essentially redundant. Article III, section 2 of the Constitution had already provided, "The trial of all Crimes, except in Cases of Impeachment, shall be by Jury." The right to jury trial in criminal cases was among the few guarantees of individual rights enumerated in the Constitution of 1789, and it was the only guarantee to appear in both the original document and the Bill of Rights.

Until 1968, the Supreme Court insisted that the Sixth Amendment afforded the right to jury trial only in the federal courts, but that year, in *Duncan v. Louisiana*, 391 U.S. 145 (1968), the Court held that the Fourteenth Amendment's due process clause "incorporated" this Sixth Amendment right and made it applicable to the states. The Court's opinion declared, "Providing an accused with the right to be tried by a jury of his peers gave him an inestimable safeguard against the corrupt or overzealous prosecutor and against the compliant, biased, or eccentric judge."

Prior to *Duncan*, every state had guaranteed the right to jury trial in felony cases. Moreover, prior to the Constitution and even to the Declaration of Independence, the First Continental Congress's Declaration of Rights of 1774 had proclaimed the right to jury trial. The right to a jury trial in America was in fact as old as James I's charter to the company that settled Jamestown in 1607. Thomas Jefferson once wrote, "Were I called upon to decide whether the people had best be omitted in the Legislative or Judiciary department, I would say it is better to leave them out of the Legislative" (Jefferson, vol. 15, p. 283). William Blackstone called the right to jury trial "the palladium of English liberty" (vol. 3, p. * 379).

Origins

In 1166, during the reign of Henry II in England, the Assize of Clarendon directed juries of twelve people in each community to reveal and accuse members of the community believed to have committed crimes. These juries, the progenitors of modern grand juries, did not decide criminal cases; their function was to serve, in the absence of professional police forces, as the king's eyes and ears. The trial of criminal accusations was by battle, by wager of law (formal oath taking by the accused and by others who vouched for him), and—most commonly—by ordeal. The ordeal took many forms—for example, carrying a heated iron a specified distance so that authorities later could inspect the wound to see whether it was infected or healed. An accused who passed the ordeal was acquitted.

In 1215, the Fourth Lateran Council under Pope Innocent III outlawed the ordeal, and in

England, jury trial emerged as its replacement. Initially, judges had sufficient doubts about this procedure that they required the accused's consent before using it, but they ordered the accused to be pressed under stones until he either consented or died. Within about a century, it was established that the common law jury consisted of twelve people, no more and no less. (Sir Edward Coke later noted the mystic significance of the number twelve, which echoed the number of tribes of Israel and the number of Christ's disciples.) It was also quickly established that a jury could convict or acquit only by unanimous vote. Traveling justices sometimes carried juries from town to town in carts until they reached agreement.

Juries initially were self-informing, relying on their own knowledge and investigation rather than on evidence presented in court. The earliest jurors thus were witnesses as much as they were judges. Even in 1671, long after jurors had come to base their verdicts on courtroom evidence, Chief Justice John Vaughan's opinion in *Bushell's Case*, 124 Eng. Rep. 1006 (Common Pleas 1671), declared that jurors could rely on their personal knowledge as well.

This landmark case arose when William Penn (later the founder of Pennsylvania) and William Meade were charged with unlawful assembly and disturbing the peace. They had preached Quaker doctrine on the streets of London, generating a tumultuous response. When the jurors refused to convict, the court fined them for disregarding the evidence and the court's instructions. One juror, Edward Bushell, was imprisoned for refusing to pay the fine. He filed for a writ of habeas corpus, and in a ruling that effectively ended longstanding controversy about the issue, Chief Justice Vaughn declared that judges could neither punish nor threaten to punish jurors for their verdicts. *Bushell's Case* established the principle of noncoercion of jurors.

Although, after *Bushell's Case*, judges could not force jurors to convict, a common law judge who disapproved a jury's verdict of guilty had an effective means of preventing the defendant's punishment. The judge could recommend a pardon with full assurance that the Crown would grant it as a matter of course. In addition, judges guided juries by commenting freely on the evidence. In America, this practice ended in the nineteenth and twentieth centuries (Lerner).

The Framers' enthusiastic support for the jury stemmed mainly from the role that American juries had played in resisting English authority before the Revolution. These juries greatly hindered the enforcement of English revenue laws and all but nullified the law of seditious libel. The jury was revered as the most democratic institution in the colonies.

The most noted of the pre-Revolutionary cases was that of John Peter Zenger, a New York printer tried on charges of seditious libel in 1735. Zenger's paper, the first journal of political criticism in America, directed most of its barbs toward the royal governor of New York. One of the governor's supporters, Chief Justice James De Lancey, appointed another supporter to represent Zenger at his trial. After the proceedings had begun Andrew Hamilton of Philadelphia, widely regarded as the foremost lawyer in the colonies, "rose dramatically from his chair in the City Hall courtroom and announced . . . that he would participate in Zenger's defense" (Katz, p. 22). Hamilton argued that the truth of Zenger's publication was a defense, and although his argument was manifestly unsound under the law of the era, he maintained that the question was for the jury to decide. The jury's acquittal brought "three huzzas" from spectators in the courtroom.

The English responded to their difficulties with American juries by extending the jurisdiction of admiralty courts (nonjury courts) and by declaring that colonists charged with treason would be tried in England. The Declaration of Independence listed as one of its grievances against George III his "depriving us . . . of the benefits of trial by jury."

The scope of the right

The Sixth Amendment right to jury trial does not extend to petty offenses. *Baldwin v. New York*, 399 U.S. 66 (1970), held, however, that "no offense can be deemed 'petty' . . . where imprisonment for more than six months is authorized." An offense punishable by less than six months' imprisonment is presumed to be petty, but sanctions other than imprisonment may be sufficiently severe to remove the crime from the petty offense category (*Blanton v. City of North Las Vegas*, 489 U.S. 538 (1989)). Many states extend the right to jury trial farther than the Constitution requires. In California, even a defendant charged with a traffic offense may demand a jury trial.

McKeiver v. Pennsylvania, 403 U.S. 528 (1971), held that the right to jury trial does not extend to juvenile delinquency proceedings,

which are nominally "civil" rather than "criminal" in character. The right also does not extend to sexual psychopath proceedings and to suits by the government to collect civil penalties.

A defendant has no right to jury trial in most sentencing proceedings (see *Spaziano v. Florida*, 468 U.S. 447 (1984)). Nevertheless, the Supreme Court held in *Apprendi v. New Jersey*, 120 S. Ct. 2348 (2000), that when the determination of a fact other than prior criminal record would extend a defendant's maximum term of imprisonment, the defendant is entitled to have that fact determined by a jury. Whether *Apprendi* will remain limited to cases in which a factual determination would extend the defendant's maximum sentence (rather than the mandatory minimum sentence, the sentence dictated by sentencing guidelines, or the actual sentence) is certain to be the subject of further litigation.

Jury size

Although the Supreme Court previously said that the Sixth Amendment required juries of twelve, the Court in 1970 declared this traditional number a "historical accident, wholly without significance except to mystics." It concluded in *Williams v. Florida*, 399 U.S. 78 (1970), that the Constitution allowed juries of six. In support of its claim that there was "no discernable difference between the results reached by the two different-sized juries," the Court cited studies that seemed to most observers to establish just the opposite. The Court declared that a jury of six was "large enough to promote group deliberation, free from outside attempts at intimidation, and to provide a fair possibility of obtaining a representative cross section of the community."

One critic of *Williams* titled his paper "And Then There Were None" (Zeisel). Nevertheless, in *Ballew v. Georgia*, 435 U.S. 223 (1978), a unanimous Court held five-person juries impermissible. A great many states now use six-person juries, especially in misdemeanor prosecutions. Only seven states expressly require twelve-person juries in all cases, but other states permit departures from this historic number only with the defendant's consent. (Miller).

Unanimity

In *Apodaca v. Oregon*, 406 U.S. 404 (1972), four Supreme Court justices concluded that conviction by a vote of 10-to-2 did not violate the Sixth Amendment. Four justices dissented, arguing that the amendment requires juror unanimity. The remaining justice, Justice Powell, agreed with the dissenters' construction of the Sixth Amendment but rejected the view that "all of the elements of jury trial within the meaning of the Sixth Amendment are necessarily embodied in or incorporated into the Due Process Clause of the Fourteenth." As a result, nonunanimous verdicts are permissible in state but not federal courts. In a companion case, the Court upheld a state-court conviction by a 9-to-3 vote (*Johnson v. Louisiana,* 406 U.S. 356 (1972)). Later, the Court held that conviction by a vote of 5-to-1 was unconstitutional; convictions by six-person juries must be unanimous (*Burch v. Louisiana,* 441 U.S. 130 (1979)).

Defendants have argued that nonunanimous verdicts violate not only the right to jury trial but also the right not to be convicted except upon proof of guilt beyond a reasonable doubt. The Court rejected this argument in *Johnson,* holding that the reasonable doubt requirement demands only that each juror be instructed to acquit unless this requirement has been satisfied. Nevertheless, both the historic requirement of twelve jurors and the historic requirement of unanimity have promoted confidence in the accuracy of criminal convictions. The unanimity requirement also has encouraged jurors to listen to and attempt to persuade one another; it prevents the majority from outvoting dissenters without considering their views. In Scotland, where juries of fifteen may convict or acquit by a simple majority vote, divided juries deliberate only if they choose. In England, 10-to-2 verdicts are permitted after the jury has deliberated two hours (Pizzi).

At the time of the Supreme Court's decisions in *Apodaca* and *Johnson,* Oregon and Louisiana were the only states permitting nonunanimous verdicts in felony cases. These states remained alone twenty-nine years later. Nevertheless, prosecutors in several other states were actively supporting legislation to allow nonunanimous verdicts. One of their concerns was that a minority of jurors might "nullify" the law by blocking conviction when proof of guilt was clear. The prosecutors may have been especially concerned that minority-race jurors would block the conviction of minority-race defendants. A later section of this entry will discuss the issues raised by jury nullification.

Vicinage

The Anti-Federalists who opposed ratification of the Constitution protested that the right to jury trial guaranteed by Article III was inadequate. Their objections led two years later to the Sixth Amendment's requirement that juries be drawn from "the State and district wherein the crime shall have been committed." For the Framers, jury impartiality did not require jurors to arrive at the courtroom wholly unaware of the circumstances of the case before them. Knowledge of local conditions and of the reputations of the defendant and of witnesses was thought to enhance the jurors' performance. Juries could serve their communitarian function only if they were local (see Abramson, pp. 22–30). State statutes now typically provide a right to trial before a jury drawn from the county in which the crime is alleged to have occurred.

Selecting jurors

Statutory eligibility: some history. At the time of the ratification of the Sixth Amendment, every state limited jury service to men, and every state except Vermont limited jury service to property owners or taxpayers. The early nineteenth century, however, saw the rapid triumph of "universal suffrage," a term used without any sense of irony to describe the enfranchisement of adult white men. Some states declared that everyone qualified to vote also could serve on juries, and in these states, affording the vote to persons without property made them eligible for jury service. In other states, however, eligibility for jury service sometimes lagged behind the right to vote. A few tax-paying and property-holding requirements persisted into the twentieth century. In 1946, however, the Supreme Court invoked its supervisory power over the administration of federal justice and struck down an exclusion of daily wage earners from jury service. The Court refused to "breathe life into any latent tendencies to establish the jury as the instrument of the economically and socially privileged" (*Thiel v. Southern Pacific Co.,* 328 U.S. 217, 223–224 (1946)). By 1946, class-based qualifications like those accepted by the Framers of the Constitution appeared inconsistent with the concept of jury trial.

Especially in the first half of the nineteenth century, formal qualifications did not always determine who served on juries in fact. The members of a group eligible for jury service might never serve, for public officials exercised "very extensive and very arbitrary" powers in summoning jurors (Toqueville, vol. 1, pp. 359–360). Moreover, statutory disqualification did not necessarily mean real disqualification. When qualified jurors failed to appear, statutes permitted court officials to impanel unqualified "bystanders," and in some jurisdictions, the use of bystanders was common.

Although unpropertied white men rapidly made their way onto American juries, the path to the jury box was vastly more arduous for blacks and women. The first blacks ever to serve on an American jury may have been two who sat in Worcester, Massachusetts, in 1860. Even when federal legislation declared blacks eligible to testify in federal courts (1864) and in state courts (1866), proponents of these measures insisted that they would not lead to the inclusion of blacks on juries.

The Fourteenth Amendment's equal protection clause (1868) was not thought initially to give blacks the same political rights as whites—neither the right to sit on juries nor the right to vote. A separate amendment, the Fifteenth (1870), therefore was necessary to extend the franchise to blacks, and this amendment did not guarantee blacks the right to hold office or serve on juries. In 1875, however, a Federal Civil Rights Act declared, "[N]o citizen . . . shall be disqualified for service as a grand or petit juror in any court of the United States, or of any State on account of race, color, or previous condition of servitude." The supporters of this measure contended, not that Congress had the power to extend "political" rights to blacks, but that nondiscriminatory jury selection would protect the right of black litigants to equal protection of the laws. On the same theory, the Supreme Court held in 1880 that a West Virginia statute limiting jury service to whites violated the equal protection rights of a black defendant (*Strauder v. West Virginia*, 100 U.S. 303 (1880)).

During Reconstruction, blacks served on juries in most, but not all, Southern states and in Southern federal courts. In some jurisdictions, color-conscious jury selection ensured that juries mirrored the racial composition of the counties in which they sat. In 1879, however, with Reconstruction at an end, Congress authorized discretionary jury selection procedures in the federal courts that were well designed to deny in practice what the act reaffirmed in theory—that no citizen could be disqualified from jury service on account of race.

Although *Strauder* and the Civil Rights Act of 1875 had effectively (if indirectly) recognized the right of black men to serve on juries, this right remained unenforced for most of a century. Booker T. Washington observed at the end of the nineteenth century, "In the whole of Georgia & Alabama, and other Southern states not a Negro juror is allowed to sit in the jury box in state courts" (quoted in Schmidt, p. 1406). Of the period from the end of Reconstruction to the New Deal, Benno Schmidt declared, "[T]he systematic exclusion of black men from Southern juries was about as plain as any legal discrimination could be short of proclamation in state statutes or confession by state officials" (Schmidt, p. 1406).

Long after *Strauder* held the statutory exclusion of black men from jury service unconstitutional, the statutory exclusion of women persisted. The first jury service by women in America (and, indeed, in any common law jurisdiction) occurred in the Wyoming Territory in 1870. A new chief justice brought this experiment in gender equality to an end two years later, and women did not serve on Wyoming juries again until the 1940s.

Just as the Fifteenth Amendment afforded black men the right to vote without guaranteeing them the right to serve on juries, the Nineteenth Amendment enfranchised women and did no more. In some states, jury-qualification statutes described jurors in part as "electors" or "voters." When women gained the right to vote in these states, they usually gained the right to serve on juries as well. In other states, however, new legislation was needed, and in 1930, the Executive Secretary of the League of Women Voters complained, "Getting the word 'male' out of jury statutes is requiring something like a second suffrage campaign—laborious, costly, and exasperating" (Kerber, p. 143).

Legislation authorizing women to serve on juries did not always guarantee them the right to serve on the same terms as men. A 1949 Massachusetts statute exempted a woman from serving in any case in which the presiding judge had reason to believe she would "likely . . . be embarrassed by hearing the testimony or discussing [it] in the jury room." Many states provided an exemption from jury service that women could claim on the basis of their sex alone. Indeed, in some of these states, women were not required to claim their exemption; they served on juries only if they registered at the courthouse or took other steps to volunteer.

As late as 1961, when John F. Kennedy was President and Earl Warren Chief Justice, the Supreme Court unanimously upheld the constitutionality of a jury system in which men were drafted while women served only if they volunteered. "[W]oman is still regarded as the center of home and family life," the Court declared. "We cannot say that it is constitutionally impermissible for a State. . .to conclude that a woman should be relieved from the civic duty of jury service unless she herself determines that such service is consistent with her own special responsibilities" (*Hoyt v. Florida*, 368 U.S. 57, 62 (1961)). The Supreme Court effectively overruled this decision in 1975 (*Taylor v. Louisiana*, 419 U.S. 522 (1975)).

The last major barrier to equal participation in jury service for blacks, other minorities, and women was (and, despite formal rulings to the contrary, still may be) the peremptory challenge. This device is discussed in a later section of this entry.

Exemption

Like women, the members of various occupational groups often have been exempted by statute from jury service—lawyers, doctors, nurses, pharmacists, school teachers, clergy, mail carriers, ship officers, airline pilots, firefighters, police officers, sole proprietors of businesses, salespeople on commission, embalmers, legislators, and others. Professional exemptions are still recognized in a great many states, but the trend of recent legislation has been to abolish them. In recent years, even judges have been known to serve on juries in courts other than their own.

Assembling the venire

Until the 1960s, most state and federal courts employed a "key man" system in which jury commissioners or court clerks asked prominent citizens, politicians, or other "key men" to nominate prospective jurors. Officials then summoned jurors from the lists these "key men" had provided. Some states in New England and the South still retain this system, and although jury selection methods must satisfy the equal protection and "fair cross-section" requirements discussed below, the Supreme Court has held that the Constitution does not require random jury selection. The Court has upheld statutory requirements that court officials eliminate anyone found not "upright" and "intelligent" (*Turner v. Fouche*,

396 U.S. 346 (1970)), and that they summon only citizens who are "generally reputed to be honest and intelligent. . .and esteemed in the community for their integrity, good character and sound judgment" (*Carter v. Jury Commission of Greene County*, 396 U.S. 320 (1970)). The Federal Jury Selection and Service Act of 1968 ended the "key man" system in the federal courts, and the Uniform Jury Selection and Service Act proposed by the National Conference of Commissioners on Uniform State Laws in 1970 was largely modeled after the federal Act.

Most state courts now follow procedures similar to those mandated by the federal statute. In these jurisdictions, jury selection begins with a "source list." Under the federal act, the basic source list must be the list of registered or actual voters, but this list must be supplemented by others when it will not assure random jury selection from a fair cross-section of the community. Partly because racial minorities, young people, and the poor are less likely than others to register to vote, many jurisdictions use lists of driver's licenses and state identification cards to supplement (and sometimes replace) voter lists. Some jurisdictions also use city directories, tax rolls, and telephone books. No source list is likely to be entirely current, however, and because the members of some groups change addresses more frequently than others, even the best efforts to ensure representative jury panels through random selection from a source list may fall short.

Under the federal statute, at least one-half of 1 percent of the names on the source list are placed in a "master" jury wheel. A judge or court clerk draws names from this wheel as jurors are needed, and juror-qualification forms are sent to the people whose names are drawn. A judge then eliminates prospective jurors whose responses indicate that they are unqualified because (1) they are not citizens, (2) they are not eighteen, (3) they have not resided in the judicial district for at least one year, (4) they do not speak English or cannot read and write English well enough to complete the qualification form, (5) they are too mentally or physically infirm to serve, or (6) they are currently charged with a crime punishable by imprisonment for more than one year or have previously been convicted of such a crime and their civil rights have not been restored. Prospective jurors may claim occupational exemptions from jury service in their questionnaires and may claim that jury service would be a hardship. (A prospective juror also may claim that serving on a jury in a particular case would be burdensome at a later stage of the process.) The names of the qualified jurors who are not exempted or excused are placed in a second jury wheel, the "qualified" jury wheel. People whose names are drawn from this wheel receive jury summonses. Some jurisdictions make systematic efforts to enforce these summonses, but in many, the sanctions authorized for noncompliance are more theoretical than real.

People who respond to jury summonses are typically assigned to a jury pool and then directed from the pool to particular courtrooms for the trial of cases. Complaints about juror waiting time have led many jurisdictions to implement "one day, one trial" systems. In these systems, a juror is excused after serving on a single jury or after waiting for one day without being chosen. The panel of prospective jurors from which a jury is selected is called the venire.

Challenges to the venire

A defendant who claims that a jury panel was improperly summoned may file a "challenge to the array" or a "motion to quash the venire." This challenge may be based on statutory grounds, or it may allege improper exclusion under either the fourteenth amendment's equal protection clause or the sixth amendment's right to a jury drawn from a fair cross-section of the community.

Equal protection.   Long before *Duncan v. Louisiana* extended the Sixth Amendment right to jury trial to the states, the Supreme Court and other courts condemned racially discriminatory jury selection in state courts as a violation of the equal protection clause. Shortly after *Strauder v. West Virginia* invalidated a statute limiting jury service to whites, the Supreme Court recognized that the discriminatory administration of a facially neutral statute also could violate the Constitution (*Neal v. Delaware*, 103 U.S. 370 (1881)).

The Supreme Court has held that the equal protection clause condemns only purposeful discrimination; a "discriminatory effect" or "discriminatory impact" is insufficient. Nevertheless, proof of a sufficiently discriminatory effect can provide a basis for inferring a discriminatory purpose. In *Norris v. Alabama*, 294 U.S. 587 (1935), the Court reversed the second conviction of one of the Scottsboro boys (a group of black youths sentenced to death by all-white juries on doubtful evidence that they had raped two young white women). The Court held that proof that blacks constituted a substantial portion of

the community and had never or almost never served on juries established a prima facie case of discrimination. Later rulings made clear that a jury commissioner's statement that he did not know any blacks or a denial that he intended to discriminate was not enough to rebut a prima facie case (*Hill v. Texas*, 316 U.S. 400 (1942); *Eubanks v. Louisiana*, 356 U.S. 584 (1958)).

The Supreme Court's statistical standards for inferring discrimination became increasingly stringent (see *Turner v. Fouche*; *Alexander v. Louisiana*, 405 U.S. 625 (1972)). In *Castaneda v. Partida*, 430 U.S. 482 (1977), proof that a county's population was 79 percent Mexican-American while only 39 percent of the people summoned for jury service were Mexican-American was sufficient to establish a prima facie case.

Some courts have used color-conscious jury selection methods to ensure the representation of minorities. They hope to increase the likelihood that the jury will represent the community, promote group deliberation, and enhance the public acceptance of jury verdicts. Some of the objections offered to affirmative action in other contexts seem inapplicable to race-conscious efforts to ensure the inclusion of nonwhites on juries (see Alschuler, 1995). A federal Court of Appeals, however, has held one color-conscious jury selection plan unconstitutional (*United States v. Ovalle*, 136 F.3d 1092 (6th Cir. 1998)).

As noted above, *Strauder* held that the exclusion of blacks from a jury violated the equal protection rights of black defendants, not the rights of excluded jurors. In *Powers v. Ohio*, 499 U.S. 400 (1991), however, the Court recognized that racial discrimination in jury selection does violate the equal protection rights of the excluded jurors. The Court held that because these jurors could not effectively challenge discrimination against them, a defendant in a criminal case could assert their rights. A white defendant therefore had "standing" to challenge the exclusion of black jurors.

The fair cross-section requirement. *Duncan*'s application of the Sixth Amendment to the states supplied another basis for challenging discriminatory jury selection in state courts. In a federal case in 1942, the Supreme Court spoke of the jury as a "cross-section of the community" and declared, "[T]he proper functioning of the jury system, and, indeed, or our democracy itself, requires that the jury be a 'body truly representative of the community'" (*Glasser v. United States*, 315 U.S. 60 (1942)).

In 1975, following *Duncan*'s incorporation of the right to jury trial in the Fourteenth Amendment, the Court invoked *Glasser* and held that a "fair cross-section requirement" implicit in the Sixth Amendment forbade discrimination that the Court had refused to condemn under the equal protection clause. In *Taylor v. Louisiana*, 419 U.S. 522 (1975), the Court did not overrule its earlier decision that the exemption of women from jury service was compatible with the equal protection clause, but it held that this exemption did violate the Sixth Amendment.

Despite its label, the "fair cross-section requirement" does not require that juries be a fair cross-section of the community. The Court reiterated in *Taylor* that defendants are not entitled to a jury of any particular composition. Indeed, the Supreme Court has said that the fair cross-section requirement does not extend to trial juries at all but only to the panels from which the juries are drawn (*Lockhart v. McCree*, 476 U.S. 162 (1986); *Holland v. Illinois*, 493 U.S. 474 (1990)). Moreover, the fair cross-section requirement forbids only the "systematic" exclusion of "distinctive groups in the community" (*Durden v. Missouri*, 439 U.S. 357 (1979)). If the luck of the draw were to yield five consecutive jury panels composed entirely of wealthy Republican women golfers, their selection apparently would not violate the Constitution.

"Systematic" exclusion need not be "purposeful" but apparently must be regular and foreseeable. The exclusion of a "distinctive group" need not be total, but the underrepresented group must be an "identifiable segment playing [a] major role in the community." When the Supreme Court held that women were a "distinctive group," it noted that with their absence from the jury "a flavor, a distinct quality is lost" (*Taylor v. Louisiana*). Lower federal and state courts have held that young adults and occupational groups are not sufficiently distinctive (LaFave, Israel, and King, p. 1034). Similarly, people unwilling to impose the death penalty in any case do not qualify as a distinctive group (*Lockhart v. McCree*).

Selecting the jury from the venire

The voir dire examination. The examination of prospective jurors by lawyers and judges at the beginning of the jury selection process is called the voir dire.

Judges sometimes require prospective jurors to complete questionnaires prior to their examination in the courtroom. In the O. J. Simpson case, prospective jurors were directed to answer 294 multiple-part questions, including: "Which tabloids do you read on a regular or occasional basis?" "How many hours a week do you watch sporting activities?" "Do you own any special knives?" "Name the three public figures you admire most." And, "Does the fact that O. J. Simpson excelled at football make it unlikely in your mind that he could commit murder?" Such in-depth questioning, however, is rare in ordinary criminal cases.

In most states, a defendant is entitled to a list of prospective jurors prior to trial, and although lawyers may not attempt to influence jurors, both defense attorneys and prosecutors may investigate them. Prosecutors sometimes use law enforcement officers for this purpose, and they typically keep records of how jurors have voted in the past. In addition, prosecutors are likely to have easy access to the arrest and conviction records of prospective jurors. Courts generally do not require either prosecutors or defense attorneys to disclose what they have learned about prospective jurors to their opponents, but some courts have required limited disclosures.

In a number of high-profile cases, defendants with means have hired jury consultants to survey community attitudes and construct profiles of jurors likely to prove favorable or unfavorable to the defense. Jury consultants use focus groups for the same purpose, and some defendants have hired psychologists to observe prospective jurors in the courtroom and predict their behavior on the basis of facial expressions and body language. Defendants also have been known to use experts to analyze the handwriting of prospective jurors.

In a substantial majority of federal courts and in many state courts, the voir dire is conducted primarily by the trial judge, who generally permits counsel to ask additional questions or else submit questions in writing for the judge to ask the panel. In many state courts, however, the voir dire is conducted primarily or exclusively by the prosecutor and defense attorney. In examining prospective jurors, lawyers probe their private attitudes and practices—asking, for example, about religious beliefs, drinking habits, reading habits, memberships, hobbies, traffic accidents, and prior experience with lawyers, and then asking about the jurors' relatives' jobs, experiences as crime victims, and arrest records as well. A lawyer usually hopes not only to gain information but also to establish rapport and to create a favorable predisposition to the lawyer's side of the case.

In *Turner v. Murray*, 476 U.S. 28 (1986), the Supreme Court held that "a capital defendant accused of an interracial crime is entitled to have prospective jurors informed of the race of the victim and questioned on the issue of racial bias." The trial court's failure to conduct this questioning, however, entitled the defendant only to relief from his capital sentence, not to the reversal of his conviction. The Court also held that a judge's refusal to question prospective jurors about possible racial prejudice violated the due process clause when the defendant was a black civil rights worker charged with a drug offense (*Ham v. South Carolina*, 409 U.S. 524 (1973)). The omission of questions concerning racial prejudice was permissible, however, when the defendant was a black charged with robbing, assaulting, and attempting to murder a white security guard (*Ristaino v. Ross*, 424 U.S. 589 (1976)).

Critics have argued that the extended voir dire of prospective jurors is wasteful, invasive of privacy, and incompatible with the democratic ideals of the jury system. Most trial lawyers, however, resist restriction of the practice and support attorney—rather than judge—conducted voir dire. These lawyers maintain that the more latitude they are allowed in examining prospective jurors, the less they must rely on hunches and group stereotypes in exercising their peremptory challenges.

Challenges for cause. Statutes typically specify a number of grounds for disqualifying prospective jurors such as prior service on a grand or trial jury in the same case or being a member of the defendant's family. The most common basis for a challenge for cause, however, is bias or an inability to try the case impartially. Judges often appear reluctant to sustain challenges for cause, and despite clear indications of bias, they may treat a pledge from the challenged juror to judge the case impartially on the basis of the evidence presented as sufficient. The judges tend to rely in doubtful cases on the exercise of peremptory challenges by lawyers to remove possibly biased jurors.

Even when jurors claim that they can render an impartial verdict, pretrial publicity can be so extensive and so prejudicial that bias must be presumed (*Irvin v. Dowd*, 366 U.S. 717 (1961)). Exposure to descriptions of a defendant's alleged crime and prior criminal record, however, does not automatically warrant a presumption of bias (*Murphy v. Florida*, 421 U.S. 794 (1975)).

In a capital case, a court may not excuse a juror for cause simply because this juror "has conscientious scruples against capital punishment" (*Witherspoon v. Illinois*, 391 U.S. 510 (1968)). A court may, however, excuse a juror whose views of capital punishment would "prevent or substantially impair the performance of his duties as a juror in accordance with his instructions and his oath" (*Wainwright v. Witt*, 469 U.S. 412 (1985)). Just as a prosecutor may "death qualify" a jury by excluding people who would oppose the death penalty regardless of the circumstances of the case, a defendant in a capital case must be allowed to ask prospective jurors whether they would automatically support the death penalty. Jurors who answer this question yes must be disqualified (*Morgan v. Illinois*, 504 U.S. 719 (1992)).

Peremptory challenges. Statutes and court rules afford prosecutors and defendants a specified number of peremptory challenges that they may exercise without giving reasons. In a federal felony trial, for example, the defendant may exercise ten peremptory challenges and the prosecutor six. Most states afford the defendant and the prosecutor an equal number of challenges.

Typically, the process of exercising peremptory challenges begins by seating a group of twelve prospective jurors in the jury box. Members of this panel are challenged initially by the prosecutor, and the jurors whom the prosecutor dismisses either peremptorily or for cause are replaced. The defense attorney then makes challenges on behalf of the defendant. Each lawyer tenders a panel of twelve to the other until both sides have exhausted their peremptory challenges or declined the opportunity to make further challenges.

A less common procedure is the "struck jury system," which begins with a panel containing a sufficient number of prospective jurors to permit both sides to exhaust their peremptory challenges and still have enough jurors for trial. The parties first make their challenges for cause, and the jurors removed for cause are replaced. Then the parties alternate in making peremptory strikes.

The right of a criminal defendant to challenge a number of jurors peremptorily dates from the earliest days of the jury, but when English and American juries were composed entirely of white male property owners, this right was virtually never exercised. Democratization of the jury, which enabled lawyers to base their challenges on group judgments and stereotypes, revived the peremptory challenge. Once the Supreme Court had condemned discriminatory jury selection by legislatures and court officials, this challenge was the last bastion of undisguised racial discrimination in the American criminal justice system.

In *Swain v. Alabama,* 380 U.S. 202 (1965), an all-white jury in Talladega County, Alabama, convicted a nineteen-year-old black man of raping a seventeen-year-old white woman and sentenced him to death. Since at least 1950, no black had served on a civil or criminal jury in Talladega County, and the prosecutor in *Swain* used six peremptory challenges to remove from the jury panel the only six blacks eligible to serve.

The Supreme Court affirmed the defendant's conviction and sentence. It distinguished between striking blacks in order to improve the prosecutor's likelihood of success at trial and striking them "for reasons wholly unrelated to the outcome of the particular case . . . [simply] to deny the Negro the same right and opportunity to participate in the administration of justice enjoyed by the white population." The Court recognized that, in the absence of tactical, trial-related objectives, the use of peremptory challenges to exclude blacks would be unconstitutional. The Court held, however, that the prosecutor's exclusion of all black jurors in a single case could not establish the proscribed motivation. Moreover, the Court concluded that the evidence before it failed to establish that the prosecutor was responsible for the exclusion of blacks in cases other than *Swain.*

In 1986, the Supreme Court overruled *Swain* and brought the unrestricted, truly peremptory challenge to an end. It held in *Batson v. Kentucky,* 476 U.S. 79 (1986), that "the Equal Protection Clause forbids the prosecutor to challenge potential jurors solely on account of their race." Later cases held that the equal protection clause forbids discrimination by defense attorneys as well as prosecutors (*Georgia v. McCollum,* 505 U.S. 42 (1992)), that a white defendant may challenge a prosecutor's exclusion of blacks (*Powers v. Ohio,* 499 U.S. 400 (1991)), and that lawyers may not use peremptory challenges to discriminate on the basis of gender (*J.E.B. v. Alabama ex rel.* T.B., 511 U.S. 127 (1994)).

In the decision forbidding gender discrimination in the exercise of peremptory challenges, the Supreme Court indicated that the Fourteenth Amendment does not limit peremptory challenges unless they are based on classifications that receive "heightened equal protection scrutiny." Prosecutors and defense attorneys, unlike others governed by the equal protection clause, need not have a "rational basis" for treating people differently. They apparently may challenge prospective jurors simply because they are overweight, ugly, physically disabled, nervous, tattooed, or former residents of New Jersey.

Some lawyers employ selection principles that savor of whimsy, superstition, and folklore. Johnnie Cochran notes that he "excuse[s] any man who shows up wearing either white socks or a string tie" (Cochran, p. 261). Unlike classification on the basis of sock color, classification on the basis of religious belief does receive heightened scrutiny under the equal protection clause. Nevertheless, whether lawyers may challenge prospective jurors on the basis of their religion remains unsettled.

Under *Batson,* a defendant who objects to a prosecutor's use of a peremptory challenge must establish a "prima facie case of discrimination" before the prosecutor must offer an explanation for this strike. When the prosecutor has not given any verbal indication of an improper purpose, the requirement of prima facie proof may effectively allow the prosecutor to exclude at least one black juror without challenge. When a defendant does establish circumstances warranting "an inference of purposeful discrimination," the prosecutor must provide a "neutral explanation for challenging black jurors." The Court emphasized in *Purkett v. Elem,* 514 U.S. 765 (1995), however, that the prosecutor's explanation need not be "minimally persuasive." The trial judge may find that an implausible explanation was a "pretext for purposeful discrimination," but if the judge regards the prosecutor as sincere, the judge's determination of credibility will be conclusive. *Purkett* allowed a trial judge to accept the explanation "mustaches . . . and beards look suspicious to me," and an earlier decision permitted a prosecutor to exclude Latino jurors because they were bilingual and therefore "might have difficulty in accepting the translator's rendition of Spanish-language testimony" (*Hernandez v. New York,* 500 U.S. 352 (1991)). A juror may be excluded either because he has failed to maintain eye contact with a prosecutor or because he has stared at the prosecutor too long (Alschuler, 1989).

Although *Batson* requires the use of cumbersome procedures, its prohibition of racial discrimination is easily evaded. Partly for this reason, partly because much invidious discrimination not based on race or gender remains lawful, and partly because lawyers' challenges generally serve partisan rather than public ends, many commentators have echoed Justice Marshall's call in *Batson* for abolition of the peremptory challenge. Defenders reply that the peremptory challenge provides a way of excluding some jurors who should not serve without calling them biased, saves judges from deciding difficult questions of what experiences, associations, and perspectives should disqualify jurors, and "allows the covert expression of what we dare not say but know is true more often than not" (Babcock, pp. 553–554).

The review of jury verdicts

The Constitution's prohibition of double jeopardy precludes the review or revision of a jury's decision to acquit (*United States v. Scott*, 437 U.S. 82 (1978)), and review of a jury's decision to convict is highly deferential. In America, unlike most European nations, appellate review focuses more on trial and pretrial procedures than on trial outcomes.

In the federal courts and most states, juries are permitted to return inconsistent verdicts. When they do, courts assume that the jury verdict favorable to the defendant reflected a decision to be merciful; they disregard the possibility that the verdict unfavorable to the defendant was the product of error and misunderstanding (see Muller).

A common law rule forbids jurors from "impeaching" their verdicts by testifying to their own misconduct. In *Tanner v. United States*, 483 U.S. 107 (1987), the Supreme Court applied a successor to this rule and prevented two members of a jury from testifying that a number of jurors had abused alcohol, marihuana, and cocaine repeatedly during a trial. Although the rule was subject to an exception for testimony concerning "extraneous" or "outside" influences on the jury, the Court concluded that alcohol and drugs did not qualify. It declared, "There is little doubt that post-verdict investigation into juror misconduct would in some instances lead to the invalidation of verdicts reached after irresponsible or improper juror behavior. It is not at all clear, however, that the jury system could survive such efforts to perfect it."

Jury nullification

In England, although jury nullification was recognized and even welcomed in some cases, juries never acquired any official authority to disregard the instructions of judges and resolve questions of law for themselves. In America following the Revolution, however, the authority of juries to resolve issue of law was frequently confirmed by constitutions, statutes, and judicial decisions.

How American juries gained their authority to resolve questions of law is obscure. When, however, Andrew Hamilton declared in the Zenger trial in 1735 that juries "have the right . . . to determine both the law and the fact," he insisted that this authority was "beyond all dispute." Hamilton's position probably reflected the practice in some colonies but not all. In the absence of law books and law-trained judges, colonial jurors may have seemed as well suited to resolve legal issues as anyone else. In 1771, John Adams called it "an Absurdity to suppose that the Law would oblige [jurors] to find a Verdict according to the Direction of the Court, against their own Opinion, Judgment, and Conscience" (Adams, vol. 1, p. 230).

Whether juries should be the judges of law as well as fact was a contentious issue throughout the first half of the nineteenth century, but over the course of the second half of the century, legal issues became, almost everywhere, the exclusive province of the court. The Supreme Court endorsed this position in 1895 in *Sparf and Hansen v. United States*, 156 U.S. 51 (1895). The Court acknowledged that federal courts in earlier decades often had told jurors that they were to judge both the law and the facts. It nevertheless held that jurors must be bound by judicial instructions concerning the law.

The constitutions of three states—Georgia, Indiana, and Maryland—still declare that jurors shall judge questions of law as well as fact. In all three states, however, judicial decisions have effectively nullified these constitutional provisions. The clear rule in all other American jurisdictions is that juries must "take their law" as the trial judge declares it.

Jurors have the practical power to disregard this rule and to acquit defendants despite unmistakable proof of their guilt. Under the "principle of noncoercion of jurors" established by *Bushell's Case* in 1671, they may not be punished for doing so, and the double jeopardy clause prevents judges from setting aside their acquittals, however lawless they may seem (*United States v. Scott*, 437 U.S. 82 (1978)).

In the late 1960s and 1970s, defendants charged with unlawful resistance to the Vietnam War frequently contended that because jurors have a right to acquit whenever conviction would be unjust, judges should inform jurors of this right and allow defense attorneys to argue in favor of its exercise. Appellate courts uniformly rejected this argument. They insisted that jurors have the power to nullify the law but not the right.

The leading case is *United States v. Dougherty*, 473 F.2d 1113 (D.C. Cir. 1972). The court did not deny in *Dougherty* that jury nullification was sometimes appropriate. Indeed, it wrote, "The pages of history shine on instances of the jury's exercise of its prerogative to disregard uncontradicted evidence and instructions of the judge." The court nevertheless concluded, "[W]hat is tolerable or even desirable as an informal, self-initiated exception, harbors grave dangers to the system if it is opened to expansion and intensification through incorporation in the judge's instruction." In the court's view, jurors should view nullification, not as a right, but as a form of civil disobedience.

Nearly everyone applauds the Zenger jury's nullification of the law of seditious libel and the nullification of fugitive slave laws by Northern juries in the period before the Civil War (although fugitive slave cases came before juries very infrequently). Some may also applaud the nullification of laws forbidding draft resistance during the Vietnam era and laws imposing harsh drug sentences today. Hardly anyone, however, applauds the nullification by Southern juries of laws forbidding the murder of blacks and white civil rights workers from the end of Reconstruction through the 1960s. The most frequent form of jury nullification probably has been, and still is, the nullification of laws against violence when juries have concluded that the victims of this violence "deserved it." Moreover, over the course of American history, many juries have seen skin color as an indicator of which victims "deserved it." For many, the 1991 acquittal of the police officers who were videotaped beating Rodney King confirmed that some American juries still tolerate violence against blacks. The King verdict triggered the worst race riot in American history, two days of violence that claimed fifty-eight lives and cost nearly one billion dollars in property damage.

In a reversal of historic roles, whites apparently have begun to fear black jurors. A controversial 1995 *Yale Law Journal* article argued that black jurors should vote to acquit black defendants in drug cases and other cases regardless of the evidence of their guilt (Butler). Although this article opposed the acquittal of black defendants who had committed crimes of violence, a few publicized acquittals and hung juries (including, justifiably or unjustifiably, the acquittal of O. J. Simpson) have prompted concern that black jurors may block the conviction of black defendants who have committed serious crimes against whites. Some members of America's majority race have begun to experience a glimmer of the fear of juries that the members of minority races have experienced throughout U.S. history.

A federal Court of Appeals declared in 1997, "We categorically reject the idea that, in a society committed to the rule of law, jury nullification is desirable or that courts may permit it to occur when it is within their authority to prevent" (*United States v. Thomas*, 116 F.3d 606 (2d Cir.1997)). The court held that, even after jury deliberations had begun, a trial judge could remove a juror who had revealed "beyond doubt" an intention to violate the court's instructions. A jury instruction approved in California in 1998 requires jurors to "immediately advise" the court when "any juror . . . expresses an intention to disregard the law or to decide the case on . . . any . . . improper basis." In 2000, the California Supreme Court agreed to consider the appropriateness of this instruction, which three districts of the California Court of Appeal had upheld.

Dougherty and other Vietnam-era decisions declining to inform jurors of a "right" to nullify had indicated that jury nullification could be appropriate. They had sought only to specify the terms on which this nullification would occur. Thirty years later, however, a juror's advocacy of nullification on the terms *Dougherty* approved could lead to the juror's dismissal. Moreover, this juror's fellows could be instructed to assume the jury's long-abandoned role as witnesses, monitoring the jury room on behalf of the court to facilitate the rebellious juror's expulsion.

Conclusion

Jury trial, once a routine, reasonably summary procedure for resolving criminal cases, has become one of the world's most cumbersome adjudicative mechanisms and one of the least accessible. In practice, this form of trial has been largely replaced by an administrative regime of plea bargaining. Jury trial now confronts some of the same challenges as other democratic institutions. Just as candidates for public office appear to be getting better at manipulating voters, lawyers, aided by professional jury consultants, appear to be getting better at stacking juries and manipulating jurors. Simplifying jury-selection and trial procedures to reduce the importance of the lawyers' maneuvering might better enable juries to speak for the community and also might make fair and workable trials more accessible to defendants and the public.

ALBERT W. ALSCHULER

See also APPEAL; CRIMINAL JUSTICE PROCESS; CRIMINAL PROCEDURE: CONSTITUTIONAL ASPECTS; GRAND JURY; JURY: BEHAVIORAL ASPECTS; PUBLICITY IN CRIMINAL CASES; SENTENCING: PROCEDURAL PROTECTION; TRIAL, CRIMINAL.

BIBLIOGRAPHY

ABRAMSON, JEFFREY. *We, the Jury: The Jury System and the Ideal of Democracy.* New York: Harper-Collins, 1994.
ADAMS, JOHN. *Legal Papers of John Adams.* Edited by L. Kinvin Wroth and Hiller B. Zobel. Cambridge, Mass.: Belknap, 1965.
ADLER, STEVEN. *The Jury: Trial and Error in the American Courtroom.* New York: Random House, 1994.
ALSCHULER, ALBERT W. "The Supreme Court and the Jury: Voir Dire, Peremptory Challenges and the Review of Jury Verdicts." *University of Chicago Law Review* 56 (1989): 153–233.
———. "Racial Quotas and the Jury." *Duke Law Journal* 44 (1995): 704–743.
ALSCHULER, ALBERT W., and DEISS, ANDREW G. "A Brief History of the Criminal Jury in the United States." *University of Chicago Law Review* 61 (1994): 867–928.
BABCOCK, BARBARA ALLEN. "Voir Dire: Preserving 'Its Wonderful Power.'" *Stanford Law Review* 27 (1975): 545–565.
BLACKSTONE, SIR WILLIAM. *Commentaries on the Laws of England* (star-page edition). (1765–1769). 4 vols. Reprint, Chicago: University of Chicago Press, 1979.
BUTLER, PAUL. "Racially Based Jury Nullification: Black Power in the Criminal Justice System." *Yale Law Journal* 105 (1995): 677–725.
COCHRAN, JOHNNIE L., JR. *Journey to Justice.* New York: One World, 1996.

JEFFERSON, THOMAS. *The Papers of Thomas Jefferson.* Edited by Julian P. Boyd. Princeton, N.J.: Princeton University Press, 1958.
KALVEN, HARRY, JR., and ZEISEL, HANS. *The American Jury.* Boston: Little, Brown, 1966.
KATZ, STANLEY N. "Introduction." In *A Brief Narrative of the Case and Trial of John Peter Zenger, Printer of the New York Weekly Journal* by James Alexander. Cambridge, Mass.: Harvard University Press, 1963.
KERBER, LINDA K. *No Constitutional Right to be Ladies: Women and the Obligations of Citizenship.* New York: Hill and Wang, 1998.
LAFAVE, WAYNE R.; ISRAEL, JEROLD; and KING, NANCY J. *Criminal Procedure,* 3d ed. St. Paul, Minn.: West, 2000.
LERNER, RENÉE LETTOW. "The Transformation of the American Civil Trial: The Silent Judge." *William and Mary Law Review* 42 (2000): 195–264.
MILLER, ROBERT H. "Six of One is Not a Dozen of the Other: A Reexamination of *Williams v. Florida* and the Size of State Criminal Juries." *University of Pennsylvania Law Review* 146 (1998): 621–686.
MULLER, ERIC L. "The Hobgoblin of Little Minds? Our Foolish Law of Inconsistent Verdicts." *Harvard Law Review* 111 (1998): 771–834.
PIZZI, WILLIAM T. "Discovering Who We Are: An English Perspective on the Simpson Trial." *University of Colorado Law Review* 67 (1996): 1027–1036.
SCHMIDT, BENNO C. "Juries, Jurisdiction, and Race Discrimination: The Lost Promise of Strauder v. West Virginia." *Texas Law Review* 61 (1983): 1401–1499.
TOCQUEVILLE, ALEXIS DE. *Democracy in America* (1835, 1840). New York: Knopf, 1945.
ZEISEL, HANS. ". . . And Then There Were None: The Diminution of the Federal Jury." *University of Chicago Law Review* 38 (1971): 710–724.

CASES

Alexander v. Louisiana, 405 U.S. 625 (1972).
Apodaca v. Oregon, 406 U.S. 404 (1972).
Apprendi v. New Jersey, 120 S. Ct. 2348 (2000).
Baldwin v. New York, 399 U.S. 66 (1970).
Ballew v. Georgia, 435 U.S. 223 (1978).
Batson v. Kentucky, 476 U.S. 79 (1986).
Blanton v. City of North Las Vegas, 489 U.S. 538 (1989).
Burch v. Louisiana, 441 U.S. 130 (1979).
Bushell's Case, 124 Eng. Rep. 1006 (Common Pleas 1671).
Carter v. Jury Commission of Greene County, 396 U.S. 320 (1970).

Castaneda v. Partida, 430 U.S. 482 (1977).
Duncan v. Louisiana, 391 U.S. 145 (1968).
Durden v. Missouri, 439 U.S. 357 (1979).
Eubanks v. Louisiana, 356 U.S. 584 (1958).
Georgia v. McCollum, 505 U.S. 42 (1992).
Glasser v. United States, 315 U.S. 60 (1942).
Ham v. South Carolina, 409 U.S. 524 (1973).
Hernandez v. New York, 500 U.S. 352 (1991).
Hill v. Texas, 316 U.S. 400 (1942).
Holland v. Illinois, 493 U.S. 474 (1990).
Hoyt v. Florida, 368 U.S. 57 (1961).
Irvin v. Dowd, 366 U.S. 717 (1961).
J.E.B. v. Alabama ex rel. T.B., 511 U.S. 127 (1994).
Johnson v. Louisiana, 406 U.S. 356 (1972).
Lockhart v. McCree, 476 U.S. 162 (1986).
McKeiver v. Pennsylvania, 403 U.S. 528 (1971).
Morgan v. Illinois, 504 U.S. 719 (1992).
Murphy v. Florida, 421 U.S. 794 (1975).
Neal v. Delaware, 103 U.S. 370 (1881).
Norris v. Alabama, 294 U.S. 587 (1935).
Powers v. Ohio, 499 U.S. 400 (1991).
Purkett v. Elem, 514 U.S. 765 (1995).
Ristaino v. Ross, 424 U.S. 589 (1976).
Sparf and Hansen v. United States, 156 U.S. 51 (1895).
Spaziano v. Florida, 468 U.S. 447 (1984).
Strauder v. West Virginia, 100 U.S. 303 (1880).
Swain v. Alabama, 380 U.S. 202 (1965).
Tanner v. United States, 483 U.S. 107 (1987).
Taylor v. Louisiana, 419 U.S. 522 (1975).
Thiel v. Southern Pacific Co., 328 U.S. 217 (1946).
Turner v. Fouche, 396 U.S. 346 (1970).
Turner v. Murray, 476 U.S. 28 (1986).
United States v. Dougherty, 473 F.2d 1113 (D.C. Cir. 1972).
United States v. Ovalle, 136 F.3d 1092 (6th Cir. 1998).
United States v. Scott, 437 U.S. 82 (1978).
United States v. Thomas, 116 F.3d 606 (2d Cir. 1997).
Wainwright v. Witt, 469 U.S. 412 (1985).
Williams v. Florida, 399 U.S. 78 (1970).
Witherspoon v. Illinois, 391 U.S. 510 (1968).

JURY SENTENCING

See SENTENCING: ALLOCATION OF AUTHORITY.

JUSTIFICATION: THEORY

Introduction

To approach the theory of justification, one needs first to understand what a justification is. A justification renders a nominal violation of the criminal law lawful and therefore exempt from criminal sanctions. For example, if the force used in self-defense against an aggressor is both necessary and reasonable, injuring the aggressor is justified and therefore lawful. Those who act in justifiable self-defense exercise a privilege and act in conformity with the law.

Claims of justification should be distinguished from two other bases for claiming that conduct is not subject to criminal liability. First, someone might argue that his conduct falls wholly outside the criminal law. Killing a fly violates no prohibition of the criminal law; it therefore requires no justification. Killing a human being, intentionally or negligently, does violate a prohibition and therefore the conduct requires a justification to be lawful. Thus, one must distinguish between conduct that violates no general norm (killing a fly) and conduct that nominally, but justifiably, violates a valid prohibition of the criminal law (killing an aggressor in self-defense). A justification concedes the nominal violation of the prohibitory norm but holds that the violation is right and proper.

A claim of justified violation should also be distinguished from the assertion that prohibited and unjustified conduct is excused by virtue of circumstances personal to the accused. The defense of insanity, for example, does not seek to justify the violation of a norm. Rather, the defense concedes that the violation is unjustified, but seeks to exempt the particular actor from responsibility for the unjustified act. A claim of justification maintains that the act is right; a claim of excuse concedes that the act in the abstract is wrong, but argues that the actor is not personally responsible for having committed the act. Injuring an innocent person is wrong, but if the actor is insane, his condition precludes his being held responsible for the wrongful act.

Thus, the issue of justification appears as the second in a set of three ordered questions bearing on criminal liability: (1) Did the suspect's act violate a valid norm of the criminal law? (2) Is the violation of the norm unlawful (justified)? (3) Is the actor personally accountable for the unlawful violation; that is, is the unlawful violation unexcused? A negative answer to any of these three questions terminates the inquiry into liability.

In addition to its function as the second stage in this scheme for analyzing liability, the concept of justification enters into the analysis of several specific legal problems. Western legal systems generally assume, for example, that self-defense is permissible only against unlawful attacks. Because the justified use of force is lawful, self-defense is unavailable against justified force. A police officer's use of necessary force to effect a valid arrest is justified; therefore, the person arrested cannot invoke self-defense to justify forcible resistance to the arrest. In contrast, the excused use of force—by an insane assailant, for example—remains unlawful. Self-defense is therefore permissible against an excused aggressor (Model Penal Code §§ 2.04, 2.11 (1)).

Of course, the law could shift its stand on self-defense so that both justified and excused attacks, or perhaps neither, triggered the right to use force in self-defense. So long as the law and our judgments of just liability remain as they are, however, we shall have to attend to the distinction between justified attacks, which undercut the right to respond with defensive force, and excused attacks, which permit self-defense in response.

Theories of complicity that distinguish between perpetrating an offense and merely aiding another's offense also require attention to the distinction between justification and excuse. Justified conduct no longer qualifies as an offense, but excused conduct might well be though of as an excuse for these purposes. If someone shouts encouragement to an aggressor later to be found insane, is the party shouting encouragement liable for aiding and abetting the offense? If the excused aggression is regarded as no offense at all, then it is difficult to regard the shouting as punishable assistance. How, after all, can one be liable for assisting that which is not a crime? On the other hand, if the assault by the insane actor is regarded as an excused offense, the party aiding the offense could be liable on the basis of his own unexcused aiding of the unlawful assault.

The law of complicity could conceivable be altered so that the party shouting encouragement would be liable as an accomplice regardless of whether the aggression encouraged is excused or justified. Section 2.06(2)(a) of the Model Penal Code seems to effect this alteration by suggesting that an insane perpetrator should be treated as an "innocent or irresponsible agent" in the hands of those aiding and directing him. This section requires, however, that for the party shouting encouragement to be liable, he must "cause" the insane assailant to engage in the assault. For encouragement to qualify as control or causation, the law would have to settle for a diluted conception of causation, which could give rise to problems in other areas. A less troublesome approach would be to treat the concept of offense

as dependent solely on the commission of an unlawful (unjustified) act. Thus, the party shouting encouragement would be liable not for causing an innocent person to act, but for aiding in the commission of an offense by the excused aggressor (Model Penal Code § 2.06(3)(a)).

The concept of justification enjoys, therefore, a distinctive place in the structure of criteria bearing on criminal liability. Of course, skepticism remains possible as to whether working out the three dimensions of criminal liability (prohibited act, justification, excuse) aids one's understanding of criminal liability and contributes to a just resolution of disputed issues. The analysis of self-defense and complicity seems to require attention to the distinction between justification and excuse. Other issues, discussed below, are clarified by the distinction between committing a prohibited act and justifying the prohibited act.

This article considers several theoretical and controversial quandaries that attend the analysis of justificatory claims. First, which issues and defenses in the criminal law are properly regarded as claims of justification? Second, what are the general criteria of justification? Third, what are the respective roles of the legislature and the judiciary in developing claims of justification?

The scope of justification

The paradigmatic claims of justified killing, according to Blackstone, are those "committed for the advancement of public justice" and those "committed for the prevention of any forcible and atrocious crime" (p. 179). The first category is illustrated by police officers' shooting and injuring escaping convicts and suspects; the second by killing in self-defense or in defense of one's home. In addition to these standard instances, most twentieth-century codes recognize a justification based on the benefit of violating the law exceeding the cost of doing so. Think of an abortion committed to save the life of the mother. Or consider the temporary taking, without permission, of a neighbor's car as the fastest means of transporting a sick child to the hospital. A justification based on these facts would typically be called "necessity." Yet, to avoid confusion with necessity treated as an excuse, this article will refer to the justification based on competing costs and benefits as "lesser evils."

One must now compare the issue of consent, which arises notably in cases of larceny, rape, and battery. There are two plausible interpretations of consent in these cases. It has been assumed so far that a victim's being alive and human is an element of the norm defining homicide. Arguing, for example, that a fetus is not a human being denies that a particular act of killing violates the norm against homicide. It is generally assumed, in contrast, that the absence of self-defense is not an element of the prohibition against killing. As a claim of justification, the assertion of self-defense concedes the violation of the norm. Now the question with regard to consent is this: Is nonconsent an element of the norms prohibiting rape, larceny, and battery, or is consent a claim of justification? In other words, is the issue of consent analogous to the problem whether the fetus is a human being protected by the law of homicide, or does consent resemble self-defense, an issue that is taken to be extrinsic to the norm prohibiting homicide?

The classification of consent has practical consequences. It might influence the allocation of the burden of persuasion or the burden of raising the issue at trial. It might lead to the imposition of certain requirements for making a valid claim of consent, requirements that are characteristic of either of elements of the prohibitory norm or of justificatory claims. These practical implications are discussed below. For now, we should attempt to resolve the problem of classification by bringing to bear our understanding of the nature of prohibitory norms and claims of justification.

The essential feature of a justification, as opposed to the negation of a prohibitory norm, is that even though the justification applies, we sense that significant harm has occurred. If we do not perceive the fetus at the early stages of gestation as a human being, then abortion is not regarded as a justified killing but rather as an operation of no greater moral significance than other operations. Yet, killing in self-defense leaves one with a sense of regret that a human being has been sacrificed to the defender's interest in self-preservation. That sense of regret testifies to the violation of the norm implicit in treating the act as justified.

If consent is measured against this standard, we should be hard-pressed to regard most instances of consent as claims of justification. In the case of consent to a medical operation or to sexual intercourse, most of us would not sense the occurrence of harm in the contact with the patient's or the partner's body. The consent in these instances does not generate a good reason for causing harm; rather, the consent seems to dissolve the potential harm into a cooperative good. The

dissolution of the harm makes it difficult to say that a consensual operation or consensual sexual intercourse constitutes even a nominally prohibited act. The notion of justification does not come into play in these cases, for there is no violation that requires justification.

Yet, there are some instances of forcible intrusion where one might well regard consent as a justification. For example, even if there is no consent to a sadomasochistic beating or to intercourse achieved by force, the prohibition against forcible bodily contact appears to be violated. Consent would seem, at most, to be a justification. If the victim wishes to be beaten or to be taken by force, then a nonpaternalist legal system might well regard the victim's consent as a good reason for the actor's using force.

Whether one takes nonconsent to be an element of the prohibition or consent to be a justification depends, finally, on how one perceives the interest protected by the legal system. Is there a general interest in not permitting forcible, nontherapeutic bodily contact? Is this interest violated even in cases of consent? If so, then consent functions at most as a justification for violating the norm protecting this legal interest. Unfortunately, the positive law supplies no answer to this basic question. The way in which the interests underlying the criminal law are perceived depends on a collective judgment of the values basic to society. However society expresses those judgments, its claims of value are open to disagreement and dispute. The classification of consent does not lend itself to clear resolution.

The distinction between claims of justification and claims of excuse proves to be easier to work out than that between justification and elements of the prohibitory norm. Two aspects of self-defense illustrate the distinction. Historically, the common law distinguished between excusable homicide in cases of *se defendendo* (personal necessity) and justifiable homicide, based on a sixteenth-century statute, 24 Hen. 8, c. 5 (1532). Both *se defendendo* and the statutory defense were versions of self-defense. Yet, a plea of *se defendendo* could result at most in an exemption from execution; the successful defendant still suffered forfeiture of his property. In contrast, a successful assertion of the statutory defense resulted in an acquittal, without forfeiture of property.

The common law claim of *se defendendo* functioned as an excuse rather than a justification. The claim did not presuppose that the homicide victim had initiated the fight. If the fight occurred as a "chance medley" and the defendant then retreated as far as he could and only then killed rather than be killed, the killing would be *se defendendo*. The claim was grounded in the necessity of the defendant's saving himself, not in the rightness of the killing. The survivor of the chance medley was not held "wholly blameless," as Blackstone put it (p. 187), and therefore suffered a forfeiture of property. In contrast, the statutory defense was grounded in a theory of justification: it recognized the right of innocent persons to defend themselves against aggressors.

Within the contours of self-defense as a justification, controversy persists whether putative self-defense qualifies as a justification. Putative self-defense arises if the defender mistakenly believes that he is under attack. He injures or kills the innocent person he regards as the aggressor and then seeks to avoid liability for battery or homicide. Both the common law and American legislation group putative self-defense with actual self-defense. West German law rigorously distinguishes between the two, and this position appears to be the better considered. It is difficult to maintain that the defender's belief by itself creates a right to injure an innocent person. Even if the belief is reasonable, there appears to be no warrant for regarding the defendant's act as justified. Justification in cases of self-defense presupposes actual aggression, not merely a belief in aggression. The more plausible view is that the defendant's reasonable belief that he is being attacked merely excuses his injuring or killing the innocent person. Under the current state of the law, it should be noted, treating the defense as an excuse does not entail forfeiture of property.

The criteria for justification

Three general questions run through efforts to understand the criteria of justification. First, is there one rationale or several to explain why the law recognizes lesser evils, self-defense, defense of others, defense of property, and the use of force in law enforcement as justified? Second, what is the point of requiring an "imminent risk" of harm as a condition for justified force? Third, what is the relevance of the actor's intent in assessing whether his conduct is justified?

Balancing interests and moral qualifications. Those who advocate a unified theory of justification take lesser evils to be the paradigmatic justification. Consistent with this view, the Model Penal Code uses the label "justification generally" to refer to its provision on lesser evils.

Taking lesser evils as the paradigm, one is led to regard other justifications, self-defense in particular, as specific applications of the principle justifying the sacrifice of the lesser interest to save the greater.

The view that self-defense is but an instance of lesser evils encounters an immediate difficulty. Virtually all Western legal systems regard it as permissible to use deadly force to prevent rape, to prevent serious bodily injury, and even, in some cases, to protect property. That is, the doctrine of self-defense permits on to sacrifice the greater interest (the life of the aggressor) in order to protect the lesser interest (property or sexual and bodily integrity). This disparity does not lend itself to ready explanation under the principle commanding sacrifice of the lesser interest.

The context of defensive force is distinguished by the wrongdoing and culpability of the aggressor. These factors lead one to discount the interests of the aggressor. If the aggressor's interests are sufficiently discounted—if they are, as it were, partially forfeited—one can perceive the interests of the innocent defender as superior. The weight that attaches to the aggressor's wrongdoing and culpability depends upon how responsible we regard aggressors for their conduct. If the aggressor is viewed as self-actuating and fully responsible, we should be inclined to discount his interest to the point that even minor interests of the defender would permit the use of deadly force, when necessary, to ward off the aggression.

This interpretation of self-defense illustrates the limits of lesser evils as a paradigmatic justification. The moral factors of wrongdoing and culpability tilt the scales against the aggressor. Yet, these moral factors themselves do not enter the scales as interests that can be balanced against other interests.

Similarly, some cases of permissible abortion, such as abortion to protect the physical health of the mother, might be interpreted as instances of lesser evils. Again, the balancing seems to be skewed against one set of interests (those of the fetus) in favor of another (those of the mother). The skewing derives from treating the fetus as a being with a legal status lower than that of the mother; otherwise, one could hardly regard killing the fetus as the lesser evil. Assessing the legal status of the fetus poses a moral question that goes beyond the balancing of interests.

In all these examples, the principle of lesser evils admittedly lies at the core of the inquiry into justification. In some cases, however, moral factors enter the analysis and skew the balancing against the victim of justifiable force.

The requirement of imminent risk. As a second general requirement, the law recognizes claims of lesser evils and self-defense only in cases of emergency. This requirement is expressed in various ways, generally by variations on the phrases "imminent risk" or "direct and immediate risk" as descriptions of the threatened harm justifying the nominal violation of the law. This requirement appears puzzling when it is recognized that the costs and benefits of the defendant's conduct might be exactly the same even though the conduct does not respond to an imminent risk. If, for example, some judges regard the blowing up of the Alaska pipeline as a lesser cost than the feared danger of the pipeline to the environment, why should a private citizen not be able to take the fate of the pipeline into his own hands? As the Model Penal Code defense of lesser evils is formulated—without an explicit requirement of imminent risk—blowing up the pipeline to protect the greater good might well be justified (§ 3.02(2)).

Yet, allowing individual judgments of costs and benefits to range so freely undermines the authority of the legislature to determine the acceptability of such acts as destroying property. Restricting the defense of lesser evils to cases on imminent risk ensures that the legislative prohibition receives due respect. Similarly, restricting the use of defensive force to instances of imminent danger ensures that self-defense does not function as camouflaged revenge or as preemptive aggression against a latent threat. The requirement of imminent risk highlights the exceptional nature of both lesser evils and defensive force.

Relevance of intent. As a third distinguishing feature of justificatory claims, most Western legal systems require that the actor know and act on the circumstances that allegedly justify his conduct. For example, a physician may be about to inject air into a patient's veins in order to kill him. Without knowing of the physician's deadly purpose, the patient strikes the physician (perhaps he is angry about the anticipated fee). In this situation, the objective fact of the physician's aggression would, if known by the patient, justify the hostile response. However, since the patient does not know of the aggression, his assault is not justified. The rationale for requiring this knowledge of justifying circumstances is that a justification represents a good reason for violating the

prohibitory norm. The actor does not have this reason; he does not, and cannot, act on the reason unless he knows of the relevant justifying circumstances.

There is thus a practical difference between an issue classified as an element of the prohibitory norm and one classified as a claim of justification. The actor must kill a human being in order to violate the prohibition against homicide. If this element is not satisfied, the actor cannot be guilty of homicide. If, for example, the actor intends to kill but shoots someone who is already dead, the actor is not guilty. It does not matter whether he knows that the intended victim is already dead. Although the objective fact of an already-dead victim precludes conviction for homicide, the objective fact of the victim's aggression does not generate a valid claim of self-defense.

The rationale for this distinction lies in the different roles played by objective circumstances in determining, respectively, whether a norm has been violated and whether the violation is justified. A prohibitory norm is not violated unless all of the objective elements of a violation are present. A predeceased "victim" objectively precludes violation of the norm. A justification, in contrast, does not turn exclusively on objective considerations. As a good reason for violating the norm, a justification requires that the actor be aware of, and act in response to, the objective justifying elements.

To summarize, three themes recur in defining the range of particular justifications. First, moral judgments about the relative worth of conflicting interests skew the balance of interests. Second, a requirement of imminent risk restricts the number of cases in which a claim of defending the superior interest is acceptable. Third, claims of justification should, in principle, consist of both objective justifying circumstances and the actor's subjective awareness of and reliance on these circumstances. The theory of justification seeks to understand why these elements are thought to be necessary for sound claims of justification.

The role of the judiciary

Western legal systems now concur in the principle that the legislature has exclusive authority to define criminal offenses. Nonetheless, there are two distinct theories for recognizing the authority of courts both to apply the general principle of lesser evils and to develop new grounds of justification. The American theory, as reflected in the Model Penal Code, rests on the judgment that the circumstances of justification are so multifarious that one cannot expect the legislature to anticipate all the cases in advance and to provide a specific rule for each case. The nature of the situation requires a delegation of legislative authority to the courts to work out particular rules for specific situations of conflicting interests. If, however, the legislature chooses to regulate possible claims of justification in a particular area, such as that of abortion, the assertion of legislative authority preempts the implied authority of the courts. Section 3.02(2) of the Model Penal Code expresses this theory by making it a condition of "justification generally" and in particular of lesser evils, that "a legislative purpose to exclude the justification claimed . . . not otherwise plainly appear."

The West German theory of justification is not based on implied legislative authority but rather on the principle that every criminal offense must meet two conditions: the offense must be a violation of a statutory prohibition, and the offense must be "unlawful." (The term *unlawful* is understood broadly to mean a violation of general principles of wrongdoing.) Since the 1920s the German courts have assumed that they have final authority to determine whether conduct is unlawful or wrongful in this sense. A justified act is not unlawful (wrongful), and therefore, the judicial authority to interpret principles of wrongdoing generates independent authority to devise grounds of justification as yet unrecognized by the legislature. In 1927 the German Supreme Court advanced this theory in recognizing a general justification of lesser evils (61 Entscheidungen des Reichsgerichts in Strafsachen 242 (1927) (Germany)). The new justification received its first legislative endorsement in the new West German criminal code enacted in 1975. With this new code now in force, some German scholars would argue that the courts no longer have independent authority to develop new claims of justification.

The American theory of "implied delegation" and the German theory of "wrongfulness as a requirement of every offense" have generated claims of justification similar in their details. Although reflecting different conceptions of judicial authority, both approaches recognize the important fact that claims of justification always operate for the benefit of the accused.

GEORGE F. FLETCHER

See also EXCUSE: THEORY; GUILT.

BIBLIOGRAPHY

American Law Institute. *Model Penal Code and Commentaries (Official Draft and Commentaries)*. Philadephia: ALI, 1985.
BLACKSTONE, WILLIAM. *Commentaries on the Laws of England*, vol. 4. Reprint. Chicago: University of Chicago Press, 1979.
CORRADO, MICHAEL LOUIS. *Justification and Excuse in the Criminal Law: A Collection of Essays*. New York: Garland, 1994.
DRESSLER, JOSHUA. "New Thoughts About the Concept of Justification in the Criminal Law: A Critique of Fletcher's Thinking and *Rethinking*." UCLA *Law Review* 32, no. 1 (1984): 61–99.
———. "Justifications and Excuses: A Brief Review of the Concepts and the Literature." *Wayne Law Review* 33, no. 4 (1987): 1155–1175.
ESER, ALBIN. "Justification and Excuse." *American Journal of Comparative Law* 24, no. 4 (1976): 621–637.
FLETCHER, GEORGE P. "Proportionality and the Psychotic Aggressor: A Vignette in Comparative Criminal Theory." *Israel Law Review* 8 (1973): 367–390.
———. *Rethinking Criminal Law*. Boston: Little, Brown, 1978.
———. "The Right and the Reasonable." *Harvard Law Review* 98, no. 5 (1985): 949–982.
GREENAWALT, KENT. "The Perplexing Borders of Justification and Excuse." *Columbia Law Review* 84, no. 8 (1984): 1897–1927.
HUSAK, DOUGLAS N. "Conflicts of Justifications." *Law and Philosophy* 18, no. 1 (1999): 41–68.
JESCHECK, HANS HEINRICH. *Lehrbuch des Strafrechts: Allgemeiner Teil*. 3d ed., rev. and enlarged. Berlin: Duncker & Humbolt, 1978.
KADISH, SANFORD H. "Respect for Life and Regard for Rights in the Criminal Law." *California Law Review* 64, no. 4 (1982): 871–901.
Note. "Justification: The Impact of the Model Penal Code on Statutory Reform." *Columbia Law Review* 75, no. 5 (1975): 914–962.
ROBINSON, PAUL H. "A Theory of Justification: Societal Harm as a Prerequisite for Criminal Liability." *UCLA Law Review* 23, no. 2 (1975): 266–292.
———. *Criminal Law Defenses*. St. Paul: West, 1984.
———, and DARLEY, JOHN M. "Testing Competing Theories of Justification." *North Carolina Law Review* 76, no. 4 (1998): 1095–1143.

SCHOPP, ROBERT F. *Justification Defenses and Just Convictions*. Cambridge, England: Cambridge University Press, 1998.

UNIACKE, SUZANNE. *Permissible Killing: The Self-Defence Justification of Homicide*. Cambridge, England: Cambridge University Press, 1994.

JUSTIFICATION: LAW ENFORCEMENT

The law recognizes a privilege for an actor to employ force to prevent crime, to effect a lawful arrest, to prevent an escape from custody, under circumstances where, without the justification of such a privilege, the actor might be charged with assault or even homicide. This category of justifications, like others, arises in cases where the law accepts that a harm is done, or may be done, by the conduct of the actor, but finds that the harm is outweighed by the need to further a greater societal interest. The availability of the justification defenses arising out of law enforcement revolves around the questions whether the actor's use of force is "*necessary* to protect or further the interest at stake," and whether it causes "only a harm that is *proportional*, or reasonable in relation to the harm threatened or the interest to be furthered" (Robinson, p. 217). These considerations are basic in analyzing justifications for actions taken in pursuance of law enforcement. The justifications for actions by law enforcement personnel discussed below are applicable to police officers, peace officers, and on occasion to military personnel when maintaining order; the scope of the coverage may vary from place to place by statute.

Arrest and attendant uses of force

An arrest, which is the act of taking a person into custody for the purposes of the administration of law, may be an assault and battery or a false imprisonment in the absence of a legally recognized basis for the arrest (*Restatement of Torts*, 2d ed.). The law of arrest is governed by the common law, as modified by statute and in the United States by the Fourth Amendment to the U.S. Constitution, which forbids "unreasonable searches and seizures" by government officials, including seizures of the person as in the case of arrest. The Fourth Amendment also provides that a warrant, including a warrant of arrest, may nor be issued by a judge except upon "probable cause." The latter is defined as facts and circumstances sufficient to cause a person of "reasonable caution" to believe that an offense has been committed and that the person to be arrested committed it (*U.S. v Carroll*, 267 U.S. 132, 162 (1925)). In general, an arrest by a public official without probable cause will be considered an unreasonable seizure of the person under the Fourth Amendment.

At common law, a law enforcement officer may make an arrest pursuant to a lawful warrant for any offense; most arrests, as a practical matter, if they are not made in the home, are made without a warrant. A law enforcement officer may lawfully make an arrest without a warrant for any crime, whether felony or misdemeanor, committed in his presence. A law enforcement officer may lawfully make an arrest without a warrant for a felony when he has probable cause to believe that a felony has been committed and that the person to be arrested committed it. Statutes commonly expand the powers of officers, to permit them to make arrests, for example, if they have probable cause to believe that a crime less than a felony has been committed and that the person arrested is the culprit (LaFave and Scott, sec. 5.10; N.Y. Criminal Procedure Law, sec. 140.10).

At common law, a private person may lawfully make an arrest for any felony committed in his presence, or for a misdemeanor that constitutes a breach of the peace (*Restatement of Torts*, 2d ed., sec 119; Dressler, p. 251). A private person can also make an arrest for a felony, even if not committed in his presence, if the felony has been committed and he has probable cause to believe that the person arrested committed it. While Fourth Amendment standards do nor limit the law of arrest by private persons, since the amendment is applicable only to government actions, the law of arrest is sometimes altered by statute to expand or limit powers of arrest by private persons. Thus, for example, the powers may be expanded to permit an arrest for any crime committed in the presence of the person (LaFave and Scott, sec. 5.10). The powers to arrest for a felony not committed in the presence of the citizen may be limited to require that the suspect actually have committed the crime (N.Y. Criminal Procedure Law, sec. 140.30).

In addition, the U.S. Supreme Court has held that a person may be detained temporarily by law enforcement officers for investigation, under circumstances that do not rise to the level of an arrest, if officers have "a particularized and objective basis for suspecting the particular person stopped. . . ." (*U.S. v. Cortez*, 449 U.S. 411, 417 (1981)).

Use of force in connection with arrest or detention

A law enforcement officer may use as much force as he reasonably believes necessary, short of deadly force, to effect a lawful arrest. In the interests of showing that the force is necessary, the officer must state his purpose to arrest the person, unless he believes that the purpose is already known or cannot be made known, for example in the case where making the purpose known would frustrate the arrest (Model Penal Code, sec. 3.07; *Restatement of Torts*, 2d ed., sec. 128). An officer may also use necessary force to prevent a person from escaping from custody (LaFave and Scott, sec. 5.10). A private person, like a law enforcement officer, may use force that he reasonably believes to be necessary short of deadly force to effect a lawful arrest, and must state his purpose under similar circumstances; citizen's arrests of this type are quite unusual.

If an officer or other person uses more force to effect the arrest than he can reasonably believe necessary or proportional in the circumstances, the justification lapses, and the arresting person may be liable for criminal charges or for damages in tort for injuries due to "so much of the force as is excessive" (*Restatement of Torts*, 2d ed., secs. 132–133). Such cases are the ones that typically give rise to charges of "police brutality." In addition, if the actor is a public official the use of excessive force will be an "unreasonable seizure" of the person within the meaning of the Fourth Amendment to the U.S. Constitution. The test whether the force was excessive is an objective one, although, as the U.S. Supreme Court stated in the leading case, "[t]he calculus of reasonableness must embody allowance for the fact that police officers are often forced to make split-second judgments—in circumstances that are tense, uncertain, and rapidly evolving—about the amount of force that is necessary in a particular situation" (*Graham v. Connor*, 490 U.S. 386, 396–397 (1989)).

Police may also use reasonable force to effect a temporary stop, short of an arrest. In connection with such a stop, police are permitted to pat down the suspect for their own safety, to determine whether he has a weapon. They may also use force to detain the suspect; for example, police sometimes draw their weapons to ensure that there is no resistance, which has been held per-

missible at least where a serious crime is suspected (*People v. Robinson*, 68 NY2d 843 (1986)).

International law standards for the lawful use of force are derived directly from the principles of necessity and proportionality that underlie the justification. The United Nations Code of Conduct for Law Enforcement Officials (*UN Code of Conduct*) provides in Article 3, "Law enforcement officials may use force only when strictly necessary and to the extent required for the performance of their duty."

Use of deadly force in connection with an arrest

As noted above, an officer may use as much force as is reasonably necessary, short of deadly force, to retain custody of a suspect. It follows that if the suspect resists, the officer may increase the force to counter the resistance. The officer has no duty to retreat as the force escalates, and if the force should ratchet up to the point where the suspect threatens the officer with death or serious bodily harm, the officer may use deadly force to retain custody (LaFave and Scott, sec. 5.10). "Deadly force" is defined as "force reasonably capable of causing death or great bodily harm" (Geller and Scott, p. 23); while it obviously includes the discharge of firearms, it may also include the use of chokeholds or even automobiles under some circumstances. Pointing a firearm without firing it or making any attempt to fire it is not in itself the use of deadly force.

The standard for the use of deadly force changes when the officer is pursuing a suspect but has not yet been able to arrest him. All the standards stated above are applicable to the use of deadly force to effect an arrest; the officer must reasonably believe that the use of such force is necessary. In addition, however, there is a further limitation under the Fourth Amendment upon the power of a law enforcement officer to use deadly force to effect an arrest. The U.S. Supreme Court stated the standard in 1985: "Where the officer has probable cause to believe that the suspect poses a threat of serious physical harm, either to the officer or to others, it is not constitutionally unreasonable to prevent escape by using deadly force. Thus, if the suspect threatens the officer with a weapon or there is probable cause to believe that he has committed a crime involving the infliction or threatened infliction of serious physical harm, deadly force may be used if necessary to prevent an escape, and if, where feasible, some warning has been given" (*Tennes-*

see v. Garner, 471 U.S. 1, 11–12 (1985)). Garner concerned the shooting of a suspect fleeing from a burglary who was not believed to pose any physical threat; in that case the Court held that the shooting was an unreasonable seizure of the person. The Garner standard is a substantial modification of the common law, which permitted an officer to shoot a fleeing suspect whom he had probable cause to believe had committed a felony, whether the felony was physically dangerous or not. The judgment that underlies the Garner standard is that while shooting a fleeing suspect may sometimes appear necessary to effect the arrest, the use of deadly force is disproportionate in cases where the suspect does not pose a physical danger to the officer or the community.

Even in a case where the use of deadly force is justified, the force used may be found to be excessive, for example, when it is not found to be necessary under the circumstances. In Burton v. Waller, 502 F.2d 1261 (5th Cir. 1974) cert den. U.S. 964, reh. den. 421 U.S. 39, the use of massive firepower in response to a suspected shot by a sniper in a civil disturbance was held to be the excessive use of force.

The standard for the use of deadly force to stop a suspect under international law, also squarely based in the basic principles of necessity and proportionality, is somewhat more restrictive than the standard under the Fourth Amendment. The United Nations Basic Principles for the Use of Force and Firearms by Law Enforcement Officials (UN Basic Principles), which are widely adopted by police throughout the world, provide in Article 9 that: "Law enforcement officials shall not use firearms against persons except in self-defense or defense of others against the imminent threat of death or serious injury, to prevent the perpetration of a particularly serious crime involving grave threat to life, to arrest a person presenting such a danger and resisting their authority, or to prevent his or her escape, and only when less extreme means are insufficient to achieve these objectives. In any event, intentional lethal use of firearms may only be made when strictly unavoidable in order to protect life." In the Case of McCann and others v. UK, ECHR vol. 324 1995)), which concerned a response to a suspected terrorist attack, the European Court of Human Rights, applying the principle of necessity, held that it is not enough to justify every use of deadly force that the actors reasonably believe that the attackers present a threat to life; in addition, the official operation in response must be organized in such a way as to minimize the threat to life.

The standards for the protection of bystanders who may be injured by the lawful use of deadly force vary. At common law, if the action in connection with the arrest was justified, then an injury consequent upon that action would also be justified, and would not be a crime or even a tort (Restatement of Torts, 2d ed., sec. 75) in the absence of negligence on the part of the actor. Although the Model Penal Code proposed the more restrictive standard that the actor may not use deadly force unless he "believes that the force employed creates no substantial risk of injury to innocent persons" (Model Penal Code, sec. 3.07 (2)(b)(iii)), the standard has not been adopted. It is not clear how such a standard could be administered as a matter of the criminal law; if the force used were truly necessary and proportional, then it would seem that an element of criminality is missing from the act.

The standards for the use of deadly force in an arrest by a private person are generally more restrictive than the standards for law enforcement officers. A private person uses deadly force at his peril; he is not privileged to rely upon "probable cause." By the general rule under contemporary law, he may use deadly force only to arrest for a felony dangerous to life when the person arrested has committed the felony (Dressler, sec. 21.03 B2b; Restatement of Torts, 2d ed., sec. 143). On the other hand, since the Fourth Amendment does not restrict actions by private persons, it seems permissible for the states to retain the common law rule that permitted a person to use deadly force to arrest for any felony; the Michigan courts have done so (People v. Couch, 436 Mich. 414 (1990)). Nevertheless, this seems to be an undesirable standard, giving justification for disproportionate force when the crime is not a dangerous felony and unnecessarily encouraging vigilantism.

Use of force for the prevention of crime

At common law, reasonable force short of deadly force may be used by law enforcement officers or private persons to prevent a felony or a misdemeanor that involves a breach of the peace. Deadly force may be used to prevent a felony that threatens death or serious bodily harm, at least if the felony cannot otherwise be prevented (Restatement of Torts, 2d ed., secs. 141–143). The standards for the use of force to prevent crime overlap with those concerning self-defense and the defense of another, as well as the standards concerning the use of force for arrest. Thus, if the actor is the victim of the crime, or is aiding a victim, then standards concerning self-defense will support his actions; similarly the prevention of the crime will often entail an arrest of the offender.

By the standards established in the *Garner* case, discussed above, it appears that the standards for the use of deadly force by law enforcement officers, limiting their discretion to use deadly force in the prevention of crime to cases of life-threatening felonies, are required by the Fourth Amendment; to use deadly force to prevent a felony that does not threaten life would be disproportionate to the crime and an unreasonable seizure of the person. The powers of private persons to use deadly force, however, not being controlled by the Fourth Amendment, may be more expansive than the powers of law enforcement officers. The common law permits an actor in his home, after giving a warning, to repel an intruder with deadly force, and some states, including Louisiana and New York, retain versions of this rule; New York, for example, permits the use of deadly force to terminate a burglary (N.Y. Penal Law, sec. 35.20(2)). The Model Penal Code permits the use of deadly force to prevent dispossession from the dwelling when the attempted dispossession is not under a claim of right (Model Penal Code, sec. 3.06 (3)(d)(i)). Some states have taken the contrary position that rules similar to the common law rule are too permissive, because they would authorize the use of deadly force under circumstances where it may be disproportionate to the crime, and have permitted the use of deadly force only when the intrusion is reasonably believed to threaten life (LaFave and Scott, sec. 5.9).

Prevention of riot

At common law, deadly force could be used to suppress a riot, after an order to disperse and a warning was given. The Model Penal Code retains the rule (Model Penal Code, sec. 3.07(5)(a)(ii)(2). The better version of the rule is that deadly force may be used only when the riot threatens death or serious bodily harm (*Restatement of Torts*, 2d ed., sec. 142). The latter rule would limit the use of deadly force to situations proportionate to the threat and comports with the standard in *Garner*. Although reported cases concerning deadly force in response to riots are rare, one leading case in the United States has

adopted the rule from the Restatement of Torts (*Burton v. Waller*). The cited case arose out of the shooting of students by law enforcement personnel during a riot at a college in Mississippi. The court accepted the standard that deadly force may be used against a riot that threatens life, but held also that the evidence showed that excessive force was used.

International law applies the principles of necessity and proportionality to the suppression of riots as it does to other actions by law enforcement personnel. Article 14 of the UN Basic Principles provides: "In the dispersal of violent assemblies, law enforcement officials may use firearms only when less dangerous means are not practicable and only to the minimum extent necessary."

Prevention of escape

At common law, law enforcement officers were justified in using any necessary force, including deadly force, to prevent an escape from prison. The Model Penal Code adopted this justification in section 3.07 (3) even though in another section (3.07(2)) the Code limited the use of deadly force in the arrest of a fleeing felon by law enforcement officers to cases where the suspect was believed to pose a threat to human life; the distinction was justified on the theory that there is a special public interest in preventing escape by persons in prison. Most states also continue the common law rule, at least when a warning is given before shooting (LaFave and Scott, sec. 5.10). International law takes the position that the use of deadly force against a prisoner escaping is not justified, because deadly force is disproportionate, unless the prisoner presents a "threat to life" (*UN Basic Principles*, Article 9, 16). Some authorities in the United States take a similar position, but the legal situation remains unclear. The Fourth Amendment may not apply, because actions against persons in prison, who are not at liberty, may not be "seizures" of the person; thus the question would be instead whether shooting a prisoner who is not reasonably believed to be a threat to life is "cruel and unusual punishment" under the Eighth Amendment. This question is unresolved at present as a matter of constitutional law. From the point of view of proportionality, the better rule would be that deadly force may be used only against a prisoner who is believed to present a threat of death or serious bodily injury, when other means of preventing the escape (such as a warning) have failed (Mushlin, vol. 1, p. 58).

PAUL G. CHEVIGNY

See also JUSTIFICATION: THEORY; JUSTIFICATION: SELF-DEFENSE; PREVENTION: POLICE ROLE; RIOTS: LEGAL ASPECTS.

BIBLIOGRAPHY

American Law Institute. *Model Penal Code, Official Draft*. St. Paul, Minn.: American Law Institute, 1962.
———. *Restatement of Torts*, 2d ed. St. Paul, Minn.: American Law Institute, 1965.
DRESSLER, JOSHUA. *Understanding Criminal Law*, 2d ed. New York: Irwin/Bender, 1995.
GELLER, WILLIAM, and SCOTT, MICHAEL. *Deadly Force: What We Know*. Washington, D.C.: Police Executive Research Forum, 1992.
LEFAVE, WAYNE, and SCOTT, AUSTIN, JR. *Criminal Law*, 2d ed. St. Paul, Minn.: West, 1986.
MUSHLIN, MICHAEL. *Rights of Prisoners*, 2d ed. New York: McGraw-Hill, 1993.
ROBINSON, PAUL. "Criminal Law Defenses: A Systematic Analysis." *Columbia Law Review* 82 (1982): 199–291.
U.N. Basic Principles on the Use of Force and Firearms by Law Enforcement Officials. New York: United Nations, 1990.
U.N. Code of Conduct for Law Enforcement Officials. New York: United Nations, 1979.

CASES

Burton v. Waller, 502 f3d 1261 (5th Cir. 1974) cert den. 420 U.S. 964, reh. den. 421 U.S.
Case of McCann and others v. UK, ECHR vol. 324 (1995).
Graham v. Connor, 490 U.S. 386, 396–397 (1989).
People v. Couch, 436 Mich. 414 (1990).
People v. Robinson, 68 NY2d 843 (1986).
Tennessee v. Garner, 471 U.S. 1, 11–12 (1985).
U.S. v. Carroll, 267 U.S. 132, 162 (1925).
U.S. v. Cortez, 449 U.S. 411, 417 (1981).

JUSTIFICATION: NECESSITY

The nature and domain of necessity

The prohibitions of criminal law apply in "normal" situations. The various criminal defenses delineate situations that are, in relevant ways, exceptional. Persons may not kill, but the defense of self-defense makes clear that they *may* do so in the exceptional circumstance of being threatened with deadly force. Similarly, one may commit harm with legal impunity if under the influence of a serious, credible, and imminent physical threat, that is, if one acts under duress. The defense of necessity alludes to exceptional circumstances in which compliance with the law is likely to involve greater harm to persons or property than would violating it.

For example, running a stop light may be justified when the passenger in one's car has a medical emergency for which every second counts. A hiker lost in the woods in a sudden ice storm or impending avalanche may seek shelter and trespass in an empty house to save her life. Or an individual fighting a forest fire may have to seize and destroy private property to create a firebreak and prevent still greater damage. In each of these situations, the defense of necessity is available to justify harmful actions when the actor deliberately chooses the lesser evil. The notion of necessity does not, as the term might imply, refer to the absence of choice, the implication that one's actions were necessitated and not freely willed. Rather it implies the actor was appropriately concerned to minimize harm, and in that sense engaged in the kind of conduct that law may reasonably encourage.

Certain limits follow from this understanding of the defense of necessity. The harm-causing violation of a legal prohibition must be the least harmful alternative. It is not available if the actor is aware of other options that would further minimize the breach. By the same token, the actor is not fully exculpated if he creates the situation of choice-of-evils out of negligence. The driver who knowingly uses a car with defective brakes will remain criminally liable for his reckless damage when he swerves to avoid a pedestrian and runs into a shop window. On the other hand, the actor who chooses the *apparent* lesser evil out of a reasonable good faith misunderstanding may nonetheless claim necessity. He may, for example, interrupt two actors rehearsing the assassination scene from *Julius Caesar* by assaulting the actor playing Brutus in the false belief that the threatened stabbing is a genuine attack.

Many recent cases have tested the limits of the necessity defense. So-called pro-life abortion protestors have invoked it as a defense for trespass on the private grounds of abortion clinics and even for killing doctors and nurses (*Wichita v. Tilson*, 855 P2d. 911 (1993)). Necessity has been claimed in euthanasia cases; defendants have argued that the perpetuation of suffering in the face of inevitable death is the greater evil (for example, *Gilbert v. State*, 487 So.2d. 1185 (1986)). Necessity is also arguably relevant as a defense for persons accused of dispensing such prohibited drugs as marijuana for medical purposes (*State v. Tate*, 505 A2d. 941 (1986)). And, for at least four decades, civil disobedients have argued that their violations of law are justified by their cause, whether it is nuclear disarmament, an "immoral" war, or the preservation of the environment.

In general, courts refuse to entertain the necessity defense when a political or moral controversy underlies the assessment of harms or when the authors of the relevant criminal prohibitions can be said to have anticipated and rejected the claim at issue. Clearly a government that has committed itself to a military campaign has made the political decision that failing to act would be worse than acting. Protestors cannot find legal cover in arguing that war is the greater evil. But courts struggle with the application of necessity to euthanasia and drug cases. Were homicide statutes and drug statutes drafted in anticipation of such cases? If not, the necessity defense remains available, if not always persuasive in particular cases.

Contours of the necessity defense

The Model Penal Code, which has generally been a template for many criminal statutes in the last thirty years, describes the necessity defense as follows:

(1) Conduct which the actor believes to be necessary to avoid an evil to himself or another is justifiable, provided that: (*a*) the evil sought to be avoided by such conduct is greater than that sought to be prevented by the law defining the offense charged; and (*b*) neither the Code nor other law defining the offense provides exceptions or defenses dealing with the specific situation involved; and (*c*) a legislative purpose to exclude the justification claimed does not otherwise plainly appear. (2) When the actor was reckless or negligent in bringing about the situation requiring a choice of evils or in appraising the necessity for his conduct, the justification afforded by this section is unavailable in a prosecution for any offense for which recklessness or negligence, as the case may be, suffices to establish culpability. (§3.02)

Statutes based on the Model Penal Code often deviate from it by emphasizing the moral underpinnings of the necessity defense. The New York Penal Law is a good example. Conduct is justifiable when

such conduct is necessary as an emergency measure to avoid an imminent public or private injury which is about to occur by reason of a situation occasioned or developed through no fault of the actor, and which is of such gravity that, according to ordinary standards of intelligence and morality, the desirability and urgency of avoiding such injury clearly outweighs the desirability of avoiding the injury sought to be prevented by the statute defining the offense in issue. (§ 35.05 (2))

The New York statute makes clear that both the actor's weighing of relevant evils and her determination about the exigency of acting must meet "ordinary standards" of judgment. It also implies that the judgment should not be a close call.

Modern versions of the necessity defense tend to follow the Model Penal Code in reaching beyond its historical limitations.

1. Current statutes make clear that the defense is available whether the choice of evils is brought about by natural events—fires, earthquakes, brake failure, shipwreck—or by human agency. For example, several widely discussed cases recognize a necessity defense in prison escape situations (*People v. Lovercamp*, 43 Cal. App 3d. 823 (1974); *U.S. v. Lopez*, 622 F. Supp. 1083 (1987)). Escaped prisoners, under threat of imminent physical assault and injury by fellow prisoners or renegade guards, have argued successfully that escape was the lesser evil. Older statutes, by contrast, limit the necessity defense to natural occurrences.

2. According to most modern statutes necessity is available to defend oneself even against such serious charges as homicide. A defendant may argue that taking one life prevented the otherwise inevitable loss of several lives. For example, homicide and cannibalism have arguably been justified within groups that, stranded in the wild or at sea, faced the risk of imminent starvation. Again, older statutes often limit the necessity defense to circumstances in which the actor brings about nonlethal harm.

3. The necessity defense is not limited to cases in which the actor is personally implicated and avoids harm to himself or his family. Nor is it limited to cases in which the actor acts altruistically. In other words, it does not matter what, if any, stake the actor had in the

harm avoided as long as that harm was arguably the greater evil.

4. Unlike duress, the necessity defense is relevant even if the threat is to property rather than to life or physical well-being.

Note that the necessity defense, as the Model Penal Code makes clear, has both subjective and objective elements. A defendant may use the necessity defense even when her assessment of the situation turns out to be wrong. It may be wrong *ab initio*, as in the mistaken belief that actors rehearsing a murder scene are in fact setting about to commit homicide. It may also be wrong as a prediction. The cannibals, having dined on one of their party, may be rescued sooner than they expect, making their "criminal" conduct unnecessary from the standpoint of hindsight. In such cases the law only requires reasonable understanding and predictive powers. The test is subjective.

On the other hand, the weighing of evils under necessity must fit the shared values of reasonable persons. The captain of a sinking ship cannot justify saving a cargo of valuable paintings at the cost of letting passengers drown. One cannot justify saving the life of a captain of industry or a rock star at the cost of numerous other lives on the grounds that the saved life was more valuable. This aspect of the defense alludes to shared values, and it seems to presume that they are objective.

The fact that the necessity defense presupposes a consensus of values has troubled some commentators (Brudner). They find a crude and untenable form of utilitarianism at its core, and they object that the consequences of our acts do not have natural moral parameters that permit an objective measure of the component of evil. These writers suggest that the underlying determinations about the scope and relevance of the necessity defense in particular cases are moral and complex, involving judgments about harm, intention, motive, and character. Thus, they criticize such formulations as the Model Penal Code for camouflaging this complexity.

Relation to other defenses

Self-defense and legal authority. Commentators have taken contrasting positions on the relation of necessity to other defenses. The Model Penal Code says that it expresses the overarching principle behind legal justification. Other commentators such as P. R. Glazebrook have argued that it is an interstitial concept, designed to fill gaps between other established defenses.

The Code position is easy to understand. If we consider harmful acts that are legally justified because of authority—for example, a policeman assaulting or wounding an escaping felony suspect—the rule that justifies the policeman's act seems to reflect a general conviction that less harm overall is brought about by the coercive acts of the police than would be caused by unrestrained offenders in such contexts. The battery by the policeman is therefore the lesser evil.

Similarly, self-defense can be redescribed as justification based on lesser evils. Less harm overall may be said to occur when persons who are threatened with harm are allowed to respond with force sufficient to repel the threat than when they are not legally empowered to do so. Arguably, even when the choice is between two lives, between the homicidal aggressor and the defending victim, the use of deadly force by the victim manifests less evil than the completion of the original aggression.

The drafters of the Model Penal Code therefore conclude that the necessity defense embodies the general principle of justification. Accordingly, a lesser evils defense should be available as justification whether or not harmful conduct happens to fall under a more specialized defense such as authority or self-defense. The difficulty with this argument, as critics such as Brudner point out, is that it is one thing to say that such circumscribed defenses as authority and self-defense are justified *at a more general level* by reference to the goal of minimizing harm, and it quite another matter to argue that the disposition of particular cases should turn on judgments about relative harm made by individuals faced with hazard. The first is a rule-utilitarian application of the lesser evils analysis to explain familiar defenses; the latter turns it into an act-utilitarian mode of justification.

It is also clear that authority and self-defense are not simply subcategories or instantiations of the general justification of lesser evils. Some situations, for example, fit the criteria of self-defense even if they are hard to justify in terms of lesser evils. In such cases, the harm to the aggressor(s) may be as great or greater than the harm threatened. A case in which self-defense is used lethally against multiple aggressors can be made to fit the necessity formula only if (a) the fact that those killed *were* aggressors is assumed ipso facto to make their actions the greater evil, or (b) recognition of self-defense as justification is said to have second-order benefits that enter in the calculus, such as the effect of discouraging other aggressors, fostering respect for law, and enhancing general security and personal autonomy. Obviously the same issues arise when persons acting under cover of legal authority appear to carry out greater harm than that threatened.

Duress.   Persons who act out of necessity and persons who act under duress do so in the face of threatened harm. Both the theory of necessity and the theory of duress draw attention to the pressure of exigent and extraordinary situations, pressure that prompts a harm-causing response. But necessity focuses on the anticipated consequences of the harming action, the concrete alternatives or choice facing the actor. Duress, on the other hand, focuses on the way in which the choice was made and the extent to which it can or cannot be said to reflect the free will of the actor.

Thus, acting out of necessity, an actor makes the optimal choice, aware that doing so entails a technical violation of the law. An actor under duress also chooses, but in a way that demands qualification. The pressure of the situation is said to be such that a person of reasonable firmness would not be able to resist doing harm. Such harmful actions, done as capitulation to threats, are not to be taken as an expression of the actor's will.

Necessity is generally held to be a justification, while duress is considered an excuse. A person acting under necessity chooses to act in a way that the law seems to approve and encourage, presumably for utilitarian reasons. The person who acts under duress, on the other hand, acts in a way that is generally regrettable and deserves to be discouraged, but the special circumstances make conviction inappropriate and unfair. Unlike necessity, excuses such as duress, intoxication, and provocation (which may mitigate rather than exculpate) refer to situations in which harmful choices may not be representative of the actor's character or desires.

The distinction between the justification of necessity and the excuse of duress has implications for accomplice liability. One who aids a principal acting under duress may be criminally liable (unless the accomplice was also under duress). Excuses are personal. By contrast, those who aid necessary conduct act with impunity. No legal blame can attach to those who help bring about justified acts.

Of course, some situations fall under both defenses. An actor may choose the lesser evil while also acting under duress. Consider, for example, a defendant forced to carry out a nonviolent act of theft by persons who have kidnapped members of her family and threatened to kill them. In general, duress rather than necessity would be the preferred defense in such cases.

Several commentators have criticized the distinction between necessity and duress as artificial and unconvincing. George Fletcher notes that the distinction is rarely made in foreign legal systems. He and others (Brudner, for example) point out that the utilitarian determination at the core of the necessity defense is disturbingly unclear. In cases of stealing bread to avoid starvation, for example, is the weighing to be done narrowly, balancing the threat of death for the starving offender against the financial interests of the baker? Or is the effect on general compliance for law and respect for law of such precedents also part of the account? Critics such as Colvin and Parry conclude if we cannot know what counts in the weighing, we cannot perform the calculus. They argue that what is really at issue is our moral perspective on the actor and a sense of his psychological characteristics as manifested in the act—and that this empathetic adaptation of the law lies at the heart of necessity and duress alike, erasing the difference between them.

Necessity: problematic aspects

The utilitarian bases of the necessity defense are problematic if it is seen as a guide for action, a rule permitting actors to choose the lesser evil even when doing so involves a violation of law. Given the uncertain nature of the determination itself, one may question whether actors will generally be able to choose the lesser evil correctly and whether knowledge of the availability of the defense will lead to its abuse. These difficulties are mooted if one sees the necessity defense, like other defenses, not as a rule of conduct directed at actors but as a rule for courts in assessing culpability retrospectively. From this standpoint, the defense of necessity seems to rest on the principle that it is unfair to punish those who violate the law with the motive of minimizing harm and in the reasonable and sincere belief that they are doing so. Whether or not the defense may be abused, elimination of it would make the law unfair and breed disrespect of it. The cost to society of such disillusionment with law is arguably greater than the risk of abuse of the necessity defense.

To see necessity and other defenses as second-order rules governing the administration of laws rather than as first-order rules directed at actors has an important implication. The first-order prohibitions of criminal law address on intent (or mens rea generally); motive is said to be irrelevant. The defenses, by contrast, bridge intent and motive. When a defendant uses the necessity defense, she concedes that she caused harm intentionally but argues that her motive was to avoid greater harm by doing so. The moral imperative of fairness that seems to underlie necessity forces us to take motive into account.

The extent to which determinations of greater and lesser evil involve more than simple calculi and are embedded in moral assumptions is clear in many examples. Cases in which taking life is arguably the lesser evil almost always go beyond counting lives. In considering cases about persons jettisoned from overburdened lifeboats or persons cannibalized to save the ravaged survivors of shipwreck, courts have asked whether the selection of the victim was fair, whether the survivor owed a duty of care to the victim, and whether the victim acceded to his fate (see *The Queen v. Dudley & Stevens*, 14 Q.B.D. 273 (1884) for a historical treatment of this issue). There is no unanimity about justified killing under necessity even when these complications are absent.

Suppose a healthy autonomous individual were the uniquely compatible donor whose vital body parts, if transplanted efficiently, would save eight patients who otherwise face imminent death. It is clear that kidnapping and sacrificing the donor cannot be defended on grounds of necessity. One moral intuition is that nothing can justify compromising so decisively the autonomy and life of the donor when, unlike the joint shipwreck victims, he has not already been compromised by natural circumstances. It is clear, from this and other examples, that the notion of greater and lesser evils is both indispensable to an understanding of fairness in applying criminal prohibitions and endlessly problematic.

THOMAS MORAWETZ

See also EXCUSE: THEORY; EXCUSE: DURESS; JUSTIFICATION: THEORY; JUSTIFICATION: SELF-DEFENSE.

BIBLIOGRAPHY

American Law Institute. *Model Penal Code and Commentaries: Official Draft and Revised Comments.* Philadelphia: ALI, 1980.

BRUDNER, ALAN. "A Theory of Necessity." *Oxford Journal of Legal Studies* 7, no. 3 (Winter 1987): 339–368.

COLVIN, ERIC. "Exculpatory Defenses in Criminal Law." *Oxford Journal of Legal Studies* 10, no. 3 (Autumn 1990): 381–407.

DAN-COHEN, MEIR. "Decision Rules and Conduct Rules: On Acoustic Separation in Criminal Law." *Harvard Law Review* 97, no. 3 (January 1984): 625–677.

DRESSLER, JOSHUA. *Understanding Criminal Law.* 2d ed. New York: Matthew Bender/Irwin, 1995.

FLETCHER, GEORGE P. *Rethinking Criminal Law.* Boston: Little, Brown, 1978.

FULLER, LON L. "The Case of the Speluncean Explorers in the Supreme Court of Newgarth." *Harvard Law Review* 62, no. 4 (February 1949): 616–645.

GLAZEBROOK, P. R. "The Necessity Plea in English Criminal Law." *Cambridge Law Journal* 30 (April 1972): 87–119.

GREENAWALT, KENT. "The Perplexing Borders of Justification and Excuse." *Columbia Law Review* 84, no. 8 (December 1984): 1897–1927.

PARRY, JOHN T. "The Virtue of Necessity: Reshaping Culpability and the Rule of Law." *Houston Law Review* 36, no. 2 (Summer 1999): 397–469.

ROBINSON, PAUL. *Criminal Law.* New York: Aspen Law & Business, 1997.

SIMPSON, A. W. BRIAN. *Cannibalism and the Common Law: The Story of the Tragic Last Voyage of the* Mignonette *and the Strange Legal Proceedings to Which It Gave Rise.* Chicago: University of Chicago Press, 1984.

WILLIAMS, GLANVILLE. *Criminal Law: The General Part.* London: Stevens, 1953.

JUSTIFICATION: SELF-DEFENSE

Self-defense and defense of others are defenses to a charge of criminal conduct in which the defendant concedes the transgression of a norm or statute against violence, for example, assault or homicide, but maintains that under the circumstances the use of force was either not wrongful (justification) or is wrongful, but it would be unfair to impose punishment (excuse). Either as a justification or as an excuse, the defendant is completely exonerated. In contrast, "imperfect" or "incomplete" self-defense, where a significant element of the defense is absent, mitigates or reduces the charge, for example, from murder to manslaughter.

That one's force is not aggressive but defensive in nature is a defense to criminal conduct in all fifty states and is recognized in nearly every jurisdiction in the world. The pervasiveness of this legal right has its root in a number of extralegal ideas. First, the use of protective force is considered a fundamental, inalienable right of natural law or morality. Second, the Old Testament demands, in the face of violence, that we take an "eye for an eye, a tooth for a tooth." Third, human psychology suggests that using force in self-defense embodies the instinctual and overwhelming impulse toward self-preservation. As the great English legal scholar William Blackstone put it, killing in self-defense embodies "the primary law of nature" (vol. iii, p. 3). Based on this principle of self-preservation, the philosopher Thomas Hobbes, in his rationale for the defense of duress, provides a persuasive account for the illogic of refusing valid claims of self-defense:

If a man by the terrour of present death, be compelled to doe a fact against the Law, he is totally Excused; because no Law can oblige a man to abandon his own preservation. And supposing such a Law were obligatory; yet a man would reason thus, If I doe it not, I die presently; if I doe it, I die afterwards; therefore by doing it, there is time of life gained. (*Leviathan*, chap. 27 (1651))

In other words, faced with certain present death at the hands of a villainous assailant or possible subsequent death from the state's executioner, the will to live inculcated in our human nature is so strong that it would be futile to criminalize self-defense. Though the inevitability and inalienability of self-defense is perhaps self-evident, and serves as a necessary adjunct to the other self-evident truths of the right to life and liberty, the right to self-defense is curiously not a constitutional right (*Rowe v. DeBruyn*, 17 F.3d 1047 (7th Cir. 1994)).

History

The origin of self-defense in Anglo-America is believed to stem from the pollination by the Normans, subsequent to the Norman Conquest of England in 1066, of the Anglo-Saxon conception of the sanctity of life with more nuanced Continental ideas. Previously, any killing, even in self-defense, was culpable. Once the accused was found liable, regardless of blameworthiness, the remedy was either monetary compensation to, or personal vengeance wrought by, the victim's family. Over time, the personal injury nature of a homicide became a public crime against the king, a breach of the king's peace. Private vengeance and reparations gave way to public punishment and forfeiture of the accused's land and possessions to the crown.

Gradually, English jurists began to wrestle with the issue of the relevance of the circumstances of a killing. The promulgation of the Statute of Gloucester in 1278 allowed defendants who killed by accident or in self-defense to apply to the king for a pardon. By the beginning of the fourteenth century, justifiable homicide preserving the king's peace—the execution of a felon sentenced to death or one resisting capture—was distinguished from excusable homicide or *se defendendo*, for example, in self-defense. In 1532, King Henry VIII's parliament enacted a statute that eliminated the forfeiture of property. In 1769, Blackstone explained that justifiable homicide could only be killings required by law that promoted the social good. Personal killings in self-defense could only be excused because they could not be absolutely free from guilt. In excusable homicide, the accused had to retreat to "the wall" before killing (except if he was in his "castle") but in justifiable homicide the accused need not retreat and could even pursue the felon.

Blackstone's interpretation was imported into the New World and became quite influential, indeed it was often the only source of law. As the frontier expanded westward, however, sentiment grew that retreat before using force in the face of a wrongful assault was cowardly and unmanly and gradually the retreat requirement dissolved. (Cynthia Gillespie contends that this male perspective infuses present self-defense law to the detriment of women.) Even today, while eastern states generally retain some form of retreat requirement, most western states do not. Gradually, self-defense became justified even though it did not further the public good in Blackstone's sense.

Theories

Various theories have been advanced, none of which are entirely satisfactory, to account for the law's recognition of the right to use defensive force.

Excuse. Under Blackstone's view, or the *social* theory of self-defense, the rights of the defender are constrained by acknowledging the interests of society; self-defense is only legitimate when it promotes social welfare. For Blackstone, the use of force in the defense of others, apprehending felons, crime prevention, and punishing convicted criminals promoted interests beyond those of who was employing the force and was justifiable. In contrast, the use of force in self-defense only promoted the interests of the defender (not society's interests) and was only excused. The basis for the excuse was that self-preservation is instinctual. The weakness of Blackstone's theory is that it failed to see that a defender vindicating his interests against a wrongful aggressor might benefit society as well.

The *causation* theory suggests that but for the aggressor's attack the victim would not have employed force and thus it is not the defender, but the aggressor who is responsible for the harm to the aggressor. Not being responsible, the defender's force is excused. Under a *character* theory of excuse, it is the aggressor, and not the innocent defender, whose acts manifest a bad character. Thus only the aggressor should be held liable and the defender is excused. Explaining self-defense as merely an excuse is typically thought unsatisfactory because of the intuition that the nature of defensive force is not wrongful.

Justification. The *private punishment* theory justifies defensive force because it inflicts punishment on a deserving wrongdoer instead of, or in addition to, the state. The theory is reflected by the common sentiment heard on the street when a robber or rapist is killed by the victim in self-defense: "He got what he deserved." The philosopher Robert Nozick partially develops the analogy between self-defense and punishment by suggesting that an aggressor's punishment should be reduced by the amount of suffering inflicted upon the aggressor by the defender. Perhaps the original source of the theory may be Blackstone's observation that if a petty thief is not executed by the state for his crime then lethal force is impermissible to prevent the theft. Analogizing Blackstone's observation to self-defense, if a minor assault is not an offense serious enough to warrant the death penalty, then lethal force is impermissible in defense of the assault. Yet the analogy breaks down because permissible defensive force fails to correspond with an aggressor's punishment by the state. For example, though lethal self-defense is permissible against a violent rape, the death penalty is a constitutionally disproportionate punishment for rape (*Coker v. Georgia*, 433 U.S. 584 (1977)).

A number of *utilitarian*-based arguments might be made to justify defensive force. In a deadly conflict in which one person will inevitably die it is better that the innocent defender live and the wrongful aggressor die. This is so because, first, an innocent person's life is worth more than the aggressor's; the aggressor's death constitutes the lesser evil. But this argument violates the principle that everyone is of equal moral worth; no life is more valuable than another. Second, it is better that the aggressor be killed because of the general danger the aggressor poses to future victims. But in many cases of physical conflict it is difficult to ascertain which is the culpable party, or alternatively both parties may be partially at fault (Garrett Epps). Third, permitting the use of defensive force will serve to preserve life by deterring wrongful aggression (lawful resistance creating a disincentive for wrongful aggression) (Herbert Wechsler and Jerome Michael). But whether violence deters violence or only begets more violence is exceedingly controversial.

The *moral forfeiture* theory maintains that by threatening to violate another's right to life or sphere of autonomy, the aggressor forfeits or loses the right to life or autonomy. Defensive force against the aggressor is permissible because it does not violate any right of the aggressor to be free from force. This is so because by the aggressor's own attack, the aggressor has lost the right to life or autonomy. The theory has been extensively criticized because it would seem to justify disproportional, unnecessary, and retaliative force. That is, force would be justified against an aggressor who abandoned the attack, was retreating, or disabled, or who no longer posed a threat to the defender. The philosopher Judith Jarvis Thomson has, in part, rehabilitated the theory to avoid this criticism. The forfeiture of the right to life is made contingent on a present or imminent threat to violate another's right to life; once the aggressor has ceased to be violating another's right to life, the aggressor regains the right to life.

The theory of *personal autonomy*, championed by the philosophers Immanuel Kant, Georg Hegel, and the criminal theorist George Fletcher, emphasizes not the devaluation of the aggressor but the enhancement of the defender's rights. The theory holds that wrongful aggression breaches the sphere of autonomy enjoyed by everyone as well as affronting the abstract concept of Right itself. Since Right must never yield to Wrong, the victim of wrongful aggression not only has the right but the duty to exercise defensive force. Or putting it in Locke's terms, aggression breaches the social contract and returns both aggressor and defender to the state of nature establishing a state of war between the combatants. Since yielding to aggression enslaves the victim, the victim is entitled to use any and all necessary force. But in its absolutist conception of the defender's rights, lethal defensive force must be employed if it is necessary to prevent even a minor assault. Critics argue that the theory goes too far in authorizing disproportional force.

Sanford Kadish's *right to resist aggression* theory postulates that everyone has a right against the state for protection from wrongful aggression. The state licenses the right of self-defense to its citizens because of practical difficulties in providing round-the-clock protection. But because the use of defensive force is only licensed or derived from the state, the state can place reasonable limits on its use and impose, for example, necessity and proportionality requirements. Though avoiding the criticisms of the latter two theories, it succumbs to a different problem. Self-defense is generally regarded as an inalienable, moral right not merely a civic or political right.

Modern law

The leading formulation of self-defense in the United States is contained in the Model Penal Code (MPC), which has influenced the criminal codes of over thirty-five states. Section 3.04 of the MPC is, in part, as follows:

(1) the use of force upon or toward another person is justifiable when the actor believes that such force is immediately necessary for the purpose of protecting himself against the use of unlawful force by such other person on the present occasion.

In the sections that follow the variations between the MPC and state law, as to the principal elements of self-defense, are discussed.

Reasonableness

American law does not require an actual threat of aggression to trigger the right to use force in self-defense, but does require a belief in the necessity of force. This has two ramifications. First, one who uses force against another without the belief that the other poses a threat, when in fact the other is a threat, is not eligible to be justified in self-defense. Second, and more importantly, a defender who mistakenly believes that another poses a threat and uses force against that threat is still eligible to be justified in self-defense. As to the latter case, at issue is just what sort of belief suffices, or alternatively what sort of mistake is acceptable.

The MPC appears to require merely a plain belief and thus allows any mistake. But section 3.09(2) provides that where the mistake is reckless or negligent, a defendant will not be eligible for the defense when charged with an offense in which recklessness or negligence suffices to establish culpability. For those offenses, only a reasonable belief or mistake will establish the defense. But if charged with an offense requiring a higher level of mens rea, even an unreasonable belief or mistake as to the necessity of using force will suffice.

The general approach of the common law and modern statutes is simply to allow the defense if the belief or mistake is reasonable. This is criticized from both sides. Glanville Williams argued for the standard of honest belief because otherwise a negligent or reckless mistake will be punished as an intentional offense. On the other hand, Fletcher and Paul Robinson maintain that even reasonable belief is insufficient; an actual threat is required.

To determine the reasonableness of a belief, the standard is whether a reasonable person in the defendant's situation would believe the use of force necessary. But how much of the circumstances, experiences, and attributes of the defendant should be attributed to the reasonable person? If too much is included—subjectifying the standard to the extent it could become the unreasonable reasonable person standard—the standard becomes meaningless, but if not enough of the defendant's situation is included, the standard may be unfair.

Consider two cases that struggled with this issue. Bernhard Goetz, dubbed the "subway vigilante," shot four African American youths after some of them asked him for five dollars (*People v. Goetz*, 497 N.E.2d 41 (N.Y. 1986)). Claiming that their conduct was the prelude to an armed robbery, Goetz claimed that he acted in reasonable self-defense. In determining whether a reasonable person would have acted as Goetz did, should Goetz's three prior muggings, the prevalence of crime in the New York City subway, and Goetz's beliefs and attitudes about his claimed attackers' race, apparel, sex, and age be included? If so, the standard risks degenerating to what a reasonable racist would have done in the situation. On the other hand, assume *arguendo* that Goetz's views on race and crime were empirically justified; does that make his conduct more reasonable?

In another case, Wanrow, a short woman with a broken leg and using crutches, shot and killed in her home Wesler, a large, inebriated man (*State v. Wanrow*, 559 P.2d 548 (Wash. 1977)). Though not presently attacking her when she shot him, she claimed that he had startled her. Are Wanrow's suspicions that Wesler had attempted to sexually molest her son, did molest her neighbor, and had been in a mental institution to be attributed to the reasonable person? Additionally, is the reasonable person a large, athletic man or a short, slight, woman on crutches?

What the defendant's situation is meant to include is, according to the MPC, purposely ambiguous so as to leave the issue open to jurors and/or courts to decide. Although most courts have avoided the complete subjectivization of the standard, a considerable amount of the defendant's situation is included. As the *Goetz* court explained, a reasonable person in the defendant's situation may consider:

the physical movements of the potential assailant [,] . . . any relevant knowledge the defendant has about that person [and,]. . .the physical attributes of all persons involved, including the defendant. Furthermore, the defendant's circumstances encompass any prior experiences he had which could provide a reasonable basis for the belief that another person's intentions were to [attack] . . . him or that the use of deadly force was necessary under the circumstances. (*Goetz*, p. 52)

Though this standard leaves open many questions, the law will continue to grapple with the issue as it lurches toward a consensus.

Necessary force

That the force used must be necessary encompasses a number of requirements. First, force may not be used unless the situation requires that some force be used. If, without retreating, the threat may be safely prevented without the use of force, then force is unnecessary. Second, the amount of force used must be the minimally necessary force to thwart the attack. Third, the amount of necessary force used

must be proportional in relation to the gravity of the harm threatened.

Necessary force and proportional force must be carefully distinguished. Force may be necessary but disproportional. For example, it may be the case that only lethal force will thwart a minor assault. Though necessary, lethal force to prevent a minor assault is disproportional. Force may also be proportional but unnecessary. Suppose a frail, old woman attempts to attack a martial arts master with a knife. Defending against a potentially lethal attack, the master's use of lethal force is proportional. But it would not be the minimally necessary force if the master could safely grab the knife out of the woman's hand.

There is some dispute as to the limitation of proportional force where to repel the aggression disproportional force is necessary. The law of self-defense must make a choice between an innocent victim suffering a comparatively minor harm from an aggressor's attack because of the inability to repel the attack using only proportional force and an aggressor suffering comparatively greater harm from the defender's use of disproportional force. While American law has chosen the former option, the moral forfeiture and personal autonomy theories, which dispense with the proportionality requirement, have chosen the latter. The argument is that if either an innocent victim or a wrongful aggressor must suffer an unjust harm, it is preferable that the aggressor sustain the harm from disproportional force. After all, the aggressor has created the situation and is responsible for the necessity of the innocent victim to use force. Furthermore, the aggressor has chosen the type of attack and the type of victim who, under the circumstances, is unable to thwart the attack without using disproportional force. As a result, it is the aggressor who should bear the burden of sustaining any unjust harm.

The limitation of proportional force is particularly problematic where there is a significant disparity in the physical prowess between the aggressor and the defender, especially where the aggressor is a large man and the defender is a slight woman. The large man may repeatedly attack the slight woman with substantial but nonlethal force, which the slight woman is unable to defend against without using lethal force. Increasingly, but not uniformly, the law has moved in the direction of relaxing the proportionality requirement in just such cases. In addition, the admission of battered woman syndrome evidence may make the defender's use of disproportional force nonetheless reasonable and justified. The continued adherence to some form of the proportionality requirement may be best defended by the need to deter escalations of violence and the view that human life, even those of aggressors, should be preserved.

Deadly force and the duty to retreat

Deadly force is eligible to be justified in self-defense against attacks risking death or serious bodily injury, forcible rape, and forcible kidnapping. The majority rule that deadly force may be employed without retreating is defended on the grounds that retreat is unmanly and thus unreasonable, Right should not yield to Wrong, and that it deters aggression. The minority rule that deadly force should not be used if the defender is aware of the ability to retreat in complete safety is justified by its placing a higher value on human life than an archaic sense of "manly" honor. Even under the minority rule requiring retreat, according to the "castle" exception, one need not retreat if one is attacked in one's home, and in some states, one's place of business. In most states adopting the retreat rule, one need not retreat if attacked in the home even if it is by a co-dweller.

An initiator of deadly aggression may regain the right to use deadly force only after completely withdrawing from the conflict. Courts are split on whether the initiator of nondeadly aggression immediately regains the right to deadly self-defense force against a deadly and disproportional response or whether the initiator must first retreat.

The MPC section 3.04(2) (b) adopts the minority rule requiring retreat, if it can be done safely, before resort to deadly force with the exception of when the defender is at work or at home. If attacked at home by a co-dweller, the defender need not retreat; if attacked at work by a coworker, the defender must retreat. In another exception, the defender need not continue to retreat once the defender has already retreated and the aggressor has pursued the defender. One who initiates a deadly conflict may not use deadly force without first completely withdrawing from the conflict. One who initiates a nondeadly conflict and faces a response of deadly force may use deadly force under the same conditions as an ordinary defender.

Unlawful threat

Force in self-defense may only be used against a threat of unlawful force. Conduct that satisfies the definition of a criminal offense or tort is unlawful. But if such conduct is justified it is lawful; if the conduct is only excused it is unlawful. The definition of unlawful force in MPC section 3.11(1) is essentially the same as the common law except for also including unlawful confinement even if it does not involve any physical force.

Self-defense force cannot be justified in self-defense then against a police officer using lawful force to make a lawful arrest. If the police officer uses excessive and thus unlawful force, nondeadly self-defense force against it is justified. At common law, there was generally a right to resist an illegal arrest due to lack of probable cause, absence of warrant, or an improperly issued warrant. However, some states have now eliminated the right to resist such technically illegal arrests (e.g., Cal. Pen. Code 834a (1985)). The MPC similarly disallows self-defense against technically illegal arrests but does allow self-defense against excessive force arrests (section 3.04(2)(a)(i)). The trend toward eliminating the right to resist technically illegal arrests may be due to the amelioration of the harsh consequences following an arrest and the increased seriousness of resisting armed officers.

Imminence

Self-defense is crucially a matter of timing. If the defensive force is used too soon in relation to the fruition of the threatened aggression, the force is a preemptive attack and unjustified. If used too late, that is, after the aggression is complete, it is retaliation and is also unjustified. The general rule is that defensive force can only be used against aggression that is imminent or about to occur (*State v. Norman*, 378 S.E.2d 8 (N.C. 1989)). The rationale of the imminence standard is that it ensures that defensive force is used neither too late nor too soon; defensive force should be used only when absolutely necessary. The rule has been heavily criticized for barring self-defense in situations where defensive force is necessary to prevent a certain, but distant (in time), attack. Supporters of the imminence rule rejoin that it insures that defensive force is used only against certain attacks and not speculative ones. But the imminence rule is overinclusive: not all imminent attacks will come to pass, even imminent attacks may be abandoned or frustrated. Richard Rosen argues that the real principle involved is that defensive force must be necessary (380). Imminence is a good proxy for the principle, but where the proxy and the principle diverge, the principle should control.

In spousal abuse cases, the imminence standard is particularly problematic. When a powerful man's attack is imminent, a slight woman's defensive response may be ineffective. However, force used at a point when the attack is not quite imminent but is nonetheless fairly certain might be effective. Joshua Dressler argues that one difficulty with relaxing the imminence requirement, for example, allowing a battered spouse to use force used against the battering, but sleeping spouse, is that it might trigger a right of self-defense in the battering spouse.

Under the MPC, force may be used not merely when the threat of aggression is imminent but when defensive force is "immediately necessary . . . on the present occasion." Though allowing force to be used sooner than the imminence standard, it may still not suffice to aid battered women or defenders in other situations. For example, suppose you are wrongfully being held captive and are told that you will be killed in ten days. Your best chance to escape is when you are brought food each day by your captor. On day five your captor lets down his guard and you kill him and escape (Kadish, p. 832). Though your force is not imminent or even immediately necessary, as under the MPC, it certainly seems necessary and arguably should be justifiable self-defense.

Risk to innocent bystanders

If a defender, who is justified in using force against an attacker, instead (or also) accidentally harms (or risks harm to) an innocent bystander, the defender does not lose the justification for harming the aggressor. Is the defender's harming the bystander also justified? Generally, the defendant's harm to the innocent bystander is also justified (*Smith v. State*, 419 S.E.2d 74 (Ga. Ct. App. 1992)). But the defendant may not be justified if he acts carelessly or endangers a large number of bystanders. Under the MPC, recklessly or negligently harming an innocent bystander would not be a justification for an offense in which recklessness or negligence suffices to establish culpability (section 3.09(3)).

The issue becomes more difficult where it is unclear whether the innocent is a bystander or part of the threat. A famous hypothetical supposes that an aggressor is driving a tank, with a baby strapped to the front, at you intending to run over and kill you. Your only defense is to fire an anti-tank gun which you know will kill both the aggressor and the baby (Nozick). While the moral forfeiture theory would not find your killing the baby justifiable because the baby has not forfeited its rights by any culpable wrongdoing, the personal autonomy theory might justify the killing of the baby so as to prevent Wrong triumphing over Right. A utilitarian theory might also find that the killing of two to save one is not justified.

Defense of others

At early common law, the right to defend others was only extended to family members and employees. In addition, an intervenor's force was only justified if the third party being defended would in fact also have been justified in self-defense; the intervenor was put in the shoes of the party being defended. These limitations on the right to defend others—the act-at-peril rule—has now become the minority rule. The majority rule, largely through the influence of the MPC, is that an intervenor may come to the aid of any person if the intervenor reasonably believes that such force is necessary to defend a third party from unlawful force.

The limitation on who may be aided may be defended by the greater chance of error when defending another as compared to defending oneself. But where an intervenor was defending a family member or employee, rather than a stranger, this risk of error was reduced. Furthermore, the efficacy of a rule prohibiting one from defending a family member would likely have little deterrent effect. The act-at-peril rule also reflects the concern that, due to the enhanced risk of error in defense of others, the preservation of life would be better promoted by restricting defense of others (Wechsler and Michael). An intervenor mistakenly coming to the aid of a criminal being lawfully arrested by undercover officers may have been a particular concern (*People v. Young*, 183 N.E.2d 319 (N.Y. 1962)).

The modern majority rule views these concerns as being outweighed by the importance of citizens not being deterred from coming to the aid of others in need. Furthermore, punishing intervenors for the use of force despite the reasonable appearance that such force was necessary might entail punishing nonblameworthy

904 JUSTIFICATION: SELF-DEFENSE

conduct. The MPC largely applies the majority rule (section 3.05).

Conclusion

The debate over which limitations should be placed on the right to self-defense arises from the delicate balancing of interests of the aggressor and the defender. The disagreement is testament to the quandary self-defense represents to the belief in the sanctity of life and the suppression of violence: The goal is to craft a formulation of self-defense that maximally protects the autonomy of innocent victims while not authorizing such excessive violence as to turn the aggressor into another victim. Another dimension to this delicate balance is the relationship between the defender and the state. Putting it in the terms of Locke's and Hobbes's social contract theory, the law of self-defense ideally should not so overly restrict the defender so as to provide less protection than would be enjoyed in the state of nature. Nor should it be so uninhibited so as to usurp the virtual monopoly power over the use of force that the defender has ceded to the state to better the dismal condition of mankind in the state of nature. The proper balance lies somewhere between the vengeance of the Old Testament and the pacifism of the New Testament.

RUSSELL CHRISTOPHER

See also DOMESTIC VIOLENCE; JUSTIFICATION: THEORY; JUSTIFICATION: LAW ENFORCEMENT; JUSTIFICATION: NECESSITY; SCIENTIFIC EVIDENCE.

American Law Institute. *Model Penal Code and Commentaries: Official Draft and Revised Comments.* Philadelphia, Pa.: The American Law Institute, 1985.
ALEXANDER, LARRY. "Self-Defense, Justification, and Excuse." *Philosophy & Public Affairs* 23 (1994): 53–66.
BLACKSTONE, WILLIAM. *Commentaries on the Laws of England.* Birmingham: The Legal Classics Library, Gryphon, 1983.
BROWN, RICHARD MAXWELL. *No Duty to Retreat: Violence and Values in American History and Society.* New York: Oxford University Press, 1991.
CHRISTOPHER, RUSSELL L. "Mistake of Fact in the Objective Theory of Justification: Do Two Rights Make Two Wrongs Make Two Rights. . .?" *The Journal of Criminal Law & Criminology* 85 (1994): 295–332.
———. "Self-Defense and Defense of Others." *Philosophy & Public Affairs* 27 (1998): 123–141.
DRESSLER, JOSHUA. *Understanding Criminal Law,* 2d ed. New York: Matthew Bender/Irwin, 1995.
———. "Battered Women, Sleeping Abusers, and Criminal Responsibility." *Chicago Policy Review* 2 (1997): 1–16.
EPPS, GARRETT. "Any Which Way but Loose: Interpretive Strategies and Attitudes Toward Violence in the Evolution of the Anglo-American 'Retreat Rule.'" *Law & Contemporary Problems* 55 (1992): 303–331.
FINKELSTEIN, CLAIRE O. "Self-Defense as a Rational Excuse." *University of Pittsburgh Law Review* 57 (1996): 621–649.
FLETCHER, GEORGE P. "Proportionality and the Psychotic Aggressor: A Vignette in Comparative Criminal Theory." *Israel Law Review* 8 (1973): 367–390.
———. *Rethinking Criminal Law.* Boston: Little, Brown, 1978.
———. *A Crime of Self-Defense: Bernhard Goetz and the Law on Trial.* New York: The Free Press, 1988.
GILLESPIE, CYNTHIA K. *Justifiable Homicide: Battered Women, Self-Defense, and the Law.* Columbus, Ohio: Ohio State University Press, 1989.
GREENAWALT, KENT. "The Perplexing Borders of Justification and Excuse." *Columbia Law Review* 84, no. 8 (1984): 1897–1927.
HUSAK, DOUGLAS. *Philosophy of Criminal Law.* Totowa, N.J.: Rowman, Littlefield, 1987.
KADISH, SANFORD H. "Respect for Life and Regard for Rights in the Criminal Law." *California Law Review* 64, no. 4 (1976): 871–901.
MAGUIGAN, HOLLY. "Battered Women and Self-Defense: Myths and Misconceptions in Current Reform Proposals." *University of Pennsylvania Law Review* 140, no. 2 (1991): 379–485.
NOZICK, ROBERT. *Anarchy, State, and Utopia.* New York: Basic Books, 1974.
ROBINSON, PAUL H. *Criminal Law Defenses.* St. Paul, Minn.: West, 1984.
———. *Criminal Law.* New York: Aspen, 1997.
ROSEN, RICHARD. "On Self-Defense, Imminence, and Women Who Kill Their Batterers." *North Carolina Law Review* 71, no. 2 (1993): 371–411.
SCHOPP, ROBERT F. *Justification Defenses and Just Convictions.* Cambridge, U.K.: Cambridge University Press, 1998.
SCHULHOFER, STEPHEN. "The Gender Question in Criminal Law." *Social Philosophy & Policy* 7 (1990): 105–137.
THOMSON, JUDITH JARVIS. "Self-Defense." *Philosophy & Public Affairs* 20 (1991): 283–310.

UNIACKE, SUZANNE. *Permissible Killing: The Self-Defense Justification of Homicide.* Cambridge, U.K.: Cambridge University Press, 1994.

WECHSLER, HERBERT, and MICHAEL, JEROME. "A Rationale of the Law of Homicide." *Columbia Law Review* 37, no. 3 (1937): 701–761.

WILLIAMS, GLANVILLE. *Textbook of Criminal Law,* 2d ed. London: Blackwell, 1983.

ZIPURSKY, BENJAMIN C. "Self-Defense, Domination, and the Social Contract." *University of Pittsburgh Law Review* 57 (1996): 579–614.

CASES

Coker v. Georgia, 433 U.S. 584 (1977).
People v. Goetz, 497 N.E.2d 41 (N.Y. 1986).
People v. Young, 183 N.E.2d 319 (N.Y. 1962).
Rowe v. DeBruyn, 17 F.3d 1047 (7th Cir. 1994).
Smith v. State, 419 S.E.2d 74 (Ga. Ct. App. 1992).
State v. Norman, 378 S.E.2d 8 (N.C. 1989).

JUVENILE AND YOUTH GANGS

Estimates of the magnitude of youth gang problems in the United States steadily increased over the last decades of the twentieth century. An unprecedented public and government response to gang problems at federal, state, and local levels began in 1989. As the century drew to a close, evidence of a leveling off of the scope of gang problems began to emerge. For two consecutive years, in 1997 and 1998, the national estimates of law-violating gangs and gang members tabulated by the Office of Juvenile Justice and Delinquency Prevention's National Youth Gang Center suggested small declines in the total number of city and county jurisdictions reporting youth gang problems. Any relief associated with observing slight reversals in the proliferation of gang problems is diminished by the levels attained by these problems between 1980 and 1995.

History

Gangs are not new, and in fact are found increasingly all over the world. Veteran researchers such as Walter Miller and Malcolm Klein suggest that the United States has experienced numerous cycles of gang activity. In response to rumors of violence against him from Baltimore gangs, President Abraham Lincoln disguised himself in his passage through that city on his way to his first inauguration. Fighting between adolescent gangs in Richmond, Virginia, trou-

bled Jefferson Davis to the point that he tried to intervene personally. When cities experienced immigration and industrial development in the latter part of the nineteenth century, organized adolescent groups heavily involved in crime can be identified as gangs were reported to be active in New York, Philadelphia, Boston, Chicago, St. Louis, and Pittsburgh as early as 1870. Disorganized aggregations of the children of immigrants from Ireland and Italy roamed the streets of their neighborhoods, largely as disorganized groups, engaged primarily in petty forms of property and crime and directing violence against one another and members of rival gangs.

As immigration patterns varied so did the composition of youth gangs. Levels of violence varied across the decades. In the 1920s, Frederic Thrasher of the University of Chicago became the best known early academic researcher of gangs. Thrasher emphasized the distinction between youth gangs and organized crime and the relationship between the changing ecology of urban areas and gang activity. William Foote Whyte portrayed the gangs of the Depression with young adult members who had few other alternatives outside the gangs of their youth. For the first time, the gangs of the 1960s were composed of significant numbers of racial and ethnic minorities. While levels of violence varied with criminal opportunities and the availability of weapons and eventually automobiles, it is important to recognize the social parallels of gang activity in the United States over the decades. Throughout U.S. history gang activity has tended to be concentrated in urban area heavily populated with families from the lower strata of the social and economic hierarchy.

Gangs are not confined to the United States. Gangs have been reported in many of the nations that emerged from the break-up of the former Soviet Union and Soviet bloc nations. Conflicts between gangs identifying themselves as "bloods" and "crips" have been reported in New Zealand. Klein has documented the growing number of European nations plagued by emerging youth gangs, including Germany, Holland, and France. The role of popular culture, particularly in the export of American cultural images through movies, music, and other forms of media, has had an important impact on this development.

Scope of gang problems

Efforts to estimate the number of gangs, gang members, and gang crimes as a national problem were not attempted until 1975. In a government study published that year, Walter Miller concluded that six of twelve major cities had gang problems. Miller estimated that there were 760 to 2,700 gangs and 28,500 to 81,500 gang members in those six gang problem cities. Between 1975 and 1995, the Department of Justice funded at least five national surveys. Each revealed the nation's gang problems to be more serious and more widespread with new problems emerging in the suburban and even rural jurisdictions. By 1993, conservative estimates for the scope of the U.S. gang problem from local law enforcement records included 8,625 gangs, 378,807 gang members, and 437,066 gang crimes. In 1995, the newly established National Youth Gang Center (NYGC) conducted its first assessment of the national gang problem. A total of 664,906 gang members in 23,388 youth gangs were reported for 1,741 jurisdictions, many of them smaller cities, suburban counties, and rural counties. By linking cities surveyed in 1995 with those surveyed in earlier surveys, G. David Curry and Scott H. Decker showed that there had been an unprecedented increase in the number of cities reporting gang problems between 1993 and 1995.

In an effort to improve the comparability of estimates of the scope of national gang crime problems over time, the NYGC National Gang Survey implemented a systematic annual sampling strategy. It was from comparisons of the 1996, 1997, and 1998 National Gang Surveys that preliminary indications of a leveling off of the great proliferation of gang crime problems were derived. The small declines in the total numbers of jurisdictions nationwide reporting gang problems do not represent uniform decreases in the numbers of jurisdictions with prior gang problems that no longer report a problem. Nor do small declines in gang members or gang-related homicides reflect across the board decreases in such statistics. The small declines in gang problems represent a greater number of jurisdictions with prior identified gang problems now reporting no gang problems, not the number of jurisdictions reporting new emerging gang problems. Likewise, more jurisdictions report declines in the numbers of gang members than report increases in gang members, and more jurisdictions report declines in gang homi-

cides than report increases in gang homicides. Perhaps most significantly, the two urban jurisdictions with the most serious gang problems, Los Angeles and Chicago, both reported declines in their number of gang-related homicides between 1996 and 1997 and between 1997 and 1998.

Correlates of gang proliferation

Still, there can be no question that gang problems had spread across the country over a period of two decades. Gangs have now been documented in every state in the nation, and throughout small-, medium-, and large-sized cities. It should be no surprise that researchers are interested in what factors may have led to this enormous proliferation of gangs in the United States.

Initially, some observers in politics, law enforcement, and journalism suggested that the spread of gangs was part of a purposeful, planned effort on the part of more established gangs to extend their influence and territory. From this perspective, one could imagine gangs in more established, chronic gang cities such as Chicago and Los Angeles looking for new territory to develop expanded membership and acquire new drug turf. The validity of this perspective was challenged by a study conducted by Cheryl Maxson and Malcolm Klein. Maxson and Klein interviewed police officials across the country to determine their perceptions of how gang members might have migrated to their respective jurisdictions. From their survey, Maxson and Klein learned that the spread of gangs, by and large, was due to movement of the families of gang members from one city to another, usually to be close to relatives or to find employment. Another source of the proliferation of symbols of gang membership and gang names is popular culture. Movies, rap videos, and television shows, symbols of gang membership, aspects of gang life, and gang style provided adolescents with models to emulate across the nation, and even around the world. In this way, gang migration can be viewed as part of a larger set of processes rather than as the purposeful movement of gangs into new territory.

A number of researchers have suggested that while popular culture and ordinary migration of gang-involved youth served as mechanisms for gang proliferation, changing social and economic conditions in the 1980s may have facilitated and accelerated the spread of gangs. Studies of gang emergence in rust belt cities such as Milwaukee and St. Louis led researchers to emphasize the importance of the presence of an economically disadvantaged urban underclass to the development and durability of youth gangs. The isolation of the urban underclass from the nation's economic mainstream was associated with another factor of some importance to the emergence and increasing violence of youth gangs, the incarceration of increasing proportions of urban minority youth. Juvenile detention centers and prisons are now very much a significant institutional feature of gang life.

Gangs and crime

A universal finding of research has been that gang members participate in a greater number of delinquent and criminal acts than youths who are not involved in gangs. While gang members are involved in significantly more delinquency than nonmembers, not all delinquency by gang members is gang-related. Klein observed that gang members engage in "cafeteria style" delinquency. That is, individual members seldom specialize in a single kind of delinquency. Still, gang-related delinquency is usually more violent than nongang-related delinquency. And there has been considerable variation across time, communities, and gangs in the scope and nature of gang-related crimes and delinquency.

Surveys of populations of at-risk youth have repeatedly revealed a relationship between gang membership and delinquency. Jeffrey Fagan interviewed high school students and dropouts in Chicago, Los Angeles, and San Diego and concluded that gang members committed more delinquent acts than did nongang members, as well as more serious offenses. Finn-Aage Esbensen and David Huizinga used a longitudinal survey of an at-risk youth population in Denver to show that gang members reported two to three times as much delinquency as nongang members. From longitudinal survey results on a representative sample of Rochester, New York, youth, Terrence Thornberry and his colleagues found that gang-involved youths were significantly more likely to report involvement in violence and other delinquency. By following youths over time, the Rochester study showed gang involvement to be a transitional process, with delinquent activity increasing during gang involvement and declining afterward. Both the Denver and Rochester research concluded that crime and delinquency increased while individuals were

members of a gang, and were lower before membership and after membership; these results underscore the role of gang membership in enhancing involvement in crime and delinquency.

Analyses of local law enforcement data have also provided much of what we know about gang-related crime and delinquency. Maxson and her colleagues used Los Angeles Police and Sheriff's Department records to document differences between gang and nongang homicides. Gang homicides were more likely to involve minority males, automobiles, take place in public places, involve the use of firearm, and include a greater number of participants. Gang homicides tended to involve perpetrators and victims with no prior personal relationship. Gang homicide perpetrators and victims were significantly younger than their counterparts involved in nongang homicides, but they were older than the typical youth gang member. Curry and Irving Spergal found that community-level variables, particularly ethnic composition and poverty, were significantly related to differences in gang-related homicide rates in Chicago across community areas and time. In another study of Chicago Police Department records, Richard and Carolyn Block demonstrated that (1) gang violence was more likely to be turf-related than drug-related; (2) patterns of violence of the four largest established street gangs and smaller less established gangs were different; and (3) guns were the lethal weapons in practically all Chicago gang-related homicides between 1987 and 1990.

For Thrasher, observing Chicago gangs in the early twentieth century, gang involvement in serious delinquency and crime was the culmination of a gang's evolution from a spontaneous "play group" to a "conflict-based" group. Gangs that became cohesive and better organized were those that survived increasing levels of conflict with other gangs and ultimately legitimate community institutions, in particular the police. Conducting research in Chicago decades later, James Short and Fred Strodtbeck emphasized the importance of the gang as a unit of analysis. Two concepts central to their analysis of gangs as groups were collective perceptions of threat and status. The importance of group factors in gang delinquency was also supported by the research of Klein among Los Angles gangs. For Klein, the key to reducing gang delinquency was helping gang members develop as individuals separate from the group context. In their field study of gang crime in St. Louis, Scott Decker and Barrik

Van Winkle described how gang structures and processes can combine local neighborhood dynamics and national-level diffusion of gang cultures. Their findings supported Klein's emphasis on the collective nature of violence and Short and Strodtbeck's focus on the collective nature of threat and status in making violence an ever-present feature of gang life. In one analysis, Decker described gang violence as a form of contagion in which the community and group dynamics produced cyclic levels of gang violence. The reciprocal nature of gang violence accounted, in part, for how gangs form initially, grow in size, and vary in cohesion among members.

Drugs and gangs

There are two competing views about the role of gangs and gang members in drug sales. The first argues that street gangs are well-organized purveyors of illegal drugs who reinvest the profits from drug sales into the gang. Proponents of this view include researchers Jerome Skolnick, Carl Taylor, and Martin Sanchez Jankowski. Several conditions are required for this understanding of gang drug sales to be operational. First, an organizational structure must be present. This hierarchy must have leaders, roles, and rules. Second, group goals must be widely shared among members. Third, allegiance to the larger organization must be stronger than that to subgroups within it. Finally, the gang must possess the means to control and discipline its members to produce compliance with group goals.

A second approach rejects this notion. Its proponents claim that drug sales by gangs are seldom well-organized and gang members often act independently of the gang in selling drugs. This approach presents a view of gangs as loosely confederated groups generally lacking in persistent forms of cohesion or organization. This view sees the link between gangs and drug sales as much more casual. Traditional street gangs are not well suited for drug distribution or any other businesslike activity. They are weakly organized, prone to unnecessary and unproductive violence, and full of brash, conspicuous, untrustworthy individuals who draw unwanted police attention. For all these reasons, big drug operators, those who turn to drug dealing as a serious career, typically de-emphasize gang activity or leave the gang altogether.

This view is supported by field research with gangs in Milwaukee, San Diego, and St. Louis, among other places. John Hagedorn characterized gangs in Milwaukee as dynamic, evolving associations of adolescents and men. In general, gangs lacking formal roles and effective organizational structures for achieving consensus among members regarding goals or techniques for achieving those goals. Hustling (including street drug sales) was seldom well organized because gangs lacked the organizational structure to effectively control their members. In St. Louis, virtually all of the gang members reported that they used the profits from drug sales for individual consumption, such as to buy clothes or compact discs, not to meet gang objectives. Few gang members reported that they joined their gang for the opportunity to sell drugs; instead they affiliated with the gang for expressive reasons having to do with prior associations in the neighborhood.

A review of police arrest records from five Los Angeles area police stations by Maxson and her colleagues examined the differences between crack sales involving gang members and non-gang members. In Los Angeles, individual gangs appeared to lack an effective organizational structure, had an absence of permanent membership or roles, and a lack of shared goals. Compared to nongang transactions, gang crack sales were more likely to occur on the street, involve firearms, include younger suspects, and disproportionately involve black suspects. However, most of these differences were small. In other words, the characteristics associated with crack sales by gang members were not much different from those of nongang members.

Gang involvement, gender, and ethnicity

From the first national survey of gang problems, Walter Miller proposed a general estimate that 10 percent or less of the gang members in the cities that he studies were females. No recent studies of police data on gang members have approached the 10 percent estimate. Surveys of police officials regarding gangs, indicate that even fewer girls are gang members than surveys show, with some estimates as low as 4 percent of all gang members estimated to be females. This set of findings has been challenged recently by school-based surveys of students. These surveys indicate that the number of females who are gang members is growing, and that they may comprise 40 percent of all gang members. In all likelihood, the difference between these two estimates reflect differences in methodology. Police statistics, gang and nongang, are more likely to represent more serious crimes and to focus on males. Surveys, almost always initiated in school settings, are more likely to capture information on less serious self-reported delinquency and usually include equal numbers of males and females. In addition to these factors, evidence has been reported by both Moore and Hagedorn that females tend to give up participation in gangs at an earlier age than males.

Research studies of Chicano gangs in Los Angeles by Joan Moore and Diego Vigil have focused on the cultural elements of gang membership and violence. (Studies of Latino gangs in Chicago by Ruth Horowitz and Felix Padilla have similarly demonstrated the role of culture in gang dynamics.) Moore and Vigil placed primary importance on the role of Chicano culture and the position of Mexican-Americans in the cultural and institutional life of East Los Angeles to explain gang formation and activities. The detachment of Chicano culture from mainstream social and political life was the foundation of her explanation of gang life and criminal involvement. For Moore, Chicano gangs: (1) were territorially based; (2) had a strong age-graded structure resulting in klikas or cohort groups; and (3) made fighting central to gang life. According to Vigil, Chicano youth are in a position of multiple marginality, with the street providing an alternative and appealing socialization path, becoming a collective solution to the problem of identity. The works of Moore and Horowitz identified links between cultures of male machismo and gang violence. For all these researchers, drug involvement among gangs played a particular role in enhancing the connection between cultural issues and violence.

Gangs and social institutions

It is important to remember that all but the most hard-core gang members lead a considerable portion of their lives outside the gang. As is the case for most adolescents, institutions such as family and school play important roles in their lives. The work of Joan Moore and Diego Vigil in Los Angeles has pointed to the need for order and regulation in the lives of adolescents. Children naturally seek these conditions, and gangs have come to fulfill these needs for a growing number of youth. In many instances, the gang has begun to fulfill many of the functions formerly held by the family. Gangs provide social cohesion and status, two functions typically fulfilled by a functioning family. As gangs proliferate and last longer, gang members become parents and raise children who are at risk for gang membership.

Decker and Van Winkle interviewed gang members and members of their families about life in the gang. They found that while gang members often characterized the gang as family, few gang members thought the gang behaved like a family and regarded their natal family in much more positive terms. Family members often were unaware of gang membership, especially at the earliest stages of membership. Few family members approved of gang membership and gang members uniformly denied that they wanted their children to grow up to be gang members.

After the family, schools are the most powerful socializing agent in the lives of adolescents. Most children attend school every day and interact with students from a variety of backgrounds. They influence each other in a variety of ways, both positively and negatively. Schools have an important impact on the lives of gang and nongang members, and provide opportunities for nongang youths to learn about and become involved in gangs.

For a growing number of youths, the criminal justice system plays an increasingly important role in their lives. The United States has come to rely upon incarceration as a means to solve the crime problem, and as it does so, contacts between gang members and agents of the criminal justice system increase. There is growing evidence that prison propels many young men who formerly were not gang members toward gang membership. And imprisonment strengthens the ties between many gang members and their gang, as the gang is one of the remaining sources of identification open to incarcerated members. Prison plays an increasingly important role in the lives of gang members.

Responding to gang-related crime and delinquency

According to Spergal and Curry, five strategies have typically been used to respond to gangs: (1) suppression, (2) social intervention, (3) social opportunities, (4) community mobilization, and (5) organizational change. Suppression included law enforcement and criminal justice interventions such as arrest, prosecution, imprisonment, and surveillance. Most jurisdictions use suppression as their primary response to gang problems. The second most used strategy is so-cial intervention, such as crisis intervention, treatment for youths and their families, and so-cial service referrals. This response includes tra-ditional social service interventions such as counseling. Organizational change is the next most likely choice as a gang intervention strate-gy. This method typically includes the develop-ment of task forces to address gang problems. Community mobilization is the primary response to gangs in a small number of communities. This strategy is deigned to create cooperation across agencies and was designed to produce better co-ordination of existing services. Social opportuni-ties is the primary response for the smallest number of cities and towns across the country; this approach stresses education, job training, and job provision as its intervention. Cities with chronic gang problems least often employ social opportunities and community mobilization. De-spite this, these were the strategies assessed as most effective by the individuals who work most closely with gangs.

SCOTT H. DECKER
G. DAVID CURRY

See also JUVENILE JUSTICE: HISTORY AND PHILOSOPHY; JUVENILE JUSTICE: COMMUNITY TREATMENT; JUVENILE JUSTICE: INSTITUTIONS; JUVENILE JUSTICE: JUVENILE COURT; JUVENILES IN THE ADULT SYSTEM; JUVENILE STATUS OFFENDERS; JUVENILE VIOLENT OFFENDERS; PO-LICE: HANDLING OF JUVENILES; PREVENTION: JUVENILES AS POTENTIAL OFFENDERS; SCHOOLS AND CRIME.

BIBLIOGRAPHY

BLOCK, CAROLYN R., and BLOCK, RICHARD. *Street Gang Crime in Chicago*. National Institute of Justice Research in Brief. Washington, D.C.: U.S. Department of Justice, 1993.

CURRY, G. DAVID, and DECKER, SCOTT H. *Confronting Gangs: Crime and Community*. Los Ange-les: Roxbury Press, 1998.

CURRY, G. DAVID, and SPERGAL, IRVING A. "Gang Homicide, Delinquency, and Community." *Criminology* 26 (1988): 381–405.

DECKER, SCOTT H., and VAN WINKLE, BARRIK. "'Slinging Dope:' The Role of Gangs and Gang Members in Drug Sales." *Justice Quarter-ly* 11 (1994): 583–604.

———. *Life in the Gang: Family, Friends, and Vio-lence*. New York: Cambridge University Press, 1996.

ESBENSEN, FINN-AAGE, and HUIZINGA, DAVID. "Gangs, Drugs, and Delinquency in a Survey of Urban Youth." *Criminology* 31, no. 4 (1993): 565–587.

FAGAN, JEFFREY. "The Social Organization of Drug Use and Drug Dealing Among Urban Gangs." *Criminology* 27, no. 4 (1989): 633–669.

HAGEDORN, JOHN M. *People and Folks: Gangs, Crime, and the Underclass in a Rustbelt City*. Chi-cago: Lakeview Press, 1988.

HOROWITZ, RUTH. *Honor and the American Dream*. New Brunswick, N.J.: Rutgers, 1983.

JANKOWSKI, MARTIN SANCHEZ. *Islands in the Street*. Berkeley: University of California Press, 1991.

KLEIN, MALCOLM; MAXSON, C.; and CUNNING-HAM, L. "Crack, Street Gangs, and Violence." *Criminology* 29 (1991): 623–665.

KLEIN, MALCOLM W. *The American Street Gang*. New York: Oxford University Press, 1995.

MAXSON, CHERYL L., and KLEIN, MALCOLM W. *The Scope of Street Gang Migration in the U.S. Presentation*. Gangs Working Group. Washing-ton, D.C.: National Institute of Justice, 1994.

MAXSON, CHERYL L.; GORDON, M. A.; and KLEIN, MALCOLM W. "Differences Between Gang and Nongang Homicides." *Criminology* 23 (1985): 209–222.

MILLER, WALTER B. *Violence by Youth Gangs and Youth Gangs as a Crime Problem in Major Ameri-can Cities*. Washington, D.C.: U.S. Govern-ment Printing Office, 1975.

———. *Crime by Youth Gangs and Groups in the United States*. Washington, D.C.: National In-stitute of Juvenile Justice and Delinquency Prevention, U.S. Department of Justice, 1982.

MOORE, JOAN W. *Homeboys: Gangs, Drugs, and Prison in the Barrios of Los Angeles*. Philadelphia: Temple University Press, 1978.

———. *Going Down to the Barrio: Homeboys and Homegirls in Change*. Philadelphia: Temple University Press, 1991.

PADILLA, FELIX. *The Gang as an American Enter-prise*. New Brunswick, N.J.: Rutgers, 1992.

SHORT, JAMES F., JR., and STRODTBECK, FRED L. *Group Process and Gang Delinquency*, 2d ed. Chi-cago: University of Chicago Press, 1965.

SKOLNICK, JEROME. "The Social Structure of Street Drug Dealing." *American Journal of Po-lice* 9 (1990): 1–41.

SPERGAL, IRVING A. *The Youth Gang Problem: A Community Approach*. New York, Oxford Uni-versity Press, 1995.

SPERGAL, IRVING A., and CURRY, G. DAVID. "Strat-egies and Perceived Agency Effectiveness in Dealing with the Youth Gang Problem." In *Gangs in America*. Edited by C. R. Huff. New-bury Park, Calif.: Sage, 1990. Pages 288–309.

TAYLOR, CARL S. *Dangerous Society*. East Lansing: Michigan State University Press, 1990.

THORNBERRY, TERRENCE; KROHN, MARVIN D.; LI-
ZOTTE, ALAN J.; and CHARD-WIERSCHEM, DEB-
ORAH. "The Role of Juvenile Gangs in
Facilitating Delinquent Behavior." *Journal of
Research in Crime and Delinquency* 30 (1993):
55–87.

THRASHER, FREDERIC. *The Gang: A Study of 1,313
Gangs in Chicago.* Chicago: University of Chicago Press, 1927.

VIGIL, JAMES DIEGO. *Barrio Gangs.* Austin: University of Texas Press, 1988.

WHYTE, WILLIAM. *Street Corner Society.* Chicago:
University of Chicago Press, 1993.

JUVENILE JUSTICE: HISTORY AND PHILOSOPHY

Ideological changes in the cultural conception of children and in strategies of social control
during the nineteenth century led to the creation
of the first juvenile court in Cook County, Illinois, in 1899. Culminating a century-long process of differentiating youths from adult
offenders, Progressive reformers applied new
theories of social control to new ideas about
childhood and created the juvenile court as a social welfare alternative to criminal courts to respond to criminal and noncriminal misconduct
by youths.

The U.S. Supreme Court's decision *In re
Gault*, 387 U.S. 1 (1967), began to transform the
juvenile court into a very different institution
than the Progressives contemplated. Progressives envisioned an informal, discretionary social
welfare agency whose dispositions reflected the
"best interests" of the child. In *Gault*, the Supreme Court engrafted formal due process safeguards at trial onto juvenile courts'
individualized treatment sentencing schema, although the Court did not intend to alter the juvenile court's therapeutic mission. In the decades
since *Gault*, judicial decisions, legislative amendments, and administrative changes have modified juvenile courts' jurisdiction, purposes, and
procedures. These changes have transformed
the juvenile court and fostered a procedural and
substantive convergence with adult criminal
courts.

The origins of the juvenile court

Prior to the creation of juvenile courts, the
common law's infancy defense provided the only
special protections for young offenders charged
with crimes. The common law conclusively presumed that children younger than seven years of
age lacked criminal capacity, while those fourteen years of age and older possessed full criminal responsibility. Between the ages of seven and
fourteen years, the law rebuttably presumed that
offenders lacked criminal capacity. If found
criminally responsible, however, states executed
youths as young as twelve years of age. Historically, when the criminal justice system confronted a child offender, it faced the stark alternatives
of criminal conviction and punishment as an
adult, or acquittal or dismissal. Jury or judicial
nullification to avoid excessive punishment excluded many youths from any controls, particularly those charged with minor offenses.

To avoid these unpalatable alternatives, in
the early to mid-nineteenth century, the first
age-segregated institutions—the House of Refuge—appeared in cities on the East Coast, and by
mid-century, reformatories and youth institutions spread to the rural and Midwestern regions
of the country. By the end of the century, the juvenile court appeared in Cook County (Chicago),
spread to other major urban centers, and completed the process of separating the systems of
social control of youths from adults.

Many legal features incorporated into the juvenile court first appeared in the laws creating
the houses of refuge. Refuge legislation embodied three legal innovations: a formal age-
based distinction between juvenile and adult offenders and their institutional separation; the
use of indeterminate commitments; and a broadened legal authority, *parens patriae*, that encom-
passed both criminal offenders and neglected
and incorrigible children. The legal doctrine of
parens patriae—the right and responsibility of the
state to substitute its own control over children
for that of the natural parents when the latter appeared unable or unwilling to meet their responsibilities or when the child posed a problem for
the community—originated in the English chan-
cery courts to protect the crown's interests in feu-
dal succession and established royal authority to
administer the estates of orphaned minors with
property. In 1838 *parens patriae* entered American juvenile jurisprudence to justify the commitment of a child to a house of refuge. In *Ex parte
Crouse*, 4 Whart. 9 (Pa. 1838), the Pennsylvania
Supreme Court rejected legal challenges to the
peremptory incarceration of troublesome
youths, noting that "The object of the charity is
reformation . . . To this end, may not the natural
parents, when unequal to the task of education,

or unworthy of it be superseded by the *parens patriae*, or common guardian of the community? It is to be remembered that the public has a paramount interest in the virtue and knowledge of its members, and that, of strict right, the business of education belongs to it . . . . The infant has been snatched from a course which must have ended in confirmed depravity; and not only is the restraint of her person lawful, but it would be an act of extreme cruelty to release her from it" (4 Whart. at 11 (Pa. 1838)).

The progressive juvenile court

Economic modernization at the end of the nineteenth century transformed America from a rural agrarian society into an urban industrial one. Industrialization rapidly displaced the household economy and separated work from the home. Industrial modernization encouraged migration from the rural countryside and immigration from foreign countries to urban manufacturing centers. These population changes weakened informal systems of social control based in extended families, communities, and churches. Immigrants from southern and eastern Europe flooded into the burgeoning cities to take advantage of new economic opportunities, and they crowded into ethnic enclaves and urban ghettoes. The "new" immigrants' sheer numbers, as well as their cultural, religious, and linguistic differences hindered their assimilation and acculturation, and posed a significant nation-building challenge for the dominant Anglo-Protestant western Europeans who had arrived a few generations earlier.

Changes in family structure and functions accompanied the economic transformation. A reduction in the number and spacing of children, a shift of economic functions from the family to other work environments, and a modernizing and privatizing of the family substantially modified the roles of women and children. The ideas of childhood and adolescence are socially constructed. Culminating a trend that began centuries earlier, during this modernizing era the upper and middle classes promoted a new ideology of children as vulnerable, corruptible innocents who required special attention and preparation for life. The new vision of childhood led parents and others to differentiate and isolate children from adults, altered child-rearing practices, and imposed on parents the responsibility to protect the child from engagement with the wider society and simultaneously to mold, shape, and prepare her to realize her potential in it.

Modernization and industrialization sparked the Progressive movement that addressed social problems ranging from economic regulation to criminal justice and political reform. Progressive reformers believed that professionals and experts could develop rational and scientific solutions, and that benevolent government officials could intervene to remedy social and economic problems. Social changes associated with modernization, such as urbanization and immigration, posed problems of cohesion, social control, and assimilation. As informal social controls weakened, Progressive reformers placed increased reliance on formal organization to govern, to maintain order, and to oversee social change. Progressives attempted to "Americanize" the immigrants and poor through a variety of agencies of assimilation and acculturation to become sober, virtuous, middle-class Americans like themselves. The Progressives coupled their trust of state power with the changing cultural conception of children and entered the realm of "child-saving." In his study of the Progressive era and policies, historian Robert Wiebe wrote that "If humanitarian progressivism had a central theme, it was the child. He united the campaigns for health, education and a richer city environment, and he dominated much of the interest in labor legislation. . . . The most popular versions of legal and penal reform also emphasized the needs of youth. . . . The child was the carrier of tomorrow's hope whose innocence and freedom made him singularly receptive to education in rational, humane behavior. Protect him, nurture him, and in his manhood he would create that bright new world of the progressives' vision" (p. 169). Child-centered reforms, such as juvenile court, child labor, social welfare, and compulsory school attendance laws both reflected and advanced the changing imagery of childhood and Progressives' special concerns about poor and immigrant children.

Ideological changes in theories of crime causation led Progressives to formulate new criminal justice and social control policies. At the turn of the century, Progressive criminal justice reformers aspired to scientific status and sought to strengthen the similarities between the causal determinism of the natural sciences and those of the social sciences. Criminology borrowed both its methodology and vocabulary from the increasingly scientific medical profession. Positive criminology rejected "free will," asserted a scientific determinism of deviance, redirected criminological research scientifically to study offenders, and sought to identify the factors that caused crime and delinquency. Reformers assumed that criminal behavior was determined rather than chosen, reduced actors' moral responsibility for their behavior, and tried to change offenders rather than punish them for their offenses.

A growing class of social science professionals adopted medical analogies to "treat" offenders and fostered the "Rehabilitative Ideal" in criminal justice policies. A flourishing "Rehabilitative Ideal" requires a belief in the malleability of human behavior and a basic consensus about the appropriate directions of human change. The "rehabilitative" ideology permeated many Progressive criminal justice reforms such as probation and parole, indeterminate sentences, and the juvenile court, and fostered open-ended, informal, and highly flexible policies.

The juvenile court combined the new conception of children with new strategies of social control to produce a judicial-welfare alternative to criminal justice, to remove children from the adult process, to enforce the newer conception of children's dependency, and to substitute the state as *parens patriae*. The juvenile court's "Rehabilitative Ideal" rested on several sets of assumptions about positive criminology, children's malleability, and the availability of effective intervention strategies to act in the child's "best interests."

Progressive "child-savers" described juvenile courts as benign, nonpunitive, and therapeutic, although modern writers question whether the movement should be seen as a humanitarian attempt to save poor and immigrant children, or as an effort to expand state social control over them. The legal doctrine of *parens patriae* legitimated intervention and supported the view that juvenile court conducted civil rather than criminal proceedings. Characterizing intervention as a civil or welfare proceeding, rather than criminal, fulfilled the reformers' desire to remove children from the adult justice system and allowed greater flexibility to supervise, treat, and control children. Because reformers eschewed punishment, the juvenile court's "status jurisdiction" enabled them to respond to noncriminal behavior such as smoking, sexual activity, truancy, immorality, or living a wayward, idle, and dissolute life. Juvenile courts' status jurisdiction reflected the social construction of childhood and adolescence that emerged during the nineteenth centu-

ry, and authorized pre-delinquent intervention to forestall premature adult autonomy and enforce the dependent position of youth. Girls appeared in juvenile courts almost exclusively for the status "offense" of "sexual precocity," and they often received more severe dispositions than did boys involved in criminal misconduct. Sexually active young women exercised the ultimate adult prerogative and posed a fundamental challenge to Victorians' sexual sensibilities and Progressives' construction of childhood innocence.

The juvenile court's "Rehabilitative Ideal" envisioned a specialized judge trained in social sciences and child development whose empathic qualities and insight would aid in making individualized dispositions. Judicial discretion, local diversity, and informal processes fostered many versions of juvenile courts that differed substantially in philosophy and practice. In a system of discretionary justice, neither procedural rules nor legal formalities constrained the judge. Social service personnel, clinicians, and probation officers would assist the judge to decide the "best interests" of the child. Progressives assumed that a rational, scientific analysis of facts would reveal the proper diagnosis and prescribe the cure. The factual inquiry into the child's social circumstances accorded minor significance to the specific crime because the offense indicated little about his or her "real needs." Because the reformers acted benevolently, individualized their solicitude, and intervened scientifically, they saw no reason to circumscribe narrowly the power of the state. Rather, they maximized discretion to diagnose and treat, and focused on the child's character, social circumstances, and lifestyle rather than on the crime.

By separating children from adults and providing a rehabilitative alternative to punishment, juvenile courts rejected the criminal law's jurisprudence and procedural safeguards such as juries and lawyers. Because *parens patriae* theory rested on the idea that the court helped the child rather than tried or punished the youth for a crime, no reasons even existed to determine a child's criminal responsibility. Court personnel used informal procedures and a euphemistic vocabulary to eliminate any stigma and implication of an adult criminal proceeding. They provided informal, confidential and private hearings, limited access to court records, "adjudicated" youths as "delinquent" rather than convicted them of crimes, and imposed "dispositions" rather than sentences. Theoretically, a child's "best interests," background, and welfare guided dispositions. Because a youth's offense provided only a symptom of his or her "real" needs, courts imposed indeterminate and nonproportional dispositions that potentially could continue for the duration of minority.

Procedure and substance intertwine in the juvenile court. Procedurally, juvenile courts used informal processes, confidential hearings, and a euphemistic vocabulary to obscure and disguise the reality of coercive social control. Substantively, juvenile courts used indeterminate, nonproportional sentences, emphasized treatment and supervision rather than punishment, and purportedly focused on offenders' future welfare rather than on past offenses. Despite their benevolent rhetoric, however, the Progressive "child-savers" who created the juvenile court deliberately designed it to discriminate, to "Americanize" immigrants and the poor, and to provide a coercive mechanism to distinguish between their own and "other people's children."

Juvenile courts resolved many cases informally and used probation as the disposition of first resort for the vast majority of delinquents. Juvenile court legislation and practice systematized and expended the use of probation as an alternative to institutions for younger offenders. Probation officers functioned as intermediaries to provide the court with information about the child and to supervise those youths whom the court returned to the community. Reformers envisioned probation as an alternative to dismissal rather than to confinement and used it to expand the scope of formal control over youths.

While probation constituted the disposition of first resort, Progressive reformers relied on institutional confinement as a disposition of last resort. Their feelings of tenderness did not cause them to shrink from toughness when required. The indeterminate and discretionary powers they exercised quickly to release some "rehabilitated" offenders also resulted in the prolonged incarceration of other "incorrigible" youths. Progressives' willingness to incarcerate some delinquents reflected their elevation of the power of the court over the family and their determination to save poor and immigrant children. They expanded the cottage-plan model in youth reformatories, used surrogate cottage parents to create a "normal" family environment within the institution, and attempted to promote a child's adjustment and development. They relabeled reformatories as "vocational schools" or "industrial training schools" to emphasize their nonpenal

character and added academic and vocational education to their "rehabilitative" program. In the 1920s and 1930s the rising influences of psychology and psychiatry prompted institutional administrators to engraft a hospital therapy regime onto the family and school models. Social workers, psychologists, and psychiatrists regarded the hospital-child guidance clinic model as especially appropriate for juvenile institutions where staff diagnosed and cured delinquency.

While psychologisms and rehabilitative rhetoric lent symbolic legitimacy to the juvenile courts and its institutions, practical programs and clinical personnel never approached juvenile justice reformers' therapeutic aspirations or claims. Progressives' rehabilitative rhetoric functioned to assert the incompetence of children, to define a relationship of dependency between juveniles and the state, to legitimate institutional practices to an uncritical public audience, and to obscure the reality of correctional practices. Historians conclude that with only a few notable exceptions, such as Denver's Ben Lindsey, most juvenile court judges and probation personnel were mediocre and their programs ineffective. Probation staff rarely possessed the resources, services, or expertise necessary to assist young people. Institutions seldom provided conditions conducive to reform and rehabilitation, and most incarcerated delinquents' institutional experiences remained essentially custodial and punitive.

In their pursuit of the "Rehabilitative Ideal," the Progressives situated the juvenile court on a number of cultural, legal, and criminological fault lines. They created several binary conceptions for the juvenile and criminal justice systems: either child or adult; either determinism or free-will; either dependent or responsible; either treatment or punishment; either social welfare or just deserts; either procedural informality or formality; either discretion or rules. Juvenile court reforms since *In re Gault* have witnessed a shift from the former to the latter of each of these binary pairs in response to the structural and racial transformation of cities, the rise in serious youth crime, and the erosion of the rehabilitative assumptions of the juvenile court.

The Constitutional domestication of the juvenile court

During the 1960s, the Warren Court's civil rights decisions, criminal due process rulings, and "constitutional domestication" of the juvenile court responded to broader structural and demographic changes taking place in America, particularly those associated with race and youth crime. In the decades prior to and after World War II, black migration from the rural south to the urban north increased minority concentrations in urban ghettos, made race a national rather than a regional issue, and provided the political and legal impetus for the civil rights movement. The 1960s also witnessed increases in youth crime by the baby boom-generation that continued until the late 1970s. During the 1960s, the rise in youth crime and urban racial disorders provoked cries for "law and order" and provided the initial political impetus to "get tough." Republican politicians seized crime control and welfare as wedge issues with which to distinguish themselves from Democrats in order to woo white southern voters, and crime policies for the first time became a central issue in national partisan politics. As a result of "sound-bite" politics, since the 1960s, politicians' fear of being labeled "soft-on-crime" has led to a constant ratcheting-up of punitiveness and changed juvenile justice ideology and practice.

These macro-structural and demographic changes eroded the rehabilitative premises of the Progressive juvenile court and undermined support for discretionary, coercive socialization in juvenile courts. A flourishing "rehabilitative ideal" assumes human malleability, the existence of effective techniques to change people, and a general agreement about what it means to be rehabilitated. Progressives believed that the new social sciences and the medical model of deviance provided them with the tools to reform people and that they should socialize and acculturate poor and immigrant children to become middle-class Americans like themselves. By the time of *Gault*, the Progressives' consensus about state benevolence, the legitimacy of imposing certain values on others, and what rehabilitation entailed and when it had occurred all became matters of intense dispute. The decline in deference to professionals and the benevolence of experts led to an increased emphasis on procedural formality, administrative regularity, and the rule of law.

During the turbulent 1960s, several forces combined to erode support for the rehabilitative enterprise and caused the Supreme Court to require more procedural safeguards in criminal and juvenile justice administration: left-wing critics of rehabilitation characterized governmental programs as coercive instruments of social control through which the state oppressed the poor and minorities; liberal became disenchanted with the unequal and disparate treatment of similarly situated offenders that resulted from treatment personnel's exercise of subjective clinical discretion; and conservatives advocated a "war on crime" and favored repression over rehabilitation. In the 1960s, the issue of race provided the crucial linkage between distrust of governmental benevolence, concern about social service personnel's discretionary decision-making, urban riots and the crisis of "law and order," and the Supreme Court's due process jurisprudence.

The Warren Court's due process decisions responded to the macro-structural and demographic changes, and attempted to guarantee civil rights, to protect minorities from state officials, and to infuse governmental services with greater equality by imposing procedural restraints on official discretion. The Supreme Court's *Gault* decision and later juvenile court cases mandated procedural safeguards in delinquency proceedings, focused judicial attention initially on whether the child committed an offense as prerequisite to sentencing, and demonstrated the linkages between procedure and substance in the juvenile court. In shifting the formal focus of juvenile courts from "real needs" to legal guilt, *Gault* identified two crucial disjunctions between juvenile justice rhetoric and reality: the theory versus the practice of "rehabilitation," and the differences between the procedural safeguards afforded adult defendants and those available to juvenile delinquents. *Gault* held that juveniles charged with crimes who faced institutional confinement required basic procedural safeguards including advance notice of charges, a fair and impartial hearing, assistance of counsel, an opportunity to confront and cross-examine witnesses, and the privilege against self-incrimination.

In *In re Winship*, 397 U.S. 358 (1970), the Court concluded that the risks of factual errors and unwarranted convictions and the need to protect juveniles against government power required states to prove delinquency by the criminal law's standard of proof "beyond a reasonable doubt" rather than by the lower "preponderance of the evidence" civil standard of proof. In *Breed v. Jones*, 421 U.S. 519 (1975), the Court posited a functional equivalence between criminal trials and delinquency proceedings, and held that the constitutional ban on double jeopardy precluded adult criminal reprosecution of a youth following a delinquency adjudication.

In *McKeiver v. Pennsylvania*, 403 U.S. 528 (1971), however, the Court denied to juveniles the constitutional right to a jury trial and halted the extension of full procedural parity with adult criminal prosecutions. In contrast with its analyses in earlier decisions, the *McKeiver* Court reasoned that "fundamental fairness" in delinquency proceedings required only "accurate fact-finding," a requirement that a juvenile court judge acting alone could satisfy as well as a jury. Unlike *Gault* and *Winship*, which recognized that procedural safeguards protect against governmental oppression, the Court in *McKeiver* denied that delinquents required such protection and instead invoked the stereotype of the sympathetic, paternalistic juvenile court judge. Unfortunately, *McKeiver* did not analyze or elaborate upon the differences between treatment as a juvenile and punishment as an adult that warranted the procedural differences between the two systems.

Together, *Gault, Winship,* and *McKeiver* precipitated a procedural and substantive revolution in the juvenile court system that unintentionally but inevitably transformed its original Progressive conception. By emphasizing criminal procedural regularity in the determination of delinquency, the Supreme Court shifted the focus of juvenile courts from paternalistic assessments of a youth's "real needs" to proof of commission of criminal acts. By formalizing the connection between criminal conduct and coercive intervention, the Court made explicit a relationship previously implicit and unacknowledged. Providing delinquents with even a modicum of procedural justice in juvenile courts also legitimated greater punitiveness. Thus, *Gault*'s procedural reforms provided the impetus for the substantive convergence between juvenile and criminal courts, so that for most purposes, contemporary juvenile courts function as a scaled-down extension of the criminal justice system. It is an historical irony that race provided the initial impetus for the Supreme Court to expand procedural rights to protect minority youths' liberty interests, and now juvenile courts' increasingly punitive sanctions fall disproportionately heavily on minority offenders.

The *Gault* decision represents a procedural revolution that failed and that produced unintended negative consequences. Delinquents continue to receive the "worst of both worlds"—neither the solicitous care and regenerative treatment promised to children nor the criminal procedural rights of adults. *McKeiver* denied delinquents criminal procedural equality with adults, but the Court could not compel states to deliver social welfare services. Although youths lack procedural parity with adult defendants, providing delinquents with any procedural safeguards at all legitimated more punitive sanctions. Once states grant a semblance of procedural justice, however inadequate, it becomes easier for them to depart from a purely "rehabilitative" model of juvenile justice.

Juvenile courts' increased procedural formality in the decades since *Gault* also provided the impetus to adopt substantive "criminological triage" policies. The "triage" process entails de-institutionalizing and diverting noncriminal status offenders out of the juvenile system at the "soft" end of the court's clientele, waiving serious offenders into the criminal justice system for prosecution as adult at the "hard" end, and punishing more severely the residual, middle-range of ordinary criminal-delinquent offenders. Recent "get-tough" waiver and sentencing policies reflect juvenile courts' broader jurisprudential changes from rehabilitation to retribution. The overarching themes of these legal and operational changes include a shift from individualized justice to just deserts, from offender to offense, from "amenability to treatment" to public safety, and a cultural and legal reconceptualization of youth from innocent and immature delinquents into responsible and autonomous offenders. The substantive and procedural convergence between juvenile and criminal courts eliminates many of the conceptual and operational differences in strategies of social control for youths and adults. With the juvenile court's transformation from an informal rehabilitative agency into a scaled-down criminal court, some question the need for a separate justice system for young offenders whose only distinction is its persisting deficiencies.

BARRY C. FIELD

See also AGE AND CRIME; CONTRIBUTING TO THE DELINQUENCY OF MINORS; EXCUSE: INFANCY; JUVENILE AND YOUTH GANGS; JUVENILE JUSTICE: COMMUNITY TREATMENT; JUVENILE JUSTICE: INSTITUTIONS; JUVENILE JUSTICE: JUVENILE COURT; JUVENILES IN THE ADULT SYSTEM; JUVENILE STATUS OFFENDERS; JUVENILE VIOLENT OFFENDERS.

BIBLIOGRAPHY

AINSWORTH, JANET E. "Re-imagining Childhood and Re-constructing the Legal Order: The

Case for Abolishing the Juvenile Court." *North Carolina Law Review* 69 (1991): 1083–1133.

ALLEN, FRANCIS A. *The Borderland of the Criminal Law: Essays in Law and Criminology.* Chicago: University of Chicago Press, 1964.

———. *Decline of the Rehabilitative Ideal.* New Haven, Conn.: Yale University Press, 1981.

BECKETT, KATHERINE. *Making Crime Pay: Law and Order in Contemporary American Politics.* New York: Oxford University Press, 1997.

BERNARD, THOMAS J. *The Cycle of Juvenile Justice.* New York: Oxford University Press, 1992.

FELD, BARRY C. *Bad Kids: Race and The Transformation of the Juvenile Court.* New York: Oxford University Press, 1999.

FOX, SANFORD J. "Juvenile Justice Reform: An Historical Perspective." *Stanford Law Review* 22 (1970): 1187–1239.

HAGAN, JOHN, and LEON, JEFFREY. "Rediscovering Delinquency: Social History, Political Ideology and the Sociology of Law." *American Sociological Review* 42 (1977): 587–598.

HAWES, JOSEPH. *Children in Urban Society: Juvenile Delinquency in Nineteenth-Century America.* New York: Oxford University Press, 1971.

HAWES, JOSEPH, and HINER, N., eds. *American Childhood: A Research Guide and Historical Handbook.* Westport, Conn.: Greenwood Press, 1985.

HIGHAM, JOHN. *Strangers in the Land: Patterns of American Nativism 1860–1925,* 2d ed. New Brunswick, NJ: Rutgers University Press, 1988.

HOFSTADTER, RICHARD. *The Age of Reform: From Bryan to F.D.R.* New York: Knopf, 1955.

KETT, JOSEPH F. *Rites of Passage: Adolescence in America 1790 to the Present.* New York: Basic Books, 1977.

KRISBERG, BARRY, and AUSTIN, JAMES. *Reinventing Juvenile Justice.* Thousand Oaks, Calif.: Sage Publications, 1993.

LEMANN, NICHOLAS. *The Promised Land: The Great Black Migration and How It Changed America.* New York: Vintage Books, 1992.

MACK, JULIAN W. "The Juvenile Court." *Harvard Law Review* 23 (1909): 104–122.

MATZA, DAVID. *Delinquency and Drift.* New York: Wiley, 1964.

MENNEL, ROBERT. *Thorns and Thistles: Juvenile Delinquents in the United States 1825–1940.* Hanover, N.H.: University Press of New England, 1973.

PAULSEN, MONRAD. "The Constitutional Domestication of the Juvenile Court." *Supreme Court Review* 1967 (1967): 233–266.

PLATT, ANTHONY. *The Child Savers,* 2d ed. Chicago: University of Chicago Press, 1977.

ROTHMAN, DAVID J. *The Discovery of the Asylum: Social Order and Disorder in the New Republic.* Boston: Little, Brown, 1971.

———. *Conscience and Convenience: The Asylum and Its Alternative in Progressive America.* Boston: Little, Brown, 1980.

RYERSON, ELLEN. *The Best-Laid Plans: America's Juvenile Court Experiment.* New York: Hill and Wang, 1978.

SCHLOSSMAN, STEVEN. *Love and the American Delinquent.* Chicago: University of Chicago Press, 1977.

SUTTON, JOHN R. *Stubborn Children: Controlling Delinquency in the United States.* Berkeley: University of California Press, 1988.

TIFFIN, SUSAN. *In Whose Best Interest? Child Welfare Reform in the Progressive Era.* Westport, Conn.: Greenwood Press, 1982.

TRATTNER, WALTER. *Crusade for the Children: A History of the National Child Labor Committee and Child Labor Reform in New York State.* Chicago: Quadrangle Books, 1970.

WIEBE, ROBERT H. *The Search for Order 1877–1920.* New York: Hill and Wang, 1967.

CASES

Breed v. Jones, 421 U.S. 519 (1975).
Ex parte Crouse, 4 Whart. p (Pa. 1838).
In re Gault, 387 U.S. 1 (1967).
In re Winship, 397 U.S. 358 (1970).
McKeiver v. Pennsylvania, 403 U.S. 528 (1971).

JUVENILE JUSTICE: COMMUNITY TREATMENT

Juvenile courts and the rest of the juvenile justice system are responsible for dealing with: (1) *juvenile delinquents,* who have committed an act, such as an assault or burglary, that would be a crime if committed by an adult; and (2) *status offenders,* whose behavior, such as school truancy, running away from home, or incorrigibility, is illegal for a child but would not be a crime if committed by an adult. The juvenile justice system has often been characterized as a series of decision points where various actors—police, court intake workers, prosecutors, probation officers, judges, treatment managers—weigh the situation and, with varying degrees of discretion, decide what to do with a child. The decision may be to do nothing further at this time, to negotiate an informal agreement with parents or others on a course of action in lieu of further formal processing, or to proceed with formal processing through the system. At the extreme, the decision may be to remove a child from his or her home, sometimes for a long time, or even to transfer jurisdiction to the adult criminal justice system. In contrast to the adult system, decisions in juvenile justice are guided by multiple goals, including treatment (sometimes termed *rehabilitation*, or *competency development*) for the youth in addition to *public safety protection* and *punishment*.

Community treatment may be relevant at any of the decision points outlined above. Community treatment in juvenile justice refers to a number of interventions whose main similarity is that they are alternatives to placement in large, secure institutions, such as detention centers or training schools. As will be discussed later in this entry, the most common of these is probation. Other community treatment programs include diversion, home detention, youth service bureaus, day treatment programs, restitution and community service, and community residential placements, such as group homes and shelters.

Communities may initiate broad-based, delinquency prevention efforts such as DARE (Drug Abuse Resistance Education) programs in schools, youth development and recreation programs, and alternative schools. Components of the juvenile justice system (juvenile courts, police, probation services, etc.) may be partners in such initiatives. These and related prevention programs, however, are discussed elsewhere in this volume. Community treatment programs within or directly tied to juvenile justice may be used to *divert* youths from further processing, as an adjunct to some other form of processing, or as the main element of a disposition. Following a description of diversion, this entry will review community treatment programs at various points in the system—*pre-adjudication* (after arrest, while waiting for a court hearing), *post-adjudication* (following the dispositional hearing), or even as part of *aftercare* (following a stay at a residential institution). A concluding section examines some major issues and trends surrounding the use of community treatment in juvenile justice.

Diversion

Diversion, which can occur at any decision point in the system, refers to a decision that neither ignores the child nor moves the child along the formal processing route. The decision normally involves an agreement between the official involved in that decision point and the youth's family to pursue some informal remedial action.

Thus, police may recommend to a youth's parents that they pursue some counseling for the youth and/or arrive at an informal settlement with victims in lieu of referring the youth to court. The court intake worker or probation officer may similarly broker an agreement as an alternative to proceeding to a dispositional hearing. At a dispositional hearing, a judge may choose to formally dismiss the case but informally direct a family to pursue treatment of some kind.

Diversion programs proliferated in the late 1960s and 1970s in response to recommendations contained in a 1967 report from the President's Commission on Law Enforcement and Administration of Justice (LEAA) (Binder). This report embraced the notions of labeling theorists, such as Howard Becker and Edwin Lemert, who argued that formal delinquency processing paradoxically created further delinquency through *secondary deviance*. That is, once a child is labeled as delinquent as a result of formal processing for a delinquent act (primary deviance), teachers, police, and others would expect him or her to engage in further delinquency and would be quick to interpret any signs of problematic behavior as verifying that child's delinquent status. Moreover, according to labeling theory, the child would come to internalize the label and act accordingly. Subsequent delinquency results from these self-fulfilling prophecies (secondary deviance). According to labeling theory, diversion programs are attractive because they provide needed services while avoiding the stigmatization associated with formal processing, thereby presumably reducing the likelihood of future delinquency. With the encouragement of federal funding, a broad and creative range of diversion programs flourished, including a network of community-based Youth Service Bureaus (local centers for delinquency prevention programming) in many states, mostly in urban areas. The federal seed money soon evaporated, and most localities did not sustain the Youth Service Bureaus, yet they are making a comeback in some places, such as Indiana.

Critics soon focused attention on some troubling, unintended consequences of diversion (e.g., Austin and Krisberg; Ezell). While intended as an alternative to formal processing, diversion seemed at times to "widen the net" of social control. Instead of "capturing" youths who otherwise would be processed further through the formal system, diversion sometimes captured youths who otherwise would have been released, thus ironically increasing stigmatization and control. Furthermore, critics argued, diversion tended to be applied inequitably, more for girls and for white, middle-class youths than for persons of color.

Evaluations of diversion have shown mixed results (e.g., Davidson et al.; Osgood and Weichselbaum; Palmer and Lewis), suggesting that some diversion programs produce reductions in recidivism while others do not. As with any other aspect of juvenile correctional treatment, the key seems to lie in the matching of the appropriate youths with well-managed programs that can flexibly tailor services to meet individual needs.

While less prominent in the "lock 'em up" climate at the end of the twentieth century, diversion retains a place in the repertoire of community-based options for dealing with delinquents, and will likely continue to do so.

Pre-adjudication

In the not too distant past, children apprehended by police were held routinely in police lock-ups and county jails. The Juvenile Justice and Delinquency Prevention Act of 1974 (JJDPA) resulted in dramatic changes mandating the removal of juveniles from adult jails and police lock-ups, requiring a parallel system of *juvenile detention centers* for those who needed to be held securely, and forbidding the secure confinement of status offenders and children in need of supervision. States' receipt of federal JJDPA funding was tied to their compliance with these provisions. Several community alternatives to detention have also evolved, as discussed below.

Shelters. Some communities have nonsecure, temporary residential facilities intended for children removed from their homes in the initial stages of child protective services investigations or for children who may be picked up by police as status offenders. In addition to these shelters, some communities also include a network of *host homes*, families who volunteer to provide temporary shelter to a child. Shelters and host homes provide a necessary adjunct to the juvenile justice system. Without them, some children might be held inappropriately in secure detention facilities, despite legislation that forbids this practice. Shelters may also be used as a nonsecure alternative to detention for allegedly delinquent youths who may not meet formal criteria for secure detention but for whom an immediate return home is not feasible. In some jurisdictions, nonsecure shelters and secure detention centers are adjacent wings of the same building, sharing some administrative and operating costs.

Holdover programs. Following the enactment of the JJDPA, as discussed above, many communities built juvenile detention centers. Small, rural communities, however, had neither the resources nor the expected demand necessary for such construction. As an alternative to using adult jails, some of these communities developed "holdover" programs to bridge the time between the arrest of a youth and transport to the nearest juvenile detention center, often several hours drive away. A holdover program requires a room (this might be located in a police station or sheriff's department, or some other public facility) and someone (either a volunteer or part-time employee) who can provide continuous supervision of a youth for a few hours or overnight pending transportation.

Home detention. Home detention serves as an alternative to placement in a secure juvenile detention center for youths who do not appear to require secure confinement but cannot just be released prior to their court hearing without some form of supervision. Home detention workers supervise small caseloads, make frequent and irregular visits to the youths' homes and schools, and may provide crisis counseling or other support. As an adjunct to, or in some cases instead of, intensive supervision of the youth by staff, some home detention programs rely on *electronic monitoring* (e.g., ankle bracelets that send electronic signals over the telephone to a central computer) to keep track of the youths at all times.

The first home detention programs appeared in the 1970s, and have become increasingly prevalent. Several evaluations suggest that they are quite effective—that is, few youths on home detention acquire additional charges prior to their court hearings, and fewer still fail to appear at court hearings (Schwartz, Barton, and Orlando). There is ample evidence that many jurisdictions too readily use secure detention for youths who do not really need confinement (Schwartz and Barton; Snyder and Sickmund). Moreover, research has shown that placing a youth in secure detention increases the probability of subsequent residential placements, even when other factors, including offense, are held constant (Snyder and Sickmund). Home detention, therefore, may merit consideration for expansion and strengthening as an alternative to secure detention.

Post-adjudication

Probation.   From its origins in Massachusetts in the mid-1800s, juvenile probation services have spread to virtually every jurisdiction in the nation. Whereas volunteers initially supervised youths, probation services have now become professionalized, staffed by graduates with bachelors degrees in the social sciences, social work, or criminal justice. Probation is most often operated at the county level, as part of a juvenile court or county executive agency. In some jurisdictions, however, such as Florida and Maryland, probation is administered by state juvenile correctional agencies.

Probation serves more youths than any other type of juvenile justice program. Howard Snyder and Melissa Sickmund summarize national statistics demonstrating how extensively the system relies on probation services. Using 1996 data, they estimate that more than half (54%) of all adjudicated delinquents are placed on probation along with an even higher percentage of adjudicated status offenders (60%). Given the numbers of delinquency and status offense cases referred to the nation's juvenile courts in 1996, this amounts to approximately 307,500 adjudicated delinquents cases and almost 50,000 adjudicated status offenders placed on probation. But probation serves almost as many additional youths who have not been formally adjudicated. Youths may be assigned to probation informally, either as an alternative to filing a formal court petition, or after an adjudication hearing even if not adjudicated. These other routes to probation resulted in an estimated 335,500 additional youths assigned to probation in 1996, bringing the total to nearly 693,000 (Snyder and Sickmund).

A youth on probation is assigned to a probation officer and usually has a set of conditions with which to comply. These conditions might specify such things as curfews, school attendance, periodic drug screening, hours of community service, making restitution to victims, or participating in various treatment programs. Failure to abide by these conditions results in a *violation of probation*, and a youth may be brought back to court and receive a more restrictive disposition. Violations of probation are misdemeanors, so that youths who are placed on probation as a result of a status offense and who subsequently violate the terms of that probation may then be charged with a delinquent offense, and thus be legally subject to such sanctions as detention or placement in training schools.

Probation officers are expected to enact two, sometimes contradictory, roles—service provider or broker and behavioral monitor. As the former, they attempt to develop supportive relationships with the youths as counselors and advocates. As the latter, they check on the youths' compliance with the conditions of probation, and are responsible for filing probation violations. As described in conjunction with home detention above, electronic monitoring may also be used, or other staff, called *trackers*, may be employed solely to check on probationers' whereabouts. In addition to supervising perhaps as many as fifty to one hundred youths on their caseloads, probation officers also may be responsible for conducting intake investigations and preparing *predispositional reports* used by the court in determining case dispositions. Thus, the amount of attention they can devote to any particular youth may be limited. Many probation departments have developed classification schemes to guide the amount of attention given to different youths, ranging from monthly office visits and paper processing to intensive probation (discussed later in this section).

The *balanced approach* to juvenile probation was introduced by Dennis Maloney, Dennis Romig, and Troy Armstrong. Beginning with a recognition of three goals of juvenile corrections, this approach requires that probation services incorporate a balance among:

1. *Protecting public safety* by effectively monitoring the behavior of juvenile offenders;
2. Holding offenders *accountable* for their offenses and to their victims; and
3. Facilitating the youths' *competency development* via rehabilitative and skill building services.

The balanced approach has gained considerable popularity, with some states, such as California and Florida, even officially adopting it in their mission statements for juvenile probation (Bazemore).

Despite the challenges posed by heavy caseloads and popular impressions that the juvenile justice system is a "revolving door" through which the same youths return again and again, probation is remarkably effective. Snyder and Sickmund estimate that 54 percent of males and 73 percent of females who enter the juvenile justice system (and remember that probation is the most common service used) never return on a new referral.

Intensive probation.   A study by the National Council on Crime and Delinquency (Krisberg, Rodriguez et al.) cataloged a number of intensive supervision programs, operated in about one-third of all jurisdictions. Intensive probation is used with youths who pose higher risks to public safety than do typical probationers. It typically involves small caseloads (e.g., ten to twenty), and frequent, perhaps daily, contact between the youths and the probation officer. Studies have shown that some jurisdictions have successfully used intensive probation as a less costly alternative disposition for relatively nonviolent youths who otherwise might be sent to institutions (Barton and Butts; Krisberg, Bakke et al; Krisberg, Rodriguez, et al.; Wiebush and Hamparian). Others, however, have suggested that intensive probation is not effective when used with relatively nonserious offenders who would otherwise receive regular probation supervision.

Restitution   and   community   service. *Restitution* refers to compensation made directly to victims by offenders. Restitution may take the form of monetary payments, services rendered, or the repair or replacement of damaged or stolen property. Because of its emphasis on atonement, restitution is often an important part of *restorative justice* models (discussed later in this entry), but may be ordered as part of an informal adjustment or as a condition of probation.

Community service, like restitution, involves the offender giving something back, although to the community at large rather than directly to the victim. Many probation orders include a prescribed number of community service hours. The service activities can range from neighborhood clean-ups to volunteering in nursing homes or other agencies, providing maintenance chores for elderly residents, or lecturing to other young people on the dangers of delinquency or the realities of correctional experiences.

Both restitution and community service have the potential to promote offender accountability to the community or to victims. The best of these activities have desirable competency development benefits to the offenders by providing meaningful, pro-social community involvement and useful skill development. A review of research suggests that restitution can reduce recidivism to some extent (Lipsey; Schneider). But restitution and community service should not be judged solely in terms of recidivism reduction—their value may lie more in their restorative and accountability enhancing functions. As with any other aspect of the juvenile justice system's re-sponse to offenders, restitution and community service orders should be tailored to the individual youths and their circumstances, and should require amounts of time or compensation that are possible for the youths to provide.

Day treatment.   Some adjudicated delinquents who remain living in the community may be ordered to attend *day treatment* programs. Those who cannot return to their regular schools may attend alternative school programs. Other programs operate in the after-school, evening, or weekend hours. Youths approaching employable age may receive job training services. Day treatment programs may include counseling services and recreation as well. They may have their own facilities or operate in a host facility, such as a Boys or Girls Club.

There are few specialized counseling models applied primarily to juvenile offenders. One of the best models is *multisystemic therapy* (MST), introduced by Scott Henggeler and Charles Borduin. MST recognizes the multiple factors presumed to cause delinquency, including the family, peers, and school, and interventions are designed to address each. Several studies, as summarized by Gail Wasserman and Laurie Miller, have shown that MST can be effective even for relatively serious delinquents. Since MST can be provided in the community, the cost is far less than institutional placement.

Community residential programs.   Not all youths who are placed out of their own homes are sent to training schools or similar secure institutions. Some are assigned to *group homes, therapeutic foster homes*, and other community residential programs. These are usually small programs, with a handful of youths living with one or more adults who act as *house parents*. In most, the youths attend school or work, partake of other services, and participate in various activities in the community. Some, like the Teaching Family homes introduced by Boys Town (Jones, Weinrott, and Howard, 1981), have well-developed treatment models. Others are less structured.

Community residential settings are intended to be less restrictive and more homelike than institutions. Some, however, may be relatively isolated from the community and resemble secure institutions in many respects. In one study, for example, Robert Coates, Alden Miller, and Lloyd Ohlin (1976) found that some group homes were indeed relatively open settings, with a family-like atmosphere and multiple community linkages, while others were more authoritarian, with few community linkages, and seemed more like institutions.

Independent living programs. While a goal of most juvenile correctional programs is the preservation or eventual reunification of families, for some adolescents pursuit of this goal is impossible or unwise. For some older adolescents, a goal may be *emancipation*, upon which the youth legally would no longer be under parental control. *Independent living programs* are designed to prepare youths for emancipation or for adult independence by housing them in apartments and providing support for them to develop basic skills such as grocery shopping, meal preparation, money management, and so on.

Wilderness and adventure programs. Many people may be familiar with ropes courses and other physically challenging programs used by some organizations to promote team cohesiveness and individual self-confidence. Not surprisingly, such programs have been used in juvenile justice for a long time. Some *wilderness and adventure programs* require relatively long stays of many months in remote locations, in camps, wagon trains, or ocean voyages, and cannot really be considered community-based treatment. Others are of shorter duration, perhaps a few days or a weekend, and may be accompanied by more traditional community-based counseling, educational or aftercare components. All rely on physical challenges to the participants. Some of the more widely known wilderness and adventure programs include VisionQuest, Ocean-Quest, Outward Bound, Homeward Bound, Associated Marine Institutes, and several operated by the Eckerd Foundation.

Albert Roberts reviewed these and other wilderness programs used with delinquent youths. He concluded that the evidence suggests that many of these programs are more effective than institutions at reducing recidivism, although evaluations are neither consistent nor definitive. A meta-analysis by John Hattie and colleagues was based on ninety-six studies of out-of-school adventure programs, including Outward Bound, around the world. Not all of these served delinquent youths. These studies documented gains in several areas, including youths' leadership abilities, self-concept, personality, interpersonal skills, and adventurousness. Like Roberts, Hattie and his colleagues noted that effectiveness varied among programs.

Wrap-around services. The youthful clients of the mental health, special education, child welfare, and juvenile justice systems are essentially the same, differing mainly in the "door" through which they access services. Yet that door profoundly influences the nature of services provided in the traditional *categorical* environment in which separate systems provide services with separate funding streams. Moreover, many youths and families become involved in more than one of these categorical systems, leading to confusion and overlap in service planning and provision. As an alternative, several communities are experimenting with *wraparound services*. Operating from a managed care framework, wraparound services involve a collaboration among service providers including schools, juvenile court, child welfare agencies, and mental health services. Using pooled funding resources, case managers coordinate the efforts of treatment teams, drawn from the collaborative partners and including the parents of the youths, to provide an array of services tailored to the needs of each individual youth. Although its origins were in the mental health arena (Stroul), the concept of wraparound services extends to youths involved in the juvenile justice system as well.

Mentoring. Mentoring programs, such as Big Brothers and Big Sisters, have a long history in the delinquency prevention and youth development arenas. While several studies (as summarized in Catalano et al.) have demonstrated little effectiveness for mentoring efforts, other research has been more promising (Tierney, Grossman, and Resch). To be effective with young people who have already engaged in delinquent behavior, mentors require special training. Mentoring may be used in conjunction with a variety of community treatment programs in juvenile justice, and may also be a component of community aftercare programs, as discussed in the next section.

Aftercare

What happens to juvenile offenders upon release from an institutional placement? For some, especially those who have been held until the age of majority, the moment they walk out the door, they are no longer under direct correctional supervision. Many, however, continue under the jurisdiction of *parole* or *aftercare* services. Juvenile aftercare may involve various combinations of transitional housing, employment training, school advocacy, mentoring, crisis counseling, behavioral monitoring, and drug and alcohol testing. These services are intended to facilitate reintegration into the community while providing a measure of surveillance and control during the transition. Resembling probation in many respects, aftercare is usually the responsibility of state juvenile correctional agencies, whereas probation is more often run by county courts. As in many probation departments, juvenile parole officers often have large caseloads that make meaningful levels of contact with individual youths impossible. Yet many would point to aftercare as the potentially most critical factor in keeping youths from reentering the system again and again.

Juvenile correctional institutions typically have high recidivism rates. Perhaps spending months or years in the company of other youthful offenders merely hardens individuals, providing them with more delinquent skills and motivations. Yet, even youths who have spent time in the best institutions, with effective rehabilitative programming producing demonstrable short-term improvements in behavior and attitudes, eventually return to the communities in which their delinquency was engendered, where the same influences persist. Moreover, their opportunities for educational or vocational advancement may be even more limited than before. Without adequate attention to aftercare and reintegration, it is not surprising that so many fail.

David Altschuler and Troy Armstrong have developed an Intensive Aftercare Program (IAP) model that carefully blends theory and practice. Key principles of the IAP model are:

1. preparing youth for progressively increased responsibility and freedom in the community;
2. facilitating youth-community interaction and involvement;
3. working with both the offender and targeted community support systems (such as families, peers, schools, employers) on qualities needed for constructive interaction and the youth's successful community adjustment;
4. developing new resources and supports where needed; and
5. monitoring and testing the youth and the community on their ability to deal with each other productively (Altschuler and Armstrong, p. 11).

The IAP model begins while a youth is still in a correctional facility, providing preparatory skills and linking institutional and community professional staffs. Following a youth's release,

the IAP model employs an intensive case management approach to provide support, surveillance, and community service brokerage. In some cases, IAP incorporates community residential programs as transitional components, like halfway houses. As with intensive probation, electronic monitoring or trackers may be used as additional control mechanisms. But the heart of the model is the individualized case planning and community support that continues when youths are returned to their families or to independent living arrangements. An IAP worker makes home visits, school visits, job visits, and the like as needed.

The IAP model is being piloted in four states, with evaluation results not yet in. Evaluations of other intensive aftercare programs have found mixed results. While some were quite successful (Sontheimer and Goodstein), others that had difficulty fully implementing intensive aftercare interventions had less favorable outcomes than regular aftercare (Deschenes, Greenwood, and Marshall; Greenwood, Deschenes, and Adams).

Issues and trends

Juvenile justice professionals and the general public continue to debate how best to address problems of juvenile delinquency. Tensions exist between those who favor a "get tough" or "lock 'em up" approach and those who favor using the least restrictive alternatives. Beginning in the late 1990s some have advocated the introduction of a radically different paradigm, restorative justice. This last section examines the role of the community in delinquency treatment in terms of these issues.

Institutional vs. community treatment. Advocates of community treatment advance several arguments in support of its use. Compared with institutional placements, community programs are less costly, less disruptive to families, and have the potential to address the youths' delinquency in the natural contexts in which it is likely to occur. Moreover, those youths placed in institutions eventually return to their communities, and, unless steps are taken to address the community context or provide community support to the youths upon their return, recidivism is likely. Community treatment rests on several values-based and theoretical assumptions—that delinquent behavior is caused and maintained by a combination of factors, including environmental influences; that the probability of delinquency is reduced through strengthening a youth's bonds to the family, school, and other community institutions; and that families or family-like settings usually provide the best context for rehabilitation.

Those who question the appropriateness of community treatments point to the increased risk to public safety, the difficulty in altering patterns of peer group behaviors, and the challenges to and limitations of some families in providing adequate structure for their children as reasons to prefer institutional placement. They suggest that institutional placements protect communities by incapacitating offenders, act as both specific and general deterrents to delinquency, and foster rehabilitation through structure and discipline. There is ample evidence that institutional placements do incapacitate offenders. There is less support for the supposed deterrent and rehabilitative effects of incarceration.

Evidence accumulating over several decades indicates that the best juvenile justice systems are those with an extensive range of options at various levels of restrictiveness, but that many states and counties have too few options and end up relying too much on institutions. States vary considerably in the extent to which they rely on institutional placements. For example, the 1997 secure custody rate of committed delinquents in Louisiana was 459 per 100,000 juveniles age ten and older; comparable rates per 100,000 population were 386 in California, 175 in Missouri, 110 in Massachusetts, and 44 in Vermont (Snyder and Sickmund). Several studies have shown that between 40 and 60 percent of youths held in training schools in several states do not appear to be serious or chronic offenders by most reasonable definitions. Many have never committed a felony-level offense, but have had difficulties in various other placement settings, frustrating local probation officers and the courts.

Early evaluation studies in Massachusetts, which closed its juvenile training schools in 1972 and replaced them with a regional network of community-based alternatives, revealed an overall higher recidivism rate, except in areas where a full array of alternatives were available (Coates, Miller, and Ohlin). A later reevaluation found that once a well-structured system of dispositional options had been developed in Massachusetts, results compared favorably in terms of recidivism outcomes with other states that relied more heavily on secure institutions (Krisberg, Austin, and Steele). Favorable results for community treatment have also been observed in several other states.

Community treatment alternatives even hold promise for *serious and violent juvenile offenders* (SVJ), those adjudicated for major crimes against persons or property, usually thought to require confinement in secure institutions. A meta-analysis of more than two hundred evaluations of interventions for serious and violent juvenile offenders shows that the most effective ones involve interpersonal skills training, cognitive-behavioral treatment, or teaching family home programs (Lipsey and Wilson). As summarized by Rolf Loeber and David Farrington, "Interventions for SVJ offenders often have to be multimodal to address multiple problems, including law breaking, substance use and abuse, and academic and family problems" (p. xxiii).

Restorative justice.   The adult criminal justice system is an adversarial system in which the state exercises its authority to exact retribution from criminal offenders whose guilt has been proven beyond a reasonable doubt. Defendants, in turn, are guaranteed certain rights or due process protections in the determination of guilt or innocence. Justice is accomplished when the punishment meted out fits the crime. The juvenile court movement at the beginning of the twentieth century, on the other hand, was based on a philosophy of *parens patriae*, in which the state assumed the responsibilities of a parent when the natural family was unable or unwilling to do so. Rather than the strict pursuit of justice, the goal of the original juvenile court was to act in the best interests of the child. During the course of the twentieth century, however, as described elsewhere in this volume, the Supreme Court recognized that the juvenile court did not always act in the child's best interest, and, in a series of decisions, gradually instituted for children many of the same due process protections afforded to adults.

Neither the adult criminal court nor the juvenile court appear to place primary emphasis on restoration, that is, repairing harm done to victims and providing offenders a way to regain full community status. The paradigm of *restorative justice* embraces these emphases. As outlined by Daniel Van Ness, restorative justice rests on three principles:

1. Justice requires that we work to heal victims, offenders and communities that have been injured by crime;
2. Victims, offenders and communities should have the opportunity for active involvement

in the justice process as early and as fully as possible;

3. We must rethink the relative roles and responsibilities of the government and the community. In promoting justice, government is responsible for preserving a just order and the community for establishing peace (pp. 8–9).

In the context of juvenile justice, restorative justice principles may be found in a variety of programs, such as victim-offender mediation, family group conferences, teen court (in which young people enact the roles of judge, attorneys, and jury to resolve cases), and some forms of restitution and community service. There is disagreement among restorative justice advocates over whether involuntary sanctions (e.g., court-ordered punishment) can play a role in restorative justice (Bazemore and Walgrave), but clearly the emphasis is on repairing harm, reintegrating offenders, and involving all affected stakeholders in the process. A national project, directed by Gordon Bazemore and Mark Umbreit, is attempting to develop and test the application of restorative justice to juvenile justice in several jurisdictions.

Conclusion

The real challenge for the juvenile justice system is to strike a cost-effective balance among the various alternative approaches. While the political climate and public rhetoric often reduce the issue to an overly simplistic battle between "get tough" conservatives and "bleeding heart" liberals, the real question is what works best, for what kinds of youth, under what conditions. The best systems seem to employ multiple response options flexibly along a wide continuum of restrictiveness, accompanied by assessment procedures that tailor responses to the unique situations of individuals, and monitored by careful evaluation of outcomes.

WILLIAM H. BARTON

See also JUVENILE AND YOUTH GANGS; JUVENILE JUSTICE: HISTORY AND PHILOSOPHY; JUVENILE JUSTICE: INSTITUTIONS; JUVENILE JUSTICE: JUVENILE COURTS; JUVENILES IN THE ADULT SYSTEM; JUVENILE STATUS OFFENDERS; JUVENILE VIOLENT OFFENDERS; POLICE: HANDLING OF JUVENILES; PREVENTION: JUVENILES AS POTENTIAL OFFENDERS; SCHOOLS AND CRIME.

BIBLIOGRAPHY

ALTSCHULER, DAVID M., and ARMSTRONG, TROY L. *Intensive Aftercare for High-Risk Juveniles: A Community Care Model: Program Summary.* Washington, D.C.: Office of Juvenile Justice and Delinquency Prevention, 1994.

AUSTIN, JAMES, and KRISBERG, BARRY. "Wider, Stronger, and Different Nets: The Dialectics of Criminal Justice Reform." *Journal of Research in Crime and Delinquency* 18, no. 1 (1981): 165–196.

BARTON, WILLIAM H., and BUTTS, JEFFREY A. "Viable Options: Intensive Supervision Programs for Juvenile Delinquents." *Crime and Delinquency* 36, no. 1 (1990): 238–256.

BAZEMORE, GORDON. "On Mission Statements and Reform in Juvenile Justice: The Case of the 'Balanced Approach'." *Federal Probation* 56, no. 3 (1992): 64–70.

BAZEMORE, GORDON, and UMBREIT, MARK. *Balanced and Restorative Justice: Program Summary.* Washington, D.C.: U. S. Department of Justice, Office of Juvenile Justice and Delinquency Prevention, 1995.

BAZEMORE, GORDON, and WALGRAVE, LODE, eds. *Restorative Juvenile Justice: Repairing the Harm of Youth Crime.* Monsey, N.Y.: Criminal Justice Press, 1999.

BECKER, HOWARD S. *Outsiders: Studies in the Sociology of Deviance.* New York: Free Press, 1963.

BINDER, ARNOLD. "Juvenile Diversion." In *Juvenile Justice: Policies, Programs, and Services,* 2d ed. Edited by Albert R. Roberts. Chicago: Nelson-Hall, 1998. Pages 231–249.

CATALANO, RICHARD E.; ARTHUR, MICHAEL W.; HAWKINS, J. DAVID; BERGLUND, LISA; and OLSON, JEFFREY J. "Comprehensive Community- and School-Based Interventions to Prevent Antisocial Behavior." In *Serious & Violent Juvenile Offenders: Risk Factors and Successful Interventions.* Edited by Rolf Loeber and David P. Farrington. Thousand Oaks, Calif.: Sage Publications, 1998. Pages 248–283.

COATES, ROBERT B.; MILLER, ALDEN D.; and OHLIN, LLOYD E. *Social Climate, Extent of Community Linkages, and Quality of Community Linkages: The Institutionalization-Normalization Continuum.* Cambridge, Mass.: Harvard Law School, Center for Criminal Justice, 1976.

COATES, ROBERT B.; MILLER, ALDEN D.; and OHLIN, LLOYD E. *Diversity in a Youth Correctional System: Handling Delinquents in Massachusetts.* Cambridge, Mass.: Ballinger, 1978.

DAVIDSON, WILLIAM S.; SEIDMAN, EDWARD; RAPPAPORT, JULIAN; BERCK, PHILIP L.; RAPP, NANCY A.; RHODES, WARREN; and HERRING, JACOB. "Diversion Programs for Juvenile Offenders."

Social Work Research and Abstracts 13, no. 1 (1977): 40–49.

DESCHENES, ELIZABETH P.; GREENWOOD, PETER W.; and MARSHALL, GRANT. *The Nokomis Challenge Program Evaluation.* Santa Monica, Calif.: RAND, 1996.

EZELL, MARK. "Juvenile Arbitration: Net Widening and Other Unintended Consequences." *Journal of Research in Crime and Delinquency* 26, no. 4 (1989): 358–377.

GREENWOOD, PETER W.; DESCHENES, ELIZABETH P.; and ADAMS, JOHN. *Chronic Juvenile Offenders: Final Results from the Skillman Aftercare Experiment.* Santa Monica, Calif.: RAND, 1993.

HATTIE, JOHN; MARSH, H. W.; NEILL, JAMES T.; and RICHARDS, GARRY E. "Adventure Education and Outward Bound: Out-of-class Experiences That Make a Lasting Difference." *Review of Educational Research* 67, no. 1 (1997): 43–87.

HENGGELER, SCOTT W., and BORDUIN, CHARLES M. *Family Therapy and Beyond: A Multisystemic Approach to Treating the Behavior Problems of Children and Adolescents.* Pacific Grove, Calif.: Brooks/Cole, 1990.

JONES, RICHARD R.; WEINROTT, MARK R.; and HOWARD, JAMES R. *Impact of the Teaching-Family Model on Troublesome Youth: Findings from the National Evaluation.* Rockville, Md.: National Institute of Mental Health, 1981.

KRISBERG, BARRY; AUSTIN, JAMES; and STEELE, PATRICIA. *Unlocking Juvenile Corrections: Evaluating the Massachusetts Department of Youth Services.* San Francisco: National Council on Crime and Delinquency, 1989.

KRISBERG, BARRY; BAKKE, AUDREY; NEUENFELDT, DEBORAH; and STEELE, PATRICIA. *Selected Program Summaries: Demonstration of Post-Adjudication Non-Residential Intensive Supervision Programs.* San Francisco: National Council on Crime and Delinquency, 1989.

KRISBERG, BARRY; RODRIGUEZ, ORLANDO; BAKKE, AUDREY; NEUENFELDT, DEBORAH; and STEELE, PATRICIA. *Demonstration of Post-Adjudication Non-Residential Intensive Supervision Programs: Assessment Report.* San Francisco: National Council on Crime and Delinquency, 1989.

LEMERT, EDWIN M. *Human Deviance, Social Problems, and Social Control.* Englewood Cliffs, N.J.: Prentice-Hall, 1967.

LIPSEY, MARK W. "Juvenile Delinquency Treatment: A Meta-Analytic Inquiry into the Viability of Effects." In *Meta-Analysis for Explanation: A Casebook.* Edited by Thomas D. Cook; Harris Cooper; David S. Cordray; Heidi Hartman; Larry V. Hedges; Richard J. Light; Thomas A.

Louis; and Frederick Mosteller. New York: Russell Sage Foundation, 1992. Pages 83–127.

LIPSEY, MARK W., and WILSON, DAVID B. "Effective Intervention for Serious Juvenile Offenders: A Synthesis of Research." In *Serious Violent Juvenile Offenders: Risk Factors and Successful Interventions.* Edited by Rolf Loeber and David P. Farrington, Thousand Oaks, Calif.: Sage Publications, 1998. Pages 313–345.

LOEBER, ROLF, and FARRINGTON, DAVID P. "Executive Summary." In *Serious and Violent Juvenile Offenders: Risk Factors and Successful Interventions.* Edited by Rolf Loeber and David P. Farrington. Thousand Oaks, Calif.: Sage Publications, 1998. Pages xix–xvii.

MALONEY, DENNIS; ROMIG, DENNIS; and ARMSTRONG, TROY. "Juvenile Probation: The Balanced Approach." *Juvenile and Family Court Journal* 39, no. 3 (1988): 1–62.

OSGOOD, D. WAYNE, and WEICHSELBAUM, HART F. "Juvenile Diversion: When Practice Matches Theory." *Journal of Research in Crime and Delinquency* 21, no. 1 (1984): 33–56.

PALMER, TED, and LEWIS, ROY V. *An Evaluation of Juvenile Diversion.* Cambridge, Mass.: Oelgeschlager, Gunn, and Hain, 1980.

ROBERTS, ALBERT R. "Wilderness Experience: Camps and Outdoor Programs." In *Juvenile Justice: Policies, Programs, and Services,* 2d ed. Edited by Albert R. Roberts. Chicago: Nelson-Hall, 1998. Pages 327–346.

SCHNEIDER, ANNE L. "Restitution and Recidivism Rates of Juvenile Offenders: Results from Four Experimental Studies." *Criminology* 24, no. 3 (1986): 533–552.

SCHWARTZ, IRA M., and BARTON, WILLIAM H., eds. *Reforming Juvenile Detention: No More Hidden Closets.* Columbus: Ohio State University Press, 1994.

SCHWARTZ, IRA M.; BARTON, WILLIAM H.; and ORLANDO, FRANK. "Keeping Kids Out of Secure Detention: The Misuse of Juvenile Detention Has a Profound Impact on Child Welfare." *Public Welfare* 49, no. 2 (1991): 20–26, 46.

SNYDER, HOWARD, and SICKMUND, MELISSA. *Juvenile Offenders and Victims: 1999 National Report.* Washington, D.C.: U.S. Department of Justice, Office of Juvenile Justice and Delinquency Prevention, 1999.

SONTHEIMER, HENRY, and GOODSTEIN, LYNNE. "An Evaluation of Juvenile Intensive Aftercare Probation: Aftercare Versus System Response Effects." *Justice Quarterly* 10 no. 2(1993): 197–227.

STROUL, BETH A. *Models of Community Support Services: Approaches to Helping Persons with Long-*

Term Mental Illness. Boston, Mass.: Boston University, Center for Psychiatric Rehabilitation, 1986.

TIERNEY, JOSEPH; GROSSMAN, JEAN; and RESCH, NANCY. *Making a Difference: An Impact Study of Big Brothers/Big Sisters*. Philadelphia: Public/Private Ventures, 1995.

VAN NESS, DANIEL. "Perspectives on Achieving Satisfying Justice: Values and Principles of Restorative Justice." *ICCA Journal on Community Corrections* 8, no. 1 (1997): 7–12.

WASSERMAN, GAIL A., and MILLER, LAURIE S. "The Prevention of Serious and Violent Juvenile Offending." In *Serious and Violent Juvenile Offenders: Risk Factors and Successful Interventions*. Edited by Rolf Loeber and David P. Farrington. Thousand Oaks, Calif.: Sage Publications, 1998. Pages 197–247.

WIEBUSH, RICHARD G., and HAMPARIAN, DONNA. "Variations in 'Doing' Juvenile Intensive Supervision: Programmatic Issues in Four Ohio Jurisdictions." In *Intensive Interventions with High Risk Youths: Promising Approaches in Juvenile Probation and Parole*. Edited by Troy L. Armstrong. Monsey, N.Y.: Willow Tree Press, 1991. Pages 153–188.

JUVENILE JUSTICE: INSTITUTIONS

The Maine Youth Center, which opened in 1854 and is one of the oldest reform schools in the United States, is home for over two hundred adolescent boys and girls from Maine who have broken the law. The campus sits high on an open hill overlooking the Fore River and looks out on the South Portland Airport. The original building, which formerly housed all of Maine's delinquent youths, is now the facility's administration building and several oversized brick "cottages," two school buildings, and a gymnasium are contained by a tall inward curving chain link fence topped with coils of wire. On one corner of the youth center campus, the brick walls of a new building rise 34 feet high, 420 feet long and 17 inches thick. After 148 years of continuous operation, the dilapidated buildings scattered across the campus will be abandoned. In the fall of 2001, when the $32 million Southern Maine Juvenile Facility replaces the Maine Youth Center, 166 young offenders will occupy a state-of-the-art facility equipped with classrooms, closed-circuit TV for monitoring juveniles, a medical health center, individual bedrooms and dining facilities—all under one roof. A few hundred

miles north in the town of Charleston, a smaller 144-bed sister institution called the Northern Maine Juvenile Facility is being constructed at a cost of $27 million dollars.

For more than a century, the juvenile justice institution has been the program of choice for juvenile offenders. Many of the institutions that were constructed during the latter half of the nineteenth century remain open today, each housing between two hundred and four hundred youths. After more than 150 years of operation, there is no research that points to the effectiveness of the institution in rehabilitating delinquent youths (Guarino-Ghezzi; and Loughran). Conversely, the harmful impact of correctional institutions on adolescents has been well documented over time. Although euphemistically referred to as "reform schools" or "training schools," large custodial institutions have been known to foster all kinds of abuses including inadequate education and counseling programs, predatory behavior by staff, and resident-on-resident assaults. Most states have not explored alternatives to large-scale institutions for less serious person and property offenders. The long tradition of institutions in America as well as the cost of constructing and maintaining an institution makes it difficult for juvenile justice policymakers to experiment with diversity in placement options.

The juvenile justice system, a distinctly American invention, got its start in 1825 when a separate institution for wayward children called the House of Refuge was established in New York City. Before the existence of the House of Refuge, young offenders were routinely remanded to the penitentiary where they were exposed to the corrupting influence of adult inmates. At the beginning of the nineteenth century, judges and juries had become reluctant to send minor offenders to prison, which resulted in the release of many young offenders and their return to the streets of the city (Feld). A reform group of the time called the Society for the Reformation of Juvenile Delinquents feared that many of these children, the sons and daughters of paupers who were regarded as the undeserving poor because of their corrupt and vice-ridden lifestyle, would themselves end up as paupers and criminals (Bernard). For the reformers, the creation of the House of Refuge was the answer to this problem, which was worsening with the migration of families from the countryside seeking work in the factories and the increase of immigration from Europe to America's cities. Other Houses of Refuge were opened in Boston and Philadelphia on the East Coast and then spread to the midwest over the next two decades.

Nearly a quarter of a century later, the country's first publicly administered training school for delinquent boys was established in Westboro, Massachusetts, in 1847 by Theodore Lyman, a philanthropist and former mayor of Boston. Lyman's cause was to end the mixing of vulnerable delinquent youths with hardened criminals in the jails and prisons of Massachusetts. He donated $22,500 of his own money to purchase the land on which the state would ultimately build the Westboro School for Boys for "the instruction, employment, and reformation of juvenile offenders" ("An Act to Establish the State Reform School," Massachusetts Acts and Resolves, 1847). The construction of The State Industrial School for Girls in Lancaster, Massachusetts, followed a decade later in 1856. Built for delinquent youths, the institutions began to receive minor offenders and so-called status offenders such as runaway youth, truants, and stubborn children. In 1862, Massachusetts passed an education reform bill that allowed the state to incarcerate chronic truants in its reform schools so as not to disrupt other children's schooling (Feld).

Nearly fifty years later in 1899, the first juvenile court was established in Cook County, Illinois, which completed the creation of a separate system of justice for juveniles. The birth of the juvenile court was based on an emerging view of children that regarded them as "corruptible innocents" who needed protection from the state (Feld). The new juvenile court introduced the concept of rehabilitation, which de-emphasized youths' offenses and focused on their treatment needs. The juvenile court, acting in the best interest of the child, would officially blur the distinction between a youth's delinquent acts and his nondelinquent status offenses. Many of the children charged with status offenses were in fact homeless, parentless, or poor and were placed in institutions for indeterminate periods of time until they reached their majority under the guise of treating their needs.

The history of juvenile correctional institutions reveals a cyclical process that has repeated itself generation after generation. When first opened, these schools enjoyed a period of calm where staff and youths interacted, and youths made progress. This was usually followed by overcrowding of the institution during periodic crackdowns on juvenile crime. Soon after, living conditions at the institution deteriorated with older, predatory youths attacking younger, more vulnerable ones, increased escapes, youths assaulting staff, and intimidated staff turning on youths. Next followed exposure of incidents and problems by the media, which usually triggered an investigation by state and federal authorities. A blue ribbon commission of elected officials and leading citizens would be convened to issue a report with recommendations for change and improvements. Reforms would be implemented ushering in a new period of calm and order at the institution (Guarino-Ghezzi; and Loughran).

Current developments and problems

During the 1990s, states began replacing old, run-down institutions and constructing new facilities to respond to the dramatic rise in violent juvenile crime throughout the country. Violent juvenile crime, fueled by the lethal combination of illicit drugs and guns in the hands of adolescents, climbed rapidly between 1988 and 1993. The proportion of juvenile arrests for violent crime grew from 9 percent in the late 1980s to 14.2 percent in 1994. Juvenile murder arrests more than doubled between 1987 and its peak year 1993 from approximately 1,500 to 3,800 each year.

According to the Census of Juveniles in Residential Placement (CJRP), there were 105,790 juveniles under age twenty-one in custody in either a pretrial detention or juvenile correctional facility on a given day in 1997. This represented a 63 percent increase in the number of incarcerated youth since 1991 when the one-day count of confined youths was 65,000. Three states (California, Texas, and Florida) that account for 25 percent of the youth population in the United States account for 30 percent of all confined youth in the country (Snyder and Sikmund). Youths in confinement facilities run the gamut from violent offenders to status offenders. The CJRP breakdown for youths in institutional placements in 1997 was:

- Violent Index Crimes—25 percent
- Other Person Offenses—8 percent
- Property Offenses—30 percent
- Drug Offenses—9 percent
- Public Order Offenses—21 percent
- Status Offenses—7 percent

This dramatic increase in the number of youths remanded to secure institutions has caused severe crowding problems in facilities throughout the country similar to the overcrowding of adult prisons in the 1980s. In 1995, 50 percent of all pretrial detention facilities and 45 percent of all correctional institutions were operating above design capacity.

Minorities, especially black youths, are overrepresented in the juvenile justice system, especially in secure institutions. Research findings show that this is primarily the result of widespread disparity in juvenile case processing. Data demonstrates that minority youths are more likely to be placed in public secure facilities, while white youths are more likely to be housed in private facilities or diverted from the juvenile justice system altogether. The custody rates for juveniles are:

- Black—1,018 per 100,000
- White—204 per 100,000
- Hispanic—515 per 100,000
- Native American—525 per 100,000
- Asian—203 per 100,000

Effect of crowding on conditions of confinement

In 1988 the U.S. Congress directed the Office of Juvenile Justice and Delinquency Prevention (OJJDP) in the U.S. Justice Department to assess conditions of confinement for juveniles and to determine the extent to which those conditions conform to nationally recognized professional standards for juvenile institutions. This congressional mandate coincided with the rise in serious juvenile crime and a flurry of legislative activity in states to increase the severity of punishments for violent or habitual juvenile offenders. Many states, in response to particularly heinous crimes committed by juveniles, also enacted laws to make it easier to try and sentence juvenile offenders as adults.

The study of 984 public and private institutions throughout the country that included pretrial detention centers, training schools, ranches, camps, and farms was conducted between 1990 and 1992. The Conditions of Confinement (COC) Report, issued in 1993, found substantial and widespread deficiencies in four major areas of institutional life—living space, security, control of suicidal behavior, and health care (Parent et al.).

The COC study found that nearly 75 percent of the institutions were crowded in some respect. To eliminate crowding in the facilities, it was estimated that more than fourteen thousand juveniles would have to be removed from the population of confinement facilities, or an equal number of new beds added in adequately designed living areas of institutions. The report recommended that large dormitories be eliminated from juvenile facilities because of the ease of adding beds in excess of the design capacity to accommodate an influx of delinquent youths. The study also found a link between crowding of institutions and a higher rate of injuries to staff by juveniles and juvenile-on-juvenile injuries. The rates for short-term isolation of acting-out juveniles were higher in crowded facilities. Poor security practices also contributed to escapes and injuries in the facilities.

The study indicated suicidal behavior to be a serious problem in juvenile confinement facilities. Ten confined juveniles killed themselves in 1990 while the COC study was underway. The study estimated that more than eleven thousand individual juveniles engage in more than seventeen thousand incidents of suicide behavior in juvenile institutions each year. Approximately 75 percent of juveniles in confinement were screened upon admission for indicators of suicide risk, and a similar number were in facilities that train staff in suicide prevention.

In the area of health care for confined juveniles, the COC study reported a number of deficiencies that included failure to complete health screenings within the first hour after admission to a facility, and failure to perform a full health assessment within a week of admission. Additionally, one-third of juvenile screenings in pretrial detention centers were completed by staff who had not been trained by medical personnel to perform health screening.

One of the limitations of the COC study was its inability to determine the adequacy of education and treatment services because of a lack of systematic empirical data on confined youth's educational or treatment needs and problems.

The COC study tested the premise that facilities that conformed to nationally recognized standards of care such as the American Correctional Association Standards, which are used as the basis for accrediting juvenile training schools, and the American Bar Association/Institute for Judicial Administration Standards (1980) would result in improved conditions of confinement. Accredited institutions scored no better than nonaccredited facilities in important areas of operation, such as safety, security, education, treatment services, and health care. The COC study revealed the shortcoming of existing standards, which was their emphasis on written policies and procedures concerning aspects of facility operation rather than specifying measurable outcomes that ought to be achieved. A major recommendation in the final COC report called for the development and promulgation of performance-based standards in all aspects of institutional life that would serve both as goals for the facilities to attain and benchmarks against which their progress could be measured.

Performance-based standards

In 1995 OJJDP, acting on one of the recommendations contained in its COC report, launched a major initiative to improve the conditions of confinement in juvenile detention and correctional facilities, now known as the Performance-based Standards (PbS) Project. For five years the Council of Juvenile Correctional Administrators (CJCA), an organization representing chief executive officers of state and large county juvenile correctional agencies, which was designated by OJJDP, developed and has been implementing a set of outcome-based standards in detention and correctional facilities throughout the country. A set of standards addresses safety, order, security, programming, health/mental health, justice of facility operations, and reintegration of offenders into the community. Each standard has one or more outcome measures that monitors performance with data and reflects improvements over time, as well as associated expected practices and processes that support performance and serve as the foundation for improved operations.

By the end of 2000, nearly sixty individual facilities from twenty-three states were implementing the performance-based system. Eight states have adopted the system in all facilities, allowing for systemic change, improvements, and management. Results of four data collections (every six months) demonstrate measurable improvements at participating sites, such as reduced use of isolation and room confinement, increased numbers of youths receiving health and mental health screenings and assessments, implementation of behavior modification programs, and reduction of assaults on youths and staff. As of 2001, the PbS project team was working to develop a software package and training model that can facilitate data collection and make the new standards system part of daily management operations in facilities throughout the country.

Institutions today

The first juvenile correctional institutions in this country were located in rural, bucolic settings based on the belief that exposure of urban youth to the wholesome agrarian environment would ameliorate the corrupting influences of the city. States continue to build juvenile facilities far from the communities where the confined youths live but for very different reasons from the founding intention. The public's fear of young offenders has been reinforced by negative media coverage and elected official's political posturing over the relatively small number of violent juvenile offenders. Facility planners are customarily confronted with "not in my backyard" opposition when searching for prospective facility locations. Consequently, juvenile correctional facilities are often constructed long distances from youths' families, their local schools' and employment opportunities, making reintegration of young offenders into their home communities difficult. This is the case in states such as California, Maine, Nebraska, New York, Ohio, and Texas. Delaware is an exception as both its pretrial detention and juvenile correctional facilities are situated on a campus in a suburban community just beyond the city limits of Wilmington where most of the confined youths live.

The first institutions were freestanding buildings that housed youths in congregate style, mixing older and younger children and criminal and status offenders. Then followed a campus setting with cottages and cottage parents to normalize the environment. Today many states, such as Colorado, Maine, Minnesota, Nebraska, and Ohio, continue to follow the campus model where youths are classified by offense type and special programming needs, such as alcohol and substance abuse, sex offending, or mental health problems and are placed in cottages or living units. Youths sleep under one roof and participate in group-counseling in the living units in the evening, but move about the campus in groups under the supervision of counselors or officers to attend school in a separate school building, eat in a cafeteria, recreate in a gymnasium or on outdoor ball fields and courts, and attend services in a chapel.

Juvenile institutions constructed since the mid-1990s are self-contained buildings that house living units and programming areas under one roof. The building design consists of administrative offices near the building entrance, a central-services area that contains classrooms, medical facilities, kitchen and dining area, and a gymnasium. Living space is divided into units or pods with individual rooms and common rooms for counseling sessions and evening-recreational activities. Most juvenile correctional institutions are now enclosed by a high inward-curving chain link fence with barbed wire or razor ribbon atop the structure.

A handful of states, such as Kentucky, Massachusetts, and Missouri, operate small secure treatment facilities for serious person and chronic property offenders in lieu of large, custodial institutions. Some of these facilities accommodate as few as fifteen youths, while others are designed for thirty to fifty young offenders. The treatment offered at these programs is much more intensive and individualized than what can be offered at institutions with two hundred or more beds. Staff has the time to get to know youths, and to learn more about their problems, offense history, and needs in order to design and carry out comprehensive treatment interventions. Small class sizes permit teachers to tailor instruction to the educational deficiencies of underachieving students, many of whom attended school irregularly or dropped out all together. Additionally, these smaller programs conduct appropriately sized group-counseling sessions that deal with a young offender's underlying issues, such as the effects of child neglect and abuse, impulsive and aggressive acting-out, alcohol and substance abuse, and other behavioral problems.

Small, appropriately staffed rehabilitation programs tend to have fewer behavior management problems. Consequently, violent incidents, use of force by staff, use of mechanical restraints and isolation, and rates of serious injury to youths and staff are significantly reduced in these facilities.

Recognizing the benefits of smaller treatment programs on youth behavior management and staff morale, administrators of larger institutions in states such as Connecticut, Ohio, and Maine, have begun to institute unit management in the living cottages or units. Under this arrangement, direct care and clinical staff are formed into treatment teams and assigned to a cottage or unit with responsibility for designing and carrying out treatment plans for the youths residing there. This approach allows the large institutional population to be broken down into manageable components. Youths are customarily classified based on the risks and needs they present at admission and assigned to homogeneous units. Classification can be based on a combination of factors, such as age, maturity, offense history and criminal sophistication or on the specialized nature of a youth's underlying problems, such as alcohol and substance abuse, sex offending and mental health problems. Unit management brings the distinctive benefits of small programs to the larger institution.

Since reaching an all-time high in 1994, juvenile crime has fallen for five consecutive years. The rate of juvenile arrests for Violent Crime Index Offenses—murder, forcible rape, robbery, and aggravated assault—declined by 36 percent in the five-year period. The juvenile murder arrest rate fell 68 percent to 1,400 in 1999 from 3,800 in 1993.

Despite this significant drop in juvenile crime, especially violent crime from 1995 forward, juvenile court judges continue to commit adolescents to state juvenile correctional agencies for placement in institutions in unprecedented numbers. Crowding in these institutions, which results in youths sleeping on floors in hallways and in gymnasiums, continues to worsen the working and living environment for staff and youths. Today, correctional administrators face a host of complex problems, such as a surge in youths with serious mental health problems, high staff turnover, and insufficient training programs for direct-care staff.

Increase in mentally ill youths. The closing of state-operated psychiatric hospitals for children throughout the country during the 1990s and the introduction of managed behavioral health care to cut the cost of providing mental health services to patients has forced many emotionally troubled and mentally ill children into the juvenile correctional system. An estimated 20 percent or more than twenty thousand incarcerated juveniles are seriously emotionally disturbed. The juvenile justice system is unprepared to care for and treat mentally ill youths. Failure to screen and assess the special needs of these youths could result in serious harm or treatment that exacerbates the illness. Co-mingling the mentally ill with serious offenders contributes to the increase in disruptive behavior in programs. Additionally, staff, unaware of the side effects of certain mood-altering medications administered to these youths, impose sanctions for their acting-out behavior, which results in unfair treatment of these youths. Many emotionally disturbed or mentally ill youths placed in juvenile correctional facilities are not receiving the specialized treatment they require, nor are plans being developed ensure appropriate aftercare services for them upon release from the institution.

High staff turnover. Direct-care staff, who supervise confined youths in their cottages or units, are called youth workers or juvenile correctional officers. These workers are assigned to one of three shifts (7:00 A.M.–3:00 P.M., 3:00 P.M.–11:00 P.M., and 11:00 P.M.–7:00 A.M.). Their starting salaries range from a low of $12,500 in Montana to a high of $30,000 in California, with the average being $20,500. The number of staff assigned to supervise youths varies greatly from facility to facility, with one youth worker responsible for ten youths being the ideal, but in most institutions the ratio is one youth worker for fifteen to twenty youths. Working in overcrowded buildings with troubled, disruptive youths contributes to extremely stressful conditions for staff. Recent surveys of direct-care staff indicated that 20 percent feared for their safety while supervising youths in living units. Absentee rates soar under such conditions, forcing staff to work extra shifts. Staff morale suffers and ultimately leads to high rates of turnover among those staff who are responsible for the day-to-day care of the youths, role modeling, and doling out punishments and rewards.

Insufficient training for staff. Training for direct-care staff in institutions throughout the country varies greatly in the number of hours of pre-service and in-service training required, the quality of the curricula, and trainers teaching the courses. In 1994 only a handful of state juvenile correctional programs had training academies. Today thirty-three states have academies that train, test, and certify staff as youth workers. The ACA Standards for Juvenile Training Schools state that all new juvenile care workers receive 40 hours of training before they supervise youths, an additional 120 hours of training during their first year of employment, and an additional 40 hours of training each subsequent year of employment. A survey of 110 juvenile correctional facilities in 1997 indicates that the average number of pre-service and first-year training for juvenile correctional workers was 102 hours. The results from the same survey demonstrate that undertrained staffs in facilities are the ones who get assaulted. In recent years, the high rate of turnover results in many youth care workers receiving a brief orientation and mostly on-the-job training until the next training for new staff is held, which sometimes is not for weeks or months.

The Kentucky Department of Juvenile Justice is recognized as a leader in its training program for juvenile correctional staff. The training academy is operated out of Eastern Kentucky University's Training Resource Center. All new direct-care staff hired at the state's thirty-five residential treatment facilities (thirty to thirty-five beds) and three pretrial detention facilities begin a ten-week cycle of training at the academy with two weeks in the training facility classroom. This is followed by two weeks on the job, two more weeks in the classroom, back to the job for two more weeks, and the final two weeks in the classroom. Research has shown that attrition rates for staff in the first year had been 37 percent. The professionally conducted training program has been able to stabilize the turnover rate.

The legal rights of juveniles in confinement

A growing body of law from past litigation against juvenile correctional facilities and relevant federal statutes specify the minimum environmental conditions that juvenile institutions must meet. Under these laws, confined juveniles have the right to protection from violent residents, abusive staff, unsanitary living quarters, excessive isolation, and unreasonable restraints. Youths in confinement must also receive adequate medical and mental health care, education (including special education for youths with disabilities), access to legal counsel, and access to family communication, recreation, exercise, and other programs (Puritz and Scali).

The sharp rise in commitments to juvenile correctional facilities during the last decade has exacerbated the living conditions in facilities where many youths are held. Investigations of these institutions by youth advocacy groups as well as the Civil Rights Division of the U.S. Justice Department have documented significant deficiencies in living space, security, control of suicidal behavior, health care, education and treatment services, emergency preparedness, and access to legal counsel. In 1996, the American Bar Association Juvenile Justice Center released a report titled "A Call for Justice: An Assessment of Access to Counsel and Quality of Representation in Delinquency Proceedings." The report revealed numerous deficiencies in both the access to and the quality of representation juveniles receive at every point in the juvenile court process (Puritz et al.). The results of inadequate representation can be seen in the disproportionate representation of minority youths and nonviolent property and drug offenders in juvenile detention and correctional facilities. As the bar association looked into the shortcomings of the process of justice for juveniles, other international and national advocacy groups, such as Human Rights Watch, Amnesty International, The Youth Law Center in San Francisco, and the Juvenile Rights Center in Philadelphia, have investigated and reported on widespread abuses of adolescents in juvenile detention and correctional facilities throughout the country.

Since 1995, Human Rights Watch Children Rights Project has published devastating reports on constitutional abuses of children in confinement facilities in Louisiana, Georgia, and Colorado. The international organization has documented abuses of youths in the Louisiana Department of Correction's four juvenile post-adjudication correctional facilities to include physical abuse of residents by staff, improper restraints with handcuffs, and youths kept in isolation for excessive periods of time.

A scathing report on abusive, overcrowded, and dangerous conditions in detention and correctional facilities, including boot camp programs, in Georgia prompted the Civil Rights Division of the U.S. Department of Justice to investigate facilities operated by the Georgia Department of Juvenile Justice. The Justice Department's investigation, conducted under the authority of a federal law called the Civil Rights of Institutionalized Persons Act (CRIPA), substantiated alleged abuses in unconstitutional living conditions and the state's failure to properly educate confined youths and inattention to their psychological and mental health needs.

In 1999, the State of Georgia avoided a lawsuit by the Justice Department and entered into a "Memorandum of Understanding" with the federal government to improve conditions in the numerous institutional deficiencies cited in the report. A monitor appointed by the Justice Department currently oversees the state's "Plan of Improvement."

The Justice department investigated very few juvenile facilities during the 1980s, but as reports of abuses that resulted from crowded conditions mounted, the federal government stepped-up its investigations of juvenile detention and correctional facilities in the 1990s. As of November 1997, the Civil Rights Division had investigated three hundred institutions under CRIPA. Seventy-three of these institutions were juvenile detention and correctional facilities. As of 2001, the federal executive or judicial branches were monitoring confinement practices in several jurisdictions including Georgia, Louisiana, Philadelphia, Puerto Rico, and South Dakota.

Distinguishing juvenile correctional facilities from adult prisons

It is becoming increasingly difficult to distinguish juvenile facilities from adult prisons. In fact, in some states, notably Georgia and Florida, the excessive building of prisons in the 1980s produced a surplus of prison-bed inventory because of either a fall-off of the number of new prisoners or insufficient operational funding from state legislatures. These states handed over the new prisons to juvenile correctional agencies to meet the demands caused by rising juvenile commitments. Spartan by design, adult prisons house inmates in cells and provide very little program space, such as classrooms, counseling areas, offices for staff in the housing units, and adequate recreational space. Until the 1990s, juvenile institutions were relatively open facilities with no perimeter fences except for secure units that had fencing around outdoor recreation areas only.

The Ferris School in Wilmington, Delaware, a seventy-two-bed secure facility built in 1997, bucked the trend of building a "juvenile prison." In 1990, the American Civil Liberties Union filed a class action suit charging that the Ferris School was overcrowded, unhealthful, unsanitary, and life endangering. In 1994, after four years of fighting the suit in court, the state decided to enter into a settlement agreement with the ACLU and to secure funds for a "new" Ferris School. The building represents an architectural breakthrough in balancing security and a rehabilitative environment that is spacious and filled with natural light. Each living area has twelve individual rooms with large outer areas for group meetings and light recreation in the evening. Correctional administrators from jurisdictions throughout the country have traveled to Delaware to obtain ideas for incorporation in their future building plans.

The reduced use of institutions

Massachusetts stands out as the state that dismantled all of its large reform schools in the early 1970s in favor of a variety of smaller, treatment-oriented programs, many of them operated by private, community-based agencies. Thirty years later, the Massachusetts Department of Youth Services (DYS) operates a balanced juvenile correctional system with a diverse network of small secure programs, group homes, outreach and tracking (intensive community supervision), and day and evening reporting centers. Each youth who is committed to DYS is assigned a case manager who will devise a treatment plan for the youth, based on clinical and educational evaluations, as well as on family history and the presenting offense. For youths initially placed in residential programs, the case manager arranges for the youth to participate in community services, such as drug and alcohol treatment and counseling, as a prerequisite of the conditions of his or her liberty. Studies have demonstrated that the recidivism rates for youths eased back into the community through a variety of residential and nonresidential community-based programs and services were below those of states that still rely solely on large, custodial institutions.

Only a few states, such as Utah, Hawaii, Kentucky, and Missouri, have followed Massachusetts' lead in either downsizing or replacing large institutions with a similar network of programs. These states as well as Massachusetts have added secure beds to their systems to deal with the rise in juvenile offender populations during the last decade but they continue to rely on small, secure treatment programs rather than return to large institutions.

Many states visited Massachusetts during the 1970s and 1980s to study and possibly replicate elements of the balanced approach but the changing picture of youth crime in the early 1990s and the media's overreaction derailed most of those plans. However, many states have developed some of the community-based alternatives, such as outreach and tracking and group homes pioneered in Massachusetts, for youths leaving the institution.

Effectiveness of institutions

Evaluations of large congregate training schools report consistently negative findings. Most state training schools do not reduce recidivism rates and fall short in reforming multiple offenders.

However, recent research on certain components of juvenile correctional programs indicates that some interventions do produce positive effects on the behavior of confined youths. Aggression Replacement Training (ART) is one of a number of cognitive behavioral interventions that tries to reduce the antisocial behavior that many youths bring into confinement programs and encourage pro-social behavior. ART has an anger control component that helps the eight to ten participants in a group session understand what triggers their anger and how to control their reactions. The "skill-streaming" behavioral component teaches a series of pro-social skills through modeling, role playing, and performance feedback from others in the group. In the moral reasoning component, participants work through cognitive conflict through "dilemma" discussion groups. Results on the studies of ART have been consistently positive for skill acquisition. Aggressive adolescents have demonstrated the ability to learn a broad array of previously unavailable interpersonal, aggression-management, affect-relevant, and related psychological competencies (Goldstein and Glick). Integrating these new skills into their overall behavior for an extended period of time and maintaining the change after returning to the community has had mixed results.

Many juvenile confinement facilities have developed a combination of clinical and educational interventions for subgroups of youths, such as sex offenders, substance abusers, and youths with mental health problems who have been committed to youth correctional agencies. Some of these specialized program components have been written up as "promising approaches" but the majority of them have not been evaluated. There is a continuing need for states and the federal OJJDP to conduct and publicize research that acknowledges how humane conditions and well-designed and managed programs can lower recidivism rates and enhance public safety.

EDWARD J. LOUGHRAN

See also JUVENILE AND YOUTH GANGS; JUVENILE JUSTICE: HISTORY AND PHILOSOPHY; JUVENILE JUSTICE: COMMUNITY TREATMENT; JUVENILE JUSTICE: JUVENILE COURTS; JUVENILES IN THE ADULT SYSTEM; JUVENILE STATUS OFFENDERS; JUVENILE VIOLENT OFFENDERS; POLICE: HANDLING OF JUVENILES; PREVENTION: JUVENILES AS POTENTIAL OFFENDERS; SCHOOLS AND CRIME.

BIBLIOGRAPHY

ALTSCHULER, DAVID M. "Tough and Smart Juvenile Incarceration: Reintegrating Punishment, Deterrence and Rehabilitation." *St. Louis University Public Law Review* 14 (1994): 217–237.

BERNARD, THOMAS J. *The Cycle of Juvenile Justice.* New York: Oxford University Press, 1992.

FELD, BARRY C. *Bad Kids: Race and the Transformation of the Juvenile Court.* New York: Oxford University Press, 1999.

GOLDSTEIN, ARNOLD, and GLICK, BARRY. *Aggression Replacement Training.* Champaign, Ill.: Research Press, 1987.

GREENWOOD, PETER, and ZIMRING, FRANKLIN. *One More Chance: The Pursuit of Promising Intervention Strategies for Chronic Juvenile Offenders.* Santa Monica, Calif.: RAND, 1985.

GUARINO-GHEZZI, SUSAN, and LOUGHRAN, EDWARD J. *Balancing Juvenile Justice.* New Brunswick, N.J.: Transaction Press, 1996.

HAMPARIAN, D.; SCHUSTER, R.; DINITZ, S.; and CONRAD, J. *The Violent Few.* Lexington, Mass.: D.C. Heath, 1978.

KRISBERG, BARRY; LITSKY, PAUL; and SCHWARTZ, IRA M. "Youth in Confinement: Justice by Geography." *Journal of Research in Crime and Delinquency* 22, no. 2 (1984): 153–181.

MILLER, JEROME. *Last One Over the Wall.* Columbus: Ohio State University Press, 1991.

PARENT, DALE G.; LIETER, VALERIE; KENNEDY, STEPHEN; LIVENS, LISA; WENTWORTH, DANIEL; and WILCOX, SARA. *Conditions of Confinement: Juvenile Detention and Corrections Facilities.* Washington, D.C.: U.S. Department of Justice, Office of Juvenile Justice and Delinquency Prevention, 1994.

PURITZ, PATRICIA; BURELL, SUE; SCHWARTZ, ROBERT; SOLER, MARK; and WARBOYS, LOREN. *A Call for Justice: An Assessment of Access to Counsel and Quality of Representation in Delinquency Proceedings.* Washington, D.C.: American Bar Association Juvenile Justice Center, 1996.

PURITZ, PATRICIA, and SCALI, MARY ANN. *Beyond the Walls: Improving Conditions of Confinement for Youth in Custody.* Washington, D.C.: U.S. Justice Department, Office of Juvenile Justice and Delinquency Prevention, 1998.

SNYDER, HOWARD, N., and SIKMUND, MELISSA. *Juvenile Offenders and Victims: 1999 National Report.* Washington, D.C.: U.S. Department of Justice, Office of Juvenile Justice and Delinquency Prevention, 1999.

STEELE, PATRICIA A.; AUSTIN, JAMES; and KRISBERG, BARRY. *Unlocking Juvenile Corrections: Evaluating the Massachusetts Department of Youth Services.* San Francisco: National Council on Crime and Delinquency, 1989.